CW00733058

THE DISSOLUTION OF THE MONASTERIES

THE DISSOLUTION OF THE MONASTERIES

A New History

JAMES G. CLARK

YALE UNIVERSITY PRESS
NEW HAVEN AND LONDON

For information about this and other Yale University Press publications, please contact:
U.S. Office: sales.press@yale.edu   yalebooks.com
Europe Office: sales@yaleup.co.uk   yalebooks.co.uk

Set in Adobe Caslon Pro by IDSUK (DataConnection) Ltd
Printed in Great Britain by TJ Books, Padstow, Cornwall

Library of Congress Control Number: 2021940111

ISBN 978-0-300-11572-7

A catalogue record for this book is available from the British Library.

10 9 8 7 6 5 4 3 2 1

CONTENTS

CONTENTS

ILLUSTRATIONS

ACKNOWLEDGEMENTS

This has been a passage through monastic and mendicant England which the Cromwellian commissioners might have recognised, except perhaps for its speed. Like their own experience, where it has brought results, it has been due to the ready guidance and willing support of those expert in the ways and means of the medieval religious houses, the later medieval church, the Tudor regime and the archives and archaeology they have left behind. I am especially grateful to John Allan, Des Atkinson, Virginia Bainbridge, Paul Binski, Julia Boffey, Tracy Borman, Clive Burgess, Janet Burton, Jon Cannon, Michael Carter, Jeremy Catto, Colman O'Clabaigh, Wendy Clarke, Martin Crampin, Peter Cunich, Stephen Fenn, Richard Fisher, Henry French, Roberta Gilchrist, Vincent Gillespie, Steven Gunn, Nick Holder, Jonathan Hughes, Ronald Hutton, John Jenkins, Eddie Jones, Charles Knighton, Julian Luxford, Jesse Lynch, Harriet Lyon, Veronica O'Mara, Ellie March, Dave Martin, Oswald McBride, Diarmaid MacCulloch, Julia Merritt, Ian Mortimer, Nicholas Orme, Matthew Payne, Rebecca Philips, Sue Powell, John Powlesland, Stephen Rippon, David Rundle, Henry Summerson, Benjamin Thompson, David Thornton and Tony Trowles. I am grateful to the editorial team at Yale University Press, especially Marika Lysandrou and Richard Mason, for their generous assistance. Sincere thanks are also due to Heather McCallum for her patient forbearance. I owe most of all to those who have shared in the journey's every turn: my parents, who unwittingly began it when they first unfolded the past time present in so many places; Henry, whose endurance was a challenge to chronology itself; Eleanor and Cecily, who alone among their generation will carry with them the capacity to distinguish canon from monk; and, above all, Katherine, as indomitable as her namesake, the Lady of Godstow. The best of this is theirs.

Cruwys Morchard, February 2020

INTRODUCTION

The week before Easter 1540 saw the end of almost a millennium of monastic life in mainland England. In the last days of Lent, the Augustinian abbey of the Holy Cross at Waltham (Essex) was surrendered into the hands of William Petre, proctor of the Vicegerent in Spirituals, Thomas Cromwell. Abbot Robert Fuller and his seventeen brother canons entered their chapter house for the final time, perhaps following their Morning Mass, the mid-point of the monastery's daily routine. There they heard Petre read out the deed that would formalise their surrender to the Crown. It opened with the common formula that their act was undertaken with their 'whole assent, consent and free will' (unanimi assensu et consensu ac spontanea voluntatae nostris); then a further twelve lines were filled with details of what they were about to give up: church, cloister, curtilage, courts and precinct, and lordships, manors, farms, tenements, granges, meadow, marsh, pasture, woodland, warren, furze and fishing waters extending over eighteen counties. Now, in descending order of seniority, they stepped forward to sign their name in the document's left-hand margin. Their signatures were well done, the lettering large; the last two of them, the 'juniors', Robert Hulle and Edmund Freke, had to fit their names onto the vellum's folded lower lip.[1] It was 23 March, a date which liturgical calendars still in use in this seventh year of the Tudors' new English Church would identify as the feast of Æthelwold (d. 699), a figure celebrated in England's monastic history. Afterwards, it seems the canons returned to their

1

convent chambers, because the king's receivers had determined not to confront their task of sequestration before the coming festival was over and (perhaps more especially) before the new financial year began in the last week of April.[2]

On the last day of the same week, Richard Rich, the Chancellor of the Court of Augmentations – the office created to take in the revenue from the religious houses – received the king's commission, written out on workaday parchment, to proceed to take the surrender of the monastic communities that were the custodians of the cathedral churches at Rochester and Canterbury. The deeds themselves have been lost and so the day(s) it was done cannot be known for certain, although it may have been before the end of the following week as the Easter octave came to a close.[3] Here too there was a pause to observe the season; no one thought to disturb the student monks at the Oxford college maintained by the cathedral monastery, until the very end of the festival. Their surrender was taken on 10 April.[4] Later pension records suggest that between the two houses there were as many as seventy-five monks; here, and at Waltham, it was almost exactly the number of men that had entered them when the Normans first made them monasteries almost five centuries before.[5]

There was no small resonance to the last acts of the religious orders being witnessed at Waltham, Rochester and Canterbury. Waltham was a royal foundation, and the church claimed to hold in its keeping the mortal remains of the last king of England, Harold Godwinson (d. 14 October 1066). Its Augustinian tradition had been the mainstay of regular religious communities in medieval England, that is to say, those foundations for men and women who committed to live communally under a Christian rule (Latin, *regula*). Houses with these customs outnumbered all others by almost 40 per cent.[6] Their cultural profile was not as prominent as that of the followers of the Rule of St Benedict, but in provincial England, where men and women were likely to be met at the parish church, hospital or almshouse, it was the dress (black cloak, linen rochet and white cassock), customs and outlook of the canon life that was most familiar.[7] For every subject of the Tudor regime, Rochester and Canterbury represented living history, the visible roots of the Church tradition in England. Arthurian legend, now finding a new audience in print, persuaded them that Christianity had come first to Glastonbury, but it was well known that it was at these Kent churches that England's long relationship with the Roman Church had begun.

After these performances, there were two delayed codas, both of them quite distinct. On 28 April the Lords and Commons convened for the third and final session of the second parliament to sit since the royal supremacy. Here, two-thirds of the way through a disarmingly diverse legislative programme, covering doctrine (a revision of the six articles), dynastic strategy (the formal annulment of Henry VIII's marriage to Anne of Cleves) and countryside crime (the stealing of birds' eggs), came an act for the suppression of the remaining eighteen priories of the Knights of St John of Jerusalem, headed by their celebrated priory at Clerkenwell, familiar to the king's subjects as a stage in the drama of the Peasants' Revolt a century and a half before.[8] It was the only instance in which an entire monastic congregation was suppressed under statute. Like the two legislative acts for suppression, it appears to have been a resolve at the eleventh hour. The rights of the Grand Prior to recover income from property were confirmed just over a week earlier on 20 April.[9] The dispossession of the preceptors (i.e. head of house) and the surrender of their sites may still have been protracted: the first pensions were not granted until shortly before Christmas 1540; the preceptory at Temple Bruer (Lincolnshire) does not appear to have been handed over until 1541.[10]

Meanwhile, there were still monks and nuns in England's westernmost territory, at Rushen on the Isle of Man, where there had been a Cistercian abbey for 400 years.[11] It seems they did not disband until 24 June 1540. Their allocation of pensions was not confirmed until the third week in April, and it seems they stayed a while longer as the house was not recorded as received into the custody of the Crown until 4 June.[12] All other island colonies of the kingdom's monastic population, from Farne in the north-east, to Guernsey, Herm and Jersey, just fourteen miles from France, had been abandoned at least eighteen months before.[13] Perhaps the persistence of the Manx population arose from that characteristic British contingency, inclement weather. By the autumn of 1540, the only regular religious communities continuing under Tudor rule were in the four counties of the Pale of Ireland.[14]

In precisely four years, from March 1536, each one of the kingdom's 850 religious houses, monasteries and mendicant convents for men and women – representing as many as nineteen different customary traditions, congregations and 'orders' – had been closed.[15] The spectacle of churches taken out of use and clergy removed or passing out of sight was not unknown in England and Wales. The effects of nationwide plague in the middle decades of the fourteenth century, localised depopulation and dislocation of labour, had caused a number of churches and convent houses to be abandoned.[16] The subjects of Henry VIII themselves had experience of change, sometimes transformation, in the landscape of their churches, driven forward by positive forces in the national economy. During the decades either side of 1500, in many centres of population, urban and rural, the old outline of spires and towers was being redrawn. In 1480 the parishioners of Chetwode took possession of the old priory church, closed these past twenty years, as their new place of worship.[17] The enforced closure of religious houses was not at all unprecedented. Their own leadership had always recognised dissolution as a necessary tool for financial administration and domestic discipline. If the material or human resources of a monastery should fail, it should be shut down. In the later Middle Ages, dissolution was also taken up as an instrument by the structures of regional and national authority that were wrapped around the congregations and orders of religious, in the secular Church, landowning lordship and royal government. During the Hundred Years War the Crown closed as many as seventy priories, which had been founded by northern French abbeys after the Norman Conquest as colonial outposts to oversee their new English lands. Edward III (1327–77) dismissed no fewer than fifty religious communities; his great grandson, Henry V, still pursuing the same ambitions in France, seized the remainder under statute, although it fell to the government of his son to complete their sequestration.[18]

The recovery and redeployment of monastic resources offered a new pattern that was followed now by prelates, nobles and successive contenders for the Crown in the conflict that preceded the Tudor triumph of 1485. One of the less familiar results of these years of dynastic battles and civil disturbance was the creation of more than a dozen new ecclesiastical foundations – chantries, chapels, collegiate churches, university colleges and schools – from religious houses that had been dissolved. At Eton, Cambridge, Oxford and on the building site of the new Tudor chantry – Lady chapel, almshouses, etc. – opposite the palace of Westminster, the generation that came of age with Henry VIII already had more than a glimpse of how the old monastic environment might be redeveloped.[19]

The closure of twenty-nine monasteries by Thomas Wolsey, archbishop of York and Cardinal legate of England between 1524 and 1528, is sometimes seen as a point of departure, perhaps even the certain prelude to the dissolutions of 1536–40. It provoked public comment: 'You do them wrong and no right / To put them thus to flyght', declared the prominent satirist, John Skelton, in his *Colin Cloute*, 'So that theyr founders soules / have lost theyr beade rolles'.[20] Thomas

4

Starkey, a commentator who, unlike Skelton, wrote from within the Tudor court circle, speculated on the potential for wealthy monasteries, such as 'Westmester & saynt Albonys & many other . . . thus use turne[d]' to 'instruct thys uthe to whome schold come the governance aftur of thys our commeyn wele'.[21] Provincial proprietors were stirred by so large a land grab. Sir Thomas Darcy of Temple Hirst (South Yorkshire) – site of a Hospitaller preceptory and a short distance from the tiny, vulnerable Augustinian house of Drax (North Yorkshire) – railed at the 'abomination, ruin and seditious and erroneous violations used at the pulling down of abbeys', as he compiled his own case against prevailing authority that anticipated his support for the Pilgrimage of Grace in the next decade.[22] At Bayham (East Sussex) there was an armed stand-off as canons of the abbey and some of their tenants refused to hand over the site and its properties.[23] The mood on the Sussex-Kent border was so febrile for a time that the king's chancellor, William Warham, feared sedition coming over the horizon.[24] '[It] was not done without some Disquiet, as everybody knoweth' was the memory that passed into the family history of the Wyatts (descendants of Sir Thomas, d. 1554) first written down more than a lifetime later.[25]

Yet Wolsey's suppressions were nothing more than a continuation of the now established pattern of redeploying the resources of the Church. There was no doubt or double-meaning in their purpose: the property and revenue of these houses were to be taken to create a new endowment for twinned colleges at Ipswich and Oxford, a Wolseyan replica of Henry VI's Eton and King's College, Cambridge. 'Exile and small' was Wolsey's view of the targeted monasteries.[26] It may be that twenty of the houses held five or fewer religious; of these some may have been effectively deserted.[27] Certainly there was scarcely the population to keep up a conventional observant routine. Some such houses had originated as outposts of French abbeys and had been left lacking purpose, and protection, when these ties were cut after the Hundred Years War. There was indiscipline that demanded decisive reform: at Littlemore (Oxfordshire) the prioress lived with her lover and their child.[28] Several of the larger houses were the dependencies of great abbeys and had long been vulnerable. As a group they were as ripe for redeployment as any of those taken to make new foundations over the past half-century.[29]

Wolsey did not plan a fundamental breach with the kingdom's monastic history. Rather he looked to the recent past, to the chantries and colleges conceived by the great and good of the Yorkist and Tudor hierarchy, and perhaps to his own personal history, as an *alumnus* of Oxford's Magdalen College, which had 'prospered and increased' him so.[30] Magdalen had been raised in 1480 on the footprint and the income of old monastic foundations whose day was deemed to have passed. '[Their] use … be converted', Wolsey reflected to Bishop Gardiner, almost at the last, 'wherof so greate benefite & commoditie shal issue unto [the king's] reame and subjectes'.[31] Clearly Wolsey planned to continue on this path when the schemes at Ipswich and Oxford were secure. In the last of a sequence of papal faculties issued to him in 1528, he was given authority to suppress monasteries of fewer than six residents and to merge those housing between six and twelve.[32]

The local disturbance in the Weald soon subsided and any alarm in political society turned on the prodigality of the Cardinal. Compiling his *Anglia Historia* scarcely five years later, Polydore Vergil (*c.* 1470–1550) bewailed Wolsey's puffed-up pride (Volsaeus … superbia elatus); he made no mention of these monastic measures.[33] Skelton, the Cardinal's former protégé, was settling his own score. There was nothing in Starkey's reflections that reached as far as a rejection of the perpetual foundation or the principle of religious vows.

What began before Easter 1536 was quite different in its reach, pace and purpose. By Michaelmas of that year almost 200 houses were in the throes of sequestration. The enforcement of the first statute was arrested in 1537 by the acute emergencies of popular protest and plague, so the number of closures fell by almost 75 per cent over the next twelve months. But the unstinting attrition of the commissioners counted its cost and before the end of 1538 more than twice that number of monasteries had made voluntary surrenders; alongside them virtually every one of the 180 convents of the friars.[34] Only fifteen houses were still standing in King Henry's fifth decade.[35] There was a chain at the western and the eastern edges of England, from Chester down to Bristol, from Thetford (Norfolk) down to Canterbury Cathedral, flanking the central and southern counties whose abbeys, priories, friaries and hospitals had now stood empty, silent and shut up for upwards of six months. Before January 1539 was out the western chain of houses was gone; then through February and March the remnant on the east, from north to south.

Ultimately, these interventions were also different in their motivation. Henry and Cromwell first framed the dissolution with the same, familiar rationale of financial efficiency and reform which had been used by Wolsey, and before him back over generations by other bishops, royal governments and the religious orders themselves. Yet even as the statute of 1536 made its way through parliament there was sharpening focus on the financial rewards of a total suppression. There was also a new conviction that monastic men and women should not be merely redeployed in houses of a better size and standard of discipline, but should 'change their coat', and 'apply themselfys', in the words of Thomas Starkey, 'to some . . . honest fascyon of lyvyng, approvyd by gud and polytyke ordur'.[36] There was no precedent in England's past for such secularisation, that is the release from vows that had been made to last a lifetime and the permitted return to a life in the world. By the summer of 1538, these outlooks were lending momentum to widespread closures of houses. For a time the king and Cromwell may have continued to ponder just how widespread they should be, but the commitment of those they charged with the task, and the constant attrition of the regulars' resources and resolve, outpaced them. To the king's commissioners, the remaining religious houses, and society looking on, the dissolution seemed a fait accompli before their actions made it so.

The removal of England's medieval religious houses was carried out against the background of an assault on the regular orders that advanced across much of north-west Europe after the outbreak of war in Saxony in 1525. The king and his counsellors were well aware of this movement and sought to know something of the principles that drove it, particularly in the minds of the ruling princes, as well as the practical measures of policy that made it possible. 'There is an abbot, whose monastery . . . has been torched and [he and his convent] cast in chains' (abbatem quoque . . . cuius monasterium . . . combustum est in vincula coniecerunt), runs a now-damaged report sent from Munich as early as September 1533.[37] Thomas Legh was dispatched to Hamburg in 1534, from where he gathered general intelligence, or 'the newes that be in this parties', of Hesse, Saxony, Denmark and 'Swevyn' (Sweden).[38] The Crown's busiest European agent, Christopher Mont, was even called upon to translate contemporary German annals, so that Cromwell could fully grasp recent acts of state.[39] By this date it was also apparent to a wider, reading public that 'these Lutheran faccyons . . . throwe downe all monasteries & churches making coyne of crosses . . . with one assent of certeyne princes'.[40] Henry saw his policy as much a part of a continental phenomenon as to pass advice on the matter to his nephew, King James V of Scotland. His chosen courier, whose own enthusiasm for reform would have lent weight to the king's counsel, was William Barlow, prior of Bisham (Berkshire).[41]

Yet in many respects the experience in England was the exception to what emerged as the European rule for the dissolution of monasteries. It was unmatched in its scale.

The monastic and mendicant presence confronted by the Scandinavian monarchs amounted to scarcely 200 houses in total between the three kingdoms of Denmark, Norway and Sweden; their population by the sixteenth century was perhaps below 3,000.[42] There were nearly twice as many in the German principalities, although the overall population may have been no larger in 1517, since a high proportion were now poor and poorly maintained.[43] By comparison, in mainland England alone there were twenty times as many houses, with each one of the orders of medieval Europe represented by several hundred men and women. The English houses were not wealthier but the number, variety and distribution of their properties made dissolution a disturbance of social and economic life in every region, urban and rural. As a shockwave shared countrywide, it recalled only moments in the remote past, the Black Death, nearly 200 years distant, or the conquest of the Normans another three centuries beyond that. The dissolution in northern Europe was also outpaced by Tudor England. Even within the crucible of reformed religious practice, of Martin Luther's Saxony, the end of regular religious life was gradual.[44] After the conflagration of 1525, houses were rebuilt, and those persisting in their vows permitted to live out their former life undisturbed. Reform was a fragile cause; some regions saw a complete reversal. Nowhere was the vowed life extinguished in just four years.

The reoccupation in England of seven conventual buildings by scarcely a hundred monks, nuns and friars of five congregations (Benedictine, Birgittine, Carthusian, Dominican and Observant Franciscan) between the spring of 1555 and the first months of 1558 can hardly be thought of as the undoing of the Henrician dissolution.[45] All but one of these new communities were gathered at the centre point of Marian authority, safely inside the curtain of royal palaces that ran across the capital from Greenwich to Westminster, and to the north and west, from King's Langley (Hertfordshire) to Richmond (Surrey). Indeed, contemporary witnesses leave the impression that it was less a corporate revival, more the resumption of a particular, metropolitan pattern of life, of Passion plays and torchlit processions described by Henry Machyn.[46] There were only two such communities that briefly flickered into life beyond this area, both when Queen Mary was already dying: at Dartford (Kent), where the Dominican women of King's Langley moved momentarily, and Southampton, where Observants lived for perhaps eight weeks. Other prospects for a provincial revival, at St Albans, Glastonbury and Tewkesbury, faded almost as soon as they surfaced.[47] There was no organic movement for the restoration of the regulars. It was an orchestrated performance, cast almost exclusively from self-conscious Catholic exiles and a handful of youngsters who had no first-hand knowledge of the monastic and mendicant experience before 1540. Fewer than twenty of the old hands who had reconciled themselves with the Tudor reforms were inclined to turn again from their pensioned life in provincial parishes. Tellingly, some were so slow to act that the scenes at Richmond and Westminster were almost over before they arrived.[48] The weakness of the queen's renewed order was conspicuous as several, including some of the leadership, did not live even as long as the queen herself.[49] The spectacle of the Marian restoration confirms that the causes of the regular religious congregations and their perpetual endowment had been defeated decisively nearly twenty years before.

The dissolution in England is the most visible drama of the Tudor reformations and stands in sharp relief on a European stage, and yet it is the least well-documented of all. There is no first-hand account of any moment in the regime's final assault on the religious houses, from the first systematic suppressions carried out under parliamentary statute in the spring of 1536, the surrender of the orders of the friars in the autumn of 1538, the execution of three abbots of prominent Benedictine abbeys in the winter of 1539, to the sudden but subdued end of the last standing in 1540. It is telling of the attitude of some of the principal actors that a unique cartoon depicting the Crown's judgement on the monasteries, drawn as a frame for a post-dissolution survey of Colchester Abbey (Essex), was made as a copy of Lucas van Leyden's 1515 engraving of the biblical triumph of Mordecai (Esther 8:15).[50] A number of the annals kept in London and provincial towns mark these moments but only baldly, as matters of fact. In his early (1543) chronicle of the reign the printer, Richard Grafton, misremembered the order of events, recording the year that 'all freers and monkes chaunged' as 1538.[51] The course of events moved quickly, too much so, perhaps, to be carefully chronicled. Thomas Cromwell was arrested nine weeks after the closure of Waltham. Much of his archive, not least his personal letters, has been lost; not, perhaps, accidentally.[52] There still remain plenty that were written to him by the agents he employed in the dissolution, but hardly any of his replies.

Cromwell was not the only principal actor to pass quickly from the scene. Three of his most diligent lieutenants, Richard Leighton, Thomas Legh and John London, did not long outlive the dissolution. In 1543 London was implicated in a plot against Archbishop Thomas Cranmer and judged with them to have become, in Bale's vivid condemnation, 'a wylye watterer of the Popes olde garden', he 'ended his naughty life in prison'.[53] Leighton was appointed the king's ambassador to France and then to Flanders where he died in 1544. Legh's loyal service won him a knighthood and a parliamentary seat, but nearly ten years as a king's commissioner took their toll and he was so sick in his last year (1545) it was thought he was already dead.[54] The same year saw the death of Richard Ingworth, the Franciscan who changed his habit to help effect the end of all four orders of the friars in 1538–39; he disappears from the public record entirely after 1540.[55] Several of the leading heads of religious houses were also dead less than five years after the last of the dissolutions. Of the 'great and solemn' monasteries, John Reve of Bury St Edmunds (Suffolk) was dead before monastic life itself was over (his will was dated 26 March 1540); Robert Fuller of Waltham died before the end of the same year; William Benson of Westminster was an invalid from 1542 and finally died in 1549.[56] There were a handful for whom the dissolution did open a career: John Scudamore (d. 1571), who led the commissions in the West Midlands and the northern March of Wales, served parliament and the Council of Wales as far as Queen Elizabeth's reign. Richard Rich (d. 1567), chancellor of the Court of Augmentations, rose to a barony and the chancellorship under Edward VI and was privy councillor in Elizabeth's first years. William Petre (d. 1572), who contributed to the dissolution commissioners in the West Country, served each of the Tudor monarchs and only retired as Queen Elizabeth's principal secretary almost ten years into her reign.[57] These long lives have yielded some personal papers, although only Scudamore can be followed closely on his Cromwellian commissions through the chance survival of one of his memoranda books.[58]

Later phases of reform robbed government departments of the little control they held over their account books. The Court of Augmentations, the instrument designed for the dissolution of monasteries, was itself dismantled little more than a dozen years after the last of the closures. Its records passed into the Exchequer, where they were placed in parallel classes and in many instances left largely untouched until the creation of the Public Records in 1838. Even then archival attention was limited to the bundling and gathering into guard books of folded parchment and paper booklets and scraps that are unusually ragged and stained, the legacy of their having been made and held together on the hoof.

Like any moment of sudden disturbance to the familiar patterns of life, those who lived through the years of the dissolution saw only a simple transaction of cause and effect. 'Suppressed and dissolved by authority of parliament and . . . the most dread and unconquered prince and lord', asserted the clerk of the Colchester Court Roll with disproportionate force, in a reference to meadowland held by St Botolph's Priory.[59] 'The abbies went doune because of their pride', ran an anonymous verse which the scholar, Stephen Batman (d. 1584), collected in his commonplace book, around the middle years of the century.[60] Early in the years of Henry's son, Edward VI, Hugh Latimer (1487–1555), bishop of Worcester, shared his memories of the monasteries now ten years past and more: 'abominable', 'foolery' and 'a mad thing'; they had disappeared because of what they were. 'Their enormities were so great . . . there was nothing [to be done] but down with them.'[61] The first printed histories of Henry's reign set this view into narrative. 'For there be houses suppressed where God was well served', Edward Hall, whose history was first printed in 1545, explained of the first act of dissolution, 'but where most vice, mischief and abhominacion of liuyng was used' and 'these were as thornes [and] the great . . . were putrified old okes and they must nedes folowe'.[62] Raphael Holinshed (c. 1525–80?) was so matter of fact that he scarcely troubled to comment on their passing at all: all 'formes of counterfeyte' and 'the cloyfters and houfes that contained them were fuppreffed and put downe'.[63] John Stow (c. 1524–1605), whose *Annales* were first printed in 1592, was still more terse: each step of dissolution was to be seen in the same way as a 'grant to the king and his heirs'.[64]

Their language echoed the statutory law that was the lever of the dissolution, and this generation, the last to have any first-hand knowledge of religious houses, fixed their fate as one scene in the general drama of the making of the Tudors' new imperial monarchy and their new English Church. They gave only glancing attention to the regulars themselves, to reaffirm what was, by the act of their dissolution, already a given fact: they were simply a 'host of Satan', in Holinshed's words, that had set against their 'liege lord'. By contrast, for those at the front line of the continuing conflict over the government of the Church and the practice of religion, the figures of the religious orders were the reason for recalling the dissolution at all.[65] 'Whoremongers, bawdes, brybers, idolaters, hypocrytes, trayters and most fylthye Gomorreanes,' spat John Bale (1495–1563) in the preface to his *Votaryes* (1551), the first printed work with a wide readership to reflect at length on the institutions that had been dissolved.[66] The 'abominable practices . . . fantasyes, and lyes' that were the cause of reformation were the 'deceytfull workemanshyp' of such as these 'monkes, with other dysgysed locustes of the same generacion' whose 'contynuall stodye, labour and sekynge was always to blynde'. Catholic opinion occupied the same ground. Nicholas Sander (*c.* 1530–81), whose *De origine* was the first Romanist history of Henry's reformation to be written (although it was not published until 1596), represented the fate of the religious houses as the king's principal crime: 'a profane carnage of this Nebuchanezzar', razing the very institution from which the English had first received their Christian faith (a quo Christianae fidem Angli acciperunt).[67]

These polemics were repeatedly reprinted during Elizabeth's forty-four-year reign but her generation, those who did not know or could hardly remember the religious orders at first hand, came to look on the dissolution in a different light. Against the background of the 1559 settlement and the later penal statutes, there was no ready acceptance of the arguments of the Catholic apologists, but both chronicles and contemporary commentary showed a degree of detachment and even expressed some regret. William Camden (1551–1623) wrote of the kingdom's medieval past from his position in the new Queen's College of Westminster housed in the refectory of the old Benedictine abbey. In his *Britannia* (1586) he described the churches and convents of the old orders free from the frame of reformist disapproval; sometimes – at Walsingham, and also in the city of London – he was moved to reflect, almost, it seemed, to mourn the dramatic change in their circumstances. Here, there was some estimation of loss that later editors and translators would amplify into outright criticism. Others around him were already more pointed. In his *Survey of London* (1598), John Stow displayed an unmistakable nostalgia for the monastic landscape of his boyhood. His descriptions seemed to dwell on the downgrade of the convents and courts of the city friaries for commercial and industrial use.[68] John Speed (*c.* 1551–1629) was the most outspoken: in his *Historie of Great Britaine*, printed in 1611 but compiled earlier, he recalled how the world had 'stood amazed at . . . the sudden deluge of those tempestuous times. . . . The waste of so much of Gods reuenewe (however abused)' was nothing less than 'this king's [Henry's] ill'.[69] Speed's judgement was not far removed even from the viewpoint of the exiled leadership of English Catholics. Robert Persons (often called Parsons, 1546–1610), rector of the English College at Rome, was not uncritical of the old orders but in his *Memorial for the Reformation of England* (written in 1596, published in 1690) he condemned 'the inestimable damage that ensued to our commonwealth', and called upon his countrymen to halt the destruction that had already occurred and 'restore and amend all that is wanting'.[70]

Nor was the public, printed discourse out of step with private and popular opinion. 'The estate of the realm hath come to more misery since King Henry his time than ever it did in all the time before,' opined Michael Sherbrook, rector of Wickersley (South Yorkshire) in a personal memoir written in 1577.[71] His retelling of the king's reformation in general, and the particular moment of the dissolution of the Cistercian abbey at Roche (South Yorkshire), was founded on family and community memories. Its disarming, embittered attack on the Tudor achievement has been read as a reflection of the continuing non-conformity of the north that would soon be transposed into recusancy and sedition. Yet it might as well be seen as a heightened expression of a nostalgia that was widespread at the close of the century. On the popular stage the cowled religious could now appear as a source of timeless wisdom and be permitted to invoke 'Holy St Francis ...!': the words of William Shakespeare's Friar Lawrence in *The tragedy of Romeo and Juliet*, II. iii. 1125 (1595). The most successful satire of Elizabeth's last decade, the anonymous *The tragedy of Arden of Faversham* (1592), skewered those who profited from the dissolution rather than those who had been dissolved. The fond attachment to their lost world deepened as the century turned and the settlement of Elizabeth's Church came under strain. John Weever's *Antient funeral monuments*, completed during the reign of James I/VI but not published until 1631, was, above all, a commemoration of the religious houses. He digressed from the advertised topic to tell the story of monasticism in England from its first beginnings to its end, 'rooted up and battered downe ... despoiled ... leaving religion naked bare and unclad'.[72] Six years later Andrew Marvell (1621–78) conjured up an image of the 'suttle nuns' of Nun Appleton (North Yorkshire) who professed to their 'happy vow', 'in shining armour white / Like virgin Amazons ... Each one a spouse, each one a queen'. Their 'instant dispossession' he likened to the end of an 'inchantment'.[73]

The first critical history to trace the course of the dissolution came only after the complete collapse of the institutional Church. Thomas Fuller's (1608–61) *Church-history of Britain* was published in 1655, as England continued under the Commonwealth. It offered not only the first full account of the fate of the religious houses but also the most complete treatment of monastic life in England to appear before the twentieth century. Fuller turned the sixth book of his history into a self-contained seven-part 'History of Abbeys', two-thirds of which weighed the causes and consequences of the Tudor suppressions. He began with Wolsey, to whom he (wrongly) attributed no fewer than forty dissolutions, that 'made all the forest of religious foundations in England to shake'.[74] He followed their fortunes through the policies of Henry VIII and each one of his children, to their final end under Elizabeth, and their new beginning in the exiled communities established on the European mainland. Fuller was well placed in patronage and proximity to the institutions of church and state, and he was able to pick over some of the principal papers of the dissolution for the first time, such as the returns of the 'Valor ecclesiasticus' (1535) and even the dispatches of Cromwell's commissioners. It seems he had it in mind to offer the first and last word on the subject: he jibed at himself that his history had expanded like the religious houses themselves, which 'engrossed the third part of the land', and judged that 'this old and trite subject is now grown out of fashion, men in our age having got a new object'. His verdict on the 'dissolving of abbeys' extended the detachment of the Elizabethans. 'The generality of monasteries [were] notoriously vicious', albeit there were exceptions, 'black swans', as Fuller called them, but their historical and cultural value had been great, and for their libraries and books alone 'Our posterity may well curse this wicked fact of our age, this unreasonable spoil of England's most noble antiquities.' The wickedness was Henry VIII's, whom Fuller depicted as 'ancient, diseased, choleric and curious in trifles', the cause of 'miscarriages and misdemenaours' and, in the sequestration of the goods and properties of the religious houses, a Danaean 'shower' of dissipation.[75]

Fuller was fearful of being found to favour 'monkery', to be no better than 'Lot's wife looking back with a farewell glance on the filthy city of Sodom'. In fact, his questioning of the case for, and the consequences of, the dissolution was matched in the most influential histories that followed. Sir William Dugdale (1605–86) and Wenceslas Hollar's title-page to the *Monasticon Anglicanum* challenged the very premise of dissolution, displaying the Ovidian tag, 'non omnia grandior aetas quae fugiamus habet' (not everything of ages past should we shun).[76] In his *History of the Reformation* (the first volume of which was published in 1679) Gilbert Burnet (1643–1715) declared King Henry's conduct of the dissolution to be 'one of the great blemishes of the reign'.[77] This historical representation of the dissolution as a matter of regret that redounded on the reputation of the Tudors shaped a social memory that surely accounts for the popularity of the unapologetically Catholic history of Thomas Ward, *England's Reformation* (1710), whose verses taught how:

Scarce stone on stone or brick on brick
Was left of any one Fabrick

Save here and there a bit of wall
To Shew a glorious abbey's fall.
Oh! Lofty towers, and sacred piles
That once adorn'd our happy iles
Who can record your over-turning
But in deep sighs and bitter mourning.[78]

These sentiments carried into the nineteenth century, still seeming to bridge the confessional divide. The Catholic Augustus Welby Pugin (1812–52) saw the Tudor dissolution as the first cause of the decline in architecture and art that he traced in his *Contrasts* (1836). Framing his history with words from Thomas Ward and documents he found in Fuller, he saw it simply as a 'fall', a 'spell ... broken'.[79] There was at least a hint of his sense of a lost enchantment to Thomas Carlyle's (1795–1881) lament, in *Past and Present* (1843), that 'the gospel of Richard Arkwright once promulgated, no monk of the old sort is any longer possible in this world'.[80] For a popular readership, Mr Punch's first *Comic History of England* (1847) reaffirmed the reputation of King Henry, drawing him as Jorrocks, the irrepressible huntsman featured in the comic novels of R. S. Surtees (see Fig. 1). It was perhaps with an awareness of a new monastic sympathy advancing into Anglican drawing rooms that the non-conformist antiquarian Thomas Wright (1810–77) presented his transcripts of letters from Cromwell's commissioners to subscribers to the newly formed Camden Society in 1843. 'The worst crimes laid to the charge of the monks are but too fully verified by the long chain of historical evidence', he urged his readership, and 'amid the religious disputes which at present agitate the world ... ought to be made public'.[81]

Wright was a pioneer of archival research, and the rise of professional academic history in the second half of the century continued to uncover the surviving documents of the dissolution. The development of the discipline occurred in conjunction with a public enterprise to organise and publish archival records and histories of national importance. From 1862 the Stationery Office began to print a calendar of the records held in the Public Records and the British Museum of the reign of Henry VIII.[82] These collections collated the surviving documents of the dissolution period for the first time and attempted to place them in a chronological order. The result was, and was intended to be, a new narrative outline of events that could be recovered from the abstracted documents alone. The first generation of academic historians, committed, *ex officio*, to the articulation of a new national history, formed a fresh account of Henry's reformation from these foundations. It was only to be expected, given the evidence before them, that they emphasised the clear direction of the policy of dissolution, its certain, uncontested, execution, and the scale, scope and sustained supervision of its material returns. Their vision of a government at work challenged the old notion of an ageing, bad king at his autocratic worst. It also tended to diminish the significance of the dissolution as an achievement of his reign. The calendared papers of the king, his counsellors and commissions appeared to show that it was accomplished speedily and with a minimum of fuss. Moreover, the relatively few dispatches from the front line that were swept up into the public records appeared only to reinvigorate the original case of the reformers, that the end of monastic life in England was not only necessary but, as their iniquities were laid bare, also inevitable. '[They] perished,' wrote James Froude (1818–94), 'of their proper worthlessness.'[83] The removal of the religious houses was itself rendered secondary to the rejection of the papal supremacy and the shaping of the new, imperial Crown.

This Reformation history found a wide readership at the end of the nineteenth century. It caused a reaction from Catholic apologists and High Church men who reaffirmed the earlier characterisations, of the religious as victims of a 'reign of terror' and Henry VIII as a 'wicked monster'.[84] In turn, this drew a damning response from academic authorities, as a challenge to the placement of the dissolution as a keystone of the Anglican state, and also because it appeared to question their professional judgement in their reading of the public records. 'A naked statement of primary moral necessity' was the verdict of George Coulton (1858–1947), a leading public historian and ordained Church of England priest; to see it differently was to be taken in by 'sentimental pictures' and worse, to fall below 'the best standards of continental [by which he also understood contemporary] scholarship'.[85] A popular, Catholic historian of the next generation, David Knowles (1898–1974), looked for common ground, drawing on a growing body of evidence discovered outside the Stationery Office calendars that could deepen understanding, both of the character of the regulars in the sixteenth century and the positions taken against them.[86] But the conviction that the dissolution was one of the more straightforward facts of Henry's reign held firm, and as the political and public force of the old confessional arguments faded fast, the focus of debate shifted sharply from institutions to individuals, to the reformation of the people.

Valuable evidence from the regions of England appeared to affirm the rightness of this new frontier, and perhaps edged the institutional story further to the margins, given how far any trace of it appeared to be confined to the State Papers.

The agency of Tudor government has since been reasserted. Returning to the great guard books (bound books designed to contain document fragments and scraps) of correspondence passing in and out of government, the origins and objectives of a policy of reformation have been re-examined. As might be expected from such a maddeningly unrepresentative muddle of fair-copy letters and scribbled dispatches, contrasting, even conflicting readings have emerged. The king himself has been redrawn but in several, quite different aspects: a ruler so determined to seize the wealth of the Church that he feigned interest in reform to reassure a conservative commons;[87] a moderate reformer who was not mutable, susceptible to indecision, distraction or undue influence as often claimed, but who from the first was after a 'middle way between Rome and Wittemberg';[88] yet one whose conviction for the case for reform was cast-iron, his particular contempt for monks years in the making, and his priority in the dissolution to compel them to confess the error of their ways;[89] a character lacking the commitment and consistency to make policy, 'liable to shift without warning', who became detached from the reform devised in his name.[90]

Cromwell, for so long monastic England's cynical, clinical executioner, has been recast in more varied roles: the natural heir to his first master, Wolsey, in his learned ability to handle the religious orders, in spite of their independent traditions, to the advantage of the Crown;[91] a religious radical and patron of radicals whose commitment to his and their cause cost him his life;[92] a believer more like the majority of Henry's subjects, whose thinking on the Church was both traditional and 'somewhat anticlerical' but not strong enough to shift the course of the king;[93] not principled at all but pragmatic and ruthless, pursuing the interest of the Crown especially where it intersected with his own.[94] An investigation of the visitation of 1535 and the origins of the suppression statute of the following year has questioned Cromwell's capacity to orchestrate policy as well as he could conceive its central theme. Perhaps it was the servants of this vast undertaking, and not its master, who first perceived its problems and proposed its solutions. It was the high-functioning cogs in the government machine, it has been suggested, who made this phase of reformation 'an extraordinary administrative achievement'.[95] Still, these fresh forays into the State Papers have reaffirmed the familiar role of the king as the principal source of inspiration and influence in the enterprise.[96] His will commanded Cromwell, himself now reduced to a 'much less unique figure', a 'conventional Tudor man-of-business' who just happened to prove an able, faithful and, above all, tireless officer of the Crown.[97]

The renewal of the debate about the architects of reformation has been counter-balanced recently by fresh research into the response of the society they ruled. While the royal regime has been represented as animated by decided opinions and plans, its subjects have emerged from the record of local and personal reactions as the very opposite: instinctively detached from causes of any kind, whether they were a matter of ideas or of institutions, and less political than practical and narrowly personal in the face of enforced change. Monasteries, like many other long-standing features of traditional culture, were more in their sights than in their minds; there was 'little clear evidence of admiration or rejection'.[98] The subjection of these houses to the Crown and subsequently their closure stirred a neighbourhood most when it seemed to threaten its self-conscious separation from government and national affairs. When, less often than not, people involved themselves in the drama, their motives were found only in a minority. For the others mere expediency prevailed.[99] The dissolution, and the transformation of other religious, cultural and social fabric, accrued meaning at a distance, as recalled by generations with little or no knowledge of it at first hand.[100]

These studies have returned the dissolution to the foreground of Henry's reformation yet they have kept the monasteries themselves largely out of view. The story of their fate still seems to be confined to the business of the Crown and its government; its impact, like so many of the changes of these years, has become a construction of those who came after rather than the lived experience – with all its undoubted turn and turnabout – of those who saw it unfold. This approach has tended to fix the profile of monasticism and its position in the English landscape in the light of its ultimate extinction: the religious houses are regarded much as the original reformers saw them, as a remnant of medieval tradition which the early modern age of the Tudors decisively cut away. The aim of this book is to trace their end from their own point of view. It recovers their people – the professed religious and those whose lives were tied to them – from the same few fragments of first-hand documents from which the characters of Henry and Cromwell have been so colourfully drawn. At the same time, it extends the field of vision following the imprint of the regulars in the archives and material record of regional England

and Wales.[101] Monastic foundations, and religious professions, were expressions of individual impulses in particular localities, and these contexts, each one not exactly the same as another, had a bearing on the manner in which both came to an end. Adopting the perspective of the abbey, priory or friary precinct and its neighbourhood is not intended to diminish the role of the Tudor regime: the purpose is not to offer a partisan rejection of the king's reformation. But it does signal that the course and consequences of the process were far less certain than that characterisation encourages, and it suggests that the agency that has been attached to policy, ideology and the government machine should be qualified. Tudor England did not stand at one remove from the monastic tradition; in many respects it was a monastic society. The professed religious were agents in their own cause, and when, how and how far they passed from the scene, in what ways they remained within it and even how they were remembered, was at least in part of their making.

This is a study of the end of the monasteries in England and Wales; Henry Tudor governed four counties of Ireland and the English presence there had shaped the history of their religious houses, but the manner of their passing, like that of their first beginning, was a uniquely Irish story.[102] The book is arranged in three parts: Part I explores the place of the monasteries in Tudor society, how and what people thought of them; why so many individuals still joined them and what kind of life they found there; and what impact these institutions and their ways had on the locality, lives and livelihoods around them.

Part II begins by exploring the regulars' relationship with the Tudor regime. Before the Break with Rome, perhaps even before the accession of Henry VIII in 1509, the terms of engagement had already begun to change. By 1534, the monastic estate had experienced searching and sustained interventions in its affairs. Henry's headship itself was no less of a shock when it came, but the monastic hierarchies may have considered their fortunes were now aligned with the king's aims. Perhaps especially for the leadership of the great independent abbeys and cathedral priories, the reforms imposed in 1535 signalled not the end of their way of life but its new beginning. Against this background, the prospect of a total dissolution in the years that followed was by no means assured; even after the closure of more than a quarter of the foundations in 1536–7, the remainder continued with little alteration to their accustomed institutional or religious operations. The drift of government policy caused a crisis of confidence in the future of the friaries that had proved fatal within a year, but it was not enough to destabilise the remaining monasteries. The timing of the final closures could not have been predicted even six months before.

Part III traces the early consequences of the extinction of regular religion. Like the Tudor government's handling of the process itself, the effects did not unfold as might have been expected – or hoped. Even as Edward VI's advisors embarked on a second stage of reformation in 1547, aspects of the old monastic England were still visible. Perhaps it was the men and women who had populated it who changed first. Most of them who lived on adapted themselves to the new dispensation of 1540, just as they had done to those changes that preceded it – far enough at least not to look to reverse it.

PART I

I

THE LEGEND OF THE CLOISTER

Sir Galahad rode non-stop for four days until his horse brought him to an abbey built from bright white stones. 'There was he receyved with grete reverence' and 'made of hym grete solace and . . . souper.' 'On the morne they aroose and herde masse.' In the abbey church 'behynde an aulter' Galahad spied a great shield, 'as whyte as ony snowe', emblazoned with a cross of red, which, he later learned, was painted with the blood of Joseph of Arimathea, 'that was sent by Jesus Christ into this land'.[1]

The tales of Arthur and the knights of Camelot, 'fresh printed' by William Caxton in the year of the Tudor succession, 1485, expressed much of what it was to be a subject of this new England: the heir to a kingdom of great antiquity; a character at once independent and indomitable; a tradition of Christianity so venerable it had been touched by those who knew the Messiah at first hand; and a landscape that was itself a treasury of true history. Caxton's preface was imperious: 'in hym that shold say or thynke that there was never suche a king callyd Arthur might wel be aretted grete folye and blyndenesse . . . ye may see his sepulture in the monasterye of Glastynburye and in the abbey of Westmestre . . . the prynte of his seal in reed waxe'.[2]

The people of Tudor England were charged with greater knowledge than their forebears. More of them were literate and learned: many of the men had acquired a formal education; well-born women were multilingual readers and writers. They were at ease with new technology introduced from the European mainland and originating in the East: gunpowder, print and double-entry bookkeeping.[3] Yet still they based their fundamental understanding of their world not on deeper study or new discoveries but simply on the impressions they absorbed from the people and places that had surrounded them since birth. Such were the unreasoned knowledge and unproven values created and conveyed by stories, sights and other sensory experiences, shared across the community and down the generations. Here began their idea of Christianity – before the teaching and worship of the institutional Church washed over them – and of kingship, knighthood and national identity. Here too was their first encounter with a house of religion. The legends of their cloisters were as extraordinary as Galahad's; and at the accession of the Tudors this was not faded, dusty history. Like Caxton's modish Malory-for-the-times, the matter of the monasteries seemed very much alive.

The Henrician Reformation is still thought of by many as the moment when the old age of medieval England was swept away. The regime of Henry VIII, his counsellors, Crown officials, most of the nobility and gentry and a good many of his subjects shook off the traditions of their forebears. Learning, literacy, at least some self-determination in their own labour and sources of income, and a line of sight to the wider world made possible not only by the success of the press but also a settled peace in the kingdom gave this generation ambition, independence and a thirst for change. When they turned their attention to the religious houses left in their locality by their ancestors, at once they concluded there could be no place for them in their new world. Their removal, however it was done, was surely inevitable.

This account has endured because it is so compelling in its perfect alignment of cause and effect. But in the light of what has survived of these people, their behaviour and, above all, their patterns of thought, it does seem at odds with lived experience. In the first fifty years of Tudor rule people did relate to monks, nuns and friars in ways which would have seemed different, and sometimes threatening, in centuries past. In their mind's eye, and in the practical arrangement of their affairs, the Henrician generation kept the regulars in their place, so as not to encroach on the domains that were equally important to them: parish, family and home. When they did do business with them they were quick to declare their rights and to demand their fair share. The Tudors' worldly knowledge and understanding did not leave them contemptuous of those living under vows but it did help them to recognise their human frailties.

Yet these new relations took shape while ideas of the religious orders which would have been familiar to their ancestors still persisted. In fact, some of the forces so often thought to have eroded old cultural and social attitudes – prosperity, travel and the availability of printed books – sometimes acted to refresh and renew them. Their survival, and even their revival, shaped the surprising course of the dissolution. It is the reason why the religious communities did not suffer the sudden severance which silenced some of Henry's individual challengers on the scaffold. It explains how the king himself was inspired to create new monasteries in the summer of 1537 after closing almost 200 over the previous year. It was why Thomas Cromwell continued to cogitate over the contribution of the largest abbeys and priories to the changing realm as late as the winter of 1538–39. And it was the prompt for those too young to have known a living medieval monastery to plan for their restoration less than a year before the accession of the monarch who would lead them into a new Protestant world.

If they were of no other significance to their Tudor neighbours, the religious houses held some meaning as features of their landscape. They were never only scenery; for many they were the very substance of their own home. The houses of religion were the oldest of all in many places and to those living among them their physical presence defined the locality as much as any natural feature. At Canterbury the precinct of the cathedral monastery and its watercourses had fixed the position of streets, shops and residential tenements for as long as anyone could remember.[4] The triangular Trinity Bridge which the community of monks constructed at Crowland (Lincolnshire) was the superstructure of the town, directing a confluence of water that made settlement possible and permanent.[5] The bridge at Burton over the Trent (Staffordshire), 'of grett length with many arches', was its lifeblood, as the monastery that raised it reminded the townspeople when it was time for its repair.[6] Out of town, the monasteries' sculpting of the land was so long-standing perhaps it was simply taken for granted. There was no sign to tell that the road which ran toll-free out of Ramsey (Cambridgeshire) had been laid by the Benedictine abbey;[7] or that the boon of a drove-way between the mill at Old Cleeve (Somerset) and the best stretch of river to wash the sheep in spring was the work of the Cistercian settlement on the other side of the hill.[8]

But it wasn't always so: no one would forget that the Mersey ferry (Birkenhead) was the work of the priory, as passengers waiting to board took advantage of the refreshment hut set up by the enterprising brethren.[9] Most often, the relationship between a place, its people and their religious house was organic; mutual. Over time, the Cinque port of Winchelsea (East Sussex) moved its marketplace willingly along with its convent of Franciscan friars as they faced the common enemy of the sea.[10] The town and Augustinian friary of Haverfordwest (Pembrokeshire) had grown together. The course of the high street still followed the dog-leg corner created by the friars' projecting precinct wall after the house itself had gone.[11] For some settlements in the provinces, the religious house had simply given them the reason to exist. Southwick, on the outskirts of Portsmouth (Hampshire), John Leland observed, amounted to no more than 'a good bigge thoroughfare ... The fame of it stoode by the priory of Black Canons'; Saint Germans (Cornwall), on the western edge of the Tamar estuary, he found 'but a poor fishar toune. The glory of it stood by the priory.'[12] Here monastic heritage and homeland were inseparable.

In spite of their shared horizons, many invested their religious houses with a special standing on their skyline. There was a common view of their practical value. In an England where cross-country routes were sketchy at best and inclined to become impassable in the wetter months of the year, the towers, rooflines and crenellated walls of the abbeys and priories mapped the countryside. The minia-tures of their spires and towers that marked the available charts and route maps were more than mere decoration.[13] As an experienced Tudor traveller, Leland with some feeling called Abbot Sebroke's tower at Gloucester 'a pharos to all partes about from the hilles'.[14] Their profile defined not only a locality but sometimes a whole region. Thomas Fuller recalled that Gloucestershire was so 'pestered with monks', it was commonly said, 'as sure as God is in Gloucestershire'.[15]

The religious houses had always been among the largest buildings anyone could see, but for the subjects of Henry VIII their fabric may have been particularly striking. The past half-century had seen a spate of ambitious new building. The church at Milton Abbey (Dorset) was recovered from near ruin, with its brand-new transepts, vaults and a decorative reredos at the high altar, all thanks to Abbot William Middleton (d. 1525).[16] Abbot Thomas Llyson's newbuild of Neath Abbey (West Glamorgan) was celebrated by the Welsh bard, Lewis Morgannwg, for its 'crystal windows of every colour' and 'vast and lofty roof' that 'sparkled like the heavens'. With a self-conscious nod to the preferred affiliations of his native land, the building was 'the lamp of France and Ireland', while, apparently, much 'talked of in England'.[17] A pink shimmer on the skyline announced the abbey of St Mary of the Meadows, Leicester – where Cardinal Wolsey came to die in 1530 – for it had recently replaced its precinct wall in bright-red brick.[18] Abbot John Vyntener's new work at St Osyth (Essex), scarcely five years old at the time of the Break with Rome, was in brick of the Italian style. Renaissance reliefs were first seen in the far south-west on the tomb of Prior Thomas Vyvyan of Bodmin (d. 1533).[19]

Monasteries now raised their towers higher and extended their boundary walls further than at any time since the twelfth century. The definition of their borders was especially conspicuous because in the past even some of the most distinguished precincts had been open-plan. The income from their religious services in and outside of their churches enabled the provincial friaries to see their principal buildings finally finished. Payments to their panel painting of the Blessed Virgin Mary propelled the Carmelites at Northampton to the completion of their Lady chapel between 1512 and 1532.[20] At the time of the dissolution the friaries of Dunwich (Suffolk) were so 'very faire churches and building ... with divers faire gates' that they were still conspicuous in the reign of James I, despite 'the greedy sea'.[21] 'The mendicants build more splendidly' was the verdict of Erasmus of Rotterdam (1466–1536), who had seen more of Europe's churches than most of his generation, and was well travelled in provincial England.[22] By contrast, in many parts of the country secular building seemed at a low ebb as old edifices were neglected and new plots were not taken up. 'Moche parte therof is desolate' ran the preamble to a bill for the 're-edification of towns' presented to the Reformation parliament of 1536, 'void groundys, with pittys sellers & vautes lying open & uncoveryd very peryllous for people too go by in the nyght'.[23] The religious houses pointed the way in the present time and to hope for the future.

The religious houses were signs and staging posts. When Sir John Arundell wrote to his wife about his tour of his estates in 1532, a thirty-mile trek over the Blackdown Hills, he described a journey from one monastery to another – Cerne (Dorset), Forde (Dorset) and Newenham (Devon).[24] The priory at Carmarthen, standing at the gateway to the west of Wales, was 'as it were an open lodging for all' because 'there is but little good lodging for noble men reasorting to these partes'; it was remembered that when Henry VII 'come to that countrey' the monks put up a new lodging 'bicause there was no house els within that shire convenient to receave his grace'.[25] It was not only personal preference that led the travelling Cardinal Wolsey to break his journey at one monastery – Blyth Priory – and find his bed at another – Rufford Abbey (both Nottinghamshire).[26] This was the most possible, practical means to pass through the realm. Even when the provinces were disturbed by dissolutions and the mustering of rebel bands in the winter of 1536–37, Thomas Howard, duke of Norfolk, was wont to 'eate or drinke in religious howses'.[27] It was a value that outlived the houses themselves. A hundred years after the last dissolution, Thomas Fuller pictured a monastery as perfect for the prodigal Roman poet Ovid: '[he] would have fancied feasting' there.[28]

The monasteries' development of the landscape extended beyond their church and convent buildings. In both town and countryside more often than not the religious house had created the infrastructure for life and work: the roads, causeways and paths that connected one settlement to another, and the bridges they passed over; the field systems, forests and parks, and the hedge-and-ditch boundaries that defined them; the waterways and their work-stations, fishery, millstream and weir; in built-up areas, the length and breadth of many plots were defined by, or in relation to, the monastery or friary that was the neighbourhood's main proprietor. Looking out over these spaces, it was their religious houses that local people might first call to mind. Even before he reached the edge of town, John Leland had been told that the trail he followed was through the woodland planted and managed commercially by Worksop Priory (Nottinghamshire).[29] It was well known to travellers coming out of the West Country that the River Severn ferries were the enterprise of the Benedictines of Tewkesbury (Gloucestershire), whether or not their route gave them a view of the abbey.[30] Bristol landlords traded tenements whose position was pinpointed from the (often larger) plots of the regulars living alongside. When John Hawkes distributed his portfolio on his deathbed in 1504, he identified three religious foundations as his immediate neighbours.[31] The connection could be a source of chronic pain. The fifty-acre enclosure around Newstead Priory (Nottinghamshire) was a memorial to the losses of their parents' generation; the closure in 1517 of the parish of Borough Fen at Peterborough Abbey (Cambridgeshire) was a reminder of what they had failed to preserve for their children.[32] The enclosure of the commons at Lytham (Lancashire) stirred the passions of the neighbourhood so much that 300 individuals marched on the priory and turned back only when the canons came out and showed them the consecrated host.[33]

Now it was a matter of public discourse. The character of Raphael in Thomas More's *Utopia* (1516), while talking with the venerable Cardinal Morton (d. 1500), thinks that the regulars' pastureland 'devour[s] even the people themselves, they despoil and destroy fields, houses, towns . . . even some abbots (holy men are they) not . . . thinking it sufficient to live idly and comfortably, contributing nothing to the common good unless they also undermine it'.[34] The naming of landmarks, for example 'Abbots' Meadow', 'Monk's House', 'Nuns' Wood' or 'Friars' Walk', is often assumed to have been a loose, Romantic expression of medievalism. Often, in fact it was an echo of the lived experience of the early Tudors. The placement of permanent boundaries, and the prosecution of trespass, gave the Henrician generation a heightened awareness of the monastic domain, and its diversity, not only 'Abbots' Meadow' and 'Nuns' Wood', but urban plots named after the officer of the monastery who held the ground rent. It lent the religious house itself associations far removed from the practice of religion: as they turned towards the priory, householders in the heart of Canterbury no doubt thought of cisterns and conduits; in the forested landscape of Fountains (North Yorkshire), it seems that firewood was never far from local people's mind.[35]

The familiarity of these sights bred a certain detachment. The first thought of many of Henry's subjects when seeing religious houses was disarmingly dispassionate: they appraised the quality of the building or the landscape, the forms, fabric and likely cost of such houses. It may be a measure of how instinctive it was in this generation that even such a bookish eccentric as John Leland, whose mind much of the time was lost in British antiquity, described what he saw in the manner of a surveyor. The Trinitarian house at Thelsford (Warwickshire) was 'butt a lytle thinge and nott perfytly buyldyd'.[36] It was an outlook that reflected the economic and social challenges of provincial life. There had been no headlong decline of towns and villages over the previous century, but nor had there been an unbroken boom. At the beginning of Henry's reign in every region, even in the largest of the cities, there were many quarters and much infrastructure in need of repair. Demands for new work, and plans made by town governors and private patrons to provide it, were in the air; they at least may have viewed the religious houses as neighbours sharing in the same challenge.

This way of seeing was encouraged by the image of the monastery they would have found in a wide variety of popular tales. Whether only a backdrop to the story, or part of the plot, invariably it was 'riche' and 'faire'. The physical fabric of the kingdom was a popular metaphor for the growing number of printed polemics on matters of religion. No lesser voice than King Henry himself worried 'what ruinous buyding ye reare vpon the false foundation of ... vnfaithfull faythe'; the failings of the clergy were as conspicuous as 'buyldyngis go[ne] vnto ruyne'.[37] Anxiety added another edge to their view. Where they saw a crazed cluster of centuries-old buildings – more gables than any young man might count on a sunny day – or discovered fixtures and fittings which had not moved with the times, their derision was unbounded. The king's commissioners conducting the royal visitations of 1535, carrying with them the yardstick of the purpose-built chambers they had known at the universities and inns of court, seemed liable to judge the future of a community by the comfort of their buildings.

Here too were the roots of a moral message to be taken up by the reformers in the decades to come, that the costly developments of the wealthiest churches ran counter to the simple clarity of good religion. In one of his published sermons, John Colet, dean of St Paul's Cathedral (1505–19), had urged the 'good bestowyng of the patrimony of Christe. The lawes that commande that the goodes of the churche be spent nat in costly byldyng'.[38] In the polemic *Rede me and be nott wrothe* (first printed in 1528) it became a bitter condemnation of 'costly bildynge' and '[of] Churches / and houses superfluous / To no purpose expedient / So that they maye satisfy / Their inordinate fantasy'.[39] Beneath such high-mindedness there was also a primitive form of envy. The 'newe werke' of the monasteries was coveted by their neighbours. At Wilton (Wiltshire) in 1520 two local men were overcome and stole specimen trees from the abbess's close.[40] The same impulse consumed King Henry himself. His first act at the suppression of the London Charterhouse was to have 'all suche rosemarie graftys ande oder suche thynges as was meyte for hys grace's . . . garden'.[41]

The material assessment of the buildings and their grounds often carried with it an aesthetic appreciation. Leland could not contain his admiration for so many of the monasteries' 'fayre villes or mannour places' and even in the smaller towns the 'fayr chirches' occupied by the friars.[42] Above all he was an antiquarian looking everywhere for relics of recorded history, yet his eye was drawn just as readily to those edifices known to be new. Abbot Lichfield's tower at Evesham (Worcestershire), whose mortar was scarcely set as he passed through, he thought 'right sumptuous and high'.[43] Leland saw far more of England than most of his countrymen, but the great beauty of these places was part of their general renown. Readers of the 1528 imprint of *Cronycles of Englonde* were advised that 'Saynt Peter's chirche at Westmynster ye is fayrer of sight than ony other place ye ony man knoweth through one all Chrystendom.'[44] Those who chose to lose themselves in verse were painted a picture that was richer still: at Canterbury, the monk Robert Saltwood described his choir so 'fayre . . . Insculped, enbosted and paynted venustly';[45] from Ely, the one-time monk Alexander Barclay (*c.* 1476–1552) wrote of a sight 'Glystring [glistening] as bright as Phebus orient'.[46] The parishioners of Burnley (Lancashire) saw Whalley Abbey as their copy-book, and set about replicating in their church the styling of the monks' Lady chapel.[47]

The wonder of their buildings aroused a general curiosity and for a growing number of people an impulse to explore them at close hand. The interest of Leland and William Worcester (d. 1482), his predecessor as explorer of provincial England, was scholarly and specialised, but it is obvious from the way they were warmly received that religious houses were used to tourism and did not discourage it. Leland learned the Welsh name for Newport (Pembrokeshire) from the monk who showed him the Cistercian abbey of Strata Florida (Ceredigion). Abbot Richard Whiting of Glastonbury opened the monastery's great library to Leland, for which privilege Leland called him his singular friend (amico singulari meo).[48] The regulars' continuing investment in their buildings and contents suggests a deliberate cultivation of outside interest. Their furnishings of porches and public altars drew attention to the history within as much as to the devotional offerings. A sculpted effigy of Osric (d. 679), Saxon king of the Hwicce, and legendary founder of the first monastery at Gloucester, was created around 1530 as a further point of interest for visitors who were now permitted to pass beyond the nave to view the tomb of Edward II.[49] Panel paintings not only depicted the patron saints of the house but also something of the story of its foundation. The board (now, although not originally, a reredos) made for Romsey Abbey (Hampshire) after 1509 depicts an abbess introducing Christianity's central tenet of the Resurrection, the monastic tradition of Benedict, and the cult of the region and diocese (see Fig. 2).[50] Often a full account of the saints, relics and miracles associated with the church was compiled, maybe as a crib for the monastic guide but perhaps for the visitors themselves. They may have been meant for display. This could have been the purpose of the 'magna tabula' made at Glastonbury, a guidebook to the abbey's sacred history pasted on oak boards the size of a door.[51] The religious were also inclined to bring out some of their most precious objects from the sanctum. The way that the Crown's agents recorded their collections of textiles, here and there throughout their inventories, suggests that some of the finest frontals and cele-brants' robes were openly displayed. Manuscript books were sometimes positioned on public altars. An illustrated book of benefactors was displayed to visitors at St Albans, no doubt to inspire them to join the distinguished roll call of donors.[52]

For very important visitors, the religious might also present a prized volume for a private view. During his Royal Progress at St Albans, King Henry VI was privileged to turn the leaves of the Passion of Alban, protomartyr of England, hand-painted by the artist Matthew Paris.[53]

Certain curiosities held a special interest for the early Tudor tourist. The tombs of royalty trumped any other shrine. Leland found that even Leominster Priory (Herefordshire), hardly on the way to anywhere, held some passing interest for its story of the monks keeping two skulls of the early kings of Mercia.[54] At Gloucester Abbey what persuaded visitors to pass beyond the nave, to the presbytery walk where an offering was required, was the promise of seeing King Edward II, and the crucifix, wrapped in the hide of a bull, tucked behind the head of his effigy.[55] St Albans presented visitors with the sword of King Offa (d. 796).[56] At Worcester in 1529 John Bale witnessed the opening of the sarcophagus containing the remains of King John, dead and buried for 313 years. 'His corpse was rotten,' Bale remembered, but he looked long enough to notice the king's gold and scarlet robes, his crown, sceptre and sword, the spurs at his feet and the ring on his finger.[57] The royal mausoleum curated by the monks of Westminster eclipsed all other points of interest in that abbey church; already, at the beginning of the sixteenth century, what the community offered outsiders may have had the air of an exhibition gallery, as the 'Ragged Regiment' of Lancastrian funeral effigies, of Henry V and his queen, Catherine of Valois, were set upright against the wall of Henry's chantry, clearly to be seen.[58] Similarly, the tomb of King Arthur at Glastonbury had something of the character of a museum installation. Fashioned from black marble, and flanked by flaming tapers, the monastery offered their guests a piece of theatre.[59] Even as harsh a critic of the religious houses as Erasmus was struck by the spectacle at Walsingham Priory, remarking drily that there was a brilliant and elegant temple (templum est nitidum et elegans verum in eo non habitat virgo) for the non-residence of the Blessed Virgin Mary.[60]

There were also the historical remains of legendary knighthood that brought the images of Thomas Malory's Le Morte Darthur into local view: the felt hat of Earl Thomas of Lancaster (d. 1322) at Pontefract Priory (West Yorkshire), and at Alnwick Priory (Northumberland) the foot of the rebel baron Simon de Montfort (d. 1265).[61] The transactions of Tudor layfolk give the impression that they invested in, and were inclined to co-curate, this living cabinet of curiosities. They made gifts of objects that they must have known were of little material value, but which would add measurably to the stock of legend, magic and mystery. In the last years of Henry VII, Thomas Thwaytes, mercer of London, gave to the abbess of Barking (Essex) something practical, a breviary, and then an object of legend, a 'sparver', valance (decorative drapery) from a bed, said to belong to 'St' Henry VI, the patron saint of the new monarchy.[62]

There was also a growing thirst for tangible traces of England's true antiquity, driven by a conviction that the great abbeys at the centre of the oldest cities were surely a gateway to it. It is apparent from his notes that Leland's quizzing of his guides often reached from the recent times as far back as to the Roman period. At Lacock (Wiltshire) he learned 'men find much Romaine mony'; at Thorney (Cambridgeshire) he was told of coins of the Emperor Trajan (98–117 CE) and whole urns 'diggid up' near the church.[63] Again, it does seem the religious communities were aware of this interest and encouraged it. The Chester monk Henry Bradshaw appeared to hitch his new history of the abbey's patron saint, Werbergh, to the public taste for Roman remains, advertising to his readers 'buyldynge of olde antiquite' and even the suggestion of catacombs, 'cellers and lowe voultes'.[64]

The fascination for the treasures of the monasteries and friaries was powerful and possessive. Their precious objects were not only seen and touched but also damaged and stolen. The accounts of the sacrists of Westminster Abbey for the century before the dissolution present a catalogue of loss, of objects that were missing entirely, and many more whose decorations, inset gemstones or silver and silver-gilt coverings had been broken, pared back and prised off.[65] It would be entirely wrong to see the mercenary destruction of the dissolution commissioners as a sudden desecration of buildings and furnishings which had never known such rough handling. The legends of the religious houses had long attracted visitors who were far from welcome. The prior of Tywardreath Priory (Cornwall) wrote with feeling of 'the pirates of the see . . . useth them self mor cruelly and mor tyrannosly towardes devoute and holy religyous places then they did of olde tyme'.[66] The aesthetic and antiquarian interest in these houses which had built up over previous generations had already made their fabric very vulnerable to desecration.

The curiosity about the buildings and their contents was fuelled by what was thought to be their history. This might have been expected to be a meeting point between the surrounding neighbourhood and the religious inside. There is no doubt that the identity of every monk, friar and nun was founded on an idea of the past. But they thought above all of the chronology of the community, the foundation of their house and the ages of each superior that led it, finally arriving at their own place in the timeline, which determined the very seat they took in the choir stalls and at table in the refectory. By contrast the annals that King Henry's subjects believed could be traced in these buildings carried them back to the furthest reaches of recorded time. It was commonly thought that monasteries had been present in the opening chapters of Britain's Christian story. Just two years after Henry's accession, the Westminster printer Wynkyn de Worde published the life story of Joseph of Arimathea, 'which buryed the body of oure lorde', narrating how 'he came into grete Britaine, which [land] was promysed to him and his yssue'.[67] The story was introduced as an 'extracte of the veraye true & probate assercyons of hystoryal men touchynge and concernenge thantyquytes of thonourable monastery of oure lady in Glastenburye'.[68] Glastonbury was given no further part in Joseph's exploits, but Wynkyn's readers were left in little doubt that their monastic history was as old as the Christian faith itself.

Stories of the Christian quests of King Arthur and his knights, two editions of which had been printed at Westminster even before Henry's accession, placed the old abbeys in the foreground of Britain's early history. In Geoffrey of Monmouth's telling of it, Arthur's court convened at Kaer Radoc in the shadow of Mount Ambrius, on the summit of which stood an abbey of 300 monks.[69] It was in the cloister that the young Merlin received his education; there too Lancelot and his brethren of the Round Table returned after the king's death '[to] redde in bookes . . . holpe for to synge masse, & range bellys & dyd odoly al maner of seruyce'.[70] Malory made Arthur the patron of monasteries, the founder of a 'faire abbaye' with 'grete lyvelode' which he called 'La beale Aduenture'.[71] In their turn, the monks were, and, the reader might infer, had ever been, faithful custodians of Arthur's memory. The preface to the printed *Le Morte Darthur* reminded Tudor readers that 'ye may see his sepulture in the monasterye of Glastyngburye' but also the 'prynte of his seale' in the 'abbey of westmestre at saynt Edwardes shrine'.[72]

There was another 'best crysten and worthy king' of Britain's early history whose story became especially resonant in Henry's reign. Lucius, whose reign was placed in the late second century, was believed to have converted to Christianity under the guidance of the pope in Rome and set up cathedrals and monasteries in England. He recovered a crucifix handmade by Joseph of Arimathea and set it in the north door of his new church of St Paul's in the city of London, and settled a community of monks at Westminster and Glastonbury.[73] As King Henry's lawyers constructed the case for his divorce from Katherine of Aragon, Lucius's story was made the opening chapter of a new history of a national English Church.[74] But also in a local setting his name was used to signal the presence of monasteries from time immemorial. Glastonbury claimed him as the monastery's first founder.[75] He was claimed in the same way at Westminster and at Winchester was invoked as the source of their sanctuary privilege.[76] Henry Bradshaw wrapped the legend of Lucius around his other claims for the special interest of his abbey church at Chester, 'a Briton kyng with great desire ... His realme to be baptize'.[77] Sir John Markham recalled, in a letter to Thomas Cromwell, a conversation with the Carthusians at Beauvale (Nottinghamshire), who wove a story about the descent of the religion of monks from 'Lucius and Eleutherius' as far as '[Pope] Gregory and Austen [Augustine of Canterbury]'.[78]

The case for the king's divorce made the matter of church history government business, but wider society looked on the monasteries equally as a portal to more worldly aspects of the nation's past. Chronicles now available in print placed the abbeys at the centre of some of the most pivotal events in the history of the realm since the coming of the Normans. Henry's subjects were perhaps especially aware of how they had been touched by the tragic history of the Wars of the Roses (1455–85) which had preceded the Tudor succession. The burials of some of the champions of the old conflict between Lancaster and York (1455–85) – Richard Neville (i.e. Warwick the Kingmaker) at Bisham (Berkshire), Jasper Tudor at Keynsham (Somerset), Edmund Beaufort at St Albans, Prince Edward at Tewkesbury – were prominent in the public spaces of their churches.[79] 'Whose dead corpses filled up our Ladyes chappel' was how it was spoken of at St Albans.[80] The abbey church there and at Tewkesbury lived in the imagination of those who had never visited them because they were the backdrop to legendary battles between the armies of Lancaster and York. The monks curated their heritage: the plating of the sacristy door at Tewkesbury with horse-armour recovered from the battlefield (of 1471) that lay to the south of their precinct may have been more than a practical measure; certainly, the resumption of the old abbey chronicle was a conscious effort to take control of the story.[81]

For these late wars, certain monasteries represented more than a mausoleum or museum. They held its living history. It was well known to early Tudors that some of the principal actors in their generation's greatest drama had visited or lived in these very precincts. The king's Yorkist grandmother, Elizabeth Woodville, had lived and died (1492) at Bermondsey Abbey (Surrey); her sister-in-law, Isabel, duchess of Clarence, had made Tewkesbury her second home.[82] Her youngest daughter, Bridget, lived still at Dartford Priory, where she had been presented as a girl of little more than ten.[83] The king's Lancastrian great-aunt and uncle, Margaret Tudor and Edward Tudor, the youngest children of Sir Owen Tudor and Dowager Queen Catherine of Valois, had also passed their lives in the cloister, Edward at no lesser house than Westminster Abbey.[84] The grandson of another great uncle, Jasper Tudor, was rumoured to be a monk of Tynemouth Priory (Northumberland), where Cardinal Wolsey – in deliberate mischief perhaps – had secured his election as prior.[85] Possibly there was a perception that there was something instrumental in the way these great houses capitalised on the history of the Roses. Gertrude Blount, marchioness of Exeter and daughter-in-law of Princess Katherine of York, gravitated to the supposed visionary Elizabeth Barton, prodigy of the Prior of Canterbury, convinced perhaps that there was a connection between the regulars and a reversionary interest in the Crown.[86]

By the beginning of Henry VIII's reign there were the first signs that people looked on the oldest religious houses as memorials for other forms of legend. Although Geoffrey Chaucer (d. 1400) was known to be buried at Westminster Abbey and the names of celebrated chroniclers – William of Malmesbury (d. *c.* 1143), Ranulf Higden of Chester (d. 1358) – were associated with monasteries, there was not yet any idea of a Poets' Corner. But there was an impulse to look in some of these buildings for a tangible trace of others famous for their words whose names had caught the popular imagination. There can be no doubt that readers of Mandeville's *Wayes* and *Marueyles* came to St Albans Abbey in search of Sir John. Wynkyn de Worde advertised the 'lytell treatyse or booke' under the name of the well-known monastery town: 'Johan Maundeuyll knight born in Englonde in the towne of saynt Albone'.[87] The public interest literally was inscribed on the fabric of the monastery, 'the inhabitants . . . lately pencilled on a pillar a rare piece of his poetry . . . [and] an epitaph for him, near to which they suppose him to have been buried'.[88]

The chroniclers' tales of 'grand batailes', and Mandeville's memoir of 'the Holy Land towarde Jherusalem & of marveyles of Ynde and of other diverse countrees', were for those with the learning and leisure to lose themselves in print, not least the monks that curated these places themselves. For many of their neighbours these houses were redolent rather of histories and memories that ran closer to their own hearth. Even beyond the big cities, in provincial centres of a few thousand people, there was a potent feeling of local identity which had grown part and parcel with their own forms of government. Wherever there was a burgess community flexing its political muscle in the face of older forms of lordship there was a view of the origins and historical development of the town. The religious houses played a leading role in this neighbourhood history, not infrequently as the villains of the piece, the malevolent captor, curbing their freedom to live and work as they would. In some places these partisan histories were centuries-old by 1509: in the boroughs of Abingdon (Oxfordshire), Colchester, Bury, St Albans, town and monastery had been contesting their history on and off since the reign of Henry III (1216–72). Leland often met these arguments on arrival in town and they coloured his record of the church and his history. At St Albans, the pages of his commonplace book filled up with the townspeople's principal complaint against the monks, that their Saxon forebears had robbed them of their very name, Warlamchester.[89]

There was a yet more personal history imprinted here. Both monastery and friary churches held family associations that were already generations old. These were most conspicuous and far-reaching for the aristocracy. For noble families of long endurance, such as the Courtenays of Devon and the Percys of Northumberland, the material and written records of a handful of monasteries contained almost all their history that was known. The religious houses held the tombs of their ancestors, any number of visual expressions of their names and titles in painted stone and glass, and often a complete genealogy, made to give the community a permanent record of the length and breadth of their patronage. These largest and most resilient dynasties traced their timelines along a chain of houses and orders which reflected almost every age of religious history. The rise of the Courtenays from the twelfth to the fourteenth centuries left its mark on six houses of four orders: Breamore and Christchurch priories (Augustinian; Hampshire and Dorset); Forde and Quarr abbeys (Cistercian; Dorset and Isle of Wight); Cowick Priory (Cluniac; Devon); and the Augustinian friars of Exeter.[90] Still, many families of lower rank and more limited lordship would see their personal history preserved in the buildings of more than one foundation in their neighbourhood. The greater space for burial available in the friars' churches had persuaded even the most loyal patrons of monasteries to branch out for recent family tombs. It was often propertied families below the nobility whose generations of patronage had just one focal point which had done most to mould the fabric of a monastery or friary church, not only marking it with their arms, in stone and glass, but also shaping the space available for worship as the choir and presbytery filled up with their tombs. In February 1512, Gyles Bull of

Chichester (West Sussex) planned a tomb in the Franciscan church, his children already lying buried in the cemetery outside.[91]

It has been suggested that family ties to the religious houses were fading fast at the beginning of the sixteenth century precisely because they were no more than a memory, any living link having been broken as personal preference, or spiritual market forces, drew wealthy and worthy families elsewhere.[92] In fact there are few signs of desertion by the oldest families. Their memories of their forebears' acts of patronage were lively. The Courtenays kept a genealogical tree and a chronicle of their ancestors which had been taken down directly from the archives of their first family monastery at Forde; in the shadow of the dissolution they commissioned a new one.[93] Elite families were continuing to create new ties to the religious houses in their neighbourhood. In the first years of the Tudors the Fitzwilliam family adopted the Augustinian friary at Tickhill (South Yorkshire).[94] With a chilling prescience, Sir John planned a sizeable tomb for himself before he rode off to fight for the king at Flodden (1513), where he fell. There was no discernible turn away from the idea that a religious house was a sure platform for a family with ambitions for power. The new stamp of the Howards on the Cluniac priory at Thetford was emphatic. The status of hereditary founder of the twelfth-century church had come to the family as part and parcel of the dukedom of Norfolk in 1483 but they made it their own. In barely twenty years the chancel was taking on the look of a Howard chantry, as a fine double tomb for Duke Thomas and Agnes, his wife, was under construction.[95]

These family histories weighed just as heavily on the monasteries themselves. Their preoccupation is apparent in the variety of records they made of their tombs and other memorials and of their lifetime acts of patronage. The only literary enterprise to have exercised the monks of Tewkesbury for generations was an illustrated register of their founding and later patrons. Their 'Founders' Book' was a communal project but the interest of individual brethren was also consumed by the families whose history surrounded them as they moved about their church.[96] The community still saw a legal authority in their link to a founding family, however threadbare their ties had run in their own time. When the abbot of Hartland (Devon) died in 1532, the first thought of his prior, Richard Tayton, was to send for Charles Dynham, his friend and the kinsman of Lord Dynham, hereditary patron, to ask him to secure the good lord's permission to proceed to an election.[97]

Monasteries were also tethered by the family ties of their own membership. For parents and siblings especially, perhaps the first thought they had of an abbey of renown was simply that there lived one of their own. Not every recruit to the cloistered life entered a house in their own neighbourhood. Among the orders of monks there was a recognised hierarchy of houses, surely as familiar to the families of prospective novices as to the communities themselves. Would-be friars submitted to the will of the provincial system, which designated particular houses as schools for the network as a whole and after the noviciate required every man to follow a rotation from house to house that could carry them nationwide. Families of girls pulled or pushed towards profession as nun were perhaps especially aware that in the comparatively narrow network of convents there were great disparities in their size, their resources and standing in the Church. It is quite possible that the only knowledge a Colchester Widow Jackson had of the august Cluniac abbey of Bermondsey was that her son, Christopher, had made his profession there.[98] Out of her sight and any first-hand understanding, sixty-five miles to the south, as she wrote anxiously to the abbot, her only idea of the abbey was that it might pose a possible danger to her precious boy. When John Hawkes, twice mayor of Bristol, dictated his will in the winter of 1503, after his own funeral arrangements his mind turned to his daughter, Anne, 'professed nun in the convent of Almesbury in the county of Wiltes'.[99] More than 50 miles' distance from his own great city with as many as a dozen religious houses within its walls, his own idea of a grand convent was where Anne might remember him in her prayers.

For their part, the men and women who made their life in these houses often felt a strong impulse to hold with them something of their former homes. Those who came to lead their monastic communities were able to use their institutional authority to reel in the family members from which their profession had distanced them. Joan Temys of Lacock Abbey made her brother Thomas steward of the demesne lands, perhaps a calculated move to channel her own career fortune into the interest of the family but surely also a demonstration of a very particular kind of attachment, of a mutual trust which can be counted in kinfolk.[100] The last abbot of Bury St Edmunds, John Reve, kept an eye on the family business, retaining a parcel of land and livestock which his brother farmed on his behalf.[101] Either way the monastery was made a family concern. Superiors also looked to project the profile of their house on the scenery of their home town. Robert Catton, whose career carried him from Norwich Cathedral Priory to the great abbey of St Albans, paid for a stained-glass image of a Benedictine to be set in the nave of the parish church of St Margaret, Catton (Norfolk) he had known as a boy.[102]

The sight of a religious house in Henrician England prompted thoughts unconnected with their original purpose, but still they were looked on as profoundly holy places. There was a view, perhaps widely held because it was so often expressed in print, that they possessed a special quality of sanctity. In part it stemmed from the understanding that they were almost incalculably old. After all, the most recent histories affirmed that houses of religion had stood for as long as the Christian faith had been known in England. Across the span of Christendom, the claim was greater still. Bishop John Alcock of Ely (1486–1500) figured the abbey as a living link with Eden, a place of pure converse with God, 'the holy place almighty god gaf to Adam forsayd & to Eue and to ther heyres'.[103] The very fabric of abbeys was spiritually charged. 'The consecrate stones . . . theyr bull warkes' was to be their challenge to the Lutherans. Even their avowed enemy, the author of *Rede me and be nott wrothe*, was distracted 'to see so many a golden ouche [i.e. arch] to make . . . sanctes for to shyne'.[104] It was also recognised that they held most of the oldest shrines and sacred objects of great repute anywhere in the realm. When this or that abbey was named, it was this 'awtyr' or that window-light, panel painting or statue that was called to mind.

The holiness of the house was focused in its physical forms. For many, the centre point was the cloister. For generations, perhaps reaching as far back as the post-Conquest period when the great stone arcades in Romanesque style had become commonplace in England for the first time, the cloister had been the short-hand term for the religious life. When he set out his plan for his funeral in 1523, John Tynmowth saw no need to be any more specific than 'every oon of the foure cloysters [of Boston, Lincs.] should accompany my body to the church'.[105] Describing the dissolution forty years on, the chronicler Raphael Holinshed knew he had only to refer to the orders 'with their cloisters and their houses' for his Elizabethan readers to recognise his subject.[106] In literature both monastic and secular the cloister had accrued a great metaphorical power. The manuals on personal piety read by many of Henry's subjects often presented the cloister as a symbol of the committed piety to which all should aspire. Bishop Alcock taught that all must 'buylde well our cloystre', its 'foure corneres' standing for purity of sight, speech, mind and heart.[107] For the *Dyetery of Ghostly Helthe*, the cloister of body and mind was a simple imperative, 'ye sholde be closed vp within. iiij. walles'.[108] It was nothing less than the threshold between earth and heaven. 'Behold there [the cloister]', taught William Atkinson's *A full deuoute gostely trea-*

tyse of imitacion . . . of our most mercyful sauiour cryst, 'heuen & the elementis wherof all erthly substaunce be fourmed'.[109] Duly cloistered as the *Dyetery* required, the nun could meet an angel at her shoulder. Bishop Alcock was in no doubt: 'A woman of relygyon or a man beynge in theyr cloyster . . . they speke with god.'[110] So potent was such counsel in the world outside that the wealthiest householders now thought to make their religious regime easier by raising a cloister in their own home. In the first decade of Henry VIII's reign it was among the most desired accessories for the grandest of private residences. The cloister symbolised the family's separation from the world, the self-contained, closed walkway, the closed way of life, as John Longland, bishop of Lincoln (1521–47) wrote, 'religious persones [should] be kepte from the sight and visage of the world . . . the more close and entyer theyr mynd and devocoun shalbe unto God'.[111]

Professed men and women added to the resonance of the cloister in their own accounts of their life. When questioned during a visitation, instinctively their estimation of the quality of their life, and the merits of their superiors, was measured by the condition of the cloister. Often the state of its own structure was taken for the whole house. Asked the familiar 'est omnia bene', their first response was to reflect on whether the cloister itself was sound.[112] If they talked of the observant life, it was to the cloister that they turned their mind. The 'keeping of the cloister' (observancie; claustrum servatur) was their measure of the monastery's well-being.[113] When the prior of Much Wenlock (Shropshire) complained that his brethren were in open rebellion, he described how they were 'rending off their rule and closing up the cloister'.[114] Their experience of the religious life was best represented by the four walls of the cloister. Richard Kidderminster, the august abbot of Winchcombe (1488–1525), lived apart from his community but when he wrote his highly personal letters to Cardinal Wolsey, he emphasised that they were 'ex claustro'.[115] When Robert Parker, recently a novice at the Cistercian abbey of Stratford Langthorne (Essex), wrote to his parents in 1519, he referred to his profession as 'the cloister'.[116] John Laurence, a would-be informant of Cromwell's sent back to his monastery, wrote of returning 'to my cloister'.[117] Looking back on the end of monastic life in England, Cistercian Thomas Clebury wrote of it as the extinction of cloister piety (claustralium religiositas).[118] The symbolism weighed heavily upon these brethren, at times in ways that challenged whatever vocation had carried them there. Young Parker confided in his parents that he was now 'a powre prisoner', where he was bound 'to keep silence and speak with no man'.

41

The holiness of the monastery was both a mental image for the Tudors and a sensory experience. Thomas More celebrated this among the Utopians:

> They burn incense and fragrant substances. They display many candles, not because they do not know that such things add nothing to God's nature . . . but they like this harmless mode of worship and people feel that somehow such perfumes, lights and other ceremonies lift up the human heart and make it rise more eagerly in divine worship.[119]

The Henrician generation were moved by visual experience, especially of the rich and rare variety of their furnishings. Even the royal commissioners charged with picking over the clutter of the convents to calculate its residual value seem to have been distracted by the colours and designs of the vestments they found. Rather than scribbling down the usual desultory note about an object, they took their time to describe the hues, the images and the fabric. At Worcester they wondered at a celebrant's suit that seemed to teem with a whole menagerie – dragons, fish, fowl, harts and lions – set in a constellation of stars and Catherine Wheels.[120]

Even before the Tudors faced the sight of the monastery they were struck by its sound. Geoffrey Chaucer, one-time resident in the precinct of Westminster Abbey, had recalled how the life of the monks announced itself to the world by the 'eek as loude [. . .] chapel belle' and 'murie orgon'.[121] By the beginning of the sixteenth century, the clamour of the religious house was as potent an idea as the cloister itself. Bells defined these spaces more than any other church because so many of them sounded so often each day. Even those now inclined to be critical of the conduct of monasteries were susceptible to their music. When Thomas More wrote of the music of Utopian religion, which 'quite wonderfully stirs up, pierces, and inflames the hearts of the hearer', he was surely thinking of practice much closer to home.[122] The Welsh bard, Guto'r Glyn (d. 1493), called the Cistercian church at Strata Florida 'teml adeilad', temple of the harp.[123] For Tudor listeners, more accustomed than their ancestors to elaborate settings and professional performance, what marked out the religious houses was the special quality of their song. John Skelton framed his picture of Carrow Priory (Norfolk) with the women's 'dolorous songs'; even as he imagined them turned out from their cloisters 'in secula seculorum', he saw them take their special sound, 'to synge from place to place'.[124] The Elizabethan, John Stow, drew on his own boyhood memory to describe the sound of London's friars: 'Aystyns ... synge the letany with faburdyn [close harmony]'.[125] Their distinctive style, tone and volume were an obvious target for mockery. 'Ornamental neighings' was Erasmus's disparagement although still he acknowledged their 'agile throats'.[126] Yet they were also widely understood to be an intimation of the divine. In Wynkyn de Worde's popular imprint of the *Myracles of oure blessyd lady*, a vision of the Blessed Virgin was conjured for a gentleman after Compline as a choir of friars sang out, 'Salve regina'.[127]

Their sensory experience at the religious houses still raised in Tudor minds the possibility of spiritual magic. The catalogue of wonders in the custody of these houses, and their potency, were still renowned. The monasteries' investment in the shrines of their patron saints was not what it had been in the past, but this was a reflection of their own shifting priorities, not those of their neighbourhood.[128] Quite apart from these main attractions, over the long centuries of their history a remarkable variety of relics and sacred objects had found their way into their care. John Bale mocked such sacred clutter as eccentric and obscure, 'a dram of the tord of swete saynt Barnabe ... a lowse of saynt Francis ... and a fart of saynt Fandingo'.[129]

But away from cities and towns, in countryside where parish churches were meagre and poorly maintained, the sacred treasure of monastic and friary churches had lost nothing of their early magnetism. An English traveller over the hills and through the valleys of remote and rural Wales in the 1530s found it to be 'alive' with 'popish pilgrimages'.[130] The legend of these churches' curiosities was so reso-nant in some regions that the religious left the neighbourhood to enact it for themselves. At Repton Priory (Derbyshire), pilgrims passed St Guthlac's bell between them, taking turns to place it over their heads; there were similar scenes at Bury St Edmunds, although what was worn was St Petronilla's skull.[131] The canons of Maiden Bradley Priory let their celebrated girdle of the Virgin Mary be loaned out; in 1535 it was still said to be 'in great request' across the Wiltshire Downs.[132] At the same time, there was a collective will to conjure magic within churches themselves. Dairywomen with an ailment waited in front of the image of St Bride at Arden Priory (North Yorkshire) for their cure to come.[133] Those with headaches camped before Cuthberga at Thelsford.[134] Around the feast of Saint Margaret of Antioch, (20 July) 1503, Richard Poell, a member of the royal house-hold under the king's father, passed through a trance in the presence of the shrine of Saint Cuthbert at Durham Priory, after fevered tears, pleas and prayers. When he came to, he was cured of the prolapsed stomach which had put him beyond the care of any physician (nullaque medicorum arte, opera sive scientia curabili).[135] The claim of a Cistercian monk of Jervaulx (North Yorkshire) to have seen the Blessed Virgin Mary and her mother, St Anne, in the pilgrims' chapel at Mount Grace became a *cause célèbre* in 1535 as Cromwell kept a watch on the northern houses' conformity to the new supremacy. He was convinced that the Virgin's mother had arisen from the 'grett ymmayge [that] doth stande in ... closyd there [where they] sayde masse'.[136]

The friars' churches were first conceived as cavernous preaching halls, but increasingly they were fitted with altar artefacts of their own. It was shortly after Henry's accession that the Cambridge Dominicans began to draw crowds to the statue of 'Our Lady of Grace' kept there.[137] When William Nicholson, his wife, their two small children and sundry livestock were swept into the River Don as they crossed the ford at Stainforth, South Yorkshire, in their struggle they recalled the image of the Virgin 'honorde and worshept in the Whyte Freeres of Doncaster', and they were able to hold fast, 'in the bothom of the water emonges his beasts feete, gate holde of a beast's heed, and thrast hymself towardes the land, and so, by the grace of God, and of this good Lady of Doncaster, was savyd'.[138]

These responses were moulded by public discussion and demonstration of the magic of monastic religion which was as widespread now as it ever had been. The seasonal dramas, often called 'miracle' or 'mystery' plays, performed publicly in provincial cities and privately in elite households, continued to represent the cowled religious as a conjurer of celestial intercession. At Holy Trinity Priory, Aldgate in the city of London, they re-enacted the Resurrection itself apparently with an elaborate stage apparatus that required the cellarer to pay for a harness.[139] They created another reality, dressing the themes treated in the pulpit in everyday clothes. But the suggestion that the cloister stood between two worlds was a feature of the telling of the most familiar stories. The fortunes of Arthur's knights so often seemed to turn on supernatural encounters in the enclosure of the monastery. There Sir Perceval met Christ himself, 'a crowne of gold upon his hede ... his body ... ful of grete woundes'.[140] Some of the first books printed under the patronage of monasteries reprised the old stories of their miraculous patron saints. The monks of St Augustine's Abbey, Canterbury, took up a little-known poem by John Lydgate and printed it for local consumption because it told of the miraculous power of their saint, Augustine of Canterbury, which had been demonstrated at the nearby Kentish parish of Compton.[141]

Some of the sacred objects in the care of monasteries commanded nationwide celebrity. Edward Stafford, duke of Buckingham (d. 1521), diverted his progress cross-country when he saw a chance to visit the Child of Grace at Reading Abbey, the subject of royal and noble oblations for nearly 400 years.[142] Even Erasmus was too curious not to visit Walsingham Priory to investigate the Virgin Mary's breast milk for himself.[143] The houses recognised that their pilgrims expected magic and they dressed the setting of these objects so it might be conjured on demand. The head relic of St Oswald at Worcester Cathedral Priory 'wore' a mitre.[144] At Boxley Priory (Kent), the canons created an automaton so that the power of their celebrated crucifix might be performed, 'certen ingynes & olde wyer . . . that did cause the eye . . . to move & stere in the hede therof, lyke unto a lyvelye thyng, and also the nether lippe in lyk wise to move as thoughe it shulde speke, whiche so founde was nott a litle straunge to [those] present'.[145] Robert Shrimton, mayor of St Albans in the reign of Elizabeth, remembered as a boy how he had marvelled at a moving statue of the ancient Christian martyr whose eyes rolled and whose head shook as the people gathered kneeling at its feet.[146]

The regulars' custody of such magical powers caused the neighbourhood to trust them with charms of their own. The canons of Little Dunmow (Essex) were made keepers of the legendary bacon flitch (i.e. joint) awarded to loyal spouses.[147] The demand of devotees of St Bartholomew at Crowland Abbey for knives to be distributed at the altar eventually caused a conflict with Abbot John Welles, perhaps as much for the cost as for the claims to spiritual power.[148]

Religious houses offered up a form of practical magic. Their sacred objects were not only borrowed from the community; they might also be mobilised to point in the direction of the religious to meet a present threat. Persistent and damaging disorder in the neighbourhood of Lytham Priory was brought to a halt in 1530 when the monks processed the consecrated host outside of their precinct.[149] The spiritual charge that their custody had given the conventual church was still understood to hold a protective power. The belief that the heart of a church offered a sanctuary inviolable even for the criminal was centuries old but in the half-century before the Break with Rome it still found many followers.[150] Public claims of sanctuary at Westminster had provoked Edward IV (1461–70; 1471–83) to strike at the exempt status of the monastery.[151] Yet at the succession of the Tudors the traffic continued. A wide variety of the regulars' churches received – readily, perhaps – the fugitive. An escaped prisoner took himself into the city church of the Crutched

Friars in London during Mass to avoid apprehension by the dogged serjeant-at-arms, Richard Cruse, who was pursuing him.[152] When Beaulieu Abbey (Hampshire) was closed in 1538, in the sanctuary of 'suche compasse', there were unnumbered 'merderers & felons ... & hopless men', who at first were apparently overlooked by the king's commissioners because they were kept within the enclosure of the choir.[153] Some were convinced that the protection of these houses covered both people and their possessions. James Huddelston seemed to be channelling some magic when he hid a coin in the post of a barn at the abbey of Stratford Langthorne (Essex), which his wife after his death then struggled to recover.[154]

The physical presence of a religious house pressed so firmly on the Tudor outlook that at times it eclipsed the community living inside. 'Those impys of anti-Christ abbaiys & nonryes', were the personification of Roderyck Mors's polemic *Complaynt* which first appeared in print in 1542.[155] For their apologists, the 'abbayes themselues were good', exemplars of the virtues of 'beneuolence', 'commoditie' and 'curtesie'.[156] The tendency to see only a corporation not a community was uncomfortably clear in the commissioners' handling of the dissolution, especially in the surprise they expressed when they met the wide variety of non-religious who depended on life inside the precinct. It may be that the outside world was generally unaware of both the variety and the number of people, not professed religious, for whom the house was a fixed (if fixed-term) place of residence. Their particular tie to the house may have been masked by the growing number of tenants occupying both residential and working buildings inside the domain of the monastery or friary on purely commercial terms. These dependents were also hidden from the public routes through the precinct, some in the departmental ranges, such as the almonry and infirmary, some given the privilege of chambers so close to the conventual centre that to all intents and purposes they were enclosed.

The public image of their institutions did not quite cast professed men and women into the shadows, but it did affect how they were perceived. Monks, friars and nuns were viewed more by what was known of them than what could be seen and experienced at first hand. The differences between their congregations and customs were commonly covered over by a blanket description, both institutional, such as 'orders' or 'possessioners', and insulting, such as 'abbey lubbers'.[157] Their outside overseers, bishops, patrons and the Crown, still recognised them as the representatives of orders that reached across the realm, and Christendom. But away from their formal acts, regulars were now spoken of as all members of the same body. The profile of a regular estate in England had first been fixed in the public mind during the anticlerical controversy stirred by John Wyclif (d. 1384) and the Lollard radicals he had inspired. By the end of the fifteenth century the characteristics of friar and monk were represented as different aspects of the same personality. The ballad of 'Robin Hood and the Curtal Friar', current before it was captured in print in 1560, saw the eponymous hero confront a friar at Fountains Abbey, a Cistercian monastery now recast as an archetypal house of religion, a haunt of the breed of the regular religious that its readership knew best.[158]

Perhaps only the rarest of religious orders in Henry's England were regarded in their own terms. In literate society at least, there does seem to have been a fascination for the monks of the Carthusian congregation and for the monks and nuns of the kingdom's only Birgittine foundation at Syon (Middlesex). The dual arrangement of men and women drew less attention from contemporaries than their separate, special characters, one a school of pastoral care, the other a template for personal and household piety, memorably visualised in the woodblock frontispiece of the *Orcharde of Syon* (1519).[159] When the last of the monasteries were closed, it was the loss of Syon alone that elicited any word of lament from onlookers.[160] The monks' presence, in robes of white (or mostly white), and their practice of contemplation, were recalled apart from other more commonplace ways of the cloister. An understanding of their differences was a hallmark of the heightened piety of an early Tudor household. A prayer in the primer of one pious family looked out across the landscape, 'convens of monkys chanons et chartrus celestynes freres pristes all . . . hermytes recuses'.[161] Their reformed performance provided the template for monasticism in its most ideal form. The monks who waited on the knights in Malory's *Le Morte Darthur* were clothed in white; when the widowed Queen Guinevere was cloistered at Amesbury she 'ware whyte clothes & blacke'.[162] Of course, it was a skewed view, as through a reversed telescope. There were fewer than 200 of these men and women in a cloistered total population of 50 times as many. Yet their influence on the expectations of elite society served to separate them from the regular estate even before 1534.

Tudors did recognise the customary differences in monastic dress very clearly. John Rudston, a wealthy London draper who made his will in 1531, showed professional care in providing for the different habits of the different members of the religious orders: long grey woollen cloth for the Observant friars from Greenwich to Newcastle (five marks); white for the Lady Prioress of Dartford and four of her nuns.[163] They were depicted in images in these years as much as if not more than in the written word, and in a variety of media – fresco, oil, stained glass and woodcut. In many of these, close attention was given to the colours and styles of their habits. The Benedictine women to whom Bishop Alcock presented his *Spousage* were drawn very correctly, with the white wimple and chemise just visible beneath their black robe. The three ages of the monk represented in a stained-glass pane from Deerhurst (Gloucestershire) depict the Benedictines of middle and old age in habits of a fine blue-black, while their novice, fresh-faced with abundant blond curls, wears the brown worsted of the youth yet to make his solemn profession (see Fig. 3). This one mark of the monks' corporate identity was well understood, it would appear, in the king's own household. In 1527, Henry himself directed a revel that satirised the great heretic Luther, in which Religion was played as a Benedictine, in a habit of black sarcenet.[164] There was something about their dress that gave justification for public suspicion and an outward sign of their deceit. Bale wrote of 'masking monks and Turkish nuns'.[165] Public attention to these details perhaps reflected the degree to which they were curated by the religious themselves. One of the stories of the Carthusian divine John Batmanson made public after his death focused on the fabric of the brothers' habits: the shade of Brother John put in the hand of one of his brothers a swatch of blanket cloth to remind him of their calling to simple clothes; the fragment was displayed at their religious house at Sheen (Surrey).[166]

Like the Church's other estate, the secular clergy of diocese and parish, the religious were recognised as persons of status. By 1509 it was usual for monks and friars to be addressed as 'Sir', the same courtesy title which was now given to secular priests. Personal references to nuns are rare, but it does appear that the generic Latin title, 'domina', was used in English translation as Lady. The social status of superiors, of male and female houses, was set ahead of any spiritual authority. This was only to be expected since most people knew of these superiors only in their capacity as proprietor or employer; if they saw them in person at all it was more likely to have been presiding at court than at the steps of the high altar. Robert Grevill and his wife, Margaret, of Charlton Kings (Gloucestershire), knew of the mother abbess of Syon not as the head of a rare community of spiritual women but as the regal personage who in 1507 held them to account at her manor court at Cheltenham.[167] Such exalted social standing did not extend to the community below the superior. Indeed, the subordinate officers of a monastery were often challenged outside their own domain. There had been some shocking instances of disrespect in years past: a cellarer of St Albans Abbey was once set in the stocks by tenants when he appeared to collect their rent.[168] Now, charges of assault on the officers of monasteries frequently came to court.

For their part, the religious of this generation appeared to be conflicted over their position in the world and the esteem they hoped to find. A new and growing taste among monks for adopting at their profession the Christian name of a favourite saint or the surname of a Christian virtue, pointed to an impulse to efface their social identity. This must also explain another novelty in their spoken and written addresses, when they titled themselves as 'trew and pore bedeman', as Nicholas Rawlyns addressed himself.[169] The label is occasionally found in the letters of nuns but generally women seem to have been less discomforted by the status of their profession; of course, by contrast with the majority of men entering monasteries or friaries, most women religious were from prosperous families and their cloistered environment may have seemed little more than a different region of the same world into which they had been born.

It is possible that the friars struggled most of all. The structure of their schooling in the order displaced them from the networks, social and regional, they had known in the world, projecting them into the neighbourhood as conspicuous foreigners, a profile heightened by the presence in most provincial convents of genuine aliens, Flemings, Germans, Italians, who were passing through. Nor were the friars set apart from their neighbours by a living of visible wealth. They were recognised for their priesthood and the services they offered in the pulpit, at confession and at the deathbed and after, at the funeral, but by their very habit they were also judged to be poor. The simple 'carving of fryer . . . shoues or knootted gyrdles' marked them for a living that was less than other men.[170] Knowing that the friars' churches stood taller and longer than the cathedrals and their precincts consumed a wide acreage of cities and towns, it might seem incongruous but the first word in most people's mouths after 'Sir Friar' was simply 'poore'. They owned the name. 'A pore friers token' was Prior Richard Ingworth's offering to Thomas Cromwell from the Dominican convent at King's Langley.[171] It was an expression of their vocation; also it reminded their patrons of their responsibility towards them.

While their clerical status and institutional home set the regulars apart from wider society, their behaviour as individuals seemed to betray traits that everybody shared. The preamble of the first statute for the suppression of monasteries (1536) accused them of 'vicious, carnal and abominable living'.[172] In fact, the most common assumption about their lifestyle was altogether less shocking: they were thought to live too well, using their unearned income to indulge a prodigious appetite for luxury of every kind. It was a perception rooted in an old tradition of anticlerical satire. Two hundred years before Henry's reign, Geoffrey Chaucer presented his audience with a monk 'faire for the maistrie' who loved a 'fat swan' best 'of any rost' and a nun no stranger to 'rosted flesh, or milk or wasstel bread' or costly finery such as 'a brooch of gold ful sheene'.[173] Chaucer's images were renewed in the new Henrician satires. In *Philip Sparrow*, John Skelton pictured a nun, Dame Margery, tempting her pet bird with 'white bred crommes'.[174] 'They eate their belies full', complained *Rede me and be nott wrothe*, 'every man as moche as he wull.'[175] At the same time new printed histories of the saints held up against the friars the standards of the past, as how Thomas Becket 'was withinforth a monke ... dyd great abstynence makynge his body lene and his soule fat'.[176] Alexander Barclay broke out of his literary frame to make explicit social commentary: 'the frers have store every day of the weke, but every day our meat is for to seke'.[177] Now these views were not confined to learned commentators and their literate audience. Everyone imagined the cloister to be a white-bread world. The Elizabethan, Francis Trigge (1547?–1606), preserved an old proverb of his boyhood: 'fat men were said to have abbots' faces'.[178] The prejudice was so deep-seated that when the king's commissioners saw the monks' kitchens and refectories for themselves in 1535 and instead met signs of a spartan existence, their surprise was almost audible: from the table at Bury St Edmunds there came the astonishing news, 'not anythynge mete for a grett man'.[179]

The accusation of greed was coupled with indolence. Anyone who had heard a preacher or read their primer knew the proverb, 'idleness is the enemy of the soul'; some were well aware it was to be found in the best-known rule for monks, that of St Benedict. And now they returned it to scold them. 'Religious folke [I] calleth ydle theves,' railed the radical Simon Fish in 1529. In the year of the suppression statute, Thomas Starkey affirmed, 'we see now reyneth ... much slothe [and] idulnes ... wherfor we cry, alter thes fundatyonys & turne them to bettur use'.[180]

From self-indulgence it was a short step to dishonesty, so there was also a ready association of the religious – men especially – with sly, swindling trickery. The deceit of the cowled man was the stock in trade of the balladeer. The earliest of the tales of Robin Hood turned on the betrayal of the hero by a 'gret-hedid munke'.[181] Among the new-minted misericords of the king's father's mausoleum at Westminster was the figure of a monk and a money bag, with a devil at his shoulder beckoning him to hell. When he wrote in favour of the prior of Launceston (Cornwall), Sir William Courtenay saw his honesty as a distinguishing feature: 'whatever people may report . . . he is guiltless of simony'.[182] Even though a staunch defender of church tradition, Thomas More, when he tried his own hand at the genre, wrote of a sergeant outwitting a merchant and thus 'to play the friar'.[183] Above all, mendacity was the special mark of the friar. Such was the premise of a *Mery geste of the frere and the boye* (1513), in which a wicked stepmother tried to turn her husband's son from his house with the collusion of a friar who 'bete hym well and gyve hym sorowe'.[184] When the spectacle of (Wolsey's) convent closures generated public and popular chatter about suppression, the *Abbot of euyll profytes* (printed in 1530) made the first of his people's commandments the 'withdrawal of the fals, flaterynge fryars'.[185] It seemed an expression of their public image that an unfortunate friar, William, was arraigned at Canterbury for 'conjuring with men's goods to the great deceit of the king's subjects'.[186] It was no less an article of faith for the noble poet, Henry Howard (1516/17–47), who himself had scarcely come of age when the friaries were closed in 1538, '[their] tongue presents the wicked sort,' he wrote, they are 'false wolves that do their ravin hide'.[187] The slyness of the friar, almost as a corporate characteristic, seemed to pass into policy. Bishop John Longland instructed the prioress of Nuncotham (Lincolnshire) 'suffre noo moo freers to serve in your monastery butt . . . vertuous honest seculer preestes'.[188] The casting of a friar as an accomplice to conspiracy in *Romeo and Juliet* (1591x1596) was no expression of reformed distaste some fifty years after their passing out of England but a reminder of an old suspicion.

There was an association of the religious with lechery too, but it was not spoken of, or shown in stories of them as a matter of course, as if it was inseparable from their status and the manner of their life. The canonical commitment of the clergy and women under vows to chastity attracted comment, critical and satirical, as much as it had done for generations, but it was neither the first nor the favourite topic when treating of the Church. Nor was there any suggestion in public and popular discourse that it was a particular problem concerning that part of the clergy professed to a rule. In his 1529 *Supplicacyon for the beggers*, Simon Fish argued against the general principle of clerical abstinence, and in the first instance for its social damage, hindering 'the generation of the people wherby all the realme at length . . . shulde be continued'; his secondary concern was that it had encouraged 'a hundreth thousand ydell hores yn your realme whiche wolde haue gotten theyre lyuing honestly'.[189] The most fully formed reflection on the life of a nun, a Middle English poem of the early fifteenth century, was equivocal about the place of chastity in the nunnery, 'sum loved [Dame Chastity] in hert fulle dere / And there weren that dyd not so / And sum set no thyng by her / But gafe her gode leve for to go'.[190] These questions conflicted with images of the monastic vocation as Christ-like. Bishop Alcock preached that the religious house might be the one heaven possible on earth. There 'a woman of rely-gyon or a man . . . they speke with God'; it is the world beyond that is haunted by the devil and a violation like that of Dinah, daughter of Jacob and Leah, in the camp of Shechem (Genesis 34:31).[191] It seems there was still an appetite for this idea. Personal seals from these years often featured a cowled figure.[192] The seal ring of an Exeter merchant showed the bust of a monk surrounded by a crown of thorns.[193]

There was a carnal aspect to representations of the religious, men in particular, although it concerned not their predilections but their physical selves. There was a ready association of the monk or the friar with the lowest forms of bestial vulgarity. The most common image of a cowled religious in a carved misericord was in a pose that was startlingly scatological: applying bellows to the anus of an ape (Great Malvern Priory) or gathering waste from beneath unidentified buttocks (St George's Chapel, Windsor). Of course, the Malvern monks had commissioned this scheme and it is clear that the professed took possession of these caricatures. A Cistercian at Cleeve drew a cartoon portrait of a brother with a bulbous nose in the frater (refectory) passageway (see Fig. 4).

Increasingly, there was another inflection to this image, that monks' humanity itself was tenuous. John Heywood (c. 1497–c. 1580) opened his *Mery play between the pardoner and the frere* (1533) with an apology, knowing that his audience would blanch at the presence of his second character: 'My friends . . . take ye heed. Beware how ye despise the poore freres. But do them with an herty chere receve'.[194] Sir Francis Bigod (1507–37) in 1535 pictured 'a blinde abbot . . . never wolde set him dwne at dyner but he wold first undo the poyn before his bely'.[195] Bishops in their capacity as king's visitors had long been struck especially by the sick, disturbed even ungovernable creatures apparently harboured in these houses. Prior William Louth of Walsingham was found in 1514 to keep an old fool (senem fatuum) in his household whom he goaded to perform.[196] Cases coming before the courts, and to the attention of ministers of the Crown, often seemed to flush out such unfortu-nates. The investigation of the suspected murder of Abbot Matthew Deveys of Holm Cultram (Cumbria) laid bare a pattern of sickness and incapacity across the monastery.[197] Quite apart from the challenge he might present to the king's Supremacy, Christopher Burrel of the Canterbury Observants was found to be mad.[198] By the time of their first visits, the royal commissioners anticipated a sorry array of inhuman specimens and they reported on them in the unmistakable tone of seeing preconceptions confirmed: 'fantasticall [and] more than half frantyke' was a canon they found at Conishead, at Ulverston (Cumbria); the visible scars of the venerable warden of the Winchester Augustinian friars were pictured in prurient detail, like 'a canker or a pock or a fistula [or] I know not [what]'.[199]

Interestingly, these savage caricatures were rarely made for religious women. Particular cases of sin, of fornication, of childbirth, were reported, but not framed by any comment on the nature of the women of the cloister. As became clear, with some bewilderment, to the king's visitors of 1535, women known to have had sexual relationships and to have given birth had held on to their places in their religious house. The tale attached to Anne Colte, abbess (1529–35) of Wherwell (Hampshire), was of two pregnancies, at the beginning and then at the summit of her monastic career.[200] Men on the outside, as well as those within the monastic establishment, spoke with some detached respect of most of the female leadership. Writing to Lord Thomas Dacre of Wolsey's meddling in the management of convents in the north, Abbot Huby of Fountains was positively defensive of 'the young sister' recently elected to lead at Newcastle. The most he was inclined to say of the women was that they were easily cowed, and vulnerable: 'they will trip and dance in the same trace as the other sisters have done'.[201]

These portraits of cloister personalities, from the life, or by repute, point to a change in outlook in this Henrician generation. They did not think at once of a corporate body of the regular clergy that 'stereth them so furiously to rage' and 'causeth insurrection ... and moveth them to ryse ... and to make havoc', as it did for the reformer William Tyndale (*c.* 1494–1536).[202] Radicals were now fixed on a fervid antimonasticism: 'oure gostly religious' were no longer vital beings but instead a litany of vice, greed, hypocrisy, mendacity, intimations of antichrist. Yet the neighbourhood at large reflected more often on the common humanity of the men and women committed to this life. Theirs was an occupation as much as a calling, to be weighed and measured for what it offered lay society and how well it was carried out. Their characters were as diverse as any in their own household, extended family or the neighbourhood beyond, and their own born nature would always cut through the uniform habit, the regular customs, and the refinement of their surroundings.

Interviewed in 1511 by their Visitor, Archbishop William Warham, the canons of Leeds Priory (Kent) spoke like the most staunch men of Kent when they complained that the head of their house had allowed a Frenchman – one William 'Parys' – to make his profession there.[203] John Heywood set a scene of contrast between his pardoner and his friar: the first stepped forward to read formulae from a papal bull, but the second put himself among his audience, to preach, 'in our English tongue …'.[204] The culture of the cloister was the 'langage maternall', confirmed Alexander Barclay, erstwhile monk of Ely Cathedral Priory, and its people were 'our natyfe nacion' no less, 'dwellers of England'.[205]

Their names were as well known to them as any in the locality, perhaps more so than any bishop or great lord. Now their personal badges – monograms, blazons of arms – framed their daily scenes, on the doorpost of the inn (Winchcombe), the middle arch of the town bridge (Evesham), and the pulpit of the parish church (Cranborne, Dorset). For the first time in the long history of the religious orders, their own, recognisable portraits were to be found in fresco, oil, stained glass, stone and in printer's ink. The chapter-house windows at Bury St Edmunds showed the superiors of the past century wearing the Canterbury cap of Tudor divines.[206] Prior William Bolton of St Bartholomew, Smithfield, pictured himself and his canons in a panel set up in the church calling upon the neighbourhood to help them with their prayers (precibus succurrite vestris).[207] Barclay, in his Benedictine habit, greeted readers of his *Myrrour* on its title-page. King Henry's subjects knew the religious orders quite differently because they could look them in the eye.

When the people of Henrician England considered the closure of the religious houses, they were still attended by their legends. Often the first thought of the old aristocracy was for the traces of their forebears. Ten days after the bill for the suppression of monasteries became statute law in 1536, Thomas de la Warr explained to Cromwell his attachment to the priory at Boxgrove (West Sussex), '[where] lyeth many of my annsytorys and also my wyffys mother', and his plan at the last for himself to be joined with that past, '[I] have made a power chapel to be buryd in'.[208] At the prospect of Thetford Priory's closure, Thomas Howard appeared almost oppressed by his sense of history, of 'the divers other duks' of his family's heritage, of the Tudor lineage (since he had brought the duke of Richmond's body there) and of his own, first marriage to the daughter of another royal dynasty, Anne of York (d. 1511).[209] Those lacking their titles and landed domains were disposed to make detached calculations of the value and use of the contents of these houses, but from Bristol to Sheppey, Cockermouth to Plymouth, it seems they also wanted the furnishings which the Augmentation agents had found to be old and worn away: bought for just a few shillings, these were not judicious investments but treasured souvenirs. The imprint of their history on the neighbourhood was so profound that the beginning of the end provoked actions, individual and collective, outside the usual patterns of behaviour: trespass, riot, petition, and even the purchase by subscription of structures beyond the scale of their own lives. Even the commissioners of the Crown who came to the closures with the most decided opinion of monastic men and women could not easily sidestep their myths. The king's visitor, John London, was disparaging of the angel's wing venerated at Reading Abbey yet he was quite distracted by the other curiosities collected there, and the stories told about them: 'the dagger that they say slew king Henry the VI and the knyff that kylled Saynt Edward with many other lyk holy things'.[210] Richard Leighton, who had visited many more houses, recognised the danger of distraction and aimed always to descend on them either very early or very late, when their cult traditions were dormant. The live charge of their daytime customs was all too apparent when his colleague, Richard Pollard, arrived at Canterbury in September 1538 to bring down the shrine of Thomas Becket. At once he seemed to forget his brief and 'buzid [himself] . . . in prayer with offeryngs'.[211]

The royal commissioners were conflicted because the traditions of the religious houses persisted, not only in sight and sound but also in widespread word and image, to the very end. Their lore was still 'fresh printed' just as many of them were being closed. In 1538, when the largest number surrendered, the London presses offered readers learning from Merton Prior (Surrey) and piety from Syon.[212] Their hold on the public scene drew much of its strength from the fact they were still closely associated with those ideas and institutions on which the new Tudor state was steadily rising: property, lordship, prelacy and the Crown. The stories of the regulars and their treasures carried with them the first beginnings of these fundamental forces that fashioned the secular world. In fact, their houses offered more than a portal to a primordial English age. Here, as Thomas Howard mused at Thetford, there was monarchy both past and present; here too was living lordship, material, social and cultural power. Cromwell's men struggled to shake off the legends of the cloister above all because they lived on. Like Galahad's White Abbey, the religious houses of Henrician England were repositories of past myth. But they were also a source of power in that present world.

II

THE RELIGIOUS PROFESSION

In the winter of 1539 five young people passed through the gates of the monasteries in their home city of Chester to begin a life under a rule. In the north-east corner of the city's Roman walls at the Benedictine abbey of St Werbergh, Richard Downe and Thomas Rutter now exchanged colourful tunics and hose for the washed-grey worsted habit and woollen stockings of the novice.[1] Richard's worldly outfit may have been finer than Thomas's because his was a family of some property and position in the region, whereas his new colleague was a city boy, 'trade'. At this great old abbey, Richard was turning sideways from one life of status to another; Thomas, on the other hand, was surely stepping up. Diagonally opposite their new home, in the city's south-west corner in the lee of the castle, at the Benedictine nunnery of St Mary, Margery Crafford, Margery Taylour and Elizabeth Whitehed were themselves settling into their novices' weeds.[2] Perhaps Elizabeth was the least perturbed by her change of state. Probably she was not the first of her family to pursue a career in the Church and her family background meant that like the new 'Brother' Richard she was accustomed to a certain status in her world. Crafford and Taylour may not have been born into a familiarity with the cloister life, and their new surroundings may have seemed forbidding, if not without a promise of a better life to come.

In the affairs of the Tudor state something of a malaise descended at the turn of this year. The truce with France had fractured beyond repair. On New Year's

Day, King Henry met his new bride, Anne of Cleves, for the first time. It was clumsy, and in an instant it seems the king was repelled.

Yet in Chester the outlook was hopeful. The religious houses gave the impression of a great energy, old bottles brimming over with new wine. At St Werbergh's an ambitious rebuild of the cloister may only now have been reaching completion; there was new work likewise at St Mary's apparently also in the cloister.[3] The cloister was the thoroughfare of a monastery, marking the route from the worship of the choir all the way out into the world. Its fabric, more than any other, was marked by the human life of the community. Here in Chester it seemed in rude health as 1540 dawned.

The arrival of five new recruits at Chester's oldest religious houses in what was to be the very last year of monasticism in England is certainly eye-catching but it was by no means unique. In 1536–37, as they enforced the statute for the suppression of small monasteries and again in 1538–40, as they brokered surrenders, the king's commissioners encountered many men and women who had only just begun their cloister careers. It had been a requirement of the king's injunctions, imposed at the 1535 visitation, for any man below the age of twenty-four, the canonical entry point for ordination to the priesthood, to be removed from the house, but it was not rigidly enforced and in many places it was simply ignored.[4] At the same time, a new generation continued to come forward to be professed to the religious life. In the first twenty years of Henry's reign, monasteries of all sizes in each congregation, and the provincial network of friaries, saw a continuous flow of new recruits. Ordination records can be used as a proxy for the admission of men to religious houses as the conferral of orders usually came in the first months after their entry. They show both great abbeys and meagre priories presenting clusters of three, five, even seven candidates every three to five years.[5] At the turn of the century bishops had shown some concern at the dwindling of regular communities under their jurisdiction.[6] The leadership of the Benedictines had voiced their own anxieties when they met Cardinal Wolsey in 1518 'for in this our tempest (the world now in its last age) they are few and rare that want to lead an observant life'.[7] In fact, the numbers recorded at ordinations and visitations indicate that by this date a recovery was already underway. The expansion may have been engineered, with communities accepting new applicants more frequently than in preceding decades. Perhaps also the regular life held a greater appeal for this Henrician generation. They were well aware that career paths in the secular world opened only with substantial patronage. If not yet committed to the cloister for the whole span of their life, they could see its unique opportunities for schooling and university.

Between Henry's accession and his headship in 1534 no fewer than seventy-one men entered Christ Church, Canterbury.[8] Of the forty-odd monasteries in the diocese of Norwich, the populations of 30 per cent males and almost 20 per cent females were larger by this date than they had been at any time since the fourteenth century.[9] Recruitment was relative to the size of the house. At the poor priory of St Mary Magdalen, Bristol, the commissioners of 1535 found one nun, 'aged and impotent', and one novice.[10] Yet it was a measure of ready supply and steady demand that small communities now saw new admissions just as often as the large ones. The turn, or return towards, the religious houses may have been a particular feature of provincial England: here as many as three adults in every 500 were professed, whereas in the widely dispersed monasteries and friaries of Wales the ratio remained as low as 1:1000.[11] The suppression of the smaller monasteries in 1536–37 did not stop the traffic. The abbot and convent of Cockersand (Lancashire) purchased their exemption from the suppression statute in recognition that their monastic presence continued to grow.[12] At the very end, novices were present at convents of every size. Three novices signed the surrender at Tynemouth Priory on 12 January 1539.[13] When the gibbeted bodies of rebel monks still dangled in 1537, new friars and monks were being professed along the routes of their Yorkshire marches, at Fountains, Pontefract and Selby. Ordinations, marking the progression of professed men into the full service of their house, were celebrated at Guisborough Priory as late as September 1539.[14] When a deed of surrender was signed there on Christmas Eve 1539, William Kirkeby alias Walton had been a priested monk of Byland (North Yorkshire) for scarcely three months.[15]

Men and women rarely came to the cloister life by force, fervour or through some other misfortune. Rather their profession was usually the result of a sober calculation of the opportunity it could offer, which they, and sometimes those around them, made for themselves. The prospect it presented was more than a pious vocation: practically, there was the opportunity for education, for both sexes, as well as other accomplishments in the performing arts and craft; socially, there was status, conspicuous in the very title of 'Sir Monk' or 'Dame Nun' but also readily apparent in the course of honours achieved by the office-holders of every house. Above all, perhaps, there was the promise of a presence not only in another, or a nether world, inside the cloister, certainly, but also in their own. The religious life was an occupation not (quite) like any other but which even so stood comparison with the other kinds of work contributing to the commonweal of the neighbourhood, the family network and the individual household.

It was a life's work and there was general agreement it should begin just as childhood was left behind. In past centuries adult converts had not been uncommon; now, they were a real rarity. This distinguished England's regular population from the European mainstream where the rise of reformed, observant congregations had acted to draw university graduates, secular clergy and laymen towards the religious life just as they had done during the twelfth-century renaissance. For most young men in Henry's England, the profession of the cloister was a prospect before them as they reached the end of their schooldays. By 1509 there was a grammar school in geographical reach of most of England's provincial population.[16] They were fee-paying but many also supported those without the means to pay, both the chartered institutions and those that amounted to little more than a master and gathering of boys at the west end of the parish church. The most institutionalised of the schools offered a syllabus of studies to occupy a pupil from boyhood (upwards of seven) to their middle teens, leading them from an elementary knowledge of letters to advanced grammar, logic and a grounding in philosophy. From here he might pass on to university if, of course, social and material opportunity allowed. But if a religious profession was contemplated, for most, this was the moment for entry.

Typically the boys were aged between fifteen and eighteen; those whose schooling had not been in a grammar school may have arrived at a religious house earlier, to take advantage of the teaching provided inside the precinct, to those monks that still needed it, and to boys admitted into the almonry. At the turn of the century, Thomas Gray was 'putt to scole' for four years at Topcliffe (North Yorkshire), under the tuition of the duke of Northumberland's steward and was 'after thys . . . wase fowlden at thabbey of Nedeborough [Newburgh Priory, North Yorkshire] where he wase chylde of the farmarye' for three years.[17] When John Cole planned a grammar school for Faversham Abbey (Kent) he expected the monastery's novices not be teenagers as they were to be taught 'as all other children'.[18] Under cross-examination, Richard Halford, canon of Bruton Abbey (Somerset), aged twenty-four 'or therabout', could not remember precisely when he had entered the house but that it was 'vii, viii or ix yeres' before; perhaps he had been only fourteen.[19]

Without an institutional setting or any common syllabus for their schooling, young women may have entered the religious life over a wider span of years. Most were in their middle teens; fifteen was the typical age.[20] But some may still have been on the borders of childhood, and occasionally there were those who stepped out of their home life at an age when family members must have thought they would stay forever. Of the cohort of women who entered Romsey Abbey in July 1534, two, Marion Goddard and Katherine Wooddam, were fourteen, another, Alice Stanley, was fifteen, and Agnes Hall, surely seeming like a matron beside them, was thirty-one.[21] Agnes may have been a newcomer but it is possible she had lived among the women for some time before making her profession. By contrast with the men, among whom, historically, the selection and timing of admissions had been strictly controlled, female houses held some women who lived for a time on the threshold of the monastic enclosure, following the pattern of life of the fully professed but postponing any commitment of their own, or seeing it postponed by kinfolk on the outside. Old Agnes herself was unusual but there may have been more like Brigid, a Franciscan at the London Minories, clothed as a novice at twenty, an age when many of her peers were already married with children.[22]

The place of school on the route to the religious house lent a particular social profile to male entrants. It was those in the middle tiers of Tudor society whose developing cultural attitudes and professional ambitions had sustained the spread of school foundations; it was they too with the money and large households that could bear the cost of boys spending years on end at their books. It was a broad social category that included city merchants, provincial tradesmen, yeoman farmers and gentry clans claiming a capital manor and a portfolio of property. This is not to say that those above and below their station, the aristocracy and the tenantry, were not to be seen at grammar school, but those of them who passed on to a monastery or friary were far fewer than in the early Middle Ages. John Bourchier, propelled into the abbacy at Leicester by Thomas Cromwell in 1534, carried a family name with connotations of the old nobility and certainly had the family capital to have come to the monastic life by way of Eton and King's College, Cambridge.[23] In a peaceable kingdom, with a rapidly expanding royal household, permanent court and widening array of offices of state there was no shortage of occupations for noble youth; meanwhile the expectation of a formal education effectively closed off the cloister to those whom school charity was unable to reach.

The female profession was a further class apart. The social composition of the larger, wealthier houses was markedly more concentrated than their male counterparts. Religious women were recruited from the top tiers of Tudor society, the elite of merchant families, the better-off gentry and, sometimes, if rarely, nobility and royalty. This was little different from earlier times. The oldest monasteries for women traced their ties to royal and noble dynasties far into the remote past; the newer foundations for newer orders were themselves the projects of elite patrons. The youngest nunneries in Henrician England, Denny (Cambridgeshire, 1342), Dartford (Kent, 1346) and Syon (Middlesex, 1415), owed their existence, respectively, to the countess of Pembroke and the Plantagenet and Lancastrian kings.[24] The conspicuous profile of the communities surely reinforced their patterns of recruitment over time. There is no record of young women of lower status being rejected by nunneries; equally there is no record that they looked to pursue a life there. Of 170 women professed to the religious life in the diocese of Norwich between 1350 and 1540 whose social status is known, only four (2 per cent) were of yeoman (or lesser) stock.[25] Seen from outside as much as within, these communities of women were socially exclusive. Isabel Stanley, prioress of King's Mead, near Darley (Derbyshire) spoke for many of her sisters across the county:

> Wenese these churles . . . overlade me? They shall not be so hardy but they shall avye upon their bodies and be nailed with arrowes; for I am a gentlewoman comen of the greatest of Lancashire and Cheshire; and that they shall know right well.[26]

The cloister profession was, above all, a matter of family. It is likely that most of the men and women who entered the religious life in the sixteenth century followed the example of kinfolk of their own and earlier generations. Everywhere there were those for whom religious houses were now an established family enterprise. For many the family concern was for the religious life in general and each generation made their entry wherever there was an opening. Still, there were some who saw the life of a particular house as their own hereditary occupation. Magnates who recognised their status as founders, benefactors and chief stewards sometimes formalised this by charter. The Courtenay earls of Devon held the right to a noviceship at Tavistock (Devon); the de Percies of Great Chalfield (Wiltshire) the same to the nearby Cluniac priory of Monkton Farleigh.[27] The names of men

61

professed at the greater Benedictine abbeys and priories bear witness to a handful of dynasties dominating admissions from one generation to another. In a little over eighty years (1457–1540) there were as many as eight Goldstons at Christ Church Priory, Canterbury.[28] Families with a history of female religious profession seem to have been less attached to a house than to a tradition of regular life, be it Benedictine, Cistercian, or that of the mendicant orders. Recruitment to the friaries, by contrast, may have been more ad hoc. There are few full lists of names before the final surrender of the houses, but their organisation may have been an obstacle to family ties: a novice friar was soon dispatched to the *studium* designated to serve the convents in his region; from there he might well move through the network of houses in a near-continuous rotation. Perhaps it was as a remedy to this drift that the patron of the Dorchester Franciscans, Sir John Byconil, provided exhibitions to support the study of their novices at the convent, with the condition that they were known henceforth as 'Byconil's friars'.[29]

Tudor families entertained the prospect of a monastic life for any of their children regardless of their sex or the order of their birth. Certainly, it was not unknown for first-born boys or girls to choose the cloister. There was no hard and fast pattern in families' placement of their women, although a profusion of daughters often led to more than one religious profession within the one family. Thomas Goddard (d. 1538) was the father of no fewer than nine girls and his three youngest, Joan, Dorothy and Maryon, were all professed.[30] He was in the best of company: the youngest royal princesses of York and Tudor had both made monastic professions. But it would be wrong to think the young people had no choice. The Campion boys, sons of William, a London plumber, made their way in the city by parallel professional routes: one was a musician, an organist; the other secured entry to the most prestigious foundation in or around the metropolis, Westminster Abbey.[31] The three Nowers sisters, Agnes, Amery and Grace, followed each other into the same Benedictine priory of St Giles-in-the-Wood at Flamstead (Buckinghamshire).[32] Thomas Burgh decided to share the religious profession of his sister, Beatrice; his support for his sister is suggested by the book he wrote out for her.[33] Just as often a family with only one living daughter led the girl to choose the religious life, or have it chosen for her. Two only daughters of well-off Bristol merchants, Agnes Hawkes and Alice Spicer, were dispatched to distant abbeys, Amesbury (Wiltshire) and Shaftesbury (Dorset).[34] The profession of Bridget Browning in the Dominican convent at Dartford was negotiated with the king's commissioners precisely because, as the prioress explained, it had been the expressed will of her mother that 'she should be a religious woman'.[35]

The determination of families to set their children en route for the cloister was driven by worldly concerns. In spite of its institutional setting, a religious profession presented the prospect of a personal status, monied and propertied, that was at least equal to those apparent in wider society, through office, business or marriage; in terms of the paths available to men in the secular Church, the cloister was a serious consideration. Thomas More thought for a monk to achieve such honours was the very curse of their soul.[36] But their immediate benefits were impossible for the incoming novice to ignore. The rebuses of successful superiors stood in relief on public-facing walls. The gold stone of Thomas, prior of Canterbury (1495–1517), stood out at the head of Burgate, the thoroughfare at the centre of the city. Their social lives were open enough for everyone to know their domestic luxuries, such as the silver cutlery for twelve place settings possessed by Ursula Gosbore, who was not even the head of house at Minster-in-Sheppey (Kent) but her deputy.[37] After 1509 there remained a collective hangover from the political and civil unrest of the last century, and the reign of a second Tudor took time to convince county society that public office, patronage or personal fortunes were any more secure than they had been for their forebears. Families whose status had been established for generations, and those that were only settling into it now may have seen some assurance in the apparently immutable outline of a nearby monastery or a friary's town-centre plot. The antiquity of these houses, their own wealth and powerful patrons might lend their support to the family of the professed. Leading courtiers often made just such a calculation: perhaps Katharine Wadham, daughter of Sir Nicholas, governor of the Isle of Wight, and step-niece of Jane Seymour, was always destined for profession at the royal abbey of Romsey.[38] Beatrice Marshal, Margaret Mounteney and Felice (name unknown) were professed at Dartford Priory after serving for a time as gentlewomen to Lady Salisbury; the social status and household culture of the Dominican convent was a satisfactory counterpart to a permanent place in the household of a great lady.[39] Sir Thomas Urswick (d. 1479), Recorder of London, went so far as to reflect the honour of his daughter, Anne's profession, in his own parish church at Dagenham (Essex), adding her portrait, in her nun's habit, to his own memorial brass (see Fig. 5).

The enduring presence of these religious houses also offered families a platform on which their own standard might be raised. For the Wiltshire Denyses it seems this was the prime objective. Their daughter, Mary, was only chosen as prioress of Kington St Michael (Wiltshire) months before its closure, but somehow money and time were found for her to insert the family blazon in the windows of parlour.[40] Personal ties to an old monastery presented families with more than a symbolic power. A kinsman or woman professed to the community held the potential to open up a host of material benefits to their family, office and properties, farmed or in grant. John Reve's appointment to the abbacy of Bury St Edmunds in 1513 brought his brother Robert into the stewardship, the primary secular office in the town, while another brother, Roger, was also a prominent proprietor. The abbot was remembered as 'kinge' of Bury and he was the head of a very visible royal family.[41] Joan Temys, abbess of Lacock appointed her brother, Thomas, to the stewardship of her house; when the dissolutions advanced, he was her first concern in making leases of convent property.[42]

Religious profession offered families another, precious capital: propriety. A house whose renown had been known time out of mind gave an identity to those whose name and origin were obscure, or needed to be concealed. As he explained at the end of his cloister career, John Musard, the son of a soldier who fought with King Henry's father, saw his entry into Worcester Cathedral Priory as the means to make good the opportunity his father had battled for at the time of Bosworth.[43] In every generation down to 1540 there were a handful for whom their religious house was the first respectable one they had known. The standing of Westminster Abbey as good as effaced the background of Thomas Pomeray, in truth the bastard son of an unnamed nobleman.[44] Cromwell himself knew well the story of Cardinal Wolsey's daughter, whose profession at Shaftesbury Abbey was under his eye in the same months that he oversaw the visitation of 1535.[45] John Walsyngham wiped his own slate clean at Bury St Edmunds; earlier he had been convicted of bigamy.[46] William Benett made an unfortunate investment in a fulling mill – perhaps a family inheritance – and retreated to the monastery to make a fresh start, although as it turned out he found it difficult to detach himself from the trail he left behind him.[47] Thomas Beche, who ended his career as the Benedictine abbot of Colchester, made his profession the moment at which to adopt another family name, Marshall, which presumably he thought better suited to his dignity.[48]

Entry into a religious house was surely as much a family decision as a personal one. Rarely, if ever, was anyone forced into making a solemn profession, but families at different points on the social scale did lead their kinfolk to the cloister for reasons of their own need: to provide an education that otherwise could or would not be found; to mark time prior to an inheritance or a marriage; or, *in extremis*, as a refuge from a volatile home. The models were no lesser dynasties than the royal families of York and Tudor. Edward IV's seventh daughter, Bridget, had been professed at Dartford Priory in her late teenage years; she remained in contact with the royal household at least as long as her elder sister lived.[49] The Queen Dowager, Elizabeth Woodville, entered Bermondsey Abbey and her daughter, Elizabeth of York, spent time with her there and at Westminster Abbey where she had her confinements.[50] Henry VII's Tudor cousins, Edward and Margaret, had both taken religious vows; a grandson of his uncle, Jasper, was a monk of Westminster Abbey.[51]

Provincial society followed suit. Brothers Richard and Robert Symondson of Helmsley (North Yorkshire) were sent to the Cistercian houses of Byland and Rievaulx under the will of their father, John.[52] In 1534 Richard Burton placed his son Clement in the custody of the prior of Markby, 'until such tyme as he comes of age of xviii yeres and longer yff they can agre' where they shall 'fynde hym meate, drynke and lernyng'.[53] The son of Edmund Yeo, a South Devon gentleman, was 'gone with the abbot of Torre' for six years.[54] At around the same time, Arthur, Lord Lisle, had dispatched his stepson, James Bassett, to Reading Abbey, where the abbot 'pleythe hym to his learnyng bothe to laten and to frenche'.[55] Here the house was held to be both a substitute for school and a surrogate family whose household ways would ease a child into adulthood. At Reading, Lisle was advised that young Bassett was in the daily care of the goodwife of his own steward because the boy was still too young reliably to dress himself.[56] 'Litle' Anne Loveday had briefly been in the train of the Queen Elizabeth of York but was then settled at Elstow Priory (Bedfordshire) with a substantial money bag providing £6 13s 4d for the next stage of her upbringing.[57] The view of the monastery as a kindergarten was shared by all those able to plan and pay for the education of their children. Some stretched its services to the absolute limit. A fourteen-year-old named Francis had been brought to Hinton Charterhouse (Somerset) by Edward Stafford, duke of Buckingham; at the latter's execution (1521) he was left there.[58] John Jerves of Thetford put his baby daughter in the care of the nuns of St George's Priory in the town and, confident of their care, he neglected to send them any payment for her stay.[59]

It was this practice, as commonplace at the end of the 1530s as at any earlier time, that encouraged a suspicion that the religious houses trapped young people into profession against their will. The king's commissioners carried this charge with them into the visitation of 1535 and were convinced that they found it confirmed. At St Osyth's Abbey Thomas Legh met twenty-five-year-old Thomas Solmes, who told him he had been threatened into the noviciate by his school-master at the tender age of thirteen and would rather die than live in that state any longer.[60] John London reported to Cromwell that women at the Cistercian monasteries of Fosse, Heynings and Irford had been professed as children.[61] The rumours were amplified in the printed polemic of reformers. *Rede me and be nott wrothe* railed that the religious now threatened the rising generation as a whole: 'Yonge laddes and babes innocent / They brynge in by their intysment / To their leawde congregacion. Whom they reccave to profession.'[62] A tract of 1531 asked if parliament might step in to prevent the profession of children.[63] Learned commentary linked the legend of coercion to current anxiety over the state of marriage in society. In his translation of Erasmus's influential *Encomium matrimonii* (1518), Richard Taverner claimed that too many girls were given to chastity 'thrugh the entysmentes of folyshe women and folyshe fryars'.[64] Real cases of coercive custody occasionally came to court. The experience of John Hawteyn alias Sharington was made the subject of a papal commission of inquiry: placed at the convent of the London Augustinian friars at the age of eight he escaped into the city; recovered by his mother he was returned to the friars and secured release only when he reached his legal majority. Mistress Hawteyn's motive is not recorded but it may have been comparable to that of John de Wessenham, a Norfolk gentleman, who placed his three half-sisters, aged seven, eight and eleven, in the custody of nuns so that their inheritance might be added to the portion destined for his son and daughter-in-law.[65] In these instances it is difficult not to detect some complicity on the part of the religious. Agnes Doryngton complained that Prioress Elizabeth Pulteney of Henwood (Warwickshire) had forced her profession 'contra eius voluntatem'.[66] John Bale, who had himself first entered a Carmelite house at the age of twelve, maintained it was their custom to trap youths into vows, by 'a clogge, a yoke, a snare of Sathan'.[67] The testimony of some of their cemeteries would seem to corroborate this. More than a third of the skeletal remains discovered from the friars' burial ground at Carmarthen were of men below the age of twenty.[68]

Outwardly, entry to a religious house appeared to be a transaction (consensual or otherwise), with solemn profession considered to be a professional occupation. Tudor satires were uncompromising in their conviction: the men and women under the cowl had made a shallow, selfish and material calculation. The only vocation John Skelton saw in the nunnery of *Philip Sparrow* (1508) was for leisure and the sensual pleasures of good food, fine clothes and small animal pets. Thomas More imagined the 'religiosi' of *Utopia* (1516) as the polar opposite of those he knew at home, for they actively looked for celibacy, fasting and worship: 'they profess,' he wrote with heavy irony, 'to be motivated by religion'.[69] The expanding shelf of popular printed manuals for a pious life carried the challenge of a pure vocation out of the cloister and into the layman's home and hearth. 'Se that with all mekenes ye submit your selves unto the vocacion of god', was the stern counsel of Marshall's *Primer*, published in 1535, 'euery man chosyng one in the which he may best subdue his rebellious membre'.[70] Learned clerks and churchmen likewise saw a slackening of spiritual impulses among the rising generation of the professed. 'Human happiness depends above all on the assumption of a . . . life suited to one's natural disposition,' warned Erasmus in his new life of St Jerome, ascetic and scholar of the early church, 'chosen by careful reflection and not by chance'.[71] His *De contemptu mundi* (On contempt for the world) affirmed 'the pleasure that is the solitary life' but warned that 'one ought to entre into religion with good deliberacion and aduisement', for 'no man is constrayned to Christis profession'.[72] A published sermon of Bishop John Longland of Lincoln returned to the image of the monastic life offered by St Benedict in his rule.[73] The script prepared, perhaps at the turn of the century, for the admission of novices at the Benedictine priory of Tywardreath challenged them very directly on the nature of their vocation and the obligations it entailed: 'Yes hit yowr wyl and yow hertely desire to be parte taker of all massis and prayers and almis dede done yn thys holy place or schall be done here after?'[74]

It is very difficult to estimate the personal impulses of Tudor religious; more so perhaps than some before them since they have left fewer words of their own. Alicia Bromfield was sixty-two years old (and a widow?) when she made her profession at St James's Priory, Canterbury, in 1493. Perhaps her choice was pure pragmatism, as it happened well judged since she was still living at eighty in 1511; but possibly it was the ultimate expression of a personal piety she had always carried with her.[75] Among the family members who arranged the entry of women into a nunnery, there was, among the other considerations, a recognition that it was in its essence a spiritual calling. Often, as they propelled them to their profession, they put books of liturgy and prayer into their hands. Elizabeth Olte received a new printed psalter on the occasion of her profession at Ickleton (Cambridgeshire) in 1516.[76] John and Margaret Edwards commissioned a breviary from a professional workshop for their daughter, Elizabeth.[77] The possession of such books, given to them or sought out for themselves, was more common for these generations of religious than ever before. It reflected a taste for private reading that was now well established in the social groups from which they had come. Even so, the surviving examples do reveal some commitment to their contents. Young Elizabeth Olte wrote out prayers of her own which she slipped into the psalter she had from home. At the Benedictine priory of Pilton (Devon), Thomas Olston took up his own pen to write a pocketbook of prayers which he signed in 1521.[78] The prayer book that came into the possession of Margery Byrkenhed of St Mary's Priory, Chester, was not a showpiece of the scribal art and had many previous owners, but she was evidently proud to have the prayer book as she saw to it that her name was written large on the flyleaf (see Fig. 6).[79] John Wheteham, a Carthusian from an unidentified house, wrote what appears to have been a practical manual to guide his monastic life, a book of (unspecified) statutes, 'old' and 'new'.[80]

These books indicate at least some interest in the practice of prayer, and some inclination to learn the pattern of life that made it possible. Some did think about the meaning of their profession. John Ramsey, canon of Merton, was a close reader of Erasmus's life of Jerome, and in his copy he underlined the passages describing the monastic life of the early Church.[81] Ramsey bought the book while he was a student at Oxford and here and at other places of learning in the first decades of the century there was an intellectual interest in early Christian models of the religious life, from the solitary, eremitic, to the communal cenobitic or monastic. It was surely stimulated by the printing of new editions of the works of the Fathers of the Church, and renewed appreciation of their teaching on the practice of the faith. The editors expressed a Christian humanism, which matched a critical view of some of the priorities and institutional problems of the contemporary Church with a researcher's zeal to recover the values and vision of its earliest pioneers. The virtue of original, pure monastic practice was presented to a general readership. Thomas Lupset (c. 1490–1530), a Christian humanist in the Henrician court, urged in his popular *Exhortation* (1534): 'For on alside you shall se menne sweatynge in a contynuall worke bothe of boyde and of mynde, to get these worldly goodes without any mention made of the soules' state: the which the verye friers car lyttel for; as it openly apperith.'[82] Those entering religious houses in the quarter-century before 1534 – men among whom there were, or would be, many graduates, and women from bookish households – may have formed as full an understanding of the vowed life as any of their kind. When, after 1535, they answered for themselves to the king's commissioners, or to Cromwell, they asserted the identity of their own monastic tradition. Richard Beerley of Pershore Abbey (Worcestershire) set himself apart from his weaker brethren (as he saw them) by his profession to the 'rewle of Seint Benet';[83] Dame Joan Fane of Dartford Priory told the vicegerent that she and her sisters were not as other women: 'we be of that profession and bait that none other be of within this realm'.[84]

Whatever the motivating force that brought these men and women to it, successful profession was not necessarily a given. Entry into a monastery of men for centuries had been subject to a test of aptitude. The procedure can only be glimpsed among the institutional records now surviving, but there can be no doubt that male candidates were assessed for their intellectual capacity.[85] It was not sufficient simply to have passed through school; the prospective monk must combine knowledge with the verbal and rhetorical dexterity of a clerk and public priest. It may be that some of the old formalities of examination had been compromised by the end of the fifteenth century. Episcopal visitors were often troubled by the rough-and-readiness of the recruits they met; their repeated calls for the provision of a teacher inside the cloister would point to a recent admission of those whose education remained a work in progress. Sometimes the visitors suspected it was less a matter of judgement than simply the will of the superior. Bishop Longland called on Abbot Richard Pexall of Leicester to see that candidates were selected only with the agreement of the greater and better part of the chapter (maioris et sanioris).[86] It appears some houses admitted candidates without a firm commitment that they could go on to make a full profession; presumably the plan was to choose only after the men or women had lived with them for some time. This might account for the youths met by the royal commissioners in 1535–36 who complained that they had languished in a limbo between the world and the cloister for years on end. A letter to Cromwell from January 1529 describes the challenges and uncertainties of gaining a guaranteed entry. Dan Halnath, a Carthusian (who did not give his first name), reached out for Cromwell's influence to find him a cell in one of the congregation's houses. He was aware of waiting to wear dead men's shoes and 'herteley recommend[s]' himself since 'the great plage of pestylence lately [claimed] iii prestis and ii lay brethren' in London. He hoped for a place in the south of England: 'I love to be sowthwardis', and not to take 'any howce of then northe contry, I may so il avey with colde and aparty northern men'. His preference was for Witham (Somerset) where he had heard 'ther be dyvers cellis wyde ther' but was resigned to somewhere as far as the north Midlands, being 'contented to go to Bevall [Beauvale, Nottinghamshire]'.[87]

Reputedly, the making of friars was a rackety business. When Thomas Manners, 1st earl of Rutland (1497–1543), was called on by Cromwell to investigate loose talk at the Grantham Franciscans, it was as though he had turned over a stone. The source of the trouble was John Colsell, a friar who was just eighteen yet 'schoolmaster' to a novice friar, William Nobul, who was a mere thirteen.[88] When he was questioned for his part in provocative public preaching in 1539, John Dove, prior of the Calais Carmelites, told how he had first entered the religious life at Hitchin (Hertfordshire) where 'he taryed from x to xiiii or xv years if age'.[89] There must be some suspicion arising from the burials of boys aged eight and ten found beneath the chapter house at Leicester's Augustinian friary.[90] There is no reliable account of the admission of any friar of the period, but the tales of teenage hostages should perhaps be offset by what few records there are of the composition of their houses, even those in the remoter provinces. At the time of their surrender in 1538 there were still university graduates distributed throughout the network; concentrations of them among the London and Salisbury Franciscans might suggest that their provincial training schools persisted to the very end.[91]

It is possible that the admission of men was now informed to some degree by a judgement of social status and material circumstances. Writing in 1535, Nicholas Rawlyns recalled that for admission to the London Charterhouse 'they made me to gyve viii pounds in money', and to surrender the income from the church living he held as a secular priest.[92] For women to enter a religious house, these had always been the main qualifications. No level of education was spoken of, although the preference for candidates from the social elite was perhaps a conscious proxy for it. Payments for the acceptance of candidates were condemned by the hierarchy of the secular Church; money to meet the cost of their material needs (clothing, bedding) was accepted under canon law, but not the setting of a price for their place itself.[93] In 1531 Bishop John Longland found it necessary to remind Abbess Joan Thomson of Nuncotham not to expect such payment, repeating the injunction that his predecessor had issued a hundred years before.[94] It seems such transactions were still widespread, common enough for an unscrupulous man like Londoner, William Paunton, to persuade Margaret Cowper to give him plate and jewels on the promise of finding her a 'competent lyvyng' as a sister of St Katharine-by-the-Tower, 'or any other place in or about London'.[95] It seems unlikely that the 40 marks paid by the king for the profession of Elizabeth de la Pole, daughter of the earl of Suffolk, at the London Minories, was simply to provide her with a good profession feast.[96] Drafting his will with two daughters still at home, another Londoner William Marowe set aside the very substantial sum of £40 each for Elizabeth and Katherine, for their marriage or their profession.[97] John Boydell added a bequest in his will, dated 1533, to Florence Bonnewe, prioress of Amesbury, so that at his death his widow, Joan, might make her profession there.[98] A place in a nunnery could be secured by a contract. Joan Lewys, prioress of Usk (Monmouthshire), dispatched such a document to Joan Haryngton in 1497.[99] Of course, legal agreements could be disputed. Prioress Alice of Stratford-at-Bow (Middlesex) went to law to recover a share in a property at Cheshunt (Surrey) in the name of Marion Kays, who intended to enter her house as a nun, but had not yet done so.[100] The Church's prohibition on payment for the profession of women was clouded by the accepted need for entrants to be properly equipped for the life of the novice. A memorandum in the cartulary of Blackborough Priory (Norfolk) set out the bed linen and clothing the newcomer should bring: pairs, and spares, of every article, enough to fill a 'cofre' and 'forceer' (travelling chest).[101] The unspoken expectation was that candidates provided for themselves.

For those unsuited to the observant regime of the choir and cloister it seems there was still an opportunity to belong to the monastery as a lay brother or sister. There was no longer the large community of these *conversi* living in parallel to the professed as there had been in earlier centuries. The Cistercian foundations had been raised and sustained through their earlier generations by the labour of their lay fraternity, but as they let out their land to tenants (which their governing chapter permitted from 1208), they allowed their numbers to dwindle and they turned over their accommodation to other uses.[102] Still, there were sometimes one or two men or women to be found in monasteries in any one of the congregations living there permanently, adhering to their customs and fulfilling some or other domestic role without having made a solemn profession. It may be that the houses no longer made a point of recruiting such members but nonetheless were prepared to accept them ad hoc. Thomas More was aware of it: in his *Utopia*, the Fool saw the solution to beggary was for vagrant men to be sent to the Benedictines as lay brothers.[103] Richard Lyst's life seems to have hit rock bottom before he turned to the life of a lay brother of the Greenwich Observants, with a debt (to his own mother) of £40 and having 'made shewre to a yonge woman by way of mariage', who in his own turn of good fortune died 'to the mercy of God'.[104] It could still be a family decision, and a solution. Twelve-year-old Margaret Fitzgared and thirteen-year-old Julia Heron lived together in a nunnery, although the former was deaf and dumb and the latter an 'idiot fool'; for their families perhaps these were the reasons they were there.[105] The life of a lay sister may have been recognised as a halfway house for women (and their families) uncertain of their long-term future. Those as yet unprofessed were sometimes referred to as 'mynchin', a catch-all term for a woman under vows. There were as many in the same position as Agnes Clement and Elizabeth Rikarde at Davington Priory (Kent), who had lived among the nuns for fifteen and ten years, respectively; clearly it was their own choice as they both told the visiting bishop, 'omnia bene'.[106]

The religious life was a path to social and public status but it still meant stepping out of the familiar environment and into another world. For most Tudor novices what they found on the other side of the gatehouse would have seemed to be an imagined land made real. Those raised under urban horizons, such as the five Chester novices of 1539, were surely surprised by the open space, extending over a large acreage – ten, twelve and more, for friaries as much as monasteries – and its green scenes, orchard, grassy meadow, pleasure and kitchen garden. Only novice women from well-off families would have found it wholly familiar. The decorated walls of the nuns' refectory at Denny (Cambridgeshire), featuring birds between fronds of ivy, would not have been out of place in a manor-house hall.[107] Between the precinct walls and the convent enclosure stood a wide variety of working buildings, both domestic and industrial. The newcomer to Battle Abbey (East Sussex) looked up at an oasthouse taller than any on the outlying manors which he may have called home, and it was flanked by two giant furnace kilns, quite possibly the first he had ever seen.[108]

For men and women, albeit in different ways, the society and manners of the place were as new as the scenery. A generational mix in itself would not have been unfamiliar but its extremities inside the monastic enclosure, gathering together those in very advanced old age with those barely into their teenage years, was surely a new experience. There was no point of comparison for the parallel communities of men and women met by the 200 or so who made their religious profession at one of the ten dual foundations of Gilbertines, and at Syon. Well-born women from great households may have recognised the principle of separate spheres, but its strict practice, perhaps especially at Syon, was undoubtedly a departure.

Given their family backgrounds, it is unlikely that male novices would have known a life so well supported by servants, which even in the smaller houses might still outnumber the religious by as many as 3:1.[109] Nor would they have met with the deliberate inversion of social norms encouraged under monastic discipline. At Holme Abbey (Norfolk), breakfast was prepared for the novice cohort and served to them by the sub-cellarer, by definition a senior already years into his profession.[110] Walsingham novices were no doubt pleased to discover that the secular master of their school was not permitted to correct them for, as clothed members of the house, they outranked him.[111] Only well-born women would have thought these customs unremarkable: an encounter with the 'day wyff' at Hempton (Norfolk), and the 'convent servante' at Sheppey – both housekeepers – for them may have been welcome reminders of home.[112]

Both sexes would have been struck by the high style of their new life. At Thetford it was the custom for novices to wear habits cut from silk with linen stockings; at Dover Priory even the novices' bedclothes were comfortable linen rather than the more ascetic linsey.[113] Young women brought up in society may have been relieved to discover at Elstow that the nuns' dress was not of the 'sadder colour[s]' and the neckline was 'deep voided at the brest'.[114] At Blackborough, the women were allowed to keep their own wardrobe of clothes, known as 'les adornemenz' in the French language that carried the familiar ring of home.[115] The novice women of an unidentified house described to Cromwell were even given to wearing their 'seculer apparell' and to have their own chambers, the 'clooss house', quite separate from the conventual range of the nuns.[116] Personal sartorial preferences were widely tolerated: at Shrewsbury Abbey, some of the men had taken to wearing breeches; at Ashridge (Hertfordshire), the novices now had a taste for berets.[117] Their vision of privilege was completed by the promise of a personal stipend. The temptations overwhelmed some: an unnamed novice of Boxgrove made off with the entire float of cash, 'robbe[ing] ... above a hundrethe markes'.[118]

Yet the mannered display masked a daily routine that offered the religious few real comforts. Not only was the physical setting out of all proportion to the buildings and landscapes they knew from home; much of it was old and unkempt. Even at the wealthiest monastery of all, Westminster Abbey, the early Tudor novice stepped around scaffolding poles needed for another phase of repairs on the south side of the church, to reach a dormitory block that was more than 400 years old.[119] Tynemouth Priory novices were taught the variety of doorways by which the church might be accessed, as the walls were subsiding.[120] At Butley Priory (Suffolk) the best lesson was to eat quickly on a wet day because the roof of the refectory was shot through with holes.[121]

In between these privations, the novice men were put to school. Traditionally, the syllabus of the novices was the substance of the monastic life, the rule of their congregation, the daily office, and its component parts, psalter, antiphoner, lectionary, and the local customs of the house. Over time it had become more bookish. The basic script for a day and night of monastic observance had come to be surrounded by commentaries and compendia of the canon laws issued from the papacy and their own governing chapters. What had been a practical training had turned into an academic test. Bishop Geoffrey Blythe was surprised by the rigour of it at Shrewsbury, where the youths were expected to study the rule of St Benedict without a translation from the Latin.[122] At Reading Abbey, the old ceremonial custom of proving knowledge of the monastic rule in front of the abbot was substituted by a full, viva voce examination by one of the monks, no doubt modelled on the practice for the taking of a university degree.[123] This reflected the influence of secular education in the houses of men. Here the novices were expected to return to the grammar school curriculum which most of them had studied before.

There seems to have been a shared ambition in the Benedictine network to carry these studies to an advanced level, from which at least some of the novices could take up a degree course at university. Reading employed a master whose accomplishments seemed out of all proportion to the task of teaching a cohort of Berkshire novices. Leonard Cox (*c.* 1495–*c.* 1549), already making his name as a classical scholar, rhetorician and translator, was a correspondent of such luminaries as Erasmus, Jan Laski and Philip Melancthon.[124] At Evesham Abbey the novice master was not nearly so exalted, but as one of the monastery's own university graduates, the syllabus may have been much the same.[125]

From the turn of the century patrons, clerical and lay, had shown an inclination to invest in monastery schools, not only for the interest of the house itself but also generally to expand local provision for education. John Cole, co-founder of the school at Faversham Abbey, conceived of a classroom equally open to traffic from either side of the wall, 'the brethren and novyces that nowe be and hereafter shalbe professede in the same monastery as all other children that be disposed to lerne the science of gramer shalbe in the seyde monastery lerned and taught in the same science of gramer'.[126] Cole's co-founders were the warden and fellows of All Souls College, Oxford, and others created at this time were likewise the work of lay and clerical consortia: the school, founded in 1519, at the Augustinian Abbey at Bruton brought together the abbot, burgesses and the bishop of London, Richard Fitzjames. Here the religious house was recognised not only as a professional occupation in its own right but as a point of entry to other clerical career paths.

There was no uniform experience of the noviciate. Anthony Kitchin, who entered the prestigious community at Westminster in 1511 at the ripe age of thirty-four and already a university graduate, was soon returned to Oxford to study theology, where he rose to the office of prior of the Benedictine students.[127] Such privilege and progression was rare. Many more found that there was some distance between the route they and their family might have looked for, and where the house chose to steer them. The daily tasks required in a busy religious house might interrupt their training, or cause it to be overlooked entirely. Nicholas Rawlyns complained that he been hurried into his solemn profession at the London Charterhouse in 'half a yere'.[128] Nicholas Ward was left to apply for a papal dispensation after his house pressed him into service as a priest below the age permitted under canon law.[129] The experience of Robert Gosfeld, Cistercian novice at Woburn (Bedfordshire) in the mid-1520s, allegedly was nothing short of abusive. He was 'used unlawfully and against kynde' by a senior monk who subsequently became abbot.[130]

At the other end of neglect, it seems novices might also be quite forgotten. After entering Winchester Cathedral Priory around 1500 Thomas Manydon (sixteen) and Fulk Hampton (eighteen) were left to their own devices for three weeks, wandering about the house, waiting to be clothed and shaved as marked members of the community.[131] Three newcomers at the canon house at Coxford were found in 1520 'professed but not [yet] in holy orders of any kind' (professi sed non constituti in sacris vel minoribus).[132] Elizabeth Burnett of Moxby Priory (North Yorkshire) was left in a limbo between the world and the veil for eight years.[133] These half-formed religious, adrift inside the enclosure, may be what the commissioner, John Tregonwell, had in mind when he considered the monks he found at Eynsham Abbey (Oxfordshire), 'a rawe store of relygyous parsons'.[134] It might explain the peculiar ignorance of professed men at Beeston Priory (Norfolk) who believed they had joined not a canon house but a friary. In provincial England it was possible for these rough edges to remain in place at the very top of the community. John Hamond, scion of Sussex farmland, secured the abbacy at Battle in 1529. To the Oxford-educated lawyer, Richard Leighton, he was 'the veriest hayne betle ... busertde and ... arrantest chorle that I ever see': a bumpkin.[135]

Novice women did not follow the same clerical curriculum that continued to command the men. Generally, they were given instruction in the rule of the life they had professed and the customs of the house. In the preface to his translation of the rule of St Benedict, published (1516) for 'deuoute and religious women in oure diocese', Bishop Richard Fox of Winchester described how the women 'teche other their sisters' and 'daily rede and cause to be reyd by one of the ... sisters' to 'the knowledge and observance thereof'. Of course, mindful of his pastoral responsibility towards them, here the bishop presented an ideal. He acknowledged, 'ee knowe by experience', that some 'wyste [know] nat what they professed'.[136] Perhaps especially in houses where a cohort of women entered at the same time, the experience of instruction may have been akin to the schoolroom. There is no clear indication, however, that this was ever taken as a framework for the formal teaching of the disciplines to which the men were almost always exposed: Latin grammar, theology and canon law. Bishop Fox judged the women of Winchester 'utterly ignorant' of the learned language; his colleague, Longland, found the women of Burnham (Buckinghamshire) unable to read or sing.[137] Anne Boleyn was remembered for rounding on the nuns of Syon for their 'ignoraunte praying' and presenting them with prayer books in English 'that they might ... understande what they did praye for'.[138]

In fact the social origin of many of the women made it possible that they made their profession already able to read languages other than English: French typically, but for some it may have been Latin. Queen Anne's own upbringing was not so different and she was 'very experte in the Frenche tounge exercising her selfe contynually in reading the Frenche bible and other Frenche books'.[139] At any rate, the household religion of their families surely ensured that the sight and sound of sacred Latin was recognisable. The books that were bought or made for their own use contained Latin text alongside those in French and (albeit less often) English.

Perhaps some were competent to read Latin at length; probably most, like their kinfolk at home, used it as a cue for devotions which they read or spoke in more familiar words. Composing Latin may have been beyond them. Abbess Margaret Tewkesbury of Godstow requested her clerk to make a translation of the charters of her house for '[she] byn excused of grete understanding [of Latin] . . . where it not her modyr tonge'.[140]

Although there is no trace of academic authorities in the books associated either with individuals or conventual book collections, it is likely that women were given a taste of learned topics in the sermons delivered to them. Preaching to nuns, certainly by their chaplains and perhaps sometimes by their own superiors (not uncommon in European convents), is hardly documented at all beyond Syon Abbey, where the stone pulpit on the women's side of the house had been renewed as recently as 1518.[141] Possibly it was a point of contact with the culture of the learned clerk. The substantial library which had passed into the hands of the former steward of Barking Abbey by 1554, and may have belonged to the house, points to a sermon cycle as clever and current as any in houses of men.[142]

The men and women inside the precinct were made religious only by the solemn profession of vows. It had long carried the secular character of a contractual agreement as the custom, derived from the rule of St Benedict, was for the candidate to write down their vows and to declare them from this script of their own in the presence of the whole community. By the sixteenth century, the legal tone of the ceremony had been amplified. At Reading Abbey, a senior member of the community was called forward formally to bear witness (testante) to the candidate's commitment to the customs and statutes of the church (quod observabit consuetudines et statute ecclesie Radingensis).[143] Tywardreath's monks examined each candidate with a prescribed sequence of questions before they could take up the script of their vows.[144] The outside world's investment in their profession was also made explicit. Episcopal jurisdiction was still acknowledged. The women of Romsey were formally received into their religious life by the bishop of their diocese or his suffragan.[145] The Cistercian *professus* (those who make a profession) at Robertsbridge Abbey (East Sussex) were required to pledge their loyalty to their benefactor, Sir John Dalingridge.[146] New friars at the Dorchester Franciscans were even made to carry their patron's name.[147]

In spite of its social frame, profession was still a spiritual transformation. Women religious were led to the chancel steps as a bride to be joined with Christ.

In the English written for their use by their supervisors, the presiding priest was to 'halow hir bed', declaring to the company, 'Behold, she will not sleep except sleeping with the Lord.'[148] The veil was truly to shut out the world, '[falling] as lowe as ther yye leddes'.[149] Men also looked on profession as a change of identity. After fighting for years to defend his property and position in provincial society, in 1528 Sir John Stanley, a Cheshire landowner, aspired to a personal reformation, renounced his marriage vows and made his profession at Westminster Abbey.[150]

Among the Henrician generation entering male houses, there was a new impulse to signal their professed status with a change of name. The names they chose were those of the saints and doctors of the Church and figures famous from the history of the monasteries in England; occasionally they chose the cardinal virtues. Most changed their first names although some adopted a devotional surname. It was the first time in England since the early years of the Christian mission that monastic profession was marked by renaming. A trend passing along a chain of Benedictine houses in the 1520s and 1530s, it was also found among the Observant Friars.[151] Religious women also carried saints' names, such as the last heads of their respective houses, Magdalen Downes of Ankerwick (Buckinghamshire) and Barbara Mason of Marham (Norfolk), although these may have been their given names.[152] The adoption of saints' names seems to have been an especially popular badge of office for the men professed in the shadow of the dissolution. All but one of the youths who began their noviciate at Westminster Abbey in 1534 took such a name.[153] The deed of surrender at Battle Abbey was signed by John Austyn, Vincent Dunstan, Clement Gregory, Thomas Cuthbert, William Ambrose, Thomas Bede and John Jerome;[154] the newest members of the community who surrendered at Tynemouth Priory called themselves 'Charity' and 'Joy'.[155] Perhaps it was an expression of a certain reformist cast of mind, forged most often by university graduates, a self-conscious response to the secular interest in regular admissions and the hit-and-miss character of the novices' formation. A Canterbury monk who had chosen to call himself Jerome grew to be an evangelical whose Lutheranism carried him to the scaffold.[156]

Between the demands and the disregard of the noviciate, there were frequent casualties. On the outside, it was generally assumed there was no more challenging start in life. In the *Mery geste of the frere and the boye* (1513), a wicked stepmother wanting to rid herself of her husband's son and heir, summoned a friar for in his custody he would 'hym bete' as much as 'hym teche'.[157] At the Carmarthen

Franciscans more than a third of the burials found beneath the cloister and chapter house were of adolescent males.[158] The sixteen-year-old John Islip, future abbot of Westminster, was confined to the infirmary for nine weeks of his noviciate in 1480–81; he passed a further five months in care before he had lived as a monk for three years.[159] As a Carthusian entrant, Nicholas Rawlyns fell sick for nine weeks and believed, 'from that tyme unto thys day I have had never my helthe a fortnet together'.[160] The resistance of the royal novice, Elizabeth de la Pole, grand-daughter of Richard III, was weakened mortally; within four years of her solemn profession she succumbed to the plague (1515).[161] Family was now well aware of the trials. When Widow Hopton sent cash to the warden of the Reading Franciscans she expected him to bring extra comfort to her novice son.[162] Another mother, Elizabeth Parys, sent her son at Stratford Langthorne a better bed from home. Too little, too late: he died anyway and the bed could only be recovered from his abbot through the courts.[163]

Profession conferred full membership of monastic society. Now, an affiliation to a house, congregation and order was recognised publicly, together with the status, authority and protection it could command. Yet for the men, whether monk, canon or friar, it did not mean the start of a life confined to the cloister. Since the thirteenth century monasteries had considered it essential for entrants to be ordained to the priesthood, first to meet the commemorative obligations of their patrons, and latterly also to ensure that the services of their church might cater for the tastes of the laity, not least for Marian worship. The cult of Mary was best honoured in a purpose-built chapel which most houses had seen constructed by the beginning of the fifteenth century. Such an extension and diversification of the traditional pattern of observance put pressure on their complement of priests. Papal reforms of the thirteenth and fourteenth centuries had also pressed the religious houses to provide their priests with the same education and formation as their secular counterparts.

By the beginning of the sixteenth century, men professed as monk or canon were at once set on a path to ordination, the length of which varied only according to their own ability. The majority were progressed through the minor orders of clergy – acolyte, subdeacon, deacon – in a matter of months, presented to ordination ceremonies in their dioceses as a cohort. Generally, they returned for their priesting in just about a year. For youths fresh out of a grammar school, this was a hard, and fast, study. Perhaps it was for cramming the rudiments of the sacraments that someone hid pages from Erasmus' edition of John Colet's *Institution of a Christian Man* (1520) in the watching-loft at St Albans Abbey.[164] It may have been the reality of this rapid course of study that persuaded men, and their families, of the rightness of a regular profession. Certainly, when it failed to follow through there was an outcry. William Wadeherst of Combwell Priory (Kent) complained to his visitor that he had been left an acolyte for six years, apparently because there was no master of the ordinands to guide them to the next stage.[165] Priesthood was always the priority and where the demand for services was high and the population was small, the canonical regulations regarding age were often overlooked. The proposal of the king's Injunctions of 1535 to eject from houses men under the age of twenty-four was not a certain prelude to their closure, but a measure of reform which had been canvassed many times before.

As they progressed towards the priesthood, men were selected for period of study at university. By 1509, the principal congregations of monks and canons each maintained colleges at Oxford; there was a Benedictine college also at Cambridge. At Canterbury Cathedral Priory, where successive priors had cultivated interest in Renaissance learning, students were also sent abroad. The spring of 1536 saw two new recruits, John Waltham and Thomas Wilfryde, studying at Paris.[166] The universities' undergraduate course required at least seven years' study; advanced study at doctoral level required another seven years. In earlier centuries, houses had been reluctant to commit their recruits to a near-permanent absence from their responsibilities in the cloister, and few saw their studies through to completion. Now, attitudes had changed, encouraged in no small part by pressure from episcopal reformers. Wolsey himself had seized the agenda of the general chapter of the Augustinian canons to call them to order over their neglect of academic study. Under his influence the Cistercian leadership reinvigorated their congregational subscription for the maintenance of student monks at Oxford.[167]

The change moulded these last cohorts of religious men. Study was made their main occupation outside the choir. Visiting Missenden Abbey (Buckinghamshire), Bishop Longland called on 'all the yong chanons and prestes to give diligent attendance . . . att theyr bokes'. He intended to fill their daytime hours outside the Office, that is before Prime, after the daily Chapter and after None.[168] Their time in some or other course of study was longer now than an entire monastic career in earlier centuries. They knew little of the traditional stability of the professed life, as they passed to and from their university colleges. Their monastic experience was perhaps too hit-and-miss fully to persuade them of its communal and disciplinary obligations. Robert Joseph, monk of Evesham, saw himself imprisoned between two competing identities, the mundanity of monastic routine (multis essem circumseptus negotiis) and Oxford and the life of the mind (at ego mallem Oxoniam, quam vel pinguissimum officium).[169] More regulars passed out of university in the thirty years after 1509 than in the previous century and a half. The crowd of graduates startled Cromwell's commissioners, not least because they wore double hoods, monastic and academic, one over the other.[170]

Those professed at houses of any size (perhaps a population greater than twelve) were pressed early into other training that required them to show their clerical skills. One of four novices at Dale Abbey (Derbyshire) in 1500 was already serving as sub-sacrist.[171] He was assigned to the office of one of the obedientiaries, to assist – sometimes directly to deputise for them in their administrative duties – the oversight of a portfolio of properties and commercial interests, and the receipts and expenditure arising from them. William Overton had taken on the roles of kitchener and sub-sacrist at Westminster Abbey only shortly after he passed out of custody as a junior monk; over the next fourteen years he held four other senior offices of the house – almoner, chamberer, infirmarer and refectorer – almost always two of them concurrently.[172] The imperatives here were practical, to respond to the pressures on departments of the monastery whose portfolios, to mitigate fluctuations in income, had been made ever more diverse; and also to assure succession into the senior roles. Yet the result was to reinforce the separation of all but the least capable in the community from the traditional life of pure observance. The typical Tudor *professus* was set on a different course that shadowed men of the world: the secular clergy, the scholar (student and master) and the *homme d'affaires*.

Professed women knew little, if anything, of these years of teaching and learning. Certainly, there was no formal expectation of continuing study. They did find time for books beyond their noviciate but in the same way as religious women had always done, in between their observance of the office and other domestic duties. It was their experience early on to take up weighty domestic responsibilities. Several women of this generation were chosen to be head of their house less than ten years after their profession. Ann Castleford was a callow twenty-seven years old when she was chosen to be prioress of Gokewell (Lincolnshire).[173] Otherwise, women found no defined route for their religious life. Its absence may account for their continuing attachment to family affinities. Perhaps it also explains episodes of irregular conduct. The king's visitors reported on women now mature in their religious life who owned up to serious breaches of their rule in years past, especially sexual offences and pregnancies. Both Margaret Studefeld, prioress of Crabhouse (Norfolk), and Barbara Mason, prioress of Marham, told their visitors of the children they had borne in earlier decades.[174]

The competing occupations of the Tudor professed might be thought to have caused the terminal decline of the traditional labour of the monastery, the continuous cycle of worship in their choir which they called the *opus Dei* (i.e. work of God). Yet there was no contemporary perception of the loss of this defining feature of their life. The complaint of the visitor at Alnwick Priory in 1488 was not that the canons neglected the office hours but that they observed them at the wrong times because their clock was broken (defectu horologii).[175] The sight and sound of observant monks and nuns was still the template for pure and simple piety. 'Placebo', the first word of Vespers, was enough for John Skelton to transport his readers to the priory at Carrow 'among the nones blake'.[176] Sir Thomas Elyot contrasted the devotion of his own peers with the 'coulde ... mounkes ... in the quier at midnight'.[177] Episcopal and capitular visitors were anxious about the observance of the monastic office but what worried them most, low attendance for Matins in the small hours of the night, and their poor performance in prayer and psalms, were perennial themes.[178] They were not symptoms of an imminent collapse.

In fact, the visitations of the years after 1509 raised as many questions about the monasteries' commitment to worship outside of their office, above all, their celebration of Mass, together as a convent and individually in fulfilment of commemoration paid for by their patrons. Bishop Longland urged the canons of Dorchester (Oxfordshire) and Leicester to witness the Mass as one community; at Leicester he made it unavoidable, laying down that daily there should be at least twenty-five present at the Mass.[179] If there was one custom of worship to which their attachment was waning, the impression is that it was this communal act, in the middle of the monastic morning. For men who had followed the same formation as any secular priest, it may have now seemed a diversion from the private masses, which were in ever increasing demand in most houses, and for which fees and even pittances were required. John Portar alias Smythe, monk (and ultimately, sacrist) of Durham Priory, kept a Latin memorandum of a dozen legitimate grounds for non-attendance at Mass. It was, perhaps, the outlook of his generation.[180]

The monks' worship can be seen only obliquely in sources now surviving, and then for the most part merely in its more material aspects, such as the number of candles they burned or the state of repair of the vestments they wore. Of course, these records alone might encourage the view that the tradition of the office lived on. It is most likely that the majority of men and women professed to the religious life after 1509 kept to the traditional routine of seven day offices and a night office in much the same way as their predecessors. A conspicuous exception may have been those houses whose population had fallen to fewer than four. It is doubtful that the three women of Davington, still more so the two women of St Mary's Priory, Bristol, took to their respective stalls and sang across to one another in the choir. Perhaps the Tavistock monk resident on the Scilly island of Tresco performed the office in an act of private reading.[181] Residents of the smallest friaries surely did the same. At Wilton Abbey, one friar lived alone in the convent, which was like a scale model of a monastery, its church just 13 feet across and its cloister 23 x 16 feet.[182]

Some of this generation knew that to perform their offices was the strictest of their obligations. The monks of Selby Abbey were so ruled by the bell that summoned them back to the choir, they nicknamed it 'Chyme'.[183] An inept monk of the London Charterhouse was deposited on a 'donge hell' (dunghill) after 'a poore seremony', that is, failing to say or sing his part.[184] Even so, they did readily give it up. When the arrest of an escaped prisoner from Newgate caused the church of the London Franciscans to be closed by the sheriffs, the convent moved to the refectory and standing between the tables and forms continued 'the servys and masse, sayd and songe'.[185] The night office was observed although full attendance was no doubt as difficult to achieve as it had ever been. William Stapleton, a monk of Saint Benet Holme, reflected that he had 'bene often ponysshed for [not] rising to matens'.[186]

The component parts of the office – prayers, psalms, readings – were no different from its early medieval origins but they may have been less demanding for Tudor religious to perform. The scale of some offices had been cut back in successive reforms; more importantly, perhaps, it was now permitted to follow them from a book. Traditionally, the office was a feat of memory, and the highest praise for any religious was that they knew the psalter well enough to chant it backwards.[187] Now, there were cribs close at hand. At Canterbury, there was a full set of service books in the choir, chained, apparently as in a library.[188] It seems the Benedictine women of Stainfield Priory (Lincolnshire) were so reliant on their choir books that they refused to rise for Matins when they ran out of candles.[189] There was also some care for the physical rigours of constant performance. In his choir, Thomas Golwynne wore his fur-lined slippers.[190] The comfortable domestication of their old duty might match what Bishop Longland felt he had witnessed in the choir at Leicester, 'laughter, joking and chatter'.[191]

Although the routine may have lost more than a touch of its original rigour, monastic leaders were showing renewed interest in their performance in the choir. While they may have shared the concerns of their visitors over the observance of custom and the honouring of their obligations to their principal patrons, a stronger impulse was to hold the attention of all the faithful in a world now overflowing with opportunities for worship. Their eyes had been trained on the rapidly developing religious marketplace for some time. From early in the fourteenth century, monasteries had responded to the rising popularity of the cult of the Blessed Virgin Mary by creating bespoke chapels and observances to draw lay enthusiasm back into their precincts.

The taste for polyphonic music to accompany acts of worship passed down society from the royal circles that had first encountered it in France; by the fifteenth century it was a focus for investment in parish churches. The regulars again followed suit: polyphonic choirs were first introduced into their Lady chapels and then passed into church itself. The new style washed over Waverley Abbey (Surrey) so forcefully that in 1526 Abbot John Browning sought to limit what he called '*Anglice* prykesonge' to Sunday masses and saints' days.[192] Early Tudor heads of house mobilised their personnel and their ready cash to produce music in the same style as the parishes and private chapels but on a scale that might outdo them. Multiple organs were installed; even a modest friary church might now be fitted with two, one for rehearsal, the other for performance. Professional choirmasters and organists were employed. Glastonbury Abbey was able to tempt into Somerset a cantor and organist, James Renynger, who had been employed at the foremost choral foundation of Eton.[193] The burgeoning talent of Thomas Tallis was bought by Robert Fuller of Waltham Abbey as late as 1538, as two-thirds of monastic England was already 'putte doune'.[194]

Professional musicians were not always the preserve of the wealthiest: a secular cantor, Robert Derkeham, was engaged at Buckland Abbey (Devon) where the revenue was a tenth of Glastonbury's. His contract required him to teach the monks not only to sing but also to play the organ for themselves.[195] The monasteries' purchasing power enabled them to eclipse the competition. Westminster Abbey diverted London's musicians – composers, instrumentalists and singers – from city patrons.[196] The cellarer of Holy Trinity, Aldgate, was able to hire out a parish's pageant paraphernalia for half the year.[197] The emphasis on professional, public performance created another career for the Tudor religious. The profile of William London of Winchester Cathedral Priory as a musician was such that he was appointed the first gospeller of the new secular cathedral; he may have been a composer.[198] Nicholas Clement, monk of Christ Church, Canterbury, mentored the early career of one of the priory's choristers, which led him towards the royal court.[199]

The spectacle of their worship challenges any general assumption that monastic observances were steadily depopulated. It is true that the superior and senior officers of any houses were unlikely to be present for every office hour, the conventual Mass, and other of the recurrent acts of observance in the church. The religious life of the head of house, like that of any prelate, was centred on their own household, and their participation in conventual performances may have been reserved for special, and seasonal, ceremonies. It was the principal complaint of Bishop Longland at Leicester Abbey in 1529 that Abbot Pescall had not said Mass in the church 'for three years and more', nor stood with his brethren in the choir.[200] Even so, the form and style of worship in the conventual church surely depended on the rump of the monastic community taking part. The multiple sets of vestments for use in the Mass, the Marian feasts and the office of the dead which are listed at length in the dissolution inventories, speak of an expectation that the whole of the professed population was prepared for these communal acts. Eight Westminster monks of the 1530s were recorded as the donors between them of three copes and as many as twelve albs for use by the convent.[201] A vision of their vocation for common worship was still invoked. Even a monk with worldly ambition such as Westminster's abbot, William Benson, was disposed to mark the passing of his predecessor, John Islip (1532), with pictures of his exequies, showing twin ranks of torch-bearing, hooded monks who processed him into his choir for the final time.[202] At the height of their confrontation with the king's commissioners in 1538, the community of Christ Church, Canterbury, expressed their sense of purpose as 'loude prease honour of God', done 'joyfully, meoldyusly and devoutly'.[203] When news came of the execution of the London Carthusians in 1535, it was the first instinct of Abbot Robert Hobbes of Woburn to call the convent together to chant Psalm 79, *'Deus venerunt gentes'* ('Oh God, the nations have come').[204]

In men's religious houses the vast stock of vestments also spoke of their canonical obligations as priests. Each canon, monk or friar who had reached the highest rank of ordination was bound, just like their secular counterparts, to celebrate a daily Mass. In practice, their houses had accepted so many donations made in the expectation of commemorative masses that they were needed at any rate to play their part in what must have been almost constant activity at one or other altar in the church. Recently, patrons with a particular attachment to a monastery or friary had gone further, to create a chantry; some of these were ambitiously complex foundations, in which the religious house acted as the principal trustee of a partnership of churches. For the religious responsible for them, these chantries presented another route out of the office routine. Friars were called upon for other sacramental roles only rarely fulfilled by canon or monk priests. It was common for testators to ask them to celebrate a requiem Mass in their conventual church at the same moment as their funeral and burial.

Friars were a presence in parishes day to day, often as a supplement to, sometimes as a substitute for, the ministry of a secular priest. It is very difficult to say just how many Tudor congregations saw them. There were ten times as many parishes in England and Wales as there were professed friars. Popular images of the public friar recall his street presence – preacher, receiver of confessions, purveyor of confraternity letters and indulgences – as much as at any Sunday Mass. The ministry of the friars may have held a special appeal because they could be expected to be only passing through.[205] Writing in 1540, the reformer Laurence Ridley knew his readers were still familiar with the prospect of 'remyssyon of synnes . . . gyven to us by Saynt Fraunces coule . . . or of fruer observantes'.[206]

Parish churches also met the pastoral ministrations of canons and monks. From the period of the papal schism (1378–1417) onward, professed men of the monastic congregations had applied for dispensations to hold a benefice. There can be no doubt their first objective was to free themselves from their conventual duties by securing an independent income; although they may have been confirmed in the title of a rectory or vicarage, it did not follow that they ever served the living. In 1520 abbots of the Cistercian monasteries urged their General Chapter to call on Cardinal Wolsey to deter the monks who flocked to him in the hope of a dispensation to be granted a benefice.[207] Occasionally they were to be found as the regular (if not resident) minister, perhaps most often when the dispensation itself was part and parcel of a formal retirement from the common life of their house. A fifteenth-century commonplace book kept by John Gysborn, a Premonstratensian of Coverham Abbey (North Yorkshire), contains both guidance for service in the monastic office and for 'ministracion' at what was presumably a parish evensong.[208]

In the volatile economic climate prevailing after the Black Death, many monasteries appropriated the revenue of the parish churches under their patronage. Now a beneficed priest was substituted with a chaplain; sometimes these were professed members of the house itself. Right up to the dissolution of the house a canon from Plympton (Devon) went out to the village of Wembury seven miles away to 'sayethe masse matynes and evensong before none and ... goeth home agayne to the priorie to dyner'.[209] The canons of Alnwick Priory seem to have shown special care for their parishioners of Lesbury, since they sent a canon who hailed from the village, George Wilkinson alias Lesbury, to serve as their priest.[210] Augustinian foundations such as these had often arisen out of parish provision, and some sense of a pastoral mission had passed down their history into the sixteenth century.

The older monastic orders did not routinely deploy their professed priests in this way. When Sir Francis Bigod condemned the practice of appropriation in 1535, his complaint was not of the replacement of a secular with a regular priest but the removal of a pastor altogether, 'a parsone ... to dwell among them and to minister unto them the pure worde of God'.[211] It was unusual for monks of the greater Benedictine and Cistercian abbeys to be committed to a parish, but it was not uncommon for them to take part in public ministry. Their first years under a monastic profession had followed the same course – university, ordination – as any high-flying secular priest and it was natural for them to be drawn into their world. Many of them may have been ad hoc celebrants, confessors and preachers in the vicinity of their house. The Benedictines of Bath, Glastonbury and Muchelney (Somerset) each secured licences for public preaching from their diocesan.[212] Richard Glastynbury, a monk of Malmesbury (Wiltshire), received confessions in the town in 1530; Henry Kyngston of Winchester Cathedral Priory was allowed (1536) to wear a priest's gown over the top of his monk's habit, hiding it.[213] When the king's commissioners came to take the surrender of Kingswood Abbey (Gloucestershire) they were told that it was 'forth ... about the ministracion of the gospell'.[214]

The contribution of canons and monks in public ministry was curtailed by the demands of their domestic administration. The majority of monasteries had been founded for populations larger than could be sustained in the later Middle Ages and endowed accordingly. Their property, agricultural, industrial and urban, was widespread and diverse; their associated sources of income, rents, customary rights, fees and fines, were complex not least because they had evolved over such a long span of time. Now, most houses held fewer than half the original number of personnel to oversee them. As a result almost all but the old, young and those physically and mentally unfit were assigned to a department of the house to do their share of such worldly tasks as accountancy, legal administration, procurement and maintenance. The first administrative duties might come to them soon after their profession.

For the able and healthy, these responsibilities might remain with them for the rest of their lives. At Leicester Abbey, William Charyte was still at work, in 1502, writing out a rental at the age of eighty-two.[215] Obedientiaries of Tudor Westminster – John Fulwell (Cellarer), Thomas Jay (Domestic Treasurer), William Marsh (Kitchener) – were still in harness when they died.[216] The demands of the institutional portfolio could mean a constant rotation of roles: Glastonbury monks served in three or four administrative departments of the monastery in a period of ten years. Edmund Bury at Bury St Edmunds kept a register of his own *acta*, which shows that in less than twelve months he had taken up two offices, in the winter, Vesterer, and the following summer, Pittancer.[217]

Office-holding was hardly a new feature of religious life, but the experience of this generation looked increasingly different from that of their forebears. In the largest houses, senior obedientiaries presided over departments each with a substantial staff of their own; some, such as their deputies, were, like them, professed men and women but most were wage employees. These departments took up a dedicated space within the inner court of the monastery, often providing domestic accommodation, even a private chapel for the use of the officer himself.[218] In their space and their time, devoted as it was to the business of the department, they were separated from the community of the house, connecting with it ad hoc as might any institution or individual on the outside. Thomas More lamented this change of occupation, from the religious observance to which they were committed as novices, as a slide towards worldly sin (e vicio in vicium prolabitur).[219] At the same time, they faced the world in their own right, seeming to many in the neighbourhood to be a manifestation of the corporate body but with an authority of their own. The exercise of their office brought them, men and women alike, a documentary identity quite different from what they might express in the books they kept for study, prayer or worship. Here they maintained rolls and registers of their tenure in their own name, and drew up deeds and dispatched letters imprinted with a personal seal. John Fulwell's fine sign of his cellarer's office might have appeared to him a rehearsal for greater preferment for in 1535 he was in Cromwell's mind as a candidate for prior of Worcester.[220] For women born into gentry society (or better), now they were behaving as their mothers and married sisters might at the head of household. Perhaps the men, most of them of somewhat lower social rank, saw themselves returning to the paths of property and trade followed by their peers.

In many respects these roles underlined the detachment of this generation of religious from the traditional monastic ideal of living by the labour of their own hands (opus manuum). Now, there could be no doubt, even in the remote colonies of congregations professing a sacred isolation, that they were regarded by many as landlords or employers. The precincts of the Cistercians may have held some stark reminders of their change of tack, the capacious fraters and dormitories raised to accommodate their community of lay brethren standing empty, or commandeered for storage now for the best part of 150 years. But in fact the practice of manual labour had not disappeared, and the principle of it, as a disciplinary and devotional tool, was still widely affirmed. At smaller, poorer foundations that lived largely from the produce of their own demesne estate, turning a hand to field and stock work may have been a necessity, perhaps especially at harvest or slaughter time. Episcopal visitors found that novices could be called away from their books to add numbers to the reapers. No exception was made for women, just as on any tenant farm. Elizabeth Burnett of Moxby Priory recalled helping at haymaking time 'to straw and cock the hay.'[221] These were, or were close to, subsistence communities and the professed members were expected to assist the food supply but also the production of goods that might be sold on.

A picture of religious in the isolation and silence of their enclosure creatively occupied in fine craftwork was fondly drawn by later antiquarians. Michael Sherbrook wanted to recall the Cistercians of Roche as 'many of them ... artificers'.[222] A century on, and John Aubrey (1626–97) conjured a vision of drawing-room accomplishments, of 'young maids ... learned needlework, the art of confectionery, surgery, physic, writing, drawing etc.'[223] These views were charged with a conviction that the dissolution of the monasteries was a wholesale catastrophe for artistry and craft. Yet there is no doubt that diverse crafts were undertaken in the Tudor houses of men and women. Parchment prickers and a stylus were found at the site of Sawley Abbey (Lancashire);[224] leather off-cuts found on the site of the Northampton Franciscans might suggest that they made their own shoes.[225]

Some of it was a commercial enterprise. The Birgittine writer Richard Whitford's condemnation of religious houses where books, paintings, textiles and musical instruments – Whitford specifies clavichords – were created for sale is surely confirmation that such industry was not unknown.[226] His view of the variety of trades can be corroborated. The scatter of pegs from stringed instruments excavated at Battle Abbey may be telling.[227] William Alynger, provisor of the Cistercian St Bernard's College, Oxford, possessed a virginal, valued enough for it to be the first item he bequeathed in his post-Dissolution will.[228] Thomas Golwynne, who moved from the London Charterhouse to Mount Grace, carried with him the tools of two trades, one conspicuously more acceptable in a cloister setting than the other: a weaving frame and a pot still from which he extracted his very own aqua vitae.[229] The suppression commissioners uncovered what amounted to an artisanal work-shop: 'we have nott fownd the like in no place,' they wrote from Ulverscroft Priory (Leicestershire), 'for there yn oon religious person thear but that he can and dothe eyther inbrotheryng [embroidering], wrytynge books with verey fayre hands making theyr own garnements karvyng, payntyng or graffyng'.[230] This could be a cottage industry but it also reflected a widespread promotion of craftwork as a creative act. Bishop Longland of Lincoln more than once called upon his regular communities to turn their hands to 'writing, paynting, kerving or some other honest study crafte', thus 'to avoide idleness whiche is the mother of all mischeff'.[231]

They returned to the traditions of their rule above all in the conditions of their domestic life. This is not to suggest that the luxuries of dress and dining arrange-ments that struck them as novices on the threshold were lost to them on profes-sion, but they were juxtaposed with privations which few would have known in their home life. There was a conspicuous clash between personal style and conven-tual custom at the Benedictine priory of St Nicholas, Exeter, monks resisting cropped hair and crown tonsures and speaking English not Latin to provoke 'Syr pryour'.[232] The scene described by king's commissioners at Beeleigh (Essex) typi-fies these tensions. Here the outer court of the house was no more than a mud-strewn farmyard, but across it strutted peacocks, reared for the entertainment of gentry patrons.[233] Beyond the cathedral cities and well-developed towns, religious houses were not always found in a safe place. Cornwall's lawless coastline assailed the Benedictines of Tywardreath: 'now adays the pirates of the see with oder men of the werres useth them self mor cruelly and mor tyrannosly'.[234]

The physical environment was old, often broken down or yet to be properly built up, and unsafe. The Cistercians of Rievaulx approached their choir with care, since the spire and part of the crossing tower had collapsed into the south transept; by contrast, their colleagues at Strata Florida may have felt safe in their choir but reluctant either to come to the common table or to return to their beds since the refectory and, it seems, the dormitory stood in ruins.[235] The buildings of Milton Abbey were in such a poor state before 1492 that the whole was exempt from taxation.[236] At Southwick the bishop intervened to begin a programme of rebuilding, after the church tower was consumed by fire (1512) and its replacement collapsed (1518).[237] The experience of these spaces can be gathered from witnesses: at Shrewsbury, 'the convent sytythe weyt (wet) in the quere as oft as hit rayns when the be at godys serveys'.[238] For those unable to live apart by means of priesthood, university study or office, there were the customary discomforts of communal living, little changed in houses that were centuries old. A single latrine bench was still in use, the only concession to progress perhaps a coat of paint in warming red. Here disease spread quickly. The entire community of Creake Abbey (Leicestershire) succumbed to the sweat in 1506.[239] The threats of the common life were often self-inflicted. Disputes were fought out with weapons as often now as in earlier times – more so perhaps in regions where patronal interest in the administration of the house was now strongly asserted. A monk of Combermere (Cheshire) named Otnell was murdered in 1520 by John Janyns, a member of the abbot's household; the claustral prior, Thomas Hamond, was alleged to have covered it up.[240] In 1535, Abbot Matthew Deveys of Holm Cultram was poisoned at his own dinner table.[241]

The degree of comfort that monks knew in diet, dress and personal possessions depended to a large degree on the income of the house they entered; it was also affected by its independence, in particular, from episcopal or other supervision. There is no doubt that at the top of the monastic orders, among the premier Benedictine abbeys and priories, and in the wealthiest of the Cistercian and Augustinian foundations, the men and women lived very well, with many of the consumables they had known in the world. Jasper Fyloll told Cromwell that a meal for twelve monks of the London Charterhouse might honestly feed twenty.[242] A diary (perhaps from the cellarer) of the foodstuffs prepared for each day of the accounting year 1536–37 at the Benedictine abbey at Tavistock – whose annual income as assessed in 1535 reached four figures – reveals a rich variety of meats: 'chekyn', 'capyns', 'byff', 'porke', 'muttyn', 'vele', 'vensen', 'wodcock'; dairy, butter, eggs, 'mylke and creem'; and fruits, both fresh, 'appylls', 'fygges' and preserved, 'prunys', 'resons'.[243] But there were fewer than forty houses that could be counted in this hierarchy and outside of it the living may have been very hit and miss indeed. 'In such bare places,' recalled Alexander Barclay, with first-hand experience of regular life, 'every day is Lent.'[244]

In fact, it would be wrong to represent the difference between these houses in absolute terms, on the one hand indulgence, on the other indigence. There were regulations of diet that were recognised in all houses of each congregation and order. The tradition of a principal mealtime, prescribed in the earliest rules, was upheld. The restricted consumption of red meat, and the substitution of fish, were still accepted in principle, although no longer applied strictly. In the Tavistock diary fish was always the principal offering on a Friday, with poultry as a secondary consideration, and perhaps available only outside of the frater itself; red meat was never served. A 1539 account of the debts owed by St Albans Abbey to game dealers and fishmongers might be taken at face value as proof of a life of excess but it does show a commitment to the consumption of flesh – herring, lark, woodcock – other than red meat.[245] On the evidence of their waste deposits the Cistercians of St Mary Graces were heavily dependent on London eels.[246] The regulation of drinking – when, where and what – was perhaps respected more for the obvious reason that there was no place for incapacity in a community where every member held at least one occupation. The variation from greater to lesser foundation owed much to the endowment of pittances, that is to say, privileged allocations of particular foodstuffs or drink, to mark particular feast days and other seasonal commemorations. At Westminster Abbey, coronation church and mausoleum, for four royal dynasties, there were as many as seventy days a year – so more than two in some weeks – on which a special platter was presented.[247]

In the unremarked religious houses of the remoter provinces, treats of this kind were scarce indeed. Here the experience may not have been very far different from the damning recollection of the Wyatt family history, 'everyone had his messe alone ... so sure they would be to loose no part of their ius'.[248] Pittances might have marked the anniversary of the foundation, or the obit of a superior, but where patronage itself was patchy there was no steady accretion of these things. In the friaries, the provision of food was quite different. '[God] knoweth better ... then we', Alexander Barclay observed, 'of some poore freers is made more curiously, then is some abbey or riche monastery'.[249] The supply of food was dependent on purchase and the (unpredictable) promise of alms. The mobility of the membership meant that a pattern of communal meals diminished and even before the dissolution began it may be that some kitchens were taken out of commission. Certainly, friars are frequently found feeding themselves, alone. Francis Lybert found a chamber cupboard (amrye) with small comforts inside, a psalter, a pair of socks, and a pint and a half of 'Romse' wine.[250]

Where famine was as familiar as feast, and the switch from one to another was under the control of a higher authority, minds were always trained on food. An anonymous scribbler at Winchcombe Abbey amused himself with a classical image: 'I thirst noe lesse than Tantalus and eke amides the fflude where water dayly tuches his chine and shunes to doe him good.'[251] Another was less subtle: 'my mowthe waterythe for etynge of a fatt capon'.[252] Well-to-do women may have marked the difference from home. 'No one in the house either eats or drinks before 12 noon' was the rueful remark of Alice Bedlingfield at Blackborough.[253] The preoccupation of John Cambridge at Wymondham (Norfolk) prompted practical action: he stole a cookbook 'librum uocatum coquine'.[254] Monks at St Mary's Abbey, York, took their pocket money into the outer court to buy bottles of wine from city merchants. But for some, no mitigation was enough. 'Y can nat awey ... the burde and stryteness,' wailed John Placett from Chester Abbey, '... theyre accustumyd abstynence, the frayter.'[255]

The extent of personal comforts, clothing, other requisites and possessions unfolded in the same way: there were expectations in each congregation governed by their original rules and later statutes that continued to be asserted by leaders of the religious house, as well as their supervising visitors, and were largely respected throughout each network. The handful of contemporary portraits of regulars that have survived observe the detail of their habits – the cowl, wimple, belt and shoes. The mural image of Prior Thomas Silkstede in the Lady chapel of Winchester Cathedral captures him simply clad in habit, cowl and hood, his pastoral staff the only distinction of his office.[256] The 'reredos' panel painted for the abbey church at Romsey depicts two nuns, both dressed in strict adherence to their own Benedictine tradition. Difference arose only around these requirements, according to the circumstances of each community, not only economic but also social, cultural and geographic. The fur-lined hoods, soft felt and velvet caps with which the heads of premier houses crowned their authority reflected the income of their households just as much as the rank of servants they were able to retain. Abbot John Islip of Westminster dressed himself as a public prelate, vested and mitred as he processed for the funeral of the first Henry Tudor; in cap and gown when he was counsellor to his son.[257] His depiction in decorated deeds wearing only the monk's habit was surely to offset his more familiar look.[258]

Monks able to stay away from their house for any length of time at university were able to cover over any conspicuous monastic austerity. William Alynger and his friends, monks of Hailes (Gloucestershire), at St Bernard's College, Oxford, were accustomed to 'rydyng clokes', 'doblets', of 'velvet' and 'saye', and the subfusc of the secular scholar, 'a studiying frocke'.[259] Yet where there was little or no freedom from the discipline of the rule, poverty was worn, unavoidably, on the sleeve. Friars attached for any length of time to the convents in provincial towns, where the pool of potential alms was limited, would see their habits run very threadbare. The reports of the king's commissioners of 1535 and later, depicting their old and greasy fabric, were deliberately bruising but it does not mean they were wrong.

The act of profession did not cause men and women to cast off the style of clothing they had known in their home life. The link was kept not least through their extended family ties which often gifted them the trappings of worldly identity – a cloak, a pair of boots – because they were considered kin. Thomas Golwynne compiled a prestige collection of outer wear, a mantle from Sir John Rawson, a pylche (cloak) from Mr Saxby and an overcoat of My Lady Conway. Clothing may have captured the conflict between outward and inward occupations.[260] Many men of this period were most attached to the vestments of their priesthood but those caught with a dagger, not a knife, at their belt, or even a sword and its sheath, perhaps still thought of the paths their brothers had taken. Women were aware of subtler distinctions in personal attire between the lady of the household and the lady superior, the chaste vowess and the novice. Dress was well understood as an instrument of monastic authority and was often varied by professed men and women as a conscious act of rebellion. Thomas Gloucester of Malmesbury was discovered to 'use a hat under his hood in the quire'.[261] Of course, challenges such as this confirm that there was no doubt about the regulation of dress, and that it was defended as a frontier of regular identity.

Possessions certainly came their way according to circumstance. Religious houses in city and town filled up with consumables. The number and very great variety of manufactured items revealed, discarded at their sites, may be taken as a snapshot of what was fetched into their living spaces. The permitted mobility of religious men, their circuit of their congregations (compulsory in the convents of friars), their periods of study and ministry, carried moveable goods through the network. Any principled objection to *proprietas* had long since been softened, for the practical purposes of reinforcing their multifarious roles as conventual officer, pastor and preacher. The old values of poverty were challenged directly by the continuing investment of family and patrons. Young men and women were sent to make their profession with a bed brought from home. Leticia, daughter of John de Preston, a city of London corder, received an income to cover her clothing and necessaries after her father's death.[262] The social custom of transferring household contents to the next generation together with property was now cemented and more and more testators thought to pass on particular books, plate and the paraphernalia of domestic altars. Agnes Bowers of Minister-in-Sheppey (Kent) was surrounded by plate metal crockery and cutlery, each piece having been given to her by one of her own network of secular friends.[263] What was most common is what emerges from excavations; the buckles and pins that held together clothing in the secular style; and a variety of boots and shoes, and the materials to make or repair them.[264] The canons of Dorchester kept the sturdy 'voyde shoes' for walking longer distances outside.[265]

The well-furnished religious life both shaped, and was shaped by, an unprecedented level of personal privacy inside the house. Before the end of the fifteenth century aspects of communal life had been recast. Dormitories had been subdivided into cells (cellae), the cavernous stone space criss-crossed with partitions panelled in timber (called wainscot) punctuated with inner doors. Each cell incorporated an integral cupboard and shelf space for personal possessions and books. It was spelled out to the contractors drafted in to refit the sleeping quarters at Durham that the windows should offer enough light for monks in adjoining cells to read and study.[266] Generally, the common refectory or frater was left as it had been built, but it was steadily surrounded by satellite spaces in which meals might be taken. The bay formed when a full-height oriel was set among the windows was almost an invitation to a prandial tête-à-tête. Office-holders occupied chambers of their own, the larger of which were surely run as separate households. Private chambers were sometimes assigned as a privilege to others among the professed, not least those who demitted senior office.

Yet, the greatest independence given to this generation was not their space in the enclosure, but their scope to enter spaces outside. It was not a freedom granted to them. The original rules of stability and keeping the custody of the cloister were never rescinded. Congregations' own statutes, and the recurrent injunctions of supervising bishops, repeatedly reaffirmed these strictures. But the precincts of these houses, monasteries and friaries were porous. Their most conspicuous feature, perhaps under the crowded skyline of a Tudor city or town, was their open space, a mix of courtyard, garden, meadow and even woodland. Some were surrounded by defensive perimeter walls, which reached around to an emphatic gatehouse. But often these were new constructions, some still being built. Westminster Abbey's precinct wall had just been built by the time the construction of the abbey was finished. Christchurch Gate at Canterbury's Christ Church Cathedral was finished within sight of the monastery's final surrender (1517). The purpose of the precinct was to be a point where the world met the cloister; in practice the traffic was always two-way. Illicit wandering was widely reported. A report from Malmesbury in 1527 may not have been especially unusual: Richard Ashton was found to change his habit so as to pass about the town unnoticed; Robert Elmore and Thomas Purton remained outside at night without permission. Walter Bristow made the fifty-mile journey to Bristol; given his toponym the pull was surely family.[267] Perhaps John Barkre of Launde had travelled as far, from Launde to Coventry, where he came to know the 'mynstral' who gave him his manuscript copy of the carols of John Audelay.[268] 'Monks prefer to live in cities', was Erasmus's decided view.[269]

But personal, social interaction in the world was also contained within the communal day. The experience of two monks of Christ Church, Canterbury, called Boxley and Goodnestone, recorded in 1533, shows how they found company, and formed friendships, in the course of their other roles. The monks began their day sharing their breakfast – in a private space of the priory – with William Gyldwyn, a tiler of the town; after the evening office (Vespers), Goodnestone returned with his colleague Boxley and sat (and perhaps ate and drank) with Gyldwyn until 7 p.m. In the small, walled city of Canterbury, where there was a chain of religious houses, it seems it was common to see friendships of this kind.[270] The wife of Thomas Haryson, 'trype berer', was said to 'suffer the Austen friars to haunt her house early and late and at all times of the day riotously'.[271] Set apart from the community they led, superiors were able to configure their life around social exchange. At Leicester, Bishop Longland saw it as a daily routine, 'Monday . . . to Friday, any day of the week'.[272]

There can be no doubt that it was the wash of contact and company that eroded regular discipline. Presumably it was her life beyond the enclosure that explains the three successive pregnancies of a nun of Lambley (Northumberland), a tiny foundation, remote from any town. This must also be the surprising story of Elizabeth Lutton of Yedingham (North Yorkshire). Professed at fourteen she lived under the veil for eighteen years before she fell pregnant at the mature age of thirty-two.[273] The names of the neighbourhood women known to Abbot John Chaffcombe of Bruern (Oxfordshire) filled four folios of a parchment booklet.[274]

More often than not, it was not circumstantial contact that called these monks and nuns out beyond the gatehouse but their pre-existing social networks. Extended family offered continuing support to their profession. For some this was seen as a necessity. Richard Ward of Christ Church, Canterbury, subsisted as a student monk at Oxford on handouts from his brother; when his brother died Richard hoped for a loan from his prior.[275] Agnes Doryngton of Henwood Priory (Warwickshire) claimed that she was dependent on her parents because her prioress denied her stipend.[276] When strict enclosure was enforced under the royal visitation, Cecily Bodenham of Wilton Abbey objected on these very grounds: 'that any of my sisters, when theire father, mother, brother or sistren or any suche nye of their kyne come unto theym may have licence to speke with them in the hall'.[277] Men who had reached the top of prestige houses also felt a responsibility to return these family favours. William Hope of Westminster Abbey bought his father a pair of shoes when he paid for his own.[278] Stephen Sagar of Hailes granted an annuity to his brother, Otho, a canon lawer.[279] Henry Parker, brother of William, abbot of Gloucester, was appointed to the office of Woodward and may have been given an abbey house at Prinknash.[280]

In many cases, the social network pressed heavily on their professional religious roles. Frequently, family and friends were preferred for material and spiritual benefits in the gift of the house. The prioress of Nuncotham was said to be given over entirely to the influence of her family, to the point that her visiting bishop commanded her that she 'give no more so liberally to your brother or your brother's children'.[281] The whole flock of Parretts came to fraternity day at Christ Church, Canterbury, at the invitation of their professed sibling, William (known in religion as Chartham), where they were able to witness Sir Edward Rugeley make his entrance into the confraternity.[282] Some of those closest to them even shared in their own monastic life. William Parker of Gloucester received his younger brother into his community and subsequently appointed him cellarer.[283] At Cerne Abbey Abbot Thomas Corton's brother 'with others of his kyndred' . . . berys under him suche rewle'.[284]

The life opportunities for men and women of middling, or better, society and some learning were widening in the Tudor realm at the beginning of the sixteenth century. For the men, there were now more schools, a greater number with an advanced syllabus and more of them well endowed than ever before. These could enable them, intellectually at least, to aspire to university, where now there were also more openings and material support: five new colleges were established at Cambridge and Oxford in the Tudors' first four decades (by 1510), although with the end of war at home and abroad, passage to a continental university, new (Germany) or old (Italy), was also a realistic prospect.[285] The teaching and practice of the law was now a serious alternative to academic study, at least as a route to patronage and preferment. The education of well-born women was already well established but now it was enhanced by the advance of print, vernacular translation and – perhaps above all – the domestication of book culture. Girls of rank who reached the age of adulthood in the year of the royal supremacy could reasonably expect a life in which letters, even independent scholarship, might find a place.

Yet a religious profession, the oldest of all opportunities for the literate, still retained a place in the plans of both men and women. Its appeal was not unequivocal – it may never have been entirely – and after 1509 it was not uncommon to find those either on the threshold of profession, or already passed over, who doubted their choice. But those who directed these decisions – family above all – were undaunted. The prospect of the religious life held out as much promise as it ever had done, and now the evidence for it was conspicuous, in the rich style of the regulars' new buildings and the secular trappings of their domestic routine. In fact, what they and, especially, their charges encountered through the wicket gate of the abbey or friary was a regime that in many aspects was still defiantly at odds with personal fulfilment – just as the ancient pioneers of their customs had conceived. There was much about the life-course of the professed canon, monk, nun and friar that replicated the 'narrow way', prescribed by Benedict of Nursia in his rule for monks almost a millennium before. There was much about it still that was, if not unworldly, then otherworldly; not least the outlandish, and probably exhausting, performance of their music. But for those who endured, and in particular those who emerged into the hierarchy of institutional offices, there was the opportunity to follow a quite different course, a counterpoint life of service and social interaction. Profession transformed Tudor men and women as much it had their forebears but their continuing presence outside their precincts also transformed their world.

III

A REGULAR WORLD

O ne Sunday evening before 1539, Thomas Warner was making his way home through the well-kept grid-plan streets of Bury St Edmunds when he was set upon by John Barnysby. Badly beaten about the head and body, Thomas was found in the street and helped home to his wife, Alice. But his wounds were mortal and he did not survive the night. Barnysby was a renowned roustabout and his 'ill-disposed and myschevous mynde brekinge the kynges peace', brutally demonstrated to Warner, was not untypical. By day, Barnysby was factotum to the sacrist of the town's Benedictine abbey whose gateway presided over the northern end of the market square. In her raw grief, Alice ran to the town's under-steward, the 'rewler' of the porters and officers of the *burgus*, to request Barnysby's arrest. They responded with a demand for payment for a warrant, knowing full well that their price was beyond her means. Barnysby was not detained. Such had been the pattern at Bury 'these x or xii yeres . . . yf such as have been porters and officers and reteynynge unto the sayd abbey', Alice later reported, 'and it ys nott to be doughted that yf it had fortuned that . . . anye other honest persone not being servant or reteynynge to the abbey . . . shuld have done suche a dede or a gretter lese offence he schuld soo never escaped but have had the utmost judgment of the lawe'. Constrained by the authority of the abbey which extended right across her neighbourhood, Alice reached out for the pity of another loyal wife. She wrote to the queen.[1]

Alice Warner blamed the loss of her husband, and her own livelihood, on the immutable presence and power of Bury's monastery. It did not take a violent hit-and-run in Henrician England to view the religious houses in this way. Their congregations may have been centuries old, and the Tudor regime itself may have been reaching out for a new, centralising authority over its realm, but there was no evidence of any diminution in the regulars' social power. In the many middling towns much like Bury in England and Wales, the outlook may have been quite the opposite in the quarter-century between 1509 and 1534. The monasteries' build-ings were not only generally taller and wider than those around them, and often far grander, but they also seemed to reach around and across the city, town or village more completely than any other. The 'Great Harry' bell tower that replaced the old angel steeple at Christ Church, Canterbury, had reached as high as 235 feet above ground in the last decade of the fifteenth century. These buildings seemed to diminish their secular neighbours, appearing at once to keep them out and confine them to their own place. In the wake of the Peasants' Revolt (1381), new, fortified gatehouses had been raised, flanked with turrets and flecked with arrow-slits. The crenellated gate (*c.* 1400) of St John's Abbey, Colchester, cautioned traffic on the southern approaches to the town.[2] The Augustinian abbey at Thornton (Lincolnshire), completed the year after the peasants were suppressed, was the best-defended building on the eighty-mile route between Lincoln and York.[3] Even the priory of tiny Tupholme (Lincolnshire) was held fast behind a moat so broad and deep that its impression is still visible four centuries after it was filled in.[4] Blazons of arms, such as those on Thomas Goldston's Canterbury gate (1521), signalled protection on earth as powerful as the monks might hope for from heaven.[5] Of course, these features were not confined to religious houses, but beyond the principal cities, where prelates and princely laymen were invested in building works of their own, there was scarcely anything in the eye-line that could compare. The impression was heightened for neighbours looking on after 1509, because so many of these buildings were disarmingly à la mode. Bright red brick (Exeter's Augustinian friary), Renaissance roundels (Waltham) and elaborate timber framing (Much Wenlock) showed that the present material wealth of the religious houses was invested in their future (see Fig. 7).[6] These foundations were known to be half as old as time. But their fabric spoke of an authority that was vital still.

In many centres of population, and middle-sized towns (3,000–5,000 inhabit-ants, such as Mistress Warner's Bury) in particular, the religious house had not only set a frame around its living space; it had possessed it. By the beginning of the sixteenth century the local regulars, friars as much as monks, had become the proprietors of residential, commercial and industrial plots. Abingdon Abbey Oxfordshire drew rent from 332 of the 445 premises within the limits of the town.[7] Just outside their gatehouses, there were whole rows, streets, even entire quarters in their possession; often they were the landlords of the largest trading concerns in the neighbourhood such as the permanent market stalls and the inns. The wide spread of benefactions they had attracted in their formative years had given some houses a proprietorial interest even in far-away towns. The residents of Tudor Kidderminster (Worcestershire) knew that their homes and businesses, and the land they stood on, were the property of a priory of canons established a hundred miles to the south (Maiden Bradley) among the Wiltshire Downs; but few, if any, would have seen the priory at first hand.[8]

Monastic lordship moulded the landscape. The house itself defined the scale and scope of the living space around it. The outline of the town and the profile of its buildings were drawn in response to the development of the conventual buildings and the precinct boundary. The expansion of Abingdon had been contained as much by the position of the abbey grounds as by the course of the River Thames.[9] The course of the monks' conduit at Sherborne (Dorset) was such a defining feature of the town that at the dissolution the stone head was set in the marketplace.[10] At Romsey, residential tenements were so tightly packed against the monastery's precinct wall that after the dissolution the quoins were assimilated into their own, to be sure they remained standing.[11] Party walls encroached, and endangered. Two fires at the London convent of the Augustinian friars in 1503 and 1518 threatened the buildings on either side.[12] The public thoroughfares of a neighbourhood were compelled to respect the perimeter of the regulars' precinct; many monasteries had been there first and the only ground to be given belonged to them. The neighbourhood made dog-leg turns to accommodate a corner; if there was a possibility of crossing the path of the professed, they went another way. A religious house defended its boundaries assiduously.

Towns where trade was lively and part of the population was always passing through – Colchester, Peterborough, Boston, Chester – witnessed many trespass prosecutions.[13] In a number of locations a commercial life of any kind had originated in the regulars' developments, such as the creation of an open marketplace at their own main entrance (Battle, St Albans), the construction of an inn to accommodate incomers (Hinton Charterhouse at Norton St Philip, Somerset), or the provision of a portway, quay or wharf.[14] Tudor neighbourhoods were more inclined to contest their control over the place and terms of their trade, but monastic development continued nonetheless. At the turn of the fifteenth century Gloucester Abbey raised new inns in the main streets of the town which fixed the orientation of traffic and trade for the next 200 years.[15] With speculative construction in the doldrums, the monastic monopoly on residential space was secure and a number of wealthy abbeys extended their portfolio of tenements. Battle created for itself an entire quarter of the town, which was returning 11 per cent of its income by 1535.[16]

Their regular landlords lent these communities their lifeblood. They provided the essential resources that established a neighbourhood and enabled it to remain. Watercourses were almost always theirs. This might be expected of old foundations whose resident population pre-dated any significant presence in the town. But institutional initiative had also served the needs of quite different and more complex conurbations. It was the conduits of the Dominican and Franciscan friars that brought water from outlying sources (at Greetwell and Monk's Abbey) into the city of Lincoln.[17] The dependence of the neighbourhood was sometimes conspicuous. At King's Lynn, the Augustinian friary set a condition on their construction of the conduit that its three pipes would be opened to the public only within daylight hours.[18] The conduit of the Grantham friars, first laid in 1314, remained the town's sole water supply until at least 1851.[19]

The role of monasteries in the creation of social communities was apparent in every region of the realm among populations of all sizes, but it is now best traced in smaller towns, villages and rural sites which saw limited later development. Winchcombe retains the imprint of the Benedictine abbey that gave rise to it, the High Street flanked by public buildings – parish church, inn – bearing the monogram of the penultimate abbot, Richard Kidderminster (see Fig. 8). The fullest expression of their formative influence was the satellite manor or grange. Here, there was a living and working environment wholly planned by a monastic proprietor. The buildings could be extensive and their facilities diverse. There were no fewer than fourteen discrete structures at Abingdon Abbey's Dean Court Farm, Cumnor, at its centre a hall fit for the abbot, its boundary marked by a moat.[20] The Chester monks raised a range of two-chamber tenements at the centre of their manor complex at Ince; its manufactory included a cheese press and the manor hall was enhanced with crenellation.[21] These were new, or renewed in the reign of Henry VIII, and although in the land-hungry south of England houses now leased their granges at least in part, in wilder country monasteries continued their development. Abbot Nicholas Pennant of Basingwerk (Flintshire) 'made a new close in the mountains' at Over Grange, Holywell.[22] These sites also declared their religious identity. At Spalding Priory's home grange, a carving over the door of the main farmhouse showed the instruments of Christ's Passion carried by a pair of angels.[23]

The religious houses provided the means to live in these places, and they also lent that life much of its rhythm. The passage of time itself was marked, and sounded, from within the precinct walls. In the close-packed streets of Canterbury and Reading, the neighbourhood might follow the monastic timetable by ear.[24] There were competing church bells in the largest cities but generally it was the regulars' that were the most assertive. For generations, priors of Leominster took steps to silence the parish bells, so that those for their own office were the only peal heard in the town.[25] The bell towers of Norwich Cathedral Priory were positioned to face on to the city, and held the heaviest bells whose peal carried to its boundary.[26] At Plymouth, no other bell demanded attention, as it was the tower of the Franciscans that stood directly over the port.[27] For many the opening of the regulars' gateway was the cue to begin their working day. Before going about their own business, the men of Canterbury stepped into the monastery's almonry to be shaved by the barber who kept a stall there.[28] The early morning task of the six-year-old John Stow was to fetch 'a halfe pennie worth of Milke' from the home farm at the London Minories.[29] At Bridlington (East Yorkshire), local agricultural work would not start until the priory had opened its doors as its outer court was used for the night storage of horses and ploughs; as the king's commissioners reported when they came to close it: '[the labourers] must have the grasse grounde within the [priory] or ells they can not tyll their lande'.[30]

The principal festivals of the house defined the profitable periods of trade. The stall holders of Lewes were bound to set up shop at the dead end of the year, 29 December, because of the customs of the Cluniac priory. In fact they faced a double jeopardy, as the monks levied pickage, a toll payable for every pitch.[31] The monasteries showed something of an imperial ambition in their seasonal markets and even communities that knew them only as a remote landlord found their commerce under their control. At the end of the fifteenth century, the market at the Wiltshire town of Marshfield was orchestrated by the canons of Keynsham, ten miles to the west.[32] Calendar celebrations created seasonal work. There was casual labour called for inside the precinct. At Lammastide the men and women of Battle came to help the cellarer shell his harvest of peas.[33] The Canterbury cellarers' custom of recruiting players for the days of Christmas was sufficient to support a home-grown troupe in the town; by 1534 they had formed a mistery (guild) of minstrels.[34]

If the routine of the regulars was unavoidable for their neighbours in cities and towns, in rural locations, principal manors or granges it was central to their lives. On the plains of South Yorkshire, from Stallingborough, across the River Trent at Burton-on-Stather, as far as Selby, perhaps the main event of the farming year was the drive of eighty head of sheep from the grange farm to the farmer proprietor at the Benedictine abbey.[35] In the isolated West Somerset village of Cleeve there can have been no sight to rival the descent of the abbey herd from the moorland to the stream of the Cistercian abbey mill for their seasonal wash.[36]

The presence of the regulars was pressed into the neighbourhood, but it was only a fraction of their neighbours who were wholly part-and-parcel of their world. The religious houses were an important source of employment; in small towns and in rural areas perhaps they were the largest employer in the district. The angry allegation of Simon Fish's polemic, *A supplicacyon for the beggers*, first printed in 1529, that the religious orders commanded the labour of a tenth of all those in domestic service, may not be too wide of the mark.[37] Yet these numbers were not evenly distributed among the different congregations and across the country. The largest and wealthiest of the abbeys and cathedral priories may have retained a permanent staff of as many as 150, a ratio of staff to professed residents of as many as 3:1. Thomas Rowland alias Pentecost of Abingdon was himself responsible for the pay of forty domestic and outdoor staff in 1533–34.[38] Fewer than fifty houses found themselves in these circumstances; from what little is recorded of their domestic arrangements, some of them seem to have already begun to reduce their wage bill. A list of in- and outdoor staff from St Albans Abbey in the mid-point of Wolsey's tenure (*c.* 1525) identifies fewer than fifty for a community of almost as many monks and an annual income in four figures.[39] In most houses of modest population and prosperity, the permanent staff may have been more in proportion to the monastic community; even so, where the numbers were already low, or dwindling, the presence of only a few servants gave the impression of a life that was extraordinarily well-served. There were only four canons at Buckenham Priory (Norfolk) when it was closed in September 1536, but there were thirty-three 'divers men resident in the priory' (diversis hominibus habitantibus in prioratu).[40]

The ebb and flow of the conventual population in the provincial friaries, and the volatility of their income, may have meant that they were no longer a place of employment for local people at all. In the capital and provincial cities, the permanent population of a religious house represented one constituency among many others, secular clergy, tradesmen, itinerants, some of which were to be found in far greater numbers. In sparsely populated places they were a more conspicuous concentration although in the absence of other employers, perhaps they were more easily integrated. The impression of a neighbourhood divided was perhaps most pronounced in towns like Alice Warner's Bury St Edmunds, where the urban community was burgeoning but still there was no other interest capable of competing with the monastery. In 1509 there were 3,000 residents; the precinct (monks and staff) counted scarcely 5 per cent of that number.[41]

The staff of a monastery of any size was led by two cohorts of lay officers, responsible in turn for the stewardship of the house and its property and income beyond. For the surrounding neighbourhood, these figures were as much the embodiment of the monastery as any sighting of the religious themselves. George Hilton of Skiplam (North Yorkshire) still remembered the seasonal visit of the 'corneman' of Rievaulx sixty-eight years after its surrender.[42] Generally, these were not outsiders, and they held some connection to the region if not the city, town or village. Robert Inglond, Lewes Priory's bailiff for Southover, was a resident of Cliffe, less than a mile from the house itself.[43] But these men were not always of the neighbourhood. The common complaint of episcopal visitors was that these responsibilities were now too often put in the hands of the monastic community's own kinfolk, ceding the proprietorial interest of the house to an oligarchy. The impression of the monastery's overmighty authority was surely amplified where the principal stewardships had been offered to noble and gentry families prominent in the region. They wielded the territorial influence of the house but seemed to stand apart from it; as men of rank, they wore no livery. The mutual assistance of the religious house and regional elite was characterised by the rebel leader Robert Aske when he challenged the dissolution in 1536: both were 'much socored in theyr nedes'.[44]

The main body of staff were waged men and women skilled and unskilled. In the monasteries each obedientiary officer – the head of the department into which the administration of the house and its resources was divided – retained a number of staff of their own. The weightiest roles – cellarer, kitchener, almoner – presided over a household of clerks, domestics and pages; most of the professed charged with some responsibility in the convent kept one or two in their pay. Henry White, cellarer at Battle Abbey in the accounting year 1512–13, retained ten salaried staff, from his factotum, Marmaduke, paid almost £1 per year, to Oliver, his egg-collector, whose annual toil earned him just 6s.[45] By comparison, the friaries may have seemed almost self-contained. As the professed population was volatile, perhaps the only permanent employees were the core domestic staff. It may have been their desperate short-handedness that led the Franciscans of Worcester into scandal (1535) when a washerwoman, known notoriously as Fair Agnes, was persuaded to take on the role of convent cook.[46] Lacking the property portfolios of their monastic colleagues, much of their external administration appears to have been handled by the friars themselves.

Largely absent from the domestic account rolls that survive is the agricultural and industrial labour that was known to be in the precinct. The abbot and convent of Selby bought and sold working farmstock on a large scale. Since the turnover in just one accounting year was as many as 400 animals, there were surely retained stockmen and ostlers.[47] Material traces show that iron was founded and forged in, or close to, the perimeter of the Cistercian Rievaulx Abbey; at Bordesley (Worcestershire) and Tintern (Monmouthshire), also Cistercian, non-ferrous metals were being cast, apparently for the manufacture of vessels for internal use.[48]

Those who did find their living within the religious houses were bound very closely to their way of life. It was not uncommon for the career to be a family tradition, with spouses and their children finding occupation side by side. Like the professed themselves, the staff often served for life and their longevity was rewarded with a pensioned retirement within the precinct. '1 very old and impo-tent creature sometime cook of the house' was found at Polesworth (Warwickshire) 'living by promise' of the nuns.[49] The king's commissioners were surprised by the extent of some of these provisions in 1536–40 when they were faced with the task of paying off the precinct population.

Their visible benefits, and the borrowed authority of the ancient foundation, may have made the staff a natural source of tension in the neighbourhood, and it does seem that for many on the outside they carried the charge of its lordship. Provincial justices, and the king's courts, presided regularly over cases of assault or damage to property in which, one way or another, the liveried servants of a religious house were implicated. Violence for some seemed to be thought a tool of the trade. When John Totyn, servant of the abbot of Glastonbury, conveyed a message to William Russell, the vicar of St Michael's, Mere (Wiltshire), he set about him with a stick and his dog.[50] These were not reliable instruments of regular authority: they weakened their house's standing, and understanding, in its neighbourhood; the volatility of such servants also threatened their houses directly. Archbishop Warham called upon the prior of Christ Church, Canterbury, in 1511 to call the staff to order in their conduct towards the monks (melius de cetero se habebant erga monachos).[51] The brawling between the old and new cooks at Chester Abbey brought them before the city's sheriff in 1511–12.[52] At Trinity Priory, Ipswich, one bullying household servant held the canons in thrall with his daily taunt, 'I shall gyff the[e] suche a strippe that thow shallt not recover a twelvemonyth after'.[53]

The staff were tied to the house but not necessarily to its neighbourhood or even its region. The monks of Durham Cathedral Priory bluntly disparaged the labour available on their own doorstep as 'personas mediocres'.[54] Casting the net wide was at any rate a practical necessity for certain roles. The competitive cultivation of complex music called for specialist professionals found only in the largest cities. Westminster Abbey filled its choir and Lady chapel with the capital's most talented musicians no doubt leaving a trail of resentment in London parishes.[55] Fewer of these itinerant professionals may have been drawn towards the remoter foundations although their generous terms might secure the contract: Robert Derkeham went to Buckland at the outer edge of Dartmoor for a substantial stipend and furnished rooms in the west gate.[56] The passage of outsiders into the precinct can hardly have helped to level the ground between the house and its neighbours, and it can be no coincidence that some of the scuffles which were carried into a courtroom saw these employees at their centre.

The houses also retained cohorts of secular clerks, those in minor orders as well as ordained priests, some occupied in the precinct, others provided to the chapels and churches under their control. The greater abbeys and cathedral priories whose spiritual jurisdiction was hedged around by papal privileges organised their clerks like the clergy of a diocese: they were summoned to synods, were addressed by the monks in sermons, and saw their further education facilitated and even funded by the abbot and convent.[57] They were visible in their extramural roles, serving the principal chapels and parishes that formed the front line of the monastery's liberty. But they were also a presence inside the monastic enclosure.

The compert (report) of the king's visitors at Durham Cathedral Priory noted the presence of Scots priests showing the titles to livings they had taken at the monastery's hands.[58] They were often at the table of the superior or one of their obedientiaries; perhaps they routinely found their meals in the monastery kitchen and took them with the professed. One of Battle Abbey's priests made a formal agreement with the monks so he might always dine with them in their refectory.[59] These secular priests attached themselves to the devotional traditions of the house and at a time when the investment of local layfolk had transferred to the parishes, for some, even prestigious houses, they became patrons of their altars and shrines. Later entries in the register of benefactors kept at St Albans show secular clergy giving generously to the church and joining the confraternity associated with its shrine.[60]

The social and spiritual affinity between the regulars and secular priests reinforced the religious influence of the old foundation in neighbourhoods that might otherwise have been inclined to hold themselves apart: in this respect the symbols of the monastery's patronal cult that appeared in parish churches at this time do not necessarily express the outlook of the congregation. They extended the clerical presence of the house to the periphery: Sherborne Abbey clerks celebrated Mass at the chapel of ease at Oborne (Dorset), six miles upriver from the town, and at the remote hermitage 'by the mylle'.[61]

Their close relationship also coloured the experience of reformation on both sides of the precinct. Often the regulars' seculars were the first to pronounce publicly on Crown policy. Thomas King, parochial chaplain at the abbey of St Albans, came to Cromwell's attention for his attack on the royal supremacy as much as a year before there was any suspicion of similar opinions inside the monastery.[62] But their public faces and voices also aroused the authorities' interest in their masters, who were reticent inside the enclosure. It was the table talk of secular clerks 'at suppor' that condemned Abbot Robert Hobbes of Woburn as a traitor in 1538.[63]

The religious houses were also a source of work and trade for those in their neighbourhood making an independent living. Their presence was a particular stimulus to specialist suppliers and craftsmen. The breeding of oxen was buoyant in the neighbourhood of the larger abbeys with extensive precincts where there was always a need for draught animals. The staff of Barking's cellaress, Mary Wynham, bought more than £50 worth of beasts at three fairs in the course of 1535; the coming of the first royal visitation had not halted the agricultural year.[64] There was enough trade for parchment-makers at Abingdon and St Albans in spite of their proximity to Oxford and London.[65] Bellfounders and glaziers prospered at Carlisle where the Augustinian Cathedral Priory and the Dominican and Franciscan friars ensured them a sustained demand.[66]

However, their neighbours could no longer rely on the regulars as a ready market for their more run-of-the-mill trade. Although many monasteries had reduced the scale of their own farming enterprise by the beginning of the sixteenth century, and let out to tenants a portion of their original demesne lands, their output was enough to supply most dairy and cereal ingredients, milk, flour and hops. They did now purchase some of their processed foods, such as butter and cream, although cheese, like bread and beer, was still produced inside the precinct. It was the complaint of the *Supplicacyon for the beggers* that the food grown on their farms was greedily garnered in their cellars and butteries so that 'they have ... the tenth part of ... hony milke ... chese and butter'. In fact, for at least half of these larder essentials, they looked to the market stall like any householder.[67] This too may have troubled their immediate neighbours. Nicholas Harpsfield (d. 1575) recalled that people carped that the prices of eggs and fish were high 'by reason of [religious people] their fasting in Advent and other times'.[68] In fact, as might be expected of any great household, with purchasing power and staff there was no need for them to limit themselves to local sources. Thomas Bolton of Selby travelled as far as London for a peck of pepper. The well-born women of Syon would only buy their bed linen at the same city's Bartholomew fair.[69] Although the town was renowned for its market, the cellarer of St Albans Abbey bought fish for the convent fifty miles away at Stourbridge Fair (Cambridgeshire).[70]

The monasteries' competitive challenge to local commerce was concentrated especially in their continuing enforcement of customary charges for trade as well as for 'piccage', the pitching of a market stall, and for the carriage of goods and for sale themselves. The flat line of their rental returns in the years either side of 1500 seems to have encouraged them to exploit these sources of income ever more assiduously. Some also tried to extend them. The prior and convent of Southwick abandoned their age-old Lammas Fair in 1514 and substituted a May Fair that would last for five days.[71] At Battle, the monastery not only owned the market and its stall but also manned them. There the cellarer offered surplus cider from his buttery.[72]

Increasingly, it was not the market of the religious houses that was good for neighbourhood business but their infrastructure. Monastery precincts had been tailor-made for a level of self-sufficiency in food and simple manufactured goods. The upper inner court at Norwich Cathedral Priory was 'teeming with merchants and craftworkers'.[73] They were fully equipped for craftwork and light industry, from brewing to tannery. As they, collectively and individually, turned to buy in from outside more of what they needed, the working environment within their walls was recognised as a source of income. Their buildings, machinery and space might be rented just as the rest of their property portfolio. The pattern of letting in the precinct suggests it was approached with a sharp eye to the commercial dynamics of the district.

Clerkenwell Priory welcomed the makers of decorative objects in horn and metal of a kind that would attract external trade.[74] Norwich Cathedral Priory aimed at the creation of a self-contained shopping centre, developing the inner court of the precinct with a series of rentable premises.[75] No doubt the abbeys of Westminster, St Albans and St Augustine's, Canterbury, saw practical benefits, as well as profit, in allowing printers to set up shop in, or on the boundary of, the precinct.[76] In parallel, many now turned over their urban property to commercial enterprises. The city and suburban rents of St Albans included both breweries and inns. The abbot and convent of Vale Royal (Cheshire) let out as many as fifteen shops in Chester as well as the superior's own hall in the city.[77]

The friaries had not been configured in the same way. They occupied a substantial acreage and their perimeters enclosed a mix of green space, working buildings and rows of residential tenements. The precinct of the London Dominicans was perhaps 'the greenest space in the whole of the walled city'. Despite the different scale of the urban environment, small town friaries could also command substantial open acreage.[78] The precinct of a city convent was now developed with property so extensive that it might be 'difficult to recognise the buildings of a religious house'.[79] Between them the five friaries established in London in the sixteenth century let out as many as forty premises in their precincts; the Dominicans accounted for as many as twenty-two.[80] Most of these had been gifted to the friars deliberately to extend their domain in the crowded urban centre and to give them a rental income. Now, these acquisitions were let out for diverse uses, and where it was seen to enhance the business potential it seems the convent was inclined to include sections of their own range of buildings in the rentable space. In 1524 in just one week in May, Prior Robert of the Norwich Augustinian Friars granted two substantial properties on the approaches to his convent to two tradesmen, one to William Togode, tailor, and one to Robert Fulsham, 'goldwyredrawer'.[81] The irregular jumble of buildings that passed into the possession of the friars perhaps were as good as any for specialist crafts that had no need for a barn. Simon Evenot, shoemaker of Lombard Street, rented a chamber and cellar from the Minories, apparently comfortably, since he held it for twenty years.[82]

The security of these sites, lacking the wide outer courts of the greater abbeys and their multiple gateways, always open in daylight hours, was well suited to the business of retail. Perhaps it was for this reason that two London haberdashers held their stock at the Blackfriars convent.[83] Even before the sudden drop in donations to them at the end of the 1530s, there is no doubt that the friars were dependent on these rents and the result was that increasingly the church and conventual buildings were encircled by tenants and their own working lives. The Lincoln Carmelites let portions of their plot to prominent citizens Henry Sapcote and Thomas Welles in 1520; their Augustinian brothers appear to have made a similar arrangement for their four acres with another leading landlord, Robert Dighton, ultimately the grantee of the suppressed house.[84] A rash of ill-advised building projects initiated by the poorer of the London friars in the 1520s offered an easy opportunity for those with the cash to lend, and merchants and the Italian banks with outposts in the city stepped in to their own, evident profit.[85]

The number of commercial tenants on monastic and mendicant doorsteps does seem to have bred a certain affinity between them. It appears that early Tudor entrepreneurs preferred religious houses for their projects, and not only perhaps for the scale and scope of their property and the stable level of their rental charges but also because of their own interest in novel sources of income. A pioneering coal magnate, William Arnold, bequeathed Beauvale Priory not only the right to mine coal from his lands but also the equipment for what appears to be underground workings, for making 'drains, punches and proppes'.[86] What began as a business partnership for some may have become a social and cultural bond. By the turn of the century, London tradesmen, long-standing tenants of St Albans Abbey, now sent their sons there to make their profession.[87] Mutual commercial interest could also breed a certain complicity. Monasteries close to the sea coast at Battle, Tynemouth and

Whitby were believed to collaborate with local mariners in the abuse of tollage, and even wrecking.[88] A meeting of five city companies at the convent of the London Franciscans appears to have fomented sedition in 1443.[89]

These ties were made where the position and property of the religious house and economic opportunity of the region naturally aligned. But there was a commercial relationship that thrived at almost every foundation, monastery or friary, regardless of location. Everywhere there was a market for the distinctive provision of board, lodging and living, known as a 'corrody' – derived from the Latin *conradere*, to scratch together – which traditionally houses had allocated as an act of charity but which for two centuries and more they had allowed to be bought and sold. Early on monarchs had demanded them as the price for their patronage, using them as a means of outsourcing their own rewards for service and political loyalty. By the sixteenth century the interest of the Crown had waned and houses now traded corrodies in their own neighbourhood. 'Spek with ye abbott of Byland for roulme for myne uncle Thomas', was the last word of Robert Lascelles in his will of 1508.[90] Market interest made the nature of the corrody ever more elaborate. At Sibton Abbey (Suffolk), John Flynn and his wife received a dwelling, grazing for a horse, use of Tylow's pond, a portion of the fruit from the 'great garden', and bundles of 200 faggots and 200 woodchips for their fires, year round.[91] Thomas and Joan Swanne of Kyme (Lincolnshire) would surely not have received a mere cash payment in lieu of the larger corrody they secured from Kirkstead Abbey (Lincolnshire), which committed to them seven gallons of convent ale and seven casts of convent bread, one mess of meat at dinner and at supper, four loads of firewood and grazing for a horse or mare alongside the abbot's in his stable. Here they were given the right to a house and garden within the precinct as well as the bounty from the cellarer's store barns.[92]

The purchase of a place in their precinct changed both the appearance of the religious house and its atmosphere. Extensions to the ranges of conventual building closest to the cathedral church at Norwich after 1500 seem to have been for the benefit of outsiders lodging there.[93] By 1516, the subprior at Clerkenwell had given up his own range to one of these paying guests;[94] at Cleeve layman Edmund Walker took chambers on the south side of the cloister itself.[95] There may have been many professed communities that suffered from this coexistence in the same way as the canons of Stone Priory (Staffordshire), who lived cheek by jowl with the Onyon family: Mr Onyon's wife and daughter were of notoriously easy virtue, while the son was known for threatening violence to the religious, and his sister, when challenged on her own conduct, for calling them Lollards (vocabat istum falsum et lollardorum vilipendendo eum).[96]

Alice Warner was unusual in thinking of her monastery at Bury St Edmunds as a distant authority. In towns such as hers, in the larger cities and in provincial centres, many knew the regulars at first hand as their own landlords. There had been enough stability over the past century for tenancies still to have passed through the generations, so that some who owed their home and place of work to their religious house had been born to it. This does not mean there were separate spheres in these places, a monastic domain and a world outside. Registers compiled after 1509 at a number of major monasteries holding substantial urban property – Bath Cathedral Priory, Bury St Edmunds, Gloucester Abbey – point to a continuing turnover of tenancies.[97] It might be assumed that their concern for continuity made the terms of monastic leases always lengthy and unvarying, but in these records there are agreements for periods of no more than ten years. Not only the scale of their portfolios and their commercial and residential variety but also their terms may have been such that the local population as a whole was forever passing in and out of their hands.[98]

'Yea happy was that person that was tenant to an abbey', affirmed Michael Sherbrook in his memoir five decades after the last of the dissolutions, recalling the tale of a gift given by a monastery to their tenant on his wedding day.[99] Sherbrook's nostalgia was not wholly out of step with his own time, which, regardless of religious preference, lamented the loss of the traditional landlord and the rise of the rapacious profiteer. While the religious houses remained in place, it was the very fact of their property, rather than their behaviour as proprietors, that provoked the fiercest criticism. 'Of this wordle they have the chefe dominion,' the author of *Rede me and be nott wrothe* reflected bitterly, 'the ryches and gooddes of the comen we all hath sett theym in their honoure full hye . . . With their temporal substanne and money they . . . supporte their foly.'[100] Their own registers, and the record of the courts, show that conflict with tenants was frequent, more so perhaps after 1485 than had been seen since the popular rebellions of the fourteenth century.[101]

Yet it would be wrong to assume that it arose from the monasteries' rigid and severe exercise of their lordship; as often as not it seems on the contrary that the loose terms of these leases encouraged their tenants to stretch their rights to the very limit. Far from 'pore people they devoure', as *Rede me* pictured them, the self-confidence of tenants steadily rose. Abbot John Prust of Hartland confessed in Star Chamber to live in fear of his leasees after they accosted him in his abbey lodging, 'arrayed in maner of war'.[102] Perhaps there was a particular wildness in the west, but Prior Thomas Vyvyan of Bodmin resigned himself to his own woodland being made into a common, while all and sundry allowed themselves to fish from his own ponds.[103] The threat of 'waste and spoyle as many tenants may do' was Abbot John Burton of Oseney's (Oxfordshire) reason for resisting the enclosure imposed under the king's injunctions of 1535.[104]

On the northern border, Richard Lighton, canon of Brinkburn (Northumberland) was cruelly murdered when he challenged Sir William Lisle's seizure of the priory's tithe-corn.[105] Their self-determination surely found encouragement in the cavalier conduct of other landlords bordering the monasteries' estates. Vale Royal's grange was invaded, very deliberately, in Easter Week 'not dreding God nor worshiping that blessed tyme of Christs passion', when the abbot and convent might not be so readily mobilised, and a herd of 160 cattle was driven away; a second wave saw the mill 'hewe[d] asunder the dores coggs and trawes'.[106] At the turn of the century, Newsham Abbey (Lincolnshire) was under siege from the Ayscoughs, a land-owning family on their border, an assault that was too frequent, and wielded too much influence, to trouble the king's justices.[107]

In regions at times unstable and violent, the regulars' exercise of their landlord-ship remained largely constant. There are few indications in the registers surviving of any sudden or significant change in the level of their rents. The accounts compiled by the king's commissioners at the moment of suppression or surrender show that arrears were common. They continued to oblige their leasees with services in-kind which for some now may have carried the smack of ancient and outmoded obligations. For the East Sussex manor of Alciston not only was Ralph Sadler required to see a 'sufficient' boar sent to Battle Abbey at Christmas and a fat cow a month before (for the feast of All Saints), but he was also bound to open his household and host the abbot and six servants for three days twice a year.[108]

Houses of all sizes did now very frequently vary the quantity of their properties they put out to farm, as they followed the fall and rise of values for food and live-stock. Thomas Cromwell himself condemned the practice at Spalding Priory where 'certen busie falowes ... be not mainteyned' because '[the prior] wol not let the fermes of his house to the greate damage of the same'.[109] Yet the constriction of leases in one region was counteracted by their release in another. Typically, less populous and poorer foundations were less inclined to chop and change their leases. The friaries, with only a handful of plots and premises from which to raise an income, let out more and more. There was such traffic in leases over the small ground the Franciscans held in Aylesbury (Buckinghamshire) that it led to bitter disputes with their acquisitive neighbours.[110]

The general reduction in the number of granges held in demesne (i.e. directly managed by the monastery) presented a new prospect to the rental market.[111] If ploughland and pasture was not so plentiful for Tudor farmers as it had been for their grandparents, there was now an abundance of infrastructure, working buildings from stables to mills, and managed landscapes such as fisheries, orchards and warrens, which previous generations had never known. It was common for monasteries to portion these out to maximise their return. The fulling mill of Stanley's (Wiltshire) home grange was tenanted separately by 1521. When Neath came to put out the majority of its grange property in 1536, the manorial centre might have been offered with a modest lot from the full parcel of land. The large coastal site at Sker (Mid-Glamorgan; see Fig. 9) was put out with just four closes.[112] At times supply exceeded demand. It was not uncommon to see monastic sites standing empty. Battle Abbey could find no tenants for its market stalls. An entire street of tenements, Well Alley, belonging to St Mary's Spital, stood empty and steadily derelict for as long as twenty years.[113]

The religious house was no longer landlord to the whole neighbourhood but it was still its principal source of fiscal and legal authority, in civil matters certainly, and for many also in the realm of the Church. Such far-reaching jurisdiction was a source of tension on both sides of the precinct wall. The monasteries' regarded their lordship as their protection in the present time and their promise for future generations; their neighbours saw it as the great threat to their livelihood. It was not, as the printed polemics claimed, their riches that made them so difficult to live with but, as Alice Warner complained so bitterly, their rule.

For generations, the greater abbeys and priories had kept chronicles of their conflict with the social community that were supposed to be subject to them. By the end of the fifteenth century there was enough of an organisation and a shared identity in some of these places for the subject community to do the same. The burgesses of Faversham, a town governed by its Benedictine abbey, made a book of their battles with the abbot and convent fought over four decades before the dissolution (1506/7–40). On the face of it, the contents are the minutes of their own council and its transactions with the monastery, but as the representatives of a subject people, it is also their story of recurrent war and treaties for peace.[114]

In fact, with the coming of the Tudors these relationships were marked more often than not by a common search for a settlement between the governor and the governed. From early in the fourteenth century, economic depression, social dislocation and war at home and abroad had combined to make monastic lordships something of a powder keg. When pressure rose to a critical level, often they were the first in provincial England to explode. Even modest towns under the authority of major monasteries – Abingdon, Cirencester (Gloucestershire), St Albans – had seen armed anarchy in their handful of streets. Yet as the fifteenth century closed, it appeared there was little appetite for those days to return. In the spring of 1492 Prior William Selling of Canterbury met the mayor and commonalty of the city for the 'appeacyng ... of suche qaurells and grugges as ... have ben in tyme past ... to thentent that love tranquilite and peace shulde be perpetually hadde and continued'.[115]

Such gestures of appeasement and times of truce were also witnessed at Battle, Coventry, Gloucester and Faversham in the early years of the Tudor regime.[116] There was a new aspect to this peace: they aimed for more than a temporary truce, rather a reconciliation of the rights of the old lordship with the community's expectations for their own self-governance. The rapprochement reflected a shift in the relative prosperity of the civic and monastic populations. Business boomed for the townsmen of Abingdon in the second half of the fifteenth century; it was natural that their abbey neighbours would now prefer cooperation to conflict.[117] The turn in the social relationship was surely also driven by personal ties. The catchment of many monasteries had narrowed down the centuries and now local families were often well represented in the house. Connections were cemented with the appointment of kinsmen as lay officials of the house.[118]

Lacking any claim to lordship, the friaries had often found themselves subject to the neighbouring commune, but in certain provincial cities and towns there appears to have been a similar affinity formed in the early years of the sixteenth century. Burgesses took their convents under their protection. The ties were strong enough to sustain some even as the pressure for reformation grew. Bishop Richard Ingworth, appointed royal visitor, reported in 1538 how many houses survived because the prominent men of the town chose to aid them in their desperate letting of conventual buildings and dispersal of fixtures and fittings for cash.[119]

Early Tudors contested the authority of the religious houses, and they would look to contain it whenever and wherever they could, but they did not wholly reject it. Their position was most conspicuous in – and surely reinforced by – their view of the regulars' spiritual leadership. The century before 1534 is now widely accepted as marking the coming of age of popular, parish religion.[120] There is a rich body of evidence to encourage this view, not least the fabric of so many city, town and village churches which bear witness to ambitious and costly schemes of new work, even at a time, between 1450 and 1485, of economic instability and civil unrest. The parish was made a 'community of purpose'.[121] The focal points of these refurbishments, bell towers, nave aisles, chantry chapels, are seen to signal a new self-determination in religious practice, enabling the parish church to contain all forms of worship, public and private. Further support for this reading of popular religion might seem to be found in the records of the religious houses themselves, as daily donations to their altars, relics and images dwindled and they allowed the old shrines which once captured public attention to fall into disrepair.[122]

Yet neither of these is a sufficient measure of monasteries' contribution to lay religious life; and it would be quite wrong to think that a prosperous and lively parish culture effectively cancelled out interest and involvement in other places and patterns of worship. There is no doubt that the religious houses retained a role in the religious life of their neighbourhoods, in spite of their competing facilities elsewhere. In some aspects of the community's Christian life their spiritual primacy was still beyond question.

In many parts of England and Wales the regulars had not receded from religious life for the circumstantial reason that their churches were their place of public and parish worship. Of the eighteen cathedral churches in England and Wales, half were staffed by monastic communities, all but one of them Benedictine; the outlier, Carlisle, was Augustinian. Here, the priests who met the laity in the nave, preached to them, and presided over public sacraments were professed under vows; in the year of Henry VIII's accession, six of them also acted as suffragans under the incumbent bishops.[123]

Of the 200 odd Benedictine abbeys and priories found in England and Wales in 1534, as many as two-thirds opened part of their churches for the use of lay worshippers.[124] In regions of the realm where towns of any size were few, there was a greater reliance on the sharing of churches. In Lancashire, a county of almost 1,200 square miles, a fifth of the parish churches were in fact monastic churches.[125]

A smaller proportion of the canons' churches were used in this way although where they were found alongside centres of population these same arrangements were made. In the busy moor town of Bodmin the people were proprietorial about their worship at the priory. The peremptory reminder to the canons was to perform the office in low voices on county days because the town would be in the nave.[126] Often the nave of a church was subdivided by length or width, to create a space for public worship on one side while the monastic community processed from their own doorways to celebrate the office on the other. It was said that packed into one end of the priory church at Bridlington there were 'a thousand and a half house-lyng people'; the same claim was made of the priory of Christchurch, Twynham (Dorset).[127] The expansion of the secular population of the precinct had placed a new imperative on these provisions, and intensified the pressure on shared space. It brought bitter conflict – Sherborne in 1436; Dunster (Somerset) in 1498 – but at the same time, new building.[128]

In the middle years of the fifteenth century a new parochial chapel was erected at St Albans Abbey abutting the north wall of the church, with connecting doorways giving them access to the altars tended by the monks in the north-west corner of their nave.[129] At Lewes, Reading and Woburn, a parish church stood on the perimeter of the precinct, although its priest and its pattern of observances remained under the direct supervision of the monastic community.[130] Only where the parish itself was free from monastery's jurisdiction, such as St Margaret's Church, yards from the north door of Westminster Abbey, might this influence be resisted.[131] In remote, rural regions of the north, west and Wales the subsidiary chapels of the religious houses remained in use. The anger in the Wye Valley (Herefordshire) arising after Abbey Dore let out the last of its granges revealed the local dependency on the grange chapel.[132]

Yet the laity came into their regulars' churches also when it was not their only option. On the face of it provincial cities and towns – Coventry, Exeter, Norwich, Salisbury – were now well stocked with parish churches, but still their space was insufficient, perhaps more so now than in earlier generations as many of them had benches installed.[133] In the century before 1534, there had been widespread adaptation of the interior space and furnishings, without doubt to draw the outside world towards their own way of practising religion.

Lady chapels may have first been created in monasteries as an expression of their own interest in Marian cult, but by the fifteenth century their furnishings and their services were styled deliberately for lay congregations. Of course, in a cityscape of multiple parish and public churches the largest and finest of Lady chapels might have been the first choice for worshippers on Lady Day (25 March). In the witness statements collected at Worcester Cathedral Priory after one Thomas Evans caused a scene, there is a glimpse of the citizens gathered to mark the eve of the vigil of the feast of the Assumption: 'entered unto our lady chappel with in the monastery . . . bendled downe and seyd a pater noster and an ave and kyssed the image [of our lady]'.[134]

The Lady chapel and its worship were elaborate and there may have been an impression of some social exclusivity. It was often the wealthiest who had claimed its space for burial. At Tewkesbury, those townspeople accustomed to worship at the parish end of the abbey nave set their sights on their own altar of St Mary while the Lady chapel on the north side was claimed by those of high status from out of town.[135] The regulars encouraged the neighbourhood as a whole to bring their worship into their church's nave. Monastic churches had not been built for public congregations, but now the space was opened up and often extended. Even at the remoter abbeys of the Cistercians, in North Yorkshire and the West Country, the surviving fabric shows that the western end of the nave was remodelled in the fifteenth century, so the laity might pass in through the north or west door just as they did in their own parish church.[136] The larger space, the greater variety of altars, their 'gyldyd images' and 'payntyd tables', and perhaps the prospect of preaching, made the regulars' nave a popular choice for everyday acts of worship.[137] Two citizens of Coventry were so at ease in the nave of the Benedictines' church that they let down their guard and were heard to share their heretical views.[138]

The churches of the friars had also been shaped by their original ministry. Only those of the preaching order of Dominicans already offered the open space for a large, lay congregation.[139] Few if any of the provincial houses could raise the money for rebuilding on the scale of the monastic churches, although it may be that because their original church was itself still unfinished some convents were able at least to alter, perhaps even to lengthen, the nave. But they too now furnished their churches to attract the devotional interest of the neighbourhood. Descriptions of friary churches at the time of their dissolution reveal a variety of subsidiary altars and devotional artefacts. The Augustinian Friars at Orford (Suffolk) attracted oblations to their 'Good Rood'.[140] Lay burials had always been accepted in the friars' precincts, although the area set aside for them was a small fraction of the whole,[141] but now they were also giving over interior space to lavish tombs, and even chantries, of their lay patrons. London's friaries held as many as 1,000 tombs by the time of their surrender; at the Franciscan convent an illustrated inventory was compiled in *c.* 1525 probably to ensure the continued use of an already crowded interior.[142] The benefactors' tombs within the church of the Bridgwater Franciscans was the abiding memory of one of the last visitors.[143] The Tudor tomb at the Carmarthen Franciscans inspired an ode by the Welsh bard, Gwilym Egwad.[144] It was a reflection of how far the friars had drawn the laity towards them in recent generations that in Lincolnshire alone their fifteen houses attracted more than four times as many bequests between 1500 and 1538 than the monastic foundations of other congregations combined.[145]

Something of the style of the public worship was now taken up in the choir of the conventual church itself. Here, in the reign of Henry VIII, there was also a growing crowd of panel paintings, statuary and tapestry to catch the eye. There was at least one, often two organs to prepare the monks for performing polyphonic music, in which they might be joined by professional singers and choristers. The five-stop organ in the canons' choir at Butley would have made music quite unlike anything heard in the small and scattered neighbourhoods of estuary and ness.[146] There was a sacring bell to signal the moment of the Eucharist's consecration to those who could not see it. Even the very space of the choir, originally configured precisely for the observance of the monastic office, might now be modified to accommodate others. At Westminster Abbey, screens were put up on either side so that members of the royal household might be spectators.[147] Sometimes it seems there was no attempt to separate monks and any laity in attendance. A chance remark from the Benedictine abbey of Burton-on-Trent conveys an impression of layfolk in devotion (indedant laici) while the monks, duly vested, celebrated (cantantes in superpelliciis tempore divinorum).[148] The trend was conspicuous enough for reformers to fear a new subjection of the laity. 'Rolled up with descant, pricksong and organes,' railed the pseudonymous Roderyck Mors in his *Complaynt* (1542) 'wherby menny hertes be rauysshed'.[149]

The regulars' churches offered more to the religious practice of the neighbourhood in space, furnishings and decorative splendour for the Mass which was their common obligation. Wherever these churches were located, they were still the natural focus for the intercession which early Tudors looked for in their lives no less than their forebears. Pilgrimage may no longer have held the appeal it had two centuries before, but devotion to saints had lost none of its energy and donations and individual acts of worship continued unchecked. Monastic churches contained more altars carrying a wider variety of dedications than any rival places of worship. Over time they had also accrued fabric and artefacts, which while they did not always have a fixed altar setting, attracted the devotional investment of outsiders. The present arrangement of these sites and objects had been shaped by time, the traditions of the house, the priorities of its patrons, and the preferences of the current monastic community who were men and women of their time like any other. There are indications that some of the cults that were their central interest no longer excited the neighbourhood. The popularity of their own patron saints waned. Oblations at Coventry's shrine of St Osburg failed to drive the cathedral priory out of its financial doldrums.[150]

The writing of new stories of saints and sacred relics in English and for the print market at Canterbury, Chester, Hailes and St Albans was without doubt a response to the eclipse of shrines which had once been a mainstay of their alms.[151] This reflected a change in the tastes of their lay visitors, however, rather than their withdrawal. Their preferences were informed by a greater choice of subjects than previous generations had known and perhaps by a self-awareness, refined by literacy, education and an exposure to print that encouraged them to follow their own path. At Battle Abbey it was the old, imported cult of St Benignus that thrived.[152] The social and cultural dynamics of the neighbourhood, stirred by well-organised parish communities, also shaped their choices. In Westminster, the laity prioritised the abbey's altar of Our Lady of Pew; perhaps it was a matter of fashion, possibly because it was practical, as the first altar encountered on entering the church from the town at the north door.[153] At Farleigh Hungerford (Wiltshire) what drew local crowds was the legendary chain of St Peter, which was claimed to ease women through the pains of childbirth.[154]

By 1509 the traffic may have been little different in the friaries. When the king's commissioners stepped into Dominican and Franciscan churches both in cities (Chichester; Salisbury) and small towns (Guildford; Ilchester, Somerset; Melcombe, Dorset), they met a crowd of 'altarys', 'tabills' and 'imagery' that reached along the length of the nave.[155] The Carmelites at Coventry were custodians of the most celebrated shrine in the city and region, centred on an image of the Blessed Virgin Mary, known as Our Lady of the Tower.[156] At Northampton's Augustinian Friary, as well as a Lady chapel, public worshippers were presented with a panel of

Our Lady of Grace and an altar in honour of the Scala Coeli, the legend associated with the celebrated pilgrim church at Rome.[157] The richness of the regulars' cult offering was unrivalled. 'Our parishe church is but a dungeon,' reflected Alexander Barclay, 'to that gay churche in comparison.'[158]

Recognition of the rare sacred space of the religious houses reinforced the old, old idea that sanctuary could be claimed there by those on the wrong side of the law. It remained the last resort of the desperate even as the independence of the monasteries faced a concerted challenge from the Crown. When grocer George Carlton's business collapsed after 1529, he suddenly slipped out of sight of his creditors, reappearing only when he was safe inside the abbey church at Westminster.[159] For their part, the religious were not disinterested in the potency of the old tradition. The principle of it might still lend lustre to their independent standing; the practice put some handy helpers at their disposal.

In a prosecution brought against the Charterhouse at Sheen it was alleged that a trespass had been committed by the steward of the house, aided and abetted by 'sanctuary men'.[160] It was a measure of the controversy they courted that when the monks of Gloucester settled their conflict with the town they agreed to drop their claim to sanctuary.[161] The Reformation Parliament regarded the recourse to sanctuary as another aspect of the case for the state's supervision of the Church. In the same session that saw the statute for the suppression of smaller monasteries, another was approved concerning sanctuarians for 'divers . . . haven the more bolde to perpetrate and committe . . . myschevous . . . dedes for that they have been always releved, ayded and succoured by the sanctuaries'.[162]

One consequence of the laity's continuing interest was the flourishing of confraternities at monastic and friary churches. For centuries, monasteries had offered to their devotees the formal award of a share in the spiritual benefit of their worship in perpetuity. At first this had been registered by the entry of the recipient's name in a volume kept at their high altar, often known as their 'Book of Life' (Liber vitae). Later a number of the greater abbeys and cathedral priories introduced a ceremony of admission, in which members were inducted in the presence of the convent at the high altar.[163] There was still a turnover in these spiritual societies as the reign of Henry VIII neared its third decade. The latest of the Canterbury registers to survive records ceremonies as far as 1526; Sir John Arundell, his wife Katherine and their children saw their names entered into the martyrology of Bodmin Priory in February the following year.[164]

From early in the fifteenth century (if not before) friaries also issued grants of confraternity. A century on and pro-forma letters were being printed for sale through pardoners.[165] Prior William Bowry of the Hounslow Trinitarians collaborated with the metropolitan printer, Richard Pynson, on two letter editions between 1519 and 1528; his colleague, Prior John Brockden of Thelsford, continued the commercial relationship with Pynson as the decade turned.[166] Monasteries may have been involved in the same enterprise although scarcely any have survived; Pynson accepted a commission from the Cistercian Abbot John Apryce of Strata Marcella (Powys) just eight years before its surrender.[167] Spiritual association was also sold in strings of rosary beads crafted and blessed by a particular house and often bearing the promise of a pardon. The trade thrived to their very end, so even in 1540 a reformer urged that 'our justificacion doth come by the grace of god' not 'by prayers beades hallowed at Syon'.[168]

The appeal of a lifetime association with the cult of a religious house was coupled with the continuing pull of its protection at the point of death. Tudors saw an attraction in living out their last days and years in a monastic setting as men and women had done since the days when it had seemed a refuge in a frontier land. The idea was most potent at the very apex of society. Henry VIII's maternal grandmother, Elizabeth Woodville, ended her life at Bermondsey Abbey. Margaret Wooton, widow of the king's loyal lieutenant, Thomas Grey, passed much of her last year at Tilty Abbey (Essex), occupying the old guest hall that was built into the west end of the church.[169] Their choices were copied by the gentry. John Clervesse, a Yorkshire landowner, decided to die in the care of the Cistercians at Rievaulx in 1505x1515.[170] Elyn Carver, a wealthy widow, chose to end her life at Combermere Abbey in 1518x1529. Widow Elizabeth Pellyham died at West Malling Abbey (Kent) in 1487 where she had occupied a richly furnished chamber and joined 'all my shepe goyng with my ladyes flekke'.[171] The future of Eleanor Togode (née Thowe) was thrown into abeyance when her late father's executors withdrew into the London Minories.[172]

The refined piety practised at this end of society was marked by an asceticism and it was not uncommon for such individuals to lodge at a religious house even when they remained in rude health. It was in his time as a law student that Thomas More lived perhaps within, certainly in the lee of, the London Charterhouse, apparently so he could learn, and repeat, their observant routine. Sir Thomas Lovell (d. 1524), courtier, soldier and one-time chancellor, made a home for himself at Holywell Priory, Shoreditch (see Fig. 10).[173] This pattern of settlement was perhaps as much social as it was spiritual; there is little to suggest that Tudor England was on the verge of a movement that might be compared to Europe's beguinage or 'devotio moderna', which saw lay households set up in a monastic formation. An exception, perhaps, were the metropolitan convents of the friars where patrons were offered the opportunity of lay brotherhood, although whether this amounted to what would later be called a 'tertiary' order remains unclear.[174]

Tudor patrons came into these churches as well to connect themselves with their public prestige. The secular forces generated by a religious house – recorded history, popular legend and the social status arising from their own wealth and that of their founders and benefactors – were sought after just as much as their spirituality. These forces were looked for in the marking of personal and family milestones. In July 1536 Holywell Priory was chosen as the scene of a remarkable triple marriage ceremony for the earls of Oxford, Rutland and Westmorland.[175] Religious houses were also chosen for local, civic and national royal and governmental ceremonies. The burgesses of Beverley (East Yorkshire) met in the Franciscan friary; their election of aldermen was run in the conventual church.[176] In provincial towns, the religious houses were especially associated with the activities of professional, spiritual and social guilds. The regulars courted their interest no doubt conscious of the prospects for patronage. There was a hint of competition in Norwich as both the Dominicans and Franciscans played host to guilds of the Blessed Virgin while the Carmelites opened their church to the guild of St Barbara, popular in a crowded city since she was the patron saint of sudden death.[177] The ties were not confined to urban centres. Forty miles from Norwich, Wymondham Abbey hosted a Watch and Play group in their chapel of St Thomas.[178]

For these communal activities, the central position and space of the friaries held a particular appeal. Parliament convened in London's Dominican church at intervals in the first two decades of Henry's reign. Under Wolsey it was almost the government's second home. It was there that the Holy Roman Emperor, Charles V, was lodged when he visited in 1522; there also that the legatine court convened to consider the case for the king's divorce from Katherine of Aragon.[179] Nor did the drift of government policy after 1534 detach the friaries. The duke of Norfolk convened the Garter Knights in the chapter house of the London Franciscans in the summer of 1538, just weeks before its closure.[180]

While they opened up their own churches more and more, the regulars were also prominent in the parish. The greater abbeys and cathedral priories were the sole spiritual authority within the Liberty – that is to say the jurisdictional boundary – of their lordship. The neighbourhood churches and chapels and many of the semi-ecclesiastical foundations, such as hospitals, where acts of worship were performed, were under the monasteries' command together with the clergy that served them and the layfolk forming their congregations. Here, the leadership of the monastery was embodied in its archdeacon, still always a professed monk, who was charged with the supervision of the priests and the pastoral care and discipline of their people.

As a figure of the ecclesiastical hierarchy archdeacons were second only to the head of their house and for many in the neighbourhood a good deal more familiar. Given their presence in every monastic lordship, the record of their role is very thin. In Durham it is possible to follow the Cathedral Priory's archdeacons' supervision of the city churches, their clergy appointments and their observance of calendar festivals; there is also a witness to the cycle of public sermons they preached, in which they attempted to promote interest in the monastery's patron saints.[181] The impressions that can be recovered from other locations are of offices firmly, even forcefully, discharged and officers who were sometimes a focus for local conflict. John Rothbury, a monk of St Albans, used his claim on the archdeaconry to allow him, with two of his colleagues, to turn Elizabeth Webbe prioress of Sopwell, out of her office and hold her in custody, an alleged misconduct that landed him in court.[182]

Whether or not they could claim the status of an exempt jurisdiction, wherever monasteries were the patrons of churches they kept them under tight control. There was a continuing anxiety in the hierarchy of the secular Church that this oversight was self-interested and that monastic interventions in their parish livings too often targeted their sources of income, to the dereliction of pastoral responsibilities. For centuries monasteries had been granted dispensations to appropriate the parish churches given them by founders and benefactors, allowing them to redivert income to their own conventual needs, and to reduce their incumbency to a chaplain, or even to one of their own professed priests. There had been vocal criticism of the practice throughout the history of these religious houses and in the sixteenth century it found a place in the litany of monastic abuses composed by the new breed of reformers. In the year before the suppression statute, Sir Francis Bigod was prompted to put the king 'in remembrance intollerable pestilence of impropriations of benefices to relygyouse persones'.[183]

Yet it does seem the effects of appropriation were very varied. There can be little doubt that some parishes saw their opportunities for worship much reduced as a resident priest was substituted by a chaplain with a stipend so low that he was likely to take on roles elsewhere. The parishioners of Wembury (Devon) complained 'ther hath byn menyone ded and hath dyed wytheoute schryftte and housel or any other sacrament mynestred'. Since they 'hath not with them no prest' they suffered 'greate labour [in] goyeng in and owte fro the sayde priore in the colde wynter'.[184] The sources of income supposed to be tied to their church were sublet for the long term. In 1530 Aldgate Priory sold on the rights to the woods at the parish of Erith (Kent) for a term of two and a half years.[185]

It was rare, however, for any church put in this position to be left untended entirely. Appropriation did reinforce the subjection to the monastery but typically the result was a different form of ministry rather than none at all. The priest presiding was in the pay of the monastic patron; as at Wembury it was not uncommon for him to come from the professed community itself. Richard Redman as visitor of the Premonstratensians discovered canons of Easby Abbey (North Yorkshire) dispersed at various churches and chapels whose cures they served (diversas habet ecclesias et cantarias quam canonici sunt curati). In 1485 his General Chapter commanded such arrangements to be restricted to their appropriated churches.[186] The priests of both parish churches at Buckenham were canons from the priory.[187] In the Liberty of Bury St Edmunds, the parishes and chapels-of-ease were served by the sacrist of the monastery and his chaplains.[188] Their service may have been kept up even after 1535 in the face of royal and episcopal injunctions for reform. The call for parish congregations to hear a sermon at least once each quarter of the year reinforced the monasteries' responsibility for pastoral care. Bishop Rowland Lee specified that religious houses with 'benefices impropriated' were to see to it.[189]

Small and remote chapels serving no more than a hamlet may have depended on the direct ministry of the monastic community. A chapel at Calbroke (Buckinghamshire) was kept open because the nuns' priests from Little Marlow Priory ministered there. When the monastery was dissolved the chapel was abandoned.[190] The pastoral supervision of their neighbours in such satellite communities remained a concern for houses conscious, perhaps increasingly so in the reign of Henry VIII, that their spiritual authority lent weight to their claim to independence. The Premonstratensian canons of Beauchief (South Yorkshire) provided new chapels in the shadow of the royal supremacy at Norton, near Sheffield, with the patronage of Bishop Geoffrey Blythe (1524) and Holmesfield (Derbyshire) also with the support of benefactors.[191] The Cluniacs of St Augustine's, Daventry (Northamptonshire), reconstituted the town's church to be the parish church for three outlying villages and appointed one of their own to be the priest, now serving a population perhaps of more than a hundred.[192]

The experience of worship in these parishes was marked by the monastery's supervision. The fabric was imprinted with its corporate identity. At Conisbrough (South Yorkshire) a stained-glass image of a habited monk prompted the congregation to remember their patrons, the prior and convent of Lewes some three hundred miles to the south.[193] At Cranborne, parishioners were reminded of the priory's authority whenever the priest climbed into the pulpit which was inscribed with the initials of the prior.[194] Those surrounded by shabbier furnishings may also have been reminded of their proprietorial relationship. In the accounting year 1533–34, Nicholas Jenney of Lewes recorded that four of the priory's local parishes stood in arrears.[195] It was surely to avoid a steady decline that in 1528 ten parishes appropriated to Glastonbury Abbey agreed themselves to take responsibility for the maintenance of their chancel.[196] The parishioners of Abergavenny (Monmouthshire) seized the initiative and started their own subscription for bells by 'going into the country with games and plays'.[197] Yet there were congregations which knew their monastery had given them a lifeline. The high altar at Sampford (Sussex) was no longer flooded by rainwater because Battle Abbey had provided a new shingle roof.[198]

Naturally, monastic patrons were most inclined to invest in the devotional life of their parishes, to fill their benches and their coffers. The Westminster sacrist paid for 'pownde tapers' to be supplied to each of the parish churches under the abbey's jurisdiction for the principal calendar festivals, no doubt so that the bright light of their own celebrations might remind the parishioners of their parent church.[199] The Cistercians of Kingswood shared their own stipendiary singing men with the parish churches in their care.[200] When a miracle cure was claimed for a panel painting kept in the parish chapel at Eldernell (Cambridgeshire), the patrons at Thorney Abbey were quick to turn it into a narrative that could be put into circulation.[201]

When not visiting their churches, the Tudor laity confronted the spiritual leadership of the regulars most often in their preaching. This was their most visible contribution in Robert Aske's North Country homeland, 'gostly liffing [of the people] by spiritual informacion and preching'.[202] Friars were familiar in a variety of guises, as confessors, vendors of confraternity proformas and other forms of indulgence, and as petitioners for alms, but it was their public, often open-air sermons that were most readily called to mind. Alexander Barclay captured the image most recognisable to his peers, 'ye olde [ofte tyme] freer that waned ... against such foyles [of man] was bodly wont to preche'.[203] Monks were thought of as preachers just as much as the friars. *Rede me and be nott wrothe*, railed at them for their avoidance of the task, 'redyr to take up tything than to prech to theym frutfully'.[204] Michael Sherbrook was too young himself to recall the life of these places but he had inherited the idea of them 'abroad, without', preaching 'faith and good works'.[205] At Battle, there was enough of a social memory in Elizabeth's reign for someone to sketch the profile of a preaching monk on the cover of one of the mayoral plead books.[206]

The preaching of the friars shaped the profile of their precincts and the identity of their churches in the public mind. Preaching crosses stood at convents of any size: at the London Dominicans the cross framed the lay cemetery; at Hereford, where the remains of a cross survive to this day, it marked the border between the convent and the social community of the city (see Fig. 11). For many on the outside, the sermon was the main draw of the friars' church. It was a familiar standpoint in a pious lifetime and a sought-after place for eternal rest. Londoner Roger Jacket requested burial before the pulpit at Blackfriars.[207]

Monasteries were not so conspicuously marked by a commitment to preaching. If there were preaching crosses in their outer courts they have left little material trace; the footprint of a cross of some purpose in the outer court at Cleeve Abbey might have been a platform for preaching, and the abbey's prominence in its coastal region might have made it a recourse for an itinerant audience. Still, monastic preachers may have been seen and heard in public as often as the friars. The independence allowed to their university graduates extended to their acceptance of invitations to preach elsewhere. At any rate, houses exercising their own exempt jurisdiction, and with a large roster of parishes, dispatched duly qualified men on preaching duty.

Returning to Canterbury Cathedral Priory from Oxford, Thomas Goldston was licensed by his superior to preach in English and Latin (and so, to laity and secular clergy) throughout the province of Canterbury.[208] Durham Priory also dispatched preaching monks to the parishes across the liturgical year. During Lent a programme of sermons was delivered, the priory's own speakers supplemented by seculars. At Rogationtide (a period of fasting in preparation for the feast of Christ's Ascension, on the fortieth day after Easter), a monk preacher represented the priory at one of their city churches.[209]

Most of the surviving sermons of monastic or mendicant origin date from the century before 1534. In itself this is no indication that the early sixteenth century saw any decline in their preaching, although perhaps the sermons were not always originals since the surviving examples are often recycled versions of much earlier scripts. Prior Thomas Mildenhem of Worcester (d. 1507) carried with him a vast compendium of sermons, some of which had first been preached in the reign of Richard II (1377–99).[210] Still, their tone and theme give a taste of what was heard by Tudor congregations. Most are written down in Latin but may have been delivered in English interspersed with Latin quotations meant to serve a mnemonic purpose. In many ways their message matched that of any secular priest of this or preceding generations: they impressed on their listeners the immutable power of sacramental practice and the imperative for the faithful to adopt a disciplined piety to drive off irreligion and heresy.

Yet there were also touches that Tudor audiences might have thought of as the characteristics of the regular preacher, whose vision was of a national community, a kingdom of Christians, in which a compact of clergy, monarch and magnates protected Mother Church. They also tended towards a homespun turn of phrase. Typically, monastic preachers were university graduates, but at the same time they were sons of the same community to which they spoke and they reached out to them with the idioms and images they all shared. At Durham, the Eucharist was presented as an invitation to take dinner at the home of a great man.[211] The audience for regular preaching cannot be known although anecdotal evidence suggests that crowds were not uncommon. In Sussex, the preacher led his audience out into the churchyard 'by cause of the wolte' which had stifled the sound of his words.[212] Graffiti on the walls of the prison at Carlisle, which are dominated by the Holy Name of Jesus, could be taken as an indication that the preaching of the friars, the chief promoters of this cult, was now reaching those who needed it most.[213]

Monastic and mendicant priests were also known to their neighbourhoods as confessors. Friars might range over a large radius from their home convent to provide a service which was for them a valuable source of income. People expected friars to pass among them, dispensing their 'religion', whether it was looked for or not. Thomas More's *A mery gest how a sergeaunt wolde lerne to be a frere* turned on a merchant being deceived on his own doorstep by the message, 'an austen frere wolde wich hym speke'.[214] Monastic confessors may have more commonly acted within their social network and it is possible that when one was specially named as a legatee in a lay will it was in acknowledgement of their role.

The ministry of regulars was also in demand for services performed at the point of death and at funerals. Perhaps the defining feature of lay piety in the century before 1534 was the ever more elaborate observance looked for at death, burial and in posthumous commemoration. The preoccupation was palpable in the parish church, where the configuration of the interior space and the decorative schemes reflected these demands. The effect on regular communities was equally profound. In the half-century before their closure, their direct contribution to the religious life of the social community came to be centred on the rituals of death. The developing tastes of this generation could hardly be satisfied in the confines of their parish church while the regulars' churches and their customs presented a larger and richer canvas that was ready-made. Here there was no indication that the parish was the limit of their spiritual loyalty. In her will of 1500, Widow Aslak of Norwich spoke first of the Carmelites and then of her parish church.[215] There can be little doubt that the Tudor art of dying breathed new life into their relationship with regular religion. The popularity of *contemptus mundi* motifs, in image and in word, naturally led the pious to look again at their monastic and mendicant neighbours. Hugh Latimer claimed that there had been a lively trade in 'coats and cowls' to clothe a burial.[216]

The capacity of the religious houses to perform a requiem Mass of a scale and style not possible in parish church had always appealed, but now testators were tempted as much by the scope offered by their cohorts of priests to provide individual observances. One or more of the professed community might be employed to follow their coffin on the day of their funeral, or to celebrate a Mass in their name for a thirty-day period from the day of their funeral, an arrangement called a trental. A London testator summoned twenty friars to his own parish church (St Michael, Cornhill) where they were to celebrate before the statue of the Virgin, to which the deceased had a special devotion.[217] Given the number and variety of houses available in the immediate neighbourhood or the wider region, it was possible for the wealthy to duplicate these performances at two, three or four houses, each one coloured by the distinctive character of its congregational customs. For his funeral John Hawkes, twice mayor of Bristol (d. 1503), arranged for a cohort from the city's four custodies to follow his coffin into the abbey church of the regular canons of St Augustine's, where they celebrated masses while the funeral ceremony itself was continued.[218]

The formation of a syndicate to offer funerary observances and subsequent commemorations became increasingly common in the first decades of the sixteenth century, no doubt encouraged by the example of the royal family itself. Henry VII's plan for his own memorial had included a scheme for simultaneous masses to be celebrated in a chain of more than twenty churches, regular and secular, that reached across the kingdom.[219]

The radical Simon Fish railed at this fashion, which he was convinced had been confected by the regulars out of mercenary greed: 'Euery man and childe that is buried must pay sumwhat for masses and diriges to be song for him or elles they will accuse the dedes frendes and executours of heresie.'[220] Yet testators' requests rarely speak of their commemorations in general terms, as some or other commodity, but express a commitment to the particularity of their customs. The executors of Sir John Dalingridge were directed to arrange for the abbot and convent of Robertsbridge to mark his obit with the monastic office of the dead, 'according to the Cistercian Use'.[221] A particular preference for their liturgical traditions may explain why a growing number of testators followed their requests with the presentation of sets of vestments for the convent's celebrants. William, Lord Willoughby's request (1526) made over (perhaps matching) sets to the friaries at Ipswich and Norwich which were to offer parallel commemorations for him.[222] There was perhaps an attachment to the monastic mode of prayer in the direction of Richard Lynge of Helmsley (d. 1531) to give family rosaries to Rievaulx Abbey, 'my grandam's bedes and my mothers, yf my brother and sister make no demand for them'.[223]

Often the arrangements made by testators reflected personal ties. John Stoner of Waltham (d. 1532) asked for a commemorative Mass from each of the canons and a special remembrance from two named individuals, Hawkins and Saunders, known to him socially perhaps, or kinsmen.[224] William Bachelor of Aston Abbots (Buckinghamshire) asked for a requiem Mass at St Albans Abbey, almost thirty miles from his home village, the celebrant to be his son, John, who was professed as a monk there.[225] The arrangements may have arisen from personal attachments but they also placed the house under a legal obligation to their neighbours. Prior William Vavasour of the York Franciscans found himself in court after failing to meet the post-mortem requirements for Elizabeth Metham.[226]

The religion of the regulars was closely associated with the rituals of death and acts of commemoration but not with burial itself. This was a change from earlier centuries. Monasteries and friaries had made space for public cemeteries from early in their history, but after 200 years and more they had filled up; and the development of the precinct left little room for further expansion. Attitudes had also altered among the laity. Since there were now so many churches of different status and religious traditions within the reach of most neighbourhoods, there was a growing tendency to connect each with a particular function: the parish church, either of the place of origin or present home, was now the most common choice for burial. The preference was at once pragmatic, responding to the parish clergy's claim on fees, and emotional, acknowledging the now lengthy tally of ancestors already lying there. In the century before 1530, nearly 90 per cent of Alice Warner's fellow townspeople of Bury St Edmunds had chosen a parish burial.[227]

The friars' spacious precincts retained an appeal for townspeople whose own parish ground was inevitably constrained, although excavated remains suggest their cemeteries saw nothing like the traffic they had seen when they were first laid out two hundred years before. The remains of women and children have been identified in the cemetery sites at Boston (Lincolnshire) and Exeter.[228] Of all outsiders, it was now the clergy that were most inclined to look for a grave in the church or cemetery of a monastery. In death, the parish priests of Bury embraced those from which they had had their living.[229] The laity were still buried in the precincts of monasteries, but considerations of space (for the religious house) and cost (for the subject and their family) meant that most often it was an opportunity or a preference only for those already resident there.

The placement of a prominent lay tomb within a monastic church was certainly less common than it had been in their early history, but those aware of hereditary ties, as founders, or substantial benefactors, still thought instinctively of burial in these oldest of settings. John, Lord Denham, declared in 1500 that the Augustinian church at Hartland – 'whereof I am fownder' – should be his resting place if he died within 100 miles of it, leaving his executors a logistical burden should he be as far as Bristol or Wells at his end.[230] The Howards of Norfolk held on to their historical association to Thetford Priory; Duke Thomas even thought to enhance the family mausoleum, persuading the king in 1536 to inter his own illegitimate son, Henry Fitzroy (1513–36). The gentry could rarely conjure a connection to the founding dynasty but they respected the patronal relationships of the more recent past. The Strangways of Dorset expressed their family attachment to Abbotsbury and Milton in a tripartite commemoration that gestured towards the grander scheme of the Tudors.[231]

Straightforward family connections within the same generation also brought a request for burial. John Moore of Evesham was interred in the monastery's chapel of St Thomas the Martyr, presumably because of the presence of a kinsman of the same name (brother, son) to whom he bequeathed a book.[232] John Audlett of Abingdon marked his own lifetime association with the abbey where he had been steward with his request for burial, as late as 1537, in the chapel of Our Lady of Piety 'within the conventuall church'.[233]

The regulars also played a pastoral role within the hierarchy of the secular Church. In dioceses north and south there were many neighbourhoods whose only contact with a prelate was the sight of a canon or monk serving as the bishop's suffragan. Priors of the cathedral monasteries acted in this capacity almost as a matter of routine, and in the scattered rural parishes and market towns of Bath and Wells, Coventry, Ely, Norwich and York the prelate presiding was typically a professed Benedictine. For the dioceses with the largest territories, such as Exeter and Lincoln, the assistance of the regulars was virtually a given.[234] Notwithstanding his personal ties to Thomas Cromwell, the promotion of William Repps alias Rugg to the bishopric of Norwich in 1536 would have been regarded outside and within monastic networks as a natural progression. Priors of the friaries had held suffragan roles for longer, and all that changed after 1509 was that their near monopoly was now challenged by the rising number of monastics alongside them. When Richard Ingworth, the Dominican who would bring about the surrender of the friar in England and Wales, was appointed to the suffragan see of Dover in the same year as Rugg went to Norwich, it was no watershed. For the prior of the favourite royal house of King's Langley (Hertfordshire) to be called upon to serve in the metropolitan see was the continuation of a tradition that was already more than a century old.

The increasingly unsettled climate of the time caused the bishops to turn to their regular colleagues more than they had done at any time since the scares of heresy at the turn of the fourteenth century. Bishop Geoffrey Blythe placed Coventry in the custody of Maxstoke Priory (Warwickshire); their children were put in the charge of the warden of the city's Franciscans, who 'straitlie examin[ed] them of their beliefe, and what heresie their fathers had taught them'.[235] In the neighbouring diocese of Lincoln, John Longland sentenced two with Lutheran leanings to terms of custody in monasteries, 'to remayne . . . in penance'.[236]

The regulars' place in the religious life of the neighbourhood after 1509 did not bring them any priority in patronage. It is often assumed that the parish was now the sole focus of lay interest, but in fact the pattern of investment shown in surviving wills reached right across the ecclesiastical landscape. The monasteries and friaries receded not in the face of the parish but in the face of a Church that as a whole was ever more diverse in its forms and facilities. The patronal ties that lasted for longest and mattered most to the religious – as a relationship as much as a material return – were grounded in family history.

It has been argued that inherited associations with a religious house held little meaning for the Henrician generation; when they were asserted it was little more than a cynical tactic to claim a stake in their real-estate value. Yet so often the impression from the sources is quite different. No fewer than twenty-five members of the families of Arundel and Warennes were commemorated at the Cluniac church at Lewes by the end of the fifteenth century. When a new range of offices for the obedientiaries was raised in 1527, the new elevations were decorated with their coats of arms.[237] The panel painting portraits of the founders of Conishead Priory (Cumbria) were among the very last furnishings to be removed at the time of its suppression and the king's commissioners grumbled at such personal mementos for which 'no man will give money'.[238]

Long-standing family affiliations reached across space as well as time. Lady Thomasina Percyval, a London widow, who died before 31 July 1513, was buried in the city parish of St Thomas Woolnoth, but she made substantial benefactions to the religious of her Devon homeland, the abbot of Hartland, some of her best table silver, and to the women of Cornworthy the weighty cash donation of £20.[239] Old patrons still identified with their houses and involved themselves in their affairs. The hereditary patron of Missenden Abbey (Buckinghamshire), Lady Elizabeth Pygot, presented herself in the chapter house to preside over the election of an abbot in 1512.[240] Even after the Crown's new authority had been demonstrated in the visitation of 1535, Lord Dynham stood ready to direct the selection of a new abbot of his monastery at Hartland.

For most of Henry's subjects, independent of an inherited tradition, patronage of a religious house was personal, circumstantial and ad hoc. The decision to make a donation to a monastic or friary church was not bound to be part of a pattern of behaviour. Typically now the object of the donation was very precise, such as a specified altar, relics, statue or image, or a Mass to be celebrated for a particular purpose. Testamentary gifts were also tied to specific acts; even where the whole convent was represented as a beneficiary, it was with the expectation that a commemorative Mass or a trental arrangement would be given in return. No doubt behind the impulse to donate there was a recognition – which as often as not may have been neutral – of the regulars' formal rights in death, burial and inheritance. Alice Warner and her Bury St Edmunds neighbours, like all those living directly under monastic lordship, were bound to present their wills in the court of the monastic sacrist.[241]

Critics seized on the transactional nature of these directions as indicative of a lack of sincerity on either side of the bargain: the laity had learned – or had been gulled into – this behaviour as a reflex and the regulars recognised the price more readily than the service it purchased. 'If the Abbot of Westminster shulde sing euery day as many masses . . . as he is bounde to do', reflected Simon Fish in his *Supplicacyon* 'M monkes were to fewe.'[242] Yet while the fastidious detail preferred by patrons may point to a heightened sensitivity about market value, there is little doubt that it also reflects a familiarity with the house, its community and their cult. The latest records of local expenditure, kept by sacrists to the end, or captured by the king's commissioners in their inventories, show that for their benefactors ancient and modern the regulars continued to enact what they had been paid to do.

While their performance of spiritual services aroused some suspicion, it was widely agreed that the religious houses still made a vital contribution to the whole spectrum of social welfare, from hospitality to charity and health care. There was a conviction voiced at every level of lay society that the regulars' provision for travellers, the poor and the sick was vital. The king's presumption that the Canterbury monks might meet the needs of his own large household was so prodigious that it provoked Archbishop Warham to make a rare rebuke, 'Spar the same from any such maner [of] extraordinary charges . . . [the] monastery hath been so burdened with receiving and intertayng bothe of the kings graces moost noble ambassitors and other princes, and of other honorable parsonages passing by that way . . . if suche charges or other lyke shuld continue, the same amongst after be utterly decayed'.[243]

The expectation of the laity was hardened by a common historical understanding that care had been their foundational duty. It was shared equally by their enemies and their friends. Robert Aske's first expressed 'gruge' against the suppressions was because they 'gaf great almons to pour men' in 'desert places, wher the peple be rud of condyccions', as well as 'refreshing ... strangers and baggers of corne' from east to west, where otherwise 'they have no such sucour'.[244] In the early years of Henry's reign these principles seemed of particular moment because of a widespread perception of a growing welfare problem. Aske himself observed that traditional forms of hospitality and charitable care had been eclipsed by commercial enterprise, 'for lucre and advantage to themselves'.[245]

He thought especially of the remote country of the north-west and north-east, but there was a rising tide of anxiety in populous and apparently populous provincial towns. When local people challenged Thomas Cromwell and his commissioners over the policy of suppression, they spoke first and foremost of the needs of welfare, and with a force in their words that suggested they had been worried for some time. 'Greate relief and conforte to that contrey' came from the Augustinian Priory at Carmarthen in Wales, claimed its mayor in 1538, '[it] being ole very pore and bare'.[246] At Coventry the citizens recalled the friars' role 'in tyme of plage', which, in the summer of 1538, was again advancing over the horizon: 'the seke people therine ... repaire and reasorte to the saide [friars'] churches there to here dyvyne service'.[247]

Of course, neither the Crown, provincial gentry such as Robert Aske, nor the mayors of cities and towns were disinterested witnesses. Naturally, they would want to see their expenditure on welfare sustained, at the same time as they wished the customary rights by which they raised income – from stallage to burial – to be curtailed. It remains very difficult to reach a reliable view of the level of welfare provided in city, provincial town or the 'mountains and desert places' of Aske's north country. The difficulty lies not only in the lack of a sequence of accounts from these places but a handful of untypical houses such as the cathedral priories and Westminster Abbey; also there is little doubt that some of the charity they offered was in a form that did not leave a record in the institutional rolls. Prior Geoffrey Shether of Little Dummow made a present of shoes for two nuns. His outlay of 4s is known only from his personal pocketbook.[248] Increasingly, the members of a monastic community made personal contributions to hospitality and charity. Superiors created a space in their own household for charity boys; obedientiaries, also keeping households, sometimes did the same. There were fourteen boys found at Darley Abbey in 1518, of whom only five served in the

Church.[249] Their stipend, and their earnings from preaching and other roles, enabled individuals even outside the hierarchy to afford modest acts of their own such as doles and sometimes even an exhibition for a poor scholar.

There were still institutional contributions made from the conventual coffers. Often these were founded on the obligations of their first founders. The Valor commissioners conducting the 1535 valuation of churches known as the 'Valor ecclesiasticus' recorded commitments of this kind reaching far back into foundation legend. The monks of Muchelney gave their alms in the name of the eighth-century monarch, Ine of Wessex (d. 726). At St Albans, the largest annual outlay down to the dissolution in 1539 was the distribution of alms said to have been inaugurated by Offa of Mercia (d. 796).[250] To these were added doles endowed by former superiors in association with their own commemoration. Valor entries, and conventual accounts as and where they survive, would suggest that the terms of these, even those reaching back over centuries, were still honoured. The reprimands of visitors in this regard may indicate that dropping them was rare. These patterns give the impression that the charity of Tudor religious was grounded in the generosity of past generations.

Yet new donations from patrons still living (or recently dead) did arise. John Musard, monk of Worcester Priory, reminded Cromwell that a dole had been instituted 'yn oure prince name unto xiiii pore people', with the effect that 'oure convent gyvyth owte of ther porcion vi tymes as moche as evyr dyd'. At Taunton Priory the Valor commissioners found the canons committed to a distribution endowed just two years before under the will of William Yorke (d. 1533).[251] At any rate, the wealthier houses were inclined to supplement their endowed doles with general distributions of alms at intervals during the liturgical year.

The record of St Albans's distributions in 1524–25 may not have been untypical: doles were on the feast of St Katharine (25 November), St Nicholas (6 December), Maundy Thursday (16 April), Rogation (25 April) and the feast of the patronal saint (22 June).[252] Anecdotally, calendared doles were not the limit of these alms. 'We may see for tyme of beyng there . . . dayly . . . be credible report iii or iiii xx [i.e. three or fourscore] pore folks of the town and cuntre,' wrote George Gyffard from the abbey of St James, Northampton. The perception of daily crowds at the gate or the precinct was widespread. Richard Ingworth said that he saw 'above iii hunderyd pore pepull' in the court of the Gloucester Dominicans, judging their reception 'a very grade ded' for the 'comenwelth ther'.[253] Perhaps the picture presented by the printer Robert Copland was not a caricature: 'dydderyng and dadderyng / leaning on their staues . . . somtyme to take in / and some to refuse . . . they be throng in many corners'.[254]

There may have been a disjunction between the distribution of what in later times would be called 'out relief' and the hospitality, charity and medical care offered inside monasteries. Here the impressions of onlookers, diocesan visitors, patrons and the Crown's commissioners are conflicting. The first of these frequently complained of the narrowness of the house's offerings and in particular of its growing nepotism, restricting board, bed and coin to their own kinfolk. Patronage, of course, took a self-centred view, welcoming its own generous reception while giving prim disapproval to the treatment of those in genuine need. The Wyatt family's mockery of how 'they [the monks] had ringes hanging over their tables to trye whether their egges had their just meaure' may have been widely shared.[255] By contrast, the commissioners' dispatches often speak of diverse and sizeable numbers supported within the religious house, in the outer court and inside the enclosure. At Ulverscroft (Leicestershire) they found both those 'of alms' and those 'living there by promise', and a crowd of children.[256]

Principled opponents of the religious orders argued that what was most conspicuous in public charity was their demand for it for themselves. In his *Supplicacyon*, Simon Fish claimed that every household (he counted 520,000 of them) was now contributing 20d annually for the support of each one of the orders of the friars.[257] The friars' dependence on alms had long been the subject of social and theological critique. In their visitations of monasteries, bishops had often found that doles funded by benefactors had been among their own kinfolk. Yet if there was a widespread suspicion that the charity of the religious orders did not extend very far from their own tables, it does not seem to have weakened the reflex to provide for them in cash or kind.

Members of the royal household, the court and the county elite can be found recording ad hoc payments to regulars, friars and monks, at least until the end of their way of life was widely anticipated. The ready acceptance of their claim on society's charity was apparent to the king's commissioners even as they sequestered their houses, and the regulars were anxious when the cash then available was not enough to meet their immediate needs.

Perhaps the most visible disinvestment was not within their walls but in the hospital foundations established under their patronage outside. At the turn of the century a number of the wealthy houses withdrew from the terms of the original endowments and re-established the hospitals for different purposes. After being left to fall into disuse, the old hospital of St Mary Magdalen at Glastonbury was finally turned over to the town as a general almshouse.[258] In Norwich, the prior and convent had left the hospital vulnerable by failing to fill the wardenship, although it was said to be the neighbourhood that degraded its buildings and drained its income: 'domus vexatur placitis et aliis injuriis plus satis'.[259]

Such was its increasing interest in the income potential of monastic property that the Tudor regime had showed some complicity in these changes. Among the property exchanges engineered by Wolsey, the monks of Bury St Edmunds accepted the revenue assigned to two of the town's hospitals as recompense for the loss of four of its manors. The money for hospital care was now to support hospitality at the abbot's table.[260] The care facilities they kept were often now confined to their immediate affinity. No fewer than seven of the in-patients found in Durham Priory's Maison Dieu in 1533 were the monks' own kinfolk.[261] When they arrived at Tilty Abbey in 1535 the king's visitors discovered a crowd of dependent relatives: at Tilty, 'Alice Mills, mother to the said abbot' and two other 'impotent parsons' have 'there fyndyng in the saye monasterye as they have hadd in tymes past'.[262]

At the premier abbeys, it appears to have been an acknowledged matter of fact that care was accessible only to an inner circle. The burgesses of Bury may have had the benefit of the abbey's own physicians from as early as the twelfth century.[263] The palliative care provided at Bermondsey to the dowager queen, Elizabeth Woodville, was exclusive; indeed it was at the same house that the mother of a monk was outraged at the carelessness of the monastic community that saw him mortally wounded by one of their own number and yet failed to nurse him.[264] Thomas Cromwell's own daughter was taken in to Wilberfoss Priory (East Yorkshire) as late as 1537 to give birth to her child.[265] The metropolitan friars were perhaps no different. At Easter 1538, Elizabeth Plantagenet, daughter of Viscount Lisle, was to be found 'sick with ague . . . in the [London] Whitefriars', just seven months before it was closed.[266]

On the rare occasions that the monastery's original oversight of public hospitals remained in place – which it appears to have done at Bury – the neighbourhood sick did depend upon the ministrations of those professed to a rule.[267] In the reign of Elizabeth a former monk of St Augustine's, Canterbury, Edward Mynge alias Bennet, testified before the city's mayor that the monks had worked as wardens of

St Laurence's hospital.[268] But the conviction and practical capacity of the religious houses to continue to commit to these ancient foundations was receding fast.

Their profile in medical care was now replaced by a growing presence in education. From the turn of the fourteenth century Benedictine and Augustinian monasteries had opened elementary schools for boys, to provide themselves treble voices for the new polyphonic performance in their Lady chapels and, over time at least, their very own choirs.[269] These schools continued into the sixteenth century and the largest of them at the wealthiest houses may have maintained as many as forty or more scholars, with teaching that took them as far as the threshold of university entrance.[270] In origin they were charity schools but in a provincial landscape in which school foundations of any kind were sparse, in time they were opened to fee payers, extending their catchment to the property-owning interest that surrounded them.

The new century, and especially the new reign from 1509, saw a further elaboration of this pedagogic relationship, as a number of urban houses entered into a compact with their neighbouring elite to create a new endowed institution. The school founded at Bruton in 1519 brought together the Augustinian abbot and convent, the burgesses of the town, and the principal land family of the region, the Fitzjames, the head of which, Richard, happened to be a former Oxford warden and bishop of London; governance of the foundation was shared between the monastic superior and the town.[271] A comparable collaboration occurred at Milton in 1521, the principal patrons of the Benedictine abbey, the Strangways, likewise presiding over a three-way partnership.[272] Prior Robert Petersen of Lewes kept up his trusteeship of the town school for seven years after the surrender of his house.[273]

The rising generation of monks, some possessing first-hand knowledge of the newer forms of schooling, made investments of their own. There may have been a number of men like Nicholas Clement, one-time infirmarer at Christ Church Priory, Canterbury, who paid for a poor boy to pass through school, only for the boy to rob him of £7 8s 10d, the reason that the arrangement is recorded.[274] Estimating expenditure on charity in the valuation of 1535, Bishop Gardiner was surprised that 'the finding of young children to scole' was 'so called as the other almes'.[275] Richard Smith (d. 1563), chaplain to the Catholic Queen Mary and presiding genius at the trial of Thomas Cranmer, recalled how he had been 'nouryshed . . . at [an abbey's] schole' and 'els I shulde never have bene learned'.[276]

The provisions of the religious houses for public education appear to have prompted patronage in the other direction. In 1526 John Cole carried property worth £14 10s per annum into a compact with the abbot and convent of Faversham and the warden and fellow of All Souls College, Oxford, to create a grammar school for the benefit of the brethren and novyces 'and all other children that be disposed to lerne the science of grammar'.[277] In his plans for post-mortem patronage, John Pulton of Lydd (Kent) combined the new value of pedagogy with the time-honoured status of his local monastery, Battle Abbey, and directed his executor, a university doctor himself, to provide the substantial endowment of £30 to the abbot and convent for the 'exhibucion and fyndyng' of one or two of the monks at Oxford and Cambridge.[278]

The patronal interest of the old monasteries in public education became proverbial. Henry, Lord Grey of Codnor (d. 1496), even tested social delicacy to entrust the upbringing of three bastard sons to the supervision of the superiors of Darley, Lenton (Nottinghamshire and Newstead).[279] Even in its savage assaults on their interest, the polemic of Roderyck Mors allowed that 'for the monkes found of their fryndes children at scole'.[280] But laymen looked also to the friars. Henry, Lord Grey, asked that Carmelite friars of Nottingham and of Lynn (Norfolk) might be found to teach poor boys their ABC and in turn to act as one-men chantries and to say commemorative masses.[281] Richard Ingworth, the last Dominican Provincial and prior of King's Langley, at the end of his life remembered the many 'such skollers as I have brought upp'.[282]

The religious houses and the social community surrounding them still met in almost every department of life. In many respects this was circumstantial. They lived cheek-by-jowl. Increasingly, it was a meeting that the neighbourhood was able to steer towards their own ends, whether it was a matter of workspace, worship or welfare. Even where theirs were the largest buildings occupying the greatest space, the regulars' capacity to control the life experience of their neighbours was not limitless; nor in fact had it ever been. Those wholly dependent upon the life and infrastructure of a monastery or friary were a diminishing band; if the regulars' own kinfolk are discounted, perhaps there were few of them at all.

The tendency might appear to be towards a relationship between religious and their neighbourhood as purely transactional, yet to accept this would be to pass over the signs of powerful social, sometimes personal and even affectionate, bonds between them. Many knew their religious house as a source of good fellowship.

Women of 'sad and of good conversation' – meaning surely of burgess families – dined with the prior at Winchester. Norwich's sacrist especially enjoyed the company of a city tailor and his wife.[283] His colleagues kept their own friends and were not averse to inviting them into their own accommodation within the conventual enclosure.[284]

The common feature of the reports sent to Cromwell of the regulars' non-conformity after the Act of Supremacy was the context in which they were discovered: in casual conversation shared sometimes outside but often within the precinct – table talk. Hugh Latimer had this in mind when he railed, 'in the court, in the noblemen's houses, at every merchant's house those observants were'; to him their good fellowship was a cause for suspicion, they were 'looking, watching and prying'.[285]

Although the neighbourhood could be seen sharing the communal life of the religious house, it does seem their sociability was sustained by traffic in the other direction. Professed men – in particular – joined their neighbours in their own communal spaces; probably sometimes in their own homes. Their regular status was recognised but it seems they were inclined to put off their habits, nonetheless. Malmesbury monks, Richard Ashton and Walter Bristow, made social visits to Bristol always 'habitu dimisso'.[286] A Norwich Priory monk, Thomas Sall, was known to pass through the city clothed as a layman.[287] Perhaps it was because he was so often among his lay friends that Thomas Gloucester of Malmesbury wore a gentleman's skullcap (pilleum) beneath his hood.[288]

This was friendship strong enough to pare back conventional separation. Thomas Towers, canon of Bayham, was living in the country household of Dr William Rootes.[289] At Walsingham (Norfolk), the prior's seneschal, John Smyth, together with his wife enjoyed a level of privilege which passed over from the fringe benefits of a close professional association into something akin to patronage: the prior passed to John's wife daily what was alleged to be an illicit monastic pittance of the best food; he lent her a horse when she fixed her mind on making a pilgrimage to Canterbury.[290]

It was a mutuality that sometimes seemed malign, especially for those who stood apart from it, locally, and as representatives of royal government. The conspiracy of Matthew Mackarell to conceal coin and plate from the Crown was made possible through his 'frendys' in the neighbourhood. The defiance of William Trafford of Sawley (Lancashire) was founded on his trust in 'as many friends as any man'.[291] It was readily acknowledged in 1537 that the prosecution of Whalley's Abbot John Paslew for his part in the winter rebellion was made possible by his confession. Had he been tried, 'it would have been hard to find anything against him in these parts'.[292]

Social ties were strong enough to encourage the professed religious and laypeople to share in each other's enterprises. Money was loaned on both sides. Thomas Mansell, merchant of Dover, made over £7 to the prior for a silver pyx.[293] Henry, Lord Grey, took his debt of £10 to the abbot of Dale to his grave.[294] Abbot Robert Frampton of Malmesbury felt his obligations so keenly that he admitted he would rather be in default of the king's fines than fail to repay 'hys fryndys' on the other side of the precinct wall.[295] Bishop Longland was alarmed at the amount of credit extended to the canons of Dorchester, fearing it endangered the very livelihood of the town.[296] What perhaps he did not recognise was the trust that was (still) established between laypeople and professed religious, raised from a personal familiarity with one or other of them and reinforced by the timeless presence of their institution. The king's courtier, Sir William Compton, expressed it in his will of 1528, when he directed that a fund 'to make defense for all such accions and suetes as shalbe wrongfully taken against my wife or executors' should be kept at Winchcombe by his old friend, the abbot.[297]

Some regulars made a very public investment in neighbourhood networks by joining their guilds. Perhaps in large urban centres with a well-organised lay elite it was understood to be a means of nurturing civic harmony. In the year of his election (1517) Prior John Webbe of Coventry Cathedral Priory joined the city's Corpus Christi and Trinity guilds.[298] But professed men outside the leadership were also drawn into these associations. Thomas Compton, monk of Gloucester, made the forty-mile journey to Stratford on Avon, where he was recorded in the register of the Holy Trinity Guild; at the turn of the century, a Cistercian, Ralph Bernys, came from as far away as Woburn.[299] The Coventry guilds attracted the attention of regulars, men and women, over a wide catchment, even as far as Waverley Abbey almost 130 miles to the south.[300]

The principal religious houses of certain cities – Bristol, Durham – gave a guiding hand to the governance of these guilds.[301] Elsewhere their part was more that of partner than patron: guilds were invited to affiliate with an appropriate altar in the monastery church or parochial chapel, or a nave altar in a friary church; sometimes they even convened their meetings there. At Bury St Edmunds,

Chester, Coventry and Norwich for a century and more the convent had been an active contributor to some of the seasonal celebrations of the guilds, in particular their plays, for which they were keepers of the costumes and sets and sometimes (certainly at Bury) the redactor of the script.[302]

These shared enterprises did not now settle any preternatural peace between the parties involved. Conflict occurred, although it was more akin to scuffle and skirmish than to open warfare. The familiar frontiers of their respective jurisdictions – the physical sites and the officers that policed them – saw the fighting that was the most serious and sustained. It was not the very presence of officers and servants of Abbot Alexander Banke of Furness (Cumbria) that provoked one William Tunstall and his neighbours to set upon them in the Lune Valley, but their purpose: they had come to fish in the open waters of the River Lune.[303]

There were also fracas which appear to reflect a more general tension between the parties. Thomas Dale, a grammar schoolboy of Ely, was passing the priory on the evening of 12 September 1527 when several young monks burst out from the building, 'not lyke any men of god relegyon, but lyke furyous persons'.[304] But these few, brief episodes do not point to an entrenched warfare between two opposing sides; rather they speak of the petty resentments and rivalries exchanged between groups whose involvement was close and whose interests, even identities, were very much aligned.

The presence of a religious house in life, livelihood and death, as Mistress Warner discovered at Bury St Edmunds, was an experience shared by many of her peers. There were larger villages and smaller towns in every region of the kingdom where a monastery or a friary defined the skyline and its people, economy, social culture, and where spirituality dominated the life of the town. Yet even outside this Tudor Middle England, in the rural landscape of the far east, west, Wales, and the north, and in the principal urban centres, the capital, the cathedral cities and the expanding provincial conurbations, where institutions had grown in number and variety just as much as the resident population, the religious houses offered not only a backdrop to life's dramas but also many of its properties and even its stage. This was not the result of an original, proprietorial, indeed feudal authority that had passed unchanged and unchallenged into the sixteenth century. The profile of the regulars in the secular world in 1509 and after was the result of give and take on either side; and the pressure for the regulars to give, and the willingness of their neighbourhoods to take, was growing. The awareness that the regulars were powerful but not always, or unequivocally, in power, was one reason for the felony of the strutting John Barnysby at Bury. This is not to suggest that in spite of their presence they had already surrendered to the world outside their walls; rather, some of the old principles and practices that had set them apart had now given way before a growing common ground. The queen had no need to answer Alice Warner with a promise to hold her monastery to account. That process was already underway.

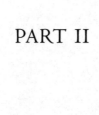

PART II

IV

THE TUDOR REFORMATION

At the height of their head-turning powers both Boleyn girls, Anne and Mary, involved themselves in the business of monasteries. In the summer of 1528, Anne, at twenty-six already secure in the royal circle and skilled in its politics, took up the cause of her sister-in-law, Elinor Carey, a professed nun of the Benedictine abbey at Wilton, where the leadership was at last vacant after the death of the aged abbess. An ancient monastery whose royal associations reached as far back as legends of King Alfred, the vacancy commanded attention at the highest level. The dauntless Anne made 'grete laboure' and 'reportyd and promised to dyversis freynds of dame Elinors care'; no doubt to the king himself, since soon he showed he had heard more than enough of 'Mr Carye's sister'.[1] Yet other interested parties were already at work. The politicking greatly animated the courtiers following the king on his country progress, and it washed over the cloister community at Wilton where the sisters were said to be 'untoward', a mood made worse because they had quarantined themselves against that summer's 'grete plage of swetyng'. Then a tale of Elinor's 'such dissolute lyvyng' was told to the king – she had confessed to bearing two children since taking her vows – and he declared that his 'mind and pure consciens' was decided that 'he wold not have her of all women'.[2]

In the very same year, so it seems, Anne's sister Mary stepped into the affairs of a distant monastery in much the same way. Tynemouth Priory, an ancient church standing sentinel over Newcastle and the location of a Saxon shrine that was still on the pilgrim circuit, was a dependent priory of St Albans Abbey, one of the prime appointments in the church held by Thomas Wolsey, Cardinal legate and the king's chief minister. Wolsey had intervened to remove an unpopular prior, leaving a vacancy. Although Wolsey claimed the authority of abbot of St Albans, the stewardship of Tynemouth was in the hands of none other than Mary's father, Thomas Boleyn, Lord Rochford.[3] He may have been the driving force behind Mary's intervention. Since her husband, William Carey, fell victim to the 'swete' and died in July, she may have felt an urgent impulse to cleave to the family interest. She now advanced the candidacy of Thomas Gardyner, a monk of Westminster familiar to followers of the Tudor household as grandson of the king's great uncle, Jasper.[4] Mary's cause prevailed, although perhaps only because it aligned with Wolsey's own. Still, Gardyner in his gratitude granted her an annuity of £100, a gesture without much guarantee of payment given that it represented as much as a quarter of the priory's income.[5]

The meddling of Mary and Anne was typical of the tactics of their ambitious Tudor family to nurture their influence and their fortune, but it was also indicative of an approach to religious houses that was made by this generation as a whole: members of the social elite, newcomers such as the Boleyns, rapidly on the rise, and established older names now recovering after years of civil war; the gentry and the urban interest, resilient through the fifteenth-century difficulties and now hungry for their independence; the hierarchy of the secular Church, closer to royal government than at any time since the reign of Edward III; and, above all, the Tudor dynasty itself. Of course, lordship and money had always had a hand in the business of monasteries; it might be said by definition, since they were founded on the endowments such people gave them, which were then protected by the exercise of their own authority. But it is possible to see a change in the character of their relationship as the sixteenth century turned and the Tudor regime took shape. The original obligations of a monastery remained in view, that is to be an exemplar of religious practice and as such to provide penitential service for the founder or benefactor, and a source of secure earthly and spiritual lordship over the territory it had been given and the people who lived there. Yet now there was a new emphasis placed on some if not all of these functions. Patrons looked for a greater commitment to their own spiritual needs, to the extent that the physical shape of the Church and the form of its observant life might be recast to match their vision of a personal, or a family chantry. They also asserted the right, by their own acts of patronage or those of their ancestors, to routine supervision of the house's administration. Now, they took up the stewardship which previous generations had left to professional estate managers and they interfered more frequently in internal decision-making, especially in the appointment of a head.

It was more than a tip in the balance of their age-old ties because these interventions appeared to be informed by a new view of the constitution of a religious house. The Crown, its ministers and courtiers, the county, city and town interest, now seemed to share a new conviction that these foundations could no longer be entirely private corporations and should be subject to public scrutiny, tested in the light of other jurisdictions, above all the 'policie' and 'grete pleasure' of the monarch. There seems little doubt that it was sharpened by a fresh estimation of the material wealth and social weight of their endowments. Perhaps the older generation that had endured the civil wars of Lancaster and York, and the younger raised in their aftermath, saw these age-old advantages with a new clarity. This outlook arose alongside a proprietorial impulse perhaps powered also by a lingering sense of the losses of the years of war. It was expressed in patronal projects on a scale not seen since the fourteenth century. In the buildings, furnishings, property and even the personnel of monasteries and friaries, changes wrought by hereditary founders and benefactors were now underway. It was also spoken of in the language of reform. The 'condicion' of the church at Tynemouth was the talk even of courtiers, like Mary Boleyn, Lady Carey and her family, who played no role in royal government. It was the religious 'lyvyng' of the candidates that swiftly settled the matter at Wilton; and the decision of the king was reported publicly as one of personal spiritual priority, guided by purity of mind and conscience.

The change appears definitive because in many respects the religious houses at this time proved to be receptive to the prospect of a new relationship brokered with the world beyond their walls. They accepted, or at least settled into, a new oversight of their affairs. Soon, it seemed as if they looked for interference if at first it was not made. Some of the monastic leadership tried to reinvent their own roles, to serve as the adjutants of royal or diocesan authority in their own regional networks or (even) their national congregation. They and at least some of their colleagues in the cloister community shared in, or subscribed to, the secular vision of observant reform and aimed at a statutory change in their codes not seen in England for two hundred years. By 1528, a year which besides the business at Wilton and Tynemouth saw the building of the king's case for divorce from

Katherine of Aragon, it might be said that a reformation of religious houses was already underway. It was not one that made a systematic dissolution more likely but it did introduce a new dynamic to their institutional lives, in which interference was more readily accepted and, crucially perhaps, its implications were not closely examined. The status and wealth of these foundations had been challenged repeatedly by secular society ever since the Norman Conquest, but in the wake of civil war and changes of dynasty there was a different mood.

It was not that the patrons, prelates and neighbours of these generations were more devout than their predecessors – although some individuals certainly were – nor that they had given way over any of the age-old arguments. Nor, for their part, that the regulars had lost any of their fight. Rather, both recognised common ground between them and on it raised a relationship of a different kind. It brought new experiences on both sides: lay men and women were drawn into the affairs of the cloistered community like never before. The traditional pattern of monastery and friary life was much altered. These changes, the result of a compact with the ruling elite they entered into readily, even eagerly, between 1485 and 1534, did as much to hasten the end of their ancient tradition in England as any of the measures of the 1530s.

From the arrival of the Tudor regime there were indications of a different commitment to the religious houses and a new vision for their place and purpose in the realm. Henry Tudor brought to the monarchy a taste for regular religion that was more sincere and sustained than any of his predecessors since Henry III. In respect of any personal religion he is best remembered for his patronage of the Franciscan Observants. The role of founder or principal benefactor is generally treated as the best measure of spiritual priorities, and it is true that in the first four years of his reign Henry had initiated investment in six Observant convents from south (Greenwich) to north (Newcastle). The plan for an (entirely new) house at Greenwich surfaced as early as his first Christmas as king.[6] This was an emphatic expression of a personal preference, yet it was also a continuation of a pattern of royal patronage begun under the previous dynasty. Observant reform had been introduced into England by Edward IV more than a decade before Bosworth (1485).[7]

Henry Tudor resumed another royal relationship with reformed regulars at the outset of his reign. He returned to the Carthusians conspicuously favoured by his Lancastrian forebears. In fact it was the house at Sheen which Henry V had founded (1415), and not any of the Observants' convents, which received the largest cash gift of the new king's first decade.[8] The church of the charterhouse of Beauvale was the subject of the first royal chantry of the reign as early as July 1486.[9] In November of the same year the king confirmed a grant of Henry V to the charterhouse at Hull.[10] This distinction was followed by the permission to purchase property from the royal demesne, and the rare privilege of a royal exemption from taxation.[11] Henry Tudor continued to favour the congregation with fiscal benefits up to the end of his first decade.[12]

His patronal interest in the fraternal orders grew more capacious with his reign. Before the turn of this first regnal year, he also confirmed the award of a £20 annuity to the provincial chapter of the Dominicans for commemoration of the monarchs past, first granted by Edward III in 1377.[13] In 1491 Henry confirmed an annuity of £10 to the Carmarthen Franciscans, burial place of his father, Edmund Tudor. Another friary of royal foundation, the Guildford Dominicans, he endowed for a weekly Lady Mass in 1504. At the same time he offered preferment to foreign friars sojourning in his realm. John de Monte Valore received the chaplaincy of the chantry of St Mary at Woodstock (Oxfordshire); Hercules de Fararia received the livings of St Michael's, Geldeston (Norfolk), and St Stephen, Lympne (Kent).[14]

Yet there was a greater break with the past, and a stronger signal of change in the Crown's approach to the religious houses, in the new king's close attention to the ancient abbeys of the old monastic orders. After decades in which it seemed to be drifting into a backwater, Westminster Abbey was returned by Henry to the mainstream of national life, as the principal stage for his coronation, his marriage, and the coronation (1487) of his queen, Elizabeth of York.[15] His public interest in the old, royal monastery was roused before there was any sign of a personal attachment, but by the second half of the 1490s it was almost beyond doubt that it would replace Windsor as the new dynasty's principal church.[16] Westminster's status was special, of course, but even in the opening months of his administration Henry revealed a protective impulse towards other monastery churches of national significance. In his second year he addressed Pope Innocent VIII (1484–92) in support of Bishop John Sherwood's petition for the renewal of the privileges of the cathedral monastery of St Cuthbert at Durham.[17] He did the same the next year in support of the campaign of William Selling, prior of the monks of Canterbury Cathedral Priory, to confirm their exemption from all ecclesiastical jurisdictions, including that of their own chapter of English Benedictines, and to be subject only to the Roman see.[18]

As the usurping monarch of a new dynasty, Henry Tudor's recognition of the status of these great houses was surely pragmatic politics. Barely four months after Bosworth he made a grant of 100 marks to the abbot and convent of Merevale (Warwickshire), west of the battlefield, to compensate them for the 'gret hurts, charges and lossis' they had suffered at his hands when 'commyng toward oure late feld'.[19] Yet in the months and years that followed, his actions also signalled a deeper, devotional interest in their tradition. Henry returned to Merevale itself in September 1503, a visit which has been connected with the commissioning of its stained-glass window in honour of the Celtic saint, Armel.[20] In addition to the regal rites he orchestrated at Westminster, Henry and the new, extended royal family soon established a circuit of abbey and priory churches for their particular attention: Bury, Walsingham, Reading and Shaftesbury. It seems that Bury was the very first monastery beyond the capital where Henry spent an extended stay in April 1487.[21] According to Polydore Vergil, the cloister was his council chamber during the months that the king anticipated a counter-attack from surviving Yorkists and their allies in Ireland and the empire. Walsingham was where he chose to dispatch the royal standard in June 1487 after his victory at the Battle of Stoke.[22] Reading, in origin a royal foundation, whose church held the celebrated 'Child of Grace', a statue of the Christ child given by the founder, Henry I, became a preferred waypoint west of the capital. The royal family were familiar enough to the monastic community for a prayer for Prince Arthur to be scribbled on a page of the abbey chronicle, beseeching the statue to make him a wise monarch (et regat hoc regnum cum senior senex).[23] In 1503, 1505 and 1507 Henry chose Reading, apparently in preference to Westminster, to mark the feast of Edward the Confessor (13 October).[24] He knew Shaftesbury well enough to issue patents from there, and, apparently, to appoint one of the nursemaids for his son Prince Arthur.[25] In 1498 he made it the site of chantry for three generations of his forebears, funded by a substantial parcel of land conveyed to the house under a Mortmain licence. Here were honoured the three Margarets in his life, his mother, her sister and his grandmother, the duchess of Somerset.[26] The monastic orders of the Western March were also wrapped around the new dynasty. Henry first visited Gloucester as king in the spring of 1486. He was certainly at the abbey for the feast of the Virgin's Nativity in 1491. Prior Thomas of Great Malvern admitted the king and his sons into their confraternity in 1496 with the promise of a special Mass on his birthday (28 January); Henry in his turn cemented the connection with the gift of a window depicting the royal family for the church's north transept; in 1502 the Cistercians at Flaxley (Gloucestershire) committed to a Lady Mass incorporating a collect for the king as 'protector omnium'.[27]

The devotions of Henry's queen, Elizabeth, and his mother, Margaret Beaufort, heightened the impression of a Tudor attachment to the monastic estate. Margaret mapped her own progresses through the provinces with landmark monasteries. She funded the repair of the 'holy' well associated with the legend of St Winifred, presided over by the Benedictines of Shrewsbury, who held her shrine; she rode out to see Crowland Abbey's legendary standing crosses in Lincolnshire; her familiarity with Durham saw her secure feathers for her pillow from the celebrated eider ducks of St Cuthbert on the island of Farne.[28] Margaret adopted a monk of Winchester as her protégé and arranged for him to return to another house at the place of his birth, Cerne.[29] She also settled Margaret de la Pole, the Yorkist heiress kept in her custody, at Syon Abbey, where she remained with her two sons until 1509.[30]

For most of her son's reign, the queen mother applied her patronal power to printed publication of Syon's devotional literature.[31] Both Margaret and Elizabeth were inclined to adopt Westminster as their spiritual home; if Margaret looked to the Birgittine priests of Syon for her Christian instruction, it was the customs of the Benedictines which she chose for acts of worship. She invested in the old altar of Our Lady of the Pew near the north door, the public entrance to the abbey; she may have been the driving force behind her son's direction to the monks to set up a new altar with the fashionable dedication to the Scala Coeli legend of Rome.[32] The statue of the Child of Grace at Reading, curated by the monks for the past 300 years, became a focus for Elizabeth and Margaret's private grief following Prince Arthur's untimely death in April 1502, aged fifteen.[33]

The new dynasty's affection to the old order of monasteries was finally consummated in Henry's scheme for a family chantry, to be centred on Westminster Abbey but syndicated to no fewer than thirty churches countrywide, which he conceived in the second decade of his reign.[34] Quite simply the most ambitious and novel plan for a memorial to be conceived in England after 1300, it required an investment of cash at least as great as the foundations begun by Henry V and the dual tomb designed by Richard II, as well as the invention of new legal instruments, multilateral indentures to tie together institutions of long-standing independence under the authority of the Crown. The king's scheme was, or came to be, a lavish spectacle, although the centrepiece chapel at Westminster was not completed until after Henry's death in 1509 and the radiating pattern of masses may never have been realised in full.

The mobilisation of monks for the production of prayers for their patron and family recalled the principal impulse for foundation in England's age of monastic expansion after the Norman Conquest. But this king's requests seemed to cut across the traditional idea of monastic occupation; indeed, they challenged the current fashions for reform. The monks were to be chosen, spiritually formed and educated especially to fulfil the duty of suffrage for their founder. Three monks were to be assigned each to say one daily Mass, a Lady Mass, a requiem and an Office Mass. It was specified that they were to be university graduates, doctors or bachelors in theology, and 'since there are no such doctors or bachelors meet for such service beside the abbot, prior and [one other]' there was to be a line of succession established as three monks at a time to be maintained at Oxford to prepare for this responsibility.[35]

But arguably it was its constitution that was of greater significance in the immediate term. Here a select group of abbeys, most of them of proven or legendary royal foundation, were designated as the dynasty's spiritual trustees. Westminster, Canterbury and St Albans were bound by a discrete tripartite agreement to supervise and execute the plan, as if the king's commemoration by the nation's monks was in itself his last will and testament. Another twenty-seven convents were co-respondents.[36] Not only did it reiterate a special duty of religious houses to the Crown, it also seemed to reassert the special value of the corporate acts of prayer which only they could offer.

Henry's commemoration represented more than an elaborate and public expression of his family's attachment to the religion of monasteries, which so often in their past had been simple and privately individual. It made plain a repositioning of the regulars in the polity, which in retrospect might be seen to have been building steadily since the beginning of the reign. Henry reached out for the counsel of a number of the superiors of the old monasteries he favoured most. The early confraternity which the Beauvale Carthusians offered the king in July 1486 was, it seems, the beginning of a personal affinity with their prior, Nicholas Wartre. John Sante, abbot of Abingdon, treated with the French in 1488; Abbot Richard Bere of Glastonbury led a royal mission to Pope Julius II in 1504–05; while the king preferred to keep Richard Kidderminster, abbot of Winchcombe, close at court, rewarding him richly for his reciprocated attention.[37]

The monastic hierarchy was prominent in the principal rites of the new royal family. The king's first-born son, Arthur, was christened at Winchester Cathedral, where Prior Thomas Hunton and Abbot Richard Hall of nearby Hyde officiated alongside the bishops of Exeter, Salisbury and Worcester; after the ceremony the royal party 'offrede' at the monastery's principal shrine of St Swithun as an 'antyme of Saint Swytyne was songen' by their choir.[38] Scarcely fifteen years later (1502) Benedictines and Cistercians of the Western March were mobilised for the funeral of the same Prince of Wales.[39]

The funeral rites of the king's queen (1503), and his own mother (July 1509) centred on monastic observance. For Elizabeth of York the monks' choir was rein-forced by the city's friars; Margaret Beaufort died in a chamber within the abbot's lodging at Westminster.[40] Henry's own funeral was conspicuously monastic: the Abbots John Thorne (II) of Reading and Thomas Ramridge of St Albans led the vigil at St Paul's Cathedral and John Islip of Westminster, Ramridge and Richard Kidderminster of Winchcombe celebrated the first masses at the burial.[41]

There was a wider network associated ad hoc with the personal and political business of the Crown. Nicholas Wartre of Beauvale was apparently a fixture at court. Prior Thomas Gudybour of Carlisle was part of the peace negotiations in Scotland in 1487 and 1490; Prior Henry Deane of Llanthony Priory (Gloucester) was dispatched as an envoy to Ireland in the wake of the Warbeck rebellion in 1497.[42] Abbot Thomas Mynde of Shrewsbury appears to have led a group eager publicly to acknowledge their political alignment to the new regime, with the creation of a confraternity in the precinct parish church dedicated to the Lancastrian cult favourite, St Winifred.[43] Abbot Sion Llwyd of Valle Crucis (Denbighshire) joined the commission charged with the confirmation of Henry's Welsh pedigree; by his son he was rewarded with a royal chaplaincy.[44]

There were several in this circle of monastics who came close to the king at any rate because of kinship. Abbess Margaret St John of Shaftesbury shared his grand-mother, Margaret Beauchamp.[45] Henry's great uncle, Edward Tudor, was a professed monk at Westminster, where his second cousin, Thomas Gardyner, the target of Mary Boleyn's patronage, would also enter.[46] Queen Elizabeth matched him in these ties. Her younger sister, Bridget (1480–1507), was a Dominican nun of Dartford, and kinswomen of their mother were in the Minories, the convent of Franciscan women in the city of London.[47]

There was more than a touch of traditionalism in Henry's reliance on prelates whose churches were the result of royal patronage and (or) whose offices were for the most part free from the influence of rival lordship. It does appear that Henry's preferences were informed by a degree of historical awareness, of the deep roots of some of these houses, and how far they intertwined with those of the Crown. With a characteristic eye for detail he cut across a whole swathe of the provincial Church to remember the royal status of the remote canon house of Blackmoor (Dorset), from where he took the prior to be his own palace chaplain.[48]

Of course, there was another motive behind his renewed affiliations beyond a respect for tradition. From the outset of his reign, Henry showed a determination to reaffirm the status of the churches that were royal foundations as part and parcel of the Crown's domain, their material resources to be at his disposal and their personnel under his direction. He supervised the election of a new abbot at Hyde, Winchester, in April 1488 and affirmed his authority of him by attaching a pension to the abbacy to be granted in the king's gift; the first recipient was Pietro Carmeliano (c. 1451–1527), his own court poet.[49] A variety of prerogative rights were reasserted after only fitful recognition in previous generations: corrodies, pensions, and even the liberty to bring a candidate forward for profession, for example at Shaftesbury, where it was exercised at a vacancy when the abbacy rested with the Crown.[50]

The greater abbeys of the Benedictines and Augustinians were barraged by Crown assigns of corrodies and pensions after 1485. In his first four months in power Henry provided more than a dozen across the country and the congregations, from Cerne to Wenlock; the number in the first decade of the regime was higher than at any point since the reign of Edward III.[51] The speed with which they were reassigned at the death of the incumbent is a measure of fiscal efficiency that might stand with Henry's legendary habit of initialling his accounts. The endowments of the religious houses were to be a vital component of the Crown's machinery to raise loyal, royal service in an unstable and provincial, society; a strategy as old as that of many of the Norman foundations it affected.

Yet it seems that Henry saw these old foundations, or came to see them, as the valuable raw materials for a clerical and religious establishment, regular and secular, that might be shaped, or reshaped, better to secure and serve his new Tudor realm.

Several houses of the old Benedictine establishment now acquired valuable new properties both directly by royal patronage – such as Tewkesbury's acquisition of the church at Marlow (Buckinghamshire) – and by licences-in-Mortmain that enabled the investment of their seigneurial patrons – such as the Throckmortons at Evesham.[52] Others saw themselves drawn into an ever expanding chain of family chantries set within a Tudor framework, where the commemoration carried a dual function, for the local founder and for the royal family: in this way the Cluniac priory at Lenton and the Benedictine abbey at Whitby came to preside over parish chapels at North Winfield (Derbyshire) and Richmond (North Yorkshire).[53]

The use of the Augustinian priory at Mottisfont (Hampshire) is indicative of the evolution of Henry's outlook over the course of his reign. Exercising the right of hereditary patron as duke of Lancaster, Henry first secured a papal licence to secularise the monastery to become a collegiate church, no doubt to be another Tudor chantry, a counterpart in the southern counties to Wimborne Minster in the west. The limitations of the endowment led him to retreat and he made new suits to the papal court to transfer its resources, first to St George's Chapel, Windsor, and second to his great scheme centred on Westminster.[54] The place and purpose of the religious house in Henry's Church was still unsettled when he died.

It might be objected that Henry's approach to the regulars was too changeable, subject to his own shifting personal impulses, to be seen as a policy, still less one that marked a watershed in their relationship with monarchy. It is true that some interventions appeared arbitrary assertions of royal authority inconsistent with any guiding principle of monastic governance, novel or otherwise. The king gave vigorous support to Archbishop Morton's battle to subject St Albans Abbey to visitation in the face of its 400-year-old privilege of exemption. Yet shortly before and after this moment he confirmed privileges and immunities to the Cistercian abbey at Titchfield (Hampshire); granted Rochester Cathedral Priory permission to refuse entry to crown officials; and enabled the abbot of Tavistock to extend his jurisdiction over the neighbouring town.[55] He took up the old (and disputed) Crown claim to the Benedictine priory of Snape (Suffolk) and, challenging the right of its parent house, Colchester Abbey, he regranted it in 1508 to Butley Priory; inevitably the rearrangement failed.[56]

Yet it is possible to see a common purpose even in the schemes bullishly begun and left incomplete, that is to establish the Crown as the arbiter of the regular estate within its dominions, its authority neither to be stayed nor diminished by any other jurisdiction, seigneurial, episcopal, corporate or even pontifical. It does seem there was rising determination to position the Crown between the regulars, both monastic and mendicant, and the governance of their congregations and orders, from within England or from presidential houses on the European mainland. Henry was the first monarch to show such a consistent interest in the congregations of monks and friars, their governing chapters and even their corporate mission, in so far as he awarded annuities to the Dominicans for their defence of the Catholic faith.[57] When in 1490 the leadership of the Cistercians looked to Citeaux Abbey near Lyon in France for a visitation of the entire congregation in England, Henry simply stifled the request, apparently concerned that foreign chapters threatened the indigenous community, 'brigas et dissensiones inter patres faciet'.[58]

The king's purpose was not only to increase royal authority: the regulars of the new Tudor realm were to be placed in the proprietary custody of an English Crown and they were to be subject to its pastoral care. The condition of observant life was now expressed as a matter of the king's high pleasure. It was not the first time that a royal regime had made the reform of the monasteries a matter for action under the king's own writ. After statutory measures to extend his authority over the money and manpower of the church, in 1366 Edward III had initiated a visitation of religious houses of royal foundation.[59]

Having witnessed the continental discussion of church reform and religious renewal at a series of ecumenical councils and the political investment it drew from Europe's princes, in 1421 Henry V convened his own forum to review and reinvigorate the observant life of the Benedictine congregation.[60] Where King Edward had left the framing of injunctions to monastic insiders, Henry pressed his own expectations in the statutes presented to the order. These earlier impulses had faded in the face of other imperatives, to suppress heresy at home, to defend the conquered kingdom overseas.

By contrast, the Tudor interest in monastic reform was evident even before the immediate challenges of the new regime had been met, and as other policy priorities arose the interest was sustained. Barely five months into his reign, Henry VII provided an annuity to the Cambridge Dominicans, not only to provide for his personal chantry but also 'for the support of the Catholic faith'.[61] The king expressed his own expectations for the monastic life more often and in greater depth than any of his forebears. He was conscious of the different degrees of observant rigour between the congregations present in England. 'The strictness of the Carthusian rule exceeds,' he wrote, 'that of all other orders soever.'[62] His instinct was to conserve them. His support for the provincial chapter meetings of monks, canons and friars might be seen as recognition of their role in defining and enforcing corporate customs; his reluctance to permit the entry of their European presidents might also reflect a determination to hold them to their own insular traditions. In 1490 he went so far as to request a papal decree to prevent the return to their former mode of life of men who had first professed in a Cistercian monastery and progressed to a Carthusian house 'again to become worldlings instead of religious'.[63]

The king's great Westminster scheme suggested a vision for the regular estate in which the intrinsic capacities of each tradition might be enhanced: the canons were called to the Mass, the friars to funerary service, and at the apex of the pyramid the Benedictines were to perform the rites with which over the course of the later Middle Ages they were most closely identified, the Marian cult, as well as to be a focus for almsgiving, with an almshouse as large as any associated with a monastery since the thirteenth century.[64]

Henry VII's pursuit of authority and reform in the regular estate was affirmed and advanced by his sons. In his short stint at the head of the Council of Wales and the Marches (1501), Prince Arthur had sought support from his father's regular ally, Henry Deane, for the abbot of Dore, whose house had suffered a 'deaulte of good oversight' and was 'gretly in ruyn and decay'.[65] Arthur's younger brother, Henry, continued in this vein. It has been said that the second Henry Tudor was 'never much committed to monasteries'; the acts, public and private, of the young king show otherwise.[66]

In the first weeks after his father's death the new king Henry VIII looked to reinforce the mendicant and monastic network he had raised around the dynasty. On 6 June 1509 by his own hand he confirmed dispatch of the 500 marks to the five Tudor convents of the Observants promised in the old king's will.[67] Henry saw the first Easter of his reign at Greenwich at the friary church and then passed on to Reading Abbey where his mother and grandmother had first mourned for his brother Arthur; for the next Easter he recruited a preacher from the abbey at Bury St Edmunds.[68]

He also followed the family's preferred route of monasteries and friaries in his first progresses west in 1510 and north in 1511, selecting abbeys, canon houses and friaries for his masses and oblations.[69] He returned to the Thameside friars for the nurture of his new family, the Christening of his son and (legitimate) daughter, Mary, taking place respectively at Richmond and Greenwich.[70] In 1518 the two-year-old Princess Mary was accommodated at Bisham Abbey and then at one of the manor houses of St Albans Abbey.[71] For his extended family the king reached for the metropolitan friars and offered the great hall magna aula of the Dominicans for the stay of his imperial nephew-in-law, Charles V, in 1522.[72]

Historic rights of patronage and claims to annuities were asserted from the moment of Henry's accession, and more systematically than before. His interventions over the status of endowments tended further, and more decisively, than his father. Blackmoor Priory was made a dependency of the Benedictine abbey at Cerne.[73] The Augustinian priory of Bicknacre was formally reconstituted as a Tudor family chantry and placed in the trust of the hospital of St Mary, Bishopsgate.[74] The Observants' presence at Greenwich was significantly enlarged with a grant of the river wharf.[75] After decades in the doldrums, the friars' *studia* at Oxford and Cambridge found the attention of the scholarly king.[76]

Henry also continued the Crown's close attention to the governance of the monastic congregations. Like his father, he did not oppose on principle the exempt status of independent abbeys, recognising the political capital to be made by representing the Crown as a bulwark between the papacy, the corporate power of the continental orders, and the local episcopacy and lordship. In his first decade he continued his father's contributions to the expenses of the triennial chapter meetings; to the capitular president of the Benedictines he appears to have been persuaded to provide venison 'to do him great comfort'.[77] In a letter to Rome in August 1512 he lent his support to the suit of the canons of Oseney for the status of exemption.[78] The following year Henry added his authority to the attempt of the Premonstratensian commissary to conduct a visitation of the English houses free from the interference of the chapter general at Premontré (Aisne, France); he also named him as king's chaplain.[79] He wrote to the king of France on behalf of the English Observants oppressed by their provincial; he took his defence of their English autonomy to Pope Leo X himself.[80]

Henry brought into his court and household a larger cohort of monastic and mendicant leaders than had been seen in his father's day; he also allowed, and perhaps looked for, the balance of their influence to shift from the personal and spiritual to the corporate and political. Some of these men he inherited from the previous reign. Abbot Thomas Ramridge of St Albans (1492–1521) continued to officiate for the family and the courtiers close to the household. He was named as godfather to Frances, the daughter born (1517) to Charles Brandon, duke of Suffolk, and his wife, the king's sister, Mary.[81] Richard Kidderminster of Winchcombe was invited to preach at Greenwich Palace; a noted scholar, his stock may have risen under the young king whose intellectual interests were strong.[82] John Islip of Westminster grew ever closer to Henry as the grand memorial for his father rose steadily on the east and west side of his abbey church.[83]

There were also new faces: monastic leaders finding favour for the first time. Abbot Thomas Rowland of Abingdon (1512–38) was among those honoured by Henry's New Year gifts.[84] Abbots Clement Lichfield of Evesham (1514–38) and Hugh Cook alias Faringdon of Reading (1520–39) shared their books with him; Abbot Richard Banham of Tavistock (1492–1523) saw his office enhanced with the right of a parliamentary seat.[85] Abbot John Newton of Gloucester (1510–14) was appointed king's chaplain; when challenges to the jurisdiction of his abbey again arose in the town, there came swift intervention from the king's council, which initiated a commission of inquiry.[86]

Together these men offered more than another thread in the religious fabric of the regime. Their connection informed Henry's interventions in the concerns of the Church. When fears of Lutheran radicalism first arose, the king turned to Abbot Kidderminster to begin a response. In 1521 he appointed him as the senior member of a commission of clergy charged with the refutation of Luther's theses.[87] At the same moment, Henry defended the Cistercians at Boxley when their local campaign 'agaynst the yul opnione of Martine Luther' was challenged by a secular priest.[88] Importantly, they acted as conduit for the monarch's control of monastic endowment. There can be no doubt that it was Henry's intimacy with Abbot Islip that enabled exchanges of property with the Crown which saw Westminster Abbey's old medieval domain steadily recede and the monarchy's presence in the territory west of London become almost unassailable.[89] These were relationships powered by the interplay of personal ties, professional service and the collateral of property, what the preceding generations would surely have recognised as an affinity. Certainly, their potential to destabilise was as great as those that prospered in the late wars of Lancaster and York.

The Crown's renewed interest in the regular estate after 1485 was matched in wider society. Secular lordship now looked for a relationship with the regulars inside or neighbouring their domain with much the same motives as the monarchy. It seems there was the same general recognition that in spite of their age and indifferent fortunes in the recent past, these houses still represented a unique collateral for their place either in this world or the next; there was also a steadily rising impulse to reach into their own affairs, even into their observant lives. It has been argued that this period saw quite the reverse, the first steps in the retreat of the magnate families whose forebears had created so many of the monastic communities centuries before.[90]

The ties of hereditary founders and principal patrons did weaken and break, of course, and these changes can be traced over a much longer timespan. Arguably, the relationship was always unstable, as susceptible to a sudden discontinuity as the fabric of the buildings or the men and women who inhabited them. Old patrons departed in every era of England's monastic past; and others arrived in their place. What appears to have been different in the five decades before the Break with Rome was that lordship, by whatever name or title, pressed its interest in the religious houses with a new insistence.

The devotional investment of this generation of magnates was very substantial. The record of the building and furnishings they provided to the regulars stands in obvious contrast to the preceding decades of the fifteenth century, when what they gave to the Church was only a taste of their guerrilla wars. Yet the scale and scope of their patronage, affecting congregations of all traditions and large and small foundations, was perhaps as great as any seen in England since Edwardian high society in the wake of the Black Death. The nobility with the longest history of monastic patronage did not necessarily honour the family tradition. They narrowed their network, turning their attention to one foundation, not always the preference of their forebears.

The Percys of Northumberland departed from the south of England churches which had known them as 'faithful protectors' and now provided for the modest houses of their own heartland, the canons of Alnwick Priory and the Carmelites of nearby Hulne, whose tower they built in 1489.[91] The Courtenays of Devon had first been patrons of the Cistercian abbey of Forde but under Earl Henry (1498–1539), created marquess by Henry VIII, they looked east, to Christ Church (Twynham) and Quarr on their Hampshire estates, and to Buckfast and Buckland (both Devon) neighbouring their lands of the ancient honour of Okehampton. The family had only recovered their estates after the succession of the Tudors and these old religious houses, whose founders were the post-Conquest lords of the West Country to whom they claimed ancestry, could still lend them legitimacy.[92] After a long career that led to Ireland, and rewards from Yorkist and Tudor monarchies, Henry, Lord Grey (d. 1496), returned to the Carmelite friary at Aylesford (Kent) founded by his de Grey ancestor some 250 years before. He called for his tomb to be set in the chancel of the friars' church.[93]

The deep identification with family was expressed in schemes as elaborate and self-conscious as the Tudor commemoration centred on Westminster, if not as costly. Henry VII's very particular vision of a network of foundations in spiritual affiliation to himself, his family and their name was replicated by a number of the aristocrats who served his regime. In his will John, Lord Dynham (c. 1433–1501), the king's Lord Treasurer, linked London's Dominican and Franciscan convents, the charterhouses of Sheen and Smithfield and Syon Abbey in common acts of posthumous commemoration.[94] Thomas, Lord Strangways, followed the Westminster model directly, binding the Benedictines of Abbotsbury and Milton to a family chantry under a tripartite indenture.[95] John Zouche (1459–1525), one of the last surviving Yorkists, long under Tudor attainder, turned Stavordale Priory (Somerset) not only into a personal chantry but his own self-imposed cell, in sight of a Jesus altar he made himself.[96] There was no aspiration so high perhaps as that of a man without noble rank, and Sir John Byconill endowed the Franciscans of Dorchester on condition that henceforth they were known as Byconil's friars'.[97] The association of elite figures with modest foundations outside the network of national shrines and with those congregations or houses that lacked a presence, through prelacy and royal counsel, with the political nation, is a striking feature of these years. Post-war, and under a new monarchy, there can be no doubt that lordship was changing, and it may be that religious houses should be seen as part of a new apparatus to support a different role centred on their own immediate domain.

This impression is reinforced by the signs of a determination to claim more than a spiritual affiliation with these houses, to be an active force in their affairs. After the waves of regular foundations had receded, by the death of Henry III (1272) the supervision of secular lordship had not been sustained, and when it had been attempted, for example at the election of a superior, or the proposed appropriation of a prize property, generally it had been resisted successfully by the religious themselves.

Yet at the end of the fifteenth century, following unstable decades not only of war but economic downturn and the depopulation brought on by plague and persistently poor agricultural yields, the distance between monastery and magnate was steadily bridged. The essential estate offices of the endowed houses were now taken by the senior members of the neighbourhood's leading families. In many regions of England and Wales it amounted to virtually a complete takeover. The higher nobility held the office of chief steward, almost always of the largest foundations and often of the entire chain of houses that reached across their territory. By the time of the 1535 valuation, Henry Courtenay, marquess of Exeter, held the stewardship of all the religious houses worth more than £200 in the hundred miles from Somerset to Cornwall.[98]

The subordinate roles of sub-steward and bailiff of the principal manors passed to men of families that were below this rank but established and already influential gentry, often socially and politically affiliated to the great magnate (sometimes strengthened by marriage ties) and with a monopoly on the Crown offices in the region – escheator, justice and sheriff. The community of Cwmhir (Powys) trusted their property on the borderland west of Hereford to the Vaughan family of Clyro, powerful in the vicinity but not yet wholly respectable gentry: Thomas Vaughan, who shared the stewardship with his father and brother, was arraigned for murder in 1536.[99]

There was a renewed awareness in regional lordship that something of the age-old territorial profile of a religious foundation might be borrowed to bolster their own. Families with growing fortunes reached out for the foundations on their doorstep to form a route to regional dominance. The Daubeneys acquired the Dorsetshire stewardships of Bindon, Cerne and Shaftesbury.[100] The Hungerfords of Farleigh, where they had been since the early fourteenth century, latterly looked south to Hinton (Somerset) and Longleat (Wiltshire).[101] In effect, the worldly enterprise of the regulars, their property and their sources of income, were now placed under the supervision of a tight social hierarchy, the source of secular power within local horizons and the sole representatives of royal authority.

It seems that many of this new breed of monastic official regarded their role as more than merely honorific. The annual fees recorded in 1535 are too slight for the responsibility to have been only an easy sinecure. Sir John Gilbert, steward of Torre Abbey (Devon), a foundation with an annual income of £700, was shown to receive just 43s 4d per annum; the Valor figures may not be the full measure of return, although there is little to suggest the total was many times higher.[102] Indirectly, the oversight of endowments that spread across counties offered substantial gains in cash, routinely the fines associated with entry into and exit from possession of a property, and in much social and political heft. Even in the patchy record of transactions that is now surviving from the majority of houses it is apparent that this generation of officers was generally inclined to intervene. Sir Richard Sutton's commitment to the cause of Syon Abbey saw him set a city draper, Walter Bettes, in the stocks to persuade him to agree to a conveyance of a plot of land at Isleworth.[103]

They also reached beyond the brief of their office to involve themselves in the governance of the house. The chief steward could now be found at the election of a superior. Here, it seems, there could be a degree of co-ordination between the different sources of secular authority sharing the aim to steer monastic affairs. Bishop Geoffrey Blythe (Coventry and Lichfield) accepted the king's recommendation that the vacancy of the Benedictine priory at Henwood (Warwickshire) should be handled by the earl of March and Sir Henry Willoughby, as auxiliaries of the office of prioress.[104] They were more likely to interfere than the other authorities. Thomas Stanley, Lord Derby, led a force into the precinct at Furness Abbey in 1514 to remove Alexander Banke, whom the monks had elected as their abbot.[105] Sir Thomas Poyntz took up arms three years later to repel the official visitors of the Cistercian congregation from Kingswood Abbey.[106]

It may have been the active stewardship of the neighbourhood nobility and gentry that reinvigorated the involvement of families claiming the role of hereditary founder. Certainly, from the end of the fifteenth century, these old ties, and the rights assumed to go with them, were resurfacing. In 1488 John, Lord Dynham, forced the canons of Hartland into a compact that protected his family's right to confirm the election of their abbot; at the next vacancy the community duly dispatched a messenger to Dynham before they notified the diocese.[107] John de Vere, earl of Oxford, summoned the abbot of Tower Hill in 1513 to do him homage for his lands held in Hertford, to come in person to his castle 'withowt further delay', observing that the neglect of this obligation 'I have long tyme forborne'.[108] In 1526, less than six months after being created earl of Rutland, Thomas Manners presented himself at Newstead Priory to preside over their election.[109] The Premonstratensian canons of Croxton Kerrial (Leicestershire) had not heard of an hereditary founder for generations when, in 1534, in the wake of the king's claim to supremacy, Lord Berkeley appeared at their gatehouse with armed retainers to remind them of his ancient right. Abbot Thomas Green was held in custody by Berkeley, who extorted from the abbot a bond to cede to him control of the house.[110]

There is some hint in their hands-on supervision that the outlook of lordship was, like the Crown, coloured by ideals of reform. Margaret Wooton seems to have wanted to govern the Cistercian abbey at Tilty in the same way that, to the consternation of the king, she governed her son by denying him funds.[111] The ejection of Abbot Banke from Furness had been prompted by his manifest misgovernment, which over the course of the decade had become the scandal of the district. This generation of patrons was now as likely as their Tudor kings to judge the quality of religious life they saw before them. Thomas, Lord Wentworth, was candid about the common reputation of the convent of Ipswich Franciscans for which he was 'their founder in blode'. They were, he wrote, 'an idell neste of dranes [drones]'.[112]

These patrons' awareness and absorption of current discourses on forms of religious life should not be underestimated; their collection of prayer and mass books, and their fastidious curation of family vestments and other chapel furnishings, combined with their private reading to create a precisely personal taste in the practice of devotion. It was sharpened further by social interaction with individual religious. Like the king and his family, their own kinsmen and women were in the cloister; and in turn they brought them into their own households. Sir Henry Wyatt created a position for a Cistercian monk of Boxley Abbey, Robert Hedcorn, at his castle at Allington (Kent).[113] What lordship looked for from the professed religious was at one and the same time idealised and highly subjective.

Much of the lordship most strongly and securely allied to the government of Henry VII shared in his taste for reformed monasticism. Westminster Abbey, the Charterhouses, Syon and the new convents of Observant friars met the same circle of courtier benefactors alongside their principal Tudor patron. Just as the young Henry VIII maintained the ties made by his father, his generation of courtiers also continued to express the preferences of the royal family. Charles Somerset, earl of Worcester, Henry's Lord Chamberlain, was patron to Sheen, Syon and the Richmond Observants; at his death (1526) he directed 'bury me in the next abby, priory or college . . . not to tarry me further'.[114] George Talbot (d. 1538), 4th earl of Shrewsbury, steward of the king's household, tied himself to the three Charterhouses honoured by the Tudors: Sheen, Smithfield and Beauvale.[115]

The press of local lordship on the leadership, property and even the devotional life of religious houses was conspicuous in provincial England and perhaps spurred other social interests to seek a new dispensation of their own. In the last decades of the fifteenth century, and especially as the danger of civil war receded, the top tier of regional cities and towns, the commanding commercial and property interest that also headed local government, were likewise inclined to assert their collective authority among their regular neighbours. Many of these places had known intermittent conflict for centuries, as the deep roots of the monasteries' endowments, or the dependency of a friary filling a large central plot, seemed to curtail their ambitions for an independent prosperity. Above all, they had known defeat, as the religious houses invariably reached out for the protection of their royal and lordly patrons.

Yet the priorities of those patrons were shifting and the Liberty of those houses, or at least its particular claims on the commune, was no longer an instinctive battleground. Now it seemed possible for urban leaders to enter into negotiation with the regulars without recourse to criminal damage or riot. Concessions which would have seemed a hopeless aspiration only a generation before were now offered. Compromise on the form and functions of communal government were agreed. At Faversham and Gloucester, the town's councils secured some freedom of action under supervision of their abbeys which, if it was no more distant, did seem to be more benign.[116] It was not that these communities became more aggressive towards the monks and friars in their midst, or that their social and spiritual authority now melted away. Rather, it seems that they had become more closely bound to one another, socially, commercially and culturally.

Increasingly, the populations of the religious houses were recruited from well-established if not prominent families within local society. Monks at St Albans named Bestney and Bodley reflected family links both inland and within the City of London.[117] Even friars, required by custom to circulate from convent to convent across their custody, carried local ties. Those who identified as gentry were not unknown in monasteries, especially at their head, as witnessed by the growing taste for blazons of arms and rebuses. Edmund Horde, prior of the Charterhouse at Hinton, belonged to an extended family network connecting him to the exalted social circle surrounding Syon Abbey.[118] The leading communities of religious women were firmly set within the tight-knit hierarchies of town and country. Abbess Katharine Bulkeley (1535–39) of Godstow (Oxfordshire) counted wealthy landowners and career churchmen among her relatives.[119]

Sharing the same networks, separated only by the religious profession and the precinct wall, the religious and local society curated their common interests. Their

169

channels of cultural and intellectual exchange have attracted particular interest from historians,[120] yet their neighbourhood cooperation in governance, commerce and welfare is just as important. The burgesses of Colchester affirmed the 'daily relefe' which their monasteries offered them; they gave a vacant plot to the Friars of the Cross to provide income for a Mass to be celebrated 'for the prosperity of the town' (pro salutari prosperitate ville).[121] Their values aligned in more than acts of worship, preaching or the devotional books they exchanged.

Within these same social ranks there was the occasional stirring of a sharper response to the regulars, a rejection of their influence and a challenge to their prevailing rights. This was not a new reflex arising with the arrival of the Tudors. Petitions for the disendowment of the religious houses had surfaced in parliament twice in the century before 1485 when (in 1385 and 1410) they had drawn support from the representatives sent there from the boroughs and the counties.[122] Such petitions were seen again in 1529 and when the Supremacy statute was promulgated in 1534.[123] The spectacle of public challenges to the customs of the Church since 1509 surely stimulated a revival of these views: first was the case of Richard Hunne (1511–14), a London merchant who when he challenged the right of his rector to charge a mortuary fee for the burial of his son, was excommunicated, imprisoned for heresy and then discovered dead; then there had been the drawn-out case of the king's divorce (1528–33) followed by his seizure of First Fruits (1534), a levy charged whenever a church appointment was taken up, previously claimed by the Pope.[124] One head of house, Nicholas Heath of Lenton on Priory, admitted to a sense of vulnerability in 1532: 'Certen men of Nottingham . . . love not my pore howese.'[125]

Yet this mood both waxed and waned. It was no coincidence that it was charged most at moments of high political drama. Perhaps all that was different between 1529 and 1534 was that one drama after another followed in rapid succession: the king's divorce, remarriage and the Break with Rome. Yet if there was radicalism in parliament it seems it was outweighed by conservatism, which may have caused the Crown to proceed with caution even as late as 1536. Away from Westminster, the pressure to topple the regular estate altogether grew most in the pages of the printed polemics, such as *Rede me* and the *Supplicacyon*. It may be a measure of the political climate that no printer was minded to reprint *Rede me* until 1536.[126]

The most sustained challenge to the position of the religious houses, and their most troubled frontier, lay closest to home. There was a rising tide of tension from their tenantry whose livelihoods were tied to the occupation of the monastery's property and the exploitation of its resources. Just as the religious became accustomed to meet the middling order at each other's tables, they met those below them in court. Between 1485 and 1534 the records of civil courts, both those under local and those under royal jurisdiction (e.g. Star Chamber), run on and on revealing cases of disputes with, and direct action against, monastic and mendicant landlords.

Early in the reign of Henry VIII, David Steward seized the oxen of Dale Abbey, left the cellarer for dead, and then hid himself in the 'hold' of neighbouring tenants.[127] The abbots of Dieulacres (Staffordshire) now went to court year after year to try to stifle the persistent threat of trespass, criminal damage and riot; once a grange was invaded and held by force of arms.[128] Abbot John Chaffcombe of Bruern was obliged to prosecute the chain of tenants that reached across his territory after repeated unrest.[129] In some of these clashes it is possible to see a new, absolute rejection of their lordship. Peterborough tenants took their stock on to the abbey's demesne pasture and then defended them.[130] The market traders whose stalls were set up in front of Chester Abbey openly flouted the terms of trade set down by the abbot and convent.[131] Here, it seems, there was an impulse to break free.

A determination to change their relationship, and to alter the religious houses themselves, was also rising in the secular Church. In the century before the Tudor succession there had been occasional signals of a new determination in the Church hierarchy to align the monasteries with their jurisdiction and pastoral authority, if not to govern them correctly. Archbishop William Courtenay (1381–96), appointed to Canterbury in the wake of the Peasants' Revolt, is best known for his role in the suppression of Wyclifism, but he also tested the exemption of the Benedictines in 1389 by a proposal to carry out a metropolitan visitation of their college at Oxford.[132] His successor-but-one, Henry Chichele (1414–43), returned to the matter of the monastic presence in the secular university, steering the Cistercians towards the creation of a conventional collegiate structure. More importantly, he lent authority to the Crown's systematic suppression and appropriation of the priories founded by French monasteries. During his term no fewer than fifty were swept away.[133]

Chichele's cohort of diocesan bishops in visitations now undertaken in recurrent cycles brought a scrutiny to cloister life which in county networks had never been seen before.[134] A series of depositions of superiors in the middle years of the

171

century saw institutions and their internal life interrupted, sometimes for years on end. The election of John Bracy as abbot of Bardney (Lincolnshire) in November 1447 was bluntly quashed by Bishop William Alnwick (1436–49), citing his unsuitability for the office.[135] Abbot Walter Newbery of St Augustine's, Bristol, was summarily removed from office by Bishop John Carpenter of Worcester in 1451; it was not until 1456 and papal intervention that he was restored.[136] For the prelacy as whole it is difficult to believe these moves were not a powerful signal of what even their existing machinery might achieve. The civil wars arrested any rising momentum for monastic reform among church leaders, as life in the cloister was paused by other means: on the eve of the second Battle of St Albans in 1461 the Benedictines of the abbey chose to close the house and leave the town.[137] Yet with the generation of prelates that entered their dioceses after the final settlement of the Yorkist regime (1471), these earlier assertions of authority were renewed and sustained.

It would be wrong to cast these bishops as 'new men', the clerical counterparts to the stamp of government servant sometimes associated with the coming of the Tudors. Some shared Chichele's profile, career clerks who carried with them a dyed-in-the-wool secular outlook and an impressive set of graduate skills. But there were still men born to high society, such as Peter Courtenay, bishop of Exeter (1478–87) and Winchester (1487–92), who were more political than ideological in their cast of mind, their administration of their sees informed by an instinctive understanding of the ambitions of secular lordship.[138] If there was a difference shaping these men it was not in themselves so much as the times. They were the first prelates of print, the first of the era of what is now recognised as a Renaissance papacy, the first for as much as fifty years, to see more frequent exchanges in education, ideas and people with the European mainland.

The prelacy following the Wars of the Roses did not act together to present a new dispensation to the monasteries but variously, incrementally, they advanced their authority over them. Their one common instrument was the Ordinary (diocesan) visitation, which was conventional, if not entirely rolling through a strictly regular cycle by 1485. The degree to which it represented common ground between prelates and the religious houses is evident from the registered records of dioceses and prelacies separated by time and space. No doubt there was some distance between the formal record of the bishop's clerks and the dynamics of the three-day visit itself, but it does at least prove that the formalities of regulation were uniform at opposite ends of the realm. The episcopal cycle even trumped the congregations' own routine scrutiny of their communities; generally now it was interrupted only by a vacancy in the see.[139] The generation that submitted to the king's visitation of 1535 were already the most visited in all of England's long monastic history.

The right of the diocesan to demand correction from a religious house and to expect its submission to visitation was now exercised notwithstanding the privilege of exemption claimed by a number of houses, some with a clutch of papal decrees dating back over several centuries. Before the new Tudor regime had entered its third year, Henry VII and his first-appointed archbishop, John Morton (1486–1500), had secured the foundations for a new framework of episcopal supervision. In August 1487, Pope Innocent VIII granted the English regime his bull *Quanta in Dei Ecclesia*, empowering the metropolitan authority to require the heads of all churches, whether or not they claimed exemption, to accept necessary reforms; only the houses of the Cistercian congregation remained outside its scope. The first test of its authority was applied to St Albans Abbey, whose tradition of papal protection could be traced back as far as Celestine II (d. 1144). The abbey's own proctors had been at the Curia in 1487, seeking to extend the independence of their church further still and it was this lobbying that prompted Morton to act. In July 1489 he issued Abbot William Wallingford with a warning, a formal notice of the discovery of maladministration and his demand that the house accept visitation and reform. Wallingford's Curial proctors won him the right of appeal, although at the same time the papal court reaffirmed the right granted Morton under the bull.[140] The archbishop never did arrive at the abbey but he turned to apply his confirmed authority at three other monasteries which had attracted similar allegations of maladministration: the Cluniac Priory of St Andrew, Northampton (1487–88), the royal abbey of Holy Cross at Waltham (1488) and the convent of the Augustinian friars at Cambridge (1494).[141] In 1490 the regime's representatives in Rome saw *Quanta* renewed.[142]

In parallel with these cases, Morton undertook a sequence of visitations of religious houses in the less contentious domain of his own diocese of Canterbury, and during episcopal vacancies in the sees of Bath and Wells, Exeter and Winchester (1492), Coventry and Lichfield (1491–92, 1496) and Worcester (1498).[143] It is possible that it was his influence that caused Henry VII to assert his authority over the Cistercians, conspicuously omitted from his bull. In the spring of 1490, after a row within the Cistercian leadership over the prospect of a capitular visitation, Henry stepped in to prohibit the entry of agents from the abbot of Cîteaux, citing the prospect of war with France.[144] In an approach that appears to be a practical application of the papal bull, in place of their congregation governors the Crown's chosen candidate, Abbot Marmaduke Huby of Fountains, was approved to carry out reform. Henry made himself the presiding authority again in 1497 when Huby fell out with others in the leadership.[145] Twenty years before his heir and Wolsey interested themselves in the internal affairs of the monastic congregations, the first Tudor king had claimed a stake in their governance.

It would be wrong to see either Henry VII or Archbishop Morton absolutely set against the principle of monastic independence. There were times throughout his reign when the king deployed his personal patronage to reinforce the status of these houses and their superiors. Less than a year before Morton intervened at Northampton, Henry had provided his letters patent to secure the prior, Thomas Sudbury, in office.[146] In March 1491 monarch and metropolitan together saw to the confirmation of the Carthusians' 170-year-old privileges, originally conferred by John XXII.[147] Henry even lent his authority to the ambitions of houses to extend their claims to exemption, enabling Tavistock Abbey to enlarge its lordship in its borough (1501), institutional support that his son continued, as he assisted the house finally to win the privilege of exemption from Leo X in 1513.[148] Morton, for his part, reinforced his monarch's diplomatic efforts for the Carthusians; he intervened when their oldest foundation at Witham was threatened by its tenants; and in his final years he championed the king's scheme to extend the network of Observant houses.[149]

The aim shared by the Tudor king and his archbishop was the renewal of monastic observance. What few records have been preserved of Morton's visitations show that his reforming vision was founded on the regulations passed down to the monastic congregations under the papal programme of the fourteenth century. Invariably, the injunctions he left with the monasteries under his jurisdiction were intended to return them to the forms of organisation and observance described in these canons, known as the Benedictina, because they had been promulgated by Benedict XII (1334–42).[150] Pope Benedict was a professed monk, the second Cistercian to occupy the papal throne; he was also a Regent Master of Theology at the University of Paris. His mixed experience, of the cloister and the secular schools, shaped his vision of reform: the regulars were to be brought into closer conformity with their secular colleagues in those aspects of their life that affected their relationship with the institution of the Church and lay society, governance, the administration of property and income, and education and ordination of their membership; at the same time the daily discipline of the cloister was to respect the precise commands of their respective rules.

Morton seems especially to have called to mind the expectations set for the superior, for competent and transparent oversight of the goods of the house, together with a commitment to an annual statement of accounts, and preservation of observance, leading by their own example. From Repton to Romsey heads faced allegations of abuse of the common seal, 'financial incompetence' and 'chicanery'.[151] He also reaffirmed the Benedictina's educational ambitions. The prior of Norwich Cathedral was challenged for his refusal to allow his monks to use the library at will and the continuing failure of the house to muster a single monk for university study; at Hyde the convent was exposed for the misappropriation of an endowment intended to provide for the grammar education of fourteen scholars.[152] At his own church of Canterbury, Morton endowed scholarships to support Benedictine students at Oxford; it may have been the influence of his scheme that caused his government colleague, Sir Robert Rede (d. 1519), Henry Tudor's Chief Justice, to pursue a comparable scheme, to provide lectureships at Cambridge which the abbot and convent of Waltham part-funded with an annual payment of 20 marks.[153]

Morton's inclination to take up the Benedictina as a blueprint for monasteries and canon houses in England was shared by a number of his peers. In his circuit of 1492 Bishop James Goldwell of Norwich pressed his houses especially over the familiar hallmarks of the papal reform, their administration of expenditure and income, their teaching and the number kept at university. He also reminded them that the Benedictina should be read daily in the chapter house.[154] His colleague, Bishop Geoffrey Blythe of Coventry and Lichfield, in his visitations seems to have held the conventual reading of the canons as diagnostic of an observant monastery. He declared Kenilworth Abbey (Warwickshire) to be a veritable model of good order for 'the Benedictine constitutions are read there, daily'.[155]

There was a viewpoint, present in Morton's immediate peer group but more pronounced in the next generation of bishops appointed in the later years of Henry VII's reign, that recognised conformity to the canons as a minimum standard for monasticism and reached out for an ascetic rigour in the observant life never featured in previous reforms. Their view was informed by a heightened awareness of the formative literature of the Church, the codes, homilies and sermons of patristic authorities such as Augustine, Jerome, Gregory and the lesser-known Greeks, Chrysostom and Basil, whose wisdom was now reawakened in new translations in manuscript and increasingly in print. This was the first full cohort of prelates whose education had been coloured by the humanist call to return *ad fontes* for the refinement of knowledge and understanding. The original form of religious life they found through the fathers of the Church was not only a subject of scholarly interest but also a prompt call to action.

The eldest among them, John Alcock, bishop of Ely (1486–1500), who had preceded Morton as the first Chancellor of the Tudor regime, recreated something of the style and much of the substance of his patristic role models in a series of homilies and sermons presented to the monasteries of his diocese. Here there was no call for the religious house to be more like the Church in the world but rather to transcend it, for 'your kynred shall be of cosynage by affynyte to the fader of heuen our lady all the angels with all the hole Genelogy of Cryst'.[156] The order of the institution of the monastery was of secondary importance to the observance of the individual religious. In Alcock's vision there was to be no diversion from its original form for 'the place of a man or woman in relygyon is beynge in theyr cloister [where] in prayer they speke with God'. There was no tolerance for the evolution or innovation of custom, 'dyspute not the rules of your relygyon / but with all reuerence and obedyence that ye may do ye take theym / obeye theym / and obserue them'.[157]

The original standard of the rule informed the approach to the regulars of William Warham, promoted to Canterbury in 1503, and Richard Fox, bishop of Winchester (1487–1528), prelates who were a generation younger than Alcock. Warham displayed an uncompromising attention to detail in his demands for asceticism. His injunctions introduced new strictures even for the nightclothes of novices.[158] Fox conceived a plan for *ad regulam* reform that reflected his commitment to the humanist conviction of the primary authority of the text. He composed his own English translation of St Benedict's rule for the Benedictine women of his Winchester diocese. To ensure that it was received at once and read uniformly 'daily . . . in their chapter howse' and 'amonges them selfe as well in . . . tyme of refeccions and collacions', he paid for its printing by Richard Pynson in January 1517; apparently a presentation copy was passed to each superior.[159]

The definitive authority of the rule was weighed as heavily by the prelates who succeeded these venerable figures, those who were the last bishops to take office before the Break with Rome. From one congregation to another across his vast diocese Bishop John Longland of Lincoln demanded the daily reading and exposition of the rule 'iuxta antiquam consuetudinem'. He circulated a commentary on the rule which Abbot Kidderminster of Winchcombe had sent him to all the houses in his diocese;[160] and showing the humanist sensibility that was now the common culture of the episcopacy, he encouraged English usage, as an aid, as some would soon argue of Holy Scripture, to a heartfelt acceptance of its commands.[161] 'According to apostolic tradition,' he counselled in one of his published sermons, 'there is no one poorer, more humble nor more foresworn from the world than the monk. Listen, listen for those that are true monks.'[162]

All of these churchmen had come under the influence of the Christian humanism which had spread through schools and universities in the second half of the fifteenth century. For them, humanism meant more than a code for a new kind of scholarship. Like the prominent public humanists of their generation, Erasmus and More, they advanced their values as the cornerstones of a new society made possible by a capable and consensual monarchy and peace countrywide. Longland looked for 'a more comen weale', through the 'redresse' of the 'ruyn and decay' in 'townes, villages, hamlets, manor places', so that it 'wuld move your harte'.[163] 'The soveraygne shall breke his faste for a straungers sake,' Bishop Fox reminded the Benedictine sisters under his jurisdiction, 'the receyuinge of pore people and peregrines must principally with all diligence be regarded'.[164] Notwithstanding his narrow view of monastic discipline, Warham kept a watch on social welfare. He exposed the withdrawal of almsgiving at Faversham in 1511 and directed that beggars at Christ Church, Canterbury, were to be separated from those waiting for confession; but they were not to be turned away.[165]

It was their interest in the precepts of the early Church that led these prelates to look to govern the regulars under their jurisdiction, reaching above and over the authority of their own superior, the customs of their congregation and their secular patron. In his English rendering of the rule, Bishop Fox affirmed St Benedict's subjection of the monastery to the 'bysshoppe to whose diocesesses that place belongeth', and reinforced it with his own reminder that the custom of the community was subordinate to 'the ordinance of the se apostolyqe which nowe be to be observed and preferred'.[166] By contrast with many of their predecessors, as much as possible these prelates addressed their houses not through a suffragan delegate but in person. Between 1504 and 1523, and perhaps as late as 1531, Bishop John Fisher of Rochester (1504–35) himself visited every house under his jurisdiction.[167] Bishop Longland dispensed with the habitual graduate master to preach for him but thundered from the pulpit as though, in the language of St Benedict's rule, he was *abba*, father to the brethren. 'I will go down,' he declared, speaking the words of the Lord God to Abraham.[168]

The prelates' claim to the headship of their houses was more than rhetorical. Repeatedly, they intervened in the identification of candidates for election as superior and where the internal selection seemed inauspicious they did not steer and make recommendations from the wings but placed themselves centre stage and called the community to order. Longland deposed the elected candidate at Sewardsley (Northamptonshire), citing the known fact that she had borne a child 'unius prolis mater'.[169] Bishop Edmund Audley of Salisbury (1502–24) summarily seized control of the election at Malmesbury Abbey in 1510.[170] Fisher did not confine himself to the headship but dictated the appointment to lesser offices.[171] Longland seems to have expected houses of all sizes to conform to an ideal of collective responsibility, in which the conventual offices – claustral prior, cellarer, sacrist, precentor – were divided among the senior members; he even took a view on the annual budgets they were assigned. Longland waged a campaign against Abbot Ricard Pexall of Leicester, which he won finally in 1533.[172]

Of Longland's peer group of bishops appointed by Henry VIII, the pre-eminent force, in practical church politics, and in the articulation of a reformist creed, was Thomas Wolsey. The careers of fellow churchmen in his generation were as long, if not longer, and far-reaching given their service in several dioceses, but only Wolsey came to influence religious houses countrywide; and only he was able to connect the new demands of the secular Church with the new dispensation looked for within government and in wider society. The anchor-hold of his career was his political service as an envoy, councillor and chancellor to the Crown. Wolsey accrued his church offices as a sure foundation in the shifting sands of court favour. Henry made him bishop of Lincoln and archbishop of York in the same year (1514); in 1516 Pope Leo X crowned him as a Cardinal, and two years later appointed him to act as his legate in England, ostensibly to implement measures of reform agreed at the Fifth Lateran Council (1512–17), which was nearing its close. In 1521, after months of persuasion, Henry appointed Wolsey abbot of St Albans, the first time in England since the Norman Conquest that a churchman not professed to the religious life held a monastic office. Two years later he took the see of Durham, leaving northern England's largest monastery also at his mercy.

Wolsey's approach to the religious houses has too often been represented as a full-frontal assault, a literal rehearsal of the programmes carried out by Cromwell, his protégé, from 1536, a lower-case dissolution before the capital event. His combination of papal and episcopal office and political authority allowed Wolsey an entry into monastic affairs at will. He made his legatine mission a platform from which to challenge the independence of the central governing chapters of the three largest monastic congregations – the Augustinian canons, the Benedictines and the Cistercians. In his first year at York (1515) he saw the Cistercian abbots agree a subsidy for the Crown, a concession which set them disputing among themselves.[173] By 1517, Abbot Thomas Chard alias Tybbes of Forde reflected that his colleagues were in fear (timore) of the Cardinal.[174] From 1517 to 1521 he pressed on each one a set of injunctions to reform their discipline.[175]

Since Wolsey had been scheming (with the assistance of his secretary, Richard Pace) to take the abbacy of St Albans into his hands for two years as the incumbent became incapacitated, his possession of it perhaps lost some of its spectacle.[176] There is no surviving record of vocal responses either among monastic leaders or his own episcopal peers. Nonetheless, by his appointment the separation of Tudor England from the practice of the continental Church was ended; and if not all at once, then Wolsey's long, almost ten-year tenure, set a template for secularisation. 'The two graces (duas deas),' Polydore Vergil observed, had been turned out (eiecit) of the monastery.[177] It is difficult not to think that it left its mark on the minds of those devising and delivering policy around him, not least, the king himself, and Thomas Cromwell. Wolsey took his tenure of St Albans as an opportunity to test both episcopal and royal supervision of a monastic empire. From here in 1524 he embarked on a sequence of suppressions and sequestrations of small and neglected religious houses (one of the priories of the St Albans network among them) to endow a twin college foundation in his name. By the time his position and his health were weakening in 1528, the scheme was almost complete.

This, Wolsey's last and most memorable intervention in monastic England, was not a blueprint for Henry and Cromwell's policy of the 1530s. The closure of these twenty-nine houses bears little comparison to what happened in 1536–40 beyond the obvious common ground that, for the most part, living communities of the professed were extinguished and their endowments were taken by the Crown. In fact, not all of them still showed very vital signs of life: the community at Tiptree (Essex) amounted to no more than a prior and a canon in 1525; at Pynham (West Sussex) there was only one professed resident; at Snape perhaps there were none living there permanently.

Unlike the suppressions of 1536 and after, Wolsey's scheme did not aim at the disendowment of the clergy. Rather it was an act of reappropriation; the transfer of temporal estates and churches from one foundation to another, in this instance colleges to be occupied by scholars and masters who themselves would be ordained priests. It was hardly unprecedented. Even the scale of his scheme, for twin colleges at Ipswich and Oxford, was entirely in step with the patronal behaviour of the early Tudor bishops. Since the accession of Henry VIII in 1509, a college at Cambridge and two at Oxford had been raised at least in part on the resources of monasteries: St John's (1511), Cambridge, carried forward by Bishop Fisher, Brasenose (1512), Oxford, whose founder was Bishop William Smith of Lincoln, and Corpus Christi (1517), Oxford, the creation of Richard Fox.[178]

Reaching the ranks of the prelacy a decade after Fisher and almost three decades after Fox, his former master, Wolsey's scheme might be seen as the expression of an impulse to stand with his peers. The reappropriation of monastic endowments for education, with the particular purpose of extending and enhancing the population of secular clergy, had been recognised as a measure of reform for more than a century. A template for such projects had been offered up by Henry VI's twin foundation of Eton College and King's College, Cambridge (1440). Their endowment was drawn from monasteries under the supervision of parent houses in France which had been seized by the Crown during the Hundred Years War. In the forty years of Tudor rule before the first of Wolsey's dissolutions, no fewer than five college and school foundations had been established in this way from the sites and estates originally given for a monastery.

The Cardinal's approach was much the same. Like every other college founder before him, he reached out for those religious houses already under his jurisdiction, or which could become so, de facto, through the assistance of his allies. A papal dispensation to appropriate was secured for each one; while the petition made much of their material condition, there was no high rhetoric, or hard evidence, representing the quality of their religion or resistance to reform. The local circumstances, economic, social and political, of each house were negotiated with notable caution, and the physical realisation of Wolsey's plan was as protracted as it had been for the founders (Fox, Waynflete) who had passed this way before. In the span of four years that was sufficient for Wolsey's master to bring an end to more than 800 religious houses, Wolsey was still wrestling over the resources of just twenty-eight.

It was a measure of how far Wolsey's scheme seemed set in the framework of familiar policy that it drew hardly any attention outside of the contexts most closely concerned. Neither of the London annalists known to be recording current events as they occurred, Charles Wriothesley (1506–62) at the College of Arms and the chronicler of the Franciscan convent, noticed it at all. Those inside, or in the orbit of, the court circle watched closely, but, as expressed by John Skelton in his poem *Colin Cloute*, their interest was in the spectacle of the Cardinal's prodigality. Wolsey's position as commendator abbot of St Albans acted to neutralise the most powerful potential source of monastic opposition; at any rate his predecessors in the abbacy had closed dependent priories in order to fund abbey projects of their own.

The closure of a chain of priories in the Cardinal's native Suffolk sparked an outcry from the nearest foundation of any scale, Butley Priory. The anonymous annalist saw it as nothing less than the declaration of war on the monastic order, which would surely bring 'the dissipation and ruin not only of our own religion but of monks, nuns and religious women more or less across England as a whole'.[179] Their words, however, did not carry outside their own enclosure. Alarm did break out in the neighbourhood in Sussex, where Bayham Abbey was seized by a band of canons and local men which then kept the Cardinal's agents at a distance for two or three days (see Fig. 12). The conspicuous figure in the fracas was a canon, Thomas Towers, but the focus of the protest was the property farmed by the religious house located among local landlords, a number of whom had interests in the burgeoning business of iron founding.[180] The hostility here was not toward the purpose of the sequestration but to the process, as tenants of long standing feared the loss of their holdings. The same anxiety was apparent at Butley, that established tenures might again be 'granted and put out to farm'.[181] Wolsey's plan was not a new departure, nor a precise blueprint for the king's reformation; but it did presage the response from the provinces which would be amplified a decade on.

Wolsey's policy for the monasteries was not total dissolution but for a new dispensation to be established by which they might be governed and reformed.

His objective in governance acknowledged the growing expectations of the Crown to exercise the authority of the founder but it did not reach as far as the formation of a state Church. When Wolsey interposed himself in the General Chapter of the Augustinian canons in 1518, one of his novel demands was for a grant of confraternity to be made to the king and queen, and to the duke of Suffolk and himself as their principal counsellors.[182] Yet for the ultimate leadership of clergy, secular and regular, the cardinal looked to the hierarchy of the Church itself, the papacy, its legates and intermittent ecumenical councils, the latest of which, the Fifth Council of the Lateran, was two years into a five-year session in his first year as bishop (1515). Wolsey was as one with his peers in their determination personally to demonstrate their diocesan authority in the face of the regulars; he differed only in the reach of his authority, since over the course of twenty years he held no fewer than four sees in administration as well as presiding over the province of York and asserting legatine authority over all the realm.

Nonetheless, Wolsey's own pre-eminence in the counsels of the king and his growing role in secular government as a conduit of royal authority created a new tier at the apex of the Church. Wolsey was an authority apart and above their own, the king's bishop, and the kingdom's principal prelate. Within four years of his promotion to York, it was spoken of in their own actions. When the abbacy of Wherwell fell vacant in 1518, Richard Fox, bishop of Winchester, was minded to permit a 'fre elecion', but he was moved to address himself to Wolsey even so for his 'gracious expedicion' of the king's assent.[183] The committed pastor, John Longland, complacently accepted his role in 1525, 'to fulfil the kings pleasure as far as all ther gudds may stretche . . . for the comen wele of the realme'.[184]

Wolsey shared his peers' impulse for monastic reform. Like his mentors, Fox and Warham, he pressed for more than a return to the baseline of the Benedictina. It seems he inclined to a vision of learned reform comparable to the celebrated congregations of mainland Europe, such as that of the abbey of Santa Giustina at Padua, which had propagated humanist standards among the Benedictines of Italy.[185] He also expressed a preference for a standard of ascetic rigour that as a manifesto for reform ran quite contrary to the spirit of the papal canons that some diocesans now sought to reinforce. Wolsey's biographer, George Cavendish (1497–1562), described the scene of the Cardinal's private visits (possible by a 'secrett gallery') to the Charterhouse at Sheen, where 'he wold sytt in contemplacion with . . . the most auncyent ffathers . . . and by ther councell perswadyd from the vainglory of thys world and gave hym dyvers shirtes of heare, the whiche he often wore'. Wolsey's monastic mortifications may have been exaggerated but that he matched Colet (whose London Charterhouse lodging he shared) in his taste for 'godly contemplacion' may be wholly authentic.[186]

It was surely this that was the source of the gulf between him and the Benedictine leadership when he pressed them to adopt a new code of discipline in 1520–21. No copy of the text has survived, no doubt because it was swiftly rejected by the monks, but an impression of its content is given in their agitated response, that it was a life harder and more difficult than their brethren could stomach, which would only cause current religious to leave and prospective entrants to recoil. To them Wolsey's discipline was out of step with the times since 'they are few, and rare, who look for ascetic rigour and the observance of rules'.[187] He wanted regulars that were different from other clergy. Urging the aged Thomas Colyns of Tywardreath to step down, he described his ideal of an abbot, 'sobre, discrete religious, polytique, & in other qualitees hable & meete', a man 'of good meryte to the pleasor of almyghty god and weall [of the] howse'.[188] As here, Wolsey's language of reform was barbed. Where heads or their houses were hostile he saw grounds for intervention, even governance imposed from outside. During the years of his legatine mission, he reached no further than interference in the business of the congregations' governing chapters. Still, the trade-off between independence and the need for reform was imprinted on the minds of those who watched him at work – King Henry from above and Thomas Cromwell from below.

Wolsey's interference in religious houses might be thought too personal and political, and perhaps simply too ad hoc to be seen as a coherent and sustained process of reform. Yet the measures of his legatine mission, and in particular his injunctions concerning internal discipline, continuing a tradition of papal and legatine canons that reached back over three centuries, offered a new template for observance to be applied across the regular estate. The impression of a programme may have been more visible if more of its paper trail had survived. His interventions among the friars, including visitations of the Observant Franciscans (1519, 1524) and the Dominicans (1524), remain shadowy; Bishop Longland encouraged the latter, 'for [they] hathe no pastor for [them] but ye noble grace as legate', but there is no evidence that it ever occurred.[189]

Yet it is clear that for the first time since the reforms of the fourteenth century, Wolsey envisaged a root-and-branch reform of the kingdom's three largest monastic congregations. To assist him he tested their own levers of governance. He interposed himself in the chapter meetings of the canons; confronted the Cistercians as legate *a latere* (i.e. standing on the side of the pope); and approached the Benedictine network by way of Westminster Abbey, recognised historically as their leading house. The first two of these interventions proved effective at least in the immediate term. The Cardinal's challenge to the canons to commit to further investment in university education, resolved for further investment in university study, appears to have carried them over divisions which had arrested their development for decades.[190] Their *studium* at Oxford, known as St Mary's College, was equipped and funded in the 1520s and 1530s like never before; its rising profile may have promoted recruitment to the congregation in these last decades. Wolsey's constitution for the Cistercians lent a canonical authority and a coherence to ideas of reform which had surfaced in a handful of houses but not spread wide.[191]

Even his abortive intervention in Westminster might be considered as a watershed, since it compelled the Benedictines to express a view of their form of religious life that distanced them not only from the precepts of their founder but also from the customs of the Benedictina. In their answer to Wolsey, they described to him their profession to a different form of monastic life which even those accustomed to the clericalism of the papal canons might have considered too much of a break with their past.[192] Polydore Vergil viewed the episode with bitter cynicism: Wolsey, he thought, was 'imperious' (imperium ostentat) almost for its own sake, and the monks were running scared (ut terreat caeteros ... ut se terribilem praebeat).[193]

It does appear that Wolsey's actions as legate, underscored by his growing presence as a prelate, brought on a more fundamental change in the leadership of religious houses. By the time his burst of legislative activity was over (1521), settling over each of the congregations was a recognition of Wolsey as the kingdom's presiding authority in their own monastic affairs. His unique position meant that it was understood to be an authority drawn equally from church and state: he was the delegate of prince and pontiff. The regulars reached out for his directions and decisions. So did their ordinaries, the bishops of their dioceses, and their hereditary founders and other lay patrons. Bishop Longland now faithfully, even abjectly, looked for his nod in all monastic affairs.[194] Between 1521 and 1529, Wolsey directly supervised, or indirectly influenced, the appointment of monastic heads from Cornwall to Cumbria. His presence expanded over the course of his ministry; he involved himself in controversies that had already begun in 1516–17 and was routinely acting as an arbiter by the mid-1520s.[195] The scale of his case-work should not perhaps eclipse its clear priority: the full force of his interference was felt at the foundations of the oldest monastic order of Benedictines – ancient, royal and accustomed to independence – such as Glastonbury, Reading and St Albans, and those allied to continental congregations, such as the Cistercians and the priory of St John of Jerusalem.[196] Wolsey's personal pre-eminence and the reach of his own affinity prompted this change in behaviour, but it was decisive. When the Cardinal was finally gone, the instinct to look to the Crown and its chief minister remained.

Wolsey carried a vision for monastic reform to the very end of his ascendancy in Henry's government in 1529. Months before, between the spring and autumn of 1528, as his agents at the papal curia picked up the last of the permissions required for his colleges, they also secured a sequence of faculties (licences) enabling further interventions in existing Church foundations. A faculty dated 31 August empowered Wolsey and the present papal legate, Cardinal Lorenzo Campeggio (d. 1539), to combine monastic communities of men and women whose populations were fewer than twelve professed with those already larger, or those that might be if they received these numbers.[197] A faculty of 12 November permitted him to enquire into the past history of suppressions and in particular if any monastery had been turned into a cathedral church.[198]

Almost all of these remained prospects for the future, but there was one initiative, given papal approval at the same time, that was followed through. The principal income arising from the endowment of the Benedictine abbey at Holme was awarded to the bishop of Norwich, in conjunction with the surrender of the First Fruits of the diocese to the Crown.[199] As an intervention it has been overshadowed by the suppression of houses for the support of the Cardinal's colleges, but as an obvious break with the past it should perhaps be seen as an indication of the direction of Wolsey's thinking at this last stage of his career. A senior see lost some of its independence as its original constitution was changed; at the same time, a 400-year-old monastic foundation was reassigned to meet the needs of the secular Church. The transfer made the bishop of Norwich de facto commendator of the monastery (i.e. the financial beneficiary of a Church foundation), an arrangement commonplace in mainland Europe where the centralising and secularising ambitions of monarchs and their prelates were already far advanced.

Perhaps the November faculty signalled further reorganisation in this vein. The August licence has suggested more closures of viable houses. But a wider plan would be a more profound challenge to the independence of congregations than had been made in the years just past, and it appears that Wolsey now resumed his bullying of their governing bodies which had marked his term as papal legate. He demanded a fine of 1,000 marks from the leadership of the Cistercians, recognising, no doubt, it was their customary right to collect fees and fines from their members that lent them any independent authority.[200] The patrons of St Mary Graces suspected the end was near.[201]

The regulars' experiences of Cardinal Wolsey, the wider prelacy, the social community, their patrons and the monarchy itself should not be seen as a succession of defeats that led inevitably to dissolution. But these exchanges did change them, to the extent that the monastic generation of the 1530s responded to state, church and society in ways that were measurably different from their forebears. It might be said that the regular religious communities that confronted the Henrician reformation were themselves (with a handful of exceptions) unreformed. It is true that they had been hardly touched by the spirit of continental reform movements, but in their relationship with what contemporaries would have called the commonwealth of the realm they had already experienced reformation of a kind.

Certainly the most conspicuous transformation was the monasteries' attitude to the involvement of external authorities in their own internal affairs, the selection of heads and other officers, and the administration of their endowments. It would be too much to see this as a definitive submission to lordship, secular or ecclesiastical. More often than not it was a reconciliation of these interests with their own; the constraint of complete independence did not mean the loss of governing authority altogether.[202] Nonetheless, the break with their past should not be downplayed. In previous generations the overpowering instinct of religious houses had been to skirmish on questions of jurisdiction with the Crown and its provincial officers, patrons, neighbouring proprietors and the diocesan. The domestic chronicles they kept recorded the battle honours of successive abbots and priors, their *gesta*, or valorous deeds, celebrated like those of a martial monarch.

Now, the first response was not to deny either the principle of their authority or their particular demands but to engage in dialogue over it and, more often than not, to come to a settlement that satisfied the external party. The role of the superior in these exchanges stood in marked contrast to past history. No longer naturally the convent's champion, now they were as likely to stand with, or at least speak for, the outsider's embassy. Some found in secular lordship a strong personal affinity and, perhaps, personal friendship. Abbot Geoffrey Barton of Lilleshall (Shropshire) looked to Sir Robert Plumpton as his mentor: 'I am a yong beginner of the world in my office, and, sir, for your good will and counsell I will . . . reward . . . you'. Abbot William Marshall of Kirkstall saw Plumpton as 'my full trusty, enterely beloved gossep'.[203]

There can be no doubt that the degree of change differed according to the source of the external authority. The monasteries' common ground with the leadership of the boroughs on their immediate horizons was expanding almost out of pace with their negotiations for the resolution of long-standing disputes over their respective jurisdictions. The family names of their leaders – Goldston, Hamond, Reve – were known before they were personally; and they were seen in their guild membership and other social contexts even before the two sides came together to treat over such matters as mayoral elections or market rates.[204] Of them all perhaps it was the diocesan bishop who was regarded with the greatest diffidence. There was no sincere or sustained reach towards cooperation. As his letters reveal, such was Richard Fox's determination to rule the monasteries that he would plan to deceive them if it was the only possible means to obstruct their plans.[205]

Above all, the regulars reached for a rapprochement with the Crown. In the last decade of Henry VII's reign and the first decade of his son, the leading monasteries and friaries cultivated royal favour at a level not witnessed since the reign of Henry III. For a fresh affinity with royalty some of these houses were prepared to reshape their lives radically. The king's mother, Lady Margaret, was allowed to sit for spiritual counsel within the enclosure at Sheen where women were strictly forbidden. For their reredos, the monks accepted the uncompromisingly dynastic symbols of King Henry's altarpiece.[206] The conduct of superiors displayed a conspicuous change, as they readily adopted the courtly currency of reward that their predecessors had once eschewed. Abbot Thomas Corton of Cerne gave a fee to John Hussee to secure the privilege of a free election from the king. As a prop for his pitch for the abbacy of Thame (Oxfordshire), Thomas Chard granted an annuity to the king's man, Thomas Fetteplace.[207] Thomas Marshall, former prior of Wallingford (Oxfordshire), was able to raise £1,000 with which he influenced Wolsey to grant him the abbacy at Chester. Steadily, these monks forged a chain of connections to the agents of royal authority, in government and the court. Four years before he became vicegerent, in 1530, Thomas Frisby, canon of Launde (Leicestershire), courted Cromwell with a gift of six cheeses.[208]

When coin, costly treasures and even property were offered up in the shadow of the royal supremacy of 1534, it might be tempting to see it as an expression of the sudden desperation and resignation of religious houses confronting their certain end. In fact, it had been their manner of business for as much as two decades; and it was understood, on both sides of the bargain, not as a concession of corporate authority but as a transaction. It was their practice in these secular political arts that persuaded some superiors to expand their portfolio of interests, or even to pull at the seams of canonical custom. The abbots of Bardney and Peterborough both tried the levers of influence to place a client of their own choosing in the priory at Spalding. Bishop Longland wrote with rising frustration how '[he] comfortithe hym with faire promes sainge he shall nott lake his helpe nor money'.[209]

There was a counterpoint to this that marked a more dramatic change in behaviour. Becoming ever closer to the social groups of town and country that traded with them and tenanted their property, the regulars took up their methods for pressing their case whenever the talking failed. They mobilised servants, at times together with professed men, to take direct action over disputed property, its boundaries, buildings and livestock, and sometimes even to take up arms against the other side. The community at Fountains Abbey were reported to be the ringleaders of a spate of enclosure riots that erupted in the North Riding in 1496 and 1497.[210] At Canterbury, the Cathedral Priory tackled the object and subject of their argument with the city over their mill: their servants attempted to change the course of the River Stour to stop the wheel, while the monks confronted the city officers and one of them, Thomas Bredgar, snatched the mace from the hands of their serjeant-at-arms.[211] The men of Leicester Abbey defended the hedges of Over Haddon with a volley of arrows.[212] When the long-running row over terms of trade in Chester broke into a brawl in 1507, the abbot and a number of his monks were among it, throwing their fists.[213]

The physical defences of monastic precincts had developed significantly since the late fourteenth century when they had been overrun in the Peasants' Revolt (1381). Now, it seems there was also a readiness in manpower and arms. The extraordinary mounted assault of Edward Stafford, duke of Buckingham, on the

Cistercian abbey at Kingswood in 1517 was repelled, successfully, by an armed force. Nor did houses always hold themselves in defence.[214] After years of oppression in their own domain, in 1532 the canons of Lytham dispatched their armed retainers to engage the Butler family on their own ground.[215]

These changes may have lent some security to the institutional position of the monasteries, but there can be little doubt that it was at the cost of their internal stability. Inevitably, the affiliations and alliances of the secular world were upheld in the cloister and inflamed the factionalism that was inherent in any monastic community. At best it made these communities more volatile; at worst it virtually destroyed them. The battle between two candidates for the abbacy of Furness led one, and four other monks, to languish in the Fleet prison for more than a year.[216] The prior of Conishead was alleged to have directed the killing of a young man whose 'hede was kyett asunder in thre peses and his legs in iiii placis'.[217] Notoriously, Matthew Deveys, abbot of Holm Cultram, a professed man so enmeshed in the social network of the neighbourhood that some of the most influential dined with him in his private chambers, fell victim to a poisoning, perhaps plotted by one of his own brethren who was himself bound to a rival clique.[218]

The allure of a royal affinity, raising with it the prospect of a higher order of patronal protection, may have served to prepare the way for Wolsey when he came to press his leadership on congregations and then particular houses. The regulars soon came to regard him as the prince's prelate, charged with a power above diocesans, rather than a prince-prelate, a concentration of all the ambition of the secular Church. The presidents of the Augustinian General Chapter convened at Leicester in June 1518 distilled this new outlook in words and deeds performed in the three days of their meeting. The Cardinal was promised the status of founder of their college; Prior Robert Shouldham of St Mary, Overy (Southwark), responded to Wolsey's call to reform with a dramatic display of compunction, crawling into the chapter house, crying and wringing his hands (contorsis minibus et digitis, miserabiliter et cum lacrimis genuflectente).[219] Before the chapter was closed, Wolsey, the king, queen and Princess Mary, along with Charles Brandon, duke of Suffolk, and his new bride, the dowager queen of France, were received into the fraternity of the congregation.[220]

By the end of the king's first decade, as often as not Wolsey's interventions were made at the invitation of the religious themselves. When they lost their prior in 1519, the first thought of the canons at the remote West Somerset priory at

Barlinch was to send for the Cardinal, a man they can only have known by reputation.[221] Wolsey formed a circle of friends across the monastic network, bound it seems by a sincere and mutual admiration. The Cardinal called Thomas Chaundler, propelled into the primacy of Eynsham, the 'flower of Seynt Benett's ordyr'; he steered the career of John Stonywell, whom he may have first met when the monk was an Oxford student, to the very moment of his downfall, securing first the priorate of Tynemouth and then the abbacy at Pershore.[222] Prior Richard Vowell of Walsingham created a chantry for Wolsey, receiving the appropriated income of Flitcham Priory (Norfolk) for the purpose.[223] Richard Kidderminster, the abbot of Winchcombe, who at court and in government was generally regarded as the best of the Benedictine divines, praised Wolsey for his pre-eminent yet pious virtues as a man and his tireless devotion to the cares of state and church.[224]

These alliances, in prospect and in practice, extended the regulars' detachment from their own systems of governance, their provincial and general chapters, and the Pope and Roman curia itself. If the Tudor regime had made clear its suspicion of the capitular authorities of the Augustinians and Cistercians anchored abroad, their members showed no strong or sustained impulse to join a battle of loyalties. The White and Black Canons were willingly steered towards insular self-governance, as if pressure from the Crown, and then Wolsey, were the prompt they had looked for to shake off a foreign influence. Wolsey's pressure on the canon houses that held Arrouaisian and Victorine affiliations to join the General Chapter in England appears to have prevailed.[225] There was a marked change in the tone of the Cistercian leadership between the accession of Henry Tudor and the presentation of Wolsey's proposals in 1521. At first, the abbots were fearful of their isolation from Cîteaux. They feared subjection.[226] Thirty years later they proclaimed with confidence their own, independent vision for an English movement for reform. The unifying force of the Benedictines' general chapter had been fading steadily for some time before these decades, but there is no doubt that the monks of the 1520s were more inclined to invoke their personal and patronal networks when internal problems arose. The mortal weakness of the chapter was revealed in 1527 when a widely reported case of maladministration at Malmesbury Abbey, of a kind which had once been its stock in trade, was settled only at the intervention of the diocesan.[227]

The monasteries' view of the authority of Rome had always been equivocal. Naturally, those houses with an historic claim to exempt status and those still ambitious to achieve it continued to regard the Curia as a bulwark against the unchecked advance of royal and episcopal authority. Yet there was also instinctive suspicion in these, as much as the generality of houses, that the papacy and its structure of government in other houses would just as readily consume the resources of any perpetual foundation for itself. This was coloured by an awareness, washed by generations of experience narrated at length in their own conventual records, that the delegates of papal authority were almost always rapacious rogues. The spectacle in 1490 of the king and his archbishop raising support for a visitation of the exempt abbey of St Albans can only have hardened the conviction that the Renaissance curia was not a reliable custodian of monastic causes.[228] Certainly, in the years that followed the traffic in petitions steadily declined. Cutting across their institutional caution was an individual outlook that still recognised Rome's primacy in their Christian world and its potential to propel their own career. John Smart of Wigmore was said to have a 'great devotion to ryde into Wales upon Lammas Daye to receive the bushop of Rome his pardone'.[229] The Cistercian leadership raised an alarm after it became clear that brethren were making a beeline there for the Papal Jubilee of 1500.[230]

By the turn of the new century, houses were no longer keeping proctors at the Curia as a matter of course, but their professed members still pursued business of their own. Those rising through the ranks of the convent or congregation continued to play its politics and pay its charges in the hope of personal reward. Alexander Barclay caught something of this double-edged view in his fourth eclogue, 'What should I travayle, in Rome is no profite . . . still catching coyne, and gaping after golde.'[231] It was through these channels that Thomas Wilkinson of Welbeck (Nottinghamshire) won himself the candidacy of provincial of his order in 1514.[232] It seems Thomas Colyn, prior of Tywardreath, planned to counter-balance the pressure from Wolsey by enhancing his own portfolio through petitions to Leo X for the grant of benefices and prebends.[233] As it happened, both men won better rewards from their dealing with the Cardinal, and as the new dynamics between regular and secular developed over the 1520s and into the 1530s, even the individual impulse to turn to Rome was undermined.

The diffidence of the monks towards Rome at root may have been a practical response to the difficulties of doing business there, but there are indications that it was now reinforced by their general view of the governance of the Church. In the years down to 1524, Abbot John Selwood of Glastonbury read a printed edition (1475) of Augustine of Ancona's treatise *De potestate papae* (On papal power), perhaps the most widely consulted exposition of papal authority before 1517. The words and phrases he highlighted in the margin – indulgentia – at least hint at a critical engagement with the concerns now rising in the secular hierarchy.[234]

The generation of regulars that rose to leadership positions in the first quarter of the sixteenth century were more closely aligned to the political, social and cultural outlook of the secular clergy and the agents of royal government than at any period perhaps since as far back as the twelfth century, when the sons of the same Norman dynasties followed parallel paths to abbey, cathedral and court. Increasingly, in the hierarchies that confronted them outside their enclosure they recognised a common social context. Such background could not be, as has been suggested, 'an unspoken factor' in their office.[235] Many of the Henrician superiors could identify themselves with the borough or county backgrounds of the coming cohort of secular prelates, Stephen Gardiner, Edward Lee, John Stokesley, and graduate-entry government servants, such as Thomas Legh, younger son of the manor house, schooled at Eton and King's College, Cambridge, who landed an ambassadorial role within a year of leaving the university.[236] Some of their family and friendship affinities, in London, the Home Counties and East Anglia intersected. A copy of Thomas von Kempen's *Imitatio Christi* which was in the hands of Abbot William Huddleston of Stratford Langthorne by 1533 appears to tie him to a network of pious Norfolk gentry into which he may have been born.[237] The common impulse for youth in this society was careerism, the conviction that office, and good service in it, was their way into the world. From their perspective, the opportunities for office within and outside of a regular profession were evenly weighed.

Above all, these seculars were bonded by their intellectual formation. Whatever their final destination, their education and professional preparation had been the same. For these men, embarking on their careers in church and state after 1509, perhaps it was a more distinctive and defining experience than ever before. They were the first to be schooled following a syllabus fully informed by humanist principles, privileging language proficiency over logic and advancing a new historical sensibility to stand alongside philosophical speculation. Many of the seculars are known to have passed through schools that now promoted teaching of this kind.

The elementary education of the regulars is generally not recorded although the subsequent academic studies of many must point to their prior experience of grammar school. Their exposure to the humanist programme continued in the universities, where, whatever their point of entry, many of them moved into the same orbit; even if they entered the university already clothed as a canon or monk, in practice there was now no great separation from the life of the secular students, formal or informal. Several of those promoted to the headship of a prominent religious house in the 1520s had been the exact contemporaries at Oxford and Cambridge of the prelates and royal clerks they met in their institutional roles. And in their common memory of colleges, faculties and academic exercise they met as equals. When in 1514 Richard Kidderminster wrote from Winchcombe to congratulate Wolsey on his elevation to a metropolitan see, he turned almost at once to the experience they shared, Oxford and its ways.[238]

The common imprint of this intellectual journey is palpable in what survives of the regulars' writing and their books. Their personal inscriptions – in the margins of books, in memoranda and occasionally in autograph letters – display the same self-conscious Roman script that set them apart from older generations. The hand of Richard Kidderminster, preserved in several epistles and personal volumes, was reminiscent of Erasmus, if a little stricter in its humanist letterforms.[239] It is not known if he made formal copies of texts, as Erasmus did, but there was a professional quality to his hand that would have made it possible. It was also conveyed in the voice of these monks, the high rhetoric of their written word, seasoned, if not always with tags, then with exotic English transliterated from their Latin. It was anchored by a common attachment to certain authorities, especially the founding fathers of the Roman Church – Ambrose, Augustine, Jerome, Gregory – whose doctrine now drew the fresh critical attention of humanist editors such as Erasmus.

Several of the seculars and regulars of this generation knew this paragon of patristic scholars personally. He corresponded with Richard Bere, abbot of Glastonbury; Leonard Cox, a schoolmaster at Reading Abbey, had known him at Basel.[240] Through the intercession of a brother of two of the nuns, Erasmus addressed himself to the convent of Denny Abbey and marked their own response with a model Latin letter dedicated to them.[241] The canons of Merton Priory may have felt a collective friendship for him following his sojourn at their Oxford *studium*, St Mary's College, which Erasmus described to John Colet as providing him with 'the company of men like yourself'.[242] His printed works seem to have been a popular purchase for regular students passing through the universities and at Reading, Abbot Hugh Cook appears inclined to have made a contribution to their transmission. Erasmus gave his patronage to Cox's *Art or crafte of rhetoryke* printed in 1532, and may be assumed to have supported the printing of the schoolmaster's translation of the *Enchiridion* which he also hoped to present to Thomas Cromwell.[243]

Their enthusiasm for the patristic age carried this generation, seculars and regulars alike, into a fresh encounter with the pioneers of Latin monasticism. The interest of the Henrician prelates in the codes and other witnesses to the earliest cenobites is conspicuous in their published works. The first sermon in Bishop Longland's *Tres conciones* (i.e. Three sermons), which he dedicated to Abbot Kidderminster, uncovered the very essence of the monastic life, that is the imitation of Christ, invoking Augustine and the authorities of the Old Testament.[244] At Winchcombe, clearly Kidderminster matched Longland's reading virtually word for word. A printed edition of the commentary on the rule by the twelfth-century monk, Rupert of Deutz (d. *c.* 1129), is marked throughout with the abbot's distinctive manicule.[245] He was not alone among monastic leaders. The only book to be preserved from the personal library of John Ramsey, prior of Merton, is a printed copy of Erasmus's life of St Jerome. Here too there are many manicules and underlines; especially, as might be expected, at the passage describing Jerome's own experience of a *cenobium*.[246]

The research of seculars and regulars alike into exemplars of the religious life returned them also to the history of their own English tradition. Richard Stone, a monk of Christ Church Priory, Canterbury, wrote, in a striking humanist script, a great compendium of the lives of the first monastic saints of Saxon England and Normandy. At the same time, 300 miles north, William Tod of Durham Cathedral Priory began an anthology celebrating local monastic saints, Aidan, Bede and Cuthbert.[247] The pioneering spirit and ascetic rigour of these legendary figures was a growing source of inspiration for this generation, perhaps especially Benedictines whose claustral formation was at any rate steeped in their historical traditions. Although Wolsey appeared to repel both seculars and regulars with his pressure for a return to primitive monasticism, they reached out for it themselves, adopting the names of the Roman and Saxon exemplars of their religious life when they made their profession.[248]

Their intellectual interests led them into common ground on matters of reform. Both secular prelates and regulars' leaders agreed on the need for advanced learning and teaching in religious houses. It was the potential for the monastery to find a place in the Church as a seminary that heads of houses held on to at the end of the 1530s, as Cromwell continued to keep his counsel as to whether all of them should close. Here, surely, they looked to the example of the monastic congregations and unions of the European mainland, led from Bursfeld, Chezal, Melk, Padua and Valladolid, which had driven a revival of monasteries and monastic recruitment with the promotion of humanist education within the precinct walls.[249] Like them, the common view of these Tudor clerics was that learning should not only renew the religious life but also lend weight to the Church Militant. This was Richard Stone's mind when he finished his compendium at Canterbury. He closed it with verses running over five leaves on the danger of Martin Luther, a dragon that 'blowyth . . . burnyth . . . glowyth agaynst al tru Chrysten men'. Here the duty of service is both to the community of believers and to their sovereign, 'O noble prince Henry', their 'lovyng king shalt be my deare derlyng'.[250]

The common experience and outlook of regulars and the clerical and lay elite forged close and effective affinities between them. Patronage, service and partisan politics had given rise to mutual associations among churchmen in the past, but rarely had there been affiliations among secular prelates and monastic and mendicant leaders, so acute was their suspicion of one another, so deep their differences of outlook on the organisation of the institutional Church. Yet now senior monks and canons joined the networks of allies nurtured by the seculars at the apex of Henry's Church. Wolsey counted Benedictines and Cistercians in his circle of partisans and protégés certainly before his cardinalate, perhaps from the time of his first promotion: John Stonywell, abbot of Pershore, was first drawn into his orbit when he was a scholar monk at Oxford.[251]

As the Cardinal secured further high offices of the church, from 1515 (York) to 1521 (St Albans), the monastic presence in his affinity expanded. His interventions in the appointment of superiors and other internal affairs might reflect a rising impulse to set religious houses under external supervision, but (in almost every case) they also reveal the range of personal ties between the Cardinal and the cloisters. Wolsey's candidates for monastic promotion were not made merely clients; many of them became his agents, charged with duties for church and state. John Islip, abbot of Westminster for almost twenty years before Wolsey's appointment as legate, under the Cardinal's direction took on an increasing number of roles for Church, Council and Crown over the course of the 1520s (see Fig. 13).[252] The abbot's affinity with the Crown was close enough to continue, after a fashion, the Benedictines' general chapter into the 1530s. That it never met after his death in 1532 was surely no coincidence.[253] By the time of Wolsey's own fall, Abbot Islip appears to have been one of the most active churchmen in government not to hold an episcopal see.

The agency of Wolsey's affinity was exceptional, but other senior prelates also made regulars active coadjutors in their own domain. The secular bishops of sees whose cathedral chapters were monastic appointed their own priors, and other superiors known to them, as their suffragans. This was not in itself a new departure, but the number of appointments, the length of their service, and the extent of their responsibility was greater than ever before. John Thornton, prior of Dover, served William Warham for most of his three-decade primacy; Andrew Whitmay, prior of St Bartholomew, Gloucester, served in the diocese of Worcester from 1526 until his house was suppressed in 1538.[254]

In the rural dioceses south-east (Norwich) and south-west (Bath and Wells, Exeter) where the incumbent bishops were of advancing years, the pastoral authority seen and heard most often was that of the heads of the county's regular houses: Bromholm, Castle Acre, Horsham St Faith, Leiston on the one hand, and on the other Bodmin, Bruton, Forde.[255] The significance of this agency given to them was heightened by the fact that these dioceses held such a concentration of religious houses. Regulars were drafted into seven out of eight secular dioceses in England, to Exeter (Thomas Chard of Forde Abbey, from 1510), Hereford (Prior Thomas Fowler of Monmouth), Lincoln (John Bransfort of Bury, from 1516, Matthew Mackarell of Barlings), London (Thomas Bele of St Mary's College, Oxford), Salisbury (John Pynnock of Edington Bonhommes), Wells (William Gilbert of Bruton) and York (Richard Wilson, prior of Drax, 1507–29).[256] It has been said that 'such numbers in early Tudor England' are difficult to explain, but it is surely an expression of a common clerical experience and cultural outlook, and shared expectations of the new regime.[257]

The Suffragan Act of 1536 served to extend regular involvement, notwithstanding its passage through the same parliamentary session as the first suppression statute. Former superiors of Breamore, Butley, Lindisfarne and Stanley, respectively, took up the suffragancies of Berwick, Marlborough, Taunton and Ipswich; the following year, surrendered heads of Margam, Milton, Sudbury and Titchfield were presented to Shrewsbury, Shaftesbury, Bedford and Thetford.[258] Robert Pursglove, only now presented to a priorate, at Guisborough (North Yorkshire), took the suffragancy of Hull; another new head, William More of Walden (Essex), was himself new to the status of regular, having been a secular clerk when he received the monastery *in commendam* (i.e. to hold the office and its income but not to occupy it); now he also held the suffragan see of Ipswich. This fresh cohort of regular prelates passed on without interruption into the clerical hierarchy that prevailed post-dissolution. In 1540 no fewer than ten men who had been professed to a rule – other than William More, all of them career religious – now held episcopal rank.[259]

Similar affinities arose among the regulars and the lay hierarchies around them, although the traces of them are fainter in the records. It surely was mutual exchanges of this kind that now saw boroughs and their neighbourhood monasteries reach a truce. At Gloucester, it does appear that the relationship was reset after 1509 by a combination of social (indeed, kinship) connections, the distribution of offices and even common interest in commercial ventures.[260]

Affinities held together by these ties were now able to steer appointments of influence on either side of the precinct wall such as the mayoralty or the stewardship; in a number of boroughs they took the position of headship of the house. The control of an oligarchy was conspicuous at Bury since the eldest son of a prominent family, John Reve, was planted in the abbacy, while his brother, Robert, and other kinsmen held office and property in and around the town.[261] The election of John Hamond at Battle in 1529 placed the house in the hands of a member of a family which had first come to prominence leading tenant opposition to the monastery's lordship.[262]

There can be little doubt that the agency of these affinities is also signalled in the instances of sudden conflict that have left a trace in the records. It was the force of one network at least, if not also its cuts across another, which explains the alarm raised over the election of an abbot at Muchelney in 1532. Unidentified 'friends' of twenty-five-year-old Thomas Inde propelled him into the abbot's seat there ahead of another four candidates. The same cross-currents were brought into focus by the Boleyn affairs at Tynemouth and Wilton.[263] The murder (by poisoning) of Abbot Matthew Deveys of Holm Cultram at his own dinner table might also be a hint that the affinities in which regulars now took active membership were at the same time closely bound to the brokering of power in regional society as a whole.[264]

The close association and collaboration of monastic hierarchies with their secular, clerical and lay counterparts directed the impulses of the Crown, Church and magnate society to supervise and reform their houses. There was no sudden surrender or complete subjection to external governance as has often been assumed. The heads of houses and other office-holders created in the course of these increasing interventions understood themselves to be – and in many respects were – not passive placemen but colleagues and coadjutors of the authorities on the other side of the wall. The circumstances of their appointments indicated that few, if any, were candidates without any context of their own. Those supported by Wolsey, any other bishop, the presiding magnate or the king himself, were already members of their own or associated networks and their arrival in the hierarchy often followed earlier exchanges of friendship, patronage and mutual service. Their relationships developed not as an unequal transaction between a subject and their lord (temporal or spiritual) but as collaborators bound by a common vision of renewal and reform.

From the first, Wolsey's entry into the matter of monastic elections was sought out, steered, and sometimes even manipulated, from within the house. He did not search the regular estate for possible points of entry; they were presented to him. Early in Wolsey's ministry, Abbot Kidderminster modelled for how the regulars' own ambitions for their houses, congregations and place in the world might be harnessed with many of those that he himself harboured for the Crown. The abbot raised with him the need for a good head at the tiny canon house of St Oswald, Gloucester, advancing the authority of his Benedictines in his own backyard.[265] His involvement in the governing chapters of the Canons and the Cistercians was also negotiated in the interest of internal hierarchies: at both, the Cardinal's presence enabled parties preferring the cause of their congregations' university colleges to prevail over their opponents; the triumph of a clique of Cistercian heads created a new governing elite, which was so well aligned to secular government that Wolsey's protégé, Thomas Cromwell, trusted them with the king's visitation in 1535.

The exchange of property and the (re)appropriation of seigneurial rights – pensions at a vacancy, for example – were more often than not settled, and sometimes proposed, on terms of mutual interest. Abbot Islip's willingness to part with Westminster's ancient freeholds in King Street, just beyond the north gate of the abbey, might be regarded as the final surrender of a defeated head.[266] Yet for a prelate who had been active in the Cardinal's affinity for more than a decade, and who represented the Crown in the supervision of regular affairs, the arrival of the king and his government at the north gate of his abbey was the fulfilment of its destiny as royal foundation. It was surely the prospect of the same special status being cemented that encouraged the priors of Beauvale, the London Charterhouse and Waltham Abbey also to agree to these exchanges.[267]

In Islip's leadership of Westminster, in Kidderminster's actions as a self-appointed spokesman for his congregation, and the positioning of the northern Cistercians at their chapter, it is possible to see the formation of a new model of governance for the regulars' estate. Each of these showed a readiness to release some of their houses' time-honoured self-determination and seigneurial independence in return for a defined role – material certainly, but also political and spiritual – in the royal programme; and, so it appeared, for the prospect that the machinery of the secular world might arrest heresy and advance their vision of reform. This was the particular vision of the leadership but there is evidence that the identification with the king and his government passed, or was passed, through the convent. In his guide to the daily service at Durham, the priory's cantor added the prayer-call, 'God Save King Harry'.[268] From Furness to Reading and on as far as Canterbury, prayers for the king were written into the commonplace books that cloister monks made for their own private study.[269]

The pioneers of a new dispensation between the regular establishment and the secular world did not live to see it realised in full. The first Henry Tudor was claimed by tuberculosis in August 1509, long before he could see how far his patronage of Westminster, the London Charterhouse, Syon and the nine Observant friaries would turn them into public churches, for better and for worse. Bishop Richard Fox died on the brink of his ninth decade (1528), apparently regretful, as he wrote in January, that he had been unable to return a greater rigour to the discipline of the regulars: the women he felt he should have seen 'mure and enclose'; the men he considered he had treated almost too kindly.[270] Since Wolsey on his deathbed was well aware that much of what he had built up, in physical fabric as well as in the practice of government, was already being taken down, he may have hardly hoped that his recipe for the rule, and reform, of religious houses might be followed by those who brought him down. Wolsey had been dismissed because the priorities of the monarch he had served for so long had quite suddenly and profoundly changed. By 1529 Henry was consumed by the case for the divorce; and in so far as he looked beyond this goal, his sights were on the garnering of an imperial power – material as much as territorial – abroad and at home.

Treaties, peace, and brokering the balance of power, hallmarks of Wolsey's policy for the Tudor Crown, were now pushed aside.

Yet in spite of the new imperatives, the Wolseyan approach to the regular estate persisted, and thrived. Here the king's outlook seems largely unchanged. It has been suggested that any residual sensibility he may have held for the religious ran dry during the case for the divorce, and as he began a new decade and a new marriage Henry's 'monachophobia' was already gathering pace.[271] Yet in the few glimpses to be found of the king's personal dealings there is no clear indication of a change of mood. He continued to honour his father's patronage of the friars at Newark.[272] His affiliations to a number of the heads of leading houses did not falter after 1529.

In these, the last years of their lives, the venerable abbots who had served his father before him garnered special praise. The king held John Islip to be a 'good olde father', for which reason he had been confident to commit the matter of the divorce to his counsel, though 'the pope may mearvayll why'.[273] Richard Kidderminster remained high in Henry's esteem to the very end: 'He who freely foreswears the honour of the world' (Qui sponte abiecit omnem honorem mundi), he reflected in 1531, weighing the abbot's monastic virtue as equal to his value in worldly affairs, 'a man of notable learning in divinitie and great experience and knowledge'.[274]

The old man himself expressed a father's affection for the king and for Cromwell, now filling the place of his former master: 'the increase off your honour and auctorite,' Kidderminster wrote, 'ys more to my confort in ihesu then I may expresse'. Perhaps it was a measure of the continuity he saw in their relationship that he felt able to affirm the compact that had been established between the Crown and his estate: 'that we may have the londe . . . we have so long possession of [as] the law ys with us [and] I and my brethren [are] all your fayzthfull bedysmen'.[275]

Henry's continuing acceptance of these 'venerandi patres' and their tradition was surely encouraged by the similarly strong attachments of some of his oldest and most loyal friends found at court. His favourite, Sir William Compton, who succumbed to sweating sickness in 1528, shared his interest in Kidderminster's house at Winchcombe where he planned twin chantries as a memorial for himself, to be placed in the trust of the abbot; a further six religious houses were to mark his obit (the date of his death) with a commemorative Mass.[276] Henry Guildford, comptroller of the king's household, who died suddenly in 1532, requested burial at the Dominican friary in London, with all the humility of a friar, 'at my burying be nother pompe nor solempnitee'.[277] George Talbot, Henry's helpmate in Wolsey's dismissal and the divorce, also conceived of a family chantry to be placed in the joint custody of Welbeck Abbey and Worksop Priory.[278]

Perhaps there was a touch of filial nostalgia in the friendships inherited from his father, but in the years from 1529 Henry also cultivated monastic allies of his own choosing. John Salcot alias Capon had, as abbot of Holm, apparently been complicit in Wolsey's annexation of his monastery's income. Through the Cardinal he was able to come close enough to the royal household to be recognised as a reliable go-between to Queen Katherine, to whom, it was reported by Charles Brandon, duke of Suffolk, he was 'alwais kind & loving'.[279] In 1531, Brandon called him a 'great clerk' for his guidance on the divorce.[280] Another of Wolsey's protégés, John Chambers, appointed at Peterborough in the closing months of the Cardinal's power, was close enough to the royal circle to receive a New Year's gift in 1532. Richard Whiting, whom old Islip had seen elected to the abbacy at Glastonbury, was also honoured with a present from the king in the same year.[281] Another seven heads of Benedictine houses were honoured by appointment as King's Chaplain.[282] It was four abbots, of Bermondsey, Bruern, St Albans and Westminster, only raised to their offices since 1528, each one under some or other influence of the king or his ministers, who presided at the christening of Princess Elizabeth in 1533.[283]

The king's outreach to these religious and their houses was affirmed, and increasingly directed, by the network-building of the counsellor who now exerted most influence on his policy, Thomas Cromwell. In the previous decade in the service of Wolsey, Cromwell had gained a ground-level understanding of monastic foundations. In 1525 he had watched over the closure and sequestration of Bayham, which had proved to be the most provocative of the Cardinal's dissolutions.[284] He had taken on the practical task of seeing Wolsey's preferred candidates into prominent abbacies. Not only did he know these promoted prelates; their relation to him – palpably so in some of their letters to him – was that of loyal clients.

Given Cromwell's historical reputation it is readily assumed that his own attitude to them was coolly detached, cynical and manipulative. In fact, their ties may have been more personable and the trade between them more mutual. The reverend fathers admired him. Old Abbot Kidderminster congratulated Cromwell on his 'honours and autorities'.[285] They also knew him for his warmth. John, abbot of Launde, recalled their 'olde acquaintaunce', and especially how 'as you and I came oon daye from Withystock . . . I fell backward in the snow [and Cromwell, so he implies, helped him up]'.[286] A memorandum, apparently of 1533, groups together senior prelates and clerks in Cromwell's service, from the archbishop of Canterbury to Richard Leighton. Perhaps they were correspondents, those with whom he had business. Among them there were three Benedictine abbots whose election he had engineered, William Edys (Burton), William Repps alias Rugg (Holm) and John Salcot alias Capon (Hyde), together with John Bird, Provincial of the Carmelites, and another unidentified 'Friar Nicholas'.[287]

As these names indicate, Cromwell was selective in his cultivation of monastic ties. The observant religious, not only the reformed Franciscans but also the Carthusians and Birgittines of Syon, were, it would seem, a cloister too far. In spite of the ties of the courtiers around him, even in 1534 he wrote a reminder for himself to 'seek owt the pryor of charterhouses name'.[288] But Cromwell's chosen monastic allies, of the Augustinian and Benedictine traditions, were close indeed. He looked for their assistance in advancing the king's causes; and he was inclined to keep their favour with special concessions from the strictures otherwise imposed on religious houses from 1535. Perhaps he also allowed himself their friendship: 'ye wolde take the payne to walke with me or my brethren abowt our busynes'.[289] His inclination to hold them apart from any general suppression persisted almost to the very last phase, in the winter of 1539–40. Certainly, as he came into his own ascendancy in the years up to 1534, he had not cut himself off from monastic England any more than his master, the king.

With a refreshed and expanding cohort of monastic leaders under royal patronage, it might be said that as the 1530s began, the compact between the regime and the regulars had found a new strength. If so, there was further rein-forcement from the bench of bishops. Wolsey's surviving peers, Fisher and Warham, were now its elder statesmen. They held to his vision of observant clois-ters but did not share his taste for constitutional change. The younger generation, Lee and Longland, were no less committed to the cause of monastic discipline but both came to cultivate their own circle of regular allies, and even turned to them as their suffragan deputies. There was also a prominent newcomer whose sympathy for the regulars was stronger than almost any of his colleagues. John Stokesley had been appointed bishop of London in 1530 for his record as an opponent of

Lutheranism; but his loyal service in this cause cloaked a conservatism. In the same year that he took his see it was said he was too trusting of friars.[290]

One of the regime's monastic affiliations new at the turn of the decade, to Waltham and its abbot, Robert Fuller, affirms the continuity in outlook at least as far as 1534. The abbey, well-placed for royal hunts in Waltham Forest, had long been a haunt of the king and his inner circle. Henry was there with Anne Boleyn before they were married and as the work for the divorce wore on from 1528 to 1530 he visited for part of every summer. In the wake of Wolsey's death, Abbot Fuller's hospitality was duly rewarded. In the new year of 1532 he received the grant of the site and principal manors and parishes of Blackmoor Priory together with selected properties of Wix Priory, both of them houses in Essex originally closed for the purpose of endowing Wolsey's college at Ipswich.[291] The grant was in exchange for the gift of the monastery's manor of Stanstead Abbots (Hertfordshire) to the king. Such transactions, which enabled the Crown at one and the same time to alter, alienate and augment the endowment of a monastery, had been pursued by Henry and Wolsey to tie a number of prestige houses in service to the regime. By this means, Abbot Islip's Westminster had been drawn under the wing of the Crown: before the old abbot died in 1532 the abbey's best properties in the town of Westminster had been traded for Thames Valley estates.[292] Westminster Abbey was already a royal chantry; in this act of re-endowment it was drawn towards a new status, that of a royal dependency.

In 1531–33 Henry continued in this vein, now reinforced by the statutory authority of parliament.[293] Abingdon, Christ Church, Canterbury, Ramsey, Reading, St Albans and Tynemouth were persuaded to exchange properties.[294] Waltham was a particular target.[295] The demands clearly strained Fuller's command over his canons, 'theyr consente . . . I do moche dought,' scribbled the anxious abbot to Cromwell, 'it may please yow . . . cum over and speke with them'.[296] His continued cooperation was encouraged with the prospect of a compensation that would be as much personal as institutional, the assignment of the revenues of the priory of St Bartholomew, Smithfield. Now Waltham appeared to be on the threshold of a transformation as a palace-monastery. Not since the new Lancastrian monarchy had repossessed Westminster was royal government so anchored to an abbey. From 1532 to 1534 the king's writ ran out from Waltham.[297] The reconstitution of royal foundations continued further. From 1533 the Charterhouse at Sheen and the abbey of St Albans were put under pressure to offer up prized properties in predetermined exchange.[298]

Henry's inclination to exercise authority over the regular estate was unchanged. In fact, interference in elections to monastic office from court and council became more frequent and the impulse came from the king. Cromwell was active but in reaction, 'to know who the king wooll have', as his memorandum for the abbacy of Beaulieu revealed.[299] They were perhaps of one mind in taking up the instrument of *commendam* that Wolsey had modelled at St Albans. Now a number of the new cohort of monastic allies were cemented in government service with these grants. Robert Fuller was given licence to petition for papal approval for holding the priorate of St Bartholomew *in commendam* in July 1532.[300] The Benedictine John Salcot alias Capon was invited to take the see of Bangor with his abbacy at Hyde in November the following year.[301]

The supervision of the wider network of heads of houses, which Wolsey had kept up from the time of his legatine mission, was now routinely exercised.[302] If there was any turning point to be noticed here, it was in the regular recognition of the interference as customary practice. When a new prior needed to be chosen at Butley in 1530, the convent acted instinctively to 'compromit' to Wolsey, not knowing that he had already been stripped of his office. Now, in matters of monastic governance, they turned automatically to the king.[303]

Henry also returned to the Cardinal's agenda of reform. The sudden decision to dissolve the Augustinian priory at Aldgate – Christchurch, also called Holy Trinity – in February 1532 has often been seen as a point of departure, the first step towards a dissolution movement that would surely sweep countrywide, a revolution 'definitely begun'.[304] This is how it might seem in retrospect, with the advantage of knowing what would be achieved by the spring of 1540. Yet it may be more accurate to associate it with the mood that carried over from Wolsey's fall: the determination to act directly under royal authority wherever corruption, neglect or depopulation had been detected. Of this, before attention turned to Aldgate, there had been other signs. When Prior Ralph Snelson of Calwich (Staffordshire) died in April 1530, he left a community of just one. As was now to be anticipated, the selection of his successor was made a matter for the Crown, notwithstanding that the house was a cell of Kenilworth Abbey. The king accepted the approach of at least one monastic candidate but held the office vacant, 'resting' at his pleasure for a full three years. Closure only occurred after the suppression statute was passed. A canon still 'abideth to supervyse' in May 1536.[305]

It seems it was in this spirit that Cromwell also now showed some credence in the proposal made by Sir Patrick Finglas for the targeted suppression of monasteries on the border of Anglo-Ireland.[306] The summary sequestration of Aldgate was a return, after two years' abeyance, of the policy that had removed twenty-eight foundations in four years. The process differed only in one respect: a papal faculty was no longer required. The sentence passed summarily on the canons was reminiscent of the fate of the Premonstratensians at Bayham seven years before.

It is difficult to see in Henry's treatment of Aldgate, any more than of Waltham, a rising impulse to destroy monastic England. Perhaps more apparent is quite the opposite: a conviction, growing ever stronger, that the collateral of centuries of regular foundations might be harnessed to the ambitions of his Crown. On the eve of the Break with Rome, the king and, probably, the Wolseyan Cromwell, looked to a future where monasteries, ever more subjected and reformed, might continue to play their part.

Five years after a Boleyn girl had tried to govern a monastery, the governors of the monastic establishment gathered to make her a queen. 'All the monks of Westminster goyng in ryche copes of golde with 13 mitred abbotts,' reported Charles Wriothesley, as the monks of the royal abbey publicly embraced the king's beloved Anne at her coronation on 1 June 1533. These Black Monks, led by their new abbot by royal appointment, William Benson, were at the head of the procession; according to Wriothesley the king's chapel, bishops, archbishops and the lords of parliament followed on behind.[307] England's monastic hierarchy had been transformed but now it appeared to be poised for a new chapter in its long history, at the heart of public affairs. On this day, the expectations of Abbot Benson and Queen Anne were surely much the same.

V

THE KING'S COMMISSIONS

A fortnight after Easter 1535, Sir John Markham, sheriff of Nottingham, set out into his county with a new commission arising from King Henry's 'supreme headship of the Englyshe churche'.[1] With two colleagues, he was charged with making a survey 'for the rate and the trew value of all spiritual promotions and possessions withyn the countie'. The valuation, which in the form of the massive ledgers returned to Westminster came to be known as the 'Valor ecclesiasticus', was intended to cover every component of the institutional Church, of which the religious houses were generally the largest and oldest of all. It was to reach across the realm. Markham's riding party of commissioners was replicated in every county. Such a survey had only been tried once, 250 years before, and then it was at the behest of the Roman papacy not an English prince.[2] Here then both the principle and the process were untried.

For Sheriff John it started badly. Just seven miles from Nottingham, at Beauvale Charterhouse, their progress was blocked. 'The proctours and others of the convent apperyd before,' reported their clerk, 'at shewyng the pryour was absent and in London.' Then they demanded that their 'facioun' of 'lay persons' should be present with them if there was to be any inquiry made of their property. 'Seyng them of such scruploisite'; they stood on their dignity. Markham thought to dismiss the stand-off with an 'exortacion frendly', and he offered them a lawyerly summary of the grounds of the headship: 'dilating the styrye true of Lucius and

206

Eleutherius and of Ethelartus and Lera his wiff and Gregory and Austen'. The Beauvale contingent was unmoved, and one of their proctors spoke for them all that they 'beleve feremly that the pope of rome is supreme hede of the church catholike', a conviction he wold hold 'usque at mortem'. Markham wondered if he should make an example of them; but for now at least they withdrew.

It was a year of commissions for different causes but under the same premise. In the summer fresh writs were issued to further teams of commissioners to carry out a visitation of every religious house in England and Wales. Now there were new riding parties passing over the same trail, sometimes at each other's heels; and the regulars gathered in their chapter houses to treat with the representatives of the Crown for the third time in little more than a year. Six months after the scene at Beauvale, at the end of September at Bruton another commission was suddenly arrested in its tracks. Thomas Legh and his clerk presented their patent as king's visitors to the canons of the Augustinian abbey. Not for the first or last time in his career there was a portentous, pompous bearing to Dr Legh. Some of the king's commissioners carried a thirst for reform but what fired Legh above all was the Crown's vision of an imperial authority. His reading of his writ was reported in a laboured Latin that perhaps captures something of the sight and sound of the moment, posturing and awkward in equal measure.

The abbot, John Ely, stepping forward (comparuit), cut Legh short, arguing forcefully (allegavit) that the house had only just received another visitor also acting under royal authority, Richard Leighton, also identifying himself (ut asserebat) and claiming to be charged with the king's commission. Legh, conscious that his own authority was suddenly undercut, blustered petulantly about the high purpose of his own commission, 'for the praise of God, the honour of the crown and the increase of the divine cult and true religion'. But the abbot deflated him again, showing the injunctions for reform which Leighton had presented to him three weeks before.[3]

These encounters seem out of step with the traditional narrative of an uncompromising assault on the religious houses advancing after the royal supremacy had been secured in parliament at the turn of 1534. Henry's new headship of the whole Church was pressed home over the next two years in a succession of royal commissions intended decisively to see them 'annexed and united to the Ymperiall crowne of this realme';[4] an investigation of the foundations of their wealth and seigneurial and social power; a root-and-branch reform of their administration, domestic and observant life; and then, the suppression of those too small, weak and unwilling to submit.

As ever in the history of Henry VIII's reign, the evidence for the effects of the commissions is not nearly as robust and persuasive as the parliamentary statutes that prompted them. Representatives of royal authority passed repeatedly through the precincts of almost 850 houses in no more than two and a half years, from the summer of 1534 to the winter of 1536–37. Yet there is some record of their presence surviving for scarcely a quarter of them; their progress through some regions – especially in the west of England and Wales – is virtually untraceable; for a number of houses right across the kingdom there is nothing documented of their dealings at all. The valuation surveys have survived well, but many of them were known to be incomplete even at the time of their submission. The course of the visitation can be followed in outline but its contents, the inquiries made, the reforms imposed, can be known in detail only for the commissioners' eastern circuits – East Anglia and Yorkshire. To a very great extent, a view of these two years relies on the broken chain of correspondence between the regime and its agents, and what, if anything, appears among the remaining archives of the religious themselves.

The impression they give recalls the scenes at Beauvale and Bruton. In spite of the supremacy, the king's commissioners were uncertain of the authority they carried. They disagreed about it with one another and like Richard Leighton and Thomas Legh in Somerset, sometimes they decided to interpret it for themselves. For their part, the religious were not suddenly cowed by the Crown's novel powers. In fact, their instinct was to lock horns with this external authority much as they always had done, with bishops, legates and monarchs in centuries past. Theirs was no simple opposition: like the monks at Beauvale, sometimes they accepted points of principle while they wrestled over procedure; there were many who, like Abbot Ely, seized the initiative from the commissioners, taking up the challenge to reform, only on their own terms. The challenge of their responses was compounded by those of interested parties that surrounded them: the 'frendys' such as those that pressed into the chapter house at Beauvale alongside the monks, and also the neighbourhood and the local diocesan authority. The king's commissions changed the religious houses' relationship with the Tudor Crown. They left their mark on their internal life, even if they did not change it beyond recognition; but they did not deliver it either to the point of complete submission or to the brink of collapse.

The Act of Supremacy, the first outcome of the parliamentary session of November 1534, proposed a revolution in the governance of the regulars in England. Since 1485 the Tudor regime had reasserted the traditional role of the Crown in the direction of royal foundations, and established a new oversight of all religious houses and their institutional affairs, from the elections of their heads to the measures of their own congregational chapters. It had also demonstrated, often verbally, but latterly with visible actions, a commitment to the cause of reform. But all of this had occurred within the time-honoured framework of state and church affairs. The regime's reaches into the monastic world had been made with some of the most traditional instruments: the chartered right of the founder; the authority of a papal legate allied to the interest of the Crown; and at least the cooperation, often the collaboration, of diocesan bishops themselves holding office and influence in royal government. In other words, it was something of a medieval reformation.

Now, the statute broke with past history; perhaps in no respect more so than in the approach to the monastic and mendicant population. It assigned to the king all 'prehemynences jurisdiccions privileges auctorities ymuntyities profitis and commodities . . . of the same church': no more might any house, whatever the terms of its original charters, its congregational affiliations or the battery of dispensations and exemptions it had built up, claim independence. This 'full power and auctorite' of the monarch encompassed both material lordship and moral leadership. 'From tyme to tyme' he might 'visite represse redress reforme ordere correct restrayne and amende.' It was a Christian duty, 'to the pleasure of Almyghtie God' and 'the increase of virtue yn Chrsitis Religion' and the measure of good kingship, to 'conserve . . . the peace unite and tranquilyte of this realme'.[5] For the Crown to sponsor a visitation of the monastery was not unknown; a nationwide visitation was unprecedented. The scale and scope of the plan implicit in the statute's 300 words resounded among those who moved in the circles around the commons and the court in the winter of 1534. Eustace Chapuys, the ambassador of the Holy Roman Emperor, Charles V, felt the febrile climate, caught 'murmur and hatred' in the air, and even sensed a certain caution in the king.[6]

Yet the first responses from the regulars suggest more continuity than sudden and transformative change. In many respects, they reacted to each intervention as they had already become accustomed to do in their dealings with the Tudor government; they recognised instinctively their own interest in cooperation with the Crown, showed an acceptance, sometimes even a ready willingness, to adapt the manner of their lives, and on matters of contention looked to activate their own local affinities. Their cohort of bishops, suffragans, provincials and royal chaplains, already closely affiliated to the government circle responsible for the King's Reformation, now exerted an influence across their congregations; some of them, such as the new mendicant and Cistercian leadership, led their colleagues into their new statutory world.

In fact, in the wake of the statute, the regime itself, the king, his counsellors and the commissioners under them, was inclined to apply this novel authority by way of the old routes of persuasion, patronage and compromise. In spite of its new powers, at the heart of Henrician government it seems there was an instinctive wariness of innovation. European printing was almost a century old in 1534 but the king's commissions were a manuscript enterprise, with all its characteristic tendencies to disagreement, error and delay. Nor did Henry and Cromwell at once turn to executive instruments; rather they looked to rule the regular estate more completely by its own means, that is to say, charters confirmed by the seal of the head or the corporate body.

Before the winter of 1536–37 summary justice was a last resort. Of the small minority of monks and friars arrested for their refusal to acknowledge the supremacy, few at once faced public execution; some submitted, some escaped, while those who were left in prison were as much the collateral damage caused by continuing indecision. It might be argued that the new relationship brokered between the Tudors and the religious houses after 1485 served to prepare those houses for the events of 1534 and provided many of them with the means to endure in its aftermath.

The imposition of this new kingship was as seismic in its execution as it was in principle. A path for the supremacy itself was prepared by the enforcement of the Act of Succession passed eight months before.[7] The submission of the entire regular estate was secured before the supremacy became law. By December 1534 out of some 800-odd houses and a population of perhaps as many as 12,000 men and women, there were just two left, amounting to sixty men (no women) who remained formally in opposition. It seems at the end the commissioners made a dash to be done by the last day of the year. The pace and reach were greater than for any other government act over the course of these years.

More significant still was the degree of coordination, which saw acceptance of the king's 'greate and invyolable' jurisdiction 'contrary' to the Roman pope, made by chains of houses, one day after another; some on the same day. In London this meant that the city's entire populace of regulars accepted the king's will in little more than seventy-two hours.[8] The commissioners who undertook the valuation, visitation and suppression of the smaller houses over the next two years not only failed to match it but fell backwards into a confusion that caused some foundations to be confronted more than once and others not at all.

The successful settlement owed much to the political compact which had formed around the leadership of the regulars at least since the beginning of the decade. The king and his chancellor and now principal secretary, Cromwell, could assume a common understanding of policy across the prelacy: John Clerk of Bath and Wells, Fisher of Rochester and Longland of Lincoln had already demonstrated their acceptance of the Crown's reach into Church foundations. Some of those more likely, at least by virtue of their age, to adopt a conservative position, Warham at Canterbury (d. 1532), Fox at Winchester (d. 1528), had passed away. A few of their older generation still lived, such as the ninety-year-old Bishop Nix of Norwich (d. December 1535), but they removed themselves from the scene entirely, taking no part either in the administration of oaths to recognise the succession, or in the parliament and convocation that approved the statute at the end of the year.

The new men now succeeding them owed their elevation to the personal favour of the king, Cromwell, or both: Cranmer (Canterbury), Lee (Coventry and Lichfield), Lee (York) and Gardiner (Winchester). Rowland Lee asserted his new episcopal dignity in directing the Carthusians of Sheen to take the oath just two weeks after he himself had taken up his see.[9] Stephen Gardiner made a most lavish demonstration both of loyalty and command of his monastic subjects by staging the submission en masse in the Great Hall of Winchester Castle (see Fig. 14), an impromptu convocation in which archdeacon and deans joined with abbots, priors and wardens of friaries, 'which al did take othes very obediently'.[10]

The king and Cromwell could also look out on appointees of their own making prominent in almost every congregation. Over the previous twelve months (1533–34) there had been government supervision of no fewer than fourteen elections of heads of Benedictine, Cistercian and Augustinian houses. Among them had been premier houses of each congregation, Westminster, Malmesbury, Rievaulx, Beaulieu and Leicester.[11] Some had seen protracted interference and palpable pressure, 'to turn the duty of the monks', as Thomas Legh had averred at Malmesbury, 'towards the king'.[12] The most prominent of all of these new heads, William Benson of Westminster, took his seat as a parliamentary abbot for the first time in the first parliament of the year.[13]

Some of these men were now conspicuously bound with the new order prevailing after the divorce. The abbots of four Benedictine and Cistercian houses, Bermondsey, St Albans, Stratford Langthorne and Westminster, presided at the christening of Queen Anne's daughter Elizabeth in September 1533.[14] The provincials of the Augustinian, Carmelite and Dominican friars, respectively George Browne, John Bird and John Hilsey, had been propelled to the top of their congregations for no other reason than their place in Cromwell's affinity. Bird had proved his loyalty by accepting the unenviable mission to persuade the divorced Katherine of Aragon to give up her title as queen. Hilsey, after all, was scarcely a decade from his first profession as a friar. In July 1533 still his name was less familiar than his rising reputation as an effective respondent to the reactionaries in the pulpit.[15] Less than eleven months later he was provincial.[16] The pre-eminence of these men exerted more than a symbolic power over their colleagues. They were travelling evangelists for royal authority, Browne covering the most ground from the eastern Home Counties to the northern province.[17]

The effective force of this affinity was arguably greater because of some notable absences. There was no Franciscan provincial in office in 1534. The capitular governments of the canons and monks had neither been abandoned nor defeated, but the new dispensation of recent years had edged them ever further to the margins of institutional life. The General Chapter of the Benedictines had been summoned only twice since its confrontation with Wolsey nearly fifteen years before. The last meeting to transact business in the customary way was held as far back as 1527; it seems writs were issued for another meeting in January 1532, although since there is no record of the presiding chair, and only glancing references to the proxy delegates appointed by some houses, perhaps it did not convene. Already it had drifted beyond its three-year cycle, which may reflect diminishing demand for its oversight across the congregation.[18] The Cistercians' Commissary General was last heard of in 1531.[19] In a way that might have surprised and alarmed their forebears, in the face of the royal supremacy, the monks gave no thought to their own governing bodies but received the king's commission directly or at the hands of their diocesan.

The apparent readiness of the regulars to recognise the supremacy may have been aided, even accelerated, by their experience of another conspicuous novelty that preceded it, the king's divorce. In retrospect some communities thought of 1533 rather than 1534 as the moment that presaged their calamity.[20] Leading Benedictine houses had surely been following the advance of the king's Great Matter for four or five years, since some had loaned or lost their books of Church history and law to the cause. Yet it seems it was not until the marriage was formally dissolved that it elicited a general response across the congregations.[21] Here there were sudden and, in houses of some importance, serious signs of strain in the loyal consensus which had so recently settled; and the capacity of the courtly clique of leaders to steer, or at least to stifle, seemed less than assured. According to Maurice Chauncy's memoir of the London Charterhouse, when messengers of the king descended (devenissent) looking for the prominent house to pledge its support for Henry's new queen, Prior John Houghton made the bluntly objective reply that it was not his concern if the king cast off or caught himself a wife (quam vellet rex repudiare aut recipere uxorem). He was smartly dispatched to the Tower of London for a month.[22] Perhaps it was indicative of a wider will to question policy that although only a handful of heads closely allied to the regime took their seats for the parliament, for the first time since the turn of the decade they packed out the March meeting of convocation.[23]

The elite of the Benedictines at their Oxford *studium* were vocal critics of the divorce and lampooned the person of the king. They made the king's marriage the subject of their seasonal skit in December.[24] Outside the university but still within its social networks, at the Cistercian Rewley Abbey (Oxfordshire), Abbot Nicholas Austen fumbled in his effort to hush a row between his monks over the rights and wrongs of the divorce.[25] It is difficult to imagine that the sharp rebuke of the king for 'bastardyng the Lady Marie', made by a Wiltshire burgess, Thomas Temys, had not resonated at Lacock Abbey where his kinswoman Joan was head.[26] It seems that casual critical chatter was widespread and communities were none too careful to keep it inside their enclosures. William Copley, a lay brother of Roche Abbey, was arraigned before the court of King's Bench after calling Queen Anne a 'bawd' and disparaging the marriage as being 'under a gusshyn [cushion]'. Copley apparently made the matter worse by absconding; he was detained at Spalding some seventy-five miles south of his house.[27]

Yet these outbursts were soon stifled. Monastic communities saw, in many cases for the first time, the direct intervention, over and above their own governance, of agents of the Crown. Conspicuous troublemakers were taken into custody and subjected to examination. There was no capital punishment except for those caught up in the cause of the alleged visionary Elizabeth Barton, but some of those detained for their criticism of the divorce were certainly imprisoned for some time. The spectacle of public execution for Barton and her supporters, in which were counted two Benedictines and two Franciscans of Canterbury, was imprinted on monastic and mendicant horizons in April 1534, at the very moment that they were called into their chapter houses to consider the oath for the succession. 'It causeth us all woofull to lament and sorow', wrote the 'congregation and monasterie' at Canterbury.[28] Nor can they have been oblivious to public calls from excited reformers for the harsh repression of 'the pope . . . his mynestres'.[29]

The sounds of dissent issuing from communities of nationwide influence caused the king and Cromwell to initiate targeted measures of reform. In the winter of 1533–34 the Carthusians in London and the Birgittines at Syon were subject to informal but persistent instruction. In a curious rotation, Bishops John Fisher, John Stokesley of London and Cromwell's clerk, Thomas Bedyll, conveyed to them 'the lernyng of theologians and that also of lawyers'.[30] The king himself may have contemplated a comparable exercise in propaganda in Benedictine circles, since he consulted his father's old ally, Richard Kidderminster of Winchcombe, in what must have been the last weeks of his life.[31]

Perhaps it was not only the quick and sharp action of the regime that curtailed criticism of the divorce. By the close of 1533 the loyalists that the king and Cromwell had found, or led into the monastic leadership, were firmly embedded. In fact, of the twenty-two Augustinian and Benedictine abbots who had lent their weight to the divorce petition of July 1530 only three – Thomas Barton of Colchester, John Islip of Westminster and Edmund Whalley of St Mary's, York – had since died.[32] The influence of this affinity was apparent both above, in the direction of the Tudor regime, and below, towards their own congregations. When a list was prepared of divines who might do battle for the supremacy, it named both the Cistercian abbot of Thame, Robert King, and Edward Baskerfield, warden of the Oxford Franciscans. It was no coincidence that the last known Chapter President of the Benedictines was John Islip, who since at least 1524 had served as an agent of royal authority in his congregation, a king's commissioner, under a cowl.[33]

The great majority of the regulars digested the supremacy and spoke the accompanying oath of succession without demur; and above all, without the unguarded opinion recently they had been given to air. In this respect, the difference between the archival record for these months and the one for the two years that followed is striking: what was returned from the visitations of 1535–36 was never quite the same from one house to another; from May to December 1534 government clerks found they could copy out a continuous list of confirmations, more or less in sequential date order. This is not to suggest that each community merely gave its nodding assent. The cases for the king's supremacy and against that of the Roman Pope were formally expounded to the professed, drawing on the discourses familiar to many of the men as career religious and university graduates: custom, history, theology and law; as one commissioner characterised it, 'diligens, resun and policie'.[34]

At times there was keen debate, some of it heated. The initial assent of the Observant friars at Richmond was secured only after their Carthusian near neighbours from Sheen had treated them to their 'exhortations'. It was not without an implicit pressure, if not intimidation. Archbishop Lee (York) and Bishop Longland referenced their visitorial powers. Gardiner's choice of Winchester Castle was not coincidental; of all the possible settings in his diocese, it most embodied the lordship of the secular arm. There was pressure applied on other matters which surely made the principle of the supremacy the least of all present evils. In June, Anne Colte, abbess of Wherwell, was suddenly swept up by allegations of scandalous conduct with Bishop Stokesley, a case confected apparently to challenge both plaintiffs. For the rest of the year she was occupied in clearing her name.[35]

Yet there were few reports of either collective or individual opposition. It may be telling that the immediate challenges reported seemed to turn on questions of procedure. There was some disquiet that the Latin of the charter confirming the assent of the religious suggested that they had acted at the behest of external authority and not of their own will; on the same grounds, there was some grumbling over the use of the convent's common seal, which by custom could only be used at their own initiative. The Beauvale Carthusians disputed the very definition of their corporation, insisting that 'lay persons', perhaps their stewards rather than their patrons, were also part of their body.[36] Their colleagues at Hinton would do nothing without their head, who in the summer of 1534 was away on pilgrimage.[37] The descent of agents of the Crown to codify the new status of the king and his successors did act to revive distaste at the divorce. The 'divers libels' of Dr Gwynborne, a Franciscan of Beverley, reported to Cromwell in July returned to the disparagement of the royal marriage heard in many houses in the previous year.[38] First-hand observations of the mood inside the chapter house are scarce, but perhaps typical was the pragmatism suggested by the Cistercians of Stratford Langthorne, who 'dyschargyd' briskly the 'busynes and controversy' (a word which baldly acknowledged the weight of the matter), for it was 'the kynges lawes and decres'.[39]

This, and perhaps a collective sense of awe at the unprecedented performance of chapter-house oath, may have persuaded some to curb the resistance they felt from within. This was the later testimony of Lawrence Blomham of Woburn Abbey, who four years on recalled, 'at the first tyme that I was sworne, I dyd not ley my hand apon the boke and kyse but whas over passyde be resound of mouche company'.[40] It may be a measure of their politic compliance that a desperate apostate monk made raucous claims in May (still six months before the statute) of imminent rebellion by 'religiouse men', the king's most 'mortalle enemys'.[41] An anonymous chronicler of St Augustine's Abbey, Canterbury, did not see this as the year's great threat to religion but worried rather over the spread of the new radicalism, voiced by 'barking heretiques in sundry places in England'.[42]

The case for the supremacy was not only accepted but also actively argued for. Thomas Reading, Cistercian monk of Kingswood, passed the closing months of the year composing a tract on the subject which he presented to Cromwell as a New Year's gift.[43] At St Albans, Abbot Robert Catton, an established member of Cromwell's affinity of regular allies, commissioned the printing of an English life of the abbey's patron saint which ended with a dedicatory prayer for the king, his new queen, their succession and his supremacy over the Church:

O protomartyr of Brutis Albion
Pray for his spouse / his louynge lady dere
His riall queen Anna / notable and famous
Indowed with grace / and virtue without pere.
Pray for our princes / that she may be prosperous
... Pray that theyr issue / haue fortunate succession.
... Pray for the princes that this londe gouerne
To rule the people by prudent policie
Pray for the chyrche that lyke a clere lanterne
By good ensample their subiectes for to gye.[44]

It seems the contents of other books were offered to lend authority to the argument, in the same way as they had been in building the case for the divorce itself. An ancient volume of papal letters in the library at Battle Abbey was given over to a government agent; a thirteenth-century manuscript containing Thomas Becket's defiant letter to Henry II reached Archbishop Cranmer's hands from St Augustine's, Bristol.[45] A record of papal privileges granted to the Franciscan friars was provided for the royal collection from the Benedictine abbey of Abingdon; at Bath Cathedral Priory, William Holwell cooperated with William Tildysleye's request to make a 'scrutynye' of the library.[46] Of course, these were the political acts of superiors, but here they may not have been out of step with their brethren. The monk John Horwood collected statements of papal authority from texts in his conventual library and scribbled a little quire for Cromwell, in front of whom he mocked his own name in religion, 'Placentius', which he described as 'secundum papisticos'.[47] An old copy of the old favourite chronicle of the popes of Martin of Troppau, either at Langdon Abbey or Merton Priory, was marked, 'Yf ther be any nayme of the bysschope of Rome or ells any other matter apertayning to his usurpide powre in this bowke contayned I doe vtterly renownce them'; a force that was perhaps self-conscious conformism.[48] An unknown Cistercian hand at Whalley Abbey scribbled his own prayer for the royal couple in a parchment booklet containing the history of the house.[49]

It was surely a reflection of the view within the convent that communal books containing the papal title were so conscientiously corrected. The fine new martyrology of Canterbury Cathedral Priory, only written in 1516, now saw every papal title erased neatly with a knife.[50] Surviving examples show more consistency in this than in the removal of the names and feast days of the calendar saints, which became a statutory requirement four years later. Someone at Crowland took the trouble to find and erase the one papal title in the rubrics of an old Gradual, a reference to the legendary patron of English Christianity, Gregory the Great.[51] The corrections reached beyond the calendars kept in the church, in the choir and at subordinate altars, the domain of precentor and sacrist, to the great cartulary volumes kept in the archives and chronicles used for instruction, communal reading and sometimes public display. The master manuscripts of the annals of the monastery at Ely and St Albans were judiciously amended. It may be a measure of their different outlooks or of their self-confidence that the papal title was erased from the convent's copy of their chronicle but not from the prior's own.[52] In a sequence of privileges copied into the Peterborough Abbey cartulary, the papal title was neatly scratched away (see Fig. 15).[53] At Shaftesbury even the inventory of the muniment room was made safe, with the heading of the list of papal bulls erased.[54] Corrections were also made to the books in their personal possession; at Woburn it was under the eye of the watchful abbot.[55] This was not mere official compliance but organic, collective will.

Persistent resistance to the supremacy was confined to just eight religious houses, of men only, out of more than 800 in England and Wales, and in each case it was shown only by a minority of their members, no more than fifty professed religious, the slightest percentage of the total population. The first indications of a significant challenge that might be sustained were seen at the London Charterhouse and Syon as early as the opening months of the year. Here discomfort over the king's headship was a direct progression from objections to the divorce voiced in the closing days of 1533.

Then, in the late spring, as the commissioners' circuit of houses and the commands of the bishops began, each one of the six convents of Observant Franciscans expressed their unwillingness to submit. The response from all parties was another demonstration of the degree of political understanding that had settled between them. There was a collective constraint from the drawing of battle lines, as the agents of the Crown most familiar with and, it would seem, friendly towards these communities entered into dialogue with them, with the neighbouring prelates, and with regular representatives joining them at intervals to amplify the message. The advocacy of the agents was orchestrated by Cromwell, perhaps with some personal oversight of the king, not lacking discomfort of his own at the spectacle of his scheme stalling in the very churches his father and he had recast as the custodians of Tudor religion. Still, the cooperation of secular and regular prelates of the front rank was secure. Bishop Stokesley's effort to reconcile the resistant was exhaustive; forever toing and froing between the city's regular precincts he confessed himself driven to 'vertigo'.[56]

The challenge of the Carthusians was spread through the congregation, north and south, but it did not command the full support of any house. The first instinct of the provincial priors was not to nurture any disturbance but to neutralise it. Seven who had toyed with refusing the oath at Hinton were found 'conformable' after their prior, Edmund Horde, returned to the house.[57] Prior John Wilson of Mount Grace put five obdurate brothers in prison; two others he let leave for a house across the northern border; at Axholme (Lincolnshire) and Beauvale, the main body of the community detached from their priors, Augustine Webber and Robert Lawrence. Both were in London by the turn of the year, a separation which may have held the mood of their houses below open rebellion.[58] Prior Henry Man of Sheen faced disorder in his house that caused him to be held in custody in the Tower but then he joined in advocating conformity to his riverside neighbours at Syon Abbey. Whether or not it was as a result of their witness to his perils, the affiliation of some of his Carthusian brothers now turned avowedly loyalist. In the months that followed, Robert Marshall of Sheen was ready to be Cromwell's informer to show himself a 'trewe subiecte' of 'our soveran prince'.[59] Under pressure only one monk at neighbouring Syon, Richard Reynolds, previously a champion of Elizabeth Barton, proved determined to resist.[60]

The response of the Observants likewise lacked cohesion. The community at Canterbury may have already partially dispersed following the loss of their prior to the Barton affair in April. The same had claimed the prior of Richmond and in their loss the remainder were receptive to conventual debate. In June it was reported that they were on the point of submission.[61] Two of the Newark convent, Hugh Payne and Thomas Hayfild, had left the house heading for the West Country, apparently preaching the papal monarchy as they went, 'yn all places wher they come they persuade the peple . . . to call[e] hyme pope and saynge they will dye in hys cause'.[62] Perhaps the Greenwich house was an exception. Regarding the fall of the Maid of Kent at a distance, their conventual rejection of the supremacy was decided at the outset and defended, 'stiffely' and 'in oone mynde of contradiction and dissent'.[63] But even here there had been evidence of division, revealed to Cromwell directly. When the marriage and succession were first matters of public discussion, the Observant lay brother Richard Lyst had warned him 'some of owre company . . . yows . . . them selfe both against god the kyngis grace and yow'.[64] Several (unspecified) friars were said to have exiled themselves already a year before the obligation of the oath arose.[65]

The supremacy presented the regulars with an unprecedented statutory requirement that challenged custom and corporate privilege as well as the tenets of their theology, but it was enforced in steps that seemed almost painstakingly in keeping with the conventions of their institutional and intellectual life. It was a self-conscious strategy. Cromwell encouraged his agents to enable communities to consult the books of authorities that could steer them towards, if not to settle, their acceptance. They were to allow them to air their own interpretation of the matter, if there was a chance that their gloss, spoken or written down, might galvanise the greater number. The dispatches of Thomas Bedyll and Bishop Stokesley passing to and fro from the London Charterhouse and Syon describe this vividly, but talk of treatises on the supremacy from Benedictine houses beyond the capital point to it being prompted elsewhere. Even the examination of the pairs of Carthusian priors and preachers of Syon was conducted in the accustomed form of a visitor's interview.[66] Cromwell's commitment to this course may have caused frustration among some of his go-betweens; what they saw at Greenwich and Smithfield were learned religious ready and resilient for a long debate.

The recourse to judicial action came so late, in the spring of 1535, a full year after enforcing the succession, that it appeared almost as an afterthought. The Carthusian priors were imprisoned but with no indication of their ultimate fate; a handful of the monks from the London house followed them but at intervals of several months over the course of the next year. It seems there was no predetermined plan. Scribbled remembrances of about this time prompted Cromwell to find out for the charterhouses 'what the kyng wyll have done'.[67]

The greater part of the Observant opposition across five convents escaped any extended period of custody. The Newark two, Payne and Hayfild, were detained in Cardiff and dispatched to London but were later released; Payne then secularised and took a parish living. He and his colleague had hoped to arrange passage from Cardiff to Brittany; at least one of their number did reach another jurisdiction, across the Channel.[68] Perhaps it was only the two London communities, Greenwich and Richmond, that were targeted for punishment at this moment. A correspondent of Lord Lisle reported seeing two carts 'full of fryars' in the city, which he 'herd sey [were] come unto the Tower' and 'more come aftur'. In his history the Marian friar Thomas Bourchier claimed 'very many' (quamplurimi) were thrown in prison (in carceres fuere ejecti); later in his text he counted thirty-two. A memorandum probably dating from some months later, if not the following year, noted six still in London but only one, John Forest, in prison, and seven of London and Greenwich who were known to be dead; perhaps having been in custody.[69] A different approach may have been encouraged by their offer, conveyed by Sir William Fitzwilliam, to make terms with the king. Cromwell contemplated licensing them to transfer to Ireland.[70] Decisive was the fact that they left their houses almost at once; according to Chapuys as early as 11 August 1534.

Still, there was no impulse to see their presence erased. A year on, when recording candidates presented for ordination, the clerk compiling the bishop's register at Lincoln still identified friars from Newark as 'ordinis de observantia' (of the Observant order).[71] Perhaps there was also a residual sense of identity closer to the centre of government at Richmond, since it was reported that in her last months Katherine of Aragon (who died in early January 1536) still anticipated burial in an Observant church.[72] In the year of its passing there was no execution purely as a result of the statute. Those of the three Carthusian priors followed in the summer of 1535, but only after the Crown had prevaricated for almost a year and a half. It would be difficult to see that the episode of the supremacy had established a decisive position on the accommodation of the regulars to the king's reform. Certainly, from the fragments of their correspondence that survives, there is little to suggest that any was recognised by the parties involved.

It might be tempting to see the collective suppression of the Observants as a congregation in August as a turning point of policy and procedure, but it was a pragmatic reaction to the deadlock at Greenwich, the painful progression of exegesis at Richmond, and the break-up of a number of the other houses. If it was a statement of intent it was one overwritten by the re-foundation of each one of the houses as Conventual friaries in the course of the next eighteen months. Their principal patron was King Henry.

The caution of the Crown was reflected in the patchy enforcement of the related requirements of the statute: to take possession of jewels more in keeping with the king's own majesty, to uphold the royal headship, and to deny papal authority in the written and spoken word. In the later months of 1534 and the first part of 1535, the precious contents of the regulars' sacristies seem to have been left largely undisturbed. The inventories compiled almost a year later in the course of the visitation cite plate and other high-value objects in quantities which do not suggest the residue of a collection already broken up.

Cromwell certainly kept monastic treasure in mind. An undated remembrance which may well pre-date the visitation was for 'all the juells of all the monasteries in Englonde', although it may be a measure of how far any plans had yet formed that the only particular object he noted down was on his own doorstep, an emerald crucifix at St Paul's.[73] It may be that before the visitation other prizes were prioritised. Cromwell was still pursuing the plate and jewels that his old master, the Cardinal, had left behind him at Ipswich;[74] he also intervened over an allegation levelled at two Cistercians of Newenham and Pipewell of the embezzlement of gold put in their safekeeping for the Chancellor of Lincoln Cathedral.[75] What came to Cromwell or the king at this time from the religious houses appears to have been more by chance than by design. Sir James Carre found he was able to help himself to plate at West Dereham (Norfolk) because the house had fallen vacant as he arrived.[76] The bishop of Bangor took advantage of the turmoil at the London Charterhouse to sue for treasures of his see which had been lodged there in 'Dr Hurdes' dayes'.[77] These were no greater losses than those of the recent years in which lordship had wrapped itself around them, many of which they had pursued through the secular courts.

There is no indication that in securing the supremacy the commissioners made a systematic search of book collections; where the supremacy was acknowledged at convocations of secular and regular clergy together, royal authority did not reach into the precinct at all. There may have been a check of books made at Canterbury Cathedral Priory, but interference in the monks' books may have been due to the arrival of Cranmer quite apart from the enforcement of supremacy.[78] The selective removal of the papal title in the surviving books adds to the impression that for now, at least conformity was taken on trust. Nor was there yet any general supervision of preaching either within the precincts or in the churches, chapels and public crosses under their jurisdiction. The reports of provocative preaching passed to Westminster in the months and years that followed may reflect a degree of frustration that the officers of the Crown had not kept it closely enough in view. Generally, the restraint of government gave tacit encouragement to individuals and interest groups to advertise conformity, or the lack of it, for themselves. The regulars joined city and town governors, local lordship and urban governors, in making representations of their own. Prior Provincial Hilsey turned from his copybook presentation of the submission to a report on the unsafe preaching of his colleagues.[79] Even at Syon, which had been under the eye of the Crown's agents since the divorce, the only report on preaching that reached Cromwell came from a member of the house itself, the confessor.[80]

Before the end of 1534 a pattern of communications in two registers was beginning to emerge: a conventual view conveyed by the superior under the common seal; and covert reports, often relayed by a third party, and always carrying some expectation of a quid pro quo. This was the tangible effect of the enforcement of the supremacy on the religious houses: not a complete subjection but a recognition of the politics of conformity and of the consequences when it was poorly played.

The events of the year, both on a public stage and inside the religious houses, had cast the supremacy as a cause of great principle. In so far as the news had passed through the regular network at all, the awareness that certain monks were in custody awaiting punishment unknown, and a select congregation of friars had been closed, seemed to affirm that the principal change to their position was in the representation of royal authority. For monks and canons, whose historical understanding of the friar drew them as a caste apart, outside of the customary jurisdiction of church and state, the extinction of the Observants perhaps held no general significance at all. The fact that there had been no widespread disturbance in their own conventual life, and that their acknowledgement of supremacy and succession had cost them nothing more tangible than the pressing of their common seal, can only have encouraged this view.

Yet as the last of almost eight months of these chapter-house submissions were made in the last weeks of 1534, parliament passed into statute the authority for further interference of a quite different order. The statute of supremacy (26 Henry VIII c. 1), which won assent on 3 November, allowed the king the right to 'visite, redresse, reforme order and correcte . . . all such abuses . . . whatsoever they may be'. There was no specific reference to a commission or its timing but the scope when it came was abundantly clear: 'any maner [of] spirituall authoryte or jurisdiccion ought or maie lawfullye be reformyd'. It was followed days later by the declaration under the terms of the statute for the payment of First Fruits (26 Henry VIII c. 3) to 'examyn serche and enquyre' for the 'true and just hole and entire yerely values' (IX) of each and every ecclesiastical foundation. Here 'commyssions in the kynges name' were promised; and by implication imminently.[81]

Beyond the parliament chamber, in the gravitational centre of the king's government, with Cromwell in attendance, the expectation of prompt action to pursue these commissions rose rapidly in the first weeks of the New Year. But for the majority of regulars this prospect, and perhaps the very fact of them at all, did not appear on their horizon much before the spring. The best informed of them, the two dozen superiors who sat in parliament, saw no reason suddenly to return home. The conventual observance of the season, and the external itinerary of the superior, seemed to have continued at many houses, perhaps even more routinely than they had done recently, given the clamour of court politics twelve months before. Of course, the questions of 1534 reached beyond the customary framework of each one of the congregations, but the fiscal imperatives of the Crown, and a visitation, were hardly unfamiliar pressures, and their closer affinity with the Crown over the past forty years had persuaded the leading foundations that loyal service was the best safeguard of their own needs. It is conceivable that some read these signals from parliament as a return to business as usual after the unprecedented dramas of the divorce. Abbot Thomas Rowland of Abingdon now looked forward to advancing his side of a long-standing argument with a local gentleman, John Audelett, which Cromwell and the king had wearily refereed.[82]

At the turn of 1535 it does appear that almost all of the pressure and anxiety raised by these commissions was experienced by the government itself. The scope of the statute for First Fruits, the urgency of the need and the limited infrastructure to carry it forward nationwide combined to undermine the valuation from the start. Instructions for the survey may have been devised at the heart of government but the drafting of them appears disorganised. Cromwell's own memoranda dated to this time speak more of discrete projects concerning particular houses – 'to shew both the bokys of the valew of . . . Cristis churche to the king'; 'the graunte of St Bartholomews' – which for the past two or three years had been his stock in trade.[83] The surviving manuscript copies have the appearance of notes made by individuals for various purposes, not blueprint copies rolling out from a single master text. Although none of the correspondence of the commissioners makes specific reference to them, their responses suggest that the instructions came to them in no common form. It seems for some they arrived first by word of mouth and they had already begun their task before any written word was received.

Long into the year, even after the first returns had been made, the commissioners continued to call for guidance from the Westminster government. In the diocese of Bangor the survey was fully underway when Sir Richard Bulkeley pressed Cromwell 'in as breve a tyme as ye convenyently maye', whether and what 'we shall tayke the valuwacion'.[84] A letter sent by Bishop Gardiner of Winchester in May implies that it is only the latest in a continuing correspondence over the precise scope of the survey and the values to be recorded. 'As I required your advise in myn entre and begynnyng therof', the bishop admits, and although he has carried it forward nonetheless, making his own judgements about what may be included, he anticipates that some 'remedy' may be needed in the return, some 'thing be otherwise thenne it shulde be'.[85] The collective voice of the Council of the North was less inclined to shoulder this responsibility, bluntly setting before Cromwell the 'certayn dowtes and ambiguities conteyned in certain instruccions'.[86]

Beyond these difficulties in the design of their brief itself, the commissioners faced practical challenges. There seems to have been no common pattern to the dispatch of the commission itself and its distribution within dioceses. It is apparent from the first correspondence on the subject returned to Westminster that it was Easter (28 March 1535) before those furthest from the capital received any word about it at all. Sir Richard Bulkeley received word at Conwy (Clwyd) only on Good Friday.[87] Their return was required by the end of May. Regardless of the pace of the communications, the common view from the regions was that the term was too short for the scale of the task. From York, Archbishop Lee was politic enough only to hint at the impossibility of a prompt return, writing that '[they] trust not to be too long behind their day'.[88] His episcopal colleague John Clerk of Bath and Wells was more provoked, complaining that the task was 'a very busye long and laboriose busynes' that would surely require 'a longer day which it may like yow to grant'; as might be expected of a leading churchman, he was also wont to remind the government that a good portion of the time available would be taken by the Easter observances.[89] The Council of the North made a straightforward plea, 'humbly besech[yng] . . . for a longer day to retourne and certifie our said commyssions wherin we shall make all the convenient spede we can or may'.[90]

Looking at Llandaff diocese Sir William Morgan measured the timetable against the terrain, and commissioners scattered '40 or 50 miles asunder'.[91] In the hill country of Herefordshire, Rowland Morton felt the same. '[The commission] requyrynge grete sirutyne and attendans,' he wrote, 'and the nowmbyr of relygyous howses in theys parties no parte off the realme lyke' and 'the teghte and weghte yn the cumpas theroff . . . shalbe as largely allottyd to my parte'. He continued, '[I] have enterprysed and entered into the saye busyness . . . alle other [causes] layde aparte according to my dute', and 'albehit that day and dyght hit befolowde and applyde as requryth . . . yett tyme wylle hartely suffice every thynge particularly to be stallyd batyd somyd engrosyd and putt in perfeccyon'.[92] In fact, Morton, could not lay all other business apart. He was diverted from the survey to investigate a murder.[93]

It was to be anticipated that regional authorities might think first of the reasons for delay given their instinctive discomfort at the fiscal reach of the Crown, but the government's most committed agents also pushed back on the pressure of time. 'I have latelye receivyedde the commisstion,' wrote Richard Southwell from Norwich in the third week of March, 'I fere me being great and full handyd with thother [commissions] . . . we shall doo little or at least not soo moche as we here desyr.'[94] The conjunction of valuation and the levy of the subsidy that burdened Southwell left the commissioners short not only of time but also of hands appropriate to the task. Morgan at Llandaff frankly admitted that his auditors were nowhere to be found. From Bath and Wells and Norwich it was reported that the other causes of the Crown, and the customary business of the county, not least the Easter Sessions of the Assize, had prior claim on all the appropriate officials. In Chichester there was precious little power in the man with whom it was charged. Eighty-two-year-old Bishop Robert Sherborne (d. August 1536) was in the last nine months of his life. 'Such . . . is his stomach to honour the king,' reflected one of his colleagues, yet 'by his great age [he is] scarce abel to bear it'.[95] The Council of the North spared nothing in its estimation of its available manpower: 'In all the cuntreys from Trent northward be but thre auditors for ingrosement of the books . . . and one of them a very old and past paynes taking.'[96]

The conditions for such a meagre force to conquer the region were also far different from the previous year. Plague had returned, patchily perhaps, but where it was found the effects were severe: in the Welsh March it was 'very sore' and the auditors were understandably reluctant to travel very far, still less to let those who had been moving in and out of houses to report to them directly.[97]

In these trying, even threatening, circumstances, the commissions reached out for reinforcements from local agency, more varied than the (largely diocesan) lordship that had secured the supremacy, and certainly less securely aligned to the interests of the Crown. Drawn into the survey of the south-west were the magnate dynasties that had extended their control over the religious houses during the course of the past half-century. Of course, any outward commitment they showed to the cause of the Crown was not the same as compliance. Sir William Courtenay, who shared a monopoly on the monastic stewardships west of the Somerset border with his cousin, Henry, marquess of Exeter, accepted the king's commission but pursued it at his own pace. In the autumn he was pressing Cromwell on a matter of personal patronage; meanwhile his return was made late and incomplete.[98] His Dorset neighbour, Sir John Horsey, charged with the commission in a county where several families rivalled one another for a controlling interest in the chain of substantial Benedictine foundations, inevitably diverted from the commission to make a personal claim for the patronage of the principal abbey at Sherborne. With the expedient fee of 500 marks paid to Cromwell, while the valuation return remained outstanding, he presided over the election of a new abbot, the candidate being described as his 'frynde' John Barnstable. 'All persons off ye monastery [are] right well plesyde and contentyde Syr,' he advised Cromwell, surely thinking as much of his own point of view. He apologised that 'Y come nott to yow at thys tyme' to settle the fee, remembering now his duties to the Crown, 'I can yn no wyse be absent for thys schyre'.[99] At Tilty, the interference of the principal patron stalled the commission completely. The residence of Margaret Grey, dowager marchioness of Dorset, was deemed an insuperable obstacle to making the return. Cromwell was so confounded that he initiated an investigation into her right to the patronage, which persisted for a further three years.[100]

Diocesans charged with the commission were likewise not disposed to carry it through with quite the same politic disinterest as they had adopted for the supremacy. In York, Archbishop Lee, whose commitment to Crown policy wavered ever more even in the summer that saw the execution of Bishop Fisher, confided to Cromwell '[I] wold have thowght you had been special good to me, if I had been lefte ouzt of it.'[101] He recited a litany of obstacles standing in the way of a return, leading with the least convincing, his own 'lytle skyll of such things'. Nonetheless declaring that 'I shall applie myself', every week or so in May he made pessimistic reports on the state of the return.[102] When at last he made the return on 'the last of June', he reiterated his 'lacke if skille' and asked Cromwell to accept 'any defaule bee in it in good parte', for 'I have for my parte done the best I coulde.'[103] The rhetoric of incapacity never left Lee's letters, but there can be little doubt that the shortcomings of the return were well managed. Perhaps the most conspicuous omission was the value of the prebends of his own Minster church.[104]

The secular and spiritual lordship of the region were the tried if not always the trusted levers of royal authority, but their uncertain cooperation and the general absence of appropriately qualified professionals caused the regime to engage the elected officers of local government. Archbishop Lee's reluctant service was reinforced by William Wright, his city's mayor, and his company of aldermen.[105] These interests may have stood at one remove from the seigneurial or material interest in monastic foundations shown as much by diocesans as by neighbouring magnates. But this did not mean that they were wholly disinterested contributors to the commission. Mayor Wright and his officers aimed to advance their own civic causes through their service, and after the submission of the return even presented Cromwell with a 'powre tokyn for a remembrance' to keep his patronage alive.[106]

The uneasiness of the Crown's collaboration was exacerbated by the role of the regulars themselves. It may have always been Cromwell's intention to realise the benefit of recent supervision of appointments to headships; the political and practical pressures made it a necessity. Abbot Robert Fuller of Waltham, now one of the most senior of his regular protégés, was charged with the commission for Colchester and the county of Essex.[107] At Winchester, Prior Henry Broke was given the delegated authority of Bishop Gardiner to supervise the valuation for his own house; the return was made in his name.[108] The commissioners may have often taken the obvious expedient of passing the task to those best prepared to complete it. The return from Goring Priory was signed 'be [by] me Dam Margarete Wodall pryorese'.[109] This seems to have been the pattern along a chain of Thames Valley convents.[110] Further west, at Eynsham, the professional script of the return perhaps points to it having been written out in the convent's chancery.[111]

It is possible that the cluster of cartularies and registers written out in fine copies at this time, a larger group than survives from any part of the previous hundred years, were a response to their part in the survey. The appearance of the commissioners' signatures of endorsement on a deed newly drawn up at Battle Abbey in July suggests that their business was carried forward alongside the routine administration of the house.[112] If so, it was a conspicuous change from the circumspection with which they had confronted the supremacy. The regulars had not submitted to the survey; they joined it. Perhaps in some places they took ownership for themselves.

In these circumstances perhaps the main achievement of the valuation was the fact that it was completed at all. Although only a handful of returns had been made by the original deadline in May, many more arrived at Westminster at or shortly after the close of Trinity Term. By the beginning of October, albeit twice the term originally intended, they had all been received. The state of completion was not what so many of the commissioners – in defeat or in defiance – had predicted; a value was recorded for the main temporal and spiritual properties of the ecclesiastical foundations of each diocese. The coverage of regular property was quite significantly more complete than for the variety of secular foundations. The weakness was not in its general coverage but in the completeness of the return for each house. The uncertainty of the instructions was compounded with the differences of the surveyors, their status, skill and quite probably their degree of disinterest, to create returns that identified sources of income and calculated their values each in their own terms.

Some were open about the omissions. Bishop Gardiner wrote that for Winchester diocese, whereas charitable expenditure had been counted in respect of cash alms, no assessment had been made of the provision of schools and scholarships, although in the regulars' rolls these were accounted for as an aspect of their charitable enterprise.[113] In Oxford diocese, the commissioners had complained that 'the bokys' (administrative records) of the colleges and monasteries were 'so longe and tedyous' they had found it difficult to extract all that was required.[114] In York, Archbishop Lee damned his own return even before it had been evaluated at Westminster. The heads of some houses 'did not apere afore [us]'; and what accounts were made were themselves defective, since they were not set out in the 'partishment' after the 'auditor's fashion'.[115]

Such a return could hardly compromise the material condition of most houses, but the scrutiny of their affairs did cause them immediate disturbance. Cromwell seems to have chosen the moment of utmost interference as the commissions began passing through the counties after Easter to secure control of the Augustinian priory of Bisham, and settle a rising member of his regular affinity, William Barlow, into the priorate.[116] Framed by the king's business of the valuation, the instinctive challenge of the hereditary founders, the Salisburys, resident there for Easter, was soon faced down.[117] The eighty-year-old abbess Margaret Tewkesbury of Godstow was edged towards resignation on the eve of the valuation of her house; the prospect of transactions of the abbey's property had been among Cromwell's remembrances for the past year.[118]

The requirements of the audit itself lent him leverage to intervene, divide and rule over a long-running dispute between Abbot Thomas Rowland of Abingdon and his Chief Steward, John Audlett. First, Cromwell pressed Rowland to accept the arbitration of the commissioners arriving to view his account. But Cromwell professed not to be ready for such a sweeping review, as 'I and my cowncell have labored continually in makyng uppe suche bokys and recompts and as yet the seid bokys be no fully made.'[119] Then, he raised the prospect of a hearing before the king himself, expected at the town in high summer.[120] Still, the abbot asked for time. In August, Cromwell directed the commissioners to cross-examine Rowland under oath. He 'utterly refused', pleading instead for a more complete examination of his accounts that had been contemplated in the spring.[121] Rowland urged the government to 'requyr[e] and command[e] theym to tary here in examynacion of the sied accompts untyll suche tyme as they have viewed the hole accompte wherby they may make a trew certifict therof'.[122] The commissioners reported that four months of persistent pressure on the abbot had disturbed local interest, his 'diverse frendys' thinke in us moche extremyte to cause thabbate to be sworne'.[123] But the attrition had driven the abbot towards a surrender of authority beyond the original obligation of the Valor. The reach into the regulars' affairs seems to have been recognised across Westminster. During the summer Queen Anne shadowed Cromwell attempting her own interference, over expenditure at St Mary's Abbey in York and an election at Vale Royal Abbey in Cheshire.[124]

Perhaps the greatest disturbance for most of the houses was the protracted process of the valuation, which left the 'bokys of accomptes' incomplete when the new commissioners for a visitation first arrived. Abbot Rowland himself saw scarcely ten days' respite in September between the last of his dealings with Cromwell over the matter with Audlett before Richard Leighton arrived carrying the king's writ to visit and impose injunctions for reform.[125] Leighton himself had carried out his duty during the dog days of summer at a speed that seems to have been too much even for his master in his chambers at the London Augustinian Friars, Cromwell. To avoid undue delay Leighton took a team of horses, although he found it difficult to find them sufficient 'barne . . . mete and litter'.[126] Already at the end of July, Cromwell had cautioned him apparently for hurrying ahead of his instructions. Leighton's rejoinder was that this was how he had understood his commission: to proceed at maximum pace and minimum cost: 'not to be by the provision of any of the harbingers [the religious houses]' and 'thynkyng that it had bene your resolute and full mynde that I shuld then depart'.[127] Leighton had passed west through the Thames Valley into Gloucestershire before the beginning of August, completed a circuit of Somerset and the Avon region as far as Bristol by the middle of that month, returning to Oxford and Berkshire before its end, turning then to the south-east, Hampshire, Sussex and Surrey. There he seems to have swept through Waverley Abbey in the space of an afternoon and 'before day' the next morning was 'ready' to make the fifty-mile ride to Chichester.[128] In an undated letter presumably from late August or September he felt confident to claim to Cromwell that the northern province itself 'we myght well finisshe by Michaelmas or sone affter'.[129] Leighton found that the superiors were surprised at the force of his coming: 'off late I have recevyd . . . your surrogate', was the disapproving response of Abbot John Essex of St Augustine's, Canterbury.[130]

Some superiors were not to be found at all: those summoned to parliament remained in session in July; others were, as would be expected given the season, at their summer manors. So sudden was the turn from valuation to visitation that even leading houses did not fully digest its import until after the visitors had left them.

Perhaps for this reason alone, the beginning of the visitors' circuits raised no general alarm. At first, superiors did not invest the visits with any greater significance than introducing further interference following the transactions of the past twelve months. There is no doubt that they felt very keenly the novelty of the enterprise: the prospect of laymen and civil lawyers put in charge of an ecclesiastical process the main purpose of which was to effect religious and spiritual reform. Yet they did recognise the principle of the visitation as an integral part of the framework of the royal supremacy, which had been set out in a parliament in which they were represented.[131] The visitors were 'deputes under your goodness beyng generall visitours', as Abbot John Burton of Oseney acknowledged in a letter to Cromwell in mid-September.[132] Although a royal visitation was unprecedented, it was not news. The monastic hierarchy had witnessed, if not joined, the discussion of the principle in the parliamentary session of the autumn just past. The leadership of the friars was firmly primed. The visitorial progress of John Hodgkin, the Dominican Provincial, had been halted by the king himself in April 1534, and Hodgkin had been ousted from office.[133] A sequence of Latin articles apparently drafted at this time set out measures to enforce the supremacy among the friars and to initiate a survey (elenchum seu catalogum) of each and every one of their properties and possessions (omnium et singulorum ... auri et argenti ... aliorum bonorum mobilium).[134] A fair draft, if not a final copy, appears, undated in a second manuscript.

It might be inferred that when the oaths were taken from them in the early summer, some form of visitation of the friars' convents was also carried out, although there are no answers to any inquiry now surviving and no mention of such a process in the letters passing to and from Cromwell.[135] It is possible that the precedent was diminished in their minds by their understanding of Church history and the stories of reforms and visitations demanded by monarchs in the distant past, and in living memory, by the first Henry Tudor. As the commissioners approached the diocese of Durham, the regulars rode out to meet them displaying attitudes of respect and duty that disarmed even the self-confidence of Thomas Legh. He was prompted to write to Cromwell about the spectacle, observing 'specially thabbots', who seemed to demonstrate how well they 'knowe ther bowden dewtye towards ther prince and suffrayne'.[136]

The palpable break with the past was the visitation's parliamentary origin. It had been the most explicit statutory power of the Crown set out in the terms of the supremacy, not only in principle but also, referencing the incidence of canonical abuse and heresy, as a pressing need.[137] The line of sight from the formulation of the statute in November ensured that this next commission was raised on foundations far more developed than the last. In fact, prospective articles of inquiry to be used in a visitation may have been prepared weeks, even months, before the parliamentary session began. The draft actions for the friaries indicate that the regime's thinking about the enforcement of the supremacy was connected to the notion of a disciplinary process at an early stage. Two drafts of articles, unattributed and undated, survive in the same anthology of government papers. The largest draft sets out a total of eighty-six questions touching on most aspects of administration, discipline and the constitution of the foundation. Seventy-four questions address aspects of any monastic foundation; a further twelve specify female communities.[138]

It may well be that they represent an early and provisional view of the necessary scale and scope of the visitation; certainly the subsequent letters exchanged between the visitors and Cromwell suggest that not all of them approached the communities on their circuits with these questions in hand. Nonetheless, the full complement can capture the expectations of the inquiry which were present at the outset. Questions of financial administration and governance were prominent but they also called attention to the performance of religious observances, and arrangements for the entry of novices and their preparation for ordination, the collective and individual discipline of the convent, and the quality of personal morality. No fewer than six questions (four of them referring to female religious) called for the evaluation of their virtues. This reached further than the customary inquiries made by episcopal or congregational visitors. Since the mid-fourteenth century the Benedictine chapters had employed uniform articles of inquiry in their triennial visitations but they were fewer and more selective.[139]

The most significant departure from custom, however, was neither the scale nor the substance of these clauses but their form. Both episcopal and congregational visitations were carried forward by interview, each professed member of the house having, for a moment, their voice heard. These articles of inquiry empowered the visitor to direct the inquiry and held them to a predetermined course, not to be diverted or deceived by their interlocutor; they also encouraged them to address themselves largely, if not entirely, to the leadership, such as they could establish it.

The questions pursued by the visitors were complemented by corrective injunctions, implemented at the end of their inquiries.[140] The surviving record of these, like the questions themselves, is only of provisional drafts; again, it might be inferred that early thinking on the injunctions never was translated into a script delivered uniformly by every one of the visitors. In early July 1535, when the circuits were already underway, Richard Leighton urged Cromwell to 'conceive a formale boke' of injunctions, suggesting that as yet each commissioner had been left to interpret the task of reform in their own way. Even so, there may not have been very much distance between their views.

The two longest sequences of injunctions, respectively of twenty-seven and thirty clauses, are almost identical, the longer adding measures for the management of outsiders entering the enclosure and the provision of a teacher of Latin grammar. The twenty-seven are written in the hand of Cromwell's legal clerk, Robert Warmington. It may be that it is a fair copy of a draft that Cromwell made after Easter 1535 when he joined the king's progress into Gloucestershire; around Warmington's script are amendments in Cromwell's own hand.[141] The thirty injunctions are in the hand of John Prise (also known as Ap Rhys), who in the spring of 1535 was a notary public increasingly employed by the king and Cromwell; within months he would act as registrar for the visitation.[142]

One other, sketchy outline appears to have been prepared by Richard Leighton, already active in Cromwell's service in the enforcement of the supremacy. It has been suggested that it constitutes a contribution to the preparations for the visitation, but it contains only three substantive clauses, all of which concern the conformity to the supremacy itself. In fact, it may belong to the efforts of 1534 rather than the preparations for the fresh commission in the following year.[143]

In the event the different drafts may not have cohered into one, common code, but this should not diminish what was a further challenge to the familiar customs. Injunctions were always issued after the event of a visitation; there might be many of them (as many as twenty-five) and they might tackle seemingly minor details of daily life in a religious house, but they never pre-empted the visit; nor were they set upon them as a fait accompli, but likely to be the subject, post hoc, of a lengthy negotiation.[144]

The clauses challenged the established principles of monastic visitation, giving authority to the king's vicegerent as general visitor, and prescribing a code to be applied to every foundation regardless of the customs of its order and the terms of its own jurisdiction; that is to say, an independent or a dependent house, and if the former, also accustomed to exemption from local (i.e. diocesan) authority. Yet in their approach to the conventual life the clauses contained few novelties. The degree of regular discipline, the adherence of individual religious to the require-ments of their rule in respect of dress, diet, the possession of personal property, the receipt of money, mobility and sociability had been the first concern of any visita-tion from its early evolution as governing machinery in the thirteenth century.[145] Establishing the profile of the professed community, its present size, and how recruitment was handled, had become a priority for an ordinary (i.e. episcopal) visitation, the written record of which typically would begin with a list of the community, specifying their office and status.[146] In the past half-century, the commitment of prelates to the pedagogic values of Christian humanism had encouraged especially close attention to the provisions for the teaching of novices and male juniors preparing for ordination.[147]

Inquiries into the fundamental terms of the foundation itself, and its endow-ment, 'how the lands given by the first founder were given, and by others' and 'by what tenor and terms they are held', certainly were not the routine business of visitors, who concentrated on the current conduct of conventual life, but they were hardly unfamiliar with the experience of any house. It had become virtually a matter of course that the formative grants and privileges of the house fell under scrutiny whenever it brought its business before the courts, whether the king's or those of the common law. In fact, these questions may have been in the front of their minds at any rate, given the renewed interest in their endowments met in recent years both from the Crown and secular lordship.

These half-dozen questions effectively synthesised what the Tudor regime had been pursuing piecemeal, as the opportunity arose, since it was first established half a century before. The interest in the personal morality of the religious has often been upheld as the signal of a new determination to do battle with the very basis of religious vows. But the behaviour of individuals, their social and sexual liaisons, had always featured in the visitations, both those carried out under the external authority of the bishop and those investigations undertaken by their own congregations.[148]

In the latest capitular visitation of the Benedictines to be documented, in 1527, eight monks were accused of disorder so violent the abbot feared for his life, while two others were suspected of 'incontinence' (sexual liaisons), one of whom was alleged to be an occasional drunk.[149] Under the traditional method of open-ended questioning in a private interview, these human dynamics naturally had tended to dominate the testimony. The subject of these articles would not have surprised any regular, male or female; the difference now being that they did not raise it voluntarily but were drawn towards it deliberately by the visitors themselves.

The injunctions have also been taken to be a transformation of the norms of conventual life. Yet even the portentous preamble that was prepared to introduce them, calling the professed to their 'hearty observance', was nothing more than a repeat of the call to accept the king's headship and reject the papal monarchy to which almost all religious houses had submitted upwards of six months before. Certainly common to all forms of the injunctions that were circulated was a clause requiring a daily prayer of intercession for the 'happy and prosperous estate' of the king and his queen, Anne. Yet this too only codified what had already been spoken in their oath, which, from the evidence of a Furness notebook, to the verses of Abbot Catton of St Albans, was already widely observed. The greater part of the proposed clauses turned sharply away from the recent upset of precedent and returned to the territory of reform repeatedly trodden by episcopal and congregational visitors since 1485; and, at irregular intervals, since the time of the papal reforms of the fourteenth century. Here were the same prescriptions for the education and preparation of entrants to the religious life, for the support of a fixed number in university study, for the due rendering of accounts annually by the superior and the obedientiaries, for the professed not to consort with seculars or the opposite sex, for their general mobility to be curbed and for all beside the superior to share in the common life of cloister, frater and dormitory.[150] In one of the drafts there was one additional requirement that gestured towards more recent concerns: it was specified that the monks of the London Charterhouse should receive claustral instruction three or four times weekly.[151]

Certain time-honoured controversies were revisited, such as the danger to conventual discipline of there being more than one door into the enclosure; and the presence of children and youths, sharing in the life of those professed to their vows. Three clauses that appear in the drafts did reflect current preferences for monastic reform: to expound the rule 'in English as plainly as may be'; for a daily lesson of scripture 'of one hour, to which all shall resort'; that no entrant be professed before the age of twenty-four 'compleat'.[152] Still, these were not new propositions.

The same vision for a monastic formation matching that of the secular priesthood was set out in injunctions issued by Archbishop William Warham in his metropolitan visitation twenty-four years before.[153] Bishop Fox had put it into effect for the monastic women of his diocese when he printed his translation of the Rule of St Benedict in 1517.[154] John Fisher had attempted to apply these strictures throughout his thirty-year supervision of Rochester diocese.[155] Looking back at 1535 from the vantage point of the Edwardian Reformation, a daily lecture in scripture might be read as a measure of evangelical reform, but the *lectura* had a long monastic history and had been part of the discourse of reform at least since the Fourth Lateran Council of 1215. There was some sincerity in the reflection in a draft bill that the king 'sent . . . his trusty commissioners . . . only intending a charitable and quyet reformation'.[156]

There were just two clauses among the draft injunctions that jarred with this conventional vision of cloister correction and reform, with the capacity to unsettle institutional and internal life. All brethren were prohibited from leaving the precinct 'by any means'. No 'reliques or miracles' were to be shown, and gifts to and for the same, and for images, were to be given instead to the poor.

The first clause, although it neither confirmed nor denied any possible exemption to office-holders, appeared to apply to monasteries of men the same sentence of permanent enclosure which under a papal decree, *Periculoso* (Boniface VIII, 1298), had been imposed (at least in principle) upon regular women for more than two centuries.[157] It was not entirely without precedent and this generation of male communities would also have been well aware of the pressure from their episcopal visitors to end the unrestricted movement of their members, but an unqualifed sanction cut through their ties to the outside world.

The second clause was yet more significant since it struck at patterns of religious practice settled in these houses since time immemorial, which is to say that the laity might secure for themselves some spiritual benefit from investment in the devotional enterprise of a religious house. Here there was a steer that it would behove them better to give alms to the poor; even without any awareness of the confessional change to come, this would have appeared a new departure in the practice of penance. In the minds of those whose thinking lay behind the drafts, Leighton, Prise and Cromwell, of course, the imperative for this particular reform intensified as the visitation gathered pace. A discrete sequence of nineteen articles of inquiry was drafted for a visitation of the Augustinian Priory at Walsingham, site of the celebrated shrine of the Blessed Virgin Mary, the focus of which appears informed by a reading of Erasmus's colloquy on the subject, first published in Latin in 1518.[158]

What might follow from the effort to enforce either the conventional or the novel reforms was not expressed. There are no grounds for thinking that the visitors started out on the commission in the late spring of 1535 with the certain understanding that the ultimate end of their inquiries was to enable the closure of the religious houses. The fragments of their letters surviving from the first weeks of their circuit show that they thought most, and most clearly, about the completion of the task, not its consequences. When an ebullient Leighton wrote to Cromwell on 4 June 1535, his vision was for the visitation as an end in itself: 'Doyng all thyngs so diligently for your purpos and your discharge forasmuch as the kyngs hyhnes hath put his onely truste in yowe for the reformacion of his clergie.' He sought out 'goode religion (if any be)' and looked 'to fynde monk chanons frear prior abbott or any other of what degree so ever he be that shall do the kyngs highness so good seruys in this matter'.[159]

Even as their reach over the regions extended and they met monasteries in an ever greater variety of conditions, still the visitors' sights were focused on the business in hand. In the course of six months of continual journeying from county to county, Leighton expressed the same commitment to 'your [Cromwell's] pleasure towchyng the visitacion'.[160] His colleagues likewise looked no further: 'I have dispeched my busyness here comittid unto me by the kings grace,' wrote Simon Haynes, a recent recruit to Cromwell's service, in the early autumn, 'as your maistership shall percive at the recepte of the said packquet, beseching yow, yf I may be advertised of the kynge his gracyose pleasor what I shalle now doo?'[161] At the year's end Thomas Legh, who had been inclined to strain under Cromwell's controlling hand, maintained that 'my only purpose and intent [is] to signyfye … that the executyon of the charge comyttyd … to me shall be so substantcially mynystred in dede'.[162]

In fact, any coherence in their commission soon fractured along the same fault lines as the valuation. The common ground between the visitors, arising from their roles in Cromwell's affinity, which forged 'familiar acqwayntance … and experiens' (as Leighton spoke of himself and Legh in early June), did not foster lasting cooperation and consensus.[163] In the eyes of the regulars, they were cut from the same cloth: 'Crim cram and Riche, with three ell and the like', as they were lampooned in a ballad composed by a monk of Sawley Abbey.[164] The opposite, increasingly, was nearer the truth. They matched one another in their record of royal service in monastic affairs, but the result was that each of them had cultivated their own connections and formed their own outlook.

Leighton and Legh claimed ties within 'x or xii miles' of each 'monasterie sell priorie [and] any other religiouse howse in the north'.[165] From the first weeks of the commission, Leighton displayed a very decided view of how to proceed. By the end of July he was pressing Cromwell for stricter uniformity, his 'formale' book – meaning both final and uniform – to be presented in the same way in 'everie place under the kinges seale'.[166] Legh was concerned less with matters of process than with the rigour of the injunctions themselves. Mindful, perhaps, of what he had witnessed as the king's ambassador in Denmark in 1532, Legh pressed for true 'reformacion'. 'In ower proceding in this hye busynes,' he told Cromwell, 'it is very necessary and convenient that all thing be don substantially, it is mete that ... these matters be not rasshely don'.[167] When it was alleged to Cromwell at Austin Friars that his own conduct was 'to rigorose to bynde them harder then other men', Legh took up the phrase for himself, wearing it as a badge of honour.[168]

The differences between them widened as the visitation continued. Leighton's eagerness to see the commission completed propelled him at a pace not seen in any of the parallel circuits. He was anxious to be on top of the task; in July he feared the year 'fast spent'. It seems he set himself to cross whole counties in the space of a day's ride, through Somerset to Bristol, from Chichester to the Surrey Hills. Inevitably, over these distances, he often arrived in the last hours of the evening or the earliest in the morning. At Langdon Abbey with John Bartlett, Leighton presented himself at the dead of night and faced the abbot in his bedchamber (where he discovered him with female company).[169]

To maintain his own speed Leighton would not always wait for the community to respond to each and every clause of the inquiry. At Leicester Abbey he looked out beyond the precinct to the surrounding neighbourhood and compiled the comperts (reports) from 'others I have learned from'.[170] His hope to make haste, and his instinctive lawyerly caution, undercut his own calls for uniformity. Where there was no ready compliance, he was inclined to move on with his injunctions 'be left ... at [the monastery's] discretion'.

When towards the end of December the Gilbertine women of Chicksands (Bedfordshire) asserted that 'they were bownde by ther religion never to confess the secrete fawtts done amongiste them but onely to their owne visiture of ther religion, and to that they were sworne ever one of them at ther firste admission', he was not disposed to challenge them.[171] For Leighton the possible scope of the visitation was limited by its scale: 'I do litel more,' he confided, than 'the redyng of the same [injunctions]'. He feared the failure this signalled and confessed, 'rather, I may be buried qwike'.[172]

For his part, Thomas Legh had no doubts, either about himself or his task; where Leighton's conviction seemed to decline over time, Legh's only hardened. He was only twenty-five but with a precocious record in government service longer than other prominent commissioners, Leighton, Prise or John London. Inevitably, Legh was headstrong. 'Butt a yong man,' as a colleague described him, and 'somewhat highe of courage'.[173] He regarded his commission as the highest of callings, his 'speciall' charge, an instrument of the king's 'supreme ecclesiasticall power', he considered it his 'very necessary' duty to see all 'hath ben ... bounded by the [king's] commandment'.[174] He interpreted his responsibility not only to be visitor but also governor of the house as if, under the terms of the commission, the authority of the superior had already been surrendered. 'I did ... upon the kings pleasure [consider] that in as much ... both the hedd and membres ... shuld be ... in strayghtnes orderdid', as he described to Cromwell after twelve weeks on the circuit.[175]

There is no copy of the injunctions that can be linked to Legh directly, but it is evident from his reports to Cromwell that he amended and added to the clauses in circulation. He told the monks of St Mary's Abbey, York, not to wear worsted (woollen cloth) as its weave was close and warm. He extended the strictures put on superiors, pressing for them to share the chambers of the conventual community. A monk of Worcester Cathedral Priory, John Musard, wrote to Cromwell to complain: Legh, he said, was an 'unresunable creature'.[176]

Legh himself was vocal in criticising the leniency of his fellow commissioners.[177] His commentaries on their conduct led quickly to conflict. The scene at Bruton was caused by his dismissal of Leighton's earlier reform.[178] The sober scholar John Prise pressed Cromwell to call Legh to order. 'In his going he is ... pompatique,' Prise complained, 'he handleth [them] very roughly for small causes ... ruffeling the hedds'. Ten years his senior, Prise mocked Legh for his self-conscious grandeur: 'Mr Doctor,' he spat his name.[179] Quite apart from the growing row between the commissioners, Legh's behaviour made every visitation a time-consuming tussle. Leighton planned his departure soon after arrival; Legh saw himself installed. His visit of Worcester lasted a whole week.[180]

For his part John Prise showed a respect for the status of the regulars that set him apart. He described them not by their family name or office, as his colleagues tended to do, but as 'the fathers'.[181] His understanding of the role of monastic superior reflected a familiarity with the language of the Rule of St Benedict himself: 'he should be mortified to the worlde [so] that no outwarde busyness shulde corrupt hym'.[182] Prise saw a special dignity in the women religious, 'for more infame and slaunder,' he observed, follows if one of them miscarries (i.e. in their disciplined conduct) than for twenty men, 'for they be of maturite before men ii yeres by all lawes'.[183]

By contrast with Thomas Legh, his inclination was to moderate his injunctions according to circumstance, to apply 'temperance', as Prise described it, and as the autumn advanced he made it his argument to Cromwell.[184] 'Your paicience not offended,' he opened carefully, 'I thinke [the injunctions] over straight.' In particular, he disapproved of the call for complete enclosure, 'for many of thes hous standeth by husbandrie'.[185] It appears Prise recognised that further repression might follow the visitation and warned that a release from vows should only be agreed if it was made known that it was a voluntary decision not to undertake the reform: 'the peple shall knowe it the better' for any that 'be straight discharged', then 'people wolde saye that we went for no other cause about than to expell theym though the trueth were contrarie'.[186]

These tensions between the commissioners were amplified by Cromwell's preference to divide them in order to rule them remotely from his position at his chambers in Austin Friars. In mid-October, Prise's rising anger at the conduct of Thomas Legh erupted after 'Mr Doctor' had again accused him of allowing the religious too much latitude. 'Boldly', as he put it himself, he protested to Cromwell and criticised his own handling of these divisions, 'howe little the complaynts of others succede at youre hands' and even 'many tymes it happeneth a man intending but well hath incurred displeasure by doing his duetie'.[187] Prise was in no doubt that their differences had already damaged the commission, 'ye shall geve occasion to somme to reken ye were too quicke in chosyng suche a one' but he observed that any recovery cast the Visitor General into a double bind since 'it wolde be thought by some that [now] all his doings and procedings were [reproved] by you'.[188]

In Wales, Cromwell allowed his protégé Rowland Lee, newly promoted to the see of Coventry and Lichfield, to use the commission as an instrument of local patronage. Lee advanced into the commission the son of a schoolfriend, Elice Ap Rice Ap Robert,[189] who soon showed himself to be conspicuously unsuitable: 'he ridethe about ... with his concubine openly whome he tok violently away from her mother at Coventry'.[190] His arrival set commissioners to 'presse agaynst' one another and raised their doubts over the intentions of the Visitor General; it also weakened the authority of the commission in the eyes of the neighbourhood, 'causethe the peple to murmur'.[191] Henry Vaughan declared angrily, 'we should have brought Wales in as good a trade as any part of England ... not to have joined such with uys that [has] his owne faults and enormities'.[192]

The regulars' acceptance of the supremacy and awareness of its implications did not mean that the king's visitors were well received. Legh complained that at Bruton Abbot Ely had 'shewed himself very haulte and obstinate' and cut him off in his speech making 'sharpe and quyk', 'litell regarding the autoritie committed to me'.[193] The abbot's lack of respect for their commission was not unique. Abbot John Essex of St Augustine's, Canterbury, lightly cloaked his contempt in 'meke commendation' and 'herty thanks' but the extent of it was clear: Leighton was a 'surrogate', the authority of the visitation was open to question in its compass of 'all relygyon exempte and non exempte', and the 'hole entente' of the injunctions was not acceptable since 'erten of them be very doubtful to us'.[194] Prior John Folkestone of Dover dismissed the commissioners as 'substytutes'. Where Ely had used the claims of one to undermine the other, Folkestone used the same tactic on the injunctions, challenging the authority of the text put before him as 'contrary commawnment[s]'.[195] Perhaps conscious of the old ties of his house to the Tudor regime, Abbot Richard Mounslow of Winchcombe reached over the heads of the commission to call on Cromwell himself, as Visitor General, to set out the Crown's demands: 'we beg your favourable interpretation of [the injunctions], especially where they seem obscure'.[196]

Even as they allowed the visitors to carry out their commission, heads and their houses continued their spoiling tactics. Frequently, it seems, they refused to respond to their questions. There can be little doubt that their silence was stage-managed. 'We did use moche diligens in oure examinacion,' Prise reported, '[but] I fermley bileve and suppose that they had confedered and compacted before oure comyng that they shulde disclose nothing'.[197] At Coggeshall Abbey (Essex), William Love schooled his monks in a script for each of them to follow when the visitors came with their questions.[198] Prior Thomas Goldwell of Christ Church, Canterbury, conceived the same subterfuge, apparently enforcing it with threats: 'to hyde and kepe secretly from hym all syche detestable abhomynable enormytys and abusyons' with the warning that the monks 'schuld be forsyd and constrayntd to take an hothe apon the same'.[199]

They also applied the lessons of affinity which their relationship with the Tudor regime had already taught. The commissioners were offered payments, privileges granted under their common seal, or the opportunity to influence some or other property transaction. There may well have been an understanding reached between Abbot Ely and Richard Leighton; without it, it is not easy to explain why Leighton, the proponent of strict injunctions, rode speedily away from Bruton with the house only nominally reformed. Leighton's praise (shared with Cromwell) for the liberality of Prior Thomas Mylne of Boxgrove, who 'kepith gret hospitalitie' and his monks 'of the same grain' (omnes sunt eiusdem farina), and his promotion of the interest of their hereditary founder, Lord de la Warr, belies a reward.[200] It is likely that the commissioners looked for these transactions. The upright John Prise pointed the finger firmly at Thomas Legh: 'His taking I thinke it excessive in many things,' he wrote in October 1535, 'besides his costes', he reckoned that he took 'rewarde unknowen'. His practice, Prise claimed, was to make a 'pretesence' of standing above bribery on arrival and then to apply pressure as he moved on: '[he] maketh theym to sende after hym suche rewardes as maye pleas hym'.[201]

To these obstructions was added the further obstacle of interference from patrons. Now houses which had seen their relationship with hereditary founders and patrons renewed in the past half-century realised their reward. The controlling presence of some made the commissioners circumspect: 'by power and might in his contrey', John, Lord Mordaunt, was said 'to use howses of religion at will'.[202] The visitors' clauses of inquiry encouraged them to engage founders and patrons, to bear witness to, or offer documentary proof of, the status of the original foundation. Too often it hampered more than helped. Leighton's plea to Cromwell from Folkestone was not untypical, 'Ther is an other priorie ... x or xii myles from Canterberie wherin is but the prior a monke sike and burston of his codds', but 'my lorde Glynton [Clinton] pretendith to be founder'.[203] Superiors acted their part in alliances that for some had only recently been formed. To challenge the 'kyngs ... clames heretofore mayde to our said patronage and foundershipe', Prior William Wode of Bridlington addressed Cromwell directly with 'substanciall evidences of recorde' of the descent of that hereditary right with Gilbert de Gaunte, 'cosyn to our orginal founder', which 'we have ever benne . . . clere withowt any interruption in this behalfe nighe this two hundreth yeres'.[204]

The seigneurial interest not only asserted status and rights; some also stepped between their houses and the injunctions the commissioners were wont to leave. The commendations of the heads of their houses sent to Cromwell by Thomas, Lord De la Warr (Boxgrove), Sir John Fitzjames (Glastonbury) and Sir William Parr (Pipewell) were surely warning shots against any severe act of repression.[205] For those who held their stewardships this was practical as well as principled action. The petition of Richard Phelyppes to exempt Cerne Abbey from enclosure, whose fees he received, carried with it a material calculation.[206]

The other source of authority in the hinterland of the religious houses, that of the bishops, also threatened the progress of the commission. In their acceptance of the supremacy the bishops had acknowledged the principle of the Crown's right to visit, but the prospect of its application barely six months later aroused a sensitivity over the status of their own powers. Their defence of their dignity had been sharpened by Archbishop Cranmer's declaration of a metropolitan visitation, which had come to them by the beginning of March. The formal appeals of such interference from senior prelates such as Gardiner at Winchester and Longland at Lincoln were still unanswered as the commission for the Crown's visitation was issued.[207]

If he did not anticipate it, Cromwell did acknowledge the challenge of episcopal cooperation. In the far west of England he put the visitation in the hands of the presiding bishops, Exeter and Hereford; for the latter, Bishop Edward Fox was underway in the Welsh March by September.[208] Yet Fox was unable entirely to escape conflict. He was drawn into a dispute with the metropolitans, Canterbury and York, which dragged on almost to the end of the year. In early June, Cranmer had appeared content to limit his own action to the enforcement of the supremacy but having watched the commission advance over his domain, by the autumn he was more defiant. In November he intervened at Canterbury itself, 'to interpetate' articles 'given in the kings graces visitacion'.[209]

Edward Lee set course for a direct confrontation, demanding the king's visitors proceed only after he had carried out his own provincial circuit. In response, Cromwell seemed to equivocate. Early in the summer Lee's understanding was that the Visitor General would stand by and let him show his own authority: 'by mowthe I had answer that your minde was now odre but I shuld do my dutie'. William Thornton, abbot of St Mary's, York, seized on the stand-off, was 'importunate', and 'pressed for ... lettres' (proof of authority) from both sides.[210] Then in mid-August, Cromwell changed his mind: 'and yet now ... you reaquyre me not to visite'.[211] Lee's own resolve wavered and now he wanted to compound his authority with the king's, 'to make redie against the coming of your commissioners'.[212]

In the course of their exchanges, the archbishop and his suffragans continued in their progress through the province; by the end of July many houses had been visited in the vicinity of York, the far north and the west, among them Gilbertine communities for which Cromwell had agreed an exemption with the new master of the congregation, his ally, Robert Holgate.[213]

Their colleagues on the bench made trouble more obliquely. Bishop Longland of Lincoln exposed the limitations of the visitors' oversight, reporting that Newstead Priory had been left without a head, ungoverned, although 'your master-shippe commanded me nott to medle with any religious houses'.[214] Stephen Gardiner questioned the status of the visitors when they came into his diocese.[215] Rowland Lee looked to have the visitors' injunctions lifted after they left.[216] Even John Hilsey of Rochester, whom Cromwell had raised to the see, was inclined to copy Cranmer and conduct his own survey of deaneries and parishes, complaining that the poverty of the see compelled it, 'for I have only 7 nobles in the world'.[217] Legh and Prise met enough opposition on their circuits that they persuaded Cromwell to pass down a general prohibition on ordinary visitation, arguing that if the prelates remained with a free rein then the royal supremacy itself would be under threat.[218]

Cromwell had aimed to pre-empt such challenges by investing the authority of the visitation in the religious themselves. The allies he had secured in monastic and mendicant hierarchies were now awarded the delegated authority of visitor for their congregation. Thomas Chard of Forde and Thomas Calne of Stanley received the commission for the Cistercian network in England; Thomas of Neath took the same authority for the anglophone houses of the Welsh March.[219] Master Robert Holgate of the Gilbertines was given responsibility for the examination of their twenty-four foundations. Abbot John Maxey of Welbeck, whose place in the regime's affinity had begun, like Cromwell's, under Wolsey, was charged with the commission for the whole congregation of thirty-four monasteries. Dominicans John Hilsey and Richard Ingworth, now promoted, respectively, to the see of

Rochester and the suffragancy of Dover, were entrusted with the largest task, to visit the convents of the six orders of friars, a responsibility which in Hilsey's own words saw them pass the year 'riding to and fro'.[220]

The effect of the strategy is not easily assessed and the reports are mixed. The Cistercian circuit has left no trace. Since the approach replicated the customs of the congregation perhaps there was no open conflict, although tensions over the observance of the injunctions erupted in the months that followed. Other than Hilsey's letter to Cromwell, the visitation of the friars is almost invisible in the archival record. He wrote confidently of the 'reformacion of old abuses', and warmly of Ingworth's contribution; another brief document notes 'praise [for] the observacion' of the friars.

The Gilbertines also accepted the authority of a visitor that was of their own tradition, although his commission appears at first unknown, or unrecognised by other of the Crown's commissioners. Both Leighton and John Tregonwell attempted to visit Gilbertine foundations in eastern counties (Chicksands, Catesby) only to be roundly rebuffed, 'the business not done' (negotio infecto).[221] The Premonstratensian foundered, apparently, on the principle of Abbot John Maxey being a provincial authority. When the abbey at West Dereham (Norfolk) was suddenly vacated as Maxey was about to begin his visitation, he hesitated, and the secular registrar, Richard Bower, lost no time in reminding Cromwell that 'the kings grace is heed of the church of englond and by the prerogatif of his imperiall crown ... ought ... by his powr and auctoritie ecclesiasticall ... to make transla-tions of abbotts and priors', while 'it was ... for the ordinaries to install them and to put them in reall posession'.[222]

The commissioners also confronted structural obstacles for which, in spite of the experience of the past year, it appears neither the visitors nor their masters were prepared. The high summer, a low season in the liturgical calendar, saw many superiors set apart from their houses at one or other manorial residence. The prior of Monmouth was reported to be 'in sentury' (sanctuary) in the Herefordshire village of Garway.[223] The absence of a leader made the completion of the visitation more difficult not least because the community disputed their own authority to submit to any binding obligation, even in the presence of a deputy such as the prior or sub-prior. In an almost empty friary it was not possible to do anything decisively. 'Ther is nor pott nor panne, nor bed, nor bed styd, nor no monke in the sayd howse,' reported John Vaughan to Cromwell, 'wherfor the contrey dothe gretly marvell ther ys no reformacion'.[224] The head and the hierarchy held the business of the house close to themselves and without them it seems some convents were simply helpless. With their abbess away, the ladies of Darley let in James Billingford, a disgraced and deranged clerk who played the visitor with them, subjecting them to questioning about 'the number of the sisters and . . . [the] view of their grain', stirring 'the great fear of the sisters'.[225]

In spite of so many obstructions, for many of the houses in every congregation the visitation brought great upheaval. Perhaps the first and greatest unrest in their life arose from the visitors' behaviour. Their commission was carried out, in every sense, on the hoof. 'He hath taken paynes divers tymes riding to and fro', was Thomas Bedyll's recollection of Richard Ingworth, Dominican prior of King's Langley, when he acted as John Hilsey's deputy for the visitation of the friaries.[226]

North and south, it seems Leighton cut his circuits according to what could be managed without a change of horses, or an extended rest period for those he had. Over the Sussex Downs the direction of his route and the duration of his visits were determined entirely by the prospects of appropriate refreshment for himself and his mounts. He decided to leave the county to stop overnight at Waverley where he was confident of board and bed.[227] Wherever he was, Leighton did not want to be detained for long. He arrived late or early, as much any other reason to be sure to be on the road to his next destination soon. He dispatched his reports 'by spedy hande'.[228]

There may have been a sly delight in the disruption caused by their sudden arrival, although the commissioners soon complained if they found the superior absent and the community unprepared to receive their writ. Their peculiar movements may have been more pragmatic: arriving at a religious house at a mealtime (breakfast or dinner) might spare their own expenditure.[229] The personal account of Prior Geoffrey Shether of Dunmow counted 57s 8d in 'costs' for the few days of the visitation.[230]

Their arrival threw the household into disarray. When he reached Waverley, Leighton planted himself in one of the principal chambers, calling for 'brede, drynke . . . and fyer', and faced with the convent, 'forgott ther names and toke from one man the keys of hys office'.[231] At Langdon in October, he would not be kept waiting. '[After] a good space knokkyng at the abbotts dore nec vox nec sensu apparuit [with no response], saving the abbotts little doge yet within his dore faste lokked bayed and barked I fownde a short polax ... and with yt I dasshede thabbotts dore in peissus, ictu oculi ... and aboute howse I go with that polax in my hande'.[232] Days later at Canterbury, the chaos that ensued after Leighton's arrival 'at nyght' placed him and the whole household in mortal danger:

> ... at one of the cloke after mydnyght one of my servaunts called me up soddenly or ells I had bene brent in my bede. The gret dynyng chamber called the kyngs logeyng where we suppede ... was soddenly fierede by sum fierbrande or suoff of sum candell that fyrste sett the rissheis in fier. My servaunds lying ryght to the saide logeyng were almost chokede in ther bedds.[233]

Even before a fire broke out, Leighton had already disturbed the household, demanding use of the best chamber and, so it seems, for candles to be relit and the fire to be rekindled, when the residents had already retired for the night. As it was, both house and neighbourhood were disturbed as he 'sent into the town for helpe [of] laddes and water' and the 'gret logeyng was past recoverie'.[234]

There remains a suspicion that Thomas Legh went further still. A century later Thomas Fuller found the impression still lingering that the visitors 'made advantageous use' of religious and if they themselves had been visited 'many failings' would have been found to match the 'infirmities of others'.[235] Rumours of this kind appear to have been current in the autumn of 1535. John Prise wrote to Cromwell on 16 October, following their visit to four houses in Somerset and Wiltshire (Bruton, Bradenstoke, Edington and Stanley), complaining of Legh's 'audacitie' and 'rowgh fasshon' with the religious which leaves them 'never so affrayed'.[236] He made one substantive allegation, of 'excessive taking' at the elections he had supervised, almost £100 cumulatively from three charterhouses and Tarrant Abbey (Dorset). Prise was not a disinterested witness, since he was 'one of those that depraved me heretofor'.[237]

Yet two letters of Legh to Cromwell survive which appear to respond to several charges put before him by the vicegerent. The direction of Legh's defence implies that some may have touched on his moral conduct. '[Of the] enormytes and abuses ... complayned of', he urged, 'I was not so adycte and given to such notabyll sensualyte and abuses specyfyed in your ... lettres'.[238]

As they wrestled over the terms of the king's writ, there is no doubt that the visitation disturbed the leadership of some houses. The commissioners did not carry with them an expressed instruction to depose the head of a house but the clauses of inquiry, and their own method of pursuing them, seem to have provoked a crisis in some communities. When the commissioners appeared at Conwy, a fearful Abbot Geoffrey Johns at once offered his resignation. They turned their attention to the installation of a successor straight away and thought 'all that matter spedd', with 'all the monkys [in] one assent and agrement'. Only as they came to leave was it discovered that the candidate, Richard Ap Rees, was a mere twenty-four years old, 'which aege dyd stay us from the confirmation'. They rode away with the house visited and put under the king's injunctions but deprived of a head, both old and new.[239]

When the same commissioners visited Valle Crucis they 'found many things to be reformed' and immediately took the abbot and one of his monks into custody, sending them under guard to Holt Castle. The remaining community of six were left alone, although the commissioners were aware that 'ther is none mete for to be abbot but only the prior . . . but abbot ther he will not be in no case as he saythe . . . the . . . housse to be all redy so farre in dett'. 'There they do remayn,' they reported, 'untill the kings pleasure', reflecting 'wherby it is not like who so ever shall have the same that ever he shall do any good upon hit'.[240]

His inquiries at Wherwell led Thomas Legh to lever the removal of Abbess Anne Colte on charges of 'incontinence', founded, it appears, on a combination of recent rumours and certain facts of her remote past.[241] Here he may have met internal divisions that were tempting to widen to bring the whole community to compliance. The convent at Hinchingbroke (Cambridgeshire) reached out to the visitors to govern for them because of their superior's perceived incapacity, confined to her bedchamber 'sore seek'.[242] Within two days of the visitation at Worcester Cathedral Priory, what appears to have been a faction within the house, formed of the prior and three monks, was sent for examination by Cromwell 'concerning causes in this visitation'.[243] Prise and Legh left Abbot Henry Emery of Wardon in open conflict with his community, in spite of his apparent sympathy for the king's injunctions.[244] Scudamore pushed his own kinswoman into the headship at Aconbury (Herefordshire).[245] There was a growing awareness of the commissioners' wilful interference and by the early autumn two senior bishops, Longland (Lincoln) and Shaxton (Salisbury), and one notable loyalist, Lee (Coventry and Lichfield), had asserted their right to see canonical, free elections occur.[246]

Yet the substance of the commission, the inquiries and injunctions, do not seem to have brought about widespread or sustained disturbance. The only imposition of the commissioners that upset the institutional routine and provoked opposition was the permanent enclosure of the professed, superior and officers together with the conventual community. For the oldest monastic congregations, it was a conspicuous challenge to custom and to the practical administration of their communal lives. Even so, there was no conspicuous display of resistance. It was only towards the year's end that a succession of Benedictine and Cistercian superiors appealed for dispensations. Months had passed since the visitors departed and the implication must be that they had already accepted the enclosure of the houses.

Most requested a particular dispensation, not a general exemption. Robert Hamlyn of Athelney (Somerset) explained that for him to 'goe abrode' was needful 'for the preservation of my bodily helthe'.[247] Stephen Sagar of Hailes, who was not prompted to write until the end of January 1536, was more specific: 'I have a desease yerelye at the fall of the leif and at the sprynge tyme . . . if I may not . . . lye in a clere ayer it will coste me my life'.[248] Anthony St Leger wrote on behalf of his brother, Arthur, prior of Leeds: 'he hathe been conselyd to doo for serten infyrmete wheche he ys owghton troublyd with'.[249] Abbot John Burton of Oseney appealed on the grounds that the particular topography of his Thameside house made strict enclosure a danger to his health, for it 'stand[s] very low, encumbered with waters' and 'if I should be constrained to tarry always . . . it would no doubt abbreviate my life'.[250]

A handful leavened the question into an assertion of their own lordship over their domain; sometimes with reinforcement from their patrons. Sir John Fitzjames set out a lawyerly case before Cromwell to secure Glastonbury's dispensation from four articles which 'shuld muche disapoynt the ordre of the howse'. He pledged himself to 'dare be suretie'.[251] But if this was a deliberate tilt towards conflict it was deflected. The first instinct of the visitors themselves was to allow the superiors their freedom, thinking perhaps above all of their own anxiety to pass on briskly from one circuit to another. But while Cromwell's own expectations were apparently still not clear enough for the visitors to be certain, from the outset he seems to have been satisfied to settle particular requests, albeit with some or other measurable obligation attached. From many religious, fines were demanded; some offered up (no doubt on request) the grant of property or office. At any rate, by the autumn a rule of thumb appears to have been recognised that communities which were otherwise 'conformable' could release their officers for 'the just and dew order therof'.[252]

In retrospect, it has always been assumed that the houses had been badly exposed by the commissioners' searches, and discoveries, concerning their personal morality. The conviction that this was, or at least very soon was made, the main target of the visitation grew as the years, and the Reformation, progressed. The polemics of the Yorkshire gentleman Wilfrid Holme (d. 1538), and Richard Morison, written in the wake of the visitations, represented the suppression of the smaller monasteries as a sentence passed on proven sin, 'vile abominacion' and 'maynteyne[d] lecherie [and] buggery' that 'stynketh to sore to be sturred to moche'.[253]

Hugh Latimer reaffirmed their reading of events in a sermon of 1549: the parliament of 1536 had responded to the 'great abominable enormities' reported to it.[254] Raphael Holinshed, the first Tudor chronicler to describe the visitation, implied that the focus of the effort had been the reform of immorality: 'they tooke order that no men should haue accesse to the houses of women, nor women to the houses of men'.[255] Three-quarters of a century later, Thomas Fuller was explicit, the visitors had been 'spies ... sent forth to make strict discovery of men's behaviours therein'; Cromwell he called 'scoutmaster-general'.[256]

For the first generation of modern historians the impression was reinforced by some of the documentary evidence that came most readily to hand. The selection of commissioners' correspondence surviving in the manuscript anthologies, and in the guard books compiled from Augmentations papers, refer frequently to the scandalous stories and suspicions shared with them on their circuits. Above all, they looked on the thirty-odd leaves of the parchment-wrapped 'Compendium compertorum', its title inscribed in an eighteenth-century copper-plate hand, a fair copy of the comperts (reports) from the circuits in the province of York, and the dioceses of Coventry and Lichfield, and Norwich.[257] The booklet sets out in summary form for each foundation the information in response to several of the visitors' inquiries: the cases of immorality; the eligible religious requesting release; the identity of the founder; the relics or shrines to be found. There are entries for 120 monasteries, reflecting the density of settlement in these dioceses. The names of as many as 670 men and women are recorded as having confessed or been convicted of various breaches of their celibacy vow. On the face of it, the booklet might seem to embody the casebook spoken of by Latimer.

Yet the status and significance of this evidence are not necessarily all that they appear. The commissioners' letters to Cromwell were not written as a verbatim account of their conduct of their visitation. In fact, their frequent digressions and often intemperate tone might indicate the opposite: that they became an outlet for what was otherwise at the margins of their main business. The compendium booklet with its own labelled cover is the only one of its kind, and it holds only a partial return from three dioceses in England and Wales. Its contents are not the original comperts but excerpts from them, with a conscious concentration on conventual discipline, numbers and cult practice. It is possible that the comperts from all dioceses were excerpted in this way but there is no trace of, or reference to, another matching booklet.[258] There can be little doubt that the visitors recorded cases of immorality, notwithstanding that their inquiries may not have followed the same sequence of questions, but only one other fragment has been found, noting eleven cases of 'incontinence' at Chertsey Abbey (Surrey) in the diocese of London.[259]

It does seem likely that the formality of the one booklet has allowed a false impression of an encounter in which each professed man and woman was held to account for their personal conduct. In this area of inquiry, as in others, the visitors themselves held quite different views. Their dispatches to Cromwell do not all share the same interest in cases of immorality. In their reluctance to press for the removal of heads of house, men and women, in the face of reported scandal, it may be that Legh, Prise and Tregonwell showed themselves to be more moderate in their judgement, or at least more pragmatic. Tregonwell judged at face value the woman of Godstow guilty of 'brak[ing] her chastytye' thirteen or fourteen years before, 'but now and ever sethens that tym she hath levyde vertuowse'.[260] It has been suggested that in the layout of the information they gathered, where 'voluntary pollution' (masturbation) is distinguished from 'incontinence' (sexual liaisons), this was a deliberate effort to draw attention to the limitations of the evidence.[261]

The exception among the visitors was Richard Leighton. For him, it seems, sexual immorality was indeed an inherent property of the monastic profession, a symptom of the human perversion of the vowed life. 'Detestable abuses' and 'all matters of mischeffe' were inevitably 'clokyde and coloryde' in the life of the cloister, he reminded Cromwell at the beginning of his first circuit.[262] He relished the self-harming claim of a young canon of Langdon, that he had been pushed into an encounter with a woman procured for him by the abbot, colouring it into a bawdy farce, as he took 'her to bed in a room adjoining [the abbot's] bed'.[263] Leighton pursued inquiries beyond interviews with the individual religious, reaching out to catch allegations and rumours in general circulation. Clearly, if he caught the thread of a scandalous story, he followed it as it wound its way around the neighbourhood. At Maiden Bradley Priory he sketched the characters and scenes for a tale that might have been told in a ballad broadsheet or on the stage:

> . . . an holy father prior . . . hath . . . vi children and but one daughter mariede yet . . . trustying shortly to mary the rest . . . and he thanks gode a never medelet with marytt women but all with madens the faireste could be gottyn and always marede them right well. The pope considering his fragilitie gave hym licens to kepe an hore.[264]

There was prurience, even self-gratification, in some of Leighton's reports. Ecstatically, he wrote from Bath Priory that '[the] monkes [are] worse then I have any fownde yet both in bugerie and adulterie sum one of them haveyng x women sum viii and the reste so fewer'.[265] His frequent use of general terms such as adultery and sodomy reinforce the impression that his judgement was founded on a categoric association between religious enclosure and sexual behaviour.

The strength of his obsession, and its sound as he spoke of it around and about, must have unsettled many of the houses he visited, but rarely did it leave a lasting impression on community life. For all of his tone of definitive judgement, the consequences of Leighton's investigations looked very much like those of any episcopal or capitular visitation in the recent past. Immorality was confessed and committed to a formal record, but apart from any measure of conventual punishment passed down, there was no further action after the visitors departed. Of course, much of what was recorded in the comperts was old news to everyone except the visitors, the story of liaisons which had already run their course and pregnancies dating back more than a decade. In the compendium, frequently heads of house are named among those guilty of 'incontinence' yet hardly any of them now faced further sanction, still less any pressure to step down. Generally, across the community, the incidence of 'incontinence' seems to have had little bearing on the number who now requested release from their vows. If the comperts caused them exposure, it was not such that it prompted them at once to choose between the cloister and the world. Nor is there any indication that they altered attitudes in the surrounding neighbourhood. In the autumn, novices still applied to enter Cockersand, Furness and Whalley, which together, in the record of the compendium, had accounted for one-third of all the cases of 'incontinence' in the county of Lancashire.[266]

The avoidance of a crisis of moral confidence within or outside the precinct wall may be due in large part to the nature of the scandal that was documented. Evidence of 'voluntary pollution', the customary euphemism for masturbation, may have troubled the virtue of successive generations of Anglican historians, but it had always featured among the minor acts of indiscipline in the institutional life of male clergy. It is very likely that the term 'sodomy' used in the comperts was another euphemism for the same act. Nearly 60 per cent of the monastic men recorded in the Compendium for the northern province and East Anglia were identified as guilty only or principally of voluntary pollution.[267]

From 170 women identified in the booklet as 'incontinent', fewer than 20 per cent were reported to have borne a child; of these several were known only to have passed through a pregnancy at one time (semel) in their past history, sometimes in the context of an earlier marriage (ex conjugato). The largest number recorded for one female house, five found at Marham, had each given birth 'semel ex conjugato'.[268]

By the measure of episcopal visitations over the previous century these patterns of behaviour were not unusual. The position of the women may reflect the forces that influenced recruitment as much as, if not more than, their experience of life after their profession. Perhaps many of these cases matched that of Joan Plumstead of Shouldham Priory (Norfolk), baldly recorded in the booklet as bearing a child 'before her entry into religion' (ante introitum in religionem). Unfortunate liaisons were not only the consequence of an enclosed life but also its first cause.

The visitors' comperts also accounted for the level of 'superstition' they encountered, but again their scrutiny does not appear to have delivered a shattering blow. In this aspect of their inquiries the commissioners shared in the same reforming zeal, although it is still Leighton's voice that is heard loudest and longest in the surviving letters. He was breathless in his boast of the book of the miracles of the Blessed Virgin Mary he had removed from the library at Bath, the truth of which he needlessly reminded Cromwell was 'such a boke of dreemes as ye never saw' and 'well able to mache the Canterberie tailles'.[269]

At Canterbury, in spite of the chaos arising from the fire that his coming had caused, it seems Leighton seized the chance to take down some part of a shrine. His target is unspecified and there is no certain proof of his success.[270] Here, however, Leighton and his colleagues have been surprised by a meeting of minds. Many of the monastic superiors had shared in their own intellectual formation, and like them embraced the Christian humanism of university theology, and the critiques of its most celebrated contemporary authority, Erasmus. Stephen Sagar, abbot of Hailes, whose church housed one of the kingdom's most celebrated relics, a vial of Christ's blood, began a correspondence with Cromwell expressing his distaste for it and his mounting doubts about its authenticity. Despite the press of lay piety on their patterns of devotion, the visitors found houses of women also willing to let go of their old cults. As they departed, Abbess Katharine Bulkeley of Godstow affirmed that she and her sisters 'ne praying to dede saints ne used ne regarded amongst hus'.[271]

By the same token, both male and female houses were receptive to the observant novelties which the injunctions prescribed. A daily bible reading was widely adopted in Benedictine monasteries. The monks of Christ Church, Canterbury, made a boast of their new custom of 'the reading of Scripture'. Abbot William More of Walden gladly delivered himself of a bible reading every day, as a demonstration against the old unholy customs of 'monkery'.[272] John London admired the provision at Reading Abbey where 'they have a gudde lecture in scripture dayly redde in ther chapitour howse, both in Inglysche and Laten'.[273] A notable exception may have been Worcester, a diocese holding four major Benedictine houses, where Bishop Latimer complained in 1537 'some of you neither have preserved the king's injunctions, not yet have them with you'.[274]

But this is not to say that any early compliance failed to effect a cultural change. When Glastonbury was visited in 1538, there were complaints from the monks because the custom of bible reading had recently lapsed. At Gloucester Abbey, it appears the reader had served continuously since the visitation and at the end the commissioners did not hesitate to judge him worthy of a pension. The bible reader at Norwich, John Barte, was retained at the creation of the secular chapter and given a house in the close, a measure perhaps of how far he had been assimilated before the closure.[275]

For the Benedictines, the injunction may have channelled a mood already current in the congregation. Biblical exegesis had become one of the hallmarks of the reforms of the Benedictine congregations in the European mainland, led by Santa Giustina of Padua, whose reputation, and tradition of scholarship, would have had some recognition value for this generation. Since the practice continued in these houses against the background of other changes in their customs, and the suppression of smaller monasteries and friaries, it may be they considered that the new biblicism might be a vehicle to deliver them safely into King Henry's new world. For the monks of Norwich Cathedral Priory the office of lector *conventus* was a tangible continuity as their transition to a secular chapter; indeed it remained as it ever had been when the cathedral was re-founded in 1547.[276]

Bible reading was adopted in other congregations although perhaps more patchily. Abbot Henry Emery of Wardon was politic enough to tell Cromwell that the daily exposition was in place but admitted that there were still two of his number who refused to engage. It may not have encouraged conformity: the friar employed at Furness appears to have stirred rebellion.[277] Certainly, the custom of bible reading was adopted elsewhere. The canons of Christchurch at Twynham (Dorset) took to their bible reader so well that he was among the eleventh-hour annuitants they attached to the foundation.[278] Religious women may have been more familiar with communal bible readings and preaching than has often been recognised, and there may have been few principled or practical arguments against compliance. There are few mentions of the arrangements in the months following the visitation, but the houses that continued with bible readings to the end of 1536 and beyond may have made the arrangements recorded at Lacock Abbey, for a 'discreet and learned priest' to come in and lecture to them. When Cromwell instructed the bishops to enforce the use of an English Bible in June 1538, it seems in the religious houses they found conformity already.[279]

In their conscientious adoption of the injunctions, some were inclined to iden-tify themselves openly with a spirit of reform. Abbot Robert Hamlyn of Athelney affected to speak for his whole house in his heartfelt declaration to Cromwell '[in] the acte of vysytation for the reformacion of good relygyon . . . be founde thankes be to gode'.[280] In a conventual letter the monks of Christ Church, Canterbury, raised their collective voice to commend their new observance as '[the] perfyt trew very synzer and goodly relygyon', in which Cromwell was their guide, the 'trew and stedfast pyller of [their] evangelicall lyberte'.[281] The women of Godstow appeared to go further, using language, surely self-consciously, of the reformed sort of religion: they urged Cromwell that they were committed to 'the trewith of [God's] holie words as farre as the fraile nature of women maye ateyne ... not dowtinge but this garmente and facion of life dothe nothinge prevaile towarde owre justifynge before god by whome for his swete sone jhesus sake we onlie truste to be justified and saved'.[282]

The same outlook was surely forming in the minds of the Cistercians of Biddlesden (Buckinghamshire) from the time of the injunctions. Their unusually personal deed of surrender, out of the ordinary not least because it was written in English, might be read as a statement of values shaped since the injunctions, rejecting 'pretensed religion', 'dumb ceremonies' and 'constitutions of Rome', preferring a 'true knowledge of God's laws' and 'the true way of living as declared by Christ and his evangelists'.[283] It seems there was some slight recollection of this successful reformation as far off as the end of the Tudor era. George Abbot recalled how their 'carnall kinde of behaviour ... was afterwarde amended in England, may bee testified by the survey, which by Visitation of the Kings Commissioners was taken under King Henry the eight of famous memory'.[284]

For the royal regime, and the diocesans who aligned themselves with it, the ready acceptance of reform appears to have refreshed the feeling of a compact with a network of houses and their heads that represented each one of the monastic congregations. As the visitors departed, several superiors came forward to reaffirm their affinity with the vicegerent. From Tewkesbury, John Wakeman sent 'intere and lovly commendacions ... all the wiche is ondeserved as yet of my part for lack of pouer but of my trew hert ye shall always be assured'.[285] His tie to Cromwell was now of five years' standing since his election in 1531, but the visitors had supervised as many new appointments in each one of the monastic congregations. Now these men and women too pledged their service.

The Premonstratensian, John Maxey, recently confirmed as perpetual abbot of Welbeck, with provincial authority over the congregation in England and Wales, wrote in early November, 'I intend to do nothinge but that shall stond with the kyngs grace plesur and yours bothe.'[286] Maxey was one of three superiors now positioned under Cromwell's influence to command their congregations according to the king's will.

Prior Richard Ingworth of the Dominican convent at King's Langley was identified as the natural successor to John Hilsey, 'right mete' to serve the king, after his 'paynys ... in the king's matters', during the weeks of visitation. Thomas Calne of Stanley and Thomas Chard of Forde shared presidential powers over their congregation in the southern province, conveying the king's injunctions to them without any immediate incident.[287] Charde's willingness to serve 'with that little I maye doo', was further demonstrated before the end of the year, as he delivered the deeds of the house's property to Cromwell, declaring himself 'reformable and conformable to that which shalbe your pleasure'.[288]

The mutual service cultivated with superiors now, after their exposure to the visitors and through them to the policy of the Crown, appears to have been sought by members of the convent. In the remaining months of the year, monks outside the hierarchy at a number of Benedictine houses reached out to Cromwell, offering their own service, and material considerations, in exchange for assuring or advancing their own position. From Worcester, apparently while the visitors were still at work, one of the monks, William Fordham, wrote to Cromwell directly offering him the extraordinary consideration of 100 marks (in instalments of 20 marks for the following five years) and 'jewels every yere after so ye have a newre yers gyft'.[289]

Internally, however, the injunctions may have had the opposite effect. The injunctions represented the first measurable change to monastic life to arise from the king's supremacy and in the months after their introduction it appears that the professed – for many of them perhaps for the first time – felt compelled to decide their own position on the matter of reform.

Divisions were visible very soon. Collegiality collapsed at Worcester on the very day that the visitors left on 1 August. That day two monks of the house addressed personal petitions to Cromwell complaining, among other things, of the conduct of their prior. Their claims echoed in a barrage of correspondence that came to the vicegerent in the weeks that followed as the customary chain of command was broken, the sub-prior and cellarer apparently acting only for the hierarchy itself, and their cloister brethren speaking for themselves. Within a week of the injunctions reaching Winchcombe, Abbot Mounslow reported that one of his monks, Dan Peter, 'cam on to me' and 'sayde ... yow have broke the injunctyons'. Peter judged him by each 'poynte' of the new code. Clearly Mounslow considered his authority to be ebbing away, as Peter 'schowyd on to me by force all my breherne to be the cause of his requeste'; at once he submitted a defence of his conduct to Cromwell.[290]

This confederation of cloisterers was found elsewhere. At Abbotsbury, a schedule of twenty-five charges was compiled against Abbot Roger Rodden, 'who doth breke the kyng's foundacons and the injuncyons of the same'. The cloister monks at Coggeshall kept a close watch on Abbot William Love, apparently with a copy of the injunctions in hand. Their report of his breaches was self-righteous in its commitment to reform, characterising his omission of the 'colet' (collect) for the king and 'hys dere belovyd spouse', as a 'tokyn of hys small love yt he beryth to his prince'.[291] Richard Beerley, a monk of Pershore, championed the cause of monastic reform when he wrote to Cromwell of his abbot, John Stonywell: 'the relygyon Wyche we do observe and kepe ys no rull of seint Benett ... but lyzth and foulysse sermonys mayd sum yn old tyme and sume ys our tyme by lyzth and ondyscrytt faders wych have ... let the preceys and coamndyments of God go'.[292]

The fervour for the injunctions did not always come from the convent. Abbot Henry Emery of Wardon eagerly reformed the daily routine, introducing a daily lecture and a 'boke of grammar' to his own brother to teach from it, but 'ther wolde come none of them to him' but two of more than a dozen in the house and the rump 'vexidde [him] with many uncharitable surmises and obprobrius words'.[293] At Furness, the monks 'murmured and grudged against' their abbot after he urged them not only to accept the injunctions but also to readopt their own congregational statutes, previously subject to certain 'relaxacions'. Later, it was suggested that the internal struggle over the old and the new had inspired some in the convent to find a place in the rebels' ranks in the spring of 1537.[294]

Some houses were split in two. At Shrewsbury a 'fallse and soyttel confederacy' settled around the abbot, resistant to the adoption of any one of the injunctions' clauses.[295] The tensions rose towards the turn of the year. In the third week of January, Prior John Sarisbury of Horsham St Faith (Norfolk) pursued his visitor of three months before, Robert Southwell, telling how a charter for 'the rewling of the howse' had been taken into the 'custodye and kepeyng' of one of his brethren who had then absconded.[296] On 4 February, Clement Lichfield, abbot of Evesham, thought he had rooted out a conspiracy, sending one monk to Cromwell, the 'princi-pall doar' in the 'king ys grace matter', and keeping one in his 'salve custody'.[297] Even at the moment of the visitor's coming to Hoxne (Suffolk) routine commu-nality had already collapsed. Southwell reported 'ravyne, spoyle and wast' among them as 'men withwote rewle or ordre'.[298]

Although the papers preserved from these months scarcely mention the friars, there is a single letter that signals divisions of the same kind arising in one of the largest convents in the southern province. In mid-November John Artur of the Canterbury Franciscans reported to an unnamed correspondent how one of their number 'callyd ... heretyke' a Dutch friar employed to 'blotte owte' the papal title from the convent's books, 'spettyng in hys face with dyvers obukill werdys', causing him to 'flee'.[299]

The experience of the visitation did affect the regulars' commitment to their profession, both individually and collectively. The visitors' inquiries compelled each respondent to acknowledge not only their position in the community but also the length of time they had lived there. Then the terms of the king's injunctions set out for them the future prospect of a regime almost certainly different in its discipline from what they had known until then, not least in the call for strict enclosure inside the convent building. Those still standing between clothing as a novice and solemn profession may have needed no further encouragement to take up the offer of an authorised departure.

John Placett wrote to Cromwell from Chester, voicing anxieties that may have resonated for others, 'Y can nat awey with the burde and srtyenes off the religion ... the frater and other observaunce off the rule.'[300] The arrival on the scene of seculars of any kind may have been enough for some to be shaken from their torpor, given the strictures under which some novices were held. Thomas Legh claimed that as many as ten canons of Merton Priory clamoured to be allowed to leave when he visited after Michaelmas.[301] A month later in East Anglia, he described men and women (of West Dereham and Denny) 'instantly knelyng on ther knees howldyng up ther handys desyr[ing] to be delivered of suche relygyon'.[302]

Archbishop Cranmer may have been well informed when he worried that the visitors were not keeping to the terms of their commission, which set an age limit on those allowed unconditional release.[303] At times, the commissioners seem to have been conscious of the sudden self-awareness their arrival had created, and they set themselves to manipulate it. From his circuit of Essex, John Prise crowed over the teenage entrants he had talked into departure.[304] By the last week of September, Leighton reported a resolve to leave in each one of the downland convents he confronted from Chichester to Waverley. Two of them he claimed were ready to close the house entirely – these were probably Easebourne and Shulbrede – 'wiche we will dispatche on Monday by the way'.[305]

In his last circuit of the year, Leighton succeeded in raising the tremors so far as to bring about an open breach. Over three days in mid-November the canons of Folkestone and Langdon, the monks of Dover and the nuns of Davington each gave up their convents.[306] Leighton and his colleagues anticipated more, not least in neighbouring Sussex, although there it was only the oncoming parliament statute that decided the matter. Yet in the febrile climate the commissioners created, not all of those who left now stayed away. Before the end of the year five women, aged between fifteen and twenty-three, petitioned to be readmitted.[307]

Yet more common as the commissioners completed their task was the sense not of an ending but of a new departure. The commissioners helped to instil this themselves. If their reports to Cromwell carry some echo of their speeches when they met regular communities, then their message was of restoration and reformation, and the task they set out before them was the settlement of the house and its members under a new syllabus set out for them by their king. The tone of Thomas Bedyll's report on Hilsey's visitation of the friars suggested that he saw the letter of their writ fulfilled: 'the reformacion of old abuses deeply roted in the mynd of many which be now brought to good confirmite'.[308]

Despite behaviour which at times seems to have been calculated to be provocative, even Thomas Legh seems to have taken care not to render a convent incapable of continued life. He told Cromwell that he had cut off any exodus from Merton Priory, 'for then I shuld have left them but eight'.[309] Their interventions in the office of the superior – the removal of one and their replacement, or where there was already a vacancy, the identification of a successor – reinforced the impression of the beginning of a new era. It was Legh's sole report from Wherwell that the former abbess, Anne Colte, was to be 'honestly ryd from thens'.[310] The fresh start was embodied in the figure of the superior. The election John Vaughan presided over at Conwy, apparently 'with one assent and without any contradiction', was Richard Ap Rees, 'saving that he was xxiiii yers of aege'.[311] Before the visitors arrived, Henry Austen had taken office at Chacombe (Northamptonshire). John Tregonwell recognised his leadership as a break with the recent past but was warily optimistic for the future: '[he] ys comptentently well lernyde . . . the chanons byn rewde and unlernyde [but] he begynneth to bring them to some order'.[312]

In each congregation in every region of the kingdom it is possible to see communities planning for their conventual future. There were new admissions. Five monks from Hyde Abbey at the beginning of their career were presented for ordination at Winchester at Easter 1535; at Michaelmas there were seven new men at Peterborough Abbey; a week before Christmas there were four receiving their first tonsure at the tiny Northumberland priory of Tynemouth.[313] Even the Carthusian communities which had watched some of their leadership at the scaffold earlier received new professions six months after the visitation. The provision to the priorate of Cromwellian appointees did not disrupt these periodical patterns of renewal at Beauvale or Mount Grace.[314] The close-bound compact between the Crown and the mendicant leadership does not seem to have deterred foreign friars from passing into the provincial network.

Three years later, at the point at which their congregations came to surrender, there were men from overseas even in the remoter convents of north and west Wales. When the Franciscan Henry Standish dictated his will in July 1535 he spoke of convents building for the future: the Carmelites of Denbigh committing to the (re)construction of their cloister; the Oxford Greyfriars repairing and chaining (locandis) books in their scholars' library, and providing for a chantry (edificatura insule) within the body of their church.[315]

Notwithstanding the gestures of subjection made by the handful of superiors in affinity with the vicegerent, generally heads and their officers continued to administer their houses, exchange, lease and purchase with only glancing acknowledgement of the expectation of government scrutiny. The survival of the registers of some of the most prominent of monastic heads, Augustinian and Benedictine, reveals how far their independent authority had remained unscathed. Some of them were moved to invest in their new world. In the same accounting year as the valuers and visitors came, Mary Wynham, cellaress of Barking Abbey, spent more than £50 on oxen at three local fairs.[316] The cloister walk planned at Chester may have been a response to buoyant admissions. Printed books taken into the conventual collection at Evesham, Hailes and Merton suggest there was surely also an investment in the new demands of observant life under the royal regime.[317] Abbot Benson of Westminster had reason to expect the distinctive quality of monastic worship to prosper anew under the king's headship, as he received licence to recruit choristers from any church in England except the chapel royal.[318]

In this regard the reach of the new provincials should not be exaggerated. The agency of Abbot Maxey at Welbeck was limited and short-lived; by August 1536 he was dead. Ingworth's promotion to the suffragancy of Dover set him apart from his congregation and his difficulty in ruling them in 1538 suggests that his was a paper authority. The commitment to a monastic future was shared outside the precinct walls. Lady Lisle brought her daughter Brigid to Nunnaminster

(Hampshire) in the summer of 1535, it seems with a view to the long term; twelve months on, her resolve was unchanged and she made arrangements to provide her with a fresh set of clothes.

The king's commissions changed the monasteries and mendicant convents. Their effect was not only visible in the final phases, when they enforced the suppression statute from the spring of 1536, or took surrenders from 1538 onwards. From the first steps to secure their compliance with the royal supremacy the regulars were aware that their terms of trade with the Crown were shifting. The feeling of affinity, and the expressions, and demonstrations, of mutual interest which they had come to know over recent years no longer seemed so assured. Their impression of an about-turn was shared by some of the clerical and secular hierarchy which had shared in the compact established in preceding decades. They too were unsettled by this new agency of royal authority and they were ready – readier in fact than the majority of the religious – to express their disquiet.

The effects were not as far-reaching as they might have been, nor as they were surely intended to be. Not for the first time, the novel ambition of the Tudor regime proved to be far in advance of its infrastructure. Plague, the changeable climate and the poor communication of a government still reliant on parchment and third-party messengers hindered the valuation and the visitation on every circuit. When the suppression statute was first presented to parliament in February 1536, the visitors were still on the road. But the force of the king's commissions was also diluted by indecision at the very source of royal policy. Even if it is heightened by the fact that only the letters written to Cromwell survive in any quantity, there can be no doubt that his own view of the scope of these new measures was unresolved, and their ultimate purpose still unsettled; and although he was adept in recruiting and retaining a network of loyal agents, his personal relations with them were somehow stilted, so much that sometimes they had no idea what he wanted them to do.

The conspicuous achievement of the king's commissions was not to carry monastic England closer to its final chapter but to deliver it to the threshold of a new beginning of observant reform. The king's injunctions described a regime of regular discipline for the leadership and the convent alike which renewed the vision of Wolsey almost twenty years before. The reports from male monasteries (especially) show that these innovations were widely accepted. On the eve of the suppression statute, there was a cohort of cloistered men and women committed to creating a new age of monastic religion. The programme of reform, and the pressure attached to it in the hands of some of the king's agents, persuaded a handful of convents, and rather more individuals, to abandon the regular life altogether. It also pulled apart the ties that bound professed men and women to one another and to their leadership.

But it would be wrong to interpret these as the first warning cracks of an inevitable collapse. The valuation and the visitation had left many, perhaps most, houses with the impression that their changed terms of business with the Crown were now settled; and some, including those prominent in their own congregations, considered that their voice might now reach further than before. Some of the old hierarchy had gone but in its place was a cadre of men and women confident of their own authority in public and political life. For the agents of the regime, at ground level, and in government office, it seems doubtful the experience of these months had set them decidedly on a different course. The tearing-down of all religious houses was certainly thought of and written about in the circles of the royal household and court where there were reformist tastes of different strengths. But the deep roots of the monastic estate had also been laid bare like never before. Cromwell may have been pensive over the prospects for the religious houses but neither he nor the king were yet to be persuaded to depart from their present course. In the wet winter months of 1535–36 the commissioners were no less delayed in their task and no less doubtful about its end. As the first year of dissolution turned, it could be said that it was the regulars who had the upper hand.

VI

THE CHALLENGE OF CONFORMITY

Around the last day of September 1536, one Mr Saunderson of Reasby, a grange of Barlings Abbey (Lincolnshire), painted the three-cornered shield of the Holy Trinity on a parchment sheet and pinned it to towelling scrap which he attached to the end of a pole. Soon after he took it in his hands and walked out in the direction of the Roman road that led south-west to the city of Lincoln. Saunderson's towel was remembered later as 'the first banner in the field' when the professed religious and the employees of four monasteries in a twenty-mile radius – Barlings, Bardney, Louth Park and Kirkstead – and their town-and-country tenants and neighbours converged on the cathedral to make an armed challenge to the conduct of the king's commissioners. It was the first act of four months of unrest. The Lincoln protest was stifled in four days but the call to arms found an echo eighty miles due north in the neighbourhood of York, where another march mustered within the week; from then until February 1537 the disturbance ran further north, east and west as far as the Lancashire coast, forming what has become known as the Pilgrimage of Grace.

The chain of challenges was easily broken and the leadership defeated before it had been able to lead decisively. Yet the turn of this year had witnessed the most emphatic resistance to the will of royal government since 1534; and the source of its manpower, manifestos and much of its rebellious spirit seemed to be the religious houses. 'Dyvers monkes, chanons and nunnes ... [have] manifest thereby their naughty mynds towards the kings maiestie', opined the outraged monarch, 'warm in their demenes and cloysters ... they may not fight for ... but against their prynce and cuntrey'.[1] Henry VIII's response was the execution of five superiors and twenty-five professed religious in eight weeks between March and May 1537, the largest number of regulars to be subject to judicial death during his reign; so many that it was reported on the day that Barlings's abbot, Matthew Mackarell, was put to death, that 'the gate of London be full of quarters'.[2] 'Reduce them to conformyte', was the king's command.[3]

At the same time as the northerners' final challenge in February 1537, the commissioners charged with the closure of southern monasteries were advancing through the West Country. After a sixty-mile sweep across Somerset and into Devon, John Tregonwell reported to Cromwell from the priory at Polsloe (Exeter), no doubt aware of the late disturbances and anxious to tell a different story of his own circuit: 'with as good expedicion as we might we have taken surrender of the [seven] howses [with] as much conformities as myght be desyrd'. Despite this confident declaration he felt bound (for it would surely be known in time) to add a caveat that altered the tenor of his whole testimony: 'Savinge,' he began, perhaps hoping that the word might somehow diminish the damage of what was to follow, 'such waste and spoyl as passed before our coming' that would be beyond their means '[ever] to be recovered again'.[4] These houses were surrendered but it seems only in the face of deliberate and widespread resistance. The scale of the spoil, which meant the leasing-out or selling of property and moveable goods to keep them from being taken into possession by the Crown, could only be guessed at, but it was certain it could not now be undone. The blatant non-conformity of the north country had blazed in the winter season, but it had been extinguished on the scaffold; the sly two faces with which the south and west responded to royal policy would not be so swiftly erased.

The enforcement of the Henrician reformation was, above all, the pursuit of conformity. Differences over doctrine, whether radical or reactionary, were tolerated to a degree, or at the least, a definitive judgement on them was deferred. Despite Thomas Cromwell's growing personal authority, and the king's own caprice, after 1534 it was still possible to challenge policy in word and deed. It was neither their convictions nor the conduct of their office that caused the executions of Bishop Fisher, Chancellor More or Prior Houghton of the London Charterhouse; rather it was their refusal to show outward acceptance of the king's authority. Conformity became the watchword of Henry's *Ecclesia Anglicana* from the time its first statutory foundations were laid at the moment of the Break with Rome. 'His maiestie more couayt[es] and desiry[es] the good obediences and conformities of his sayde subiectis', explained the earliest (1533) in a succession of royal proclamations, printed for consumption nationwide, to 'establishe ... one conformable and vnyforme order'.[5]

The royal commissioners sent out to the churches of the kingdom to administer the oath of succession in the summer of 1534 were charged to seek 'a good conform-itie'.[6] Now all of the statutes that issued from the ongoing session at Westminster demanded the same obedience, in the words of the king's writ: 'By your truth, plain-ness and conformity show yourself a personage of wisdom and gravity in the tolera-tion and furtherance of such things passed ... in our high court of parliament'.[7] Lords and commons, court, county magnates, and the commissioners carrying government's programme into the provinces were called to set an example to the community of the realm, 'joyned in oon conformytie to serve the king'.[8] In his *Exhortacion to the people*, commissioned by the government and published between the close of the Reformation Parliament and the outbreak of unrest in October, the humanist Thomas Starkey cast this practical necessity as a principle of kingship: 'a Chrystian prynce ... studyeth [no thyng more] thane to conserve concorde and unitie'.[9]

The capacity to conform was made the principal measure of the fitness of monas-teries and friaries to fulfil a satisfactory role in the new state Church. Cromwell commanded his agents always to weigh their willingness to accept the king's will whatever the matter of business might be. Soon, houses of each order came to be marked out as either 'conformable' or otherwise, and the most loyalist of their heads had been set on a new *cursus honorum* that propelled them, via royal patronage and prelacy, to a new status as avowed servants of the Crown. Perhaps the most successful of these new conformists, Robert Fuller, abbot of Waltham, saw the changing circum-stances very clearly: 'I suppose all thynge will prove the betre to suche conformyte'.[10]

The challenges to conformity with Henry's reformation are generally under-stood to have been concentrated at opposite ends of the governing process, on the one hand among the counsellors and courtiers closest to the king, and on the other in provincial society among those whose livelihoods were affected by government policy but who lacked the status to influence it or its enforcement in their own locality. The institutional clergy, secular and regular, have long been seen as decid-edly docile in the decade after the Break with Rome, standing in contrast to the lively debate and even violent direct action that arose from cathedrals, churches and religious houses in some regions of mainland Europe. The conspicuous, fatal conflict of a tiny minority of the total population, often represented at any rate as the result of personal struggles with the regime, has tended only to heighten the impression of an otherwise collective calm.

The reception of the royal supremacy in 1534 in every congregation, and the apparent readiness of communities to accept institutional closure and individual secularisation from 1536, has suggested that the regulars were almost meekly submissive. Two monks of Canterbury Cathedral Priory defended Elizabeth Barton to their deaths in 1534 but sixty-eight of their brethren detached themselves from the drama. Three Carthusians refusing to acknowledge the supremacy were hanged as traitors in May 1535, but as many as 100 of their colleagues, resident in nine houses from south to north, came to accept it and lived on. The Birgittine Richard Reynolds died with them but as many as eighty men and women of Syon lived on. John Forest, Observant Franciscan of the Greenwich convent, was burned as a heretic in May 1538, but he was the only member of the congregation in England to be publicly executed. Perhaps thirty were imprisoned between 1534 and 1540, but perhaps up to fifty remained within the network until the general surrender of friaries in 1538.[11] Seven abbots and priors, and some monks and canons, were counted among the executions that followed the dispersal of the Pilgrimage in the spring of 1537, but they died alongside five times as many laymen. The abbots of Barlings, Fountains, Jervaulx, Kirkstead, Sawley and Whalley and the priors of Birdlington and Guisborough were condemned to death although Thomas Bolton of Sawley may have died before the sentence was carried out.[12] Finally, four abbots, of Benedictine Colchester, Glastonbury and Reading, and Cistercian Woburn, were convicted of treason and condemned to death between June 1538 and December 1539. Glastonbury and Reading had an immense public profile, being ancient, with royal associations and on the main routes of public devotion; the others did not. Each case arose from the personal position of the superior, two of whom (Glastonbury and Reading) had been, like others of his victims, previous intimates of the king.[13]

The few contemporary accounts from these years do not argue greatly with this view. The testimony of laymen taken in the aftermath of the Pilgrimage scarcely registers the presence of the religious orders; their part in the rising is known mostly from the tales they told themselves. The earliest history of the decade, Edward Hall's chronicle first published in 1545, recorded the sequence of executions as the downfall of individual dissidents.[14]

In fact, it seems likely that the responses of the religious orders to the king's reformation have been underestimated and oversimplified. The view has been obscured by the limitations of the surviving evidence, for the commissions of 1533–35, the risings of 1536–37 and their repression, and the treason cases of 1538 and 1539. There are few first-hand accounts of the acts of the religious at these moments, the best of them concerning the place of Barlings in the Lincolnshire unrest, and the resistance of Robert Hobbes, abbot of Woburn. Many of the fair copies of the confessions of the suspects of the Pilgrimage have been fragmented by tears and damp. If it was notarised at all, not one word of the show trial of Glastonbury's abbot, Richard Whiting, has ever been found. Here, perhaps more than on any other aspect of their reformation history, the record has been distorted by the dependence on the narrative that is threaded through the HMSO calendar of state papers, which by its nature, and the priority of its Victorian editors, gives the greatest emphasis to the steady progress of government policy. Much of what is contained there about the challenges and conspiracies of the religious orders they chose not to transcribe.

There are strong grounds for suggesting that monasteries were more committed to, and complicit in, the unrest not only in Lincolnshire and the northern counties in the autumn and winter of 1536–37 but also in East Anglia, Oxfordshire, Kent and Somerset in the months after those pilgrims had been punished. The impulse to protest may have been more collective in some of these locations and if not quite coordinated, at least somewhat less ad hoc and headstrong than has often been assumed. The common cause between a monastery and the employees of their grange, which inspired Mr Saunderson to down tools and take up his makeshift banner, may have arisen in many places. The bellicose behaviour that burst onto the Lincolnshire roads at Michaelmas 1536 should also be seen in the light of the long history of direct action on the borders of monastic estates. The landowners of Henrician England would not recognise history's portrait of a monastic estate that was always apprehensive and ultimately submissive. Apart from the Pilgrimage, it does appear there was more, varied and widespread non-conformity among religious houses after 1534 than historians have recognised, or indeed was registered by the royal government at the time. The superficial compliance that Tregonwell met in Somerset and Devon, which thinly disguised a pattern of deliberate and damaging resistance, was widespread in England and Wales.

There are so many instances in these years before 1540 where there is evidence to prove, or to suspect, covert action of this kind that it might be said to have been the typical response. At the same time, the disturbance spilling out of many houses may have been higher also because of the presence of conformists, self-conscious and vocal in their loyalism to the Crown and their taste for reform. Their interests have often been interpreted as only personal careerism. Rather, it may show that far from being cowed by the king's reformation, some communities pursued the central arguments within their precinct walls. That they might act as a crucible for conflict was itself a threat to the new conformity.

There was no strong tradition of political and public radicalism in monastic England. Passed down to them from their forebears was a simple loyalism, sustained by the verbal and visual reminders of monarchy as founder and protector that surrounded them. Looking up at the ceiling of their chamber, priors of Carlisle were reminded daily 'to lofe God and thy prynce'.[15] In this respect the English religious orders were quite unlike their European counterparts, where for generations the clerical and scholastic authority of convents, and their neighbourhood ministry, had drawn them towards the controversies of state, church and commune. Especially in urban centres, the religious houses, their precincts and their personnel, had become the centre point of critique and popular protest.

The coming of the printing press had only heightened their leadership in public discourse since they were its principal patrons.[16] Of course, England's religious could not claim the same pre-eminence in cities and towns crowded with parishes with a material, social and cultural agency of their own. Print had not spread very far or very securely into provincial England, although when and where it did it was almost always under the patronage of the monasteries.[17] English monks and friars did command the same position in public ministry; indeed, the familiarity of monastic and mendicant preachers and pastors may have been much more akin to the European experience than has often been appreciated. The structural differences were significant but perhaps above all the prevailing culture of their communities did not propagate political engagement.

At a time when the English language was established as the medium of political and popular critique, the regulars continued to hold it at arm's length; their increased investment in university education in the half-century before 1534 only reinforced the distinct, Latinate identity of their leading spokesmen. Their intellectual enterprise did inspire them to court public attention but the audience they aimed at was the clerical and scholarly establishment. The most celebrated scholar monks of Henry's early years, Richard Bere of Glastonbury and Richard Kidderminster of Winchcombe, concentrated their speaking and writing energies in papal, episcopal and courtly circles: among their own kind. Bere (d. 1524) is not known ever to have referred to the Church controversies rising around him in his last decade; Kidderminster only turned his mind to Luther at the instigation of the king.[18]

Certain monastic prelates were drawn towards public debate over the authority of the Church: Thomas Goldston of Christ Church, Canterbury, aligned himself to the secular prelates that challenged Henry VII in 1497;[19] Abbot Kidderminster joined the seculars who spoke out on the Hunne case.[20] But these were two moments in more than twenty years and their contributions were Latin sermons which they might have presented in their own chapter house. It is possible that there was a social dimension to the regulars' diffidence towards political discourse. Religious men were not from high society; their horizons were provincial, their family experience of court and parliament at the level of petition not participation; it may not be coincidental that typically Tudor superiors did not take up the seats in the House of Lords to which they were summoned.

Not being natural insiders in the political and public spheres, the regulars were inclined to respond to current affairs according to the dynamics of their immediate neighbourhood. Through the years of conflict between Lancaster and York called the Wars of the Roses, religious houses had tended to catch, and sometimes to channel, the mood that surrounded them. At St Albans, first in 1455 and then in 1461, the monastery joined their tenants and townspeople in condemning the royalist forces for bringing the battle into their streets and in the lee of the abbey.[21] There was a Lancastrian loyalism just below the surface in the counties of the south-west and it was natural for Roger Bemynster, a local man and newly elected abbot of Cerne, to allow Queen Margaret of Anjou to convene her council of war in May 1471.[22] In 1498 Athelney Abbey and Beaulieu offered temporary respite to Perkin Warbeck, whose local popularity had not dimmed after his humiliation at Taunton; Athelney was still paying the fine for its partisan moment when the Valor commissioners arrived in 1535.[23] Historians have appeared surprised at the Canterbury monk Edward Bocking's defence of Elizabeth Barton but such an absorption of a popular, neighbourhood cause – which initially Bocking shared with his Augustinian (Leeds Priory) and Cluniac (Monks Horton Priory) colleagues in the county – was an instinct common to all religious houses.[24]

Their ties to the social community of their small townships and the surrounding countryside also gave them an understanding of, and even a taste for, pursuing their causes through direct action. It is possible that this was also a particular legacy of the civil strife of the fifteenth century, when factional conflicts caught local communities in their path, even the walled precincts of wealthy monasteries. Just as the regulars came to recognise the institutions of communal authority so it seems they adapted to the more immediate practice of politics in the open street and the common field. In the seventy-five years after the first battle of St Albans had marked the beginning of the Wars of the Roses, the involvement of religious houses in acts of public disorder rose steadily. When the jurisdiction of a monastic proprietor was challenged, now they were as likely to make an immediate and public demonstration of their authority as they were to fight their cause formally in a civil court. After their tenants of Over Haddon had torn down their boundary hedges, men from Leicester Abbey showered them with bowshot.[25] Employees of Chester Abbey were prosecuted for affray in the city; their targets were typically tradesmen whose guild grip on the market steadily eroded the monastery's dominant influence.[26]

Increasingly also they found (and perhaps looked for) a shared cause with other local interests against a common threat, such as the expanding reach of a neighbouring landlord or the diocesan bishop. Fountains Abbey was widely believed to have led the six successive attacks on field enclosures that erupted in the North Riding in 1496–99.[27] On the Sussex Downs, the prior and convent of Lewes were suspected of stirring the tenantry persistently to threaten neighbouring landowners in the 1510s and 1520s. Prior Robert Croham of Lewes lent the weight of his office to the support of eighty-year-old John Walcock, when his landlord saw him summoned to Star Chamber for taking gulls and their eggs from the cliffs at Borne.[28]

Houses equipped themselves for active protest. They maintained a store of weaponry; they may have retained men in their precincts who might serve in an impromptu defence force. At Kingswood in 1517, the monastery faced troops in the pay of Edward Stafford, duke of Buckingham, and they held them at bay.[29] The canons of Lytham Priory held the wherewithal to launch an offensive raid on their neighbours, the Butler family.[30] The professed were known themselves to take part. The fight between Peterborough Abbey and its tenants in 1517, remembered locally as the Battle of Borough Fen, saw Benedictine habits on the field.[31] This was a generation of religious men as familiar with feats of arms as any seen in England since the battle-hardened monks of Norman times. There were

271

killers, proven and suspected, behind the cowl: an allegation of murder in 1533 did not displace Thomas Lord from the priorate of Conishead.[32] The shock, in 1536, of the king's commissioners at the spectacle of professed religious at Sawley wielding 'bows and spears' surely spoke only of their own inexperience.[33]

Their active, often aggressive reach into local arguments did not diminish as the Tudor regime matured. In fact, as Henry's reign entered its second decade, in some parts of the country it appeared that the monastic estate was increasingly preoccupied with seigneurial and popular politics. As the 1520s advanced, the leading houses in each of the congregations were increasingly inclined to respond to the government in two quite different registers: by their superior and as a corporate body they showed their willingness to accept the principle of royal oversight, even as bluntly applied by Wolsey and his agents, and the emerging proposition for a divorce and dispensation from Rome; at the same time, in their own domains they mobilised their material and patronal resources to defy the interference of the Crown.

Their most conspicuous challenge in this mode was to Wolsey's plan for the suppression and sequestration of monasteries for his twin college foundation at Ipswich and Oxford. The parent houses were not cautious in challenging the cardinal's terms. Prior Richard Vowell of Walsingham outmanoeuvred Wolsey when he cast his eye over Flitcham by publicising anxiety over heretical preaching in the vicinity.[34] St Mary's Abbey, York, countered his claim on their dependent priory at Rumburgh with a demand for a payment of 300 marks which would obviously curb his ambitions.[35] Lewes Priory defended its claim to the principal manors and churches of Stanesgate Priory (Essex), diminishing its potential as an endowment for the colleges. It caused such a delay that the remainder of the priory's property finally passed to another religious house in 1531.[36] At Bayham Abbey, the canons in company with their tenants and neighbouring proprietors took up arms.[37] It is possible they planned a series of risings over the Weald. Archbishop William Warham was so worried by the rumours that he would not press them to pay the subsidy recently granted to the king.[38]

A more insidious challenge to the aims of the Crown was building in a number of major friaries and monasteries over the course of the decade. There was a rising interest in the radical theology of Martin Luther. By the mid-1520s there was a circle of Lutheran friars at Cambridge whose influence radiated outwards to other of their convents. In May 1528 four Augustinian friars of Clare (Suffolk) were forced to abjure the heresy they had learned, apparently, from the university masters, Miles Coverdale and Robert Barnes.[39] William Roye, erstwhile Observant friar and confederate of William Tyndale, had been followed intermittently by the authorities for much of the 1520s. He was still being tailed from Westminster to the Norfolk coast in 1529 where the fact 'he doth speke all maner of languages' made him conspicuous. Now two further Observants of Greenwich, John Lawrence and John West, were also known to the regime.[40] Their radicalism was matched in the convent of the Augustinian friars at Cambridge and it transmitted to points north, east and south as far as the Home Counties and London.[41]

By the mid-1520s, such radicalism was not only harboured in-house but was leading some into cross-Channel contacts and a traffic in books. The movements of the Carmelite Laurence Cooke were reported from Flanders as far as Walden Abbey.[42] The literature of reform, if not outright radicalism, reached the Franciscan women at Denny, just eight miles north from Cambridge, where it was reported in May 1528 that Abbess Elizabeth Throckmorton had asked to borrow a copy, perhaps in manuscript, of William Tyndale's translation of Erasmus's *Enchiridion militis Christiani*.[43] Perhaps as early as the turn of the decade these friars were also beginning to test their ideas on lay audiences in the towns and villages where they served as preachers and pastors. Reports of the provocative preaching of John Bale, 'the hyst prichynge of a whyght freer', which reached the government only in 1533, give the impression he was already something of a veteran radical in the countryside around Ipswich.[44]

The reception of reformation ideas was not confined to friars influenced by Cambridge University and its traffic in continental books. Luther's arguments were familiar to many, if not fervently followed in the monasteries. John Skelskyns returned from Cambridge to Ely Cathedral Priory with one of Luther's pamphlets just two years after the publication of the theses at Wittenberg (1517). Perhaps his reading brought about a Damascene conversion. He had abjured the monastic life by April 1536.[45] In 1521 the Cistercians of Boxley had made a sufficient study of Luther's 'yls' to put up a refutation of them for locals and pilgrims to read.[46] John Bateman, a Carthusian of Hinton Charterhouse, knew Lutheran theology well enough to compose his own refutation.[47] Houses sending students to university were also exposed to the radicals' ideas. At Evesham Abbey, Luther was taken as a nickname by one of the monks exchanging letters between the cloister and their college at Oxford.[48]

273

Among these academic cohorts there was an intellectual curiosity amounting almost to commitment to the radical cause. In February 1528 a secular scholar, Thomas Gerard (also called Garret), who had been covertly circulating copies of the reformers' pamphlets in Oxford for some time to 'the grette corrupcion of yuogeth ther', was taken prisoner on university premises. He was first confronted at the city's Benedictine Gloucester College, where three apparent accomplices were also detained. Two of them were monks of Bury St Edmunds, one was from Glastonbury.[49] Within weeks it was revealed that Gerard had already put a cache of his illicit imprints, 'three score or above', in the hands of the prior of Reading, John Sherborne.[50] Another Bury monk at the university, one Dr Rougham, was reported for expressing radical opinions; his colleague, William Blomfild, was called to London for questioning about his radical views. He later turned to Calvinism and so these early suspicions may not have been groundless.[51]

In 1531 the warden of Canterbury College told Cromwell about two student monks who had a collection of suspect books which were then surrendered into his hands.[52] Two canon students of St Mary's College, the Augustinians' *studium* at Oxford, were found in possession of suspect books in 1532; one of them was Robert Ferrar, a future bishop executed under Queen Mary, whose reformed convictions may have begun here.[53]

It does seem there was more to the monks' involvement with underground groups of religious radicals than mere student misbehaviour. When Archbishop Cranmer's metropolitan visitation uncovered a cell of 'heretiks' at Sandwich (Kent) in 1534, the evidence led him to the Benedictine abbey of St Augustine's, where one of the monks, William Wynchelsey, was said to have acted as their self-appointed patron, providing them with game from the convent's larder, 'to make mery'.[54] Testimony from his own cloister colleagues suggests they were well aware, and weary, of his avant-garde views. Meanwhile Cranmer's informants from the continental mainland found the Cistercian Gabriel Donne in Louvain with Dominicans and other English clerks surrounding William Tyndale.[55]

The king's visitors of 1535 were often struck by the expressions of enthusiasm for reform, and sometimes downright radicalism, they heard inside the monastic enclosure. From Walden Abbey, John Prise reported that Abbot Robert Baryngton 'in his lecture ... kept dayli [persuaded] ... that there was no sanctimonie in monkery'.[56] Of course, it is unwise to project back from the middle of the decade; on the other hand such points of view did not arise overnight. By the time of the

Break with Rome, monastic interest in, and sympathy for, the case for reform should not be underestimated, perhaps especially in those houses closely bound to the universities. It may help to explain the hesitant, at times conflicted and inconsistent responses made to the royal supremacy, both at the moment at which it was first enforced and in the months and years that followed. It might also offer another reason for the limited showing of collective acts of resistance, as the Crown's interventions in their affairs intensified. Perhaps it was not that these religious lacked a response to the reformation argument; rather that they could not arrive at any common ground.

Given the Crown's small cohort of committed monastic and mendicant allies in 1533, the king and his counsel might have anticipated a challenge to the Break with Rome and the enforcement of its central legislation, the succession and the royal supremacy. Their pressure on the diocesan bishops to administer the oath and to compel conformity perhaps reflected their underlying caution. Yet as it happened, the divorce of the king from his Catholic queen and his kingdom from its Roman pope met with the least challenge from the regulars, and the most lasting conformity of any measure of the decade. The end of one royal marriage and the revelation of another did not provoke a principled response from any congregation or house, and certainly not a theological one. Criticism from individuals was reported from time to time but most of it was aired only after the Boleyn marriage was already two years old; without exception, it turned on the propriety of the match, and the queen's personal reputation, not on the matter of reform. In fact, there was an impulse to isolate those who were not inclined to conform. The anonymous chronicler of Canterbury condemned the 'marvelous hypocrisy' of Elizabeth Barton and her supporters, and cast his monastic colleague Bocking as a conspirator, 'chiefe author in her dissimulation'; their separation from the community of monks was conspicuous when they were 'grevosly rebuked … at the sermon time'. Theirs was a 'disobedience towards the kings majestie' quite distinct from the mood of the house.[57]

Nor did the rejection of papal authority disturb the congregations en masse. The leaders of the reformed orders, the Birgittines, Carthusians and Franciscan Observants, held it to be incompatible with their corporate mission. But they could not easily convince each one of their brethren that it compromised their own vocation. Their personal – perhaps consciously exemplary – stand against the royal supremacy worked against the creation of a wider opposition.

William Peto, the Observant Provincial, exiled himself at the beginning of 1533. John Forest and Hugh Rich, wardens of the Greenwich and Richmond Observants, and John Houghton and Humphrey Middlemore, prior and sub-prior of the London Charterhouses, were taken into custody before the supremacy statute even came before parliament, each before the examination of their communities had been completed. The warden of the Southampton Observants also held himself apart. He made a peculiar public appearance in the pulpit of Winchester Cathedral Priory, apparently intending to play the critic rather than the traitor. He condemned the 'diversitie' of clerks, urged the people to 'stond theyr faith constantly and humbly obedyently use theym selfe towards their prynce'; but at the same time he held before them a book, 'which ley upon the pulpit', which 'theryn five or six place approvynge *primatum Petri*, and Englyshed the same'.[58]

From the remaining Greenwich Observants, Cromwell was able to recruit two, John Lawrence and Richard Lyst, as advocates for the cause of the Crown among their colleagues. The convent of Newark showed itself conformable enough, for Forest was released into their custody.[59] The conformist, even reformist, mood of some of the congregation propelled Observants to apply to change their habit and serve as secular priests from February 1535 onward.[60]

There was the same impulse for complicity passing through the chain of charterhouses. Prior Houghton's stand seems to have stirred only those who were already members of his own circle of corresponding friends. The outlook of Brian Bee, monk of Axholme, was the opposite of his martyred prior: in December 1535 he purchased a licence to withdraw and live as a secular priest.[61] The rump of the community at Hinton Charterhouse roundly rejected murmurings of rebellion from one or two of their elders. Their prior, Edmund Horde, was commended to Cromwell by Archbishop Lee: his presence shall 'more worke in them than anye lerneng or autoritie'.[62] At Mount Grace Priory the generational dynamics were the other way around, as the prior stifled stirrings from his juniors. Robert Marshall from Sheen presented himself to Cromwell as an informant. Here a demonstration of conformity may have been the strategy devised by the governing authority of La Grande Chartreuse.[63]

The general conformity of 1534 fractured; almost, it seems with the final passage of the statute for the royal supremacy in November. By the time that crown commissioners set out on their circuits to begin the valuation, the list of oaths uniformly sworn six months before already seemed like a chronicle of another age. A rising number of reports reached Cromwell of religious houses where some or other of the professed had spoken against the king's headship, his marriage, and their loss of the beneficent authority of Rome. On the very doorstep of the king's new archbishop of Canterbury, there were tales of regulars preaching publicly against the new world.[64]

A royal injunction for the preaching of the royal supremacy published in June 1535 returned public attention to the case for the headship, and for regulars much employed in the pulpit this introduced a new aspect to the assent they had given previously behind closed doors. The executions of the Carthusians (May), John Fisher (June) and Sir Thomas More (July) may well have proved a catalyst for more outspoken criticism. For some perhaps it was a turning point in their relationship with the Crown. There had been a conscious effort for the convictions of these few professed men to leave their mark on their congregation. John Houghton's dismembered arm was set over the gate of his own house.[65]

Annalists recording these events as they happened appeared to notice a change in mood, as they described the executed not as errant individuals, as they had done Elizabeth Barton and her defenders, but as officers of a religious house and representatives of an order.[66] At Woburn Abbey the spectacle of the scaffold prompted a novel response to royal policy of the Crown, as the monks marked the deaths with a liturgical commemoration.[67]

Now, it seems there was a shift in the presence and performance of monks and friars in the pulpit. Previously, in public addresses they had been in the shadow of their secular colleagues. Yet as the year turned there were widespread reports of what they had been heard to say in parish churches and at outdoor preaching crosses. Some of them seized these pulpits with a coup de théâtre. The monk of Syon Abbey (Middlesex), David Curson, stirred his audience with a verbal sleight, appearing to speak for the royal supremacy then suddenly crossing himself and saying 'Mea culpa'.[68] His colleague Richard Whitford preached the Sunday sermon, publicly enough for Thomas Bedyll to hear it and report it to Cromwell, passing over any invocation of the king and his headship now expected. It may not have been Whitford's only display, since Bedyll spoke of him as a known quantity, 'one of the most wilful of that house', a man of 'but small lernyng' but 'a greate rayler'.[69]

At Syon, if not elsewhere, they were now taking up the same theme week on week. Edmund Horde, prior of the Charterhouse at Hinton, also appears to have been preaching on controversial topics at this time, since his surviving commonplace book carries notes on prayers for the dead and the king's own refutation of Luther.[70] The chaplain of St Albans Abbey's precinct parish was reported for his disloyal preaching, 'defacyng of the kyng' to 'make ... much sedycon and stryffe'; he was a secular priest but his position meant his outspoken behaviour must have been sanctioned by the monastic employer.[71] In Bristol, the Dominicans and Franciscans were said to have seized control of the city's public sermon cycle.[72]

Further signals of agitation reached Cromwell's chambers at Austin Friars as the royal visitation was underway. They came not from the commissioners for the most part but at first hand from inside the religious houses, from superiors (at Kingswood, Woburn) and those outside the ranks of office-holders (at Stratford Langthorne, Waltham).[73] Correspondence with ministers of the Crown, and with the king himself, sent from inside the monasteries, was not new, but there was now a frequency and a tone to the dispatches which had not been there before. John Placett alias Horwode wrote to Cromwell from Waltham at least four times in the summer and early autumn of the year, in a manner so familiar it is certain these were not his only letters. 'Papysche munkyshnes be ... so exalted', he confided.[74] 'Our suffran lord ... most catholyke ... hede and supreme hede next gode to whom we owe feyth and fydelyte ... ys nat sett furth so dylygently so hertelly as it shulde be'. He begged 'Master Secretary' for 'suffycient auctoryte' to 'sett further the supremyte ... evry Sunday' that 'y may call evry monke to preche and tech to other and to wryte hyte and ofte to repet and nat tepide aut frigide sed totis viribus'.[75] The shallow conformity now exposed scarcely six months from the passing of the statute might suggest that their submissions of the previous year had been no more than short-term expediency; even that they had been deliberately stage-managed displays.

The tales told at Woburn trace a steady erosion of the consensus the community had shown when they first submitted in 1534. One of the monks, Lawrence Blomham, claimed that he had opposed the king's purpose from the outset and when he spoke the oath his hand had not touched the Bible. More straightforwardly, his colleagues suggested they had since changed their minds as they turned from the principle of the supremacy to consider its practical enforcement. They had spoken of the headship in their sermons but had not been prepared repeatedly to expound the justification for it by scriptural exegesis. The sub-prior admitted to adopting a neutral position and in his preaching now neither commended the king's headship nor condemned the papacy.[76] This account of submission is unusually vivid but it may not have been unique. Anecdotes of this time told a year or two later at Worcester Cathedral Priory are very similar. There it was said that monks had taken the oath 'for fear' but on reflection afterwards could not in all conscience conform.[77]

For many who had subscribed to the succession and supremacy it may have been the upheavals of 1535, locally, in visitation, and nationally, in the spectacle of executions, that laid bare the power of the policy which previously had not been clearly perceived. The annal for the year kept by a Canterbury monk appeared to recognise a conflict between principle and practice: now the name of the pope was 'utterly renownced', and preachers rightly 'bark against his [the pope's] power', but Bishop Fisher and Chancellor More were put to death although 'being excellent well learned men'.[78] Returning to the realm in 1536 after a decade in Italy, Richard Morison, an apologist for the king's reform, recognised the conflict with a sudden clarity: 'Sorry I must nedes be to se monkes, friers, and priestes whyche so longe stode doubting whether they myght aknowledge our soveraygne lord the kynge to be theyr heed.'[79] Their difficulty in digesting what was now unfolding is focused in further scenes described at Woburn: the community watched as their abbot now 'liynyn[ed] [learned] in reasons and bokys' somehow to recover the case for 'the maytenance of his proposition [of papal power]'.[80] His sub-prior Dan Raffe looked to his books for the opposite remedy, to persuade himself of the case for reform, by reading William Tyndale's *Obedience of a Christian Man* (1528) and the anonymous *The Glass of Truth* (1532).[81]

The communities that had wrestled most with the royal supremacy saw doubts resurface at this time. The tentative conformity achieved in the majority of Carthusian houses by the end of 1534 steadily eroded in a wave that passed from the south-west (Hinton Charterhouse) to the north-east (Hull). A vision experienced by one of the remaining monks at the London house, John Darley, about one of his colleagues now in prison, challenged him, 'why do ye yet not follow our father (i. e. Prior Houghton) . . . for he is merter in heven'; it was perhaps a symptom of what was now emerging as a party line.[82] Pressure to turn from conformity to resistance split the community. One of the monks, Peter Wattes, appealed to Cromwell, 'if the men of my order . . . get me, they would make me agree to their sprites, or else imprison me that I should never see the sun'.[83] Another, William Marshall, attempted to make the case for religious reform, receiving and circulating radical pamphlets imported from the European mainland.[84] It seems there was a similar conflict at Mount Grace, where the prior's plan for the whole convent to abjure the oath they had made six months before was confessed to the king's commissioners.[85] At Syon, it was reported that now 'muche evyl and . . . muche treson . . . hath been sowed abrode in this mater'.[86] One of the former Observants now broke his cover at Southampton and spoke out against the king, recalling the claims and cause of Elizabeth Barton from two years before.[87]

In these expressions of resistance it does seem there was now a level of planning and a sense of purpose. At Syon Abbey, those who were decided against the royal supremacy used their established channel of print publication to set out their position. 'No temporall lawe maye bynde any spirituall persone,' declared the monastery's prolific author, Richard Whitford, in his *Pype or Tonne*, 'exepte it be graunted or ratified by a decre of the Pope and his Cardinalles or by a general counsell'.[88] If this was intended to overturn the supremacy, the text also threatened the person of the king, calling them 'greate herytkes' that 'saye and wryte . . . that . . . all maner of personales as well spirituall as temporall shudle be obedient unto the prophane and seculer princes'.

Syon's location and profile assured access to metropolitan printers but in provincial monasteries it seems there was some effort to restate the case for papal monarchy in more traditional forms. Monks at Pershore Abbey, under the direction of their abbot, John Stonywell, appear to have displayed or distributed manuscripts. One of their brethren had set himself against them and appealed to Cromwell, 'sumwatt . . . relygyus men . . . kep yn puttyng forth of books the beyshatt of roms userpt power'.[89] A planned, passive resistance to the removal of the papal title from public view may have spread wide. It was reported in the summer from Chichester diocese that 'books are not well razed or cancelled with diligence'.[90]

There was also some effort to recover control over the spoken as well as the written word. In Worcester diocese, where Hugh Latimer, a reformer rising under royal patronage had just taken the see, neighbouring monasteries at Hailes and Winchcombe seem to have coordinated a campaign of public preaching consciously to provoke the new regime. Anthony Saunders, a secular priest dispatched to promote the royal supremacy, complained 'if [the abbot of Hailes] favered ye word of God so moche as he hinder yt yt might be unto me a great furthere and help. Of truth what communycatyon so ever any man use in hys company the monastery or nyghe to hyr yt may be allowed of hym so yet be not. Ye gos[ell of our savyor Crist that he and hys name new lernynge and full of heresy.'[91] In Somerset, where the diocesan (Bath and Wells) was in his dotage, Abbot Richard Whiting welcomed a Franciscan, John Brynstan, to stir audiences against any 'who support the new fangles'.[92]

In many cases the agitation of these houses was spread, or spilled out, into the neighbourhoods that surrounded them. Thomas Bedyll feared that the priests of Syon Abbey had shared their doubts over the royal supremacy when they received the confessions of the layfolk who came to their church: 'uttward confessiuns of al commers ... hath been the cause of muche evyl, and of muche treson which hath been sowed abrode in this mater of the kings title'.[93] The pointed omission of the supremacy from the liturgy at Sheen was observed by 'straungers in the church every [week] and holyday'.[94] At times, clearly it was a two-way exchange. Brother Raffe of Woburn said that his rejection of the supremacy had been encouraged by a priest from a nearby parish, himself a former friar. Another, the incumbent at Toddington, five miles away, presented the abbot with a book of statements in support of the plenitude of papal power.[95]

Some superiors looked to assert their leadership in the local community. From his pulpit at Stratford Langthorne, Abbot William Huddleston called on his neighbours to recall the old sentence of 'excommunycacon, as we know right well ... optayned by non other power ... by yonde the see ... then of certen bishops of rome' and challenged them that by conformity to the new ways 'bothe we and they that eate or dryncke with us be also a curste'.[96] Sir Piers Dutton, patron of Norton Priory (Cheshire), suspected that the prior and canons were conspiring acts of sedition with prominent citizens of Chester.[97] Actions of some kind seems to have been anticipated in the neighbouring county, as the new abbot of Vale Royal (Staffordshire), John Harware, was made the subject of a popular prophecy.[98]

It was a reflection of the conflict inside the houses, however, that some heads became active in the enforcement of conformity and the exposure of potential sedition. Prior John Draper of Christchurch at Twynham (Dorset) won the approval of Thomas Legh for his display of loyalism 'in the parishe churche in the pulpit to the multitude of the parisshe wher by was declared that the kings grace is emperor of this his realm'.[99] Abbot John Reve of Bury St Edmunds rooted out and reported a spinster from the Bradfields, villages under the abbey's jurisdiction in the orbit of the town. Margaret Chanseler alias Elys had challenged the conformist calm of her neighbourhood with her colourful slanders of the king's new queen, 'a goggyll yed hoore', and her heartfelt plea for her predecessor, 'God save queen Katherine'.[100] When Richard Marshall began preaching against the royal supremacy in Newcastle, the prior of the Dominicans was the first to report him.[101]

Before the suppression began in earnest in the summer of 1536 a potent partisanship was building in towns and villages with or within the reach of religious houses, their inmates and staff. They were not always the first, nor the only causes of it, but there is no shortage of accounts – first-hand testimony as well as witness statements – that demonstrate they were often deliberate and determined contributors. They stepped into public arenas to speak their minds. A Canterbury friar, named only Arthur, chose the Sunday sermon at Herne, six miles to the north, to condemn preachers of reform as 'Judas fellas'.[102] Prior Edmund Harcocke of the Norwich Dominicans made first Easter Monday, then Ascension Eve, the platforms for his protest, apparently to the embarrassed surprise of the city's governors.[103]

These provocations did not stop at public rhetoric. The tendency of certain regular communities to sponsor local violence now seems to have strayed into some of these locations. There seems to have been fear of a fracas at Norwich, which persuaded the mayor to allow the preacher to finish his rant.[104] Sir William Stonor reported that the regular houses from Oxford downriver to Thame were stirring outlawry.[105] A dispatch from Cromwell to an unidentified abbot demanded his descent on certain manors and farms to remind them of his authority, 'so that no common bruit be raysed therby'.[106]

The commissioners completing the visitations met some rough handling. In July 1535, John Prust, abbot of Hartland, put out of office by the commissioners, battled his way back into the abbey, as the retainers of his patron, Sir John Arundell, acted to deter any immediate reprisal.[107] The following February at Exeter the visitors approaching the Benedictine priory of St Nicholas walked into pitched battle. They were pelted with missiles from the tower and pushed back from the precinct walls by an armed crowd, dressed to deceive, 'disguysed ... in womens appareill'; later it was remembered that their threats with 'spykes ... and some ... suche tooles' and 'hurled stones' caused one of the party to suffer 'brake ... rybbes'.[108] It was a public spectacle that was surely planned, the defenders' costume designed to bring humiliation together with defeat. The street assailants were the priory's neighbours, protective of its popular church, but those on the tower were surely members of the household.[109]

The readiness of some religious themselves to press their case with physical force became more apparent in the course of the visitation, as several avowedly conformist superiors reported fears for their own safety. Abbot Henry Emery of Wardon now faced a faction that declared 'openlie that I hadde no aquctorite to correcte ... and stirryd them sediciousle a genste me [and] thretenidde me'; at Pontefract, Prior James Thwaytes uncovered a conspiracy of three of his brethren who were planning his own murder.[110]

These episodes show that communities were generally agitated and increasingly divided among themselves, but they do not reveal clear evidence of coherent conspiracy. Even so it would be wrong to infer that their reactions to royal policy were in every case nothing more than a reflex, an unreasoned outburst in the heat of the moment. Intelligence gathered into Cromwell's hands at Austin Friars in 1535 and early 1536 was beginning to point to something more. In West Sussex, Sir William Goring was anxious about the atmosphere at Tortington, and the book of prophecies which he heard that the prior there had read out to his canons, predicting the downfall of the king; he had also learned that letters talking of treason had passed between a canon and his kinsman in Southwark.[111] One hundred miles west, whispers of treasonable words had prompted a canon of Bruton to be taken as far as the Fleet prison for interrogation.[112] A cache of counterfeit coin, an essential resource for any ambitious uprising, was uncovered at Norton where there was already suspicion of an alliance between the canons and certain citizens at Chester.[113] At the centre of royal government, the court ambassador to Emperor Charles V, Eustace Chapuys, reported an encounter with a monk – his order and house unnamed – who asked him if he might put him in touch with his imperial paymaster, and to school him in the use of a secret code.[114]

Then, in September 1536 the evidence of an escalation in resistance inside the houses seemed suddenly unequivocal. When the commissioners approached the Augustinian priory at Hexham (Northumberland) to enforce its closure under the statute, the news reached them that 'the said religious persones had prepared them with gonnes and artillery mete for the warre' (see Fig. 16). 'Riding towards the said monastery', they were met by 'persones assembled with bills halbartts and other defencable wepyns redy stondyng in the strets like men redy to defend'. At the sight of the commissioners, the 'common bell' of the town was rung, then answered by the priory bell. The gates of the house were 'fast shut' and canons 'stode apon the steple heade and leades in the defence of their hous', firing 'with bowe bentt with arrows'.[115]

Just two days later there began the most serious and sustained challenge to be made by members of the religious houses at any time before the dissolution was completed in 1540. Between October 1536 and February 1537 armed uprisings erupted in four counties of central and northern England, Lincolnshire, Yorkshire, Lancashire and Cumbria. The true size of the rebellions can only be estimated. There were certainly not the 20,000 or 30,000 spoken of by the loyalist lords sent to quell them. But there seems little doubt that in the course of these five months some hundreds of the king's subjects, churchmen and laymen of all social ranks, from labourer to aristocrat familiar at court, had shown support for the cause. The rebel bands of these last three counties were well organised and won control of a swathe of territory stretching coast to coast before they were dispersed. They styled themselves as pilgrims and their rebellion has been remembered as the Pilgrimage of Grace.

The disturbance started at Louth (see Fig. 17), one of the smallest of the county's towns, but standing less than a mile from a Cistercian monastery, Louth Park, which had been closed by force of the statute only days before. It was one of twelve within a thirty-mile radius which had been suppressed in the month of September. After the first Evensong of October in the town's parish church of St James, a mix of clergy and layfolk shared their anger at the coming of the king's commissioners, their closure of monasteries, and collection of another subsidy granted for the king. Their outcry in the open air seemed to summon up a sense of common purpose and they decided to register their distress by marching on their cathedral city. They covered the thirty miles at speed and with rising support; by the time they reached Lincoln there were thousands of them. They occupied the cathedral and its chancellor, who tried to disperse them, was cut down. They held it for forty-eight hours before they were driven out and captured or dispersed.

The Lincolnshire rising lasted less than a week but before its end their cause was carried across the county's northern border. Now, there were copycat musterings passing up through Yorkshire as far as Northumberland, and to the west as far as the gateway into Wales. In mid-October there was an attempted mustering of men at Norton Priory where the abbot and canons had been under pressure to surrender to their patron, Sir Piers Dutton.[116] In retrospect, it was alleged that Abbot John Harware of Vale Royal, fifteen miles from Norton, made gestures of support during this Michaelmas, and let it be known that if any tenant were to join the king's forces, 'he wold not take hym [again] for his tenaunt'. The main bodies of men marched on York and took control of the city for almost a month, until the principal captain, Robert Aske, was granted safe conduct to present grievances personally to King Henry. It proved to be no more than a midwinter respite, however, as after Pentecost two rival captains, Sir Francis Bigod and John Hallam, again raised the rebel standards with the aim not only of retaking York but there proclaiming the princess Mary as England's queen. They failed to break out from the north (Scarborough) and east (Hull) of the county, but thousands had mustered and it was almost a month before the disturbance ended and the leaders were taken.

The rebellions did not present a direct threat to the king and his personal authority; nor did they destabilise his government. But they did throw obstacles in the way of Crown policy and its enforcement, and it did so over a large region (some 8,000 square miles) of the kingdom. The Tudor regime had faced armed rebellion in its Irish domain which had left its authority over church and community very weak, but this was a fraction of the territory touched by the Pilgrimage of Grace.

When the first histories of these years were published towards the end of Henry's reign the rebels were briskly treated: for Edward Hall they had demonstrated only that 'the inhabitauntes of the north partes [were] very ignoraunt and rude ... altogether noseled in superstition and popery'; although they had 'ioyned into an Army' as 'men apte and feete for the warre' in the face of the 'kynges royal majestie ... furnished with a ... warlike armie', he saw 'sodenly they began to shrink'.[117] To Richard Grafton it was but 'a folyshe commocion'.[118] This dismissal passed down the generations. 'A distemper ... seasonably cured', was Thomas Fuller's description, a perspective not so far removed from the view that settled in modern histories, a 'grass-roots, peasant rising' whose 'dynamic heart lay with the commons'.[119] The trouble in the north was a late example of a medieval form of popular protest; there was nothing here to threaten the march of early modern rule.

By contrast, the profile of the religious houses has receded only in recent times. Eustace Chapuys was certain that at the heart of the rising were 'well-armed ... priests, monks and religious persons'; 'over 10,000'.[120] Those caught in the net of the counter-attack were quick to confirm the contribution of the cowled. There were so many of his brethren in among the host that was raised at Louth, claimed William Burraby alias Morland, that he could hardly count them.[121] The Crown's captains in the region shared the conviction that 'naughtie religiouse persons' and 'traitorouse monkes' did 'eyther set them on or aydyd them with money or men'.[122] King Henry readily received their verdict: 'these troubles have been promoted by the monks and canons of these parts'.

The first narratives of events left no doubt that the monasteries were not only the central scenes of the unrest but also the sources of its inspiration. At a distance from Louth of 150 miles, Charles Wriothesley in the College of Arms saw a rebel army led by two captains, a shoemaker and a monk.[123] Half a mile away from him, the city's anonymous Franciscan chronicler reported it as 'a rysyne for the taske and talenge of an abbe'.[124] Richard Morison, whose *Lamentation ... what ruyne and destruction cometh of seditious rebellion* was printed in 1537, was certain that regulars were the ringleaders: 'spirituall traytors ... in harneys agenste theyr countrey' with 'coules [turned] in to iackes, their portessis and beadis into billes [and] bowes [they] come nowe harneist into the field, ayenst God, their king and bothe their lawes'.[125] In his public history Edward Hall agreed, '[they were] not a little stirred and provoked ... by the meanes of certayne abbottes and ignorant priestes'.[126] Only Richard Grafton, writing in 1543, was inclined towards other influences, and 'ye meanes of Lord Darcey, Lord Hussey, Sir Robert Constable, and Robert Aske'.[127] Yet it is this instinct that has grown over the generations. In the continuing debate among modern historians, the regular communities have accrued no greater agency; indeed, the argument has turned on the relative investment in the cause of secular constituencies, conspiratorial courtiers, gentry and the commons.[128]

In fact, the religious were neither at the margins of the trouble nor were they its originators or its mainstay. Involvement of any kind was concentrated in two clusters of houses, in the East Midlands and in the north-east and west in the regions beyond the Mersey and the Humber. There was no direct contact between them; in fact, there was little indication of clear or effective communication within their own networks. What they shared was some or other encounter with the rebel bands, but it was each in their own way. The muster at Louth and march on Lincoln touched only six of the county's sixty-odd religious houses. The Benedictines at Bardney, the Cistercians at Louth and Kirkstead (among them three former monks of Vaudey) and the Premonstratensians from Barlings each joined the rebellion in numbers; several came from Revesby and a former canon of Welbeck, now a curate at Snelland (twenty miles from Louth), was recognised in the field. There was brief contact at Legbourne Priory, four miles south from Louth, but it was with crown agents engaged in survey work; Cistercian women were already dispersed.[129]

The monastic response represented an axis reaching no more than twenty miles either side of Louth itself. Larger monasteries to the south of Lincolnshire, such as Crowland and Spalding, and the urban communities of friars at Boston and Stamford, remained unmoved; although there were four houses of Gilbertine canons less than twenty miles from Louth, only a handful of men from Watton – sixty miles to the north across the Humber – were mobilised.[130] The short-lived mustering at Norton Priory (11 October), more than a hundred miles west from the trouble at Lincoln and the same distance south from the Yorkshire marches, can be connected to the unrest only in its timing; its cause was local.[131]

The rebel forces that set out from the North and West Ridings to march on York scarcely a fortnight after the Lincolnshire rising did not sweep up many of the religious houses in their path. At no point in almost five months of unrest was there any reaction from the largest monastic communities in the province, at Durham Cathedral Priory, Rievaulx, St Mary's Abbey at York, or Selby. In fact, it was three months, and the tail end of the whole episode, before any religious of the large monasteries showed a sustained commitment to the cause. The first response of Abbot Adam Sedbar of Jervaulx was to resist the pressure of the rebel band that arrived there on 11 October. He fled, leaving the rebels to remove two of his monks as hostages. It was only when facing the threat of summary deposition that the abbot returned and was persuaded to join their march to Doncaster. When the first protest dispersed and pardons were promised he resumed his position at Jervaulx; it was six weeks later, as the rising revived in February 1537 when, under the influence of William Thirsk of Fountains Abbey, Sedbar showed more decided support for the rebels, providing them with supplies.[132] Prior William Wode of Bridlington was remembered in the spring trials as the 'great procurer' of the first rebel bands of the autumn, but like Abbot Sedbar he seems to have been more decisive in his involvement during the second wave of February, when it was said he put his servants and tenants 'into harness'.[133]

No other Yorkshire heads or houses stepped so far into the foreground of the trouble. There was mustering of armed bands close to the priories at Marrick and Nun Appleton, fewer than five miles from rebel focal points such as Bolton Percy and Tadcaster and on the route to Robert Aske's family seat at Augton, but their communities kept their distance.[134] William Todde, prior of Malton, dined with Bigod en route for York, but he did not join him.[135] The Bowes, Percy and Stapulton bands were billeted briefly in the precinct of Hampole Priory, but by invasion not invitation.[136] It was the renewal of unrest in the new year that finally stirred William Thirsk, the deposed abbot of Fountains, to stand with the rebels, joining his brethren from Jervaulx and Sawley, but their colleagues from the county's five other Cistercian abbeys held back.[137] During this short coda to the Pilgrimage of Grace, the remaining seventy-odd religious houses of Yorkshire did not stir at all.

The rallying of the rebels by Robert Esch, 'Friar of Knaresborough', was reported repeatedly in dispatches to Westminster, but he was a conspicuous exception to his kind.[138] Two displaced friars, Thomas Johnson, former Observant, and John Pickering, deliberately came north in October 1536 to connect with the rebel band, but it may be a measure of their detachment from their colleagues that the support they found was for the most part among gentry and townsmen. Pickering penned a rousing rhyme for the latter, 'chief bellicose champions . . . of god his elect'.[139] Despite the spectacle of the convocation convened at Pontefract by the rebel leader Robert Aske, there was no support from the neighbouring friars; the populations at Richmond, York and Hull also stayed away. At Tickhill, near Doncaster, the friars responded to the unrest only to tell of their suspicions of their colleague, the prior of the Augustinians at Grimsby.[140]

Of the twenty friaries standing between the Wash and the Tyne, only two, Beverley and Knaresborough, were roused by the movement. Beverley's involvement was almost entirely circumstantial: the rebel band mustered in front of the house; inside they found a supporter in an Observant Franciscan who had been relocated there.[141] Knaresborough it seems was unusually disturbed, distributing 'bills and proclamations' from the start of the 'laste [i.e. October] insurrecion'.[142] Despite the Crown's repression, there were still 'false tales to move the people to new commotion' sent out from there as the winter of 1537 approached.[143]

The Yorkshire risings inspired resistance to royal authority in the coastal region of the north-west. Here the religious houses were the scenes of the worst unrest: early in the second week of October the priories of Cartmel and Conishead and Sawley Abbey were taken forcibly from the custody of the king's commissioners and reoccupied by some of their former residents (see Fig. 18).[144] In the weeks that followed, the Cistercians at Furness and Whalley expressed their support for the cause and seem to have put themselves out to link local outbreaks of unrest with the movement to the east of the Pennines.[145] In spite of their conspiracies, the trouble was concentrated, and confined, in their respective neighbourhoods, the twenty-five miles of coast between Cartmel and Furness, and the fifteen miles of the Ribble Valley that separated Whalley and Sawley. It seems the agents of royal authority in the region, Derby and, latterly, Norfolk did not expect these houses to serve as platforms for further protests, as they allowed the returned religious to remain for the three-month duration of the trouble.[146]

No more than eight monasteries or friaries across the same number of northern counties were associated with any of the protests seen in the six months between October 1536 and March 1537. The judicial process itself appeared to acknowledge that the rebellion had been among individuals more often than institutions. Four houses were summarily suppressed: Barlings and Kirkstead in Lincolnshire, and the canon house at Bridlington and Cistercian abbey of Jervaulx in Yorkshire. Yet other houses, the origin of those who joined the marches, or which had given a word of support (or something more practical) to the rebel leaders – such as Revesby and Welbeck, Fountains and Malton – were left undisturbed. Even Bridlington's sentence of closure was suspended for a year. Commissioner Richard Bellasis saw no reason for urgency: 'I have doyn nothing there as yet, but spayrethe itt.'[147] Perhaps as many as thirty regulars were arrested on suspicion of rebellion, imprisoned and interrogated, but fewer than half that number were executed. The fate of some is obscure but without records it would be wrong to assume that they still suffered in gaol or at the scaffold.

The convicted canons and monks claimed their connection to the rebellions was circumstantial. The men of Bardney, Barlings and Kirkstead all maintained that they were found among the rebel forces because they had been pressed into their service. They told how the bands had descended on their houses, demanding provisions and priests to attend to their spiritual needs on the march and at the battlefield. Their counterparts at Jervaulx spoke of much the same: in the October rebellion they had carried letters to the muster at Doncaster being fearful if they refused, although they admitted, 'this ys no ansure, for I knowe no man that whas hurtyd yn the compuleyon therof'.[148]

The following January, again they argued that their part in the drama had been forced upon them. The professed religious also suggested that they had faced pressure from the laity of their own precincts, their domestic staff, and the labourers and tenants of their outlying properties; men such as Mr Saunderson of Revesby. The testimony of witnesses gathered by the Westminster government lends some weight to their claim, showing that the lion's share of those from the religious houses who took up arms were their employees. The reoccupation of Sawley Abbey and its armed defence was led by its former staff; there may have been monks among them but they were not in charge.[149] Several houses saw their servants take off on their own to join the marches elsewhere, perhaps making the judgement that action from inside the monastic enclosure was unlikely. Two of the serving men from the Bardney refectory were appointed petty captains of the band that mustered nearby; they absented the monastery by day but returned (for dinner service?) at night.[150] Prior Todde of Malton was confronted by one man of his household hungry for revolt, seized by 'the mysordre of his tonge'.[151]

But the religious were rarely, if ever, in thrall to their staff. Far from falling under the influence of those in their pay, often it does seem that they acted to mould and mobilise their rebellious spirits. At Watton, the Yorkshire house nearest the Lincolnshire border, Canon Thomas Asheton wrote a tract 'touching the supreme headship', no doubt intended for an audience, whether inside or out. The sub-prior, the nuns' confessor and another canon named only as Anthony were known for their hostility to the royal supremacy.[152] It was reported in the region of Beverley and Hull that before the bands began to muster, the Knaresborough friar had 'sente lettres to all the township';[153] when they marched, the agent provocateur himself disappeared over the Scottish border. A westward chain of Yorkshire convents, Newburgh, Byland and Whitby, resisted the call to arms but were ready with cash payments, each of 40s;[154] the abbots and some of the monks of Rievaulx and Guisborough were inclined to join the marches in person and only Robert Aske himself dissuaded them. The religious from Bardney, Barlings and Kirkstead were not captured by the rebels; they pursued them. Henry Jenkinson, cellarer of Kirkstead, opened his stores to them and then joined them on their march; several of his brethren followed after other bands, to give service as priests voluntarily but apparently also to act on previously formed alliances.[155] The vicar of Snelland (Lincolnshire), whose voice had roused the rebellious parishioners at Louth, was a former monk of Welbeck Abbey who had been moving through the district over the previous month mixing with the religious of houses recently dissolved with the responsibility of dispensing licences to wear a secular habit. Final confessions of three of the Jervaulx monks each corroborate that contact with the rebel musters was coordinated by no less a figure than their abbot, Adam Sedbar.[156] It was he who asked the armed band to assist, and defend, his reoccupation of the abbey, a conscious act of defiance of the king's supremacy.

Further west, the monastic interest in the cause may have been geographically contained but it surfaced quickly and was sustained. Less than a week after the march on Lincoln, those religious restive in Lancashire were reported to be purchasing arms.[157] A further five days and three religious houses closed for three months had been reopened. The Sawley monks may have been pressed into their return to their house but it seems one of them was sufficiently committed to the cause to compose and circulate a ballad calling 'god that right all redresse now shall . . . by this viage and pylgramage of yong and sage in this cuntre'.[158]

The communities of Cartmel and Conishead themselves chose to reoccupy their houses having learned of the events at Sawley.[159] Once there they made every effort to stay. Before Christmas 1536, the Cartmel canons disconcerted the neighbourhood when they claimed produce from their former fields that were now in other proprietors' hands.[160] While the local representatives of royal authority vacillated, these communities were not to be moved. It is perhaps a measure of how far they remained in command of themselves that the moment of their final dispersal in the spring remains uncertain; what is clear is that their return had lasted the best part of six months. As the year turned, several monks of Furness Abbey raised their voices, if not expressly in favour of rebellion, then against royal authority. Henry Salley and others made the familiar complaint against the supremacy. John Broghton ran to his brother's house to share a prophecy 'a mervelous and a daungerous word'.[161] Their independent action is affirmed by the desperate attempts of their abbot, John Paslew, to prove otherwise, as he tried to reimpose the injunctions of two years before.[162]

There are hints that the rebels' musters acted only to accelerate plans for resistance among the religious which were already taking shape. The interrogation of Abbot Matthew Mackarell of Barlings and his canons revealed that over the preceding two or three months the monastery's coin and plate had been concealed from the king's commissioners, for the most part, passed among a local circle of clergy and kinfolk, among them the abbot's own sister. Cash had also been passed to gentlemen leaders of the rebellion. Edward Dymoke claimed to have had £200 from the abbot, a substantial sum and a resonant one since it had spelled the end of so many of the neighbouring monasteries. Mackarell may even have begun to consider a higher political conspiracy: by birth a Scot, the crown's inquisitors wondered about cross-border communication, and being aware of Bigod's abortive usurpation, they could not have doubted the possibility.

A further indication of the regulars' complicity may be found in the traces of their efforts to carry the cause outside of the region. After their failure to hold on at Lincoln, the rebel leader, Thomas Kendall, vicar of Louth, fled almost a hundred miles to the south-west to Coventry, where he seems to have persuaded the monks of the Charterhouse to help him. 'He made instant labour to have byn receyvd into oure religion,' recalled the prior when he reported the incident in January, and although they refused him this request, Kendall 'sometymes resortyd to oure howse for loggyng'.[163] A 'bill of Robert Aske' was in circulation at Reading in the last weeks of 1536; it seems to have come from a traveller as it first fell into the hands of one William Wyre of the Cardinal's Inn, but one of the monks secured a copy and carried it back to the abbey.[164] After his arrest, independent witnesses were found to show that Abbot Paslew of Whalley had written to his colleague at Hailes, Abbot Stephen Sagar.[165]

The Crown's agents caught whispers of contact from north to south elsewhere in the Cistercian network. There was a suspicion that fugitive monks from Yorkshire had reached as far as Cleeve in West Somerset. John Estgate, a monk of Furness, did find refuge 300 miles to the south-west at Neath Abbey.[166] Words of sympathy for the so-called pilgrims were reported at houses in the south-east, at Cistercian Woburn and Benedictine Reading, where copies of a manifesto associated with Aske were in circulation.[167] It is possible there were thoughts of conspiracy behind them; no doubt it was this that created such hearsay as recorded at Austin Friars.

It does seem there was a growing atmosphere of agitation in the southern counties at the very moment in January 1537 when Yorkshire rose for a second time. There had been prophecies of rebellion in Dorset the previous spring, one of which made explicit mention of a connection with the northern rebels.[168] There had been an abortive attempt to extend the protest southward in the weeks before Christmas 1536. Four Lincolnshire men had appeared at the public shrine at Walsingham Priory, speaking openly of carrying the cause 'goon through the realme', if Norfolk and Suffolk were 'rysen' with their northern neighbours.[169]

Their obtrusive provocation was resisted and reported but in a little over a month there was a local conspiracy to challenge the enforcement of the dissolution statute. Perhaps it was first conceived by two laymen of Walsingham, but the sub-prior of the Augustinian priory, Nicholas Mileham, gave it enough of a fair hearing for him to be judged 'infetyf'.[170] Like a number of houses, including those implicated in the northern rebellions, it seems there was a division between the prior, a self-conscious conformist, and his canons, who may have feared that in spite of an income easily exceeding the £200 threshold, they were certain to lose their livelihood under a Cromwellian prior. The plot attracted two Carmelite friars from the convent at Burnham Market (Norfolk) but it found no wider support, perhaps a reflection of the region where wealthy houses were still confident of their continuation.[171]

There was a plausible prospect of a regional rising in the south-west. The Westminster government itself had unwittingly created a channel of communication with the northern counties, recruiting forces to put down the rebels from as far away as West Devon.[172] An armed march for monasteries was planned at St Keverne (Cornwall) modelled very deliberately on the Yorkshire pilgrimage, repeating the schedule of grievances presented by Aske. Large-scale support was anticipated as the ringleaders purchased 200 jerkins for a presumably liveried march.[173]

The feeling of something significant about to happen was strong enough to unsettle William Lord Godolphin, who confided to Cromwell the ominous calm: 'the country is in a marvellous good quiet'.[174] After an outbreak of disorder at Taunton in May, the mood was less ambiguous. 'My lorde this is a perillose contre,' wrote Simon Heynes, dean of Exeter Cathedral, 'for godds love let the kyngs grace look to it in tyme'.[175] Laurence Colyns warned Cromwell of the 'plaint or tresouns . . . not openlie knowen', and of the need to find 'the verie trew and hooll knowledge therof'.[176] Sir Thomas Arundell reported treasonable talk at Shaftesbury and the communities there and also at Cerne.[177] It was perhaps a measure of how powerful the portents of a southern rising were that a canon of Carlisle, Richard Huttwythe, should openly advertise the possibility again in the summer of 1539; two years after the pilgrims' defeat he was taken seriously enough to be convicted of treason and executed.[178]

Eight weeks of executions north and south, between the beginning of April and the end of June, demonstrated the defeat of the enemies of the king's supremacy. The early chronicles recalled it as a decisive conclusion: 'these thynges thus ended,' Edward Hall wrote, and now 'all thynges [were] in quiet'.[179] Not only had the 'horley borley' of the autumn and winter now passed, he seemed to imply, but also the disquiet provoked by the royal headship which had persisted for two years. Writing half a century later, John Stow conveyed an image of a collective pause, describing how the body of a Yorkshire rebel, William Haydock, 'there hanged long time after'.[180] His implication was that the public mind as a whole was arrested by the awe of the spectacle. Even as far away as London, and at a distance of forty-odd years, he was able to name the field where Haydock's scaffold had stood. Hall claimed that the repression of the rebels turned the climate among the religious to a new conformity: 'those which before were bent as hote as fyer to fight ... went now peaseably to their houses and were as colde as water'.[181] Stow himself did not pass comment on their condition but now narrated nothing more of the religious houses than the last of the suppressions and the suffering of the notorious non-jurors, the friar, John Forest, and the Benedictine abbots of Colchester, Glastonbury and Reading.

It is possible to perceive a change in the mood of monastic and mendicant communities in the wake of the rebellions, but it was the opposite of Edward Hall's cold-water calm and peace. The dangers of the unrest, both the immediate threat and the prospect of a judicial response, appear to have aroused the conformist religious into conspicuous acts of service to the Crown. It was the cooperation of Richard Vowell, prior of Walsingham, that saw the plot there stifled when it was no more than a plan on paper. The prior of the Burnham Carmelites was the 'very taker of one of the most rank traytours that were privy to the conspiracy', one of his own friars, and was commended 'in good words of thanks ... for the doing of hys true dute and service to the kings mageste'.[182] In October 1537 Prior Jonas Badcock of Barnwell (Cambridgeshire) came forward with the offer of assistance in the arrest of rebel suspects. William Walle, abbot of Kenilworth, was even more demonstrative, despite his advanced age, and with his own armed troop, mobilised himself at Coventry and showed 'good and trewe servyce at the insurreyion'.[183]

In several houses, the voices of conformity now seemed impatient at their own partisan divisions and determined openly to challenge their colleagues. The prior of the Burnham Carmelites presented himself to the vicegerent in person at Austin Friars.[184] Prior William Castleton of Norwich introduced the radical preacher, John Barrett, a former friar who had rejected his Carmelite vocation, as the convent's new lector.[185] At Wardon Abbey, the customary daily reading in the refectory was changed for excerpts from the *Homilies* of the Ingolstadt reformer Johann Eck.[186] Where the conformists were a minority, their desperation drove them even to invite acts of repression against their brothers. A Worcester monk, John Musard, sent sporadic dispatches to Cromwell over the course of six months or more, 'concyence compellyng' him 'to schew ... the serves of god ... hath be[en] clene abusyd'.[187] Loyalist monks at Abbotsbury and Cerne made their own *comperta* of the indiscreet words and works of their colleagues and sent them on to Cromwell.[188] From Pershore, Richard Beerely informed on his superior and his fellow monks and pressed for his own release.[189] At Southwick, canon John Gunwyn did the same.[190] Winchcombe's new parochial chaplain, dedicated to 'scrape the sure of rome owt of the harts of men', now spied on 'ther popysshe servyce'.[191]

Behind these hurried and heartfelt expressions of conformity, there arose another, new proposition: the creation of a reformed religious house, allowed to continue its closed life in church and convent in return for its acceptance of the principle of the royal supremacy and the practice of its administrative and financial control. It was at the start of the unrest of 1536 that the cellarer of Evesham, Philip Hawford, first came to the attention of Thomas Cromwell, and it appears that it was Hawford's willingness to contemplate the Crown's supervision of property and income that set him on a path to being offered the abbacy.[192] Hawford had been remembered as one of a number of collaborators content to act as placemen, to secure a disproportionate pension at the moment of suppression. In fact, up to the final moment of surrender, it does seem that Hawford's collaboration was driven by a different impulse. Two letters to Cromwell survive in which he set out his vision for a convent reformed not only in its governance but also in its social purpose.[193]

These efforts were found alongside a quite different form of resistance, with the potential to threaten the ambitions of the Crown far more than mustering and marches. In many, perhaps most, of the monasteries and friaries still in place, there were now manoeuvres to put their possessions and properties beyond the reach of the Crown. 'Concealment' was the charge made with growing frequency by the king's commissioners, meaning the illegal grant, exchange or sale of any property, by a transaction that would not be recognised in law, such as a cash sale without a written record, or a conveyance that was forged or falsely authorised. The commissioners used it as a byword for all manner of illicit transactions intended to thwart their interference in the houses' property, suspected as much before a surrender as after the process of sequestration had begun. The drawing-up of fraudulent deeds was perhaps the most audacious of these acts, but the officers of the Crown also alleged that properties had been hidden or deliberately damaged or destroyed, 'waste and spoyl', as John London and John Scudamore called out on their circuits in the Cotswolds and the West Midlands.[194]

295

The royal supremacy had made a sweeping declaration of ownership of all commodities in the possession of the Church. The next year the king's visitors were empowered by writ to search for them, count, value and compile an inventory; as many as a fifth of the eighty-odd clauses of inquiry addressed the status of leases, grants, corrodies and annuities, together with 'corne, cattalls and other commodities'.[195] Even as the commissioners set out on their circuits in the summer of 1535, there had been some alarm that the claim of the Crown would be challenged. Richard Leighton sensed 'secret . . . matters of mischief' at the beginning of June, in particular the selling of jewels and plate 'at half their value for ready money'.[196] In North Devon it was discovered that John Prust, just deposed from his abbacy at Hartland, had somehow spirited away a herd of sheep said to have numbered 1,000, leaving 'not above four'.[197] Before the first phase of £200 suppressions had begun in 1536 it was reported that the prior of St Radegund's, Bradsole (Kent), had seen to it that the priory's woodlands, now destined for the king, were cut down.[198]

From these first confrontations it was clear to the commissioners that the determination to deny the Crown its acquisitions was not confined to the religious themselves. Neighbourhood resistance was widespread and strong and not always allied with the house. After the fire at Canterbury Cathedral Priory in October, Leighton was alarmed to find fixtures 'in the cloister and other placeis . . . convayede away and imbeselede by poire fooks wiche came rather to spoile then tin helpe'.[199]

Among the questions drawn up for the visitation were several aimed at uncovering any abuse of possessions and properties: a superior's use of the common seal of their house without the consent of the convent; their making of grants to 'kinfolk, allies and friends'; the conscious undervaluation of a lease. His Majesty's mandate to the visited themselves took a knowing tone: 'Show yourself a personage of wisdom and gravity in the toleration . . . of such things passed in this session of our high court of parliament [and] conform yourself without reluctation, concealment or refusal.'[200] Here, at least, their instructions responded directly to what was known about the current state of the house. The injunctions laid down by the visitors included a minimal defence against these dark arts, commands to make no lease of property without the consent of the whole community, and to keep a register of all transactions which saw the use of the conventual seal (20-21).

Yet these injunctions carried no great conviction. In the parliamentary session in the new year the present danger of the spoliation of the Crown's commodities was among the arguments urged for starting the suppression of foundations: there was 'utter spoyle and dystruccion' of the 'king's . . . cattalls', which suffered 'great decay and dymyncyon' voiding 'his owen propere use'. The problem was said to be of long standing and so parliament proposed to make the force of its statute retrospective: the suppressed monasteries were to surrender all moveable goods which had been in their possession for as long as thirteen months before (March 1535), at the beginning of the valuation, and to present the portfolio of properties as it was a year earlier, in advance of the visitation.

The effect was not to end this form of resistance but to extend it, as houses so far exempt from suppression now committed to it in earnest. 'After my imedyat coming [I] perceyve[d] rawyne, spoyle and wast [and] conveying onye wyse plate money stuff,' reported Richard Pollard from Norfolk on the first day of 1536, setting a tone for the year three months before the suppression statute.[201] The advance of the suppression circuits incited some of those anticipating closure into sudden and desperate manoeuvres, many of which were soon discovered by the commissioners. The actions of the religious were matched by opportunist snatches by their tenants and surrounding neighbours. The suppression statute itself was scarcely two weeks' old when Sir Francis Bryan advised 'dyvers and sounder persons make sute and labure . . . for the lesses of dyvers farmez appertayneng to the abbeys'. There was no doubt such 'sutes' were intended to circumvent the Crown, Brian confessed, 'for the Wyche I have byn offeryd myche monye'.[202] The change in the mood of the houses above the £200 threshold was marked. Their heads seem to have been quick to take up the dispersal of their prized possessions; the number of their brethren inclined to conform to the king's injunctions made the management of property another source of division. The cellarer of St Albans, Richard Bourman, alleged to Brian in April 1536 that Abbot Robert Catton was now acting to 'destroy' or 'wast . . . oure monasterye [with] any other unlawehfulle act[s]'. He and his brethren hoped for its business to 'be well meytenyd and orderyd', so 'that ye monasterye myght prosper'.[203]

Remarkably, the defeat of the rebellions and the destruction of the rebels did not stall or even slow such activity. The reports of Cromwell's agents give the impression that the dispersal of property grew steadily in the year after the execution of Matthew Mackarell. If there was now a surge it was prompted as much by practical needs as by a principled rejection of the royal supremacy. Investment in religious houses declined as the dissolution statute was enforced. Donations to the convents of the friars ebbed away, receding almost exactly along the path of the commissioners' circuits. By the spring of 1537 when at least a dozen monasteries in every English county had been closed, cash gifts to the friars had all but collapsed. Some communities may have now disbanded, preferring the challenge of their own living rather than keeping up a whole household. But most held on and began to let out or sell anything that could raise cash. 'Spoyle and grett ruynne ... [there] hath been ever sins mid Lent', was the reported state of the Blackfriars of Lynn just after Easter 1538 (21 April).[204]

The greater monasteries did not find themselves suddenly vulnerable when the smaller houses were suppressed; indeed, for a time their status as survivors of this measure of reform may have strengthened their relationship with their patrons. But by 1538 it was clear that their own continuation, whether formally under licence from the king, or informally under the patronage of Cromwell or one of his agents, could only be purchased. The constant demand for protective payments compelled them to pursue property transactions which challenged the general principle of the headship and the precise terms of the visitors' injunctions of 1535. As the pressure for surrender mounted from the summer of 1538, the remaining monasteries continued down this path, now with another motive: to provide for themselves and their membership in the post-dissolution world. 'The abbot hath made money of all,' reported Richard Leighton from the reconstituted community at Bisham, where he claimed there was scarcely any food or furnishings; a bed for himself and his colleague had 'to be borrowed in the towne'.[205]

From the testimony of the commissioners it seems that by the end of 1536 the dispersal of moveable goods – from livestock to liturgical vestments – had become systematic countrywide. During his rout of the rebel bands that winter the duke of Norfolk repeatedly reported that he had met with scenes of spoil.[206] When he finally reached Bridlington after the defeat and execution of the rebels, Richard Pollard discovered 'afore my coming [there was] gret spoyle and robery'.[207] Of course, there was a deliberate rhetorical colour applied to these dispatches and the images of 'spoyl' and 'waste' were deployed as much to describe the general disposition of these dissident houses as they were to declare any individual crime. Yet many of the reports carried precise charges, such as the absence of cattle, sheep and horses, or the disappearance of a celebrated gilt crucifix, in a level of detail that is difficult to doubt. Spoliation was not seen as solely a matter of monasteries but, now under its new royal headship, of church property as a whole. Taking possession of the see of Rochester, John Hilsey was dismayed at the condition of its lucrative woodland: 'the byggyste ys karyd away'.[208] Their claims were also echoed by local officers engaged to support the suppression and often to keep the buildings and contents in their custody.

In the wake of the rebellions there was a widening suspicion that waste and spoil were practised now on all sides. Those charged with the king's commissions themselves came under scrutiny. 'My lorde, whatsoever other men do,' postured Richard Lee in February, 'it shall never be proved that Richard Lee shall consume the kyngs goods wherewith he is put in trust ... nor agenst his ... pleasure or profit'.[209] Archbishop Lee was moved to warn his congregation 'in no wise meddle with any such goods ... neither embezzle nor alienate'. There was a hint of a cultural memory. 'Like stout fellows [they] stood out against any that thought to enrich themselves,' recalled the antiquarian John Weever (d. 1632), with a touch of nostalgic approval.[210]

Most goods were sold. There was a predictable pattern, treasured objects of conspicuous value being the first priority for sale; then livestock, produce and stocks of raw materials, such as timber and even wax; household furnishings and utensils were a last resort, albeit one which many of them reached. It is very diffi-cult to quantify the plate, jewels and other precious objects put beyond the reach of the Crown. The surviving inventories compiled at the time of suppression and surrender show that houses had not been stripped entirely of their costly decora-tions; nonetheless the total value of the objects still present is often in the range of £20 to £50. Presumably the most prized pieces were plucked out for sale as commu-nities left themselves with sufficient church furnishings, cloths, candlesticks, Mass chalice and paten, to keep their altars functional. It may have been different in the friaries. The inventories of their furniture are well preserved and they show that at the point of their closure, in the second half of 1538, there was scarcely any plate at all. Perhaps any pretence of the possibility of continuing communal worship had passed out of sight months before.

Precious objects of obvious high value were not always easy to sell. This may explain the comical contrast in the inventories between the few remaining pots and pans found in the domestic chambers of a tiny friary, and the full stock of priests' vestments, in silk, 'tissue' and velvet, and decorated with embroidery still stored in their church or sacristy. It must also explain why the commissioners found that more mundane fixtures and fittings, and even the very fabric of interior chambers, were stripped out for sale. An eyewitness at Dover Priory described it as ransacked: 'the dores be broken up . . . beds, burds wood cocks of brasse, boltts of yron, glasse and diverse other things are broken up and caryd awey'.[211]

The illicit transactions of livestock were on a large scale. Substantial demesne herds (rising well above four figures) were still held by religious houses in the southeast and west of England (East Anglia, Wiltshire) and in the northern counties from east (Yorkshire, Northumberland) to west (Cumbria, Lancashire).[212] It does seem that many were dispersed in whole or part before they could be claimed for the Crown. John Smythe was startled to discover 500 sheep missing from the home farm at Launde. Prior John Lancaster claimed their sale was made to meet the cost of continuation fees and fines, 'to the intent to have redeemed the house', but as Smythe could see, the effect was to deprive the house of its value to the Crown.[213] The duke of Norfolk thought it inevitable that 'cataill . . . will not come all to light so well' at the North Yorkshire monasteries unless he himself presided over the process of suppression and sequestration.[214] The dispersal of such numbers, and their disappearance from the sight of crown officials, could not be managed through the customary seasonal sales and was surely dependent on the collaboration of the neighbourhood landowners and farmers. Norfolk knew this: 'the cuntrees abowth them be popelouse and the howseds greatlie beloved with the people'.[215] The hiding of all the animals in the possession of the Trinitarian Priory at Ingham (Norfolk) hours before the arrival of the commissioners could only have been possible with the cooperation of those outside the house.[216]

These manoeuvres continued down to the last of the dissolutions. Just weeks before he surrendered his house in 1539, Prior William Kingsmill of St Swithun's, Winchester, somehow concealed away 'six-score' (i.e. 120) sheep assigned to his office; it must have been an illicit sale since the Chancellor of Augmentations could only recover them on payment of £4.[217] The subversion of the king's will became ever more obvious to commissioners who had come to know these houses, their precincts and nearby manors and farms very well from their repeated visits. Their contempt for authority was sharply signalled by the unreal sight of their twelve-to-twenty-acre precincts empty of animals save for the monks' meagre palfreys, perhaps a swannery, and ornamental birds and fish.[218]

From 1535 onwards, possessions were also hidden away. Abbot William Love was bold enough to conceal chalices in the plain sight of the visitors, and to 'cownsel' his monks 'not confesse to have any knowlege of one great chalesse'.[219] During his visitation, John London claimed that the 'substance', that is to say the cash wealth, of Prior John Bochard of the Coventry Charterhouse had been 'part hid in the earth'.[220] At first it may have been intended to be a temporary expedient, to ensure there was a stock of valuables for potential future sales; yet increasingly there was an impulse to place precious objects out of sight for the long term. At Ludlow (Shropshire), a large haul of altar plate was stowed 'in the backside of the ... house in an olde [pair of] hose'.[221] According to old John Lorymer, long-time servant of the women of Sheppey Abbey, much of their church plate had been hidden so well that even he, who knew the house better than anyone, was at a loss to help the king's men in finding them. In the undercroft to the chamber of the sub-prior, 'in a drye draught', were found 'certen peces of peutre ii clothes of diapere certen books and ii lathers [ladders] for the goyng up in to the house ... it appereth ... mych stoff hath bene covayed [there] for the staye wheroff'.[222] After the surrender of Glastonbury Abbey, pieces of plate were found 'hyde and muryde up in walls, vaultis and other secret placis'. Here there was a suspicion of a wider network in operation, these treasures being 'convaide to diverse placis in the contrye'.[223]

Often the intention may have been to put items out of sight until they could be sold without interference, but it is possible that for some it was an act in defence of the convent's survival, to hold objects invested with monastic as well as market value in safekeeping. It seems almost an act of memorialisation that caused the Woburn Cistercians to place a crozier and cope morses (clasps) into the ground, and persuaded a monk of an unidentified house onto the Rhinogydd mountains of Cwm-yn-Mynach (Gwynedd) to bury a thirteenth-century chalice and its paten. It was not uncovered until 1890.[224] When a stash from the Maison Dieu was discovered elsewhere in Dover, it was suspected that this was in defiance of royal authority: 'stoff hath bene convayed ... that masse maye be said eons or twyse in the weke for the stope of the brute of the people which is mych'.[225]

More commonly, however, there was a determination to challenge the Crown through the damage and destruction of the monastic estate it was about to claim. The particular concern of the visitation clauses over the custody of woodland points to the suspicion if not the proof that the spoliation of timber sources had already occurred. Here it may have been the tenants of the monastery that were directly culpable; again, they may have shared their landlords' antipathy towards the advance of the royal domain in their own locality, and they were not unused to collaboration in outlawry against particular targets. On the Ramsey Abbey manor of Woodhurst (Huntingdonshire), Ralph Claye was accused of wasting the wood, 'thyking that the said monastery schulde not continue but to be suppressed and come to our seid soveraygn lorde hands and possession'.[226]

The houses' disposal of their farmed resources was held in check by the continuing need to support themselves. As a tactic to spoil the Crown's profit, there was greater scope in their portfolio of income-bearing properties, from manors to tenements, church rectories to fractional portions of their tithes. Changes to the tenure of these, the building blocks of their endowment, had been encouraged by the Crown for the past twenty years, with a level of interference that had already passed from patronal persuasion to royal imperative even before the passing of the statute of supremacy. During the valuation and visitation of 1535–36 it had intensified, and as the £200 houses were suppressed in 1536–37 the greater foundations faced a barrage of petitions for particular properties from Cromwell's chambers at Austin Friars. The commissioners' dispatches that spoke of the houses' own covert spoiling of their property were sent just as the superiors of the same received demands to present some or other property to a crown nominee. In the second half of 1536 it seemed to have become a general policy, and Cromwell appeared to be targeting the premier houses in each monastic congregation.[227] If monastic England now used the distribution of their property as their primary means of resistance, it was a weapon they took from the Crown itself.

It was not, at least not at first, an effort to prevent dissolution. The first and foremost intention was, in the words of the St Albans cellarer, to 'meytene' the house, to enable the continuation of the community day to day. Yet as further sequestrations were anticipated after the repression of the northern risings, there was also an impulse to make a stand against the upheaval of the economy and society of their locality as a whole. The rapid grab and regrant of the estates of the houses attainted for their part in the trouble of 1536–37 revealed what the supremacy empowered the Crown to do with their endowments. The commissioners charged with administering the attainders did not tread lightly around local interests, so that further outbursts of protest were feared at Furness, for example: there as late as July, Robert Southwell met apprehensions 'yff the people wolde rysse a gayne'.[228] Now, this highly charged mood seemed to spread, wherever the agents of the Crown appeared to interfere with local property and livelihoods.

The response of heads of houses was to turn to the tactical manipulation of their portfolio for two purposes: to limit the reach of the Crown into local landlordship and to hold out some hope of provision for themselves if, or when, they had been dispersed. The incidence of lease agreements endorsed around the time of the suppression is generally high. 'I doe perceive verrey latly that ye monasteries of Rumsey rekyn to be in daunger of suppression,' wrote Richard Lyster to Cromwell in September 1538, 'and by reason of such ... thei begyn to make graunts and leases and to put good of their hows from them and so will doo dayly more and more'.[229]

In many instances the number of lease agreements rises near to the known closure of the house. Among the remaining houses in Lancashire and Yorkshire, leasing rose to three or four times the typical annual rate in the spring and summer of 1538.[230] Some cluster at the time of the suppression or surrender itself. A surviving book of rentals from Kirkstead Abbey shows a succession of leases made from the summer of 1535, after the departure of the king's visitors, most of them grants to new tenants, including of portions of pasture in the monastery's demesne. Even on Michaelmas Day 1536 (29 September), the day before the parishioners of Louth took up arms, another new grant was made.[231]

Every category of property beyond the site of the church and convent itself was vulnerable to these manoeuvres. They were most common among tenanted properties – farms, mills, portions of land and urban tenements – outside of the demesne but within a relatively narrow radius of the religious house. At Dale, Abbot John Bebe appears to have been acting to safeguard the new industry on the monastery's lands. Having purchased exemption from the 1536 statute, less than a year from final surrender, he made over the Dales manor of Griffe to Ralph Gell for a sixty-one-year term but with a peppercorn rent for the first six years.[232] But the demesne itself was not always left untouched. 'They leave neither demesnes unlet', John Freeman found on the Lincolnshire circuit, '... but also minisheth the greater part'. It was claimed at Whitby that Abbot John Hexham alias Topcliffe 'hathe made many secret leases of those thyngs that can not conveynytly be forborne from the demeanes'.[233]

Even the infrastructure inside the precincts, the barns, gardens and orchards, were not always what they appeared to the commissioners as they stepped inside. In a number of provincial towns the friars had leased out not only the working buildings but also some of their communal spaces, such as the refectory. The survival of so many of these clusters of buildings and the precinct spaces surrounding them at least to the end of the sixteenth century was a direct result of these preventative measures by the convent. There was also some effort to place spiritual property beyond royal authority. Under the shadow of the commissioners, a number of advowsons were reassigned; there was also a presentation to parish benefices, among them the professed themselves who were awaiting the faculties to allow them to act as secular priests.

It is difficult to estimate how many of these transactions were made by means of consciously concealed grants, endorsed under a seal applied outside of the law (i.e. when it should have been surrendered) or one that was itself counterfeit. The widespread belief, both at Westminster and in the regions, was that there were concealed grants connected in some way with most of the foundations suppressed from 1536, especially among the 'great and solemn monasteries' but also those, such as the largest establishments of the four mendicant orders, which had held acres of space in the greatest cities and towns. Formal inquisitions were initiated by the Court of Augmentations from as early as 1537.[234] After Henry VIII's death in 1547, concealment still held the attention of Edward VI's regime, heading a memorandum listing 'pointes' for attainder.[235] A fresh commission was begun in the second year of Mary's reign (1555), and throughout Elizabeth's reign county concealment inquisitions became a sought-after privilege for the enterprising gentry.[236]

The firm evidence of flagrant law-breaking before the last of the suppressions is limited. In April 1537 Cromwell himself found that a monk of Much Wenlock had aided two of the priory's present grantees to fabricate a renewal of the lease of the vicarage of Clun, having 'stolen owt the Covent seale' and the new document 'cownterfetyd and forged'.[237] There is one lease surviving made by Prior Richard Jenyn of Maiden Bradley for a prize property in Beckington (Somerset) that carried a date of 1537, more than six months after the house itself was suppressed.[238] The deed of grant of the Fountains Abbey grange of Bramley is dated 2 January 1540, just over four weeks after the house was surrendered on 26 November 1539.[239] At Tywardreath it was suspected that Prior Nicholas Gyfte continued to make transactions under seal after he had left the premises. John Whytney, brother of Thomas, abbot of Dieulacres, told the commissioners he had noticed sealed charter blanks in his chancery. In fact, formal accusations of the distribution of blank sealed deeds to allies, implicating both Abbot Whytney and his predecessor, had already surfaced.[240] It seems they were too widely dispersed for the commissioners themselves to recover the full extent of the damage; post-dissolution grantees were left to challenge counter-claimaints through the courts.

Some forty-five years after its suppression, the young Lord William Howard challenged the veracity of leases connected with his inherited manor of Axminster (Devon); over the course of a two-year investigation (1582–84) it was revealed that the Abbot of Newenham had recovered the conventual seal, 'glewed and sett' it together and used it to grant out at least two properties.[241] A quarter-century after its suppression it was made clear that a row of almshouses at Bury St Edmunds had been covertly conveyed from the abbey, an indication that it was not only commercial property that was diverted from the Crown.[242] Nearly fifty years after its suppression, a county inquisition uncovered evidence of a campaign of concealed grants carried out by the sub-prior of Newenham in the vicinity of the abbey after the convent had been dispersed.[243]

Perhaps more common were transactions that challenged the Crown and its commissioners in plain sight. Grants were made between 1535 and 1540 under conditions intended to confound the intentions of the Crown. New tenancies were established, or existing ones renewed; terms were generous, often far beyond the customary duration. John Reve of Bury made a series of new leases of properties within a short radius of the town in 1538–39, each of them at a forty years' term (see Fig. 19).[244]

In the eighteen months before his surrender of the house, Marmaduke Bradley of Fountains granted a number of the abbey's granges on equal forty years' terms; the last recorded of these apparently at the time of the surrender itself.[245] Prior William Holeway of Bath made a succession of new leases in the three months before the surrender of the community in January 1539, of valuable mills on the Avon to local proprietors including one of the city's aldermen; and just nine weeks before the end, of an annuity to his organist.[246] Prior James Thwaytes of Pontefract conveyed land and tithes just eight months before his surrender, in March 1539, for a term of forty years at combined rents barely above £2 annually.[247] In 1537 the Abbot of Dunkeswell (Devon) leased a farm at Bolham for seventy years; in 1538 he leased a tenement at Uffculme for ninety years and rights to pasture for ninety-eight years.[248] Joan Temys, abbess of Lacock, in 1537 again let out one of her more valuable assets, a fulling mill at Bishopstrow, for the remarkable term of ninety-nine years.[249]

Grantees closely connected to the community, stewards and other paid officials, kinfolk, were named as beneficiaries of some of the choice properties in the locality. The traffic in transactions increased after 1536, and in some instances continued to within days of the final surrender. Deeds were still endorsed under an authentic seal long after the house had been instructed to close and to surrender their matrices. Here, of course, the Crown suffered more damage than any obvious fraud: a legal obstacle to its hopes for sequestration. In frustration, Sir William Parr wrote from Titchfield Abbey, 'How many late grauntes be passed under convent seale of trewth.'[250]

There was much complicity in these transactions. Richard Leighton was so convinced of the neighbourhood's abetting at Westacre (Norfolk) that he addressed superiors of the surrounding houses to condemn their 'briberie, spoile and ravyne with crafty colours of barganes contrived by thynhabitantts'.[251] The most committed accomplices were those closest to home. Abbot Richard Mounslow of Winchcombe planned grants with his brother, William, and another man, perhaps also a family member; just four months before the surrender he granted William his own residence in London.[252] Naturally, Abbess Joan Temys of Lacock turned to her elder brother who had for several years held the abbey's stewardship. No doubt fearing the encroachment of royal authority, neighbouring proprietors offered to purchase monastic rents above the market value. Simon Catesby committed a sum of £40 for Lenton Priory's rectory of Wigston (Nottinghamshire), the 1535 value of which was only £22 7s 4d.[253] There was also a suspicion that cash was now committed simply to keep it from the Crown. From Lincolnshire, John Freeman reported that bailiffs and other lay officers were now retained in numbers, 'thies superfluous ffees given . . . to robe the kinge of part of his revenues'.[254] The commissioners were too set apart from the neighbourhood, and perhaps too briefly in it, to track all these transactions, their intent, and their implications for the interest of the Crown. William Parr spoke for many of his colleagues from St Andrew's Priory, Northampton: 'we fynd . . . muych tangullyng'.[255]

The rising number of suppressions and the dwindling network that remained seems not to have stifled conflict but rather sharpened it. Acts of opposition were more overt. The impulses to challenge or confront, which before had been a running tension within the professed community, now cut loose, reached across superiors, and was projected outwards. In a number of houses there was perhaps still a trace of the two opposition parties which had brought internal battles between the visitation and the first of the suppressions. Some of those sympathetic to reform had still not forsaken their vows. James Gunwyn endured the abuses of his abbot at Southwick and took his pension with his brethren.[256] But it was those who had long been set against the royal supremacy who now broke their cover. According to the testimony of a passing secular priest from Chichester, John Roke, there were monks at Reading Abbey who openly showed and shared texts asserting papal authority; the clergy of Chichester itself were not themselves above suspicion and so Roke's word may be trusted.[257]

Perhaps it was at this time that Thomas Epsam, said to be a monk of Westminster Abbey, was taken into custody for speaking against the headship; there seems no doubt that he was a Benedictine since the public stripping of his habit in June 1540 was remembered as a singular spectacle, but there is no documentary record of him at Westminster.[258] At Hinton Charterhouse in Somerset, Steward Sir Walter Hungerford was called upon to enquire after monks who had spoken out against the royal headship.[259] Nicholas Baland was arrested, convicted and only spared execution when his community claimed he was mentally unstable. Their prior, Edmund Horde, declared his resistance to surrender and 'declaryd himself to be . . . rather more styffe' than before. As these two monks openly challenged the Crown, it appears that a covert effort was in motion to convey the titles to some of the monastery's properties into neighbourhood hands.

In February 1540, Cromwell called on Walter Hungerford to 'excogitate and devyse' precisely what had been 'ymbestyd and conveyed away'. Here, to the best of Cromwell's knowledge, there was a collaboration between the house, secular clerks and a local man of means, a clothier called Thomas Horton.[260] At Glastonbury, there was also a combination of personal challenges and communal plots. Like so much, they can only be read in retrospect, from Richard Leighton's report to Cromwell at the very end of the year. From this it appears that members of the community were acting in opposition independently from their abbot, Richard Whiting. 'Thabbot and the monkis . . . have ymberelyt and stollyn as much plate and adornments as wold have sufficide to have begone a new abbay. What they mentt thereby we level itt to your indquitull [inquisition].'[261]

At both of these West Country sites, there was a suggestion that the impulse to challenge the Crown's authority was also to be found beyond the precinct walls. Provocative prophecies had been coined in the vicinity of Glastonbury. Perhaps they had originated inside the abbey, like the Sawley ballad, but as there they circulated far enough to be recorded later. A popular prophecy also became attached to Abbot Harware of Vale Royal, whose opposition to the royal supremacy was now exposed by what may have been a body of reformed opinion both outside the monastery and within.[262]

Tales of a new agitation were spoken of elsewhere. Nicholas Harpsfield heard it 'constantly affirmed' by Kent 'men of good honesty and credit' that in Canterbury there were provocative visions of the tower and church of St Augustine's Abbey 'lift up on high in the air, and suddenly falling down to the ground'.[263] An assembly of shoemakers at Wisbech (Cambridgeshire) in the summer of 1538 appeared, in the eyes of the bishop, to hold troubling undertones, since one was brother to the ringleader of the Louth rebels of Michaelmas 1536, and another took a primer from his jerkin and swore an oath on it.[264] Gentry in the Thames Valley were said to have expressed their sympathy for the regulars recently dispersed. Sayings such as 'I am sorry for the monks for they go down so fast' may have been proved innocuous, but these were the first of the kind to be heard since the spring of 1537 and it does seem that the commissioners, and Cromwell, were set on a new alert.[265] There was a stronger impression of passive criticism in the declaration made at Chester at the turn of the year when the coming of the annual mystery plays was announced, 'devised and made by one Sir Henry Frances, somtyme moonck of this monastery dissolved ... obtaynyng [authority]' of Clement 'then bishop of Rome'.[266]

The suspicion that a substantial number of religious houses still standing might harbour opposition both within themselves and towards the communities surrounding them must explain the sudden and severe repression carried out at Woburn in the early summer of 1538, and at Colchester, Reading and Glastonbury in the autumn of 1539. Woburn was the litmus test for the diagnosis and the remedy. Doubts about the conformity of its monks were first raised with Cromwell two years before when the sub-prior, Ralph Barnes, had submitted to Cromwell a confession of 'untowardnesse and lothenesse' in the face of the royal supremacy and 'alledge[s] [of] scriptures of doctors for [the bishop of Rome]'.[267] His revelation may have been prompted by his encounter with William Shelburn, the parochial chaplain at Woburn whose 'poer service' as a conformist Cromwell himself had engaged.[268] A continuing conventual debate over the rival claims of the Crown and Rome glimpsed in Barnes's testimony of 1536 did not subside; and Shelburn kept up his watch.

Shelburn was surely the prompt for Thomas Legh, John Williams and William Petre to subject Woburn's abbot, Robert Hobbes, and nine of his monks to examination in May 1538. The common thread between their testimony was wound tightly around Hobbes, showing him to be at least as equivocal over the royal supremacy as the sub-prior and receptive to another reactionary, the chaplain of the hospital at Toddington, whose preaching and writing in defence of papal authority was well known.[269] Hobbes, Barnes and the sacristan, Lawrence Blomham, whose own retraction of his conformity had originally been confessed by the sub-prior, were condemned and summarily executed, perhaps on 20 June, within the abbey's open court.[270] It was a measure of the regime's apprehension at the capacity of non-conformity to be networked through the monasteries that the Toddington chaplain was left alone.

Abbots Thomas Marshall alias Beche of Colchester and Hugh Cook alias Faringdon of Reading were arrested on suspicion of treason in November, examined and tried before juries in their own towns. Convicted, they were executed, Cook on 14 November and Marshall on 1 December. Abbot Richard Whiting was arrested, held in custody in the Tower of London, tried at the diocesan centre of Wells, and executed the day after Marshall.[271] The response of the Crown was quite different from the earlier, and, arguably, greater challenges. These episodes did not receive the same contemporary coverage as the risings of 1536–37 or the challenges of the Observant Friars and the Carthusians. They were recorded as little more than matters of fact in the earliest national histories. 'Attainted of high treason, for denyng the Kyng to be supreme head of the churche . . . and other gret treasons', was Edward Hall's report, adding only a glancing estimation of Whiting, 'a stubborne monk and utterly without lerning'.[272]

Thomas Fuller noticed only the execution of Richard Whiting at Glastonbury, and then only as an entry in his catalogue of predictions and prophecies 'wherein monks . . . did drive a great trade': 'current in the abbey' was the saying that 'a whiting [will] swim on the top of the Torr' and 'it happened that abbot Whiting . . . was hanged thereon . . . and waved with the wind of the place'.[273] The book said to have been compiled by the commissioners at Glastonbury has been lost; likewise the record of the examination of Hugh Cook; only the depositions of Beche's accusers survive.[274] The view has always been clouded by the sensitised, sometimes tendentious narratives of Catholic martyrologists, which dramatised their deaths as the height of Henry's Reign of Terror as much as they doubted the grounds for their treason.[275]

On the face of it, the charges against each of these men were no different from those voiced at the same time against the prior Edmund Horde and Abbot John

Harwood of Vale Royal, and other superiors and communities over the previous two years. Had the same charges been made in 1534 a dramatic confrontation might have been expected, but since the second half of 1537 the regime had seen steadily rising opposition from the houses that had escaped the first suppression; when brought together from the scattered correspondence and royal acta, the substance and reach of this opposition seems very significant indeed. The prompt for proceeding against Beche and Whiting was their refusal to cooperate in the managed surrender that was now the commissioners' preferred approach, in which the formalities were concluded at an agreed date with an outward display of complicity. They were by no means the first to obstruct the commission, but that was not the grounds for their treason because allegations were also made of their rejection of the royal supremacy.

Hugh Cook was accused of the covert conveyance of livestock, grain and timber, 'wherof he may make monie, wherbie the less advauntage ... to the king'; an act which at the very same moment commissioners were reporting in every region where religious houses still held their stock in demesne.[276] If there had been an effort to confound the commissioners' sequestration it was limited since Cromwell's agents reported the contents '[found] all thyngs according to the inventory', and the demesnes were in the hands of the abbot's own accuser barely a fortnight after the accusation was first aired, a speedier transaction than at many other monasteries.[277]

An anonymous tract, now badly damaged, composed after the conviction of all three abbots, connects Cook with the conspiracy surrounding Henry Courtenay, marquess of Exeter, and also with a chain of secular priests who spoke out against the royal supremacy at Reading.[278] The first may amount to no more than an attempt to use the coincidence of these two cases to amplify the danger of both. But the association with agitation in Reading may reflect a real anxiety since the town had been the subject of recurrent rumours of sedition for more than a decade. In an aide mémoire, Cromwell remarked on the need to proceed not only against Cook but 'others in [his] countrey'.[279]

No less an authority than Commissioner Leighton admitted to 'marvail' at the revelation of Whiting's treason, that his 'outward appearaunce' might mask that he was 'inwardly cankired'. Leighton's politic conclusion was that his own 'excessive and indiscrete praise' reported 'at the tyme of vysitacyon' resulted from his own 'great folye and untrewthe', which would surely now 'dyminish my credytte'.[280]

Evidence of Whiting's resistance to reform seemed to gather around him, not least a text asserting the primacy of the papacy said to have come from, or in some other way be associated with, the late Queen Katherine, and a life of Thomas Becket, which were found in the chamber he had abandoned at Glastonbury. This last is an anomaly, and not because the cult had been condemned but that no life of Becket had been printed by 1539.[281] It is conceivable that Whiting contributed to his own case. He had been alleged to have conspired in a deception of Lord Lisle three months before his arrest and was subject to examination by Sir William Stourton; he was also sick, having excused himself from the April parliament.[282] Perhaps his withdrawal to his manor at Sharpham four miles away was to allow them to build their case.

Beche had been known for more than a year to be among those monastic leaders whose grudging acceptance of the royal supremacy in 1534 was now wearing thin. Sir John St Clere had informed Cromwell in late November 1538 of Beche's dinner-table defiance of the principle of the headship: 'for I know by my lernyng that [the king] cannot take [my house] by right and lawe wherfor in my contyens I cannot be contente ne he shall never have yt with my hart and wyll'.[283] Beche had continued to cooperate with Cromwell's growing demands for lucrative leases but his suspect loyalty was a spur for those with an interest in the region and in Colchester. Of those whose information led to his arrest at the surrender of the religious house in November, the fullest and most exposing testimony came from the town's tradesmen, Thomas Nuthake, mercer and physician, and Robert Rouse, also a mercer.[284] They were not only Marshall's neighbours but also guests at his table. They were members of a social community whose attachment to the institution of the abbey was now weak and whose appetite for reform appears to have been rising for some time. Ten of the town's aldermen joined the jury at his subsequent trial.[285] By the spring of 1539, even the clerk of the town-centre parish had been prosecuted for his suspected heretical sympathies.[286]

The speed and the spectacle surely reflected a conscious effort to realise the political capital of the public defeat of leaders of the oldest monastic tradition in England, associated with the legendary beginnings of the church known to be among the wealthiest of them all. 'The abbot of Reading' was placed fourth in a list of abbots that appears on the back of a letter Cromwell received in mid-April 1539; the abbot of Glastonbury also appears next to last.[287] Certainly Cromwell considered the cases in parallel and with some degree of design as they appear in one of his aides mémoires as tasks still to be completed; in the same list is a note to consider the grant of Mount Grace Priory, not suppressed until December.[288] It is difficult not to perceive a form of provocative theatre in the executions at Glastonbury, as the abbot, stripped of the trappings of his power, was taken in procession to the Tor outside the town – standing five hundred feet above sea level, the tallest landmark in the west – to be put to death with two accused of thievery, albeit professed monks of his own house. Perhaps this was an appropriation of Gospel imagery to affirm that by punishing traitors to the king, the kingdom could be redeemed. The performance was also proof that it was the threat of a continuing challenge to the royal supremacy that finally decided government policy. The legacy of these abbots was the dissolution of monasteries.

According to Edward Hall the challenge to the dissolution was finally defeated in the late summer of 1540. On 4 August, Thomas Epsam, apparently languishing in gaol for as long as three years, was brought before the public to be scourged: 'his monkes coole was plucked from his backe and his body repried till the king was informed of his obstinacie'.[289] In Hall's chronicle, Epsam's punishment was itself a coda to the performance of royal justice seen at Colchester, Glastonbury and Reading in the winter just passed. Hall's judgement would have been shared by many of the king's subjects: now the religious houses could be seen standing empty and the clothed religious had passed out of sight. But conformity on the matter of the monasteries was not settled. Regulars who had not renounced their vows were passing out of the kingdom, north into Scotland, and east into Flanders. There was enough awareness of a sensitivity over the appearance of cowled religious in the realm for the Scottish king to seek safe conduct for friars travelling to their Chapter General in the winter.[290]

The threads of old conspiracies continued to be exposed. In October 1540 the Privy Council examined one John Barkley who had a tale of a book of treasons alleged against Thomas Goldwell, the prior of Christ Church, Canterbury, who had resigned his office only seven months earlier; it was claimed that the treasons had been made known at Cambridge by another monk studying there.[291] The government also listened out for new agitation. A former friar, Anthony Kyngston, now vicar of Stroud, was accused of 'yll' preaching and gaoled in Gloucester Castle awaiting examination.[292] There was still a residue of lay interest in the cause of the religious houses. Popular attachment to the shrine at Walsingham Priory resurfaced early in 1540 when a 'pore woman' of Wells proclaimed a new miracle for the image of the Blessed Virgin taken down almost two years before. After examination in London she was returned to the custody of the constable and 'sett in the stokkes ... wyth a papire sett aboute her hede' declaring her 'a reporter of fake tales'.[293] Also in Norfolk, there was rising tension over the distribution of the property of Wymondham Abbey, in which a certain landowner, Robert Kett, was already prominent.[294]

Prophetic rhymes and ballads on the subject of dissolution continued to circulate after the last of the commissions had departed. In York a secular priest, John Whaplod, was brought before the Council of the North in March 1540 for speaking an 'abominable' rhyme abbot Adam Sedbar, abbot of Jervaulx.[295] They point to opinions polarised, between Cromwell a 'false traitour', and monks, friars and nuns as 'rotten sqyers' of the Bishop of Rome. On either side treason, past and yet to come, was the common fear.[296] The double edge to the discourse was sharply exposed in the broadside *Complaynt of Roderyck Mors*, printed in 1542, which welcomed the dismissal of those 'impys of Antichrist Abbays and nonryes' and their 'false religyon' of 'sprytuall fornycacyon or idolatry' yet struck out at the 'extorcyon, oppression and brybe ... of the augmentacyon', the cause of 'urgent damage of the common welth'.[297] The two views were apparent even at court: shortly after Cromwell's execution in July, an exchange between the duke of Norfolk and a clerk of the exchequer was overheard: the clerk was said to have married a nun, and Norfolk rebuked him. The man defended himself since there were 'non nuns nor religious folk in this realm ... seing as God and the King have made them free'. Norfolk replied, 'By God's body sacred, it will never be out of my heart.'[298] They did not fade further until after the trouble of 1549 was put down.

VII

PUNYSSHID, SUBPREST AND PUT DOWNE

In the last week of August 1536 four gentlemen, two of them local and two courtiers, rode into the coastal village of Ingham (Norfolk) with a commission from the king to close the monastery. It appeared that they had come too late. 'The howse was founde wyde [empty] of any religious persons', one of them later reported to Cromwell. More than this, there was not a trace of the domestic doings of the place, the usual huddle of working men, women and animals. The church, whose tower they had spied several miles away, the cloister and compact precinct seemed to have been abandoned. 'A bargayne [was] made with the hedde of the same', a bystander had volunteered, doubtless enjoying their bewilderment. True to his report, when the commissioners had 'repaired us' to Coxford Priory more than forty miles to the west, Sir William Woodhouse MP paid his respects, as the new proprietor of Ingham. He told them how the prior had indeed given up his religious house to him, on the grounds that it belonged to the European order of the most Holy Trinity (Trinitarians), and that the prior and his brothers were 'no monke nor chanon' but friars 'withoute [beyond] the case and daungier of the statute of suppression'.

Despite having devoted themselves for some weeks to the king's business with the monasteries, this caused the commissioners to 'peruse and scanne the words of the statute [of suppression]', to 'perceive [the priory was] without the compass of the same', and finally to pronounce that any further action 'as we take it [the statute] will nott warraunte us'.[1] It was only their first embarrassment. Even as a report was being made to Cromwell, their priggish colleague, Thomas Legh, had already provided the proof that they had been gulled. The prior had prepared his house for sequestration and sale, in cooperation with his own immediate network of patrons, lay officials and principal tenants, but he had done so only 'condycionally'. The friars might 'styll contynew' and 'have all in theyr hands'.[2] The king's commissioners had been double-crossed – to buy the community time, or perhaps only to make a point.

The closure of religious houses was recalled in Tudor England as a short and sharp act of state: the authority of the Crown had suddenly descended and, in the words of Raphael Holinshed, 'all the orders ... with cloisters and their houses were suppressed and put downe'.[3] The first printed history to narrate the events, the chronicle published by Edward Hall in 1548, offered an image that many kept in mind, of a forest being felled.[4] Memory distorts: time is compressed and events are selectively preserved. Perhaps the only really reliable insight to be taken from these original witnesses is of the pace of the episode: between Easter 1536 and Easter 1540 – four years, five festivals – the 660 monasteries and 180 friaries of England and Wales were closed, their communities dispersed, and their assets taken into the ownership of the Crown.

The overall pace of the change leaves a trail of false impressions: of the momentum from year to year; the clarity and certainty of the policy; and its completeness even at the very end. The scenes at Ingham, where the impotence of royal authority was almost comic, were by no means typical, which, of course, is one reason why the king's men seemed so hapless, but they place centre-stage tensions that were present to a greater or lesser extent at almost every location and continuously over the course of these four years.

The first cause of the dissolution of the monasteries was a parliamentary statute, but what followed was directed as much by other forces, including the response of the regular estate itself. In the first place, the modernising ambitions of the Tudor regime were not matched by its machinery of government. This was less a matter of its continued reliance – increasingly out of step in the Europe of the 1530s – on spoken and handwritten commands. In fact, the government's capacity to mobilise people and resources, and to manage the communications that saw them effectively deployed, was impressive given the perennial, practical challenges of provincial England: the roads, weather and recurrent outbreaks of plague. Rather, the pursuit of abstract aims, whether it was the appropriation of monastic wealth, or the creation of a chain of new cathedrals and colleges, was held in check by the realities of holding the balance of power between interests which had not receded purely because of the Break with Rome: lordship; provincial society; prelacy and, still, the regular religious themselves. Just as the commissioners discovered at Ingham, the imperial kingship claimed in the act of supremacy did not necessarily mean the ready compliance of subjects, clerical or lay.

The aims of the regime were abstract and ambitious, and hence they were often not readily understood either by those called upon to carry them out or by those who confronted them. The commissioners at Ingham were uncertain of their brief; and time and again, from 1536 to 1540, so were other agents of the Crown. It may be that the loss of Cromwell's half of his correspondence has amplified the tones of hesitation, sometimes exasperation, that resound from the commissioners' surviving letters, but it is difficult to argue away the countless times they begged 'to know your masterships' pleasure'.

Perhaps the course of these years was influenced principally by the role played by the regulars themselves. Rarely were they passive. Nor did they respond in a unified way as a corporate body, religious congregation, or an order; in this respect even the Franciscan Observants, most of whom finally accepted life under the royal supremacy, reacted contrary to type. What Wolsey, Henry and perhaps even Cromwell thought of as the inherent characteristic of the professed religious proved to be no more profound than the colour and style of their habit. Each religious responded to the Crown's pressure for closure according to the particular circumstances of their house and of themselves – material, social and patronal. Consequently, more of them were inclined to wrestle with the regime's policy, to negotiate, even to try to direct its terms, than simply to concede or to oppose. Some of them had reason to think that there was a role for them in the government's new plans. Here the dissolution appeared to promise a beginning not an end. There were more, perhaps, like Ingham's prior, who shared their sense of opportunity but under local horizons. The commissioners could hardly have credited it in the high summer of 1536, but the prior's manoeuvring was an indication to the Henrician government of what was to come before the last of the religious houses was closed.

The one factor that influenced the course of events above all others was that the dissolution of religious houses was never a fully formed policy. Of course, closure was a central proposition in Henry and Cromwell's thinking from the beginning of the 1530s, just as it had been for Wolsey in the previous decade. Clearly, it was a prospect that appealed in the outer circles of government, and in the Commons in particular, where at least the outline of a policy came into view, albeit briefly, at the height of the divorce deliberations in 1530, and at the moment of the Break with Rome in 1534.[5] Yet at both levels, executive and legislative, it was a proposition that was constantly in competition with others, a good many of them concerning the reform of the Church and religion but which did not include systematic suppression and sequestration of all perpetual foundations.

The draft of a bill that never reached the statute book at this time was intended to tackle the cult of saints head-on; support for it may explain the concentration on relics and shrines in Richard Leighton's early sketch of possible visitation injunctions.[6] It implied significant interference in the rites and riches of religious houses but it did not spell their end. It may be a measure of how far an impulse for reform of the Church in its present form persisted at the heart of government in the aftermath of the royal supremacy. The object of an observant monasticism in the longer version of the visitation injunctions is another. This is not to suggest that the design of a dissolution policy was held in check because of a sincere reinvestment in the monastic principle. The vision of a pure yet evangelical monastic religion was another of the many moods that washed over policy at this time. It is revealed, above all, in the commendations of houses and their heads that run as a counterpoint through the correspondence of 1534–35.

If there was a guiding principle that was held to during these years, it was not for the complete extinction of religious houses but their total possession by their king-governor. If Henry and Cromwell had anything approaching a plan at the mid-point of the decade, it was for piecemeal intervention in foundations large and small, just as they had done already at Waltham and Aldgate.

Early in 1536, there was no indication of imminent action nationwide. The visitations had brought about a handful of closures. The Kent houses of Dover, Folkestone (both Benedictine) and Langdon (Premonstratensian) surrendered their common seals in mid-November, although the houses themselves may not have emptied before the turn of the year: 'chanons and monkes [were] still in ther houses withoute any clere discharge', although 'the key [was kept] in [the visitors'] custody'.[7] Yet these events were viewed as confirmation that the policy of the Crown was to prune the religious establishment, to remove those houses found to be no longer viable, or those irrevocably corrupt, rather than to begin dissolution.

The visitation had dragged on to a ragged conclusion. There were still houses to be examined, but six months into their circuits and confronting the usual challenges of winter travel, the commissioners were railing at a responsibility that, from the wording of their reports, seemed to grow with each new route. The burden of unfinished business only raised their tendency to act on their own initiative; it also aggravated the divisions between them.[8] Late in the year John Prise seemed disinclined to press his inquiries, or the king's injunctions, with very much force. Where 'this house was of . . . good name' he was satisfied to report 'we have no comperts'; elsewhere '. . . because of confederacions', he settled for frustration: 'we found litle allthough there were muche to be fownde'.[9] Legh's tendency to act at the very limits of his commission had not diminished. '[In] my opynyon,' he wrote on 27 October, '[it] war better [they were] dymyssed from ther bondage then so unrelygiously to remayne', for 'that blyndenes that ys rotyd in them ys impossybyll . . . to eradycate and plucke awaye'.[10] Yet still his business was done only at the behest of the king's headship, not in preparation for some new purpose. 'My hole proceeding hath been . . . to the honor . . . of the kyng's hyghnes'; 'I wold do [as] yff your mastership was present with me.'[11]

It does seem there was now some momentum in the release of regulars, the young, elderly and sick, from their vows. Perhaps it is an accident of the retention of some letters rather than others, but as the visitation continued through the winter the commissioners spoke more of the numbers that would, and should, be allowed to leave. Legh claimed that at West Dereham they were abject 'instantly knelyng on ther knees and howldyng up ther handys'.[12] It was enough to encourage some to think beyond the visitation. Richard Leighton was weary when he reached Syon after weeks of cross-country circuits: 'suche religion and feyned sanctitie god save me fro', and it appears he saw his own weariness reflected back at him, claiming to Cromwell that the brethren and sisters all 'wold gladly depart hens'.[13] Thomas Bedyll, sensing a stalemate, imagined a more sweeping transformation, sniping at the committed Syonist, Richard Whitford, 'that he might be the occasion that shrift shalbe layed downe through England'.[14]

Local interest had been stirred by the passage of the visitors, but there was no indication of a demand for a new policy. At the turn of the year, West Country gentry, Richard Phelyppes and Sir John Fitzjames pressed Cromwell for a repeal of the changes which had already been made.[15] The neighbours of religious houses looked for an end to the recent disruption, not more of it. From York, Laurence

Colyns called Cromwell to appoint 'some discreit men' to oversee especially the 'powre religious howses'. He was concerned about the custody of their 'plait or tresoures', and to see them accounted for, '[as] verie trew and hooll knowledge therof', not sequestered.[16] For the most part, after their challenge to the authority of the visitation, the bishops held back from the business of the king's commission. John Longland's careful treading may have been typical: he wrote to tell Cromwell of 'voyde' of Newstead Priory since October but was at pains also to acknowledge, 'your mastershippe commanded me nott to medle with any religious howses'.[17]

The winter of 1535 saw no decisive turn in the thinking of either Henry or Cromwell. The compulsion to destroy his most determined opponents, from the Carthusian priors in April to Bishop Fisher and Chancellor More in July, may have left the king cautious about his capacity to sustain his political support. The terminal decline of the deposed Queen Katherine, and the deterioration in his relationship with Anne at the end of the year, can only have amplified the uncertainty over the effects of his policy. The pressing business of the New Year for Henry was to manage the news of the queen's death and its diplomatic impact, advising his ambassadors to 'temper [their] doinges' with 'discrete wisdom'.[18] The start of parliament's next session was delayed until February.

From the fragmentary record of business, in the months either side of the new year the attention of the king and his chief minister was diverted from domestic to foreign ambitions. It was the king's ambitions in France and his anxiety over the emperor's actions in Italy that preoccupy the papers filed at this time.[19] Cromwell did turn his mind to the resumption of parliament and perhaps in response to the present stasis sketched out a plan for a full and far-reaching programme for legislation. But what was written into his November memoranda were great causes not of the Church but of the commonweal, of the prosperity of provincial towns, of customs and domestic effects of foreign trade.[20] The church business that concerned him at this time assumed no sweeping change in the structure of the institution. In the final days of the year, as the Church marked the feast of the Holy Innocents (28 December), the matter of the monasteries uppermost in Cromwell's mind was how to secure a sufficient quantity of timber from Bath Cathedral Priory for ship-building.[21] The only mention of dissolution on a government agenda was a measure to enable the Crown to add or subtract holy days from the liturgical calendar.[22]

The undated remembrances which the HMSO editors have connected to the year's end do find the religious houses on Cromwell's horizons. 'Of the religious in divers places,' he reflects in one; in another there is the tone of a new resolve: 'the abhomynacion of religious persons' is listed thirty-fourth among forty memoranda, 'and a refformacyon to devyse therin'.[23] On the reverse side of a reminder to find a preacher for Queen Katherine's funeral are the names of twenty-one bishops.[24] These are scarcely suggestive of an emerging strategy, still less the first steps of a fully formed plan. In fact, if Cromwell had in mind practical measures for the regulars at this moment it seems they concerned his affinity of allies, which the visitation had served to reinforce. It was the identification of further loyalist superiors that the commissioners were eager to report now as their circuits came to an end. Leighton and Legh steered Abbot William Thirsk of Fountains towards his resignation in January and advertised to the vicegerent the credentials of Marmaduke Bradley, the 'wysyste monke within Inglonde of that cote ... wiche will gyve yowe syx hundredth marks to make hym abbot ther'.[25] Cromwell himself was busy with the deployment of patronage and conspicuous responsibility to ensure these heads were set in authority over their congregations. The Dominican provincial, John Hilsey, was given no lesser prominence than to preach the funeral sermon for the dead queen.[26]

If major change was anticipated at the turn of the year it appears to have been within the religious houses themselves. It seems the visitors' injunctions had begun to drive sharp divisions through some of the larger monastic communities, as the professed openly declared themselves for or against reform. The heads of these houses became the target of attacks from both parties. William Ripon of Quarr Abbey feared a rebellion inside the enclosure. 'Sume who is not my best frendes wold be very glad to see and make busyness between other and me,' he wrote. '[They] make exclamacion apon me to my no litull perturbacion and hevynes.'[27] At Winchcombe Abbey, it seemed the authority of the abbot simply ebbed away. 'In no maner wyse wold [they] obey,' reported Abbot Richard Mounslow; even 'shownyed prysynment they lytull or notyng dyd regarde hyt'.[28]

The atmosphere was surely another spur to those who now looked for a release from their vows or a faculty (i.e. archiepiscopal licence) to change their monastic profession for the secular priesthood. Between October and December 1535 no fewer than six monks from the Cistercian abbey of Roche applied to change their habit for a secular one; a further five sought permission to take a benefice. Two of these, John Waren of Monkton Priory, Pembroke and John Amery of Missenden, hoped to continue to wear their habit beneath their secular robes. It seems they were certain of a change coming but not at what pace.[29]

For several smaller and (perhaps especially) remote communities the passage of the visitors prompted a decision to disband. Now it seems the presence of regulars – Franciscan and perhaps Augustinian at the tiny chapel of Saint-Tugal – at Herm (Channel Islands) was abandoned; the canon houses off the coast of the Llŷn Peninsula (Ynys Lannog, Ynys Tudwal) had been included in the valuation survey but may have been given up soon after; and the one Benedictine minding the cell at Tresco returned to the parent monastery at Tavistock.[30] The monks of Monmouth, perhaps no more than three or four, now gave up any pretence of a permanent presence, leaving 'nor pott, notr panne, nor bed not bed styd not no monk . . . but one the wich doth goo to bord in the towne'.[31] It may be that the residual number of friars found in the poorer provincial convents also began to break up, preferring, and finding it more profitable, to remain in circulation in the neighbourhood than to be confined in such meagre surroundings. Precisely when 'most part of the frers be rone awaie' from the Augustinian house at Grimsby (Lincolnshire) cannot be known, but the certainty of the report in 1538 perhaps shows that it had happened many months before.[32] When it was targeted for surrender in the spring of 1538, it was discovered that the convent of the Winchester Carmelites had been standing empty for many months.[33]

The coming of the statute 'whereby all relygeous houses . . . whiche may not dysend . . . above the clere yerly value of £200' (27 Henry VIII c. 28), one of sixty-three bills to win assent when parliament resumed in January, is one of the most poorly documented moments in the history of the dissolution. No papers have survived that might stand as evidence for its preparation, and there is no reliable account of the precise timing of its presentation to the Lords and the Commons and its final approval. News of its passage and its principal terms was made public by 13 March when a secular priest, Thomas Dorset, sent a letter setting them out to the mayor of Plymouth; the imperial envoy, Eustace Chapuys, reported it to his master five days later.[34]

Rumours of a parliamentary measure for the suppression of religious were in circulation as much as ten days before. Sir Richard Whethill told Lord Lisle that it was 'bruited' on 3 March.[35] Less than a week later, on 9 March, another of Lisle's correspondents was able to pass on almost the final details of the statute, that there was to be a suppression of monasteries of 300 marks or less, and already 'diverse have forsaken ther houses'.[36] An Elizabethan copy of a list of houses suppressed under the statute carries a date more than a month earlier, 4 February;[37] yet at the end of that month Cromwell's agent, William Popley, apparently well informed, was telling Lisle that parliament was less likely to repress than reform: 'for at the session of this parliament they ordeyne statutis and provisions for the mayntenaunce and good order of the clergy, as well religious as secular'.[38] Perhaps the matter was raised in parliament at the beginning of March and the statute passed into its final form in a little over a week.

Even without a transcript of what was said and done in parliament, or a sheaf of papers showing government preparations, there can be no doubt that the statute responded directly to the commissions of the past year, the valuation and the visitation. In spite of their late delivery and the incomplete account they returned, the Valor books, the collated returns of the valuation of surveyors, had satisfactorily described the spectrum of religious foundations and distinguished those lacking 'manors, granges, meases londs tenements revercions rents servyces tythes pencions procions churches chapelles advowsons patronafes annuyities rights entres condycions and other heredytaments . . . in large and ample maner'.[39] The seventh clause of the final form of the statute confirmed, 'foreasmoche as the . . . value of all . . . relygyous houses . . . is certefyed into the kyng's escheker amongst the bokes of the yerely valcuacions'.[40] Where the valuation defined the scope of the statute, the first clause declared unequivocally that its need was determined by the revelation of the 'abhomynable lyvng . . . dayly usyd and committed', derived 'as well by the comperts of [the] late vysytacions as by sondry credible informacions'.

It might be questioned whether February or early March was too soon for the king, Cromwell and any who assisted in the drafting of the bill that was the basis of the final statute, for this to be a response to the visitors' comperts. In a sermon delivered some thirteen year later, Hugh Latimer referred to the moment when the 'enormities of the abbots' were 'first read in the parliament house', the members crying out 'nothing but down with them'.[41] The scene Latimer depicted was a neat illustration of his text: Romans 15:4, 'Whatsoever was written afore was written for our learning, that we might have hope.' It is hardly proof that *compendia compertorum* (collated records of the reports on each monastery), such as those collected for the province of York and the dioceses of Coventry and Lichfield, and Norwich, were presented. The enormities and the outrage might as readily relate to the opening clause of the statute itself, which certainly would have been read in the house. By contrast with the Valor books, it is unlikely that all of the returns from visitors' circuits had been received, still less that collated compilations in a fair-copy script had been prepared. John Prise had advised Cromwell in late October 1535 that what he would send him while still on circuit was 'thabridgment of the comperte'.[42] William Blitheman wrote of the dispatch of a 'cleane boke of the compertes' for the northern province from Ludlow on 28 February; 1536 was a leap year but still it is doubtful that the comperts were in London sooner than 2 March.[43]

The surviving compendium and fragments are not an exact match for the propositions set out in the statute. They count cases of apostasy and immorality but also provide details of relics, shrines and other devotional artefacts, which find no place in any of its clauses; nor do they record the total population, or the services, pensions, annuities and other rights they 'spoyle dystroye consume and utterly wast'. Yet it may be a mistake to think that such slight and incomplete evidence as survives of the comperts can confirm any position on the preparation and presentation of the statute. It is hardly persuasive that the comperts to which the statute referred were no more and no less than the parchment booklet now surviving; but it is plausible that the reports which Cromwell's commissioners had committed to paper in a variety of forms, including their dispatches sent on the hoof, since the late spring of 1535, had informed the case that the statute now made. But to call them 'an offical exhibit' may be too much.[44] The memories of the Wyatt family, woven into a chronicle only at the very end of the sixteenth century, carry a ring of truth: that the statute was prepared by some of those who had undertaken the commissions, John Audley and Chancellor Richard Rich, but what they presented was 'towched . . . by generall words [and not] then declared in particularitie'.[45]

The timing of the statute, its preparation and the evidence that supported it have been debated primarily because of what they might reveal of Cromwell's outlook and his development, such as it was, of a policy for reformation. The only substantial evidence for his thought and action at this time is the final form of the statute itself; otherwise, there are only the snatches of memoranda scattered through the anthologies of surviving government papers, and the drafts of bills (also undated) mooted between 1533 and 1539, but which did not reach the statute book. There is just the one memorandum, perhaps dating from February, contemplating 'the abhominacyon of religious persons of this realme and a refformacyon to be devised therein'.[46]

Demands for such decisive and definitive action against all the religious houses had been aired around Cromwell at court and in the Commons since at least the time of the deliberations over the royal divorce. A draft of a bill that appears to be associated with the sessions of 1529 proposed the conversion of monasteries into other forms of clerical foundation.[47] 'Nothing else but plain invective against all monasteries' was how the Catholic opposition assessed the climate around the king.[48] Yet it is difficult to see this as a steadily rising clamour; the turn-of-the-decade proposal neither made an immediate nor an intermittent return in subsequent sessions of parliament.

In and around the court, the chatter about reform for the sake of the commonweal – if not outright anti-monasticism – was steadily rising in 1536, perhaps due in part to the personal outlook of Queen Anne, which her allies deliberately amplified when her position came under assault early in the year. Her almoner, John Skip, seized the opportunity of the Passion Sunday sermon (2 April) to stir up the household.[49] The humanist scholar, Thomas Starkey, reached the high point of his royal service in the first months of 1536, and in a letter (again undated) to the king urged him to 'converte thhys acte to the welthe of your subyectuys now lyvyng', and 'wherin we see now reynyth ... much solthe, idulnes ... blyndnes and hypcrysye' to 'alter thes fundactyonys and turne them to bettur yse ... as commyn scolys to the education of youth in vertue and relygyon out of ... wych you may pyke ... byschoppys and prelatys', so 'they may be some ornament to the commyn wele'.[50]

Yet there is little trace of such a bold scheme in the final statute. While it did decide that 'lytell and smale' monasteries showing 'lytel or no amendment' were to be 'utterly suppressed', and 'beyn spent spoyled and wasted [the houses] shuld be used and coverted to better uses', the statute also committed to the continuation of monastic religion, and to 'conforme' the regulars now displaced to the 'observacion of good relygyon [in] great and honorable monasteries of relygyon in this realme'. The language used here echoed the royal supremacy statute of two years before. The suppression of these houses was not to set the foundations of the commonweal described by Starkey, but to progress the general aims of the royal headship, 'the increase advauncement and exultation of true doctrine and virtue in the ... church'. To this end, as the first articulation of the supremacy had signalled, monasticism was to be reformed: 'relygyous persons ... to be compellyd to reform ther lyves'; and 'dyverse and great solemp monasteryes', known to be 'destytute of such nombers as they ought and may kepe', but whose observance was unequivocally endorsed as 'relygyon right well-kept and observed', were to be revived.[51]

The representation of the statute as the royal supremacy in action was reinforced, and surely self-consciously so, by the presence of the king at its reading: the only direct evidence of his involvement in any part of the process. In a rare comment that dates from July 1536, Cromwell explained the purpose of the statute 'to take Refformacion of all and singular howses off relygyon'.[52] In this there was a distinct echo of Wolsey's scheme, prepared with papal licences in the summer and autumn of 1528 but then aborted when he was ousted from government.

Cromwell's first-hand familiarity with the old cardinal's monastic policy may explain not only the particular emphasis on the redistribution of the regular population but also the general hesitancy in pursuing a more radical plan. It was remembered in the Wyatt family that Cromwell had 'feared' the consequences of a dramatic move against the religious houses. He had witnessed the local unrest unleashed by the suppression of Bayham Abbey in 1525, and the political opposition mounted against the endowment of Wolsey's colleges. According to the Wyatt tradition, Cromwell accepted the balance of opinion in the council that 'it should be done by acte of parliament'.[53] It was his caution that caused Cromwell to 'think better', according to the Wyatt account, than to lay bare any comperts before the members and to confine himself to 'generall words'.[54]

The view of the monastic estate which had emerged in the 1520s, and endured even in the wake of Wolsey, was again apparent in the legislative interventions that followed the statute. The same parliamentary session saw the approval of new restrictions on the self-government of large monasteries, as cathedral priories and their heads were deemed subordinate to their bishops (27 Henry VIII c. 45); and exchanges of monastic property (27 Henry VIII c. 33, 42, 53), which applied the principle the cardinal had pioneered, of the Crown's claim on endowments which were otherwise perpetual, 'for suche purposes and intents as his grace entendyth'.[55] Yet it also enacted measures to safeguard the presence of regulars for the foreseeable future: a statute for the punishment of beggars and vagabonds (27 Henry VIII c. 25) was explicit in its exclusion of measures 'prejudiciull or hurtfull' either to the friars or to the monasteries' traffic in alms and oblations; another for exoneration from the obligation for First Fruits (27 Henry VIII c. 42), whereby the Benedictine colleges at Oxford were finally recognised 'as other colleges' in the university, a status denied them since their foundation; regulations for sanctuarians (27 Henry VIII c. 19) also showed some solicitude for the monastic interest, since the concern was expressed that 'divers hath ben ... bolde to perpetrate and committee ... myschevous ... dedes', which would have been recognisable to many monastic superiors.[56]

The first published histories presented this parliamentary moment as a decisive and speedy end to the greater part of monastic England. For Richard Grafton, Edward Hall and then Raphael Holinshed it was the pivotal moment of the dissolution.[57] What followed thereafter they treated as the removal of a handful of remaining prestige foundations; the final surrenders of 1540 they passed over entirely. These accounts coloured later histories, clouding what may have been the authentic reaction in the weeks and months that followed. The defined terms of the statute were well understood, and under discussion even before the parliamentary business was done. Across the country, there was chatter concerning foundations about to be 'putte downe' but not in anticipation of a sweeping suppression of them all. The questions the statute raised about the value, viability and virtue of particular houses were echoed in these exchanges. The speculation on the future of the priory at Frithelstock (Devon), which spun on through the letters of Lord Lisle to his agent John Hussee for nearly six months, may be only the most extreme example of debates that were now spread wide.[58]

The immediate reaction of the regulars themselves can only be caught in passing comments, but they do point towards the same reading of the statute, not as repression but as a necessary measure of reform. Katherine Bulkeley, abbess of Godstow, probably reflected the view of most heads of the greater foundations, in regarding her own house as unaffected by the legislation, 'hav[ing] never offendyd gods lawes, nother the kyngss, wherebie [otherwise] ... this poore monasterie ought to be suppressyd' above such 'punysshment'.[59]

The effort to implement the statute began at the same rapid pace as its parliamentary approval. In keeping with the speed at which the proposal had been made, Cromwell instructed commissioners continuing the visitations to take up this new task. It seems he had sent this new commission northwards to Richard Leighton and Thomas Legh as early as the beginning of February. Leighton confirmed the suppression of the priory of Marton, near Hull, on 9 February;[60] any message from Westminster must have taken at least three days to reach him. Leighton suggests as much in a letter to Cromwell sent from York, reporting that on receipt of his master's letters, Legh 'keppes oute oure apointement in visitacion and [is] goyn forwards styll . . . wels [he] go aboute thes matters'.[61] From there the two made the eighty-mile journey due north to suppress Hornby (Lancashire) on 23 February.[62] Their effort, for two tiny communities separated by such a distance, must have been motivated by the knowledge that there was a readiness to reach terms.

Yet Cromwell also made a beginning southwards, although perhaps after he received news of the outcome in Yorkshire. Robert Southwell arrived at Bilsington Priory (Kent) in the last days of February; the extant deed of surrender is dated 28 February.[63] Richard William effected the suppression of the Cistercian house at Tilty on the same day.[64] A Friday, still this may have been as much as a week before the bill first appeared in the House of Lords.[65]

The statute passed with the crown commissioners already on call and from the third full week of March circuits were underway in several directions. The visitors had only recently departed when the Augustinian priory of Shelford (Nottinghamshire) was apparently suppressed before 23 March, less than a fortnight after the passing of the act.[66] There was one further suppression in Kent before the end of the month at Minster-in-Sheppey (27 March); again, like those in February, perhaps brought on early as much by the will of the women religious themselves.[67] It seems even in February there had been an anticipation of closures as far from Westminster as Wiltshire, where John Tregonwell speedily signalled his interest in Ivychurch Priory.[68] No documents survive but it was surely surrendered in March since the site was the subject of a grant made in the last days of the month.

In Sussex the imminent descent of the commissioners was known before the end of March as Thomas, baron de la Warr, appealed to Cromwell for the preservation of his patronal priory at Boxgrove.[69] As it happened, it seems there was no decisive action across the county before the summer. The closure of pairs of priories both east (Hastings, Michelham) and west (Shulbrede, Tortington) was confirmed only in, or after, June.[70] In Wiltshire it seems there was a similar pattern: after Ivychurch, four further houses, Kington St Michael, Maiden Bradley, Monkton Fairleigh, Stanley, standing in a thirty-mile chain to the south of the county, were suppressed, but at least not until June.[71]

It has been assumed that days or weeks after Hornby there followed a series of suppressions in the north-west, where the visitation circuit had continued in the opening months of the year. Yet there is no documentary record of any activity at the priories of Burscough, Calder, Cartmel or Conishead as early as March or April, and it may be that the summary record of the visitors' *comperta*, which was written at this time, has been mistaken for the surrender itself. Thomas Legh, with characteristic self-interest, broached for his brother the tenancy of Calder in a letter to Cromwell that is undated, its assigned date only assumed.[72]

The sense of purpose that followed the passing of the statute seems to have faded in less than a couple of months. Easter was late (16 April) and, even when it had passed, fair copies of the instructions for the commissioners were probably still being prepared.[73] A commission was in train in Northamptonshire but it seems no earlier than the second week in May.[74] Perhaps the main cause of any hiatus was the conclusion of the parliamentary session and the unexpected announcement of its successor, accelerated by the new priority to reconsider the succession after the sudden end of one royal marriage and the beginning of another. If it was that the drama of a nationwide dissolution was edged into the wings by the public spectacle of Queen Anne's arrest and trial, there was still a trace of this impression over a century later when Gilbert Burnet wrote his history (1679): 'the great concussion and disorder things were in by the Queen's death made the commissioners unwilling to proceed in so invidious a matter'.[75] Practically, perhaps there was no time for the now routine but necessary bureaucracy of commissioners' writs. Sir Richard Page was surprised on 14 June when he received a summons to 'repayr unto' Waverley, for 'I dydd nott know tyll now that I was in any such commyssion'.[76] The next dated examples to survive were issued for Leicestershire on 24 June, after the new parliament had been in session for three weeks.[77]

Superiors may not have been conscious of any immediate prospect of action as some took the opportunity to pursue their affairs elsewhere. Even visitors in the vicinity did not dissuade Prior Peter Prescott of Upholland (Lincolnshire) from remaining in London at least until the second week of May.[78] On the other hand, those worn down by wave after wave of intervention, and having only recently undergone the visitation, with some desperation demanded to make an end of it. Prior John Matthew of Coxford (Norfolk) wrote to Cromwell on 30 April begging to settle terms now so that he might escape any more 'vexacion or trobyle'; in fact, there was no action for another six months.[79]

The sense of anticipation was enough for some local lordship to set a limit on their patience and to start the process for themselves. In Norfolk, the duke was soon minded to seize control. It appears the Benedictine women of Bungay were given an understanding that the duke was ready to take the house from them and in April (or perhaps even earlier) they duly withdrew. 'I require you to show his grace,' the duke boldly declared in an undated letter to Cromwell, 'before the passyment of this act I had in my lawful possession the priory off nunnys of Boungay'.[80]

The change of pace in government, as well as the lone action of local lordship, bred uncertainty and resentment among those who had viewed the statute from the outset as a familiar redistribution of old resources. In early June, Lisle pestered Hussee for news of potential property prizes such as Nunnaminster and Waverley. '[They are] like to be of the number,' he reported, but any hurry on the matter 'would be but time lost'.[81]

In fact, it was only in June that something approaching a connected pattern of suppressions began. Now, in the fortnight between the execution of Anne Boleyn (19 May) and the public acclamation of the new queen, Jane Seymour (4 June), the pursuit of the policy became visible from south to north. It can be no coincidence that now, after months of uncertainty, a suppression bill was presented to the king's parliament in Ireland.[82] The work of the commissioners was already underway in Essex on the first day of the month, when an inventory of the choir of Leigh (Leez) Priory was written out and signed.[83] Within three weeks another six houses were closed. Probably over the same period a further half dozen were suppressed in Kent and Sussex. Now it seems there was a sequence of closures also to the west in Hampshire and Wiltshire, and into the Midlands, in Leicester and Nottingham.[84]

Northwards, in the East and West Riding of York, the commissioners had taken up their task before the end of May, adopting an approach not seen (at least not systematically) elsewhere, initially taking each eligible house into their custody to be kept under supervision, the formal suppression being set for a date between four and twelve weeks following. By mid-June almost all of the eligible houses in the lower-lying districts were now under supervision; by the last day of August they were gone.[85]

Yet the activity of these three summer months, from June to August, proved to be the high-water mark of the year's suppressions. September saw new commissions set off into the west, to Gloucestershire, Somerset and Devon, but they were slow and scarcely half of the eligible houses had been closed before the turn of the year. Elsewhere, in East Anglia, the West Midlands, the Welsh March and the northern counties there was no further action before the spring of 1537. Although there were closures in the bordering counties of Bedfordshire, Cambridgeshire and Essex, the remaining houses falling under the terms of the statute in the eastern counties were left until the following spring.[86] It is difficult to date the closures northwards in Derbyshire, Lancashire and Cumbria in the absence of any deeds, but it does seem doubtful that they had begun in earnest until after the Pilgrimage of Grace (October–February) and its repression (February–March), which ran on into the early months of the new year.

The most complete and concerted enforcement of the statute that occurred in any region after the end of August appears to have been in Lincolnshire, where 'ther be more of great howsys ... then be in Englonde', as the circumspect John Freeman reflected just before he took up the task.[87] Here again there are no formal records of the closure of houses, but the dated dispatches of the commissioners trace a course through the month of September.[88] Certainly they had completed their task at the Cistercian abbey of Louth Park before the end of the month, as some of its dispersed former monks were among the crowd outside the parish church where the Lincolnshire rebellion erupted on 1 October. Yet the job had not been done either at Bardney or Barlings where the monks and canons later testified that rebel bands had come to recruit them.

If the suppressions were already slowing by Michaelmas, the rebellions brought them to a stop. In the north and west of Lincolnshire the task of the commissioners was overtaken by a new priority just it had been in the spring, although the matter now was not the legislative capacity of parliament but the pressing need to assert royal authority. Even far from the affected regions it appears commissioners were inclined to watch and wait. John Hussee wrote to Cromwell at the end of October that the religious house in his charge would be 'soon despatched ... I hope, if the rebels were once subdued as I trust they will be shortly'.[89] To Lord Lisle, still hoping for Frithelstock, as he had been since the spring, Hussee wrote, 'I cannot do nothing therin till such time as these rebels and traitors be subdued'.[90] Yet caution of this kind was perhaps the worst effect of the risings. The last of the closures in Lincolnshire had been completed at least a week before the first signs of protest were seen at Louth Park. Other than at Bardney and Barlings, no suppression and surrender secured before Michaelmas had been challenged. The same was true in the North Riding of Yorkshire: what had been secured, as recently as the last week of September at Easby, remained settled for the time being despite the disarray sixty-odd miles to the south.[91]

There were other obstacles. The unfinished business of the visitation continued to hobble the new commission. The visitors' determination to take down objects of veneration had provoked a pitched battle with the citizens of Exeter just at the moment when the suppression bill was passing into law.[92] The closure of the

Benedictine priory of St Nicholas was put off until Michaelmas; neighbouring houses were now given a receptive hearing when they requested dispensations. Most, in the immediate vicinity – Polsloe, Canonsleigh – and at a wider radius in Somerset and Wiltshire, had been dispensed by the end of January 1537.[93] Here there may have been a recognition at Westminster that the goodwill of the chief steward of the region's monasteries should be maintained: Henry Courtenay, marquess of Exeter, was expected to field no fewer than 5,000 'picked men' to put down the rising in the north.[94]

The collision of the two commissions was compounded by the government's preparation of new measures for enforcement of the statute, which seemed to sweep aside much of what had been done only months (in some cases just weeks) before. There are three fair copies surviving of 'instrucions' intended for the king's commissioners for 'a newe survey and an inventory' of any 'howse of religion' specified in their commission. Each is written in a different clerical hand, one of which is that of the Elizabethan historian John Stow; the others appear to belong to the date of the statute itself.[95] They carry the same twenty-three articles of inquiry applied at each house. As many as half of these call for the very same information which had been the subject of the two investigations of the previous year: the yearly value of the property, including demesne lands and woodland, the sight of the common seal, the status of the foundation (i.e. independent or dependent on another), the size of the professed community and, among the men, the number of ordained priests. To these repeat inquiries were to be added new information on 'grauntes bargaynes sales gufts alyenacions leases' of any property made in the year since the valuation and visitation themselves had begun (to be counted from 4 February 1535), and the value of lead and bells to be found there.[96] The commissioners were also instructed in the steps to be taken to empty the house of both occupants and contents, the making of an inventory, the confirmation of the destinations of the religious (i.e. to go to another house or to be released, if they were men with a 'capacity' or licence to act as secular priests), and the obligations of the superior, to sue for a pension themselves, and, at the king's pleasure, to see to it that their lands continued to be sowed and tilled.

On the face of it the clarity, consistency and coverage of these instructions was in marked contrast to what had been written in advance of the visitations. Writing four months after the passing of the statute, Cromwell seemed self-conscious of the difference, boasting to the prior of Horsham St Faith of a process that was following a plan held at the very apex of royal government, the 'howse[s] byllyd and namyd . . . [within] the kynges bokys'.[97]

But the administrative foundations were more apparent than real. Repeatedly, the articles required the commissioners, those they engaged to assist them, and the superior of the house to refer 'under a greate payne' to the Court of Augmentations. Yet this novel office of state was devised only after the statute won parliamentary approval; its personnel were gathered only as the circuits were already underway, and the precise definition of its practical role only came to be clarified in a slower time. In the meantime, the commissioners responded to their instructions each in their own way. George Gyffard, making a circuit of the west and the Midlands in the early summer, maintained a scepticism about the Court: 'Mr Chancellor and Mr Attorney of thaumentacions . . . have written . . . we be returned in to Northampton . . . where we must begyn our suppression', he reported, questioning 'whither ther letters subscribed with their honds be a sufficient warrant . . . in that behalf'.[98]

As late as November, when the commission was already interrupted by the northern rebellion, John Hussee still lamented to Lisle, 'The court is new begun, and no men knowe the order thereof'.[99] As much as two years later, Richard Rich, chancellor of Augmentations, would complain that he and his office were left at the margins. Standing on the dignity of his office did not build a relationship with agents on the ground. 'I fynde very small frendship,' John Hussee confided to Lady Lisle. He spoke for many on the circuit.[100]

These questions of process, and of the authority that steered it, were amplified by differences of outlook and personality among those charged with the commission. Just as at the outset of the visitation, Richard Leighton and Thomas Legh were each of them inclined to seize their initiative of the suppression for themselves. Both had been on the road, visiting the northern province, since Epiphany, but still they were brimming over with energy for 'what policie and meanes' Cromwell would pursue. Leighton encouraged him to be 'assured unto yow', in matters 'whatsoever they be concernyng hygh judgment [and] parliament'.[101]

Their enthusiasm galloped at a furious pace, and fellow commissioners were left pressured and pushed out of their path. By December, their claim on the circuit of Chester diocese provoked an appeal from Thomas Evance, 'you had assigned me your deputy and commissary there'.[102] Legh pledged himself to Cromwell in February as 'most yourers and redyest at any tyme', reminding him that he 'hathe said at dyvers tymys that I shuld be your chauncelor'.[103] As during the visitation, they were ready to interpret the instructions for themselves. This might explain the position of houses such as St Mary Magdalen, Bristol, undoubtedly closed in the late summer of 1536, but apparently without any documentation. Since there was only an 'aged and impotent' prioress, and a novice, and an income of £21, perhaps it was thought to be beneath an entry in their 'book'.[104]

Richard Southwell was fearful of such impatience, and before the end of March had sounded the alarm for Cromwell at the sacking of Marham Priory, which 'noo doubt of it hathe and dothe giff great encouragement unto others to make such licke entreprise'.[105] Yet as the circuits advanced it was for him that the trust was eroded. Before December he was the subject of the king's 'late conceived displeasure; bad enough for its passing to seem as if to 'restore and yeve unto me my life'.[106]

John Prise, whose first experience of the Crown's monastic policy had been in visitations in the west of England during the previous summer, had first seemed subdued by the forceful Thomas Legh, but as the circuit continued he had distanced himself from the man he nicknamed 'Mr Doctor', taking a more concil-iatory tone in the imposition of the injunctions where he found 'no excesses' and 'the house in good state and well ordered'.[107] Now, a year on, Prise's instinct to judge a house as he found it was foremost. His approach to each head was particular and personal; so much so that sometimes he took them into his counsels. In August 1536 he trusted Prior Griffin Williams of Carmarthen with a personal letter destined for Thomas Wriothesley.[108] George Gyffard, who had joined the commissioners in the West Midlands by the beginning of May, showed signs of the same readiness to consider each house in their own terms. 'A right discret man a singular good husbond ffor ye howse,' he reported on Prior James Dasset of St Andrew's, Northampton, when he arrived to effect the suppression, 'and wellbe-loved of all his neighbours.'[109]

The superiors of houses in the scope of the statute made no easy submission. It seems they knew and understood its terms well enough before the commis-sioners brought it to them. Joan Missenden, prioress of Legbourne, was ready to challenge the contention that her house was due for punishment. 'Whereas we doo here that a grete nombre of abbyes shalbe punysshid, subprest and put downe, bicause of their myslyvyng ... yet if it may pleas your goodness we trust in God ye shall here no complayntes agaynst us nother in oure lyvyng.'[110] It may have been a defiant demonstration of their virtue that led George Gyffard to praise the art and craft of the canons at Ulverscroft.[111] Prior Richard Hudson of the Augustinian foundation at Beeston tried a more obvious evasion, asserting that his community were professed as friars and so exempt from the present legislation.[112] Margaret Vernon of Marlow pre-empted the commissioners' process, dispersed her nuns, and stayed herself 'to maynteyne it withal' until the coming of the king's men.[113]

A number of superiors deflected the commissioners by taking up their tools of patronage, both traditional and those to which the regime itself had recently introduced to them. Their aim was not to argue with the commission per se but to appeal at once for their own exemption from its terms, that is, to save their house from the sentence of suppression. The conspicuous proof of their efforts is the licence to continue that some in time secured, although it seems very likely that more of them employed these persuasions than succeeded. Cash was the most common currency. The sums that secured a licence were very high relative to the reported value of the house. Abbot Robert Pulton and his convent of Cockersand first offered 1,000 marks, more than three times the abbey's annual income; it was doubled before their continuation was confirmed.[114] Abbot John Norman of Bindon (Dorset) paid £300, 50 per cent more the yearly revenue of the house.[115]

Payments on such scale almost certainly were possible only because of the activation of their own affinity of patrons. Some reached instead for the resources in their own hands, offering up property from their portfolio with a proven return. The prospect of cash payments prompted something approaching market pressure, however. It was made clear to Abbess Clemencia Stock of Delapré (Northamptonshire) that her grant of woodland at Hanslope (Buckinghamshire) was not enough to be sure of a licence; £266 was also required before her licence to continue was sealed.[116] The trade not only distracted the commissioners in their task, it also threatened to disempower them, as the negotiations urged from both ends obliged them to act as a go-between. It also left them vulnerable to allegations of venality. Chancellor Richard Rich was convinced they 'receyve rewardes which causeth [them] to wright as [they] do'.[117]

A handful of superiors succeeded in keeping their houses open at a much smaller material cost, through their personal ties of clientage. Prior Thomas Manning alias Sudbury of Butley now profited from the patronage of Bishop William Rugg of Norwich, himself from the beginning of the decade one of Cromwell's most prominent monastic allies. Rugg appointed Manning as his suffragan in March 1536, surely, since he had witnessed the proceedings in parliament, in anticipation of the prior's likely need for preferment. In fact, when the commissioners' circuit reached the county, Butley itself was bypassed. It was not dissolved for another two years. Rugg appears to have provided the same to another of his suffragans. Prior John Sarisbury of Horsham St Faith, Rugg's deputy in West Norfolk, saw nothing of the commission. The most spectacular prize for a game of politics was taken by Robert Holgate, prior of the Gilbertine house at Watton. In the months before the passing of the statute he had already seen Cromwell turn his 'good mynde' towards him and enjoyed no less a name than John Hilsey, the new bishop of Rochester, to make his own 'power suites' on his behalf. Hilsey was a close enough ally to carry to Cromwell the prior's request to 'enjoy hys office withal yn commendam'.[118] Before the turn of the year the exemption of his entire (Gilbertine) congregation was confirmed.

The superiors reached out for these fresh contacts within, or close to, the Cromwellian circle, more readily than they did for their hereditary founders and principal patrons. Their involvement in the affairs of their foundations may have become closer since the turn of the century but so too had their interest in their property, its income, and even their standing buildings. The superiors that received rough handling from secular lordship – for example, at Hartland, Kingswood and Lytham – naturally now did not think of them as a defence against the Crown. Given the weave of social networks surrounding them, there can be little doubt that the religious were aware of the early and eager seigneurial interest in the passing of the statute. John Hussee's gathering of news for Lord Lisle of the prospects for houses in the south and west was only possible if he found a large number of informants. There are no fewer than five letters surviving from those claiming founders' status sent between the close of the parliamentary session (14 April) and the beginning of June. They represented the length and breadth of the kingdom, from Northumberland (Henry Stafford) to Sussex (de la Warr), Essex (Henry Bourchier) and Devon (Sir Piers Edgcumbe).[119]

If this can be a measure of the attention to the statute and its implications then it is possible that these survivors are just a fraction of the inquiries now made at Austin Friars. Most did not attempt to challenge the principle of the suppression but aimed only to register their own interest in what they regarded as a property about to be taken into the king's hands. Lord Essex looked only for a straight-forward transaction. Writing while parliament still sat, he set down the price he was prepared to pay (1,000 marks) and his preferred terms, three instalments payable over three years.[120]

Six months on and with the circuits of the commissioners underway, Edward Stanley, earl of Derby, would not accept the accuracy of their survey and pressed for Burscough Priory (Lancashire) at an asking price of his own estimation, since their valuation of 'even the glass and bars in the church windows', led them to a figure 'higher ... than they be well worth'. As founder, the earl was minded to challenge the purpose of the Crown: 'forasmoche as my auncester, sumtymes founder therof, lye buryed there, I wold be right glad that the said church might stand in good reparacion'. He contemplated its conversion as a chantry, 'as it is, suppressed; intending ... to fynd summe preist'.[121] Lord De la Warr likewise tested Cromwell on the force of the statute, raising the prospect of preservation, secularisation (as a collegiate church), as well as the assign of the endowment to him as founder, 'to have the prefarment with all suche other thyngs that the pryor yn his tyme had'.[122]

There were as many powerful individuals, both prominent courtiers and those whose influence was confined to their own counties, who entered into correspond-ence only after they had taken direct action to conserve their interest. 'I am steward and fownder of the most part of the howses of religion and under me many of the jantlemen have the rewles of them,' Thomas Howard reminded Cromwell at Michaelmas.[123] As the circuits of the commissioners advanced in the summer and early autumn, Howard had – often, it seems, in person – moved to place his hered-itary houses out of their path. He suppressed Bungay and Sibton himself; at the latter the abbot, William Flatbury, was left to look for 'sum person in the cuntrey to take his resygnacion'.[124] For Thetford Priory, where many of his forebears lay buried, Howard saw an opportunity when the king was sick to oversee the burial arrangements for the duke of Richmond and 'at my sewte' to send the body 'wrappd in ledde and a close cart ... theer unto Thedford'.[125]

The high status and regional heft of Howard favoured his approach, but lesser men also looked to the same methods. Sir Piers Dutton represented his interfer-ence in the suppression of Norton Priory in October as the loyal defence of the king's writ: 'Thabbot gedred a gret company to gedder to the nombre of two or thre hundred persons so that the ... comyssioners weare in feare of there lyves.' Dutton and retainers of his 'came suddenly apon them', and although 'it was so derke' he 'used some polax' and 'it was thought of the matter hadde not ye quykly handlet it wolde have growen to forther unconveniunts'.[126] Dutton reported that he had seen the commissioners 'and theyr stuffe' safely into the custody of Halton Castle, but he took possession of the priory itself, planned the summary execution of those resisting the commission, among whom were neighbouring landholders, and proved reluctant to stand down his own force.[127] Dutton was already sheriff of Cheshire and the first result of the affair appears to have been to take much of the rest of the local authorities, including the governors of Chester, into his service.

Far from Westminster, there may have been a general view that lordship might interpret the statute for itself. Two hundred miles from Cromwell's chambers at Austin Friars, Edward Grey, Lord Powis, secured the abbey of Strata Marcella into his custody in October and only then turned to Cromwell for confirmation of his de facto possession.[128] The commissioners found themselves oppressed by the forceful claims of local proprietors: 'I have sene none', came a report from the Western March, 'butt that they were promysyd unto suche persons'.[129]

How these challenges were 'handlet' – as Dutton phrased it – is rarely described in any detail. For a number of houses in East Anglia and North Yorkshire it is possible to trace the steps of the commissioners as they attended to each of the articles of inquiry. Their surviving, soft-bound paper record books bear witness to their effort to search out the required information about people, money, high-value raw materials and conspicuous furnishings. Their entries begin in neat and well-spaced lines but are often amended and annotated in an untidy scrawl. Often, it seems the scale of the task, even at a tiny, rural foundation, drained or frustrated them. The repeated cancellations and corrections might suggest that answers to inquiries seemed unreliable at the time. That these working documents were preserved, and even copied by later generations, might indicate a general shortage of final fair copies; the nagging suspicion is that they were never completed.

It may be because the commissioners often left with the task unfinished that much about what they found and what they did with it is recorded only in their personal dispatches to Cromwell. These men whose experience was clerical and educational, legal and theological, self-consciously applied themselves to the task of the surveyor. They estimated the extent of a building's lead by eye and committed to a rough-and-ready calculation of its fother weight: from Buckenham, Cromwell received a full account of the metal although his keen eye can hardly have missed

the salient detail that it remained 'on the churche'.[130] Some now showed the attention to detail so often lacking in the Valor returns. At Crabhouse the common
names of each field in the priory's demesne were documented, notwithstanding
the obvious danger that the similarity of 'Olde Field' and 'Pasturefield' might lead
to confusion.[131] Reporting from Warwickshire in July, George Gyffard gave the
impression he had spent several weeks walking the fields of the nuns of Polesworth,
to be able to advise Cromwell that 'the pasture is either a heth grownd or els itt is
a very dire and a hard spieri grasse'.[132]

It was in their handling of people that the rough edges in their process were
most sharply exposed. In this respect the efforts of the visitors over preceding
months do not appear to have passed on very much advantage to the new commission. Youths below the canonical age of twenty-four, and the sick and elderly incapable of a fully observant life, had not been removed entirely from every house.
The response to the different approaches of the commissioners to this measure was
mixed. Thomas Legh claimed that he found them desperate to leave. No doubt
many went, although it seems likely that Legh, and others among the visitors,
acted as agents provocateurs. The record of established religious, men already
ordained to the priesthood, seeking licence to secularise in 1535, may be an indication that opportunists seized an opening intended for the more vulnerable. In just
about a month between the first week in June and the second week in July, the
Faculty Office issued licences to nine canons and monks representing each one of
the congregations.[133]

The surviving books of the suppression commissioners that do contain lists of
the professed confirm that residents at opposite extremes of the age range were
still in residence. These lists, and the commissioners' letters, also draw attention to
the presence of the chronically sick. So often was it reported that at least one of
the monastic community was an invalid or insane, it may be assumed that the visitors, or the superiors after they left, had baulked at the prospect of re-homing
them. Of course, the late visits of the northern counties, not completed until early
February 1536, may have prevented very many departures of any kind before news
of the statute was widely known.

The suppression books show the commissioners following their instructions in
determining the intentions of the professed, to remain in the monastic life at another
foundation or to be released and, for the men, to be licensed to act as a secular priest.
Yet, these decisions were not so readily enacted. A later, Elizabethan copy of a ledger

that must have originally been written out in the summer of 1536 records the names of 387 houses whose suppression was anticipated, together with a figure for the professed intending to continue in religion and the names of houses to which they might be sent.[134] The list and its calculations must be prospective, since it includes several that were later exempted from the terms of statute.[135] It cannot be certain that the figures recorded stand for the number of religious to be transferred elsewhere, but it is likely given that several houses are named without any figure, signalling that none there had chosen to continue. The value of this late copy is that it incorporates a note alongside the names of houses of women in East Anglia and the archiepiscopal province of York, stating that since the suppression has removed nunneries from the region, there is nowhere in the county to where they can transfer (nullus extant ibidem monasteria ad quem transferrantur); the women of Essex, Suffolk and Norfolk are signposted to London; no alternative is given for those in the north.[136]

There is scarcely a glimpse, either in the government papers or the fragments from the houses themselves, of the transfer of religious from a suppressed community to another still standing. The relocation of two complete communities of religious to two new royal foundations, the women of Stainfield (Suffolk) to Stixwould (Lincolnshire), and the men of Chertsey to Bisham, were stage-managed by King Henry himself.[137] They were not completed until months after the first suppression, although even at distance they must have drawn attention to the drift of other communities in search of a new cloister.

The evidence of the Elizabethan ledger suggests at least initial planning of what was an unprecedented migration. The provisional numbers counted here were high indeed: more than 1,200 men and just over 600 women. Where there were houses remaining nearby to be identified as potential destinations, it seems the compiler held nothing more in view than a general sense of the geographical vicinity. Other practical considerations, such as distance and – critical for any institutional life – the capacity of the new house, were overlooked. Nor was there a consistent attention to the differences of congregation and order.

The provisional allocation for the ten Benedictine monks of Earl's Colne (Essex) was to travel nearly thirty miles south to the Augustinian house at St Osyth.[138] Here there were already as many as fifteen canons. The descent of the Colne contingent promised to push them towards a population the house had not been able to support for some 300 years. No fewer than thirty-one Augustinian and Benedictine women at houses in the Welsh March in this list were destined for Wilton Abbey, more than 120 miles to the south, where they would have doubled the community in size.[139] In the event, it is very likely that the transfer of such cohorts was more dispersed. It seems the men of the four suppressed houses in Derbyshire spread far and wide, and beyond the county, as only one of them arrived at the largest remaining monastery of Dale.[140] Six displaced canons arrived at Nostell Priory (West Yorkshire) from three different houses, three of them travelling almost seventy miles from Bridlington.[141] The crowd of displaced religious in houses ill-equipped either to accommodate or occupy them may explain the number of men who applied for licences to secularise after 1536 but before their house itself surrendered. By December 1537, Wybert Gilboye, who had joined St Mary Graces (London) after Stratford Langthorne closed, had found a preferment that persuaded him to purchase a licence to live as a secular, ten months before St Mary's was shut down.[142]

There may have been no more assurance for those who now wanted to leave their religion behind. Men looking for a licence to secularise were made to wait. It may have been the delay in Lincolnshire in September that led released canons and monks still in limbo into the path of the rebellion. The Faculty Office registers show that the applications from canons and monks whose houses were suppressed in the spring of 1536 were not issued until the following spring. The Lincolnshire men who took no part in the rising, such as Abbot George Walker of Louth, and a dozen monks of Kirkstead, did not receive their capacities until early May.[143] The position of Richard Smyth, Thomas Herman and Thomas Hoth of Buildwas Abbey (Shropshire) was especially weak: their licences, which arrived six months after they were sent out from the house, would not overcome the obvious obstacle that none of them was yet an ordained priest.[144] The elderly and sick surely faced a different practical challenge: for some, unable to ride or walk, perhaps it began with how to leave the precinct at all. In the face of these difficulties, it does seem the commissioners were inclined to limit their own actions to the formal closure of the community and securing the custody of buildings, property and the corporate workings of the house. They left the priory at Coxford with the house and its furnishings still in the care of the prior.[145] The anonymous monk chronicler at Canterbury noticed over the wall of the women's priory that 'the monyalls niot-wythstanding at that tyme were not removed . . . they abyde[d] until Easter'.[146]

At their government masters, however, the commissioners were aggrieved. Their persistent complaint was the sheer scale of their task. After the first twenty miles of their circuit and just three houses, the Northamptonshire commissioners already sounded weary of their 'tarreying'; a week later, and a further twenty miles, and already they were admitting to shortcuts because they could not 'certefie' every aspect of each house until 'the fynyssyng of the ... other howses'. Their dispatch was signed off with the barbed comment that their own task could have been easier, 'yff every man had done his partie at the firste commission' (i.e. the visitation of 1535).[147] Once he was out of the office confronting the task for himself, Robert Burgoyn, auditor of Augmentations, considered it 'painful and long' which he could complete only 'as best he may'. He was soon overwhelmed: 'my paynfull and long circuite ... [is] my greate and intolerable buysnesse,' he confided to fellow commissioner, John Scudamore.[148] If they had each of them received a version of the articles of inquiry, they were unprepared for the effort they required. Those who had served as visitors may have not had a full set of injunctions when they faced each house and their passage through the circuit had been rapid and often self-consciously cavalier. The process of suppression was not to be pressed so readily into this pattern.

The surviving account of the expenses of the commissioners in East Anglia attests to their attempts to contain their time at each house within the span of a working day, from their 'fyrst breakfast' – perhaps taken as soon as it was light – to dinner time in the mid-afternoon; still they were obliged to stay overnight at least a couple of times in a given week. They were pained as much by the effort of it as the cost. Passing through the eastern counties the commissioners were paying for food and drink three or four times each day. Their charges for two days at Crabhouse and Thetford (thirty miles apart) in Norfolk stood at a sizeable £2.[149] Richard Leighton demanded his 'mete and drynk was at the abbot's cost', but even so by later in the year he admitted to Cromwell in cod Latin: he was broke.[150] George Gyffard reminded Cromwell that his commitment to the cause was a burden to others: '[I am] more chargeable unto my pore father ... by reason of this office' and 'have no howse wytyn the lymytis of the circuyte'.[151] His colleague, John Freeman, feared for his very survival: 'my desyr is to leve and to have some mene leven to mayntayne the lyfe withal wyche cannot be had without yow'.[152]

The pressure they felt was made worse by the limited personnel. In the draft instructions for the commissioners it was envisaged that six – three government officers, three gentry of the region – would serve on each circuit. In the event it was often four (as arrived at Ingham) that were the most to be mustered; in the

West Midlands and Yorkshire the circuits began with six but they were soon broken up by the piecemeal process of the suppressions.[153] In Wales, and its northern marches, able and willing hands were in short supply. John Vaughan found, 'Y was constraynyd to apoynt days for the determynacyon of ... matters' for 'the people do say ... they had no law mynysteryd to them in the spyrtualyty thys meny yerys'.[154] Bishop Rowland Lee doubted the fitness of Cromwell's choice, John Scudamore, who 'dwelling nyghe the Welshery' was 'greatly kynned and alyed in the same'.[155] Still Scudamore was chosen for a circuit that extended over 100 miles of difficult terrain and unstable society. At once he begged Cromwell to let him employ as his assistants 'too yong ladds' fresh out of schools in England. When suppressions had turned to surrenders his son William was recruited so that the receiving of houses, contents and property might be handled more 'fully'.[156] The task in Wales and the Western March was almost beyond endurance. Cromwell rebuked his commission for complaining; in return there came only a hangdog response: 'we will make as much haste and use as great dexterite in our further proceedings as your good lordeshipe vouchesauede to admonyshe us by youre lettres lately directede'.[157]

Cromwell's chivvying perhaps spoke more at this particular moment of his standards of administrative efficiency than of his unshakeable commitment to a policy of dissolution. At the head of the regime, the onset of a statutory process for suppression did not represent a resolution of the matter of the monasteries. Not for the first time, or the last, the king's personal priorities were unpredictable. In the months either side of the passage of the statute, Henry had made some public displays of enthusiasm for religious houses and their role. On progress the summer before with Queen Anne he had visited Syon Abbey, Winchcombe and Hailes, places of monastic worship favoured by his father and grandmother.[158]

The encounter at Hailes was later remembered by Anne's personal chaplain, William Latymer, to have prompted thoughts of a grand programme of reform. This has been read as proof of her influence on a deepening distaste for the tradition in the mind of the king. Yet what Latymer remembered was not the total suppression of the monastic estate but rather a judicious reform: 'from that tyme forwarde she advertised all other preachers of goddess worde ... towching the subverting of any howses of religion but rather to make continyall and earnest peticione for the staye of the same'. Latymer claimed that 'The swete sownde

1. John Leech's cartoon 'Henry VIII Monk Hunting', in which the king is shown as a huntsman; Archbishop Thomas Cranmer joins him mounted on a donkey. An illustration for Gilbert Abbott à Beckett's *The Comic History of England* (1847–48).

2. Detail of a panel painting from Romsey Abbey (Hampshire) now used as a reredos. Here an abbess proclaims Christ's Resurrection; her image is framed by a row of the saints venerated by the women of the monastery, among which was a figure perhaps meant to be the founding abbess.

3. Stained-glass window at Deerhurst Priory (Gloucestershire) depicting the different ages of monastic men: the middle-aged, the elderly and the young novice.

4. Graffito showing a tonsured monk drawn on the plaster wall of the passageway leading to the refectory of Cleeve Abbey (Somerset).

5. Brass figures from the tomb of Sir Thomas Urswick (d. 1479) in the parish church of St Peter and St Paul, Dagenham (Essex), showing the first of his nine daughters in her nun's habit (lower section, far left).

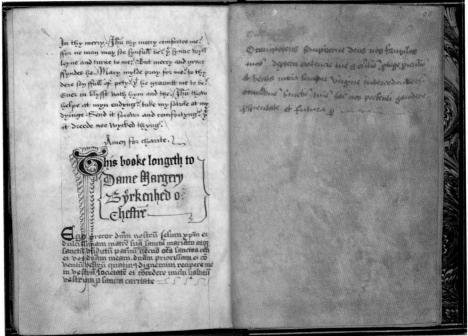

6. A processional and prayer book which at one time belonged to Margery Byrkenhed, a Benedictine nun at St Mary's Priory, Chester (Cheshire).

7. Panels carved with a Tudor rose and a medallion in the Renaissance style, part of a sequence made for a chamber at Waltham Abbey (Essex).

8. The initials of Abbot Richard Kidderminster (d. 1533/34) carved in the door frame of the George Inn, Winchcombe (Gloucestershire).

9. Sker House, near Porthcawl (West Glamorgan), originally the hub of a grange farm of Neath Abbey.

10. Stained-glass window showing Tudor nuns in prayer, installed in memory of Sir Thomas Lovell (d. 1524), originally placed in the church of Holywell Priory (Essex), now in St Andrew's Church, Enfield.

11. The preaching cross of the Dominican Friary at Hereford.

12. Bayham Abbey (East Sussex), one of the twenty-nine monasteries closed by Cardinal Wolsey between 1524 and 1529. When Bayham was shut down in 1525, one of its canons led a small band to reoccupy it, holding out for more than a week before they were overcome. Five centuries on, a tree is rooted in the wall of the chancel behind the high altar.

13. Abbot John Islip of Westminster (1500–32), depicted in the illumination of the initial capital letter of the royal indenture (dated 1504) that confirmed the monastery's part in an elaborate commemorative scheme for Henry VII and his family, centred on a new Lady Chapel to be constructed at the abbey church.

14. The Great Hall of Winchester Castle, where Bishop Stephen Gardiner gathered the clerical leaders of his diocese to give their assent to the Act of Succession in 1534.

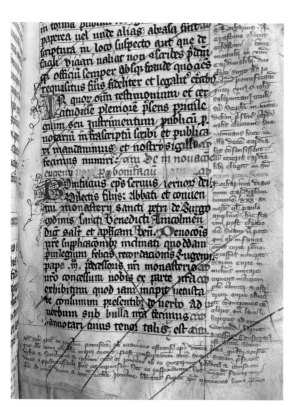

15. A thirteenth-century cartulary from Peterborough Abbey showing the title of pope scratched out from the text of a privilege granted to the monastery, an act of conformity with the terms of the royal supremacy. The text of the document itself has been crossed through, perhaps by a later hand.

16. The priory gateway at Hexham (Northumberland), where the crown commissioners met armed resistance in September 1536.

17. The parish church of St James, Louth (Lincolnshire), where the call to armed protest over the closure of monasteries was first raised after Evensong on 1 October 1536.

18. Passageway within Sawley Abbey (Lancashire), which after its suppression under the statute of 1536 was reoccupied by some of its monks and held by them from 12 October until early in the new year.

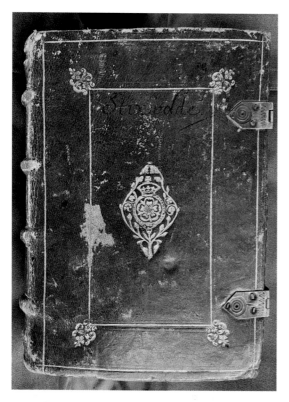

19. A thirteenth-century cartulary from the Cistercian abbey of Stixwould (Lincolnshire), rebound and stamped with royal insignia at the time of Henry VIII's refoundation of the monastery, for women under Premonstratensian customs, in July 1537.

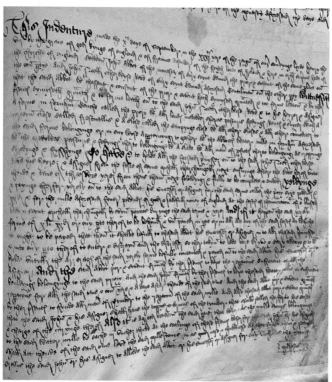

20. A copy of an indenture recording the lease by the abbot and convent of Bury St Edmunds (Suffolk) of a farm at Fornham just two and a half miles to the north, to the reeve of the town, John Noell. It was dated 10 September 1539, little more than seven weeks before the abbey's final surrender to the crown.

21. The font from the parish church of Dunster Priory (Somerset) carved with the badge of the Five Wounds of Christ, a motif also carried by those that joined the 1536 uprising known as the Pilgrimage of Grace.

22. Deed enacting the surrender of the Cistercian abbey at Biddlesden (Buckinghamshire) dated 25 September 1538. It was one of only a handful to be written in English. It was unusual also because not only did it describe the buildings and property to be transferred to the Crown but also made an apology for the form of life, the 'pretensed religion', which had been followed in the monastery.

23. Guisborough Priory (North Yorkshire) seen from the east end, where the last recorded ordination of regular religious men occurred in September 1539.

24. Letter from Giovanni Portinari, the Italian military engineer employed by Thomas Cromwell to demolish the Cluniac Priory at Lewes (East Sussex). Writing on 20 March 1538, Portinari reports on his assessment of the proportions of the church, his essential preparations before setting his explosive.

25. Memorandum written in a twelfth-century bestiary from Newark Priory (Surrey) allocating the manuscript to one of the canons, John Rosse, on 6 October 1538, just weeks before its final surrender at the turn of the year.

26. Memorial brass of Prior Thomas Nelond (d. 1429) of Lewes (East Sussex) which was recovered from the priory church and carried twenty miles inland to Cowfold in the west of the county, where it was installed in the parish church of St Peter.

AGATHA·BARLOW·WI·DOW·DAVGHTEROF·HVMFREY·WELSBORNE· LATE·WIFE·OF·WILLIAM·BARLOW·BISHOP·OF·CHICHESTER· WHO·DEPARTED·THIS·LIFE·THE·13·OF·AVGVSTE·ANNO·DOMI·1568 AND·LETHE·BVRIED·IN·THE·CATHEDRALL·CHVRCHEOFCHCHESTER BY·WHOME·SHEE·HAD·SEVEN·CHILDREN·THAT·CAME·VNTO·MEN AND·WEMENS·STATE·TOO·SVNNES·AND·FIVE·DAVGHTRS·THE SVNNES·WILLIAM·AND·IOHN·THE·DAVGHTERS·MARGARITE·WIFE VN·TO·WILLIAM·OVERTON·BISHOP·OF·COVENTRI·AND·LITCH·FILD ANNE·WIFE·VNTO·HERBERT·WESTFAYLING·BISHOP·OF· HEREFORDE·ELIZABETH·DIED·ANNO   WIFE·VNTO· WILLIAM·DAY·NOW·BISHOP·OF·WINCHESTER·FRANCES·WIFE VNTO·TOBY·MATHEW·BISHOP·OF·DVRRHAM·ANTONINE· LATE·WIFE·VNTO·WILLIAM·WICKAM·DISCEASED·BISHOP·OF·WINCHESTER·SHEE BEIN·G·A·WOMAN·GODLY·WISE·AND·DISCREETE·FROM·HER·YOVTHE MOSTE·FAYTHFVL·VNTO·HER·HVSBAND·BOTHE·IN·PROSPERITE·AND·ADVE RSITE·AND·A·COMPANIONE·WITH·HIM·IN·BANISHMENTE·FOR·THE·GOSPELL· SAKE·MOSTE·KINDE·AND·LOVING·VNTO·ALL·HER·CHILDREN·AND·DEARLY BELOVED·OF·THEM·ALL·FOR·HER·ABILITY·OF·A·LIBERALL·MYNDE·AND PITIFVIL·VNTO·THE·POORE·SHEE·HAVEING·LIVED·ABOVTE·LXXXX· YEARES·DIED·IN·THE·LORDE·WHOM·SHEE·DAYLY·SERVED·THE·XIII· OF·IVNE·ANNO·DOMINI·1595·IN·THE·HOWSE·OF·HER·SVNNE·WILLIAM BEING·THEN·PERSON·OF·THIS·CHVRCHE·AND·PREBENDARY·OF WINCHESTER·ROGATV·ET·SVMPTIBVS·FILIE·DELECTÆ· FRANCISCÆ·MATHEW·

HIC·AGATHÆ·TVMVLVS·BARLOI·PRÆSVLIS·INDE EXVLIS·INDE·ITERVMPRÆSVLIS·VXOR·ERAT PROLE·BEATA·FVIT·PLENA·ANNIS·QVOS·MARY·N

27. Memorial tablet for Agatha Barlow (née Wellesbourne), a former nun who married William Barlow (d. 1568), bishop, successively, of Bangor, St David's and Chichester, who himself had begun his career as an Augustinian canon. The couple had seven children; Agatha died almost thirty years after her husband in 1595.

28. Memorial brass for Ann Boroeghe, a former nun of St Mary's Priory, Clerkenwell, found at All Saints Church, Dingley (Northamptonshire), where she lived for nearly thirty years after the surrender of her community in 1539.

29. The Cistercian abbey of Valle Crucis, near Llangollen (Denbighshire), backed by the black hills which for the Tudor traveller John Leland underlined the landscape's desolation after the closure of the monastery and the loss of its grange farms.

30. Among the furnishings of the cathedral church at Winchester, which were inventorised when the monastic chapter surrendered, were two pastoral staffs said to be made from unicorn's horn. Curiosities like these were later to be found in the king's own collection of treasures.

31. The church of the Dominican friary at Brecon, where the former Augustinian canon, William Barlow, bishop of St David's (1536–48), established a school under the terms of a charter dated 19 January 1542.

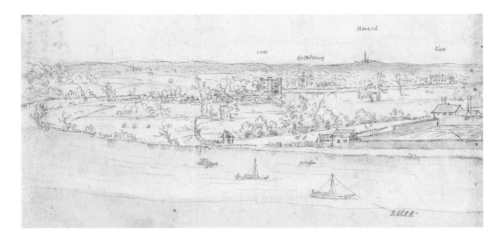

32. Anton van den Wyngaerde's panoramas of London and its outskirts from the River Thames (*c.* 1562) provide views of the Charterhouse at Sheen, the Birgittine convent at Syon and the Observant Friary at Greenwich, whose communities were re-established from 1555 and came to reoccupy their former buildings.

33. The cadaver effigy of William Weston, last Grand Prior of the Knights of St John of Jerusalem, from his tomb at Clerkenwell Priory. He died in the spring of 1540, apparently on the very day that the act for the suppression of his order passed through parliament.

wherof, after it came to the eares of the governor of other religious houses wonderfully revyved them and gave them good hope.'

In Anne's 'godly enterprise' their houses were not to be suppressed but to join her in the patronage of doctrinal instruction, 'liberally offering . . . large stipendes and exhibicions to be distrybuted yearely to preachers and scollars'. According to her chaplain, she urged Bishop Latimer to 'dissuade the uttere subversion' of religious houses and to 'induce the kinges grace to the mynde to converte them to some better uses'.[159]

It seems the mood of the royal household persisted into the New Year. In January 1536 the funeral and burial of Queen Katherine was entrusted to the prelates of old monastic England: the lady's coffin had been attended by the abbots of Crowland, Ramsey, Thame, Thorney and Walden. A pre-burial Mass had been celebrated at Sawtry, prior to the interment at Peterborough Abbey. The king had rejected her hope of burial at one of the churches of the Observant friars, but the arrangements he did allow could hardly be said to be hostile to the religion of the regulars.[160]

In the spring Henry was suddenly receptive to petitions for exemption from the conditions of the suppression and to the award of licences to continue. Some of the houses that appear approved for continuation without any word in the surviving record as to when, why or by what means, such as the tiny Cistercian community at Heynings (Lincolnshire), may reflect the king's own hand. There is no doubt that the most conspicuous proposal for the continuation of houses scheduled for closure was Henry's personal project. The conversion of Stixwould Abbey, a house of Cistercian men, for the Cistercian nuns of Stainfield was passed to Cromwell to put into effect in early summer. Henry orchestrated the enterprise from another monastic setting, Waltham Abbey, where he stayed for much of June. Before the unrest at Louth and Lincoln at the beginning of October their continuation was settled. A thirteenth-century cartulary containing the foundational grants to the house between 1171 and 1263 was restored with a new leather binding stamped with the royal device of the Tudor rose and the garter motto (see Fig. 20).[161] It was in the same month as the removal from Stainfield began that the Augustinian priory at Bisham was suppressed and it may be that Henry had already conceived a plan for another conversion here, now (in contrast to Stixwould) a change of and rise in status to a Benedictine abbey. The buildings were occupied eighteen months later by the brethren of Chertsey Abbey, who had stayed on at their old house after it had been suppressed in July 1537. Here too there was a self-conscious statement of continuity with the ancient past, the statutes headed 'uppon the foundacion of William Montacute earle of salysbury', the original fourteenth-century founder.[162]

The summer after his removal of Anne, and the spectacle of armed risings against him, Henry's instinct to reach for monastic religion seemed little changed. He even appears to have permitted the burial in a church of the friars of the courtier who had betrayed him for the rebel cause, Thomas Lord Darcy; Greenwich was denied him as it had been to Queen Katherine, but Darcy's body went to the Friars of the Cross at Tower Hill.[163] The birth of the king's son in the autumn of 1537 did not bring any change of tack: his christening was entrusted to three Benedictine abbots, of St Albans, Waltham and Westminster.[164]

In so far as Cromwell's outlook can be recovered at all from so few surviving papers, it does seem that the passing of the statute did not propel him rapidly towards a plan for total suppression of the monasteries. Like the king, as the commissioners set out on their task in the spring of 1536, Cromwell continued to cultivate his relationships across the monastic hierarchy. Generally, these attachments have been read retrospectively, as manipulative manoeuvres aimed only at preparing particular houses, targeted for their influence, regional significance and wealth, for eventual closure. Their superiors were drawn into Cromwell's affinity, like any other, as dependents, knowing that this continued favour was dependent upon their service. Yet still, like the king himself, he looked for them to serve him as heads of living religious houses. Rather than a temporary contingency his patronage of them appeared to be directed towards a new configuration of the regular congregations. The Benedictine prior of Horsham St Faith, John Sarisbury, was presented as *commendam* abbot of Titchfield, the wealthiest Cistercian foundation in the south-east of England; around the same time, William More, a Cambridge secular priest, was promoted as *commendam* abbot of Walden.

When these appointments were made it seems Cromwell envisaged an extended role of regular prelates in the new state Church. In the year from March 1536 no fewer than seven heads of monastic and mendicant heads of houses, each one of them already with a place in the Cromwellian circle, were appointed to suffragan sees: John Hodgkin (Sudbury; Bedford); William More (Worcester; Colchester); Richard Ingworth (King's Langley; Dover); Thomas Manning (Butley; Ipswich); John Bird (Coventry; Penrydd); Lewis Thomas (Cwmhir; Shrewsbury); John Sarisbury (Horsham St Faith; Thetford).

In the same period, four regulars took full bishoprics: Augustinian William Barlow (St David's); Benedictine William Rugg (Norwich); Gilbertine Robert Holgate (Llandaff); and Cluniac Robert Wharton (St Asaph). A reaffirmation of the place of the regulars in the regime's reforms was apparent in prospective bills prepared for and perhaps put before parliament at one or other of the sessions of 1535–36 and 1536–37. A proposal for new welfare provision for the elderly (over the age of sixty) echoed Queen Anne in its vision of a monastic foundation (at Coventry) as the ideal infrastructure for such a 'Court of Centenarians'. Another draft asserted directly that 'all houses not yet suppressed shall stand and abide notwithstanding the said act', as if to codify that the rump of the regular estate might now be enshrined in the Henrician Church.[165]

How far Cromwell's hand was in this putative legislation cannot be certain, but another paper that surely passed close to him at the same time, a summary account of the revenues of Walsingham Priory, is indicative of the same pattern of thought, an appraisal of the possibilities of monastic foundations.[166] It is possible that the commissioners on their circuits in the second half of 1536 had detected a certain diffidence over the direction of policy. Their letters fizz with their frustration. Their appeals for decisions on the future of sites, properties and the regulars themselves seemed more often than not to meet with delay, evasion or no answer at all. John Hussee, charged by Viscount Lisle to press his case for the grant of Frithelstock Priory, returned to him month after month to report he 'hath not [anything] certified yet'.[167]

Looking back almost a decade later, Edward Hall recalled there was public disquiet at a suppression that seemed to have been halted almost as soon as it had begun. 'But even at that tyme,' he claimed, 'one sayd in the parliament house these were as thornes but the great abbottes were putrified old okes and they must nedes folowe.'[168] The case was pressed on the reading public of 1536. 'Consider ye princes,' commanded the translation of Philip Melancthon's defence of the Augsburg confession, 'the unshamefastnes of our adversaries', that is 'the monasticall lyfe' and its 'abbeye workes'.[169] It was also audible from the pulpit. 'How religious, howe mocking howe munking so ever they be,' Hugh Latimer reminded the first Convocation after the winter's unrest in a sermon that saw two print runs in the same year.[170] Latimer's interventions in his diocese suggest he had already decided not to accept the terms under which the visitors had left the religious houses in 1535. It may have been the climate that his influence created in the Marches of Wales that accounts for a report received by Cromwell that 'the voyse of the contrey ys that whylle ye have monks ther ye schall have nother good reule nor god ordre ther.'[171] Yet there was no ground-swell of pressure for further suppressions. In keeping with the sight of so many monastic suffragans in the provincial Church, monastic voices of reform were given a platform by London printers: now there was a 'newely corrected' edition of *Werke for housholders* by Richard Whitford of Syon Abbey, and a refutation of the Protestant theology of John Frith by John Gwynneth of St Albans.[172]

The 'greate' abbeys had not been, as Hall remembered it, unaffected by the enforcement of the statute. A number of independent abbeys and cathedral priories faced an immediate collateral challenge as their chain of dependencies was caught in the commissioners' path. Eleven fell by March 1537.[173] Some pre-empted a confron-tation by recalling the resident communities: the outposts of Durham, Evesham, Lenton, Norwich and St Albans were emptied in the months that followed; at least twelve were now leased out.[174] Battle in Sussex accepted the loss of its distant Devon cell, but Bath Cathedral Priory and Tewkesbury Abbey fended off the interference of the commissioners, or their masters, in spite of their priories (Dunster, Bristol) showing incomes scarcely a quarter of the £200 threshold of the statute.[175] In parallel with the passage of the commissioners in the first phase of suppressions, Cromwell now brought the hierarchy of Benedictine cathedral priories and independent abbeys under closer supervision. Between Easter and Michaelmas 1536 three houses saw their headship changed at the hands of the regime: Walden, Winchester and Worcester. Henry Broke was removed from Winchester under Thomas Legh's duress before news of the statute itself had spread countrywide.[176] William More of Worcester followed him three months later. Robert Catton, whom Cromwell himself had presented to St Albans after Wolsey's death as a prospective protégé, was ousted, ostensibly by a faction of the monastic community but almost certainly with the vicegerent acting as agent provocateur.[177] The heads of two others, Chester and St Albans, came under sustained pressure to step down, which they duly did before the end of the year.[178]

It has often been suggested that such interference, reaching further and further into the monastic establishment, was only in preparation for their certain suppres-sion. Yet the removal of these incumbents had been prompted not by any general challenge to the royal supremacy but by their particular resistance to the reforms of the previous year. In 1536 at least the role of their replacements was no more than to recommit their communities to the king's injunctions.

To the same end Cromwell now provided new superiors to the leading abbeys of the Augustinians and Cistercians: of the former, Guisborough (February); Leeds (September); Kenilworth (December); St Andrew's, Northampton (July 1537); and the latter, Coggeshall (June); Fountains (September); St Mary Graces (January) and in Wales successively Cwmhir, Conway and Dore.[179] His chosen candidates were commended for the conformity to the observant norms which the visitation had defined. Marmaduke Bradley, now presented to Fountains, won praise even from Richard Leighton as the 'best monk of his coat in England'.[180] Here there was no hint that the 'old okes' were about to be felled; rather they were pruned better for the king's service.

There was one territory of monastic England that was left largely untouched at this time. The friars are almost entirely absent from the papers that passed in and out of government from the closing weeks of the visitation in 1535 to the last of the statutory suppressions almost two years later. The keeper of the chronicler of London Franciscans looked on the closure of the monasteries with some detachment, 'also this yere was alle the placys of relygione . . . subprest in November'; that he saw it as a winter happening might suggest that the sweep of suppressions seen in the east of England since the spring had passed him by.[181] The Dominicans of Derby perhaps literally stepped out of the path of the commissioners in the summer because 'pestilence in the towne was mervelous fervent', and there were 'x or xii howsis sore infected within ii butts length'; their colleagues to the east, at Nottingham and Newark, and west at Lichfield and Stafford, may have also been affected.[182] The mendicant congregations might have been inclined to conclude that the acts of the two parliaments of 1536 carried no particular challenge for them. Indeed, one of their statutes, for the punishment of beggars and vagrants, offered the reassurance of nothing 'prejudiciall or hurtfull to mendicant friars'.[183] Here the Commons may have acknowledged a provincial point of view that their convents were the mainstay of social welfare in urban centres. At the head of government the mood may not have been quite so benign. John Hussee confided in a letter to Lisle that 'Mr Secretary [Cromwell] wold they were all at the devyll.'[184] Yet for now he only held his ear close to reports of their preaching.[185]

The few glimpses there are of friary life suggest a certain confidence in the future. In August 1536 a Ludlow barber, John Tomlyns, gave to the town's Augustinian friary a substantial plot adjoining their boundary just outside the town gate, certainly to extend their rental income but perhaps to allow their expansion.[186]

The Crutched Friars of Colchester now took possession of a new common hall, an ambitious development best justified if numbers were rising. Candidates presented for ordination from friaries of the four largest congregations in 1536–37 are certain evidence of new admissions over the course of the two years since the royal supremacy. Their capacity to accept new recruits reflects a sustained demand for their spiritual services. The taper lit in perpetuity at the Dominican church of Haverfordwest drew such attention that the new bishop, William Barlow (himself an Augustinian canon), was minded to make an early demonstration of his zeal for the policy of the Crown and 'done reformacion'.[187] It has been suggested that the friaries of Wales 'faded away'; yet the surrender deeds of two years later show that their numbers remained at least in proportion to the size of the houses.[188] At Easter 1537, Lord Lisle was anxiously seeking confirmation that the Carmelites at Calais had remembered their obligation to offer commemorative masses for the duke of Richmond; the friars were so sure of their patron's attachment to them they demanded payment for the proof.[189] At Michaelmas, the king made a new grant of an annuity of 20 marks to his most favoured Dominicans at Guildford. His eldest living child, the twenty-year-old Princess Mary, spent the Christmas season in the enclosure of the London Dominicans.[190]

The thriving of the friars, and the government's apparently arm's-length stance, heightened tensions in provincial towns where partisan positions on reform were becoming more pronounced. As parliament remained in session in late March, the bailiffs of Ipswich raised concerns with their MP, and Commons Speaker, Humphrey Wingfield, over covert communication between 'a freers concubyn' and an unnamed friar of Canterbury, a city of suspect regulars after the notorious treason of the Holy Maid.[191] In the first week of the June parliament the sheriff of Gloucester agitated over the 'mysorder . . . colourable and payntyed prechyng' of friars protected by the patronage of Bishop Latimer of Worcester. The scenes in Gloucester seem to have been part of a wider pattern as, for the first time on any scale since the passing of the royal supremacy, preachers from all four of the principal friars' congregations appeared active in public pulpits.

These friars took up the matter of reform from both sides. Radiating out from Ipswich, the radical Carmelite John Bale regaled country people and a 'dayly lecture' was reportedly packed with 'dyvers erroneous opinions'. At Salisbury, a Franciscan William Watts spoke up for the old ways, even, it was alleged, for the authority of Rome, provoking a royalist townsman to post bills condemning him.[192] In Bristol the Dominican and Franciscan priors entered into a public contest, the former declaring that 'x carte lode of cowls or freers habits ... could not avayle without faythe', as the latter 'perswaded [that] Chryste and John the Baptist to be of lyke sortt as freers be'.[193] Perhaps it was the sudden dominance of friars on these public stages that roused the remaining Observants, out of sight for nearly three years; in Durham diocese it was feared they were again 'sowers of sedicion amoinge thar people'; two were said to have returned across the Scottish border; one, William Robinson, read the mood as 'yff it wold pleasse hys grace to restore ... agan the ... observaunts'.[194]

Tudor historians were sure that the events of 1536–37 were a watershed. The end of the monastic estate was begun in earnest; what came after was the destruction of particular churches and cults and the defeat of inveterate traitors to the king. For Edward Hall, the closure of the friaries in 1538, and the surrender of Colchester, Glastonbury, Reading and St Albans in 1539, were codas to a performance otherwise played out as far as the defeat and execution of the northern rebels. Hall made no mention of the passage of a second statute concerning religious houses in April 1539; for him the striking business of that parliament was its 'whip withe six strynges' (i.e. the Act of Six Articles).[195] Neither he nor Richard Grafton gave notice of the final dissolutions of Easter 1540. It was almost half a century after the events that Holinshed first reflected on the significance of the suppression of 'the religion of saint Johnes' and the passing of the last of the regular leadership, Prior Provincial William Weston.[196]

No doubt the regulars recognised the turbulence of the time, but there was little that had touched their lives since the passing of the suppression statute that was entirely without precedent. Only those just now beginning their noviciates had not already seen the closure of convents considered too poor, too small and too undisciplined to continue. Even the awful authority of a king that took clergy to the scaffold was not unfamiliar, and the fate of Matthew Mackarell of Barlings and others may well have been met as matter-of-factly as that of Elizabeth Barton and Edward Bocking three years before. Quite possibly, the divorce of one queen and the execution of another made a deeper impression on the mood in the cloister. In fact, in the wake of recent events, the outlook in religious houses appears to have been not of any likely end to their lives but of prospects for a new beginning. The declaration in the summer of a royal dispensation to allow the eating of white meat in Lent – not a trivial concession given the traditional custom of a Lenten

349

fast – seemed to signal a new understanding of the regulars' lives, greater perhaps than had been shown during the visitation.[197]

Especially in the hierarchy, there may now have been an expectation that the compact between the Crown and the monastic Church could be renewed. The monks of Canterbury were given an early opportunity to perform their new part when the king and 'the lady Jane the qweene' were 'reseaved very honorably' at St Augustine's Abbey, in the company of the Christ Church prior.[198] In the last week of October 1537 monastic London came together at St Paul's to celebrate the birth of the future king, Prince Edward: 'all the orders . . . of London standing about Paules in rich copes . . . and the abbot of Westminster mitred'.[199] Henry, prior of the Charterhouse at Sheen, was so confident of a new dispensation that he shook off the restrictions left by the visitors and encouraged his colleagues to 'goo and ryde abrode' and to 'preach . . . in churches where they come'.[200]

The air of renewal was potent enough to persuade some superiors to make fresh investments in their house. In the year from Michaelmas 1536, Prior Robert Gybbes of Montacute committed to what appears to have been comprehensive works of 'repair and improvement' (reperacionem et edificacionem) requiring plasterwork, carpentry, tiling, glazing, plumbing and 'other mechanical works' (aliis mechaniis operibus), amounting to the lion's share of some £260 10s 8d.[201] Now the new crossing in the church at Milton was completed; among many projects, Syon's sacrist paid for the painting of a chapel.[202] Richard Bourman alias Stevenage, installed as abbot of St Albans just as the suppression statute appeared, spent heavily on the working buildings and accommodation of his demesne lands.[203] Prior William Smyth of Stone bought timber from his diocesan although the bishop was reluctant to deliver it, apparently because he did anticipate closure.[204] The prior and convent at Dunster provided a new font for their parish church, carved with the badge of the Five Wounds of Christ, reflecting popular tastes but perhaps also stirring rumours rife in the region of covert correspondence with the northern rebels (see Fig. 21).

New building was a symptom of a greater investment in the future evident in 1536–37: the admission of new cohorts of novices. This traffic can be clearly traced at the houses of men in the record of candidates presented for ordination at diocesan ceremonies. The abbots of St Albans and Waltham, both of whom felt the benefit of Cromwell's patronage, between them sent as many as eleven recruits to receive orders from Bishop Stokesley of London in February and March

1537.[205] In Lincoln diocese between 11 March 1536 and 22 December 1537 candidates for minor orders (likely to be recent entrants) were presented from five Franciscan convents (Bedford, Leicester, Lincoln, Oxford and York) and one Augustinian friary (Northampton). In the same timespan nearly thirty candidates from Augustinian and Benedictine monasteries received minor orders and thirty-seven completed their probation in their ordination to the priesthood.[206] Leonard Pope joined the Franciscans at Hereford in the winter of 1537–38; in March he became acolyte, and looked forward to his progression to the priesthood.[207]

There is no directly comparable signal of new entries into houses of women but there are novices identified in the later deeds of their surrender.[208] The value of pensions assigned may be a proxy for the identification of novice women, where there was a wide distance between the value of the lowest and the next.[209]

The confidence of the friars was misplaced. Perhaps John Hussee's ear to the ground did not betray him: Cromwell's resolve over their future may not have been as mutable as for the great and solemn monasteries. The persistent reports of vexatious preaching in provincial cities and towns, which may have appeared a more pressing matter after the recent trouble in the north, and the particular challenge of the Observant John Forest, who 'doth boste . . . he may and wyll reull [and] put ye kyngs grace besides hys purpose', acted together to propel him towards decisive action.[210] Now, there was no parliamentary process, for their foundations lacked the endowments that stirred the proprietorial interest of Lords and Commons. Instead, the principle of the royal supremacy was reasserted, that the head of the Church held the right to visit, reform and repress. The regime took up the template of 1535, adapting it only in now giving overt encouragement to the visitors to consider suppression as the necessary measure of reform.

In early February 1538, Richard Ingworth, the Dominican suffragan of Dover, received the king's commission as principal visitor.[211] The writ charged him with the correction of abuses, but after three months a second writ added the obligation to capture a complete record of plate and other valuables.[212] Ingworth's first circuit in East Anglia prompted pre-emptive action, houses hiding or selling their treasures. Suppression was suspected although turning west Ingworth still announced himself only as visitor. He appeared cautious, even uncertain. The more impoverished and sparsely populated the house, the more hesitant he was to declare its summary closure. By the summer, as Ingworth turned towards the south-east, several of Cromwell's long-serving agents were given the commission to visit Wales and the Midlands.[213] Here, as Cromwell had surely hoped, the visit and closure of convents were made to coincide. By Michaelmas the friaries outside of the south had been closed. Ingworth's prevarication left several to linger to the end of the year. 'Ye be yet styll standyng aboute x houses in these partes,' he admitted, 'besides iii or iiii in Barwyk [Berwick-upon-Tweed].' The bishop was overwhelmed: 'I perfytly knowe nott whether [a commissioner] hath recyvyd them or no.' He was sure, however, that he could not go on: 'Yf yt I shulde ryde ye were aboute an hundreyd myle owt of my waye, so that I shulde nott be able to come home before ester.'[214] In the last week of November, John Hussee noticed 'as touching the friars ... there is small despatch of the same'. John Dove, prior of the Carmelites at Calais, in the same month signed himself 'prior as yet'.[215] The brethren of Lewes were left waiting as late as St Stephen's Day.[216]

As Henry's thirtieth year as king ended, for the first time his regime had removed religious orders entirely. The collapse of the friars' congregations in scarcely nine months may have been formalised by the king's commissions but its cause lay in their local circumstances. Across the country, their income had suddenly melted away. From the winter of 1537, the laity stopped providing them with alms. 'Judas,' a friar was heard to rail of the citizens, 'for they will not geve almesse'.[217] 'The peple had no devotion to geve them a lyvyng,' Richard Ingworth discovered as he made his first circuit as visitor.[218] It does seem to have been a sudden about-turn. There were still acts of patronage witnessed in the summer of 1537. Alice Lane of Ludlow included the convents of the Augustinian Friars and the Carmelites in her ambitious arrangements for commemorative masses for herself and her late husband. She saw the friars' houses as the best hope for the keeping of the obit, and required them to repossess property granted to the warden of the Palmers' guild should that society fail to continue the commemoration.[219] When Ingworth arrived at Gloucester the following year, the mayor boasted that the townspeople would provide for the poor just as well as the friars to the number of 'above three hundred daylye'.[220]

The turn was too rapid plausibly to be explained by the spread of reformist piety, although the friars' preaching against the royal supremacy may have set more of their neighbourhood against them. Diocesan bishops had undoubtedly reacted against their pulpit troublemaking. In their neighbouring dioceses, Hugh Latimer and Rowland Lee published new injunctions for regular and secular clergy in the summer of 1537, prohibiting friars from officiating in any parish church.[221] In Hereford and Salisbury, injunctions issued in 1538 expressly forbade any preaching by friars.[222] The suppressions of 1536–37 had fixed in the popular imagination the possibility of more.

A pragmatic caution over giving to convents with an uncertain future could have grown quickly; and as alms, donations and bequests began to dwindle it would also have been self-fulfilling. Even in London, where the largest churches of the friars (Dominican and Franciscan) had been crammed with lay burials, there came a sudden decline in the course of 1537. Margaret Fynche, dowager countess of Kent, had provided for a range of almshouses for poor widows of the Clothmakers' company in 1536, but the transaction carried a caveat in case of closure.[223] With no cash to meet their everyday needs, in the spring and summer the visitors found friars already giving up their buildings to tenants and selling any contents that might command a price. 'In every place [there] is poverty and moche shiffte,' Ingworth reported to Cromwell, 'seling and other shiffte by leasys.'[224] At Ipswich he learned that the prior of the Franciscans had leased the convent refectory and its adjoining solar for a term of ninety-nine years.[225] Perhaps in greater need, the Dominicans of the town made a permanent grant of their ground.[226] Neighbours were ready to help them raise money through these transactions, and perhaps not all of them did so from self-interest.

In Gloucester, the former mayor Sir Thomas Bell stepped forward to accept a lease of a garden from the Franciscans; he also redeemed their plate from the pawnbroker at his own expense.[227] Their destitution eroded their resolve to continue as they were. The Carmelite prior of Calais now wanted relief from his 'terrybul burden' which had made him a public spectacle, wishing for a time that 'the pepull shall not wonder at me'.[228] Their desperate disposal of their own property threatened to interfere with the suppression itself. In the third week of September Norfolk called on Cromwell for 'some streit commandment [to be]sent to the . . . freers that doth stande to make no more waste then is done allredy'.[229] John London discovered that the Oxford Carmelites were bargaining with the abbeys of Eynsham and Westminster for the sale of annuities.[230] Meanwhile, the city's Franciscans had turned to the consumption of their own fabric, 'by necessitie as they do saye', having 'taken upp the pypes of ther condytt lately and have cast them in sowys to the nombre lxvii', although when the commissioner arrived they had only sold enough 'for the costs in taking uppe'.[231]

The extinction of even the largest convents of the friars was accelerated also by the final assault on shrines and their associated cult objects which began in the summer of 1538. Relics and other artefacts that attracted devotional interest had been taken into custody by crown commissioners in their earlier circuits of the religious houses. The injunctions introduced at the visitation of 1535 had required the communities to end their observance of the cults connected with them; a number of the diocesan bishops had reiterated their command in their own injunctions of 1537–38, calling for all such 'stinking ... mucky ... filthy rags, gobbetts of wood ... and such pelfrey' to be surrendered to them.[232] That they had thought it necessary to do so is an indication that cult interest had not been stifled. It may be that its driving force was found in the neighbourhood and not in the professed community, but their churches, still fitted with a wide variety of altars, even if with fewer furnishings, remained their focus. Yet what prompted the regime to act now was not the reform of popular religion but rather the defence of the royal supremacy.

In April, Thomas Becket was confirmed in council as an enemy of the English kingship; the verdict was made public in June.[233] Cromwell did combine the two objectives in devising a public spectacle for the execution in May of John Forest for his denial of the supremacy. The timber effigy of the Celtic St Derfel, venerated at Llandderfel (Gwynedd), was ordered to London to create a coup de théâtre that testified to the vicegerent's antiquarian fascination for church legend: there was an ancient prophecy that the statue would one day burn a forest. Three weeks after Forest's death a royal proclamation directed that Becket's shrine at Canterbury was to be dismantled and for all associated relics to be destroyed. It was more than two months before the order was carried out at Canterbury.[234] There may have been the usual summer slowdown; in the south-eastern counties there had also been the resurgence of plague. But from Becket, Cromwell directed his commissioners to turn their attention to other popular cults and prominent shrines.

An undated letter confirms that they targeted Bury St Edmunds and then Ely Cathedral, advancing cautiously because of the contagion.[235] The Marian shrine at Walsingham may have been broken up in the course of the same circuit. The canons of the priory had remained under suspicion following the abortive rising of the previous spring and had surrendered themselves to the commissioners in early August. Winchester's shrines were taken down in the third week of September; Gloucestershire was reached a month later, Sussex in the last weeks of the year.[236] It may be assumed that other shrines of national renown were also removed in the autumn and winter, including those in the custody of leading monasteries, Durham

Cathedral Priory, Glastonbury and St Albans, but no record of this is known to survive.

It has been thought that the loss of their principal, patronal and most popular shrines was the certain prelude to the final collapse of monastic life. Writing in 1538 itself, Laurence Ridley 'reporte me unto you that be awake, your dreme is gone, your eyes be open ... you be fully awaked thanked be god and our moost soveraygne lorde kynge'.[237] The first Tudor historians described it as a dramatic demolition; indeed, it was only in the dismantling of the shrines that they pictured the destruction of monastic buildings at all. Edward Hall recalled fabric 'utterly taken awaye' by 'speciall mocion' as much from friaries as monasteries, Ipswich, Worcester, Wilsden, as well as Canterbury 'and diverse other'. John Stow saw, at a distance of six decades, 'the spoyle of which ... fill[ing] two great chestes' such as '6 or 8' men could carry only one at a time.[238]

In fact, the effects, at least on the leading monasteries, may not have been profound. Hostility towards their old cults was hardly new in 1538. It was three years since they had been compelled to alter their own patterns of observance, and more since the crown commissioners had first confiscated cult objects. Some of them, at any rate, shared a distaste for these traditions. Devotional interest had moved with the times within the monastic precinct as much as outside. Regulars had not detached themselves from the cult of saints entirely, any more than had their neighbours, but like them they were more selective in their attachments: the Blessed Virgin Mary, above all, and the pioneers of Roman Christianity. An unnamed monk of Christ Church, Canterbury, might well stand for most of his generation in that his travelling coffer carried clothes, printed books and a single panel painting for his private devotion, in his case depicting St Dorothy, patron of gardeners and brewers.[239]

In recent generations regulars had been less than conscientious guardians of their churches' original shrines, some of which had already been damaged and robbed of their decorations before 1538. Since the passage of the visitors in 1535 some had removed them from public view. At the Lady chapel of Worcester Cathedral Priory the long-standing clutter of devotional objects was cleared away in 1537, leaving only a panel portrait which worshippers were wont to kiss. Here, on the eve of the feast of the Assumption, one of them, Thomas Evans, spoke out to his fellow citizens, declaring 'thowgh our ladyes cotte and youalls be taken away from there the symyllitude is no worse to pray unto havyng a remors unto here above than hitt was before'.[240]

Stephen Sagar, abbot of Hailes, reached out to Cromwell for moral support as he shared his own distaste for the relic of the Holy Blood of Jesus Christ which had been presented to his church almost 300 years before. He represented himself as caught between the continuing popularity of the relic in the wider public and his own thirst for reform. 'Thancked almighty god that ever I was born to lyve to this tyme of light and knowledge,' he declared, 'that hit hath so perchyd in my very hart . . . moving me to set a parte all . . . superstycon or ydolatry'. His monks, he claimed, now self-consciously neglected the blood relic, which in the lifetime of the oldest of them, 'ny lxxxx yeres of age', had not been 'chaunged, renewyd or ever lokyd upon'.[241]

Sagar pressed his case repeatedly in the early autumn of 1538, but Cromwell appeared unresponsive. It was not until the very end of October that Bishop Latimer was called upon to lend his authority to Sagar in removing the relic from sight. It is difficult to explain the delayed response in the absence of Cromwell's own letters. There may have been some hesitancy where there was still such a public following for the cult. Prior Thomas Hore of Cardigan explained to his diocesan, William Barlow, that he had tried to deter his parishioners from their devotion to the taper of the Blessed Virgin Mary that was venerated in his church but he would not preach to them that their custom was 'abhominable idolatre . . . of old rotten tymber', unless he was bound to by an injunction.[242] The shrine of St Cuthbert at Durham was decorated as late as the autumn, and oblations continued to be offered.[243]

A degree of diffidence in the face of popular devotion was shown by the commissioners themselves. John Hussee told Lisle how Richard Pollard, arriving at Canterbury to dismantle the shrine, 'has byn buzid both nyghlt and day in prayer with offeryngs unto "S T" . . . and [his] hedd'.[244] Even with the full gaze of the government trained on Canterbury, Prior Thomas Goldwell seems to have been reluctant to remove every last trace of the church's most popular saint. Archbishop Cranmer was outraged when he heard that Goldwell had 'commanded [a selection of the relics] to be set forth as usual'.[245]

Goldwell was closely watched but elsewhere it seems it was possible for the fabric of the shrine and furnishings to be kept, out of sight. This may explain the presence of the jewelled skull of St Osyth in the inventory compiled in 1539; and the preservation of the principal pieces of the plinth from the shrine of Alban at his patronal abbey.[246] The cult tradition was not effaced at the end of 1538. Even the king's accounts for the year's end recorded that the customary payment for a candle at the shrine of the Blessed Virgin Mary at Walsingham was kept up.[247]

What drove the monasteries towards surrender in 1538 was not religious reform but the continued rule of their administrative lives. Now the king and Cromwell governed the greater part of them just as they had done the royal foundations at the beginning of the decade: properties were demanded both by exchange and as a direct grant; there were repeated interventions in appointments to offices and the award of annuities; and cash fees for continuation were levied even for those whose revenue was far above the terms of the statute. The Court of Augmentation's account for Michaelmas recorded payments from as many as thirty monasteries for 'toleration and continuance'.[248]

The sums were very variable and were no doubt subject to individual negotiation and to the resources available in each instance. Polsloe Priory on the edge of Exeter was a small community of women but with wealthy manors and it was able to manage the staggering payment of £400; the women of Polesworth raised only £50, still almost 50 per cent of their income as assessed at the valuation three years before.[249] Those who might have been suppressed in 1536 and paid for their exemption were among the first to give way in the face of these demands. Abbess Clemencia Stock of Delapré confided to John London that she could not go on, not least given her own age and infirmity.[250] As it had done among the friars, the attrition threatened to undermine the Crown's own interest in their dissolution. The monks of Shrewsbury complained to Cromwell that their house was now barely habitable: they 'sytythe weyt' while '[the abbot] pullet downe the howse dayly to the bare grownd never to be bueldyd agayne and whether he have sold the tymbor tylle and stos as yet no man can tell.'[251]

Superiors bore the brunt of the persistent interference. While many of the Crown's commands came to them by patent, letter or by word of one of the king's commissioners, from 1536 it was not unknown for them to be summoned to answer for their house in person. The physical toll of cross-country travel itself would have wearied them but it appears that some were treated with deliberate rough handling. Despite having been approved as a candidate for the abbacy of St Albans in 1536, Richard Bourman was threatened with imprisonment.[252] No doubt they suffered the more insidious injury of the watch that was kept over them. When Thomas Legh renewed old allegations of a sexual relationship against Prior Alvered Comyn of Nostell, it seems it was the final straw and he withdrew to his chamber, 'bedridden and sick and powerless to stir hand or foot'.[253]

It does seem that some responded to these waves of attack by actively embracing reform. The self-conscious critique of the regular religious life contained in a handful of surviving surrender deeds has been taken as indicative of the prime motive of the Crown.[254] Yet the words and phrases of these statements carry an echo of the reformist chatter recorded in a number of monasteries in the months following the visitation. It may be that the statement signed and sealed at the Cistercian abbey of Biddlesden in September 1538, which expressed in English, rather than the customary Latin, contrition for 'pretensed religion' and a preference for the religion of the Gospel, spoke for Abbot Richard Green and his monks themselves (see Fig. 22).[255]

Nonetheless, there were monasteries in each congregation and of all sizes and wealth that still strived to survive. The leadership of these houses used every lever possible to raise the funds required to stay afloat. Prior William Holeway of Bath now issued a flurry of leases no doubt to encourage some cash flow.[256] New rental income was generated, as the friars had done, from buildings inside the precinct. At Hailes Abbey, the butchery was now given over to an external tenant.[257] Also, as with the friars, treasures were sold. Abbot Henry Davell of Whitby emptied the sacristy of its plate.[258]

Credit was raised from every possible source. In February 1538 Robert Blakeney, prior of Tynemouth, committed to a two-year loan.[259] At his parent house of St Albans in Hertfordshire, the usual source of loans may have been exhausted, as Abbot Richard Bourman now prevailed on the brother of one of his own monks.[260] Prior John Reading of Leominster, a dependent cell of Reading Abbey, tried to persuade his abbot that a speculation on his own lands might turn a profit. His bailiff wrote to him: 'Yf ples your lordship to be good to the pryor and geve ere to hym he wyll show your lordship of large mony.'[261] Margaret Vernon of West Malling Abbey simply appealed to Cromwell's pity: 'For as moche as I perceived ... that ye were somewhat yn a love toward my howsse,' she wrote, 'I entende to stay.'[262]

Despite these desperate measures communities still seem to have maintained their usual administrative and domestic routines. The abbot and convent at Merevale made a lease shortly before Christmas 1537 that was quite the opposite of a calculated act of pre-emptive concealment: there was a timeless quality to the terms of the grant of their grange, to maintain a monastic chaplain on a substantial stipend, and for the leasee to perform a boundary walk every four years, and make customary payments at the election of a new abbot. In the past year, the demesne estates of as many as 150 foundations had passed into the possession of the Crown and yet here was an expression of monastic lordship which would not have looked out of place in the fourteenth century.[263]

There was a similar air of unbroken tradition when Abbot Sagar of Hailes purchased books, copies of Bede and Denis the Carthusian (d. 1471), for daily collations in the chapter house.[264] Prior Holeway of Bath settled terms for his organist and one of the priory's professional singers; perhaps there was just a hint of circumspection in another transaction over the rectory at Walcot (Somerset), as he referred to the priory 'or to ther successors or to certeign attorney'.[265] One monk of Much Wenlock was sure enough of his staying put to stand as a godparent at a christening in the parish church.[266]

Their perseverance was given encouragement by their government masters. Even in 1538, thoughts persisted of reform and retention rather than repression. Edward Hall remembered that the king had greeted the defeat of the northern rebels with the declaration 'no houses [would be] suppressed where god was well served'.[267] A year later, still it seemed his pledge held true. In January 1538 he honoured heads of the hierarchy of monasteries with New Year gifts as he always had done: Canterbury and York, Reading, St Albans and Waltham had long known this distinction, but now Peterborough and Ramsey were also remembered for their role in the funeral rites of his queens, Katherine and Jane. Throughout the year, Henry also continued his customary quarterly payment of £200 to the Franciscans at Newark, an obligation inherited from his father.[268] At Michaelmas, even as the fabric of shrines was broken up the royal accounts recorded the latest instalment of a customary payment of 100s to the prior of Walsingham for the king's candle to be lit before the shrine of the Blessed Virgin Mary. At the same time he reimbursed Thomas Wriothesley for his payment of 'king's rewards' to 'sondry' monks at Christ Church, Canterbury, while paying the labourers for their 'disgarnishing' of St Thomas's Shrine.[269]

Henry may have had a taste for reform not unlike those who led his government but it seems he also held a powerful attachment to the traditions he inherited, perhaps especially those of his own pious forebears. For now at least, he imagined abbeys and priories retaining a place in his Church, albeit on his terms.

Cromwell now wrestled with competing priorities. First was the conformity of the professed population, perhaps especially of those independent abbeys which had held themselves apart from the rebels. Cuthbert Tunstall recalled in January 1538 that he had advised him 'that whensoever any suche cankered malice shall either chaunce to breke oute or any to be accused therof, his highness wold have the same tried and thoroughly perused with as great dexterite and as litill favour as their demerytts shall require'.²⁷⁰ In that month alone Cromwell demanded inquiries into suspicious activity in monasteries from north to south, at Newburgh, Peterborough, Reading, Westacre and Wymondham. At the same time, he tightened government supervision of the regulars' routine administration, in order to seize opportunities to secure influence and income for the Crown. Thomas Legh was commissioned in January to begin a new visitation of houses in the West Country, 'according to your ... instructions'.²⁷¹ The commissioners were in no doubt as to the object of their inquiries: 'what hold [of the house, property or office, even the headship itself] was mot lyke sone to be [had]'.²⁷²

Nonetheless, it seems that Cromwell was at pains to dispel rumours of a general dissolution. Just a fortnight after Legh had been dispatched to Somerset, Richard Leighton reported back to Cromwell at Austin Friars on an 'expedition' to quell the rumours 'bruted' that 'I wolde go from thens ... and suppres where soever I came and that the kings hyghnes was fully determynede to suppress all monasteries and that Mr Southwell and I were sent into Northfooke onely for that purpose'. Leighton claimed to have visited unnumbered of 'thabbays and priores calling unto me all such gentilmen and honeste men as were nygh inhabitans there and opynly in the chapitre house commanded and charged thabbotts and priors ... that they shulde no in nowysse ... fere of any such brute or vayne babullyng of the people'.²⁷³

In an undated letter from the largest surviving sequence of his own correspondence, which the HMSO editors positioned in 1538, Cromwell appeared to offer a candid explanation of his own position. It had not shifted far from that of 1536: there was no place for religious houses resistant to the royal supremacy, but he did not look for, nor expect, a general suppression:

His majestie signified unto you that using your selffes like his god and faithfull subiectes his grace wold not in any wise interrupte you in your state and kinde of lyving ... and you wold hold so firmely repose yourself ... ne mans words ne any voluntary surrender made by any ... religious house sithens that tyme shall put you in any dowte or feare of suppression or change of your kinde of lyff and polycie ... knoyng aswell that of theonside feare mey entre where ... some malicious and cancred hartes ... wolde perswade and blowe abrode a general and a violent suppression ... onles there had ben ofertures made the seid howses that have resigned his grace wolde never have receyved the same and that his maiestie entendth not in any wise to trouble you or to devise for the suppression of any religious howse that standeth.[274]

His caution was clearly revealed at the turn of the year when he intervened to stop John London from coercing Abbess Katherine Bulkeley of Godstow into an immediate surrender of her house. She launched into a tirade at Cromwell: 'Like my mortal enymye, soddenly [Dr London] is cummyd unto me with a greate rowte with him,' she wrote, 'to supress the house in spite of my tethe.' 'He dothe threten me and my systers,' she added, and '[he] intreate[s] and inveigle[s] ... otherwise than I ever herde tell that any of the kynges subiettes hath been handelyd.' Giving glancing reference to the statute of 1536, she asserted that since she and her sisters were committed to 'the maytenance of God's honoure with all treuthe and obedience to the kings majestie', they should 'never [be] movyd or desired by any creature ... to surrender or gyve upe the house'.[275] If there were no abuses to be punished, and the royal supremacy was upheld, there should be no suppression. Cromwell agreed. London was evidently disabused of his plan for further dissolutions. 'Speciallie [I] thank you ... for the staie of Dr London,' the abbess acknowledged 'spedelie' and with your 'contrarie commawn-demente'.[276] To be sure he bore no grudge she gifted London a mallard and a 'gudly' heron.[277]

John London was not alone among the commissioners in trying to seize the initiative. That they did so increasingly in the course of 1538 may be another indication of Cromwell's own caution. Their commitment to the repression of religious houses had hardened after three years of repeated circuits. Cromwell's continuing circumspection must have seemed an obstacle to the cause of reform. Thomas Legh was ever the opportunist: he exploited circumstances to extend his commission from visitation to suppression. Arriving at Muchelney as a visitor, he persuaded the abbot to agree to give power of attorney to his patron, Richard Phelyppes. Now, with the superior's authority compromised, he pressed for punishment of the community which he judged to be 'all war ignorant and unlernyd'. London argued that the remaining regulars were a source of subversion: 'I fynd so moch dissymylation as may be ... [your] grace knwerth what beggarly and crafty merchants I have be occupyd withal.'[278]

By the summer of 1538, the commissioners' repeated free-wheeling was alarming Chancellor Rich. In July he complained to Cromwell that he now learned of the closure of a monastery only 'by comen repot', and that the sites and properties were being taken in hand ad hoc, locally. 'The survey of the possessions ... apperteyn[s] to myn office,' he wrote in pique, 'I as one that wold not neglect or be remysse in doing my deuty and yet loth to enterprise in anything further than your most hereley desyryng', but 'lacke of further knowledge' now 'the lymytacion of myn owne office.' Bluntly, he begged to know, 'Els what be your lordship do appony for the disolucion?'[279]

Between the urgency of the commissioners and Cromwell biding his time there grew rumour and suspicion. In the second week of January 1538, John Hussee was confident to advise Arthur Lisle that the suppression of the greater houses, such as Canterbury and St Albans, although 'not yet' done, was 'looked for daily'. Less than a month later George Rolle declared 'the abbeys go down as conveniently as they may'. By Easter, Hussee would 'think not the contrary but the most part will down'.[280] The wash of such common knowledge may have driven houses to surrender in the second half of the year, notwithstanding the strictures of the Crown and the harassment of the commissioners.

The surrender of a religious was quite different to suppression. Now the rhetoric, verbal and visual, was not of punishment but of patronage. The passage of the corporation into the possession of the Crown mirrored the substance and style of lay benefaction: the foundation itself became the subject of a grant, released by the corporate authority of the superior and their convent convened in chapter. The grant was signed, witnessed and sealed. The lay grantee was represented with well-chosen trappings of their worldly power: just as benefactors had in earlier centuries presented their endowments clothed as prince or magnate under the panoply of a retinue, here the representatives of the Crown came in number and, surely deliberately, they did not spare the symbols of the secular arm. No fewer than eight of the most experienced commissioners were present at Hailes in January 1540.[281] A description of their coming to Carlisle recalled how they were 'garnished and accompaned with a goodlie sighte of horsmen and speres'.[282] Even for Muchelney in the middle of the desolate Somerset levels, no doubt waterlogged on 3 January, there were 'dyvers knyghts and gentilmen there then being'.[283]

Perhaps this was typical. A caravan of courtier life came to St Albans, and they were received, with costly 'vytals' and wine, as benefactors had always been, with the resources of the conventual cellar given over temporarily to an entire household. The religious wore the robes of their congregation, their leaders distinguishing themselves for their office. Thomas Woodcock, prior of the Beauvale Carthusians, put on his precious 'velvytt cappe redy before [their] comyng'.[284] Ceremonial acts, performed by both parties, reinforced the agreement. The commissioners seem to have swallowed their dislike of monastic ceremonial, and witnessed Mass. At the Reading Franciscans John London presented himself at Mass, and then steered the brethren into the chapter house to make an end of it; perhaps this was the pattern he followed elsewhere.

Communities do seem to have made a conscious effort to coordinate the chapter house proceedings with a service of some significance. At Lewes Priory, they opted for the final feast day of the year (St Stephen: 29 December), after which there was a natural pause in the observant cycle between Christmas and Twelfth Night.[285] The canons of Bradenstoke (Wiltshire) ended their conventual life on the morning following the feast of St Anthony, the final celebration of the extended liturgical period of Epiphany.[286] Perhaps it was pure coincidence but the women of Brewood, Lacock and Marrick each made their surrender on the feast day of a female calendar saint (respectively, Hedwig, Agnes and Hild).[287] The monks of Battle must have known their calendar, so surely they saw and seized the opportunity to steer their surrender to fall on 27 May, the feast of Augustine of Canterbury, evangelist of England and miracle-worker of their own weald.[288] At the Bonhommes house at Ashridge, the connection with the liturgical calendar was acknowledged with some formality as an anonymous member of the house made a fresh, final entry in the manuscript annal, 'Hoc anno nobilis domus de Asserugge destructa fuit et fratres expulsi in die sancti Leonardi'. The self-conscious vision of the convent 'in choro' was heightened by the fact that the same volume held the customary and martyrology of the house.[289] In a copy of Miles Coverdale's English Bible (1537), which appears to have been salvaged from Evesham, someone wrote an account of the convent's conduct of their day of surrender, suggesting it was stage-managed: first they performed vespers, and 'at thys verse, deposuit potentes, (Magnificat), [they] wold not suffer to make an end'.[290] The echoes of a deposition in the deep past of monastic history are strong enough to suggest that these performances were studied: in Wulfstan's life of

St Æthelwold, when the seculars were driven from the church at Worcester to make way for monks, they chanted a final Mass.[291]

The performance of the grant itself was a matter of moments. The placement of names on the deeds confirm that each individual came forward to sign as part of one act; few of the women signed themselves but their presence was recorded by the commissioners.[292] On occasion, although not often, further names were added after, but the ink and pen strokes show that it was after some hiatus.[293] However, the brief act itself may have been the last rite of a lengthy visit, or even the culmination of a succession of audiences. A scrap of paper that clearly relates to a monastic cathedral chapter is a memorandum of questions to be answered in connection with its potential transformation, including whether the diocesan should be compensated when a dean is appointed. The implication is that the commissioners came prepared for a negotiation.[294]

The accounts from St Albans give the impression of the latter. From Michaelmas to Advent, the sub-cellarer paid £14 7s 7d 'for sondry necessariis for the king's servants', as well as £5 expressly for malt; the buttery was put under strain, as Thomas Kyng, 'copar', was called in to mend the 'vessels'; finally, the vast sum of £16 2s 6½d was paid for 'vytalls' as far as 5 December, the day of the surrender itself.[295] In the case of the independent monasteries, the commissioners were somewhat circumspect. It might always have been anticipated that the approach to a house such as St Albans would be cautiously incremental but even at provincial foundations of far lesser prestige their instinct was for caution. This may have allowed the religious some latitude to choose their time of surrender. At Muchelney the community appears to have been allowed to review the surrender deed for two days before they signed it and it was sealed.[296]

Still such care could cause confusion and uncertainty. A month after he presided over its closure Prior John Wilson of Mountgrace complained that 'yet was never none that ever gave unto hym ... any conseyll ... to surrender it but [one] ... said that they shuld not', and he hoped to 'suffer his majestie to take by his own autoritie'.[297] Years later Abbot Thomas Whytney wrestled because the loose ends remained untied.[298]

On some of the friars' circuits it seems there was an attempt to coordinate the closures by agreeing a period of notice for due preparation and, no doubt, the return to the house of those members at remote parishes or dioceses. At the Ipswich Franciscans an indented agreement between the warden and the commissioners was sealed on 28 March; the act of surrender followed on 1 April.[299] Of course, the approach was not fail-safe: at the Cambridge Dominicans none of the friars had returned to the house to meet the commissioners; at Winchester, Richard Ingworth seems to have been so overwhelmed by the rows of friars in front of him that his determination to take their surrender faded away.[300] The convent of the Carmelites at Calais had been broken up by the end of 1538, but their prior was still present and a cause for concern.[301]

The fact that the circumstances of many of the surrenders seem to have been negotiated by both parties is a reflection of how far the pattern of mutual exchange established even before the royal supremacy persisted even after the passage of reformation statutes. For their part, the king's agents, many of whom had themselves contributed to the cultivation of the new relationship with regular leadership, continued to act just as they had done as much as a decade before.

By the beginning of the fourth year of the commissioners' circuits, however, there were signs of their own strain and antagonism. At Dunkeswell, John Tregonwell arrived in February 1539 with an armed escort, although his anxiety may have been as much about the region, where rumours of a rising had circulated for more than a year.[302] He was in no mood for monkish ceremony, though, and took the abbot's seat in the chapter house for himself.

By the time the thirtieth year of Henry's reign turned, three-quarters of the religious houses in England and Wales had been closed. There were now fewer of these churches and convents than at any point since the death of the last Norman king, Henry I, some 400 years before. Yet there is no indication that at the beginning of 1539 Henry VIII was unequivocally committed to the extinction of the old tradition. His affinity of monastic heads again received his New Year gifts. Abbot Robert Fuller of Waltham was considered close enough in the royal circle to have his own New Year present to the king's baby son Edward recorded alongside those from his father and sisters.[303] The king enjoyed his hospitality at Waltham just before the beginning of Lent in early February; it was not his only visit of the year.[304] Henry's devotions during Lent took on a distinctly regular colour as his chosen preachers were the Augustinian canon William Barlow and the Dominican friar John Hilsey.[305]

On the face of it, Cromwell's winter months were much taken up with the business of reform. In early December 1538 he received word from the printer Richard Grafton of the efforts in Paris to prepare an authorised English translation of the New Testament.[306] William Barlow, promoted to the bishopric of St David's for his loyalism, urged on Cromwell the need for appropriate schooling in Wales.[307] George Lawson, JP of the North and West Riding, reported on the raw materials now awaiting recovery from the Cistercian abbeys of North Yorkshire.[308] Chancellor Rich reminded him of the ready return on monastic properties, promising to pay 3,000 marks to the Crown by Pentecost for the grant of the abbey of St Osyth.[309] At the same time, dispatches from the Councils of the North and of Ireland signalled the danger of those opposed to any policy of change.

Still, Cromwell was not inclined to hurry surrenders. Requests to continue received from Cerne, Shaftesbury and St Swithun's, Winchester, were accepted, and these communities carried on for almost four months. Robert Ferrar of St Oswald's Priory, Gloucester, found reason to thank him for his reasonableness.[310] It might also be inferred from some of his correspondence that there were some contexts where Cromwell's interference had divided but not delivered rule. In January two monks of Winchcombe batted back to him what seemed to have been thinly veiled threats when they hesitated over granting a lease. They seemed aware that Cromwell was not sure of himself and his commands, 'shoulld nott be surely certyed how that the kyngs most gracyus hygnes shulld be dyscharged'. It was confidence of their own independence that saw Winchcombe continue until the very end of the year; confident enough to share the words of a seditious song with a fellow who landed in Gloucester castle for his pains.[311]

Even beyond these venerable houses of the Benedictine establishment it seems there was no rising feeling of vulnerability. Early in the year, Dunstable's Prior Gervase Markham saw no danger in rejecting Cromwell's demand for the grant of part of his demesne with the simple defence 'yff I shuld . . . I wernet abbell to kepe & maynten my pore howse' and the airy promise, 'I wuld be as glade to accomplesshe your lordsheps desyre as any man lyvyng'.[312] In Boston, a town of four friaries, the friars of at least three were still in residence.[313] At the turn of the year the commissioners themselves had no clearer vision of the future. In mid-January, William Petre was uncertain what his next command would be and when it might be 'declared'.[314] There was perhaps more anticipation of completion of the process than was signalled by Cromwell himself. William Basing, prior of Winchester, thanked him in the last week of January for sparing him so long.[315] His response at the end of February was to continue to demand fines for continuation.[316] A letter from Abbot William of St Mary's, York, in early March responded to

Cromwell's case for the closure of their Lincoln cell, on the grounds that there were 'one or two monks at the moste and somtyme non no hospitalite kepte ne all myghtie god served not any religious ordre'.[317] Cromwell's reasoning was little different from three years before. He was continuing on a course that called for the closure of monasteries, but there is still little to suggest that there was a single template as to how many and how fast.

The statute presented to the parliament that assembled at the end of April 1539, enrolled as an 'acte for the dissolucion of abbeys', was misnamed and as such has often been misinterpreted. It did not initiate the closure of all remaining religious houses; nor was it intended to. It was pragmatic, even an urgent intervention to recover a degree of order and oversight over a movement whose momentum was in danger of exposing the limitations of the government machine. 'Diverse and sundrie abbotts priours abbesses prioresses and other eccliasticall governours and governesses' were now responding to the challenge of crown supervision and continuous uncertainty by giving up their houses 'of their owne free and voluntarie myndes good willes and assents'.[318]

Tacitly at least, the terms of the statute were an acknowledgement of what the papers of commissioners and convents reveal on the ground. The attrition of persistent fees and fines, and indecision and delay over matters of governance, from faculties for secularisation to the headship itself, eroded the substance and structure of corporate life; and while their future prospects remained unconfirmed, local interests stepped in to exploit their painful limbo. The first two of the statute's nineteen chapters affirmed, defensively, that all houses, 'seites and possessions', 'be vested in and deemed in the actual seisin of the king and his heirs'.[319] The main body of the statute, from chapters three to fifteen, aimed to clarify and confirm the status of leases, grants and sales of monastic property, applying the force of parliamentary law to those transactions made in the past year as 'utterlie voyde and of none effecte'.[320]

But in itself the statute made no measurable difference to the houses still standing. On the face of it their future was no less assured. There was rumour of panicked pre-emptive action against an imminent closure: in March it was said of Henry Davell of Whitby that he had suddenly 'solde and put awaye ... the store of the greate cattell and a great numbre of the sheep' (i.e. the demesne herds), made 'many secrete leases of those thynges that can nott be easily forborne from the demesnes', and 'made divers graunts of annuyties for somes of money'.[321] But there was no flurry of such stories now. These charges directed at Davell were formulaic, largely because of their frequent use by the seigneurial interest in the neighbourhood. Certainly, superiors contemplated surrender but what we can detect of their motives was not tied to the statute. John Stonywell admitted that he 'desired . . . that I wolde resygne my monastery' as long ago as 'afore the last cristmasse'; in fact, he resented that from Michaelmas to the Annunciation (September to March) he had 'borne all the charges'. Perhaps this was both rhetorical and signified real intent. He remained in office for another three months (until June).[322]

A chain of West Country houses did seek terms with the commissioners' circuit passing eastwards from February as far as Easter, but some also challenged them. The abbot of Bruton took himself off to London; Joan Darrell, prioress of Amesbury, faced them down.[323] William Thornton of York was enough at ease with his present position to make a trip to France.[324]

Perhaps there was a noticeable change in the superiors' public position by the autumn. In London there were no professed religious involved in the exequies for Bishop Stokesley in September 1539. Anne of Cleves stopped at Rochester but this was circumstantial rather than a monastic welcome. Yet there was still some sense of uncertainty on both sides.[325] In the summer of 1538 it seems there was more certainty in the provinces than there was at Westminster or Austin Friars. 'We lacke many books of accompts court rolls and rentals which are supposed to be in . . . custody,' wrote an alarmed Chancellor Rich from Abingdon. 'He hathe informed me [of] the possessyons of Abyngon', but 'I wold be right glad to knowe'.[326]

Sir Thomas Audley was aware not only of 'such bruits' that 'runne' through Essex but prospects well focused enough to be talking about the conversion of monasteries into mansion houses, prompting him to point out that such a plan for St Osyth would hardly be auspicious, for it 'stondith in the marshes not very holsom as yet fewe of reputation as I thinke will kepe continual house in any of them save it be a congregation as ther be now'.[327] The discussion of possible reformations continued. Audley argued for the 'contynuans' of Colchester and St Osyth 'not as they be religious but . . . to translate them in to collegys'. Audley's correspondence bears witness to a direct conversation with Cromwell on the subject, 'for the which I seyd to you afore his grae may have the gyft of the deans and prebendaries at his owne pleasure'.[328]

From north to south (especially) on the eastern side of the kingdom, communities of a cross section of congregations continued to function as before. Here the familiar signs of the cycle of institutional life can be found from the spring to the autumn. The profession of new monks, canons and nuns continued: in March another canon joined the community at Nostell Priory, now larger than at any point in its 400-year history.[329] Four men from Thornton Abbey were presented to the bishop for ordination as deacons in early April.[330] At Michaelmas the rites of ordination were performed again at Guisborough Priory (see Fig. 23), under the direction of its prior, and the suffragan bishop of Hull, Robert Pursglove. Among the candidates were a Cistercian from Meaux Abbey (East Yorkshire) and two Benedictines from St Mary's Abbey, York.[331] In December, five new recruits, three men and two women, were received by the Benedictine monasteries at Chester.

At the turn of the accounting year, there was a commitment at St Albans to purchase 'cots' (coats, habits), apparently for the full complement of professed men since the cost was a substantial £3 12s 9½d.[332] Abbot Richard Stevenage seemed to have the economy of another year clearly in his sights since he also paid almost the same sum (£3 12s 8d) for a flock of twenty sheep.[333] Stephen Sagar of Hailes had done nothing to end the habit of husbandry, as Robert Southwell ruefully observed, 'as thoo he had lokyde fore no alteration of hys howse, hys arable londe … husbondyd … acres redy sowen … and the tylth seasonablie orderyd'.[334] That winter he saw three of his monks return to the Cistercians' St Bernard's College in Oxford. The University's regular students continued to act as if they could expect to be there for months to come. Thomas Potter of Durham College took out a loan from a (secular) colleague, which he would later struggle to repay.[335] At Westminster, there was even a commitment made to a major fabric project, a replacement pair of bells (to be cast at Reading), presumably for the precinct tower.[336]

These continuities surely reflected the superiors' reading of the outward intent, and perhaps also the inward impulses of the regime. Just as the object of the statute itself was foundations already surrendered, it does seem that at least as far as the summer of 1538 Cromwell's mind was open as to the future of the others and any plan was still unformed. It may be telling that the one reference to a religious house in his remembrances at the turn of the year was Syon Abbey, whose continuance had been challenged for five years because of the community's reluctance to reconcile to the royal supremacy. Now Cromwell noted 'the king may dissolve that by praemunire and he will'.[337] It seems, perhaps, that something of the outlook of 1534 persisted. On the back of a letter received from Sir Philip

Draycott on 16 April 1539, Cromwell wrote out a list of nineteen abbots (by their offices, not their names), all but one (Waltham) Benedictine monasteries.[338] None had surrendered by the date of the letter and the snatches of evidence from several, such as St Albans, St Mary's in York and Westminster, suggest a general stability and the maintenance of routine. It is possible that the vicegerent continued to envisage the survival of this group, at this moment the largest of the surviving monastic communities other than the cathedral priories.

The summer manoeuvres of a number of superiors, none of whom were new either to Cromwell or to the volatility of policy, do point to a conviction in their minds that there were futures to be negotiated. In May, Abbot William Thornton of St Mary's, York, pressed for Cromwell's help in securing protection for his possession of its dependent priories, 'my trust is grete in your lordshipes goodnes'.[339] There was less conviction in the mind of Gabriel Morton, prior of Gloucester, at the beginning of June when he made supplication on the convent's behalf for an election of a successor in the abbacy. 'We do as yet remayne ignoraunt and inconsulted howe to behave us,' he confided, 'and offre our true herts and faithfull obedyence conformable to the pleasure of our moost drad and derest sovereign.'[340] No response survives and the vacancy continued, although this may prove nothing more than that plans for the future were very slow to form. Barely a matter of months before his arrest, Abbot Hugh Cook of Reading seems to have had in mind securing a guarantee for the future of his house with the present of almost six pounds of gold for the king.[341]

An appeal to Cromwell made by Abbot Philip Hawford of Evesham at the end of June does attest to the fact that Thomas Legh pressed for the closure of the dependent priory at Penwortham (Lancashire), but his tone of surprise – 'I know not what is meanyd' – would suggest that from Cromwell (whom he had hosted recently) he had anticipated quite a different steer.[342] What Legh responded to here, it seems, was more than just a hint. Soon after – weeks perhaps, rather than months – he petitioned Cromwell 'in consideracion of the promysses and otherwise herin not mencyoned to have your seid pore oratours in remembraunce', that his house 'maye be one of those monasteryes which [the king] entent to dispose and reserve as to his princely wisdom ... for any such princely and godly purpose'. He commended its 'goodlye logynge and buidyngs well repayred with all necessarye howses of office' and its 'pleasaunt scytuacyon', observing that at Evesham '... there is a greate thorough fare and passage in to Wales ... the redye wey to receave and

370

lodge all suche noblemen as cause to resorte towarde or frowarde the . . . counsell [of the West]'. He offered its 'alter and change . . . for the true and syncere preaching and teaching of the word of gode unto his pore loving subiects', for the 'educaion and bryngyng up of yowth in virtue and true knowledge of the same as also for the releavyng and succoryng of the pore nedye lame and impotent persons'.[343]

Hawford's certainty that the king and his minister had in mind 'those monas-teryes' is given some further credence by the series of similar petitions Abbot Thornton sent in the second week of November, that St Mary's, York, might be 'the kings bedehowse hable to kepe and continue such poore hospitalite as hath ben in tyme passed with such possessions as it is endowed'. Like Hawford, Thornton had taken his cue from Cromwell himself, 'bicause I may ponder and gather of your lordeschip most loving lettres so much . . . goodeness and towarde-lines towards me and this poore hows'.[344] A scheme for the secularisation of Thetford Priory is set out on an undated paper, assigned by the archivist to 1539; Prior Robert Ferrar, closer to Cromwell than any of these others, pressed the case for the transformation of Nostell Priory into a college as late as the summer of 1539.[345] It has been suggested that in these months the monastic leadership suffered an attrition of importunate demands and intimidation leaving them largely pliable and vulnerable.[346] Yet in Ferrar, Thornton and Hawford there was no recognition of an end to negotiation; their propositions still carried a trace of the feeling of opportunity which had risen in the wake of the visitations.

The autumn saw a shift in the view of what was desirable, and practically possible, on both sides. There is no dated paper of Cromwell's that might be proof of a change, but another remembrance which the HMSO editors assigned to 1539 prompts 'touching the suppressions' of Canterbury (Christ Church), Leeds, Rochester, Waltham, St Albans and Westminster; a following entry reads 'touching Winchester'. The same memorandum refers to the marchioness of Exeter, Gertrude Blount, who had been taken into custody in the Tower of London in July, which may point to a date no earlier than the late summer of that year.[347] The response of a commissioner, Philip Paris, to a lost letter of Cromwell's from early December signals a new urgency to see the closures completed: 'We will make as moche haste and use as greate dexterite in our further procedings,' Paris assured Cromwell, 'as your good lordeshipe vouchesavede to admonyshe us by your lettres'.[348]

Perhaps for Cromwell himself the most important turn in his train of thought was on the balance between the reformation of regular foundations and the total reappropriation of their sites, buildings and endowments. The ambition of creating new cathedrals and colleges had never been in doubt but it may have required the spring statute's sober summary of the potential losses arising even from a surrender to clearly focus the costs. There can be little doubt Cromwell's decision hardened as accounts of non-conformity suddenly came in to him thick and fast, and even in the Benedictine hierarchy, until now the anchor-hold of his authority in the monastic estate. The news from Glastonbury may have unsettled him more for its signs of the impotence of the commissioners. His summary demand in September for the St Albans printer John Herford to be given up to him for interrogation suggests that Cromwell's trust in his old alliance was now worn.[349]

For their part, superiors, at the start of another financial year, recognised that unstinting demands of the Crown could not be sustained. From Malmesbury at the end of September, Robert Frampton reported that if he complied with another request for a further grant of demesne 'I shall not beable to contoynue the charges that am dayly charged withall'.[350] Richard Stevenage did not himself petition Cromwell, but the account drawn up at his December surrender shows the house holding huge cash debts. The spectacle of executions between Michaelmas and Advent can hardly have encouraged the superiors' continued forbearance. Less dramatically, some may have reflected on their own age. John Reve (Bury), Thomas Rowland (Abingdon), John Bryggys (Crowland) and John Lawrence (Ramsey), who surrendered in succession between November and December, were all of them at least in their sixties; within eighteen months, all of them would be dead.

In the last weeks of 1539 there are signs that the anticipated closures would come soon. Robert Pursglove's grant on 10 November of his priory's valuable nearby vicarage of Stranton to a consortium of locals looks very much like a sly manoeuvre made while he still had the chance. Even so, the fact that the grant was made in the traditional manner, in the chapter house, without any commissioners' counter-signature, suggests that there was still no continuous supervision, no coordinated constriction of their corporate freedom.[351]

If there was now a clarity of purpose at Austin Friars, or indeed in the mind of the king himself, it was not clearly communicated at the turn of the year. Chancellor Rich and his staff were no more certain of their next task, or the timetable for it, than they had been at any point since suppressions had given way to surrenders eighteen months before. There is no documented direction surviving to explain the sequence of surrenders that followed, and it is difficult not to conclude that it was still a matter of contingency. Four houses may have already agreed to surrender after the celebrations of Christmas and the New Year. It seems unlikely that the surrenders of Newenham on 2 January 1540, or St Bartholomew's Priory, Newcastle, Egglestone (Co. Durham) or Hailes on 3 January, were unplanned; at Hailes they seem to have been better prepared than the commissioners had expected: '[they] dyde surrender with suche discrete and frank maner as we have sen no other do better in all ower iorney'.[352]

After these, it seems, surrenders were ad hoc, with weeks passing between them: Chester was closed in the third week of January, but Shrewsbury and nearby Much Wenlock continued on to the end of the month; it was another three weeks before there was any action at Thetford. It may be a measure of the continued improvisation that several of the convents closed during these weeks have left no record at all. The fifteen men at Leeds Priory left the house, certainly, but whether or not it was before or after the remainder of the county's religious cannot be known. Their pensions were not approved until Lent.[353] There seems to have been no notice of the writs sent to Chancellor Rich to take the surrender of Waltham, Christ Church (Canterbury) and Rochester. Yet suddenly they were in hand. Perhaps he carried the writs personally to Canterbury because he had been ready for the moment; equally, he may have gone without them and just dropped everything to go.

Even in this latest iteration of a process of statutory enforcement that had first been tried for the royal supremacy six years before, the commissioners, and their masters at Austin Friars and Westminster, seemed unable to arrive at a definitive conclusion. After their surrender, the professed communities at Christ Church (Canterbury), Rochester and Waltham returned to their chambers. There is nothing to suggest that they did not enter their churches for the Easter observances. Prior Walter Phylypp remained at, if no longer formally in, his office at Rochester perhaps for the remaining months of the year. Surely the prospect of his succession as dean was signalled well ahead of the writ of appointment; there were no other candidates. Prior Thomas Goldwell at Canterbury was disappointed in the deanship but it does not follow he was displaced, at least not from the precinct where he occupied a prebendary until his death.

Beyond these scenes of the last surrenders, there were continuities even more conspicuous. Philip Brode, provisor of St Bernard's College in Oxford, was new in post.[354] He and his colleagues entered the new academic year apparently in the same way as the last; the provisions of the previous year's statute concerned the disposal of properties and rights; the religious had changed their habit as and when they were secularised and since the provisor and scholars had not secularised, perhaps they acted and looked the same as they had done before. That the Prior of Students, Edward Hindmarsh, opened a new account book in September 1540 suggests that at Durham College the new year opened just as the last.[355] Their counterparts at the Benedictines' common *studium*, Gloucester College, and at the Augustinians' St Mary's College, appear also to have remained in residence.[356]

It may be the lack of a clear-cut end to the matter that can help to explain the absence of comment from the wider public. The laments of the losses came later, many of the most influential a generation later, in the words of those too young to have any real memory of what they now so readily recalled. One of those contemporaries who did comment was in a position to be a first-hand witness. Charles Wriothesley was pushing thirty-two and herald at the College of Arms. He noted the suppression of Syon in November as the passing of 'the vertues howse of religion that was in England'.[357] There are grounds for thinking that Wriothesley's comments were made close to the events themselves. It is a lament, but offset by the very matter-of-fact notice he gives to the passing of every other house; like many of his contemporaries, perhaps he saw the royal house of Syon as one of a different order. Certainly, this was not a unique lament for the loss of monasteries. The passing of old Bishop Stokesley weeks before had roused Wriothesley to greater heights of praise – 'the greatest divine that was counted in this realme of England'.[358]

The first signals of a decisive end to the dissolution were visible only in the summer of 1540. The very first did not concern a religious house but Cromwell himself. In the second week of June he was arrested, just days after his confirmation of properties in possession of the Clerkenwell hospitallers had seemed to hint that their own history might continue still. Cromwell's appearance on the scaffold on 28 July was evidence enough that this was indeed the watershed. Charles Wriothesley saw not only the vicegerent dispatched but also all his works: 'condemned by the whole bodie of this last parliament ... [his] heresie, treason and fellonie, and extortion'.[359]

Now, in the remaining weeks of the summer, the surrender and sequestration of the hospitallers, the last of the orders, were put underway. Finally, on 4 August, Edward Hall remembered that a 'sometyme monke of Westminster', one Thomas

Epsam, was removed from Newgate where he had been held for three years and set before the justices; when he 'would not aske the kynges pardon nor be sworne to be true to him ... his Monkes ferment was plucked from his backe, and he repried till the king knew his malicious obstinancie'.[360] There is no record of Epsam at Westminster, nor of the detention of a monk of the house in 1536–37. Whoever he was, Hall was surely right to regard his reprise as a meaningful performance: 'this was the last Monke that was seen in his clothing in Englande'. The printer, Richard Grafton, considered that this was the moment to give an account of the king's reformation:

> His grace hath done a great and infinite nombre of most prudente and beneficial thynges ... laste of all the dissoluynge of cloisters and suppressynge all conterfete and false religion, which so long as thei continued, wer not only teachers and preachers of false and supersticious doctrine but also wer euer the autours and bgynners of all mischiefs and commocions. For reformacion I saye of which thynges, who is haible to render worthy thankes and prayses to his highnes?[361]

Yet outside the circles of eager reformers like Grafton the sense of an ending was not nearly so well defined. In the course of 1540 the balladeer William Grey published a fresh assault on the monasteries' shrines that were causing 'roning hither and thither ... offryng candles and pence to stones and stockes and old rotten blocks'.[362] An anonymous author of the *Balade agaynst malycyous sclaunderers* railed again against the religious, apparently suspecting some counter-action: 'For here though upholdest both monkes and fryers / Nunnes and noughty packes / and lewd lowsy lyers.'[363] His printer, John Gough, was persuaded enough of a ready audience to run off sheets before the turn of the year. With good reason. Even close to the centre of government in the capital, there had been recent preaching against reform by a former Franciscan, William Wattes, which had 'converted many from the new opinions'.[364] When Wattes was arrested for similar sermonising in Canterbury, it was said that a force of 10,000 were prepared to spring him from gaol, 'with strength'.[365] Another former friar and an accomplice with their 'sediciouse ... prechynge ... sett the best of the town of Glouc. one in a nother is toppes'.[366] Rumours of an uprising surfaced at Norwich. In the East Midlands, some hospitallers remained in their preceptories, apparently not persuaded to leave as yet. In the Pale of Ireland, the Crown's battle for the extinction of regular religion had only just begun.[367]

Perhaps not far from Ashridge, a member of the house of the Bonhommes now standing empty still held the customary and annals of the house in his hand and he now added a further entry with a faint hint of victory, however pyrrhic: 'Hoc anno decapitatus fuit ille eximius haereticus et proditor Thomas Cromwell, qui causa fuit destruccionis omnium domorum religiosorum in Anglia' ('In this year was the beheading of the notable heretic and traitor, Thomas Cromwell, who was the cause of the destruction of all the religious houses in England').[368] The last of the commissions had run their course and the institutional presence of the religious orders had been removed, but many of the trappings of their life remained; as did the men and women themselves.

PART III

VIII

NOTHING ENDID

During the morning of 21 March 1538 the church of the Cluniac priory of St Pancras at Lewes was suddenly shattered and broken by an explosion. Perhaps the sound of the blast was muffled by the walls of the chancel which the military engineer who laid the charges of gunpowder had calculated to be at least five feet thick, although there was surely some reverberation in Southover, the hamlet of a few dozen souls, and an almshouse of fourteen residents, that had hugged the precinct wall since the twelfth century. It was a Friday, still formally a day of observance, and among the startled passers-by would have been some hurrying to or from the parish church of St Thomas. The Italian engineer, Giovanni Portinari, preferred for the job because of his knowledge of what could, and could not, withstand artillery, had attracted no great attention when he arrived with seventeen skilled tradesmen recruited in London, 'moch better than the men fynd in the contrey'.[1] Lewes was a prosperous trading place accustomed to traffic from out of town. The last prior was himself the son of a foreigner whose profits had helped him purchase one of the best town houses. But the detonation of high explosives, the heavy fall of dressed stone and the rapid rush of rubble that 'putt the hole down to the ground' forced an impression on their business minds.[2]

The scale of the destruction, the felling of thirty-two Romanesque pillars, the least of which were 10 feet in diameter and 25 feet in height, and a steeple standing

90 feet high, was no more startling than its speed.[3] Portinari had estimated eight days to raze the church; in fact, he completed it in five. It presented the town with more than a passing spectacle: it provided a vision of Tudor industry, as a furnace, built for the purpose, and fuelled, with some improvisation, with joinery from the church and melted old lead, into new 'pigs' for sale.

If the labour of Portinari's men roused their commercial interest it also stirred social anxiety. The almsmen and women of the priory's hospital of St James were left exposed; the absence of responsibility for welfare in the town was made unusually urgent by reports of plague in the poorest parishes and the rabble-rousing return of a displaced monk, compelled perhaps by news of the demolition to return to the site of his old home. Now, for the first time in more than 400 years, nothing stood between the town's southern rooftops and the sea estuary six miles away. As Portinari's *grande chiesa* fell, it seemed the townscape of Lewes was in every sense transformed (see Fig. 24).

This is how the Tudors remembered King Henry's dissolutions. The generation that witnessed them at first hand thought above all of decisive change. 'All was suppresside furisly under footte,' recalled Hugh Latimer, in a sermon of 1549, 'evin as tholly temple of Hierusalem was handylde when the Chaldees had dominion thereof.'[4] John Foxe, a twenty-five-year-old Cambridge MA when the last of the convents was closed, wrote at a distance of two decades, 'The late kyng of moste famouse memory [had] taken away and ... defaced all monasteries,' reflecting that in their place was 'ful libertie, as though those vnwittie and supersticious vowes had neuer bene made'.[5] The memory of provincial England was of no lesser transformation, although it was measured more prosaically: 'all religious men ... changed their habits,' recorded Robert Yowle MP, keeper of a chronicle for his city of Worcester, 'and wore secular men's raiment'.[6]

The children and grandchildren of these eyewitnesses, who reached adulthood after a second royal supremacy statute had claimed to settle Church affairs, and stifled the tentative revival of regular religion, saw more romantically what they had never known themselves, and were inclined to conjure a melodrama: an old civilisation vanquished, its citadels swept away. Michael Sherbrook, rector of Wickersley, in 1577 retouched his boyhood's tales of the fall of the nearby Cistercian abbey of Roche with vivid colour: 'it would have pitied any heart to see what tearing up ... there was ... all things ... either spoiled, plucked down carve away or defaced to the uttermost'.[7] Ten years later William Camden chose the imagery of the battlefield: 'Henry VIII conquered (profligaret) superstition 'and everything [of the old order] disappeared (haec disparuerunt omnia)'.[8]

The Elizabethans' fascination for the drama of these scenes carried with it a new attention to their effects. Sherbrook grieved for the loss of great buildings, 'so that in most places it cannot be perceived where they stood'.[9] Camden remarked on the sharp turn in fortunes for settlements where so recently they had been: 'Now the crop is the best crocuses', he saw at Great Walsingham, the site of the premier Marian shrine in monastic England, 'formerly, it was pilgrimage'.[10] 'Where wonce was some praier', ran a catchphrase which Stephen Batman, Archbishop Parker's personal chaplain, copied into his commonplace book, 'now places for swyne'.[11] As the Tudor age itself passed away, these themes thrived in the historical imagination. The generation that in 1642 confronted the outbreak of a religious war of three kingdoms saw in the dissolution nothing less than a social revolution: 'the wasting cloister with the rest / was in one instant dispossessed'.[12]

The theatre of destruction at Lewes was a unique performance. The felling of the priory church was Cromwell's personal enterprise. The thirty-nine-acre precinct was intended to be the site of a new mansion house. The vicegerent had engaged Portinari at great expense, the business done between them perhaps the most emphatic demonstration of Cromwell's Italian experience and linguistic skill of his public career. The possession of the site, its survey, the demolition, extraction of raw materials, and their sale and distribution were subject to an extraordinary degree of organisation and supervision from his chambers at Austin Friars. His son Gregory was sent to Lewes while Portinari worked; and, wisely perhaps, his father called in other contacts to keep him informed.[13] The pace of the work, the product of Cromwell's scrutiny and Portinari's skill, was unparalleled. The priory was not the first medieval monastery to be taken down in Henrician England but it was the first and only one to pass out of sight in the space of a working week. Its sudden felling drew attention, no doubt, but it was followed by a singular calm. Days later dependents of the former monastery questioned their future status; but that was all. The spectacle at Lewes was also exceptional for being so well documented, the written record led by the letters (in his native language, and in an English transcription) of the foreman Portinari himself.

Across the kingdom, the act of dissolution did not match the extraordinary spectacle that Cromwell orchestrated on the Sussex coast; nor was it very much like the drama of despoliation that came to be written into communal memory. In truth, precisely how it was performed wherever there was a religious house, near or far from places of settlement, remains very difficult to recover. The most detailed of contemporary accounts do not always carry as much authority as might appear.

The ruin of religious houses was described by a succession of witnesses in the half-century after 1539, well travelled and knowledgeable antiquarians such as John Leland (d. 1552), William Lambarde (d. 1601), John Stow (d. 1610), William Camden (d. 1623) and John Speed (d. 1629). But their primary purpose was to catalogue, not to provide a running commentary on, history in the making. Their sense of the passage of time was as loose and as liable to distortion as any account reliant on memory as much as the written record. When they described a location as the site of a monastery of the past, not always did it mean that all visible trace of it had passed away. Typically, these authorities described the history they held in their heads, not the sight in front of their eyes. The danger of misunderstanding their testimony is underlined by the example of Hyde Abbey, which was assumed to have been effaced within a year only because of the tense of Leland's note that 'in this suburbe stoode [a] great abbay'; in reality at Easter 1539, the bishop still convened an ordination ceremony there.[14]

The primary sources for the course of events after the formal suppression and surrender are not chronicles reporting action as it happened, or was said to have happened, but books of accounts – many of them patchily kept and poorly preserved – that offer only a static record of the people, possessions and the physical infrastructure. Payments made to tradesmen and received from buyers of discarded furnishings and dismantled buildings were not routinely dated; rarely is it possible to piece together a complete sequence of events. Framing these documents are sporadic dispatches from commissioners, busy with tales of their transactions with people, property and the raw substance of the monastic world, from the precious metal of the sacred interior to the marketable practicality of sheets of roofing lead. They are not a reliable record of what was done and when; nor, arguably, were they intended to be. Their picture of a great government enterprise was self-consciously created to respond to a rising tide of criticism about their conduct. Notoriously, of the taking-down of the city-centre religious houses at Coventry all that now survives is an angry correspondence from the king's commissioner and their local opponents; how much was demolished and, crucially, when, remains unclear.[15]

It has been argued that a more reliable guide to the scale and speed of the dismantling of monasteries is to be found in the material remains. The record of excavated sites is rich indeed and it is only because so many archaeological reports have been left unwritten that much of what they might reveal of the dissolution remains as scattered data in the Historic Environment Record, for the most part undigested. Sadly, much of the spoil of churches which was exposed when excavations were funded well enough to be frequent, between the 1930s and the 1970s, may never be seen again as it has been overlaid with development. But even when it has been properly documented, the evidence does not reveal the course of events much more clearly than the letters and papers in the archives. Broken glass and stone are always labelled as dissolution-era and the traces of lead working are said to be 'indicative of the . . . processes taking place immediately following the closure[s] . . . across the country'.[16] In fact, there is nothing in these shards that can fix them to a precise moment in time.[17] The mode of destruction, such as the snapping of glass panes to free their lead fixings, or the rubbling of mouldings to make lime mortar, might belong to any part of the Tudor period or beyond. Ironically, it may be the standing remains of the religious houses, imprinted with the new purposes to which, in time, they were converted, which may provide a more precise record of their transformation.

It was natural for contemporaries to represent the putting-down of religious houses as a cataclysm. Images of churches, and comparable ancient edifices, felled or fired, had animated public, printed and popular discussion for as much as a decade before the act of supremacy. What was best known to Henry's subjects of the Reformation in the German principalities was the widespread ruin of places of religion, and the settlements that surrounded them, by warring bands. The dedicated language of deliberate damage and organised demolition, 'deface' (v.), 'defacement' (n.), was new in Henry's England (first recorded in this context in Robert Fabyan's chronicle of 1516),[18] and it was taken up rapidly in public and private to the point that by the middle years of the decade other terms were being eclipsed. In the first summer of suppressions, its novelty was noted: 'or as he callyth it, defased,' wrote a parish priest, Robert Colyns of Tenby, in a letter of 22 June.[19] 'Defausyd and pullid downe' was soon adopted by Cromwell's commissioners as shorthand for their efforts to strip religious houses, by whatever means, of their viability and visible identity.[20] The repetition of the phrase in their dispatches was used by them, and perhaps understood by Cromwell, as a measure of their success.[21]

Wolsey's suppressions of 1524–28 had proceeded only in fits and starts, but by the time of his own fall from power populations in the south and east of England were faced with the unfamiliar sight not only of churches stripped out and unroofed but also of domestic and working buildings deliberately put out of use. In the Cardinal's service, Thomas Cromwell himself had watched the dereliction of the twelve-acre site at Bayham, which included a forge standing yards from the chambers of the canons.[22] The spectacle left its mark. Even after a decade of reformation policies, a summary of the suppression written in 1539 by an unknown government hand still set the removal of the religious houses in a Wolseyan frame: 'the houses and churches [were] diffaced after the sorte and fashion as other houses of religion by the bishops of Rome's authorite in the cardinal of York's tyme had ben diffaced afore'.[23] It was not just (perhaps not especially) the suggestion of social revolution that made these viewpoints so unsettling, but rather the threat they seemed to pose to their own daily grind of getting by. Such thoughts were well formed some time before the first house fell under the statute of 1536. *Rede me and be nott wrothe* vividly described:

> I am sure thou hast hearde spoken
> what monasteries he hath broken
> He subverteth churches and chappells . . .
> He plucketh downe the costly leades
> that it maye rayne on saynct heads
> whereas they red service divine
> there is grountynge of pigges and swine . . .
> the aultres of their celebracions
> are made pearches for hens and capons.[24]

For Cromwell, for his commissioners, for the regular communities and for the society that looked on, the narrative for a dissolution of monasteries was ready-made.

In fact, the treatment of houses and their populations at the time of closure was approached with far less clarity and direction from the regime than any other measure since 1534. The fair copy of the instructions given to the commissioners of 1536 did not address what was to be done with the buildings and the site. Their charge was introduced self-consciously as a departure from the recent commissions: this was to be altogether 'a new survey', and they were commanded to begin their task by declaring 'the cause and purpose' of 'desolucion'.[25] Yet their instructions extended no further than the removal of the resident population and the recording of the site, its buildings and their contents, 'the state and plytt of the same'.[26] The principal machinery of a living monastery, such as its seal, were to be in 'suer' and 'save keping', until they 'knowe further of the kings pleasure'.[27] But there was no word about the church, the convent buildings and wider environment of the precinct. From the first weeks of the suppression in the late spring of 1536, some commissioners reported briskly that they had seen to it that houses had been 'defacyd' even, in one instance, 'to the ground'.[28] Yet in doing so, it does seem that they acted at their own initiative, to interpret commands that were far from clear. This impression is reinforced by the fact that just as many reports spoke of houses untouched, 'ther to remayne till they knowe further of the kings pleasure'.[29]

There was no greater guidance three years later. The prospect of change, of conversion in the use of the house and its 'scites circuits precincts', in the repeated formula, was signalled in two chapters of the Act of 1539, but there was no explicit acknowledgement that any action beyond the transaction itself had already begun.[30] There was only a slight implication of such in the second of these chapters, the last of the statute, in specific references to the purchases of Norfolk (Sibton Priory) and Cobham (Cobham College) 'nowe beinge utterly dissolved'.[31] No instructions for the enforcement of the second act are known to survive; there are indications that none were issued. John Prise, receiving surrenders in Glamorgan, seemed entirely at ease in advising Cromwell that 'I shall devyse the commission for the dissolution and other things perteynyng thereto, I shall . . . I wait not on you myself'.[32]

In the absence of Cromwell's correspondence with the commissioners, and the scarcity of statements of intent among the royal letters, the precise expectation at the point of dissolution can never be known. Given the attention not only to the discharge of the professed members of the community but also, among the men, to their secularisation, it might be assumed that there was always an expectation the house would be put beyond their use. From the concern for certain costly fixtures of the buildings, of lead, bell metal and timber, apparent in the instructions of 1536 and the Act of 1539, it could be inferred that a campaign of demolition was anticipated as soon as it was standing empty.

Yet the first-hand witness to suppressions and surrenders so frequently shows otherwise. Clearly, there had been no defacement begun at Louth Park and Sawley in September 1536 since the former monks remained close to the precinct and at

Sawley they were successfully reinstated.[33] It is evident that local officials, almost always informed about, and engaged with, the closure of their neighbourhood houses, did not expect any immediate demolition, given their fierce protest when certain commissioners acted on their own authority. Coventry's mayor and aldermen called for the convents of the friars to stand and remain precisely because as yet they had '[no] further knowledge from your good lordesipp'.[34]

The persistent uncertainty of the government position is clearly revealed in the commissioners' own dispatches. In the absence of any certain command, written or spoken, they pressed their own opinion on possible approaches to the churches and conventual buildings. As early as 4 June 1536, apparently less than a week into his circuit of Kent, Anthony Aucher wrote to advise Cromwell that at Langdon Abbey, 'the cloystar . . . is easy to be taken downe and the dortar also, whiche is a great house'.[35] Two years later, and still there was no instruction for Richard Rich when confronted with the precinct of Abingdon Abbey, and so, unbidden, he made his own assessment of the 'state and plytte' of the place and what might, 'the most parte of the [precinct] houses', and might not be defaced, suggesting to 'excepte the churche which assuredly ys a great and goodly thing well repayryd'.[36]

As the closures continued, and the traffic in people and possessions necessarily drew neighbourhood attention, the commissioners were more direct. Pleas for confirmation of 'the kings pleasure' were made repeatedly. 'The resydew of the howse I have left hole,' wrote John London in September 1538, 'tyl I knowe your farther pleasure.'[37] Yet still they found it necessary to seek guidance in the fourth year of closures, in what would prove to be the final six months of dissolution. In January 1539, John London was cautious, if not grudgingly so: 'Iff I sholde have defacyd the churche and the howse and solde the hole . . . I cowed nott have made xx pounds' yet still 'all [is] standing as it dothe.'[38] After another house was emptied of its residents in November 1539, Rich again asked how he should proceed, 'yf the same shalbe by your most gracious commawndment defacyd'.[39]

Committed to their circuits and constrained by the speed of communications, which was always dependent on another agent being en route 'to thausten fryers', some simply lost patience with the uncertainty of the situation and took action at their own initiative. Those involved in the visitation who had been inclined to impose restrictions on the religious more rigorous than the king's injunctions again seized the initiative for themselves. It appears Richard Pollard had set out to raze houses recently suppressed in Lincolnshire when his free hand was suddenly restrained. In March 1537 he wrote urgently to the receiver at Kirkstead: 'immedyat upon sight herof . . . deface nothing of the said monasterye'.[40] Thomas Legh decided himself to direct the demolition of a chain of houses in Midland counties in the course of 1538. It was conspicuous enough to provoke a sharp rebuke from Cromwell. In late October, Legh acknowledged 'your lordshyppes letters the contents wherof admonysshith us'; at Pipewell Abbey, he was commanded 'in no wyse to deface the monastery'.[41] Richard Poulet hoped to halt Thomas Hill in Hampshire when he opened the signet letters 'uppon the sight hereof ye cease to rase or deface any ferther of the howsyng . . . beynd as yet the kynges possessyons'.[42] Chancellor Rich, apparently more cautious than his colleagues in the interpretation of their commission, rounded on them with a mix of anger and angst: 'I am credibilie advertised that [Bordesley is] defaced and plucked downe . . . enquyre of theym that so hath defacid [it and] of their auctoritie [for they] will answer at their perills.'[43]

The vicegerent vented his greatest anger at John London whose free-wheeling through the Thames Valley, Gloucestershire and Warwickshire caused a formal complaint petition to be presented at Westminster. Cromwell's letter expressing his outrage is now lost but it was surely a blistering broadside, as London dispatched a defence of his conduct at each location in his seventy-mile progress from Aylesbury to Coventry. He began with awkward evasion: 'I have not so moche rasyd the howses I have be[n] at as I percyve the kings grace and your lordshippe ys informyd', and again, 'I dyd not extremely so do'. But he followed with the admission that he 'partly rase[d]' at Aylesbury, Reading and Coventry. Evasion became excuse: 'necessitie compellyd me,' he suggested, 'by reson of the importunyte of the people. The wiche els wold have pullyd all so the kings grace shulde have had no profytt of these houses.'[44] This was at the very least disingenuous given that the towns through which London had passed had been surprised and outraged by his behaviour. For him, and perhaps for Legh, the first impulse to fill the space left by their masters' silence was personal, an intellectual distaste certainly but also it seems an emotional outrage over regular religion. Even in his letter London confided that at the Reading Franciscans 'I dyd only deface the church [for] all the windows being full of fryers', no doubt a history of the order told in a sequence of stained-glass scenes. Downriver from the town at Caversham near Reading he appears to have been roused to a furious tearing-down of 'lights, shrouds crowchys and images of wax' he found in a Marian chapel maintained by the canons of Notley.[45] Their fury at discovering what he had done was charged by a feeling for the present political danger. London insisted that he had feared some counteraction: 'I pullyd doune no howse thoroughly at noon of the fryers butt so defacyed them as they shuld nott lightly be made fryers anew.'

The commissioners' sense of righteous self-defence was heightened by conspicuous contradictions in the dealings of Austin Friars. It does appear that in a handful of instances there was a clear instruction to begin to take the buildings down. John Freeman gave an account of five unidentified houses 'defausyd and pulld downe to the grownde'.[46] The document, much damaged, is undated, although the HMSO editors of the printed calendar entry attributed it to the early months of suppression in the summer or autumn of 1536. That such immediate action was out of the ordinary was perhaps implied in his endorsement of his paper 'boke': 'this besynes is truly doon'.[47]

It does seem that those dispatched to Lincolnshire and the northern counties in the spring of 1537 to take into custody the houses associated with the recent rebellions carried with them an expectation of imminent demolition; certainly there was a view among those now taking depositions from captured rebels that the continued use of sites which formally were closed weeks before the first of the marches, had served to propagate the unrest. Still, there seems to have been some hesitation to make any sudden demonstration of the Crown's claim on the substance of these houses despite the summary justice shown to their members. Reportedly, at Furness Abbey the king's men remained 'put only in trust to pluck downe'.[48]

There may have been a greater degree of decision in the handling of the friars' houses in the summer and autumn of the following year. In his response to Cromwell's admonition, John London implied that a certain level of demolition had indeed been his instruction, and that he 'hadd rasyd noon saving for the words of such commission as I have to schew'.[49] Given the particular acts of defacement which London was willing to own, of church windows, altars and furnishings, it may be that there was a command to ensure conventual churches were left unusable.

But the letters of Bishop Ingworth, the Crown's principal agent in securing the surrender of the friars, convey a quite different view, of such uncertainty surrounding the scope of his authority, and persistent silence from Austin Friars, that it was scarcely possible to take any decisive action. 'I artely beseche you send to me yowr pleasure whether ye will have ye ... freers styll ... or nott,' he wrote in July 1538 in the early weeks of his six-month circuit.[50] In the last week of August, he reached out to his fellow prelate, Hugh Latimer: 'sende me sum word how yt my lorde privy seale take ye mater'.[51] Nothing came, and by the turn of the month his exasperation was palpable: 'I had no worde from you thys v wekes'.[52] Richard Ingworth also weighed his own commission with the climate of the local community. From Shrewsbury he warned Cromwell to be very circumspect over the houses of the Dominicans after confronting the town bailiffs, 'for ther shall be gret suite made'.[53] His letters reveal a further obstacle that may have dissuaded all but the most vehemently anti-fraternal to remain at any house long enough to deface it. 'In many howseys I am fayn to pay alle my costs and receive never a peny,' he complained, time and again, 'wherefor I so lefte.'[54]

The commissioners were not alone in their struggle with the uncertainties of the Crown. The absence of decisive action over their churches, surrounding buildings and precinct sites stirred neighbourhood agitation, and not only in the regions that witnessed the rebellions of 1536–37. It would be wrong to suggest that the mood of the social community was now wholly partisan. At the height of the marches on Lincoln and York, it was conspicuously clear that even in the path of the pilgrims there was a majority of clergy and laity that looked on in different states of nervous detachment ranging from favour to fear. But there were pockets of powerful feeling that were directly focused on the monastic and mendicant infrastructure. The Crown's agents, not only the commissioners, but also the courtier captains dispatched to repress the rebels, reported widely on an almost frenzied anticipation of a general campaign of demolition. As early as February 1537, when scarcely two-thirds of the houses subject to the suppression statute were standing empty, it appeared that the talk of the provinces 'from towne to towne' was of nothing more than 'pullyng downe of the churches'.[55] The Buckingham JP, Sir John Baldwin, blustered that the country for eight miles around was ready to 'rayse' as soon as the demolition, certain to happen, was to begin.[56]

It is possible that some neighbours now seized the initiative. The pattern of the shattered pieces of moulded stone recovered from inside the church at Torre Abbey might point to deliberate destruction for its own sake, although the original shape of these pieces remains unclear and the destruction itself is impossible to date precisely.[57] Here, among those who lived alongside the religious houses, there may have been a surge of the same fervour for reform that fired certain commissioners to overreach their authority. John London claimed at Coventry that the citizens 'layd so sore uppon' the church and convent buildings of the Whitefriars, although the mayor and alderman claimed the contrary.[58] The 'pluckyng down' of the paraphernalia of the shrine at Boxley Abbey was more or less superfluous according to Jeffrey Chamber, 'for [the people] wold either plucke it down to the ground or ellse knowe off it for they have the sayd matter in wondrous destatacion'.[59]

More commonly perhaps, it was both a practical, and also consciously a political, act to pre-empt any action of the king's agents either in demolition of the site and disbursal of its materials or in its complete repossession. John London felt both impulses at Reading, where 'the peple wold . . . pull all downe so the Kyngs grace shulde have had no profytt of these houses' and 'moch powr people . . . fell to steling so fast in every corner of the howse'.[60] The Carmelite and Dominican convents at Norwich appealed to the duke of Norfolk to arrange their swift surrender because already they were 'inquity[d] by lyghte persons . . . now often tymes' with 'brekyng of glasse wyndows' and 'deffasyng off manye other thynges'.[61] At the Franciscan convent, his defence of the Crown's interest had been roundly defeated: 'for as soon as I hadde taken the fryers surrender, the multitude of the poverty of the town resortyd thedyr and all things that myzt be hadde they stole away. Inso myche that they hadde convayd the very clapers of the bellys'.[62] This illicit plunder had begun before houses were taken into custody: in Norfolk it was reported at the point of the formal suppression that 'parte [of the building] was gon' when the commissioners arrived.[63] The robbing of rubble-stone from the Augustinian Friary at Shrewsbury appears to have started as early as 1536; by the time of its closure in 1538, it was already judged to be 'ruynous'.[64] Their wait for further instruction, or, like Ingworth, their failure to wait, left sites vulnerable to further waves which demolished them by default. At the Cistercian house of Hailes they had even prised the locks from the still-hanging doors.[65]

The threat to the largest sites and to concentrations of buildings in urban centres turned the commissioners from the prospect of demolition to the immediate problem of defence. At Coventry, John London made hasty arrangements but, perhaps because of the difficulty of securing cooperation locally, he confessed that he could 'not long contain the spoil'. 'The pour people thorowly in every place be so gredy upon these howsys when they be suppressyd that by nygt and daye nott oonly of the townys butt also of the countre they do continually resort as long any dore, wyndoes, yren or glasses or lowse ledde remaynthe in any of them. In every place I kepe wacche as longe as I tary and prison those that do thjis abuse.'[66] John Scudamore paid for watchmen wherever he could; inventories show an immediate expenditure in bolts and chains. It was of limited practical use. 'The dore was broken up' at Carmarthen, 'and certeyne stuffe taken owt';[67] at Evesham, exceptionally the decision was taken to begin wholesale demolition because so much, so quickly, had been brought down by such 'spoyl'.[68] Excavations at Lewes Priory revealed evidence of forced opening of graves in the floor of the crossing and the Lady chapel.[69] The tomb slab of Abbot John Ripon of Fountains Abbey was removed and smashed, apparently at a point when the site was still occupied as there is evidence of a makeshift repair.[70] This was a sign of desperation. A skeleton found beneath a fallen pier at Rievaulx, since it was left, may be the remains of one who was on the site illicitly.[71] The looters were men both of action and means. As houses remained in custody, claims to their fabric were brought before the courts. The removal of marble from the nave of the Dominican church at Derby was defended as justifiable in no lesser court than Star Chamber.[72]

The potential of monasteries and friaries for plunder was the primary – and arguably the only well-developed – viewpoint of the Crown at the moment of their closure. The first responsibility of the commissioners, and the guiding principle of their conduct on site, was to determine the value of everything, from the fabric of the church and connected buildings, to their furnishings, other extraneous moveables and finally the site itself. It was from this and, so far as Cromwell and the king were concerned, only from this, that an early move to demolition might be considered; even then, the letters in response to Cromwell suggest that any hint of such an intention he offered was always hedged with caution, subject to a better knowledge of the king's will and of the character and condition of the buildings in view. The only acts of demolition carried out under royal authority directly after the closures were for the recovery of particular elements of the fabric. The accounts of the agents suggest an almost clinical operation in which certain components were extracted while the structure as a whole was kept intact. In the earliest instances, it seems it was prompted only to answer a particular need; in no case is there a clear indication of a scheme in place already at the moment of closure to mine a site for materials to be sold on the open market.

The only locations where activity can certainly be documented in the days and weeks immediately following a suppression or surrender are those in the vicinity of other of the king's works. The fabric of a handful of houses was consumed in a matter of months. The demolition of Chertsey Abbey began three days after the surrender of its former inmates, who were relocated to Bisham.[73] Elevations at Merton Priory were taken down in a little over twelve weeks after its suppression in April 1538 to supply the building site of the new palace at Nonsuch just five miles away. Given the gang of bricklayers passing to and fro in August and September, it seems it was not the imported stone of its oldest buildings that was wanted first but its fresh red brick; the stone came after too, more than 3,000 loads before mid-September.[74] The buildings of the Cistercian Abbey at Quarr were commandeered as a quarry as soon as the monastic occupation ended and all of its facing Purbeck stone was carted across the estuary to the king's new blockhouses on the coast at Cowes.[75]

Correspondence from the commissioners' circuits suggests that the only roofing lead that was lifted and dispatched from sites soon after closure was to answer a specific call from elsewhere in the Crown's domain. Chancellor Rich instructed the commissioners passing through the Welsh March to proceed with the removal of roofing lead, its smelting and recasting ready for the repair of castles right along the route, from Brecon to Holt (Chester), a hundred miles of March.[76] The need was urgent, 'for the tyme of yere', that is to say, the season for building, was so short, and 'there is more of Breknok castell fallen and a nother pece at Chyrke and all must be doyne gode'.[77]

Generally, as the closures progressed from the first phase in the spring of 1536 to the end four years later, the first, conspicuous activity at monasteries and friaries was not the taking-down of buildings but the removal and redistribution of a great variety of their contents. Their growing awareness of the pre-emptive leasing of properties encouraged the commissioners to concentrate their attention here; it may be that their tales of suspected concealment led Cromwell to make it a matter of formal policy. Letters to him became more and more a matter of 'moveable goods'; it is possible that his lost letters gave a steer in this direction.

The first priority of the commissioners was to record what they found – and to locate and recover what was known to be among them by common report. But entries in the inventories they were bound to compile show that they began to

disperse them at the same time. Buyers were soon found both for household furniture and utensils and for the special objects of the sacristy and vestry, candelabra,
crucifixes, altar cloths and complete Mass suits for a celebrant. Given the tempta-
tion to plunder present in many neighbourhoods, it is likely that as the commissioners worked over a number of days, they drew a willing market around them.
They sometimes settled on a single day of sale, to speed the clearance certainly but
also no doubt to enable prospective buyers to make the journey to the house. Thomas
Legh dispensed with almost all 'implementes or houshoulde stuffe corne catell
ornamentes of the churche and suche other lyke' from Dieulacres on 21 October
1538, the day after the monks' surrender.[78]

The commissioners do seem to have felt some pressure to see the contents
cleared. Robert Southwell held a hasty sale at Hempton on 25 January 1537, the
morning after he took the surrender; the next day he moved on.[79] Titchfield Abbey
was said to have been left 'barren' in four days.[80] The interest in the sale stirred
tensions within the neighbourhood and between the king's men themselves.
Reports from Lincoln told of a dispute with one agent complaining that 'Mister
Sesel dyschargyd my folks from sals of the gray and whyt fryars by a byll of his
owne'.[81] The scale of their circuit, and its costs, which many of them, like Ingworth,
bore themselves, called for them to move on. Also, there was the widespread alarm
at the possibility of popular spoliation. At Dunkeswell Abbey, John Heydon left
nothing to chance. He put a heap of unsold furnishings against the wall of the
cellarer's chamber and set them on fire; the scorch mark was still visible in the
twentieth century.[82]

In the agricultural economy of Henry's England, it was the livestock and food
stores of each house that held the immediate attention of the commissioners as
well as those in the neighbourhood who watched what they were doing. The
demesne herds of the great churches were the largest in the kingdom and their
dispersal must have amounted to a greater movement of animals and redistribution
of rights over them than had ever been seen. The sale and transfer of the principal
herds is not well documented in the commissioner papers that survive. In part
this may be because herds had been exchanged or sold some time in advance of
the closure. The ready cash raised by houses of all sizes from 1535 onwards
was not only from the sale of treasures from their altars and shrines. There
were also covert transactions. The disappearance of livestock from the demesne
pastures was discovered by the commissioners at Ingham Priory, but unlike the

apparent transfer of the deeds of the house it is not known if the beasts were ever recovered.[83]

But the inventories, which provide more consistent information on what was in a religious house than what was sold from it, show that among the independent abbeys at least there were significant numbers still standing in and around their own farms. William Griffith, prior of St Katherine's, Lincoln, took it upon himself to press Cromwell directly over the quality of the livestock there, 'the shepe, cattell, for they be very good. I think ther will be labour for them ... I have here 1400 shepe yong and old'.[84] The sale of the stock at Leicester Abbey raised £228, more than 20 per cent of the annual revenue of the house as assessed in 1535.[85] At times there was as much stock taken into the precinct of the house. The commissioners who came to Butley Priory counted no fewer than 120 sheep, an impressive sight that left the stock of the prior's household seem more than a little threadbare. Here they saw 'a lytll nag to ride by the cart'.[86] There may have been a recall of livestock in anticipation of the Crown's sale; perhaps also to pre-empt it. Yet there were times when the commissioners found the seasonal cycle unbroken. The rapid suppression of Dover Priory left them with the task of retrieving fifty cattle that were pastured on Romney Marsh. 'The catall all to be sold to theym that shall have the growndes', the decision at Bridlington, may have been most common.[87]

As the hub of the houses' economic and social networks, there was a mix of animals in the precincts themselves. There were as many as fourteen riding horses stabled at Dover Priory when the commissioners arrived. There was also a variety of stock farmed in situ for the refectory table: pigs, poultry, among them, swans and, apparently on a larger scale than the rest, pond fish such as pike, tench and roach. John Crayford told Thomas Wriothesley that there were 100,000 carp and pike at Titchfield.[88] Even in the smaller monasteries there were animals associated with the leisure of the social elite. At Beeleigh, the commissioners took possession of the prior's peacock and peahen.[89] Perhaps in every monastic precinct beyond urban centres there was also a kennel full of hounds.[90] Most of the animal stock from a religious house was sold upon its dissolution, even the palfreys that were somewhat out of place in a secular world that did not share the regulars' preference for the humble mount of a churchman. The rest of the stock was disposed of on site. Excavations have revealed high deposits of the bones of mammals, rather more than might be expected of a priory's kitchen. At the site of

Norton Priory some 12,400 bone fragments were found. Possibly there was always an abattoir there but perhaps it was that one was improvised at the time of the house's dissolution.[91]

At the moment of closure, the stores of many monasteries were found to be filled with food. There is the slight hint of surprise in some reports to Austin Friars of granaries replete with grain. Those houses standing outside the terms of the 1536 statute had made no significant change in their accustomed, seasonal pattern of provision as the pressure to surrender intensified. The food diary kept at Tavistock Abbey from Michaelmas 1536 is redolent of the cellarer's stores being stocked much as they always had been.[92] Of course, even the prospect of enforced closure in the future did not displace the need to keep the community, the professed and their employees, fed until such time as they were led out of the precinct. By the same imperative monasteries that were closed in the first year of suppressions may well have been emptied of their residents when the barns, bakehouse and buttery remained at least half full. The mustering rebels of October 1536 and February 1537 fully expected the houses nearby and on their marching route to be able to feed them. These were local men, well aware of the recent passage of the suppression commissioners, and the terms under which the houses had been placed in custody; they were well informed.

Generally, the situation of the friaries may have been very different. The inventories suggest that kitchens had been all but decommissioned, the combined effect of the diminishing numbers keeping residence in the convent itself, and the necessary sale of furniture and utensils for cash. It was empty platters, as much as empty coffers, that contributed to the cold comfort of Richard Ingworth as he passed among the provincial friars. The Shrewsbury Augustinians, he reported, could not even count on a cup to celebrate the Mass.[93] A handful of the convents in towns and cities whose numbers had always been larger and where local support had always been strong may have held supplies not unlike a self-sufficient monastery. At least, the comparatively high numbers of convents present not only in cities – Exeter (14), Salisbury (14) – but also small western towns – Carmarthen (14), Truro (11) – that signed the surrender, point to a conventual kitchen that was still open.[94]

Dry-stored food carried a high face value and the commissioners were inclined to deploy it like coin. The price of wheat reached its peak of the decade in 1536 and as the domestic economy of monasteries continued unchecked up to the moment of closure, they held it in quantities both severed and unsevered, that is, the produce of their own demesne as well as the tithe portions they had taken in. A portion of the store of unmilled grain was sometimes allocated to the superior as part of their personal settlement. Abbot Henry Cundal of Roche was told to take 'a convenient porcion of corne at discreasion'.[95] Where one member of a male monastery was to be presented to the parish living, an allocation from the granary store might also be offered. Larger quantities were appropriated to meet the Crown's needs, to supply the stores of a nearby garrison, or one of the provincial palaces. Where there was scope according to trade in the region, it seems grain was sold to merchants. The eighty quarters of wheat kept at Butley were dispatched to a Spanish merchantman off the Suffolk coast.[96] Of all the houses' contents, here there was a need to act quickly. 'If the corne be solde now', the commissioners said of Bridlington, 'it wilbe the most profyte to the kyngs grace.'[97] At Sawtry Abbey (Cambridgeshire), the unsevered grain was valued at £39, more than a quarter of the total value given in 1535.[98]

The stores of the 'great and solemn' abbeys also held some costly specialities. All of them were supplied with tuns of beer; at Glastonbury they were matched with mead.[99] The contents of their wine cellars are a conspicuous absence from the surviving inventories. It must be assumed that the best of it was appropriated for the Crown, if not always to pass into royal cellars, then to be expended as a source of patronage. Other rare treats may have been taken for the king. There was imported marmalade at Westminster Abbey, reputedly a particular favourite of King Henry.[100] The compilers of the inventory at Peterborough Abbey may have had a particular recipient in mind when they recorded in the fish house, 'one old drie ling'.[101] They were also surprised by the richness of the fresh produce. At Reading, John London found 'a fruyt orchard full of gudde fruyte'.[102] There was some interest in the abbeys' ornamental gardens too. Specimen bay and rosemary trees, or grafts from them, together with grafts 'of all sorts' taken from the ninety-one trees of their apple orchard, seem to have been among the first of anything to be removed from the London Charterhouse.[103]

The church furnishings were not a general commodity. Many of them were marked with expressions, in word and image, of the traditions against which the king and his government had turned: the Roman papacy, the cult of saints, and the history and authority of the religious orders themselves. There were times when the commissioners could not contain their contempt for the content of some of this artistry. John London was enraged by the stained glass in the church of the Reading Franciscans, apparently depicting the serried ranks of their order and, perhaps, their papal protector. 'The inward part of the church thowrolye dekkyd with grey fryers ... in the wyndoes,' he reported, and decisively, 'I have defacyd.'[104]

The commissioners' reaction reflected a rising antipathy to some of the central features of traditional religion, especially any references, verbal or visual, to the Church of Rome, and the cult of saints, their relics and shrines; but it did not reach as far as rejection of the essential ritual of their Church, the celebration of Mass at an altar duly decorated for the sacrament by a priest dressed in fine vestments. Men such as London were opposed to the presence of the religious orders in a church; but they were not Protestants. They, like most of the secular clergy and laity of their time, considered monastic religion to be quite different in style from the practice of their own parish, but they knew its substance to be the same. The rich and diverse array of ornaments that commissioners came across in monastic and friary churches they recognised as being valuable for more than the costly materials from which they were made, as they might still be used in other churches. In their inventories, they described these 'special implements' in careful detail. They also consulted experts. 'Sum goldsmyth' was found to look over the plate at Bridlington.[105] Their concern for the details of fabric and design and the quantity of the vestment suits may be a measure of a lively second-hand market for unique pieces, made from costly, imported materials, from the best workshops. The descent of duplicitous jewellers to remote, rural churches suggests the rumours of rich pickings had carried far.[106] A Cheapside dealer made off with an emerald and a ruby from Fountains Abbey, having persuaded the abbot that the stone was a mere garnet.[107]

The release of such artistry on the open market was unprecedented and there was a sudden clamour. 'Be so good to ... fynd any ... vestment or copys,' urged James Leveson at Lilleshall.[108] Despite his own damages, John London found a buyer at Reading for stained glass, 'and yet [I have] made som mony for the kings grace use'.[109] He could not contain his admiration for the fine textiles he found and begged Cromwell for some for his own parish church. 'We have very few ... vestments and oon awter clothe ... and thes very olde.'[110] His colleague, Richard Leighton, looked out for his church, purchasing a chalice and two altar basins from Westacre Priory.[111]

The very best of the church ornaments were routinely reserved for the king. At regular intervals from the summer of 1536 onwards the accounts of Augmentations recorded the delivery of church decorations, jewels, gold and silver plate and vestments, either into the hands of gentlemen of the Privy Chamber or directly into the custody of the Keeper of the King's Jewels, John Williams. At Michaelmas 1538, from Abingdon Abbey alone, reserved for the king there were two mitres, two gold pontifical rings, a jewelled crucifix containing a relic of the true cross, altar cloths of cloth-of-gold and a six-yard piece of the same fabric.[112]

The royal collection continued to grow up to the very last of the surrenders. Cromwell's remembrances for the winter of 1539 include a reminder about 'the ryche cops from Glaston'; the inventory of vestments at St Albans Abbey made in early December was marked up with as many as nineteen destined for the king.[113] The constant cross-country traffic in luxury objects for which, for any ordinary subject, duty would be owed, left some in the wider public somewhat askance. William Wodlow of Winchester spoke out when he saw 'two malt suffes full of plate' carried out of the city and conveyed as far as the tollbooth at Tewkesbury.[114]

The religious begged to keep some of the church furnishings for themselves. Most of the men expected to act as priests in the secular church; a small number had been presented to benefices at the point of departure; some anticipated a cathedral appointment. The commissioners acknowledged these prospects: sometimes they added vestments, altar hangings and other ornaments to the settlement they offered superiors; just as often they gave them the option to buy them.[115] Henry Cundal of Roche Abbey was presented with a chalice, vestment (unspecified, but presumably his Mass robes) and a selection of books, some if not all of which may have been liturgical.[116] Surrendering as abbot of St Albans, Richard Bourman was permitted to purchase five copes of white damask embroidered with daisies for which he paid the surprisingly small sum of 33s 4d.[117] To his new parish church at Kingsclere John Norman of Bindon seems to have carried three 'hole sutes' of vestments, one black (funerary), one green and one blue velvet which, with an altar cloth, he asked to be sent back to Bindon.[118]

They wanted to keep more than these tools of their vocation: the religious hoped to recover, perhaps to reuse, some of the fixtures of the church buildings. Prior John Lancaster of Launde Priory pressed Cromwell for much of the interior of his church, including a pair of organs, 'lately' provided at his own expense and 'one gret grave stonne lieng in the churche . . . which he bought to lye upon hym

... when it plesed god to cal hym to his mercie'.[119] It seems their priorities were always personal and pragmatic. They looked to take away the objects they thought of as their own, the result of their individual acts of patronage, for which they had paid. Once his own needs were provided for, Prior John Draper of Christchurch at Twynham was quite prepared for the commissioners to lift the tombstone which had just been laid in his church for Margaret Pole, countess of Salisbury, mother of the future cardinal, and to put it up for sale.[120]

There were contents of the church and convent buildings to which the king's commissioners were inclined to turn a blind eye. Books, especially, often seem to have escaped their closest scrutiny. This was something of a change from the mood at the visitation, when the commissioners appear to have been on the alert to appraise the contents of all institutional libraries. Famously, at New College, Oxford, Richard Leighton encouraged a dramatic purge of manuscripts from the library which saw leaves of Duns Scotus's medieval philosophy scattered from its first-floor windows.[121] At the monasteries he visited, Leighton had picked out volumes of saints' lives and miracle stories and dispatched them to Cromwell as evidence of their superstition.[122] It may be that months later, as the suppressions started, this interference was remembered as a sufficient purge of monastic and mendicant books. It is just as likely that the sequestration and sale of commodities, church ornaments, and ultimately the fabric of the buildings simply overshadowed objects which were among the least conspicuous of all their contents.

Typically at this time the core of a monastery or friary library was kept chained in a library room to which access was controlled by keyholders; the library was not one of the communal spaces of the house through which all members might pass at least once on a given day. In addition, a disparate selection of books was dispersed through the community itself, assigned to them because of the office they held or as part of a reading collection in perpetual circulation. The smallest and poorest houses may not have held enough books to maintain a recognisable conventual collection. Many of those suppressed in 1536–37 may have revealed to the commissioners a meagre stock like the 'xiii olde bokys of smale valwe' found at Coxford Priory.[123]

Yet books of whatever number, age and condition, both manuscripts and printed editions, carried a market value: the best of them might have commanded a price comparable to the vestments which the commissioners did put up for sale. There may have been book sales. A canon of Oseney acquired two books from

Thame Abbey, less than twenty miles downriver, one from the choir and one from the library; of course, such local transmission may be a sign that they could be more casually acquired.[124]

There may also have been a rough-and-ready removal of books. The Portable Antiquities Scheme record of the clasps and studs from book bindings found in Norfolk have been mapped, although they indicate the 'ubiquitous distribution of books' rather than a certain tie to a monastic site.[125] More suggestive is the scatter of brass book clasps uncovered within the site of the Carmarthen Franciscans.[126]

More often than not, however, it would seem that books were overlooked; and the religious were left to decide their fate for themselves. Some continued the old custom of allocation under licence of the superior. At Aldbury, New Place (Surrey), a very old manuscript, a bestiary, and a very new printed Bible were assigned to individual canons in October 1538 (see Fig. 25).[127] Abbot Thomas Gyllam of Pipewell made over a volume to his monk, John Webster, just hours before the deed of surrender was endorsed and sealed on 5 November. It was a thirteenth-century manuscript psalter; surely the sign was a conscious act of conservation.[128] These may have been deliberate, pre-emptive grants intended to secure conventual property away from the Crown.

Books were also carried away by monks without any of these formalities. Often office-holders held on to the books associated with their roles. The customary of the shrine of Thomas Becket seems to have been saved by its custodian.[129] Academic scholars and others with a taste for independent learning seem to have been able to hold on to the pick of their personal libraries. The Syon Abbey writer, Richard Whitford, left with enough of his working collection to be able to prepare a new publication which appeared in 1541.[130] Some of this may have been illicit but given the large share that such men took away with them it is more likely that it was with the knowledge of the commissioners. Edward Heptonstall of Kirkstead kept a chestful of books.[131] From Monk Bretton, Prior William Browne and two of his monks carried away more than a hundred of the convent's volumes.[132]

The richest resource of the religious houses was their own fabric. Here there was no real difference between the monasteries and the friaries, or even between the greatest establishments and the smallest. In the half-century since the coming of the Tudors foundations of every status and size had seen new building; in fact, it was only in these recent times that some of the smaller friaries had found the investment to develop something approaching a suite of conventual buildings, including such facilities as a library. Some of this work had been among the very finest architecture undertaken at the beginning of the sixteenth century. But what may have been most striking about the majority of the buildings was not the high style but the bright new currency of their materials: exterior timber frames and plasterwork, interior panelling, windows never shuttered now but glazed and, above all, clay tiles and brick cast from English clay. 'Yt ys universally,' observed John London, that 'the people be this gredy for yren wyndoes doors and ledde.'[133] A Boston man confirmed this, 'consyderyng howe barron our cuntre is bothe of stone tymber and tyle'.[134]

The determination to document these resources, to investigate the scope for their removal, and to estimate their market value stifled any idea of simply taking them down. Much was expected of the commissioners, almost all of them university men whose practical education was primarily legal. Some took up the charge with an amateur enthusiasm. Perhaps John London drew on his dozen years of experience as warden of New College, Oxford, a fourteenth-century foundation with its own share of ageing fabric, as he offered detailed accounts of the scale of buildings and their state of repair. Confidently, he confirmed that the 'old tile' on the roof of Warwick's Dominican convent 'ys very gud', although 'els all ys old and little worth'.[135] For twelve friaries from Bedford to Stamford he made painstaking reports of their roof covering and rain gear; then he turned clerk of works, advising, 'the winter is the time to make ready for summer building'.[136]

Richard Rich was also ready to act as surveyor, to direct what might be extracted by 'masons, carpenters or other devysers', and he was audibly bruised when he believed Cromwell did not credit his authority, 'I as one . . . wold not neglect or be remise in doing my dewty and yet loth to enterprise . . . any thing . . . than . . . your most hertey desyryng.'[137] Thomas Legh, as ever, was more inclined to argue with his brief, maintaining that the fabric should be left alone for the time being, as it was 'moche the better because they war not easy to be alienate sold or caryed a waye'.[138]

The principal materials of walls and roofs – stone, timber, brick, tile (clay, slate) and lead – together with that of fixtures and fittings – iron, glass, marble and other decorative stonework – were all appraised for their potential reuse and sale. The systematic survey was carried out in full view of the neighbourhood, although it does seem that locals were held at a distance and the tradesmen who cast their expert eye on this brickwork or that joinery were often recruited from out of town. The talk of the suppressions turned to the precincts' raw resources; speculations over the title to outlying properties were, for a time, almost entirely eclipsed. Certainly, in the course of 1538, as the first of the greater houses gave way to the pressure of the Crown, Cromwell's unsolicited correspondence was all about construction. The burgesses of Boston promised him the town's 'immortale memorie' should he 'stay the tymber, iron and stone' of the friaries to repair the sea walls; if this was not sufficient cause, he was also warned that the advancing sea would soon waste the Crown's new property, to their 'utter deslacyon' and the loss of 'agrete dele of monye'.[139] The mayor of Worcester reached for the same lever in October 1538: 'the amendemente of the wales [walls] and the brugg [bridge]' would be for the 'high comoditie' of what now, with the seizure of the friaries central sites, was 'the kyngs said citie'.[140] Local pleas, even couched in the corporate authority of a mayoralty, did not move government policy in this matter any more than it did on the final destination of sequestered property.

There were one or two instances where the intercession of the most influential of the Crown's agents saw selected materials released to meet local needs. It seems Chancellor Rich was responsible for the removal of stone from Abingdon Abbey for the repair of roads running south of the town to Culham, and those downriver to Reading, Henley and Marlow.[141] It was possibly the power of Robert King, *commendam* abbot of Thame and ally of Cromwell, that saw the abbeys of Bruern and Rewley given over to building sites before the end of the same year.[142]

But in general there was an early recognition that the value of the raw materials might best be realised if they were not broken up for sale as soon as the buildings were empty. The commissioners recognised the insecurity of a site given over to demolition. At Austin Friars, there was a rising awareness of the immediate costs. The concession of Abingdon stone to the towns of Berkshire committed the Chancellor of Augmentations to a great enterprise: fifty skilled trades were needed on site together with thirty-two jobbing labourers and no fewer than seventy-eight carters.[143] Soon there was a preference to pass the responsibility for extraction and removal to the beneficiary – grantee, or purchaser – of the particular materials. Of course, such terms served to raise the value to the Crown, as the right for salvage and sale commanded a price of its own.

In these transactions attention was always paid to the structural stone, brickwork and timber, and to roofs robust enough for reuse, such as clay tile and oak shingle. Decorative stonework was overlooked, leaving it vulnerable to illicit removal. The appearance of carved stonework in the elevations of buildings at a radius from a former religious house speaks of unofficial preservation, certainly, but also of official neglect. The exception in interior stonework were flagstones which could be lifted and carried as a complete floorspace. The timber wainscot of internal walls and partitions lent itself to reuse, although, joined with pegs more often than nails, it was also prone to damage when taken up and so was rarely stripped out completely but harvested according to demand. The Crown was still selling expanses of panelling from St Mary's Abbey, York, and Dunstable Priory in October 1550.[144]

Glazing, it seems, was not considered to be a general prospect for sale. Where demolition was a deliberate, directed undertaking, it appears glazing was discarded. Excavations have revealed refuse pits packed full of glass fragments. At Thorney Abbey it seems that all of the painted window glass was sacrificed for the fret of lead that held it.[145] The painted glass was also discarded at Bardney Abbey.[146] The preparatory survey gave close attention to significant and structural metalwork but only select elements were extracted and sold.

Bell metal was of interest everywhere. The full complement of bells was usually discovered, weighed and valued. Some were promised to named buyers at the same time as the other contents. Their healthy market value, however, was matched by the high cost of removal, and as more churches were taken into custody there was less of a readiness, among the commissioners on the ground and at Austin Friars, to bear the cost. One solution was to subcontract to speculators. The sale of some 60,000 lbs of bell metal from the monastic and friary churches of East Anglia was settled with a consortium of London merchants; the price of £600 carried with it the responsibility to remove and ship the spoil the hundred coastal miles to the capital.[147]

Increasingly, bells were left in place while other things were taken down; long enough for there to be some dispute as to their future use. Some items were not the Crown's to claim. Those in the church of the Trinitarians at Easton had been purchased by the parish and they were obliged to leave them in place. The iron-work of doors and windows perhaps was deemed too intricate. John Crayford did select 'a few wyndowes glass irone' at Southwick for his patron, Thomas Wriothesley, to use at Titchfield, but it seems there was no call for them because he had them 'chepe ynowgh'.[148] Excavations have shown that at the time of demolition much of the ironwork to doors and windows was allowed to be discarded among the general refuse; sometimes it seems the ironwork was tidily buried.[149] The decorative ironwork of church interiors, such as the perimeter railings of a tomb, were left in place for a time. John Weever saw some standing still when he entered former monastery and friary churches at the beginning of the seventeenth century.[150]

The material of most interest to the Crown was lead. The instructions issued to the commissioners for the suppression in 1536, generalised and evasive on much else, had been straightforward on this point: the 'quantitie or value of the leade' to be found was to be the first priority of the fabric, in fact it was the only building material to be mentioned in the twenty-three clauses of their brief.[151] Among the diverse resources of the monastery or friary precinct, lead was naturally pre-eminent. Its price was strong and, relatively speaking, stable, and since production of the raw ore in England had dipped sharply in the course of the decade, demand was rising; by no means the least was the demand from the Crown itself, on the one hand to meet the needs of its expanding network of fortifications, on the other to equip them, and any offensive force, with artillery.

Cromwell was fixed on the dual reward from his first comprehensive view of the monastic and mendicant infrastructure provided by the valuation commissioners. Lead was the first asset he asked about in his correspondence with his agents, at least, so it appears: on the subject of lead there is such precision in their replies that it must be assumed that his questions were searching and persistent. The call to calculate lead stocks shaped the layout of the summary reports that the commissioners returned. Set out in columns on unfolded foolscap letter paper, lead was given an entry of its own, whereas compound figures were recorded for 'stock' and chattels.[152]

These papers, which are better preserved for the £200 houses and friaries than others, and for north-eastern England than for any other region, record the quantity of lead in fother weight (1 fother = 2,184–2,520 lbs). The calculation at Buckenham was perhaps not untypical for a house whose annual revenue like many suppressed in 1536–37 stood midway between £100 and £200. Here there was as much as 61 fother covering church, crossing, steeple, choir, aisles and adjoining chapels, cloister and domestic chambers.[153] Such measures give the impression that the lead had already been lifted, if not also already melted down and recast into the ingots, at the time often called 'pigs', that were the customary unit of the raw materials. Yet the instructions for the suppression did not specify the removal of the lead; on the contrary, their implication was that, once quantified and valued, it should, like the contents of any value, be 'put in sure kepinge'.

The lack of clear direction over the very commodity on which they were so continually quizzed was keenly felt by the commissioners. In their reports they pressed their own proposals, observing somewhat sourly that 'as yet noo suche commission cummyne to owre handes'.[154] Certainly some of them anticipated the command to strip off the lead which they assumed would come in time. Although John London denied it in his defensive letter to Cromwell, the mayoralty of Coventry testified to the fact that he had overseen the removal of the lead from the roof of the Carmelite church and convent. Others were impatient only to press ahead with their commission, and of all the uncertainties surrounding their charge they were inclined to accept this one.

The delayed response from Austin Friars was surely deliberate. It was essential that the value of lead, above all, was defended, and by the time, in the early autumn of 1536, that it was being assessed in circuits across the country, it was apparent that the greatest threat to the Crown's purpose would be the illicit plunder of houses by the local populace. The impulse to preserve lead stocks was greater perhaps than the impulse to prevent observant life returning to the precinct. There was also a growing awareness that of all their material features, the right to the roof of these foundations might raise as many questions of title as that of any messuage. Some lead roofs were the result of acts of patronage; for a number of the provincial friars this was well within living memory. The roof of the church of the Augustinian Friary at Rye (East Sussex), the gift of a local merchant, William Marsh, was just over ten years old.[155]

The roofs of churches that were the shared place of worship of a monastery and their neighbouring parish could not straightforwardly be said to be part and parcel of the monastery alone. Bridlington Priory church was reportedly 'all covered with lead', but 'the better part of it perteineth to the parochians', who were quick to press their particular case with the commissioners: 'it wyll pleasethe parysshe better to have the part that the prior and convent had'.[156] Generally, the locality could not remain onlookers as the Crown circled the largest supply of a valuable commodity ever seen within their horizons. At Newcastle-under-Lyme (Staffordshire) it seems there was soon deadlock over the lead of the Dominican friary. The Bishop of Coventry and Lichfield urged its immediate removal, to be sold to settle the debts of the friars, an obligation which he was anxious to avoid himself; Henry Broke, the king's commissioner, and also a local man, held the house in his custody and kept the roof in place, clearly hoping that an extended delay might see the grant of the lead come his way.[157]

It is also possible that by 1539 the caution about removing lead had been reinforced by recent experience. Where the recovery of some quantities of lead was underway, it had stumbled under a host of practical problems. Recasting the lead consumed large quantities of timber which was not always readily available on site, at least not without the complete demolition of the standing buildings that was itself costly and time-consuming. Without recasting, carriage was impossible; and with it, it was still costly and timebound. The dispatch of 'pigs' down the coast from the Suffolk friaries was delayed for want of ships and standing on the quayside it was looted: 'all thys lythe ner ye water mete to be caryd to London', it was reported, but 'such as lay in dyspayer and parte was gone', despite 'such ys in slabbys and markyd with a crowne for yet king and indenturs of the same'. No one in provincial England was cowed by the stamp of royal authority on raw materials.[158] Where it had begun to be pared back it was an invitation to thieves. Word from Lincoln was that the commissioner 'want v or vi pounds towards 'chargys of myltyng and carage of led yf I had taryd v days lyngar they had ryn to other costys and the king had lost all thys as he is lyk to do of the rest'.[159] From Bridlington, the contractor said he was 'doyn nothing there as yet', but 'sparethe itt to March, bycause the days are now so short'; the decision to build a quay may have added to the delay.[160] In regions away from the transport routes of south-east England, it seems the market was uncertain. At Merevale Abbey, there was no buyer to be found for £32 of lead; in the West Midlands lead still lay at eight houses as late as 1553.[161]

The summary reports should surely be read as they appear, that lead was lifted, to allow for an accurate estimate of quantity and value. These documents are not routinely dated, however, and given the vocal expressions of doubt and dispute coming from the sites it may be that very little was done very quickly or systematically. It is also possible that the figures from the returns represented only a portion of the full complement of lead to be found at a given site. Some do seem to have been visual estimates. At Blackborough, the report was nineteen fother of lead 'at lys [at least]'.[162] At Abingdon it appears the first assessment offered by Chancellor Rich referred only to the conventual buildings, because, in his own mind at least, the church itself was destined to stand. Here it does seem that only a sample of lead had been lifted, to diagnose the condition of the full load. 'Waryn thyn' was the verdict, so perhaps nothing more was taken for a time.[163] Excavations have revealed evidence of lead melting and ingot casting at monastic sites large (Rievaulx, Kenilworth) and small (Ixworth), and at several of the small-town friaries (Haverfordwest, Northampton), but rarely have they provided firm evidence for a timeframe. It may be telling that a 2012 dig at Thorney Abbey uncovered a smelting hearth cut through layers of deposits clearly post-dating the dissolution period itself.[164]

Generally, the earliest instances of the comprehensive recovery and removal of lead occurred where the principal buildings of the precinct had been granted to a new proprietor at the point of suppression. Edward Stanley, Lord Derby, began to take down the lead from Burscough Priory less than a month after the departure of the canons. The situation reported from Bardney Abbey may have been typical: 'the bells lede and superflose byldyngs . . . hathe stoud hole thys xii monthys and the fennys butts one yt; the lede ys letyllysee [at the least] werthe a thousand mark'.[165] The first sight of the dissolution was not unroofed religious houses, although its first sound may have been of constant discussion as to their condition, value and future ownership.

It is the terms of the grants of churches and convents made by the Crown that offer further proof that typically the lead remained in place long after the house was emptied. Sir Arthur Darcy was granted the 'goodes praysed at Sawlaye', both the paraphernalia of the church, 'vestymentes and copes', and the bells and lead, in May 1538, more than a year after the abbey had been taken into the king's hands.[166] It was almost eighteen months after the execution of Abbot Adam Sedbar at Tyburn that there was any move to recover the lead from Jervaulx Abbey, and even then Cromwell's contractor wanted to wait for another season because 'the ways . . . are so foul and deep that no caryage can pass in wyntre'; in the event the lead was taken down from the buildings but not fetched from the site. It was finally removed, for repairs at York Minster, four centuries later in 1923.[167]

Of course, there were conspicuous advantages, on both sides of the ledger, to the Crown making grants inclusive of the lead: the sustained losses to theft, the costs of carriage and the contingencies of onward sales could be avoided. To offset the inherent deterrent to prospective grantees, the conditions set for the use of the lead gave some allowance of time. Sir Henry Long, granted Bradenstoke in August 1539, was required to 'rase' the church there by Michaelmas 1540 but the materials, the lead among them, might be removed piecemeal, within a maximum term of seven years.[168]

As many grants were made with the right to the lead reserved for the Crown. These had the general effect of slowing the stripping of the site, and sometimes of stopping it short of structural demolition. By contrast to the conditions set for grantees, the claim of the Crown was open-ended, defined by the timeless 'pleasure' of the king. A Winchester gentleman, William Lambert, charged with the custody of the lead at Nunnaminster, understood that the whole would remain simply 'until such time as he is discharged of this duty'.[169] For as long as the lead was claimed by the Crown, the church and principal conventual buildings could only stand, hollow, but still roofed. The reservation of lead gave the Crown a paper fortune with each grant made under these terms. In a letter to Cromwell in May 1539, John Freeman shared his assessment of the market advantage: if sales began without delay by his estimation there were four years of 'goodlye payment', perhaps £20 per fother. If the stock was withheld from the market over the same time then the value might fall to 20 nobles (£6 13s 4d). Freeman added, clearance of the stock 'wold qwyken ... agene ... the myndes of his leade'.[170]

Cromwell may not have accepted Freeman's analysis and at any rate as he entered this final year of closures there were conspicuous obstacles in the way of such a clearance sale. For lead stock to be left in situ was hardly adequate custody of a Crown asset. Looting continued, and the scope of the reservation was repeatedly challenged, both by opportunistic individuals and by local authorities impatient for their own infrastructure. A decade after the last of the closures, the Court of Augmentations commanded civic officials to account for the lead removed from the churches within their limits.[171]

In 1556 one Edward Pryn, executor of Nicholas Thorn, former master of customs at Bristol, wrote despairingly of the demands to account for lead that had been left in Thorn's custody at the time of the suppressions. 'Be I not bordened for that I have never had neither can come to the knowledge therof, as god knoweth', he begged, having 'travailled to come to the knowledge therof.'[172] At the time of his writing, Thorn had been dead for ten years. The slow dispersal does not appear to have stimulated market value as has sometimes been suggested. Above all, the accounts of Augmentations bear witness not to steadily climbing values but stock that was 'regarding superfluous'.[173] The 3,000 fothers prised from St Mary's Abbey, York, did not find a buyer until the end of 1550, and then this individual, a factor for the Vivaldi, appropriately named Senor Salvago, would only take three-quarters of the whole.[174] Scudamore's notebooks show stock piled high at Bristol.[175]

Due to the patchy preservation of inventories, to offset the unreliable rhetoric of dispatches to Cromwell, it is difficult to arrive at an estimate for the total cash gain to the Crown at the moment of these dissolutions. Raphael Holinshed recorded that the 'moveables' from the £200 houses alone raised £100,000 for the king.[176] There was obvious variation in the value of contents although even at smaller monasteries and friaries it may have reached as much as £200. Not every inventory is valued, which may say something about the status of the inventory but it may also signal that valuation and sale was never completed. Only a handful of surviving inventories record not only values but also sales made. The day sales made only modest sums. At Sawtry Abbey no more than £115 5s 5d was raised from the sale of the contents.[177] At any rate, much of the cash that came into the hands of the commissioners was spent again to meet the cost of rewards (for the professed) and wages (for employees). What was certainly sent to Cromwell at Austin Friars was not necessarily what readily represented a cash gain, but objects of interest and presumed value. A cabinet of curiosities would not pay for the king's wars.

At the time of the closures, and in the aftermath, as much of the talk and the action was not of demolition and destruction but of conversion and continued use. It does seem that the first thoughts both in government and beyond it, among patrons, civic authorities and parish communities, were of the new purposes the precincts might serve. The lawyer Richard Rich turned surveyor for two days when he went down to Abingdon and excitedly appraised the abbey as a future palace for the king. Cromwell contemplated palaces of his own. 'Myselff for Launde,' he affirmed in his remembrances.[178] 'Those that be gaye', recalled a doggerel, took 'these howses of pompe.'[179] Whether the thought was his own response to the prospect of the twelve-acre precinct at Glastonbury, or it had been primed by Cromwell, Richard Leighton conjured the image of a palace, 'great goodly and so pryncely as we have not sene the lyke with iiiior parks adjoynyng'.[180] It was not only the new materials in evidence in conventual buildings but their very configuration, for domestic living in some style, that caught the creative imagination of ambitious men and women.

Many of the earliest to move for the grant of a suppressed monastery carried with them a plan for their conversion that was already well advanced. Here the king and the vicegerent led by example. The scheme for the recasting of St Augustine's Abbey, Canterbury, into a royal palace, was started on site as the closure of the monastery was taking effect. There were as many as 300 labourers on site by October 1539, working day and night down to 21 December; they needed 372 extra candles to see them through their night shifts, with braziers kept alight to speed-dry the new plaster. The residence was required to receive the new queen, Anne of Cleves. Cromwell's agents surveyed Launde Priory in preparation for the raising of his mansion house before the resident community had left the premises.[181]

The earliest visible interventions in the fabric of the religious houses were reconstructions. Stavordale Priory was occupied as a gentleman's residence before the end of 1536.[182] Thomas Wriothesley's contractors at Titchfield pressed ahead at remarkable speed during the winter of 1537–38, turning the refectory into a great hall; he had already 'laydyn sarteyne stonne' there.[183]

These early conversions did not abruptly or brutally strip the structures of their monastic or mendicant character. The neighbourhood would have been first struck not by the truncating, or the taking-down, of the familiar ranges and roof lines, but by the new outlines that now jostled with them. At Amesbury, a new house was arranged around the church and convent of the nuns. The mansion raised by Sir William Paulet at Netley (Hampshire) stood only feet apart from the monastery and in time its living space literally absorbed the transepts of the church.[184] There was perhaps more activity early on at subsidiary buildings, hardly surprising given the sheer complexities of converting precincts, large and complex, which had accrued over several centuries. Thomas Savile lost no time in rebuilding the rectory house he secured at the suppression of Kirklees Priory. In a matter of months, new barge-boards carried his monogram and the date, 1540.[185]

Residential conversions remained more a matter of discussion than action for years after the closures came to an end. At many sites, there were significant structural constraints. Buildings that had developed episodically – often paused for decades on end – over several hundred years, had not made for easy living in their original institutional condition, and rarely could be directly translated into the nucleated household of a layman. The cloister range of a religious house positioned the spacious chambers – dormitory, refectory – on the first floor and the internal access, passage and doorways were wholly oriented towards a church standing at right angles to the whole. The structural and social alignment of the Tudor mansion could not be achieved except for near total reconstruction.[186]

The attempt at raising a mansion house at Sempringham (Lincolnshire) was made at the end of the century but then abandoned after about twenty years before completion.[187] At Titchfield, Sir Thomas Wriothesley retained the cloister but as an unnecessarily elaborate frame for his house's water conduit.[188] Other conversions were highly selective. At Spye Park (Wiltshire) and Hinchingbrooke (Cambridgeshire) just the gatehouses were of monastic origin, respectively from Stanley and Ramsey.[189] The churches of modest foundations may sometimes have offered an exception to the rule. Sir Richard Lee formed the hall of his new mansion house at Sopwell near St Albans from the nuns' church. The relatively short nave of the Carmelite friary at Hitchin made it a viable full-height hall for the Radcliffe family.[190]

The pleas of prospective grantees to Cromwell sound very loud in the letters that survive, yet as the closures continued equally there was mounting pressure to recognise the public need. Civic authorities addressed Cromwell directly on the poverty of their infrastructure for communal governance and the administration of justice. Watching the work of sequestration, and sometimes assisting it directly, at the same time they lobbied the commissioners, with some success. 'Admytt me a powr sutar for theis honest men of Redinge,' wrote John London in September 1538:

> They have a fayer town and many gudde occupiers in ytt butt they lack that howse necessary of the wich for the mynystration of iustice they have most need of. Ther town hall ys a very small howse and standith upon the river wher ys the commyn wassching place of the most part of the town and in the cession days and other court days ther ys such betyng with bateldores as oon man can nott here another … the body of the church of the grey fryers wich ys solyd with lath and lyme would be a very commodiose rowme for them.[191]

For the mayor and aldermen of Norwich it was a matter of defending the status quo: '[we] have accustomably used to mete in common counsell wythyn the church off the blak fryers'. Their separation of the fraternal community from the infrastructure was clearly expressed: '[it] stondeth in thee mydde parte of the said citie to the bewtifieng of the same'.[192] Civic interest in these central spaces was sustained and does seem to have acted as a check on complete demolition or redevelopment.

It was more than two years after the Franciscans had left Chichester that their whole precinct was confirmed in the possession of the mayor and aldermen of the city.[193] Petitions came forward to the end of Henry's reign. The mayoralty of Newcastle secured the Dominican convent six years after the friars had vacated it.[194] Conversions for public use continued to the end of Elizabeth's reign. By the turn of the century the town prison at Bridlington occupied the gatehouse of the old priory.[195] In 1596 the London actor-manager, James Burbage, purchased the upper refectory of the Blackfriars for use as a theatre; the plan was opposed, but on grounds of ungodly playing, not the proposition that the friary should be turned to public good.[196]

The social community thought as much of their spiritual needs. The closure of monastery and friary churches not only raised the prospect of new facilities but also revealed the shortcomings, and essential contingency, of their present circumstances. A significant number of closures challenged parish identity itself. Here, the church was a subdivision of the conventual church of monks, canons or nuns, the north or south side of the nave, or a contiguous chapel. These arrangements often originated in the distant past and as much as their communal identity the parishioners expressed a powerful sense of history. At Cartmel their share in the canons' church had been confirmed by its founder, William the Marshal, 400 years before.[197] Some churches may have been allowed continued use. The parochial chapel of St Andrew, on the north side of St Albans Abbey, stood in the precinct perhaps as late as 1551.[198] Others were quickly given clearance to take possession. The truncating of the priory church at Leominster began right away and the new east window may have been finished by 1540.[199]

But there were some parishes that were locked out of their place of worship and were left to look for its recovery. Down to the dissolution of the abbey the parishioners of Romsey held their services in the north aisle of the nave and its nearest transept; but then they were locked out for six years.[200] The church house built by the people of Weston to accommodate their priest was lost to them for twenty years, as the proprietors of the former Glastonbury Abbey manor assumed it was part of their domain.[201] It appears the people of Twynham were worshipping in the former church (Christchurch) of the canons only because the former prior himself had led the campaign for the right.[202] Their assimilation of the priory was played out over a century and a half; it was after the Restoration that they secured permission to make use of the old chapter house.[203]

For some, if not parishes, then at least their leadership, possession was a political act. At Binham the wardens were quick to paint over the saints of the chancel screen with passages of scripture taken from the 1539 King's Bible. However, the motive for most appears to have been practical continuity. At St Nicholas, Yarmouth (Norfolk), they were pleased to continue to worship as they had done before the commissioners arrived, and the grave slabs of the old priors were left where they lay. The parishioners of Kidwelly kept the alabaster statue of the Virgin Mary and the infant Jesus which had been the focus of intercessory prayers. It was not until 1865–70 that it was taken down and buried in the churchyard, from where it was swiftly recovered by popular demand.[204]

There were small and widely dispersed communities which had not benefited from the new church building witnessed in urban and suburban parishes in the generations after 1450. The sudden, visible vacancy of church buildings stirred some opportunism. The suppression of Titchfield Abbey stirred enterprising parishes from across the Downs. They came from East Meon and Overton (both Hampshire) to pick over the church and even its heaviest furnishings, 'marbles stones auters'. Excited, they 'promysed to retorne and bye'.[205] Bath's citizens recognised their opportunity in the priory church but were captive to caution 'that they might be thought to cosen the king if they bought it so cheape'; it was forty years before they committed to taking it on.[206] Even in the City of London, two parishes were combined into one to take possession of the Greyfriars church while a third, the parish of St Nicholas, was itself dissolved. Arguably, the availability of churches remade communities in Wales, as much in the English south (Chepstow, Kidwelly) as in the Welsh north-west (Cwmhir, Llanllugan).[207]

More parishes were prompted not to look for a new church but to complete their own. Perhaps the most remarkable refit was of the parish church of Morley (Derbyshire), which was embellished with glass, decorative stonework and tile from Dale Abbey, perhaps under the patronage of Sir Henry Sacheverell, possibly through his purchases from Sir Francis Pole, who had bought the fixtures from the Crown apparently as a commercial speculation.[208] Few parishes were favoured with such lavish patronage and most made only piecemeal and practical acquisitions: above all, a bell-peal. The parishioners of St James at Bury made use of the abbey's Norman gate tower for their bells.[209] A generous testator of All Hallows, Lombard Street (London), provided for the purchase of the full peal of bells from the priory of St John of Jerusalem, Clerkenwell, although his son was unwilling to extend the support to pay for the frame, John Stow recalled, and so just one bell was raised on it, 'as friars were wont to use'.[210] At Waltham, the parish claimed 'suche povertye that they be not able to bye one good bell'; bells from the abbey were bought by subscription: eighty-two people gave between 1d and 6s 8d, raising a total of £35, enough to pay carpenter Thomas for 'the trussyng [there]of'.[211] At Watford, the wardens called for a bell, claiming the king's ancestor and namesake, Henry II, had promised it to their forefathers nearly four centuries before.[212] Unless they were the legacy of ages past, bells were beyond the means of many. The parishioners of Stanley St Leonard (Gloucestershire) aimed just for their continued use of the two amenities of the tower of the former priory church, its bells and its clock.[213] Dorset parishioners at Combe Keynes, Fordington and Wool reputedly stole the bells from Bindon Abbey, an act commemorated in a rhyming couplet.[214] Those whose needs were met already thought more of aesthetics. The wardens of St Nicholas, Kenilworth, purchased a Norman stone doorway from the Augustinian priory still visible in their own south wall. A nearly new stained-glass Jesse Tree was carried from the Cistercian abbey at Basingwerk to the parish church of St Dyfnog, Llanrhaeadr (Powys). The quality of the abbey's interior decor was well understood, it would seem. The choir stalls were claimed by the city parish of St Mary-on-the-Hill, Chester.[215]

Parish outlooks were not only practical. There was an impulse to preserve, perhaps to honour, their monastic past. Some glass from Furness was recovered and set in the windows of the churches at Dalton and Urswick (all Cumbria); here perhaps the last abbot, Roger Pele, had a hand, since he held the vicarage of Dalton.[216] Memorials were moved: Abbot John Penny's alabaster, less than twenty years old, was taken into the parish church of St Mary, Leicester. This was the preservation of the men and women whom they had known. But sometimes there was an historical imagination at work. The parishioners of Cowfold (West Sussex) moved the tomb and brass of Prior Thomas Nelond of Lewes some thirty miles across the weald (see Fig. 26). Perhaps it was this impulse that led to an image of Christ being recovered for the bridge at Crowland. It is mistaken to see this as an act of opposition and resistance.[217] At Coventry, there was a battle over principle, perhaps in some unformed sense, to hold on to the status of a cathedral city, as 'principal see and head church'. It succeeded in so far as the church was left untouched to the end of Henry's reign; its two towers stood for a century after the closure.[218]

The earliest changes of use most clearly visible across the kingdom as a whole were neither residential, parochial nor public, but commercial and industrial. The infrastructure of the religious houses was commandeered to provide workspace for a very wide range of trades. In this respect, the buildings of the friaries were a particular draw because of their position, standing either inside the boundary of a city or town, often in a quarter close to one of the principal points of entry, or on the main road outside. In a number of towns, there had been a deliberate effort by the burgesses to connect the convent to the commercial centre, for the mutual reinforcement of their material and spiritual trade. Now, at the prospect of their final closure, it seems there was a powerful impulse to see that principle of civic benefit preserved. The scale of the church, refectory and dormitory of Dominican and Franciscan convents made them ideally suited to the storage of trade goods.

In the winter of 1544, scarcely six years after the surrender of the friars, the anonymous annal of the London Greyfriars witnessed the old church, as well as that of the Blackfriars, in use as a warehouse for (presumably salted) 'herrynge and other fiche' and wine tuns, 'tane on the see goynge into France that came from Anwarppe [Antwerp]'. 'All the church was fulle,' observed the annalist, 'in every place of it.'[219] At Coventry, the Franciscan precinct was made the principal store of materials for the repair of public buildings, including the city walls and gateways. Timber was dry-stored in the tower.[220] At Newcastle no fewer than twelve craft companies shared the Dominican church; at Bristol the Bakers' company, sitting tenants of the Dominicans' infirmary hall, put down their roots.[221]

These spaces were not only wide but also well built and from the outset they were seen as a potential shop floor. Less than eighteen months after it was emptied, the London printer, Richard Grafton, set up his press within the walls of the Greyfriars. There was irony, and no small poignancy, that his first print was a combined epistoler and gospeller for 'sondayes and festyvall holy dayes' which might have seen much use by the friars.[222] At the time of the surrender in the autumn of 1538, John London wrote from Oxford with the proposal to transform the Dominican precinct into a fulling mill for 'the water be convenient and commodiose ... to sett ... mills upon'.[223] The corn mill of the canons of Beauchief at Bradway (South Yorkshire) was converted to drive a cutler's grinding wheel.[224] At Lincoln, the vacant church of the Franciscans was taken in hand by the city to serve as a shop for wool spinning and knitting where the able-bodied poor might be productively employed.[225] As early as March 1540, Sir George Lawson was planning a 'great garner [granary]' at York's Augustinian friary, so as to begin the production of malt.[226]

Only the largest monasteries could match the nave-space of friary churches but there was often a larger cluster of working buildings already standing in their precincts. The warming-room at Robertsbridge was turned over to the oast, to dry hops.[227] Space on the west side of the cloister and beyond at Holy Trinity, Aldgate, served as the workshop of the London mason, William Kerwin, well into the reign of Elizabeth.[228] By that time, the buildings were also occupied by a dealer in delftware. William Stumpe, clothier of Malmesbury, took the old conventual buildings of the Benedictine monastery for his weaving shop. John Leland saw 'at this present tyme every corner of the vaste houses of office that belongid to thabbay be fulle of lumbs [looms] to weve clooth yn'.[229]

Outside cities and towns, the wide precincts of monasteries in rural regions had seen some industrial production before their closure. Here there were purpose-built workspaces, some of which may have seen very little hiatus at all. The tannery shop at Rievaulx fell silent when the surrender was made in early December 1538, but in a matter of months it was in the hands of a local iron entrepreneur, who transformed it into a furnace and foundry.[230]

In general, the physical presence of the religious houses endured. The change in local horizons was slow enough in some locations that it seems barely to have registered even in living memory. When Sir John Oglander came into his inheritance at Quarr in 1607, he met men who remembered it but not 'whoe pulled [it] downe'.[231] In the seven years between the final surrender and the death of King Henry the greater part of the regulars' infrastructure, churches, conventual buildings, workshops, gatehouses and precinct walls remained in place. It seems there was little difference in the pace of change between those houses retained in the king's hand and those subject to early grants.

Grantees who set off straight away in pursuit of grand plans were exceptional. Some retained the site but did nothing for years after. Thomas Cranmer kept West Malling Abbey in his hands for twenty years and went to the stake with the site still mothballed. Even the roof of the church was not removed until the property passed to his brother-in-law.[232] The reservations under the terms of their grants sometimes constrained comprehensive redevelopment. Although the demolition of Stanley Abbey had begun weeks after its suppression, it stalled and in 1565 the church was still standing; the north transept and its adjoining vestry had simply been turned over to other uses.[233] At Waltham, Anthony Denny was forced to wait for five years before he was awarded the right-in-fee to raise a mansion of his own.[234] Many more held their religious house as an asset temporarily and then traded it on.

Even the beneficiaries of grants for the salvage of stone, timber and metals did not snatch their reward but mined it slowly. Sir Richard Gresham took lead from Fountains Abbey over a period of five years up to 1544; the same, judicious retrieval of raw material was managed at Rievaulx by the new proprietor, Thomas Manners, 1st earl of Rutland, 'althynges fastened and . . . not rehersed . . . to remain fastened styll'.[235]

Several of the city convents of the friars, and a higher number of those in provincial towns, were held by the Crown to the last years of Henry's reign before they were first granted. They may have suffered some dilapidation in almost a decade of custody but the terms of the grant indicate that they had not been demolished. It is tempting to think that new proprietors were defeated by the practical challenges. It is also striking how many sites that have been excavated have revealed bodies beneath fallen masonry.[236]

Even under the gaze of the reformed metropolis, the steeples of the London friaries stood for almost as long as the king himself lived. The keeper of the Greyfriars chronicle noted the loss of the Carmelite church and the pinnacle of the Dominicans in the same year that Henry lost his flagship *Mary Rose* (1545).[237] Many neighbourhoods knew their houses to be empty of their former communities but in all other respects remarkably complete. The monastic or mendicant shapes in the landscape may have looked more unkempt than in the past but they endured. The kitchen fishponds at Garendon (Leicestershire) were so unchanged that when a mansion was built there nearly a century later, they were kept as ornamental ponds for the garden.[238]

As a three-year-old, Michael Sherbrook said he remembered seeing the bell still swinging in the tower of Roche Abbey. John Leland saw a panel painting at Flaxley 'hanggid up in the abbey church'. He was still able to admire the portraits of bishops in the chapter house at Sherborne.[239] The stained glass in the empty abbey church at Reading was untouched ten years after its closure and raised £6 13s 4d when it was sold.[240] A sketch of the skyline at Shaftesbury made in 1553 shows the tower of the abbey standing still.[241] With no one there to wind it, the clock at Rievaulx had stopped, but since the 'deskes' (i.e. benches) of the refectory were also in place, it seemed as if the monks were only away on an afternoon's recreation.[242] The ferryboat remained tied up in the boathouse at Birkenhead Priory as if the service the monks had supervised for four and a half centuries was only temporarily suspended.[243] Inventory lists of church and household furnishings removed for sale divert attention from the conventual chambers and contents that for a certain time at least may have been left as they were. There were thirteen celebrants' suits still in the Lady chapel of Milton Abbey when an inventory was compiled in 1549.[244]

It does seem that some libraries were not dispersed. There can be little doubt that books remained in the presses at St Augustine's Abbey, Canterbury, beyond the death of King Henry, where John Twyne, former schoolmaster at the house, was able to consult them.[245] There may have been continuity at the Oxford college of the monks of Durham Cathedral Priory. As many as eight of the former monks returned there after their surrender.[246] When Bishop Longland died in 1547, he bequeathed a set of law books there, naming it still as Durham College.[247]

At Syon Abbey the strangest possession of all was still unclaimed in the reign of Elizabeth: the corpse of King James IV of Scotland, vanquished at the Battle of Flodden a quarter-century before the closure of the convent, but still recognisably Celtic to John Stow who remembered his red beard. Syon acquired a peculiar, purposeful emptiness. In the winter of 1541 it was made the last lonely home of Queen Catherine Howard before her execution the following February. Later her royal husband's body was placed in vigil there in April 1547.[248]

The lack of speedy conversion or systematic demolition left infrastructure of religious houses to stand as a scarred and hollow backscene to the continuing reformation drama. The people of Arundel, Lichfield, Warwick and Winchelsea looked out on the preaching churches of the friars as late, perhaps, as the early 1550s, the last years of Edward VI. Cloisters, anomalous and, presumably, inaccessible, were still standing in the old mendicant quarters of the cities – Chichester, for example – and the smaller towns – Sherborne – until after King Henry's death. This strange limbo of imposing buildings became the subject of comment. Arriving in London in 1554, Venice's ambassador remarked how the city appeared 'greatly disfigure[d]'.[249] The view from the provinces was much the same. Looking out from his Kentish home, William Lambarde lamented 'places tumbled headlong to ruine and decay' and a 'general desolation, not only in this shyre but in all other places of the realme'.[250]

The first, visible and most meaningful effects of the Crown's policy for the religious houses concerned their material. This was apparent as much as a year before the first of the statutory suppressions, when visitors, reaching beyond the terms of their writ, confiscated treasured artefacts treated locally as relics, and, occasionally, books from their libraries. Royal rule of the neighbourhood priory touched residents of the north-west quarter of Exeter, at the moment when the Crown's commissioners thought to remove the ancient crucifix in the church where residents were accustomed to make their oblations.[251]

When the closures came, from the early summer of 1536, the conspicuous consequence as much for the resident community as for those looking on was the change in the site, the standing buildings and all they contained. The visual presence of the religious house, monastery and friary had defined its legend on local horizons and even the slightest change might have left its mark. It is clear that closure itself, the shutting-up of precincts that had never been completely closed at any point in their history, challenged the neighbourhood, causing many – perhaps for some as a matter of principle – to force their way in. The clearance of contents of a variety, if not a scale, unrivalled in any locality, could scarcely fail to capture attention. Regulars reached out for something of the fabric of their lives before they thought of their status and occupation. It was not that the trappings of the religious orders were now passed on to the society that supported them; often they were shared among those who knew them best.

Some did experience the sudden shock of demolition weeks, or even days, after the living community had been dispersed. The deliberate despoiling of churches was not uncommon, it seems, especially in cities and towns where there was a concentration of houses, those of the friars proving perhaps the most vulnerable in the aftermath of suppression given their prominence on the skyline, their structure making partial removal practically possible, and the slighter attachment of patrons lessening the political risks. Total destruction was rare. In an urban environment it was hardly seen at all: what disturbed the citizens of Coventry, Leicester or Lincoln was the spectacle of such substantial building stock left in limbo, neither standing whole, nor falling. Yet the few sites – Merton, Lewes – that were cleared completely before the eyes of those who had witnessed their closure conveyed an unequivocal meaning: dissolution was the seizure of material wherewithal for the purposes of the king and his principal ministers.

The Henrician regime succeeded in emptying the religious houses but not effacing them. When the old king died in January 1547, he left a monastic and mendicant landscape which in its principal features was for the most part unaltered from the scene he had stepped into thirty-eight years before. This is not to claim that certain buildings had not been taken down. But they were the smallest fraction of the whole, and in most of the major centres of population, the essential ensemble, the placement of conventual buildings within a wider residential, commercial and industrial setting was little changed. In outline they still appeared as the cornerstones of their neighbourhood just as they were known before the royal supremacy. The distinctive domestic spaces of the cathedrals' old monasteries did not begin to disappear from their city's roofscape until the third decade of Elizabeth's reign.[252] Reassimilation and recycling unfolded so slowly that it was surely imperceptible to the passer-by. The abiding impression would not have been of savage ruin but strange abandonment. John Leland observed how Henry Bourchier's efforts at Markyate (Hertfordshire) 'did much coste in translating of the priory into a maner place but nothing endid'.[253]

IX

CHANGES OF HABIT

At the turn of 1540, when fewer than twenty religious houses remained in England, Thomas Goldwell, prior of the premier monastery of Christ Church, Canterbury, was moved, above all, to address Thomas Cromwell on the matter of their habits:

> Ther is a comen spekyng here abowte as that religiouse men shall leve or forsake their abitt or go as secular prists doo. Whether they mynde of some certen religion or of all I knowe nott as conserving this mater ... ye have sent me word before this tyme that I and my bretherun shuld nott be constrained so to doo. And as for my part I will never desire to forsake my abit as long as I lyve for dyvers consideracions that movyth me to the same. One is because religious men have ben and continued in this oure cherche this ix hundred yeres and more. Also I made my profession to serve god in a religious abiit as moche as lay in me to so to do. Also yf we that be religious men do forsake ower abitts and go abowte the worle we shall have meny moo occasions to offend god and to comytt synne than we have nowe.[1]

After the legal extinction of the corporate body, the re-clothing of the professed members of the religious community was the primary responsibility of the king's

421

commissioners. They were to ensure that each religious cast aside their old habits before they were turned out of the precinct. It was the principal reason for their payment of cash 'rewards', that appropriate secular apparel might be purchased, if it could not otherwise be found. Then their re-entry into the world might begin at the gatehouse. Also, there could then be no doubt of their standing as loyal subjects of the Crown: the loss of their habits was as much an expression of their personal acceptance of the *ecclesia Anglica* as the submission they had all made in 1534. The coerced change of clothes became a visual shorthand for the cultural transformation brought about by the policy of the Crown. 'Al freres, monkes, chanons and non chaunged their new-founde garments and so came home again to their mother church', narrated the new edition of Robert Fabyan's chronicle, printed in 1542.[2]

Resentment of the religious orders is thought to have been provoked above all by their displays of wealth, in their buildings and their domestic comforts. But there was also a rising tide of anger over their clothing. Perhaps the politics of Henry's reign, which saw the conventional understanding of rank and authority repeatedly challenged by the comings and goings at court – not least of the sons of an Ipswich butcher (Wolsey) and a Putney blacksmith (Cromwell) – cast a new light on the traditional markers of their congregations. In the first half of the century, the differences of dress across the social order were not as strictly defined or regulated as they came to be by the end of Elizabeth's reign.[3]

The Reformation Parliament (1529–36) had attempted a 'reformacyon of excesse apparrell' under statute (1533), but within a decade it was acknowledged to be a dead letter.[4] The secular clergy, in particular, were more readily identified by the services they performed than the clothes they wore. In this landscape, the dress of professed men and women left them standing apart. It seemed to signal not only that their life was different from their neighbours but also their interest: 'theyr dysguysed cotes', in Taverner's 1536 translation of Erasmus, 'wher by they be chefely knowen from the temporall'.[5]

For Richard Morison, writing in the same year, monastic dress was nothing less than the sign of their deception of the world: 'these holy hooded religious . . . need none to accuse them, except they change their apparayle'.[6] 'Dowst thu not se how I in my colours jette,' confided Dyssymulacyon in John Bale's *Kynge Johan*, performed before Henry VIII as early as 1538, '[I] blynde the people' and 'have yet further fette'.[7]

As the Crown's new governance of their lives extended, the clothes of religious came to be fixed on as visible proof of the challenge they presented. When two Observant friars, wanted for the rejection of the royal supremacy, were chased into Wales in 1534, the greatest alarm was raised when it was said they had 'caste off ther clothys' and 'yn secular rayment' were invisible to passers-by.[8] From their encounter with Abbot William Thornton of St Mary's York, the lasting impression of the king's visitors was of his silk-lined, velvet hood.[9]

Those on the inside of the enclosure with a taste for reform now turned on the traditions of their dress. Contempt for their coat acted almost as a password to open a personal correspondence with Cromwell. 'Off truth my lord, I putt no confydens in my koote,' confided Thomas Chapman, warden of the London Franciscans, 'neyther in the coolor nor ffacyon'.[10] 'That clokyd abytt,' spat Robert Myllys, monk of Winchester, in his missive, 'the monkys cote [is no] more holyer then the cortyers cot [just as] the brod croune and the scot dockyng more then cumly here [hair].'[11]

The case for a religious 'reformacyon of apparel' found expression in the formalities of surrender, no doubt under the influence of the talk on both sides of the precinct wall. 'Weryng of a grey black whytt ... cloke frokke or cowle', ran the statement signed by the Reading Franciscans, is 'peculiar', an 'inverntyon ioff mens wytt' and removed from 'unyforme laudable and conformable maner of lyving off all other christen men'.[12]

But the marks of profession were not easily shed, voluntarily, or by force of parliamentary statute. Prior Goldwell's scruples were not the principled preserve of the superior of England's pre-eminent church. Right across the country the commissioners found regulars readier to agree to the suppression or surrender of their collective selves, their *conventus*, than their own, visible identity as professed religious. William Burraby, the former monk of Louth caught up in the rising of October 1536, had already received his faculty for secularisation two weeks before the trouble but was still wearing his monk's scapular.[13] Even after the defeat and dispersal of the rebel bands, the awful sight of the Crown's capacity to repress, and their own submission to the commissioners' suppression of their house, in February 1538 the remaining canons of Lanercost (Cumbria) '[did] confeder and flok to gither there in their chanons cots very unsemely'.[14] In the spring of the same year, Richard Ingworth petitioned Cromwell for the speedy dispatch of faculties for secularisation, pressed by convents surrendered but whose religious were still clothed as friars, 'I praye yow ... yt ye warantts for ther [secular] habetts may be had ... for they may not be suffereyd'.[15] Warden Chapman had claimed that Charles Wriothesley recalled the sight in the City of London of dismissed friars still wearing the clothing of their original profession: '[they] goe abroade in theyr religious habyts ... such other as used to live of the charitie of the people'.[16] It provoked a preventative measure, at least in the capital.

In the summer of 1538 the order was put out for former regulars to remove habits or face the capital punishment of felons. Anecdotally, Cromwell met Alexander Barclay – formerly a monk, now a friar – at a bookstall by St Paul's and told him that if he did not take off his habit he would be hanged, 'for example to all other'.[17] Beyond London and the vicegerent's gaze, it proved more difficult to prevent. Sir Piers Edgcumbe caught up with two Plymouth Franciscans still clothed as friars. 'Wolde [they] by them new hobyts or naye?', he challenged them. 'They bowthe sayed that they wolde not for a yere or tow and by that tyme perchance ther wylbe aouther change and then oure olde hobyts wyll serve agayne.' One Sir Robert Elys, resolutely uncooperative, was 'carried hym to the joyell [gaol]', declaring, 'he trustyd within tow yeris he mought weer his clothyng agayne ... [and] that he had red in a pronunsticacion that ther shulde be a kyng in yglond that shulde do gret wrong to his comynaltie to ther semyng and that within tow yeris after he shulde take gret repentance for the same.'[18]

Like the matter of their habits, the transformation of the men and women of the religious houses did not follow as readily as was hoped by the Tudor regime. From the first months of 1536 to the Easter of 1540 as many as 10,000 professed religious in England and Wales saw their settled pattern of life suddenly interrupted.[19] Much of the daily routine of the life they had known within the precinct of their houses was rapidly dismantled, in a matter of days, certainly, for some perhaps in no more than a few hours. The most conspicuous change was the end of their monastic and mendicant rituals. Each community, of every congregation, experienced a final, communal performance in the choir of their church, although the uncertainties over the movements of the commissioners and their own membership meant they may not have known it to be their last at the time.

Monastic communities also witnessed an ultimate corporate act in their chapter house when either they received the patent for suppression under statute or they enacted their own surrender. These were moments in time as much for a great old abbey or cathedral priory as for a sparsely populated friary in a provincial town. The notary's paper records of their submission made their way to the Court of Augmentations where they were bound together. They capture something of the action of the moment as each man signed his own name, some showing that they were used to pen work and proud of their skill, some seemingly unfamiliar with such a mundane skill. Monastic men and women saw an end to other occupations that had defined their day: the administrative work which they had led, or assisted, in one or other departments of the house, or the practical care they had taken of church, chapel or the unprofessed men, women and children who had lived with them.

Yet there were as many features of their monastic life that saw no sudden shift. Their habits were the slightest trace of their old life that lingered on. In the immediate aftermath of the institution's end many of the men may have been occupied much as they were before. Some heads of house secured permission to remain in their suite of chambers. A number of those who were priests continued to officiate at the same parish altars they had already served under the authority of their monastery. Students returned to the universities. Those lacking any such status or defined study often stayed within a narrow radius of their former house, sometimes together, recreating a communal life in a residential, suburban setting. If Henry VIII had in mind the instant creation of new subjects of the Tudor Crown, no different from their neighbours and all under the sole authority of his supremacy, he was to be disappointed. The machinery of monasticism had been silenced but its workforce remained standing, recognisable still. Change also washed over the other populations of the monastic world, those inside the gate, employees, pensioners, family and the dependent poor, and those tenants whose lives were tied to their outlying territory. When the saleable contents and treasures were gone and the sites placed in secure custody, on the skyline and at ground level, the face of the neighbourhood looked much the same. The anticipation of some dramatic disturbance remained in the air and there were as many in wider society who shared the 'pronunsticacions' of the former friar, Sir Robert. In fact, what was most noticeable after all the religious houses were emptied was a scene that seemed to be very much the same.

In the few first-hand accounts that survive, the human experience is largely obscured. The commissioners reported on the condition of the buildings more often than on their residents. What they did write was brief and business-like. The professed populations were confirmed as 'dispersyd', 'dischargyd' or 'put forth'.

Interestingly, there was rarely any of the aggression which animated their dispatches about the churches and their altars. These attracted the language of punishment. Their people did not. It was only those who joined the risings of 1536–37 that were 'put down'.

In a rare moment when the correspondence captures the scene it is one of mutual respect and ready compliance. 'With moche quyetnes and contentacion of the cuntrey,' wrote Thomas Legh from Holm, 'the monckes in secular apparell having honest regardis in their purses be disparsyd a brode and . . . be so ordferyd that they thincke them self in better case then ever they war'. 'They weras they . . . war ever more bounded . . . to pray for the kings hinges maigestye and your lordshiups honour . . . they have now more cause then ever they had.'[20] Social memory soon painted over this impression of peaceable acceptance. 'Toren and rent . . . by violence' was the recollection of a popular verse of the middle years of the century, 'the[e] furneshe with ragges'.[21] By the reign of Elizabeth, amid a rising tide of Reformation narrative, recent history was recalled as melodrama. 'It would have made an heart of flint to have melted and weeped to have seen the breaking up of the houses,' declared Michael Sherbrook, fifty years after the event, 'that they could this day . . . be the House of God and the next day the House of the Devil'.[22]

The closure of each religious house disturbed the lives of its residents and those who depended on it for their livelihood, but it did not destroy them. For most there was no single moment of sudden drama but a performance that unfolded over days and weeks and for some even months. In the first weeks of the enforcement of the 1536 statute the commissioners beginning the circuit through the northern counties put houses under notice of closure and then moved on again leaving them to their own devices for weeks or months on end. The six women of Nunburnholme first confronted the king's men on 22 May but then continued their routine for another eleven weeks before they saw them again.[23] Nor was there any personal peril except for the handful who consciously challenged the regime, or were suspected of doing so. The majority suffered only from the attrition of an enterprise that rarely found clarity or consensus in its aims and met practical challenges at almost every turn.

It would be wrong, at any rate, to think of suppression, in 1536–37, or surrender thereafter, as causing a wrench in communities that had lived up until then as a complete and cohesive whole. By the spring of 1536 there were many monasteries and friaries that had experienced major upheavals for upwards of two years.

Some twenty-six houses, a cross section of monasteries, cathedral priories, 'great and solemn' abbeys and nunneries, had been subject to the sudden substitution of their superior as a result of the interference of the royal regime.[24] Since the beginning of 1534, the Franciscans had witnessed no fewer than seven re-foundations as the Observant houses were assimilated into the Conventual congregation. In the year of visitation, 1535–36, communities of all kinds saw their stability shaken. At Sawtry Abbey, Thomas Legh claimed to have 'given libertie to halfe the house'.[25]

It was not only the youngsters who left; well-established religious had also reached out for the opportunities apparent outside. Two canons of Buckenham had abandoned the monastic routine but remained on site. One of them tended to the organs but the other was unoccupied.[26] Prior Thomas Mundy of Bodmin 'restrayned' one of his brethren fearing an 'yl example to others', but at Bury St Edmunds some of the professed did abscond.[27] Less than twelve months later the reverse happened as men and women displaced from suppressed houses were sent to or searched for another house so as to continue to live under vows. There can be no doubt that the scale and speed of the new admissions seen in 1536–37 were unlike anything in living memory. The new arrivals may have also caused further disruption. This may explain why there appear to have been more canons and monks outside the precinct, in parishes and 'about the ministration of the gospel'.[28]

Perhaps the sudden influx was the prompt for the increase in the number of students' houses supported at the universities from 1536. In the winter of 1538–39 the commoners at St Bernard's, the Cistercian College at Oxford, included monks from each one of their remaining houses.[29] The following winter, the last of monastic England, at the Benedictine Gloucester College, Oxford, there were still four monks each from Evesham and Gloucester abbeys.[30] On 18 November 1539 two student monks of Ely made the sixteen-mile journey from the university at Cambridge to the cathedral to sign the convent's deed of surrender.[31]

Ironically, the most immediate disturbance of the dissolution may have been that it compelled men and women to come together as a corporate body in a manner they had not experienced for many months. For those monastic and mendicant men already following an independent life at a college or in a parish it was perhaps an unwelcome reminder of their original profession. Robert Southwell seems to have had this in mind when he wrote to Cromwell about John Sarisbury,

427

nominally prior of Horsham St Faith, but since his appointment as a suffragan bishop out of touch with the life of his house and lacking 'neyther place whereunto to make certain repaire nor lyvyng ... to maynteyn hym'.[32] For those of both sexes who only months before had moved in from a suppressed house it required the expression of an identity they had hardly had time to grasp. Thomas Alban was one of the final four signatories of the surrender deed at St Albans Abbey; he had been a priest for less than eighteen months.[33]

The commissioners arrived thinking of the community in quite different terms. The visitations of the previous year, with their ever-lengthening schedules of inquiry and sheafs of comperts, gave them a confidence that there could be nothing more to be discovered about the people of the precinct. Rarely, it appears, did they consider the possibility that the comings and goings of 1535 would continue, or that the routine traffic of study, parish duty or administration might resume. In fact, the anxieties they spoke of as they approached a house to close it concerned the legal and material business of its sequestration. By contrast with the custody of the site, standing buildings and contents, the instructions that the commissioners carried with them for the treatment of the resident population were unequivocally clear: the professed religious were to be removed from the house, receiving a cash payment or 'reward', to meet their immediate needs, not the least some appropriate clothing to wear at the removal of their habit.

No draft or fair-copy guidance for the surrender of houses has been found, but apparently from the first of these in the winter of 1537–38 it seems there was a general understanding that each professed religious was now to receive not only a cash reward but also a pension to be drawn from the income of the founda-tion itself. References to the assignment of pensions first appear in Court of Augmentations records for houses surrendered in the early spring 1538.[34] The statute of 1539 confirmed that the liability for all such 'porcions and pensions' was, like the revenue of the house, vested in the Crown.[35]

But the principle was quite different in practice. Coin for the rewards was not always readily to hand. The first suppressions in the spring and early summer of 1536 were of foundations still following their routines to the very end. For them it seems there was a money supply just as much as there was an impressive store of food. Houses that continued after 1537, however, were drained of any remaining reserves and many of the valuables that might be converted into currency had already been sold, often by the religious themselves. Sir William Cavendish had tried to 'discharge' the monks of Bruern 'with suche money as [we] receyved', with an airy promise 'untill a nother tyme'; it failed to persuade them and they stayed put.[36]

The shortfall was felt acutely at the friaries, as the collapse of public donations had already caused them to sell almost anything that might be taken away. Richard Ingworth, their principal visitor, grew steadily agitated as his tour progressed. By the time he reached Sussex, Bishop Ingworth was determined only to 'put forth' the friars of Lewes, where he knew there was the wherewithal to provide for them.[37] There was more than a touch of congregational loyalty to his reluctance to force the friars to leave when there was nothing to give them. At first, he does seem to have reached into his own saddlebag, after which he pestered Cromwell for some recognition of his increased outgoings, for 'I schall have neyther money of my owne nor of the kynges money'.[38] By the end of the summer of 1538, it seems Ingworth preferred to alter the terms of the surrender at Lewes: the formalities of closure were followed and in all probability the friars signed their name on the surrender deed, but then the bishop allowed them to stay, leaving them with the vague hope that, between local sales of the remaining assets of their house and his own urgent dispatches to Austin Friars, something would be done for them: 'I schall kepe styll [for] I do them much good for they be not abull to leve.'[39] It seems very likely that surrendered friars were still to be found on site at Lewes early the following year.

Even where rewards were distributed without delay, the commissioners did not find it straightforward to see the regulars re-clothed and made ready for departure. Despite facing the threat of summary justice after the defeat of the Pilgrimage of Grace, it was reported that the monks of the suppressed abbey at Furness still milled about in the precinct dressed in their Cistercian habits.[40] Quite apart from the uncertain promise of their petty cash, monastic and mendicant men were wary of losing their regular identity as long as their future status as secular clergy remained unconfirmed. From the first enforcement of the 1536 statute, the commissioners understood that they were to determine which of these men intended to change their status to that of a secular clerk; this would allow them to serve a benefice if they were already ordained and if they were still only in minor orders (as any novice might be) to arrange for their ordination to the secular priesthood.

Such a conversion required recognition in canon law, conferred only by means of a faculty, that is a formal licence, granted by the presiding authority which, after the Break with Rome, was now the archbishop of Canterbury. The responsibility had been passed to Canterbury barely three years before, and the office charged with the administration of the faculties and its operation was not well established. It was further complicated by the matter of cost: the Faculty Office called for a fee of between £8 and £12.[41]

The commissioners were not told to meet the fee from the same petty cash they relied on for rewards and other immediate expenses, and generally they left the applicants to find it for themselves. That many applicants did so may be an indication of how far their departure was assisted by their personal networks outside the precinct. Yet there were also those who could not, or would not, find the means. John Barrett, a Carmelite, haggled with 'your good lordships', the commissioners, that the charge of £8 might be halved.[42] Whether his request was born of need or stubborn refusal, it merely added to the delay.

The men of the houses suppressed between Easter and Michaelmas 1536 who did not migrate elsewhere were left waiting for their faculties for weeks on end. Unsure what to do themselves, the commissioners at Berden Priory (Essex) encouraged two of the canons to set off for Canterbury to seek out Archbishop Cranmer himself. They sent their own dispatch appealing, 'they complain . . . fail ye not!'[43] A faculty was their licence to look for a clerical living and until they could hold it in their hand they would not stray very far from their former house.

The depositions of the canons and monks arrested for their involvement in the Lincolnshire rising in early October reveal that their communities, suppressed in September, had been left in suspended animation as they stayed within easy reach of one another waiting for the faculties that would not come.[44] William Burraby, who led some of them into the march, had been well placed to rally his troops as he had taken responsibility for the distribution of licences to his colleagues when they were delivered.[45]

The threat of agitation from these restive groups of men, and, after October 1536, the spectacle of armed protest, made no difference to the delays. As the closures continued the demand overwhelmed the capacity of the Faculty Office.[46] 'Master . . . make owt dispensations for these persones as shortly as ye maye conveniently,' urged Wriothesley from Billesden at the turn of the year.[47] When the five former monks of Birkenhead Priory finally received their licences in May 1537, almost a year had passed since they had submitted to the commissioners for the suppression.[48]

Another year on, and the closures of the friaries advancing in the summer and autumn of 1538 pushed the system to the point of collapse. Bishop Ingworth's response was to question the case for closure itself. 'I koulde by juste and fayer menys (and do no wronge) dyspache a great parte off ye fryers in Ynglonde or [the year] were endeyd,' he wrote to Cromwell, 'so yt I might have sum lyberte to lycens them to change ther habetts.'[49] His deliberate pausing of the dissolution naturally projected him into a head-on collision with Cromwell. The anger of the vicegerent's letter to Ingworth can be guessed from the bishop's reply: 'Ye juge ... I have changeyd my habet [but] ... not ... my fryar's hartt ... For god shall be my juge my fryers hart was gone ii yers befor my habet.' His defence was to avoid 'to moche ... praty besynes' ... 'ye favour yet I have schewyd is but to brynge all thyngs with ye most quiet to passe'.[50]

Their bruising exchange did not blunt the bishop's criticism. The following March, Ingworth was still complaining of the bottleneck, now noting the further difficulty that bishops, alarmed at the prospect of new secular priests passing into their diocese seeking benefices, now required each former religious to present documentary proof of their priesthood. Perhaps even Cromwell himself could have admired the bishop's ironic jibe that faculties issued from the king's grace 'with not so much favor' as they had once won from the bishop of Rome.[51]

A friar himself, Ingworth may have felt some responsibility for his former colleagues, but by 1538 less sympathetic commissioners were likewise reluctant to release the religious until their new status was confirmed. John London complained that as the wait went on, he was obliged to become the de facto warden of the ten Augustinian friars at Oxford, and 'ayt the chardge in fyndyng them mete and drink'.[52] His discomfort continued for seven weeks of high summer, from early July to the last day of August. The Carmelites, on the opposite side of the city, were left waiting in the same way; they were still there in September.[53]

The only shared experience of departure from the religious life for men and women may have been a nagging uncertainty as to when they would finally pass out of the gate for the last time. Perhaps those for whom there was always a clean break in their current occupation were the handful of foreigners, almost all of whom were to be found in the houses of the friars.[54] The commissioners were not disposed to test their jurisdiction over men whose entry into their orders had been made overseas; Bishop Ingworth did not detain the 'ii eryschemen' he found at Shrewsbury's Augustinian friary, returning them to what he called their 'owen cuntrey'.[55]

Women, without the prospect of any future occupation, may have left without delay. 'My lady and the other religious persons ... takith the matier very well,' advised Sir William Cavendish from Little Marlow Priory. The implication was that it was briskly done, Prioress Margaret Vernon acting 'lyke a wyse woman'.[56]

There were reports of religious trying to force the issue. Richard Leighton claimed that he could hardly contain the surrendered canons of Bisham who were so 'desierouse to be gone' that they took their re-clothing into their own hands and 'creyde a new marte in the cloister' every man 'bringyng his cowle ... to be solde'.[57] At Vale Royal Abbey the commissioner Thomas Holcroft lost control. It seems the abbot, John Harware, harried him to 'disspatche all the monks oute of the howse as hastely as I canne ... to lette never one tarre ... bot [himself]'. As soon as the house was empty, Harware held himself fast inside, declaring his intention to continue the monastic routine by which he 'shuld say masse'.[58] Holcroft's attempt at dissolution was suddenly halted.

No doubt for the avoidance of such a farce, the commissioners' common preference was to keep the community under their watch and to make their removal as gradual as the decommissioning of the house and its contents. For as long as he followed up suspicions of their covert grants of property, Richard Leighton would not disperse the prior and canons at Westacre. 'Kepyng both the head and body yet together,' he explained to Cromwell, was 'no moche to the kynges' charge'. He judged the prior himself to be a 'feble heade' and it would be only with the whole community that he would get to the bottom of what had gone on, 'diligent phesicians ... so well expert and accquaynted with ther diseassis [will] in shortte tym ... have cured theym cleane'.[59]

At Calwich Priory, Richard Strete 'left such as be husbands', by which he may have meant the obedientiaries bearing administrative responsibilities, and 'dischargyd such persons as were not mete to be there', perhaps the young and old conventual monks with nothing left to do.[60] Prior William Holeway of Bath appears to have been co-opted to assist the commissioners in their task, staying there for many weeks after the last of his monks had departed, and continuing to make entries in his register. A grant of the valuable manor of Weston (Staffordshire) was written out in September 1539, nine months after his surrender in the chapter house.[61] Like Leighton, Richard Ingworth chose 'to kepe both the hede and body yet togyther'. After securing their formal surrender he left the Bristol Carmelites in situ, with sufficient books for their worship and a daily allowance of 20d, while he continued his circuit around the region.[62]

There may have been some present in many professed communities who, whether by command of the commissioners or their own inclination, were simply unable to leave. When these men and women came under their scrutiny again a year or more after the Valor and the visitation, the commissioners were often surprised to find some who were completely incapacitated. Cases of extreme old age were most common but there were also those found to be blind, lame, mute and mentally confused.

Three of the convent of seven at Langley (Leicestershire) were found in the summer of 1536 unfit to be let out on their own: the prioress was aged and 'impotent' (presumably unable to walk), another was almost eighty and one was 'in regard a fole'.[63] At Esholt (West Yorkshire) the commissioners deliberated what might be done to move old Elizabeth Pudsey and Joan Holynraker but they admitted defeat, noting in their book that 'neither riding nor walking would be feasible for either woman'.[64]

How and when regulars such as these, wholly dependent on those around them, passed out of the convent buildings is never recorded in the commissioners' notebooks. Perhaps they let them be until all other business was done. The incapacitated monastic superiors may have been saved by their status, as even under the 1536 statute the commissioners were expected to provide them with a pension, and sometimes it was supplemented with the right to accommodation and other benefits in kind. For the rest, the commissioners, assuming that family or the neighbourhood might step in, simply moved on. Old Joan Holynraker, who had chosen to 'contynew', it seems was left to the care of her friends. Of course, the oldest may have had the least family to fall back on. The commissioners at Langley were told that the eighty-year-old Prioress Dulcia Bothe was sister to the local MP and Royal Justice Sir Richard Sacheverell. This may have been enough for them to move on, notwithstanding that old Sir Richard had died two years before.[65]

When at last these men and women left their religious house, whether in the wake of the statute or later, they each of them went on different terms. The prospect of the secular world that lay before them was by no means the same for each member of the same community. Their cash reward, where it was available, was the only step out of the regular life that they may have experienced in the same way. Even the change of clothes differed one from another. For the suppressed of 1536–37, part of the community now put off their habits while their colleagues who had chosen to continue their monastic life looked on. There may have been even greater variation within the surrendered communities, where some of the men at once put on the gown of a beneficed priest or the canon of a secular cathedral chapter. At Montacute, Prior Robert Gybbes faced a journey of just two miles outside the precinct to the manor house of East Chinnock, which had been granted to him because, as the commissioners noted, 'he himself built [it]', while John Walles was to take up a living at East Holme (Dorset). Ranked twelfth in a community of seventeen no doubt it was Walles's good fortune, not the prior's, that nonetheless seemed stark on the day of departure.[66] Such contrasts were not unknown among the friars: at the Oxford Franciscans, Warden Edward Baskerfield put himself apart from his seventeen colleagues as he persuaded John London to let him stay in the city in the confident expectation of picking up a benefice of his own.[67]

The communities closed under the statute of 1536 saw the most dramatic divide, as they had been compelled to choose one of two opposing paths, to continue the cloistered life or to try to make their way somehow in the world. At this distance it seems inevitable that there would have been no pattern to these choices, as they would always be made according to the personal circumstances of the individual. It does seem, however, that the king, Cromwell and, under their influence, the commissioners, had anticipated that a greater number of communities would want to leave and, for the men at least, to secularise. The commissioners' experience of the visitation may have encouraged this view, as on some circuits there had been a high proportion of the total population ready to accept the promised unconditional release from their vows. The commissioners may have also held a distorted impression of how many inside these houses were unfit for the religious life because of age, sickness or mental capacity. There can be little doubt that they were unprepared for the number deciding to continue and needing another monastic home.

An inventory originally compiled in the summer months of 1536 but now surviving only in an Elizabethan copy gives the name of the houses suppressed in thirty-eight counties of England, the dioceses of Carlisle and Durham, the archdeaconry of Richmond and two dioceses of Wales; alongside many of the names in adjoining columns are a number and the names of further religious houses, which can be identified as those that stood outside of the terms of the suppression statute.[68] Brackets align these names to some of the 387 entries. It may be inferred that unbracketed numbers stand for the population at a suppressed house where no individual has chosen to continue and bracketed numbers the opposite, the proportion that will continue and their potential destination. The inventory was evidently only a provisional document as several of the houses listed ultimately secured exemption from suppression; there are also mistakes, as the affiliations of abbeys and priories are muddled.

Nonetheless, it may be read at least as a rough indication of the transfers which the commissioners, and their masters, now found themselves having to fix. From just seven houses in Norfolk, no fewer than eighty-four women were recorded as intending to continue; from the seventeen nunneries now closed across the Province of York the total given in the inventory was 131.[69]

In this document, the number of women choosing to continue in religious service is consistently high: thirty-seven from Worcestershire; forty-five from Devon and Somerset; fifty from just three priories in Yorkshire, Marrick, St Agatha's and Swine; from Denny Priory alone the figure was twenty-five.[70] By contrast, the numbers given for the houses of men are evenly balanced. The eleven religious at Little Dunmow Priory were recorded as not choosing to continue; twenty miles away at Earls Colne Priory it appears that all but one of the monks looked to remain in religious service.[71]

Among the men, there are also differences between the congregations. The Cistercians are recorded as continuing apparently en masse in each county of the south-east, south-west, Thames Valley and the Midlands; only for those in Lincolnshire and in Wales is no destination noted in the right-hand column.[72] The suppressed houses in Wales stand apart from the other regions in this document as there is no destination indicated for the total population shown of twenty-seven houses in the dioceses of Monmouth and Llandaff.[73]

The inventory also indicates that, in their choice to continue, the religious were further divided. At whatever point in the planning it was compiled, it seems it was already apparent to the commissioners that these men and women could not be transferred as a cohort. For the transfer of the women there was an obvious obstacle, that the suppressions had removed the only houses for female religious in the same county. 'There is no nunnery in these counties' (nullum extat monasterium monialium in hiis comitatibus), the compiler noted by the entries for

Norfolk, Shropshire, Staffordshire, Hereford and Worcester, Yorkshire, Durham diocese and Richmond archdeaconry, together with the note that 'therefore they are to be transferred to monasteries in other counties' (igitur transferantur ad monasterium), respectively 'near to London' and to Wiltshire.[74] For the nearly forty nuns from Worcestershire, their transfer would be over 150 miles. There were many more male monasteries still standing after the enforcement of the statute but their capacity, and their inclination to accommodate, would surely have differed one from another.

This same compiler envisaged that men from the same house had to be sent in different directions: the seven monks at Tilty were noted as destined for Stratford Langthorne, St Mary Graces (London) and Croxden.[75] Those intended for the latter faced a cross-country journey of some 160 miles. The compiler also planned to send men of one congregation to houses of another. The Cluniac monks from Prittlewell were destined for the premier Benedictine foundation at St Albans. Likewise, the jurisdiction of the greater abbeys over their dependent priories was ignored. The monks of Binham Priory, which had been governed by St Albans since its foundation in the twelfth century, were to stay within their county and to continue their monastic careers at Wymondham Abbey.[76]

The final record of the decisions of the suppressed communities, which survives only from parts of East Anglia, the West Midlands and Yorkshire, suggests that as it finally turned out the patterns among men and women were not so different. When it came to confirming their position only half the women of Carrow and Marham wanted to find another house; at Blackborough, Bungay and Crabhouse, in the same county, all looked to be dispensed and to depart; at Bungay there was 'not one none left therin ... before it was suppressed'.[77] All nine men at Ulverscroft committed to continue; their near neighbours, the fifteen Cistercian sisters living seven miles away at Gracedieu (near Thringstone), made the same unanimous decision.[78] Of the eleven women at Esholt, nine would 'contynew', among them women aged between their mid-forties and late fifties; however, the prioress, Joan Jenkynson, a relative youngster of just forty, would not continue. The Cistercian prior of Sibton, Robert Sabyn, and the monk next to him in order of precedence, John Fawkes, elected to continue their monastic life elsewhere; three juniors, listed last in the community, also left.[79] The new sparsity of the monastic landscape in this area may also have influenced the choice of these East Anglians. At the last only one canon of Langley (Norfolk) confirmed that he 'desyrethe to continue'.[80] His destination is not recorded but as a

Premonstratensian his nearest new religious house would have been West Dereham almost sixty miles to the east.

Those who chose to continue in the monastic life in 1536–37 did so for no more than three and a half years before again they stood on the threshold of departure. Ultimately, the enduring divide in their experience of the dissolution was their material position. In the suppressed houses of 1536–37 the head was set apart from the body of the community as the sole recipient of a pension. At the outset, the Crown committed to the obligation for the lifetime of the superior, to be met from the income of the portfolio of properties now taken into its own possession. The overall value of the endowment did not determine the value of the pension, however. If there was a formula for the calculation no record of it has survived, but it seems likely that the income of the house was weighed along with the extent of its debts as well as the length of service, age and prospects of the individual head. The men who led abbeys recording a revenue above £150 could receive upwards of £20; the superiors (of both sexes) of priories returning less than half that figure typically were assigned less than £10. It seems very possible that some acknowledgement was made of the local, social standing of these superiors and the kinfolk and patrons known to be at their back. Young Mary Denys of Kington St Michael, whose election as prioress the previous year was probably the result of her family ties, was awarded £5 although her house returned annually only £38 3s 10d.[81]

Clearly, there was a will to reward those who had assisted, even accelerated, the closure. Abbot George Walker of Louth Park received one of the most generous pensions (£26 13s 4d) of all the suppressed heads, perhaps for no other reason than that he cooperated with the commissioners within a week of their arrival in the county.[82] William Sheppard, who had held the priorate of Mottisfont only since the visitation and had steered it to suppression scarcely a month after parliament rose, was rewarded with a pension £20 out of an endowment worth £167 15s 8½d.[83] The commissioners encouraged the expectation of special treatment in many more than ultimately received it. John Mathew of Coxford appealed to Cromwell, claiming Thomas Legh had given him to understand that he might expect as much as £20, about one-sixth of his priory's total value.[84]

For some of the heads, both men and women, the pension itself was only one component of the settlement offered them by the Crown. When he submitted to the suppression of Breamore, William Finch was appointed as suffragan bishop of Taunton; the prospect of the office, and its attendant fees, may account for a pension sum (£18) somewhat below what might have been expected from the value of the endowment alone (£200).[85] Preferential settlements created a hierarchy of former heads who emerged from a process which to the general public was represented as a punishment in fact as premier prelates with substantial personal wealth. The impression of double standards was deepened by the award at the same time of even more generous pensions to a number of heads of greater abbeys and priories whom Cromwell had wanted to substitute with his own allies. Prior Thomas Day of Leeds complained that his house had been committed to £40 in pensions to his predecessors, one of whom had also passed on debts of £950.[86] William Thirsk of Fountains Abbey faced pressure to step down in this way; the price for the Crown was a pension of 100 marks, in other words more than £65, three times more than for the best-rewarded heads of the suppressed houses.[87]

No doubt aware of the differences, a number of the heads attempted to haggle over the terms. Prior Richard Harwell of Brooke (Rutland) went so far as to claim that his house, a dependent priory under the jurisdiction of Kenilworth, was in fact an independent foundation. His superior soon weighed in and wrote with no small satisfaction to Cromwell that he would now be due 'not such [a] profitable and commodyous pencyon' as 'he and his consell wold devyse'.[88] Nicholas Austen, abbot of Rewley, laid himself bare to Cromwell, begging him to 'direct your favourable letters' to the burgesses of Burford (Oxfordshire) that they might offer him a chaplaincy in their gift to supplement his pension of £11.[89]

Without supplementary income, or other benefits in kind, the pensions below £12 were not enough for these former superiors to live nearly as well they had done before. By 1540 a benefice with an annual value of £6 was thought to be too poor to afford the sole living of a secular priest; towards the end of Henry VIII's reign, in a season of stable prices a farm labourer might earn almost as much for their annual wage.[90] Of course, it is very difficult to calculate the true value of what a head of house received not only in the cash made available to them but in the accommodation, food and clothing that were the trappings of their office. Probably only those provided with a package of benefits, including the office and the use of this or that residence, could hope to continue living in their accustomed style. A good many of these men and women had long experience of the administration of a large household. It was surely the shrewd judgement of some who migrated to another house rather than trying to make their way in the secular world.

The members of their communities who decided to go now were sent away with cash that would last them no more than a few weeks. The commissioners were charged with providing 'sum reasonable reward' sufficient to see them re-clothed and removed from the vicinity; the commissioners were advised to decide the amount 'accordinge to the dystaunce of the place'.[91] Where cash could be counted on, it seems there was some determination to take account of status, and perhaps age and personal prospects. At Arden Priory old, deaf Elizabeth Johnson received twice as much (40s) as her sisters (20s). It may have been because she was newly professed at Flamstead Priory (Hertfordshire) that Alice Whytley was given 20s, a noble (a gold coin valued at 6s 8d) less than any other nun.[92] The sole lay sister at Gokewell (Lincolnshire) was paid off with the sort of token (4d) that might otherwise have been seen by a kitchen scullion. Where cash was scarce it seems the commissioners' practice was to count what remained after outstanding charges were met and to divide it evenly between those electing to leave. There were £6 remaining at Royston Priory (Hertfordshire) and accordingly the six canons each received 20s.[93] At Barlings and Kirkstead abbeys the share was meagre indeed, as only £20 was found to settle on twenty-four religious and their full complements of resident staff.[94]

These sums may have been enough to provide them with some secular clothing although perhaps not a complete suit of 'apparel', as the sightings of dispersed religious still wearing some part of their old habits would suggest. It hardly held out the prospect of cross-country travel. At the end of the decade a traveller would have to pay 8d per mile for the use of a good horse and the commissioners' own accounts confirm that respectable board and lodging required an outlay of at least a few shillings. That some religious still haunted their precincts months after the house was taken from them may indicate that they had found themselves marooned. Certainly, the cash put into the hands of these men could not have covered the likely cost of securing a faculty, least of all if the continuing delay required them to take their application to the Faculty Office itself. It is noticeable that former religious emerge as beneficed clergy only at the end of Henry's reign, more than a decade after some of them had left their monastery. Of these, almost all were from the (later) pensioned ranks; those left without remained also outside of the Church.[95] This may not reflect a mood of reformation but rather the practical challenge they now confronted of making their way in a secular world.

The terms settled on the monasteries that surrendered were far better. Each member of the community received a pension charged to the income of the house that was now in the hands of the Crown. There was no exception: even novices yet to make their solemn profession and, in the case of men, not yet priests, were also granted an annuity. Yet this was the community's only common ground. The sums were awarded according to their office and their years under vows. After the superior, the prior or prioress received the next largest allocation. Where there was no great difference in age or degree of responsibility the same or a similar sum was given to each member, but in the largest communities with a variety of roles the sums were strictly graduated.

Just as in the suppressed communities the superior was set apart from their colleagues. The difference in their pensions had formerly been that of a modest annuity – between £5 and £25 – as opposed to a one-off cash reward. Now, however, it amounted to a huge disparity in the value of the pension. In many cases, the superior was awarded a sum ten times that of the next member of the community, £100 to the prior's allocation of £10. In a handful of cases the multiplier was even more. Abbess Katherine Bulkeley of Godstow (Oxford) was awarded a pension of £50; her prioress, second only to her in seniority, received just £1. The superior's share represented at least 10 per cent of the annual revenue of their house as assessed in the Valor; for some, such as the Lady of Godstow it topped 15 per cent (£50 out of £325).[96]

Previously in 1536–37, the commissioners had considered that their charge was to punish the houses, and heads were expected to earn their rewards. Now, however, they saw these superiors in a different light and were disposed to show them some compassion. John London persuaded Cromwell to be generous to Clemencia Stock, elderly abbess of Delapré, 'for surely she cannot long enjoy this pension'.[97] London extended his sympathy as far as Polesworth, nearly sixty miles to the north-west, where he argued that Abbess Alice Fitzherbert was worth 'more than less' for her good husbandry of the house in the four years since the visitation. She received £26, almost a quarter of the abbey's total income.[98] A minority of superiors received a far lower allocation simply because the revenue of their house could sustain nothing more. The superiors of Chatteris (Cambridgeshire), Poulton (Gloucestershire) and Taunton, whose houses had been on the margins of the £200 threshold for suppression, each received pensions of just £15 or less.[99]

Ostensibly dissolving their community at their own volition, many more of these superiors were inclined to bargain over their terms. It seems some began a correspondence, perhaps directly with Cromwell, over the value of the pension. There were times when the commissioners were obliged to leave a space in their book of papers alongside the superior's name because the matter was still unsettled when they were ready for the community to leave. At Bury St Edmunds, Abbot John Reve seems to have remained for the best part of a week, as the commissioners worked around him, while they awaited word from the Court of Augmentations or the centre of operations at Austin Friars.[100] By contrast with the challenges made by their suppressed colleagues, frequently the expectations of these superiors were met in full. Bartholomew Fowle of St Mary Overy (Southwark) lobbied successfully for his pension to be raised from a healthy £80 to a prodigious £100, nearly 15 per cent of the total annual return from his foundation.[101]

It was surely a reflection of the occupation and lifestyle experienced by these superiors of large and wealthy monasteries that they applied as much pressure for the award of property and associated chattels. Many of them, men and women, looked to retain one of the manors that had always been allocated as part of the superior's portion, together with its furnishings and household servants and a modest demesne that would enable them to live there independently much as they had done before.

Abbess Cecily Bodenham of Wilton secured the manor house at Fovant, seven miles from the house, where she would have lived at least for part of her year during her tenure of office.[102] John Stonywell, abbot of Pershore, chose not the most prestigious of the superior's residences but the manor closest to his own family home, at Langton (Staffordshire); a university graduate, his priority was not having domestic servants but that he should 'have his books'.[103]

Some hoped to recreate in perfect miniature the status and comfort they had known. Prior William Gryffyth of St Katharine's Priory, Lincoln, sent up to 'my lord privy seale' a costed schedule of his expectations for a fully stocked farm, including five score 'schepe', four score 'lambes', four score 'hogges' and three score 'wedders', as well as twelve swine and five oxen, the whole to be held with the priory's grange at Bentham, which, he reminded him, needed new 'dores and wyndowes'.[104]

Prior John Lancaster of Launde did not look for the life of a country squire but rather to enjoy the comforts of his priorate in every last detail, 'all such stuffe standing within the chambers in which the servaunts that do wayte appon [him] do lodge and lie in', 'one hoggeshed of red wyne leying ... in the celler with iii other vessels that wyne was in', 'ii peyre of organs with the lofte they stand in', 'the paving tyle being within the chaple called Thomas Beckets chaple', 'one of the ii furnessis standing in the ketchyn', and 'wher the seid prior hath boght 7 payd for iii stonne troughes standing in the kecheyn he desirith to have one of them', and 'one Glasson window standing in the newe fratrie'.[105]

The cloister community was well aware of the other world inhabited by their superior, but these transactions must have set it in sharp relief. Their own allocated annuities were set at a value generally below those awarded to the superiors of the monasteries suppressed in 1536–37. Only those at the wealthiest abbeys received sums in the region of £10. The canons of Merton Priory, the Valor assessment of which was over £1,000, were distributed pension sums descending from £10 to £6.[106] The highest value awarded to the women of Godstow, whose revenue was less than half that of Merton, was only a tenth of this sum.[107]

The size of the monastic community pressed down on pension values. Selby Abbey had received novices in its final year and at its surrender there were twenty-four in the community: all but the three senior officers (abbot, prior and sub-prior) received a pension of £5, the sum for six of them enhanced by one noble (6s 8d).[108] At Hartland, where there were just four canons at the surrender, each one of them received a £5 pension.[109] The calculation was not easily made. 'Owre tyme is to[o] schort,' complained Philip Parys at Ely Cathedral Priory, 'fayen [we are] occupyd tell x of the cloke in the nyt'.[110] John Freeman left the canons of Leicester with some ready money and departed with a dispatch to Cromwell 'to knoe what they have to doo ... for the chanons pencions'.[111] Chancellor Rich, who saw the situation from both points of view, from his chambers at Westminster and standing with the commissioners on their circuit, warned that the delay in deciding pension values threatened the advance of the dissolution.[112]

The distinctions made for seniority by office, age or years spent in religious service were only slight. The prior of Kingswood Abbey received £4 13s 4d, just a mark more than his colleagues, who were pensioned at £4.[113] Although difficult to trace by name, there is no record that those who had joined a community now surrendering from one that had been suppressed were left at any disadvantage. In a letter of late 1538, Cromwell himself had advised Thomas Legh and William Cavendish also to give some consideration to the conduct of individuals, what he called the 'towardnes of the persones there'.[114] This might account for allocations that otherwise cut across office and age. Young Agnes Snayton of Nun Appleton received £1 per year more than her sub-prioress, Elinore Normavell.[115]

It appears that an upper limit was applied for allocations to novices and to professed men not yet ordained as priests. Given that so many who were identified as novices received a pension of 40s, it does seem that on some circuits it was adopted as a flat rate. These meagre awards were already apparent in the course of 1538 and were presumably common knowledge within the monasteries' own networks. It is doubtful, then, that any of those who entered a religious house in the last eighteen months before Easter 1540 did so for purely material motives.

In the monasteries the terms were altered where a benefice in the assign of the house was available to be filled. William Philippes, canon of Cirencester, was presented to the town's vicarage with the sole right to its tithes (a source of income which previously may have been subdivided); in return he resigned his claim to a pension from the revenue of the house.[116] Not all of the available benefices were nearly so comfortable. The trade that Philippes made was unusual, the result surely of the value of the particular living. John Rodley of the Gilbertine priory at Marlborough was presented to the church at Kenes and awarded a pension which, accounting for his seniority, was just one mark more than all of his brethren.[117] The prospect of a benefice depended on the circumstances of the house, the presence of a precinct parish or another church under its patronage and standing vacant. Richard Wodhill, monk of Quarr, was confirmed in the living of the parish church of Binstead when the monastery closed but largely, perhaps only, because he had held it for some time as part of his reward for his role as second sub-prior. For the commissioners, continuity in the current arrangements, in this as in other aspects of the closure, appears to have been the guiding principle.[118] It was rare for any more than one or two individuals to secure a living at the very moment of departure. The distribution of benefices to most of the canons of Lanercost, an exercise of local patronal power by Lord Dacre, was reported to Cromwell as an act of provocation, 'so that by his maintenaunce the hole covent do confeder and flok togither'.[119]

The majority of the professed community received pensions no higher than the annual income of working men and women. Only those men who passed directly from their place in the monastery into a benefice might have known a standard of living that set them apart from their neighbours. For the rest, to continue the life they had known in the cloister would require another source of income: for the men, this meant an occupation; for the women, since marriage was forbidden them as long as the king lived, it meant relying on family and friends. Some of the commissioners do seem to have acknowledged the challenges now confronting these cloisterers and agreed to pay them the first instalment of their pension in advance of the next quarter day when it would otherwise be due. When St Andrew's Priory, Northampton, was closed at the beginning of March, Sir William Parr paid the monks 'mony in honde' for the three weeks before their first portion on Lady Day.[120] The monks of Lewes were shown great good cheer in mid-November 1538, as their first instalment due at Christmas was brought forward by six weeks and paid to them before they left the precinct.[121]

It would never be enough. From the moment of their release there were former religious seeking to raise income from their pension patent through transfer or sale; many petitioned the Court of Augmentations to complain of arrears, although an analysis of the Augmentations accounts for 1552–53 shows that there were wide regional variations in the experience of the pensioned religious: fewer than 15 per cent were owed all or part of their pension in the East Riding of Yorkshire, but nearly 60 per cent in the same county's West Riding; in Cambridgeshire and Gloucestershire it seems there had been no defaults of payments at all.[122] The limitations of pension income must account for the number of men and women from the same community who arranged to live in the same household in the years that followed.

The poorest to pass out from the surrendered houses were the friars. Since their houses held no endowment but had been established only on the grant of the site on which the buildings stood, there was no recurrent income of the scale required for lifetime annuities. Most of these houses had accrued a handful of nearby rental properties over time as a result of bequests, but the total return on these scattered holdings of tenements, orchards and meadow land was very limited: in the few instances where it was recorded, rarely more than about £20. A conspicuous exception may have been the friars at Calais where there was some anticipation at the prospect of their 'lands' coming on to the open market – until word was out that the whole would be taken into the king's hands.[123] Notwithstanding their limited means, the commissioners found that some houses were already charged with annuities to secular beneficiaries, obligations which no doubt had been accepted for some short-term cash contingency. In the immediate term these annuities seem to have been respected by the commissioners, although in the months that followed alternative grants were provided to pensioners willing to surrender their claims.

The majority of friars received nothing other than petty cash that might see them out of the precinct. If Bishop Ingworth's constant complaints are to be taken at face value, even this very limited support was often in very short supply. Alone among the five orders still present in the kingdom in 1538, the priors of the seven Trinitarian convents received modest pensions, all at the very lowest end of the scale of rewards made to male monastic superiors, between £5 and £10.[124] The patchy correspondence of the commissioners would suggest that similar arrangements for the priors of the principal convents of the regional grouping of friaries – London, Oxford, York – were contemplated at first but in each instance they were left unconfirmed. Some of these heads, Dominicans and Franciscans, were given some other small compensation: at Exeter it was a velvet cope; at Reading, use of the lodging they lived in.[125] Still, of the number of superiors who surrendered between Easter and Michaelmas 1538, perhaps 80 per cent departed with no secure income at all.

With or without money, what they did when they first left the precinct is difficult to establish. If any religious men and women did record their subsequent experiences those memoirs have not survived. The closest to a personal memoir of the dissolution is the history of the martyrs of the London Charterhouse and the exile of some of the remaining monks, composed at a distance of four decades by Maurice Chauncy. Although he described the arrest and execution of the community's prior in 1534 and the search by some of the survivors for a safe haven in Flanders, the act of surrender itself is described in one allusive phrase: 'we were all expelled . . . and led into Babylon'.[126]

The majority of the men, monastic and mendicant, did not move very far in the weeks and months that followed. The unfinished business of their pension, either the patent itself or receipt of the first quarter payment, and their application for their faculty, were persuasive reasons to stay in sight of their former house. The witness statements taken from the canons and monks arrested after the Lincolnshire rising indicate that the men from the houses suppressed in September had moved no further away than the surrounding villages and towns. It seems they stayed in touch with one another as they waited for the formal right to secularise; they were a captive audience for the rebels' call to arms, and the ringleader of the regulars that joined the rebellion, William Burraby, had been one of those responsible for the distribution of the faculty grant. Set apart from the punitive measure of the suppression statute and with the threat of popular protest diffused, it seems some of the surrendered communities stayed close by and for longer in a state of suspended animation. Loitering 'together in their chanons cloths very unsemely' at Lanercost, suppressed in the spring of 1536, was reported in London. Of course, at least half a day's ride from the nearest urban centre (Carlisle) and from the Scottish border, their best option was to stay put.[127]

For the unpensioned friars, a faculty was the only route to an independent life and until it came their own locality was the best source of temporary support. Perhaps because so much of their site, the precinct and outlying buildings were already occupied by tenants, there was not the same urgency to put them into custody and the professed residents were not summarily turned out. At some of the substantial urban houses, friars may have remained in residence for some time, at least as late as the turn of the year. In a letter dated 31 January 1539, John Hussee reported that the London friars were about to be sent abroad – in other words, out into the world – which would suggest they had stayed where they were throughout the Christmas period and well into the New Year.[128] Charles Wriothesley saw the city's friars standing in limbo, 'they change theyr habettes', but they waited to 'knowe the kings further pleasure'.[129] Prior John Dove of the Calais Carmelites was still seen as a cause of 'trouble' in the town as late as June 1539.[130]

Reformers frustrated at the pace of change condemned the prospect of 'covent monckes . . . to be spiritual pastours' now 'admitted to have cure of soules . . . over a hundredth and meny mo'.[131] In fact, it seems most of these men, as and when their secular status was confirmed, did not step directly into clerical roles. This may have been as much because of a lack of opportunity as of will on their own part. Those with a patent for a pension worth less than £10, at any rate paid to them in quarterly portions, or with none at all, would have held no better prospect for their living long-term. Some, presumably younger, men presented themselves for ordination to the priesthood within a year of the surrender of their house, of course to position themselves to secure some or other preferment.

For centuries, the monasteries had played a central role in the careers of secular clergy, providing candidates for ordination to the priesthood with the necessary title, that is to say the specified location of their ministry. This had been a transaction, a lucrative source of income for the monks, and by the beginning of the sixteenth century most of those entering the secular priesthood took their title from a religious house. When the Crown took possession of their patronage of the provincial church, the old approach persisted – and the candidate's title was recorded as conferred by the former (nuper) monastery – only for a matter of months. Thereafter, as the ecclesiastical domain of the monasteries was redistributed under crown grants and sales, the provision of titles for new clergy, and the presentation to benefices more generally, moved at a markedly slower pace. Perhaps the first conspicuous casualties of the change were the former religious themselves.

Of course, as long as King Henry lived there remained other opportunities in the secular Church, a chaplaincy associated with foundations, including secular colleges, guilds and hospitals, as yet untouched by reformation and chantries established in parish and cathedral churches. The surviving records of these roles is very sparse indeed and it would be impossible to arrive at a plausible estimate for the number that included former religious between 1536 and 1547. The province of York is better documented and understood than other regions and here there were only forty-three canons and monks (7 per cent of the total population) and thirteen friars (6 per cent) known to have held chaplaincies up to 1547, most of them in the city of York itself.[132] Perhaps this is indicative of what would have been the pattern countrywide, that a handful found clerical employment in urban centres where these roles in place remained for another decade. For the rest, dispersed between rural isolation and smaller market towns, these opportunities extended too far beyond their local horizon.

If not in clerical employment, it must be that these men lived with what means they had. Like women religious, their main source of support may have been family and friends. The early records of their receipt of pensions suggests that in their first years the surrendered religious remained in the town nearest to their former home. Eight Cirencester canons whose pension receipts survive from 1542 obtained them in the town.[133] Brother Dunstan, former Benedictine of Faversham, seems to have found a place in his family network. When he had surrendered in the chapter house he had given his name as Chartham, a toponym no doubt given him when he had been professed. Now he collected his pension, still with his name-in-religion, Dunstan, but signalling his new means of supporting with the family surname, Goodhewe.[134] It seems that John Coxeter of Evesham now shared a home with his married sister since his pension was collected at Oxford by his brother-in-law, her husband Matthew.[135]

In the wake of the dissolutions, only a minority of monastic and mendicant men took office in the secular Church. When the last communities surrendered at Easter 1540, probably they amounted to fewer than 10 per cent of a total population that may have topped 12,000; by 1542 perhaps they had doubled, but still this meant that most of the men who under vows and habits had ministered daily as priests at least for a time were not working clergy.[136] Membership of this select cohort was not a consequence of suppressions and surrenders themselves. The majority had passed into the ranks of the secular clergy when their convents were transformed into secular chapters, nine cathedral priories and six abbeys and priories re-founded as cathedrals at Bristol, Chester, Gloucester, Oxford, Peterborough and Westminster.

Their entry into these new communities was circumstantial. Recruitment to the reformed chapters of the existing cathedrals began with the incumbent community. There was no guarantee of selection and it does appear that the merits, or otherwise, of candidates were appraised.[137] Nonetheless, between a half and two-thirds of the men who had lived as monks in these churches were now given the opportunity to remain. The new cathedrals also drew from the monasteries that now formed their foundation and from those within their regional network. The inaugural bishops at Peterborough and Westminster had been the abbots of the Benedictine monasteries; those at Bristol, Gloucester and Oxford had each been heads of houses nearby.[138]

The secularisation of the old cathedrals was not done at a stroke, at least not in the formality of a legislative act. Norwich was the first to be confirmed as a secular chapter in May 1538, but it stood alone for almost two years. The new status of the remainder, including the metropolitan see church of Canterbury, was confirmed in piecemeal fashion from March 1541. The last of the conversions, at Worcester, was formalised in March 1542.[139] What was noticed first in these places was the absence of the former chapters; perhaps especially at Bath and Coventry where the churches also fell into disuse. There is very little in the surviving records to explain how the religious occupied themselves in what was, for some, a hiatus of as much as eighteen months. 'I am in no suretie,' wrote Prior Goldwell of Canterbury, almost a month after he had surrendered the cathedral priory to the Crown.[140] The men at Carlisle were given petty cash by the commissioners with the command to buy themselves surplices:[141] clearly, it was expected that they would continue to keep the liturgical routine in the church during the interregnum, but not to do so making use of the vestments of the old monastery, if not for reasons of political sensitivity then for the practical reason that they had already been sold.

Presiding over these new secular chapters was a smaller but more conspicuous cohort of former religious appointed to episcopal office. Yet their presence for the most part was not the direct consequence of the dissolution. All of those holding episcopal titles in the spring of 1540 whose careers had begun under regular vows had been appointed when the religious houses remained in place. Five had been advanced in the wake of the 1535 visitation; a further six had been created bishops under the terms of the Suffragan Act passed the following year.[142] Each one of these prelates was an established or emerging member of Cromwell's clerical affinity, their careers both a cause and consequence of the regime's close supervision of the regular congregations and their hierarchies prevailing since the years of Wolsey's ascendancy. It might be said that regulars in the hierarchy of the Henrician Church represented no change but rather the culmination of a relationship which had been cultivated for as much as twenty years.

A handful of monastics outside of this clique found another route into the secular clerical establishment. They returned to the universities where the student communities of their congregations had thrived even to their very end. John Hopkys of Much Wenlock Priory chose not to make the 100-mile journey home from Oxford – challenging in winter time – for the surrender of his house in late January 1540 but secured Commissioner Scudamore's agreement for his assigned pension to be collected by a proxy.[143] Three Cistercians from Hailes had returned for their surrender on the last day of 1539 but then found their way back to Oxford. In the deed of surrender Philip Brode, Richard Eddon and Roger Rede were each designated bachelor of theology; presumably they intended now to proceed to their doctorates. The monastic community of their college, St Bernard's, was dissolved in the spring of 1540 but the buildings and their contents remained in place and perhaps their now secularised students also stayed.[144] Rede was still at Oxford at the death of Edward VI in July 1553; Eddon departed for the re-founded Westminster Abbey in 1555 but returned to the university again in 1559.[145]

A university life, with which many were already familiar, may have seemed a more possible path at the moment of dissolution than the pursuit of preferment in the church. Also, there may have been something of a demand for such trained scholars to return. It does seem that teaching masters were in short supply in the years around 1540. There were perhaps more openings in Oxford and Cambridge colleges than there had been for a generation. Certainly, two former superiors found places in them: Prior John How of Plympton at Exeter College, Oxford, and Abbot Nicholas Austen of Rewley at Trinity Hall, Cambridge.[146]

In the aftermath of dissolution very few regular men resolutely refused secularisation and attempted to retain the identity of their original profession. English Catholics of the next generation created a legend of courageous escape and exile.[147] Their claim that the expatriate communities of Birgittines and Carthusians, later established in Flanders, had crossed the Channel as early as 1539–40 was unfounded. Neither in fact left the country before King Henry's death. The Privy Council first voiced its concerns over the 'conveyaunce over the sees of sundry suche popishe persones late religious' in the summer of 1547.[148] Reports of 'friends' of former religious now abroad, and collecting their pension portions to be sent to them in exile, surfaced at the same time.[149]

In fact, the most traffic in exiles was seen before the last of the houses was shut down and across the Scottish border. Carthusians and Observant friars had first fled north at the time of the royal supremacy in 1534, and others followed, albeit no more than a handful, after the unrest of 1536–37 and as the surrender of the friaries advanced in the spring and summer of 1538.[150] In early March 1539 the Council of the North reported to Cromwell on the capture of a ship which had run ashore at South Shields and was carrying a papist priest of Chichester, two religious from Ireland, and the survivors from another wrecked vessel whose passengers had included an English Observant.[151]

At the beginning of the following year, eight former regulars – two canons and six friars – were named among nearly fifty English rebels known to be sheltering in Scotland.[152] Those who remained under the Tudor regime did not hide. They bound themselves together, some of them in the same shared household where it may be assumed they continued to observe a form of common life; and it seems they were recognised for their monastic identity by their neighbours. Yet rarely did they challenge their new condition. In almost a decade between the closure of their house and their decision to leave, only once did the diehard Carthusians draw wider attention: in May 1545 one Selby was dispatched to the Tower for a 'lewde wrytyng against the primacy of the kings highness which he subscribed to his own hand'.[153]

In fact, the first and most committed monastic exiles were those who had adopted the other side of the argument, absorbing the message of the radical reformers. These men had almost all left their houses before 1536. Augustinian friars of Cambridge were in Germany before 1530.[154] John Bale had taken up the life of an itinerant preacher by 1534 and finally threw off his priorate two years later.[155] But some of them stayed, and some of them returned. William Jerome of Christ Church Priory, Canterbury, was condemned as a Lutheran only three months after the surrender, in the summer of 1540, and burned alive at Smithfield.[156] The radical former friars John Cardmaker (originally a Franciscan of Exeter) and John Lawrence (a Dominican of Sudbury) were visible and vocal enough in their regions to fall foul of the Marian persecutions.[157] The reformist preaching of the ex-Dominican John Rough may have caused him to flee his native Scotland but he had gone no further than Yorkshire; he left for Germany in 1553 but returned again to London in 1557 where he was finally caught.[158]

The departure of religious women may have been swifter than that of the men only because there were fewer prospects for them in the outside world. In principle they were expected to apply for a licence or 'capacity' to permit them to change their habit just like the men. Some 100 of them did so in the first two years of closures, 1536–37, fewer than 50 per cent of those who were eligible; later the licence was ignored.[159] For the women it was no licence to earn a living. After their cash 'reward', or, from 1538, their pension allocation, there was nothing to keep them in the precinct. The minority of women in the suppressed monasteries who chose not to continue their life in another community were left with no visible means of support. Where their age and years in the cloister are recorded, it is often the case that they were either the elderly or the young, and it seems likely that their choice was influenced by the impression of a better prospect beyond the monastic network.

Some women seem to have thought first and foremost of marriage; perhaps they were encouraged to do so by their kinfolk outside. John London claimed to Cromwell that the ladies of Heynings Priory had lived in 'unperfytt chastitite' and were 'wonderfull gladde' clamoured to 'be at liberite to marye if they will'.[160] In fact, only those recently professed under the 1535 age limit (21) were free to wed; all others were at liberty in everything but their chastity vow. Twenty years on, under Queen Mary when the marriages of former regulars became a matter of public interest, rumours circulated of the early, illicit alliances of monastic women. It was suggested that Agatha Wellesbourne, the legitimate wife of Bishop William Barlow, had first been married to him in secret before it was legal (see Fig. 27).[161] The number of unpensioned women passing out into the world in 1536–37 was perhaps less than

10 per cent of the total whose houses had been suppressed, and of these perhaps as many as half were said to be sick and elderly.[162] Still, to dismiss the possibility of common-law liaisons would be naïve. The practical case for them was strong.

Like the men, only those women with a pension at the upper end of the range – £5 and upwards – might comfortably manage to live independently. Jane Forget of Wilton Abbey found enough in her pension for modest furniture – a bed, chest and a couple of coffers – and for kitchen utensils – 'to cauldrons one crocke one frying pan one grydeiron one broche a skillet and one posnet'.[163] It seems kinfolk regarded a royal pension, in its security if not its scale, as a living that was good enough. William Martyn of Wokingham, father to ten children, considered that his daughter Elizabeth, 'that was professsyd nonne', had been provided for by 'our sovereign lore the king', and so he bequeathed her an annuity of 20s from the rent of one of his mills only 'yf she fayle of her pencion' but 'or ells nott'.[164] Perhaps it is possible to read a shrewd assessment of the cost – and opportunities – of living in the settlement of many of them in the nearby towns. Women from Norfolk's rural priories, Campsey Ashe and Shouldham, migrated, respectively, to Dunwich (6 miles) and Lynn (10 miles).[165]

The force of family ties was as variable then as at any time: Ann Boroeghe, former nun of Clerkenwell, took herself a hundred miles north of her old religious house to live alongside a married sister and, it seems, at or close to the former Hospitaller commandery at Dingley (Northamptonshire), which may have become a focus for locals attached to its religious traditions (see Fig. 28).[166] Not all religious women were reeled in by parents and siblings. Some also chose a more independent path. George Norman saw that his daughter's monastery, Handale (North Yorkshire), might close when he made his will in January 1539, and so he directed that 'Isabel shall have her part of my goods if the house be suppressed . . . or elss not.'[167] Despite her kinsmen being close by, Katharine Neudyke of Wykeham Priory (North Yorkshire) made her new home as much as a day's ride from her former religious house, near Kirkbymoorside.[168] Mary Pomeroy of Canonsleigh (Devon) chose to return to the original site of her profession, at Cornworthy, the priory which had been closed in 1536, and lived there until her death in 1566.[169]

The majority, men and women, pensioned and unpensioned, continued to live very close to their old communities. Those whose houses had stood in or close to a town centre stayed there; those whose houses had been self-contained and cut-off rural oases moved within a radius of no more than perhaps twenty miles.

Three monks of Bury St Edmunds moved no further than the boundary of the old abbey precinct, in the parish of St Mary, where they were buried, one after the other, in 1540, 1542 and 1545.[170] John Peryn, abbot of Tavistock, made his residence a town house just 350 yards from the abbey precinct, remaining there until his death in 1550.[171] Richard Hempstead alias Hart of Lanthony Priory, Gloucester, crossed to the opposite bank of the River Severn where he took the living of the parish church of St Nicholas.[172] At least one of the Cistercians of Rushen remained on the Isle of Man, where their pension entitlement was still recorded in 1552.[173]

A surprising number never left their premises at all. Of course, the hundred or so men whose foundations were secularised between 1538 and 1542 experienced no greater change in their living environment than a temporary pause as they waited for their new status to be confirmed by charter. Yet even at the majority of sites where the old community was dispersed and the church left standing derelict, some of its members were still to be found. The settlement of a broad range of superiors included the right to occupy some portion of their own precinct. In spite of its suppression under the 1536 statute, and meagre rewards given to her sisters, Prioress Grace Sampson of Redlingfield (Suffolk) was permitted to stay in the same lodgings she had entered at her election a dozen years before, apparently at the indulgence of the new proprietor, and former patron, Edmund Bedlingfield.[174] Abbot John Ely of Bruton received a grant of a space known as the Palm Chamber together with a responsibility not far removed from those of his former office, as under-steward of all the abbey's former manors.[175]

No member of the convent community is recorded as having received a grant of accommodation either inside the monastic enclosure or within the precinct, but it is possible that some informally took possession, perhaps by no other means than staying put. In 1602 it was remembered that Joan Spylman of Swaffham Bulbeck Priory (Cambridgeshire) had made herself a cell in a 'cave' on the site of the old abbey and remained there for as much as a year after its closure.[176] The low-lying landscape of Swaffham hardly lends weight to the legend but the general recollection that the religious did not stray very far from their former house carries a ring of truth about it.

That entries continued to be added to the chronicle of the London Franciscans creates the impression that at least one of the twenty-four friars who signed the surrender stayed on there in some capacity or other. Of course, the manuscript itself might have been carried away but the later entries are striking for their observation of events in the neighbourhood of the old convent. From 1547, three of the former friars later served as priests in parishes adjoining the precinct; one of them, John Baker, requested burial in the cloister.[177] To secure a chantry appointment or benefices upwards of a decade after the dissolution nearby might suggest they had been living in the vicinity for some time. It may be that they had found lodging in the precinct, not least because some of the tenants of its tenements were known to have sympathies with the old religion. A request for burial in the parochial chapel adjoining the abbey church of St Albans, made by a former monk, John Albon, less than six months after the dissolution, might certainly be an indication that he was then living within the precinct, which was the centre of the chapel's parish.[178]

The continuing presence of religious within or under the shadow of their former home was only fleeting. It may be that those who stayed there were those close to the end of their lives. Some died within a year of their departure. John Reve, abbot of Bury St Edmunds, was dead before the last of the monasteries was closed down.[179] John Albon of St Albans was buried there roughly when the Canterbury and Rochester monks made their surrender at Easter 1540.[180] Richard Leitheley of Byland must have died around the anniversary of the closure of his community (November 1538), his will being proved on 29 December 1539.[181] A record of pension payments compiled in 1565 shows that ten of the monks of Crowland Abbey, pensioned in 1539, had died by 1546; four had not lived beyond 1540.[182]

For the others there was less a tie to the site of their house itself than to their former colleagues. When Thomas Ringstead of Bury St Edmunds wrote his will in 1548 he was confident that the men he still called 'our brethrene' were nearby and would attend at his deathbed, 'beinge at my dyeing'.[183] William Edys of Burton-on-Trent saw enough of his former brethren to borrow a horse from one of them, Robert Heithcote.[184] Richard Barwicke, from St Mary's Abbey, York, perhaps was not on such everyday terms but knew enough of their whereabouts to imagine 'iff it be so that any of my brethren of the house of religion come to my buriall'.[185] The presence of signatures by the abbots of Rufford, Roche and Rievaulx and eight of the former religious on the same deed of 1554 suggests a network with a remarkable 100-mile reach along the Pennines.[186]

As property deeds and personal wills have been investigated it has become increasingly clear that these continuing ties created a framework for their life in the secular world. Some small groups of religious from the same house not only lived nearby one another but shared the same household. The example that has attracted much attention is the arrangement of William Browne, former prior of Monk Bretton, who lived with two other former monks of the house at Worsborough about four miles from Monk Bretton, together with more than a hundred books which came from the conventual library and vestments and other furnishings which may have been salvaged from their house.[187] A 'full choir' of former monks of Llantarnam (Gwent) was said to have congregated at the site of the abbey grange at Penrhys in 1550 about forty miles away, in plain sight of the surrounding neighbourhood.[188]

There are other instances, not all of them so self-consciously monastic but no less marked by their continuing conventual ties. Joan Kyppes, former prioress of Kirklees, took a tenement at Mirfield a dozen miles to the north, and kept it together with four of her former sisters. Their life together reputedly was commemorated in the naming of an inn built on the same site, 'The Three Nuns'.[189] The shared household of former Syon nuns at Denham matches the men of Monk Bretton in hinting at some form of continued observant life. Each of the four former sisters who lived together with their former prioress Agnes Jordan kept a furnished altar in their chamber. Their former chaplain lodged in the same village; perhaps he too reprised something of his old role, as celebrant, confessor and preacher.[190]

Wherever they settled, it is striking that these men and women, though they wore a new habit, still owned their old identity. Many monastic men carried to their grave the toponym given them at their profession. Thomas Ringstead died under the name of the Norfolk village that had once formed part of the domain of the great abbey of Bury. Those who had held office in the monastery often spoke of their old titles. Ringstead called on the clerk who copied his will to record his title as 'subprior and cellarer of the dissolved monastery of Bury'.[191] Twenty years after the house had passed out of sight, Richard Page still wished to be known as prior as well as Prebendary of Upavon (Wiltshire).[192] When he made his first will in 1551, John Stonywell used the suffragan title 'in partibus' which he had won from his patron Thomas Wolsey before 1530.[193]

Their attachment to name and place touched the neighbours they now lived with cheek by jowl. Whoever inserted the memorial stone to Clement Lichfield in the porchway of the school building at Evesham in 1546 knew him still as 'Abbot Clement'. Benefactors remembering the household of the former Dartford nuns living at Denham referred to them as 'sister' in their wills.[194] Isabel Sackville, prioress of Clerkenwell, was commemorated by her adopted parish community in a memorial tablet set above the high altar at the church of St James.[195] The same was true of small country parishes: at Dingley and Mere former women religious were laid to rest under their original title.[196]

The recognition of the neighbourhood around such men and women owed much to the fact that they too had been touched by the time of closure. Suppression and surrender had uprooted a resident population of seculars and layfolk. The paid staff may have been the very first to be turned out of a religious house. Certainly those who continued in 1538 only by raising cash from their furnishings may have reduced their numbers in advance of the final surrender. Reports of friaries found already deserted in the summer and early autumn of 1538, even if exaggerated, may indicate that the domestic staff had already begun to be broken up.

By contrast, at the wealthier abbeys and priories that continued in 1539 and 1540, it seems there was no piecemeal retreat from the full service of the foundation. At Westminster, the obedientiaries continued to budget for the liveries of their servants at the beginning of the new accounting year, 1539–40.[197] In fact, it appears few of the £200 monasteries had experienced a disintegration of their staff before the suppression began. The fact that the musters of October 1536 and February 1537 called on them to supply bread, ale and other necessaries suggests that it was well known that institutional life was still in place.

Where staff lists survive, in the 'books' compiled by the commissioners, they record a number that was sometimes twice, even three times, the size of the professed community, whether it was itself small (e.g. fewer than twelve) or large. There were seven women religious at the priory of Redlingfield in the summer of 1536, but there was a resident staff of forty-four.[198] There were as many as fifty-one domestic staff serving sixteen canons at St Osyth's at the end of July 1539.[199] At Dieulacres there was a staff of thirty in service to the abbot and only two professed monks.[200] Those houses that remained large living communities to the end, such as Westminster, presented the commissioners with a retained population larger than the total number of people they had met at any point on their rural missions. The commissioners were obliged to settle their wages and outstanding debts. The numbers meant that their immediate outlay exceeded the sums paid to the professed.

The women of Blackborough received cash rewards of 26s 8d, their staff of fourteen some £11. The canons of St Osyth carried £20 between them when they left; their staff took £35 5s 4d.[201] Where there was ready cash, they were well satisfied. At St Osyth, William Woodcock was provided with £2 for debts unpaid over and above his 'reward'.[202] The workers of Nuncotham received the full complement of 'rewardes conveyent' and wages for the half-year.[203] However, where the house had already raised all the cash it could and seen it spent, and the furnishings offered a meagre return, the commissioners offered only partial payments. Or they simply let them go. No doubt it was down to their meagre prospects that former employees of Tintern Abbey appear to have crept back to the precinct after the commissioners had passed on, and made their home there.[204]

The profile of the staff was as mixed as the professed community in respect of age, occupation and future prospects. The need for new employment may not have greatly unsettled the (unnamed) shepherd at Blackborough or the four kitchen men at St Osyth, but the four women who waited upon the five professed ladies of Crabhouse Priory may not have known where they might offer their service.[205] The commissioners seem surprised to find former staff still supported in their dotage. There was an old and impotent *quondam* cook living alongside the women at Polesworth.[206] Certainly, some may have welcomed the enforced leisure that came with a cash reward. John Spyard, domestic to the monks of Ely, was 'old and blind'; now he clutched two marks in his hand.[207] At Lilleshall the commissioners it seems were surprised to find among the household servants four who were gentlemen. It was perhaps with some embarrassment that they offered them rewards of one mark.[208] There were two 'little poor boys' among the fifty-seven staff at Dale Abbey.[209]

Not all domestic staff were obliged to look elsewhere. At the nine monastic cathedral priories, there were new roles to be taken. Designated the dean of the new secular see of Winchester, Prior William Kingsmill was assigned twelve servants of his old household.[210] Some of the best rewarded of the abbey superiors may have held on to staff together with the chambers, chapels and household furnishings they bargained for. When Katherine Bulkeley at last left Godstow it seems possible that her maidservants stayed with her.[211] The household of women who lived alongside Cecily Bodenham at Fovant (Wiltshire) were not former nuns; they may have been those who served her when she was abbess of Wilton.[212] The monks of Lewes kept close to their former servants, living nearby one another in the suburb adjoining their old precinct and supporting one another in their wills.[213]

The staff of the house were the most conspicuous secular presence, but they were only one part of the permanent population of the precinct. There were laypeople living alongside the enclosure not always in large numbers but certainly in a wide variety of capacities. Some enjoyed the in-kind benefits of corrodies (the right to annual benefits provided by the monastery in cash and in kind) purchased or granted to them, chambers somewhere in the outer courts, and doles of food, drink, firewood and sometimes clothing.

How many of these stayed on to the moment of suppression or surrender can only be counted for the houses whose surviving accounts run down to the last financial year. But their witness, combined with the observations of the commissioners, would suggest that some were certainly still in situ. The foundations' liabilities in this regard had been researched during the 1535 visitation and some were understood well enough for the Crown to take its own advantage of them, as grants, in the years following. However, the commissioners were not given explicit guidance on the cancellation of these arrangements at the point of closure nor on the circumstances in which the benefits might be commuted. There seems little doubt that there was immediate disruption to the lives of these laypeople.

Dr Mychell was turned out from his chambers at St Mary Overy (London) before the canons had left the precinct; they were passed to the prior as a supplement to his pension.[214] Nicholas Gilbert had only moved into the range known as 'Doctor's Commons' at Glastonbury Abbey in the previous year and when the surrender was made he was minded to challenge his removal. The matter was not settled for another year, during which time he may have stayed put.[215] Alice and Philip Myllet found that their custody of the chambers in the gatehouse of Chichester Greyfriars was challenged almost immediately.[216]

There were others in the precincts who were there neither through payment nor privilege. From his viewpoint in the city of London, Charles Wriothesley believed that from the houses suppressed under the 1536 statute there were 'pore people . . . kepit among theim' numbering some 10,000 who 'lost their living'.[217] In the houses of men there were sometimes members of their own extended family. It may have been extended family who were among the 'sundry poor folk' that received 47s at Gracedieu Abbey (Monmouthshire) in lieu of corrodies they had held.[218] To these the commissioners seemed to show some discretion. The aged mother of Abbot William Bewdley of Kingswood received a reward in her own right albeit surely at the intercession of her son.[219]

There were larger numbers of the incapacitated poor, beneficiaries of what the post-Reformation Poor Law would define as 'in-relief'. '[There are] old and impotent persons [here] lyvyng by promise,' reported the commissioners at Ulverscroft; at Erbury (Staffordshire), there were 'other impotent persons . . . fwnd of alms'.[220] Alongside them there were also children, whose social status is unclear except that they were set apart by age from the boys and girls old enough to be employed in the household. Over the past 150 years several abbeys had come to claim the right to give fugitive felons permanent sanctuary, that is, protection from the forces of the law so long as they remained inside. At Beaulieu Abbey, these were overlooked entirely by the commissioners, who after closing up the precinct were embarrassed by a petition from thirty-two agitated men languishing inside.[221] Even in the very conspicuous environment of Westminster Abbey there may have been no assured dispersal of the sanctuary men. When the monastery was recreated in November 1556, at three weeks' notice there were enough of them nearby to assemble a procession.[222]

The presence of these people is recalled for the most part in anecdotes and so at best the numbers can only be estimated. In a professed community of twelve or fewer, perhaps their number was matched by a mix of kinfolk and disabled and poor dependents; in the larger communities, there may have been several dozen. There was no transaction with which the commissioners could see them off the premises. Perhaps, as at Beaulieu, they did not.

There was an obligation to settle a payment on non-resident secular officers, among them the magnates who held principal stewardships. Here the sums were modest, no more than a few pounds; but, of course, for many of them they were repeated at several houses given their monopoly of these offices. Those receiving an annuity at or soon after closure were acknowledged and provision was made for the Crown to recognise their obligations. It is apparent, however, that there were eleventh-hour annuitants, and those whose claim was more dubious, who continued to emerge making claims in the months and even years that followed. Already in 1542 the Augmentation accounts spoke of 'travail' in the trial of information and 'hearing of reckonings' to which its officers were repeatedly called.[223] Some turned on their superiors who had made undertakings to them. John Stonywell of Pershore was pursued by a disappointed annuitant who had been promised a chamber and garden in the former house.[224] The continuity of such payments must have eased the passage of some of these individuals to new employment. The professional singing man from Quarr Abbey was still receiving his annuity in 1543.[225]

Annuitants, corrodians and pensioners held parchments to prove their right at least to a final payout. There was a far larger cohort of all ages who received reward from the monastery in much the same way, in cash and kind, but without the security of a document that might be defended in law. Those who received doles at the gate and in the court of these houses across the liturgical seasons of the year suddenly saw the practice end, without any ceremony, certainly without any challenge. For these beneficiaries of 'out-relief' the cut-off was complete, and comparable to the collapse of oblations made to the friars after 1536. Perhaps as for them, they simply stopped coming to and through the gatehouse. The smaller number who received their bed and board inside the precinct, some inside the enclosure itself, may have received some provision from the commissioners, although it is noticeable that their reports speak of them, and their infirmities, but not of what was offered to them. A good proportion were kin to the religious, and they may have passed out of the precincts with them.

Those who were resident as schoolboys, often under the direction and cost of the almonry, presumably, were disbanded. The five schoolboys present at Lewes Priory before 1534 had passed on by 1537, a year before its surrender.[226] The children who caught the attention of the commissioners tended to be those claimed to be the regulars' own.[227] The tenants of Furness remembered still sending their children to school in the monastery at the time of the dissolution and their taking their dinner and supper there.[228] The absence of references does not prove that the schools were closed in anticipation of the end. That Arthur Lisle was anxious over his schoolboy charge, James Bassett, at Reading in 1537 suggests no sudden upheaval.[229]

Perhaps the one relationship with the regulars that did change suddenly was that of their commercial suppliers. Given what appears to have been a wide, perhaps a widening, catchment of their purchases, it is doubtful that many manufacturers or traders saw their market entirely extinguished at the disappearance of the religious communities. The August fair in the precinct of St Bartholomew's, Smithfield, continued, and from 1541 the former prior held the right to the stallholders' customary fees.[230] An exception may have been city merchants trading in luxury goods – from imported wine to furs – the scale and value of whose business was surely constrained, at least in the short term. Craftsmen whose workshops existed to meet a very particular local demand – such as the glaziers' workshops in Carlisle – must surely have seen a permanent contraction in their market.[231]

Yet all of them may have experienced a novelty that was entirely beneficial: their debts were paid. The commissioners may not have been instinctively open-handed since creditors seem to have come to the monastery gate on spec. The Reading fishmonger Mr Badesdon waited there, apparently until the sum he was owed was entered into their book.[232] But where there were ready resources payment was also prioritised, perhaps to the detriment of the 'rewards' settled on the religious themselves.[233] Many, perhaps most, of these payments had been years outstanding. The account of debts compiled at St Albans in December 1539 records creditors whose claims dated from three or four abbacies past, in the first years of King Henry's reign.[234] The spectacle of old debts settled prompted some creditors to pursue the heads of houses for themselves. Thomas Wytney of Dieulacres blamed the commissioners' hurry to move on.[235] John Stonywell of Pershore faced a claim in the last year of his life.[236]

The movement of people out of and inside the precinct at the point of closure and in the weeks and months that followed may have stood in sharp contrast to the atmosphere in the satellite communities, the manors, granges and farms which recognised the religious house, directly or indirectly, as proprietor. There is no direct word from these places in the correspondence of the time, which turns always on the transactions at the precinct centre of the monastic enterprise. Their experience in the days, months and years following can only be estimated from the routine record of their annual administration.

By their very nature, the annual Ministers' accounts of the manors, that is to say the accounts of their principal officers, tend to construct a picture of continuity. But it would be a mistake to doubt or dismiss their testimony purely for this reason. Some properties of the houses suppressed under the 1536 statute saw a singular continuity, as they were regranted to another monastic proprietor. The Vaudey Abbey grange at Burton (Lincolnshire) passed into the possession of the neighbouring preceptory of the hospitallers within weeks.[237] Even as surrenders were made, heads of houses negotiated to retain some modest portion of their original holding for themselves. Thomas Legh granted Abbot Robert Watson of Lilleshall the former abbey manor of Longdon-upon-Tern, ten miles to the west, together with an acre of land adjoining.[238] The houses recast as secular cathedrals retained, or were regranted, the greater part of their property. Carlisle even benefited directly from the dissolution of other houses, being granted the properties of Wetheral Priory.[239]

Grants to new proprietors preserved the integrity of the original endowment. Tenure was conferred with the common formula, 'in as full a manner as the late abbot [or other superior] and their predecessors'.[240] Sir William Fitzwilliam took possession of Durford manors that reached in a chain across the South Downs from Petersfield to Brighton.[241] The pattern was often the same even as the Crown released the property under lease. Sir Edward Clinton took up the tenancy of the whole parcel of demesne meadows of Barlings Abbey, its orchards and fishery for a term of twenty-one years.[242] This continued at the surrenders, at least where there was prominent lordship in the locality which to a greater or lesser extent had presided over the process of closure. Charles Wriothesley secured each of the three grange farms in the vicinity of Beaulieu Abbey.[243] Often outlying properties were made the subject of discrete grants. Thomas Adyngton, city of London tanner and Serjeant of the Royal Peltry, received the grange manor of Chigwell (Essex), the former possession of the monks of Tilty, some forty miles to the north of the county.[244] Yet some grantees in these circumstances offered continuity of a kind. Miles Borne, who received the Crowland Abbey out-of-county manor of Morborne (Cambridgeshire), had been among the bailiffs of the abbot of Peterborough.[245]

The form of these transactions ensured continuity for those dependent on, and those responsible for, these properties. Some of the continuities they record were of no small significance to those who earned their living there. The ministers themselves were not much changed. More often than not the incumbent bailiffs were kept on. There was no fixed pattern to the Crown's transmission of seques-tered property but often these satellite properties were retained for some years after the suppression itself. A new proprietor, John Henage, arrived at Markby Priory's grange only a little over two years after the canons of the house had departed.[246] The Crown claimed chief stewardships but then granted them out often to those prominent families which had claimed a share of them when the monasteries were still in place; the tenure of lesser stewardships was not always challenged, at least not in the short term. The seasonal rhythms were uninter-rupted. Seigneurial courts presided at the same time, in the same way, as they had ever done; only the source of their lordship had changed.

There was also a tangible continuity in that the existing court books and rentals were taken up and continued, in the first accounting years, on the self-same parchment which had originally been purchased by a monastic obedientiary. There was an immediate change to the structure of an annual account since the subdivision of income by obedientiary office was ended, but this was invisible to those who generated and returned this income.

In general, those who rented premises, land and other amenities from religious houses at the time of their suppression or surrender were not immediately displaced. It does seem that they had anticipated a quite different experience. From early in King Henry's reign there was public and popular anxiety that a past harmony between landlord and tenant had been broken and the husbandman was now in plight. It was heightened by the broadside ballads coming into print: 'the worlde is changed from that it hathe beene; not to the better but to the warsse farre', shouted one anonymous sheet, 'unto the riche it makethe the greate deale, but much it marrethe to the commoune weale; to reyse his rent alias it nedeth not; or fine texacte for teanure of the same'.[247]

Such scares were as likely to be read inside the monastic precinct as on their tenanted properties. The canons of Butley Priory watched the closure of the neighbouring priory at Snape, rueful at the rumour that 'all their lands and rents are to be put into the hands of the laity'.[248] Pre-emptive interventions – and naked opportunism – were seen even before closures were confirmed. William Griffith of St Katherine's, Lincoln, reported 'ther is dyvers men that doth fewe [view] diverse thyngs her: the schepe, catell for they be very good'.[249] John Ferreys of Waltham seems to have assumed that he could withdraw from the agreement of a new lease that was at the point of completion when the abbey was finally closed in 1540, when the leasee, Richard Connydewe, had already 'paid the price to the servant of the cellarer'.[250] For as much as a year after its suppression, the tenants of Combwell Priory did not meet their suit-of-court obligations (a cash fee), an act of resistance which was slow to be noticed by their new royal proprietor.[251] The common pattern of a marked increase in new and renewed leases issued by houses still standing in the spring and summer of 1538 where records survive, north and south – Bolton, Bury, Chester, Fountains – may itself represent a sharp pang of anxiety among tenants.[252]

In fact, the commissioners' judgement of the circumstances of the neighbourhood was not to unsettle the present pattern of tenure, and to suppress any impulse for redistribution. Some careful stock-taking is apparent in the surviving documents: soon after the surrender of St Augustine's Abbey, Canterbury, a list revealed

132 tenants living in fourteen parishes in and about Canterbury.[253] A rare glimpse of their dealings is given in a letter reporting the suppression at Furness Abbey: 'at [the commissioners'] first cummyng [they] assembled all the tenants before [them] and declared [that they] shall see due and indifferent justice mynystered to every of them in all matiers of controversy .. or chance . . . and that there shalbe no exaction rent or knowledge taken of any of them but onely such ordinary rents and dewties as they have been accustomed heretofore to paye to the abbottes'. The tenants were assured that 'the kings highe pleasure is . . . that they shalbe at all tymes rather better used and ordered no thay be his graces tenantes thenne they were when they were tenants to the abbottes'; the secular officers of the domain, the stewards and bailiffs, were likewise advised of the Crown's commitment to its subjects, that 'in no wise [to] take any other fees . . . then they have been accustomed', not making charges 'further than their habites may susteyn'.[254]

Three weeks after the suppression of Abingdon Abbey no less a figure than 'Mr Chancellor Augmentations', Richard Rich, 'apon Sonday . . . rode' to 'view and surveye the manors . . . wich be within iiii or v myles'. There it was reported he secured the 'contentacion of the kyngs people'.[255] Sometimes the commissioners pressed for precise reassurance to be forthcoming from Austin Friars. From Bridlington, they called for confirmation that the tenants' customary use of the precinct for the custody of their ploughs would not be challenged by any grant of the site of the monastery, 'and thereby many men shalbe relyved'.[256]

The leases issued in the last months of the houses were not always respected. It does appear that the commissioners tended towards a blanket assumption that tenures recently entered into were legally dubious and a likely breach of the terms of the injunctions of 1535, and the subsequent statutes of 1536 and 1539. Where there were thought to be general grounds for suspicion, such as in Somerset and Devon, where they were first raised during the visitation, all leases were 'stayed and called in again'.[257] The illegal alienation of property and moveable goods was foremost among the allegations made against the heads of houses that lent support to the risings of 1536–37, and here tenures were discontinued as a matter of course. The grants and leases made by many of the friaries as their income fell away after 1536 were also frequently challenged. Henry Broke of Staffordshire, who had built up quite a portfolio from the Dominicans of Newcastle-under-Lyme, made an ineffectual protest to Cromwell as the commissioners took his tenancies away: '[they] hath answered me that [they] hath no right or authority to ratify nor to confyrm my seyd leasses'. He knew he was beaten, begging the vicegerent to 'take peyne to rede thys letter forth to the ende'.[258]

Yet the settlement of the friars' surrender by the end of 1538 appears to have seen the beginning of a change. Closure, or steps in preparation for it, now seemed to be reaching beyond the oversight of the commissioners, the Court of Augmentations or Austin Friars. The principal ambition of the new statute of April 1539 was less material than practical, that the Crown might recover control over property transactions. The approach to the sequestration of the estates of the three houses whose heads received sentences of attainder – Colchester, Glastonbury and Reading – was quite different from the rebel houses of the north. Three months after his former landlord, Abbot Cook of Reading, had been hanged from his gatehouse, William Biriton saw his old lease of land in Reading renewed by the Crown.[259]

The parcels and periods of existing tenancies for the most part were not challenged as they came into the Crown's possession. There were many leasees like Thomas Glover, only two years into a forty-year term for the Lilleshall Abbey grange at Willmore (Shropshire), for whom the closure of the convent changed nothing other than the recipient of their rent.[260] When tenures came to term without any interference, it does seem the typical response of the new royal proprietor was to renew with the same rights and responsibilities as before. The Crown's new tenants at the old manors of Westminster Abbey were under the same obligations to offer hospitality to the officers of their landlord as their predecessor had accepted over the past several hundred years.[261] At Leicester, for a time the Crown retained the identity of its last tenant for the administration of spiritual property, and as late as October 1540 it presented clergy to benefices under the 'abbot and convent of the abbey of St Mary de Pré'.[262]

In many cases the only conspicuous change in tenure at the point of closure, or in the months following, was the letting-out of those lands and buildings which had been held as the houses' demesne. Perhaps because it was late September, the harvest was over and the time for ploughing almost arrived that the commissioners distributed the demesne fields at Glastonbury even as the attainder of the abbot was being confirmed.[263] For the neighbourhood this may have represented a change in the arrangements of the most recent years, but this generation was accustomed to change in the status of this land. From as far back as the Black Death, houses had varied the proportion that was farmed directly according to fluctuations in the

465

market and the conditions – climate, disease – of their own husbandry. The availability of meadowland at Glastonbury in the autumn of 1539 would not have been considered unprecedented any more than it would have been unwelcome.

The continuity was reinforced by an inclination to retain the monasteries' own paid officials. It may have been a response to pre-emptive pressure from the present cohort. Cromwell's papers include several such as that from John Pakyngton of Worcester, explaining 'I am understeward [in his case, to the prior of Worcester] ... and have had the surveying of copylands, and desire to continue in the same. It is in my native country.'[264] Certainly, the consistent steer from the commissioners was to settle with those tied, by tenure or office, to the monastic domain. Some were confirmed. At Plympton, each of the priory's bailiffs was reappointed as soon as the domain was surrendered to the Crown.[265]

Perhaps more bailiffs were permitted to make suit for their role at relatively reasonable terms. John Collins, who had been bailiff of the manor of Leigh (Kent) under the abbot and convent of St Augustine's, Canterbury, was offered the office for a life term for a fine (fee) of £1 6s 9d. There was some awareness of the value of stewardships as patronage. At Chatteris, John Goodryke, confirmed for life as steward by the last abbess, Anne Gayton, was first accepted in the role for one year only after the suppression of the house.[266] Yet at Glastonbury, notwithstanding the stain of attainder, no new bailiffs were appointed until the year of King Henry's death (1547).[267]

Roles with lower status, it seems, were of lesser concern. The Chatteris rent collector, Ralph Johnson, was not interrupted in his duties at all. Richard Iver, parker (keeper or warden of parkland) of the former St Albans manor of Tyttenhanger, held his role until the end of the Crown's tenure of the estate, some eight years after the suppression.[268] It was perhaps proof of an unbroken tradition that men who had been boys when their local monastery was closed could recall who had managed their manors, and how.[269] The novelties in the administration of estates were not of manpower but of method. The receipts from the Westminster estates were recorded by county not obedientiary office. But the change was invisible to those whose graft generated them.[270]

Here the landlordship of the king and his agents appears to have contrasted with those to whom monastic estates were granted. This, at least, was the perception of tenants; and certainly the first complaints arising over challenges or changes to the established terms of their holdings concerned the second or subsequent proprietors, after the estates had passed from the Crown. Scribbled into the old rental book of Kirkstead Abbey is a new plea from the tenants of the manor of Gayton regarding their new proprietor, Sir Edward Dymoke. 'Ryght abote a yere last past [he] dyd inclose yn the said maner . . . and toke from the tenants suche common as they have ever usyd to have yn pasture to the greate damage and he hathe also increasyd and plowyd ther also of the kyngs lands abote xx acres [which] afore tyme [the tenants] dyd use to plowe'.[271] The tenacity of the new tenants of monastic estates was tested within weeks of their transfer at Conishead in October 1536, when the canons returned to their house after the suppression and tried to reap the corn from what months before had been their own fields.[272]

Those who had been the indirect beneficiaries of monastic landlords, depending on the pasture and woodland forage they permitted for common use, may have experienced a far more definitive change in their circumstances. Remote tenure, either of the Crown, or of the Crown's grantee, did not favour the conservation of these rights. Whoever was their new proprietor, the usual priority was to raise the annual return on estates that carried with them the high cost of paid officials and infrastructure always in need of maintenance. Muchwood, the customary common of the Ramsey Abbey tenantry, was earmarked for enclosure as soon as the new proprietor took possession.[273] Naturally, tenants represented – and remembered – these developments as evidence of how the dissolution had trampled over custom. Yet more often than not there were no mass protests here. The volatility of agricultural production and prices had long persuaded monasteries to experiment with enclosure. Battles – more often in the fields than in the manor court – had been fought with tenants in many regions for much of the past half-century. The last great cause to preoccupy the prioress and convent of Nuneaton (Warwickshire) and their chief steward in April 1538 was a protest from the parishioners of Nuneaton and Chilvers Coton concerning the common pasture there.[274]

The Catholic polemicist, Robert Persons, was born in the last year of Henry VIII's reign and held no personal memory of religious houses to colour his view, but when he surveyed Elizabeth's England he saw many signs of the old world. 'The sweet and high providence of Almighty God hath not been small in conserving and holding together a good portion of the material part of the old English catholick church.'[275] Parsons's view may not have been skewed by nostalgia but, of course, it was driven by his confessional preference and his commitment to a papal mission. It was only to be expected that he would claim there was 'little means [required] to raise them up or repair them again'.[276] Naturally, in the face of an apostate and excommunicate monarch, Persons was wont to provoke: 'there wanteth nothing but a new form to give them life and spirit'.[277]

His confidence was unfounded. The regulars had been reluctant to change their habits and many of them held on to a memory of their old profession. Men and women alike were attached to the social experience of their cloister life, the fraternity they had found in an institutional setting. But none of these things amounted to a corporate self and when Queen Mary and her close circle of coun-sellors thought to recover monastic life in England, they found no groundswell of support either from former religious or those who remembered living alongside them. Yet Persons's witness should not be dismissed purely because it was partial and political. He knew provincial England well, and at close quarters when he had travelled as a missionary through the Midlands back in 1580–81. Perhaps most suggestive was his perception that 'the matter went as a stage-play, where men do change their persons and parts, without changing their minds or affection'.[278] A new world had not, at least not yet, effaced the old.

X

THE OLD WORLD AND THE NEW

In May 1540, barely a month after the last monasteries were dissolved, 'a lytll broken byll' bearing 'straynge words' was dispatched to Sir William Kingston, comptroller of the king's household and Gloucestershire MP. The source of the words was alleged to be one John Plommer of Wotton-under-Edge, in Kingston's county. He himself 'steffly denyd' the claim, although his neighbours in the parish readily confirmed it. 'Ther shall be a new world [af]or mydsummers day,' Plommer was said to have declared. And he 'hopyd that ther shole be a new order menyng . . . that the kyngs hyenes . . . wold mak sum order of ponysment for such persons that wold nother fast nother pray'.[1] Over the past year old and new worlds had been spoken of and scribbled about across the kingdom, from provincial parishes such as Wotton to the Privy Chamber and secretariat from which government policy emerged. The drafts of bills planned for Henry's parliament had included such new-age ideas as statutory social welfare for the elderly and a standing army.[2] One popular rhyme saw Church reform as just the beginning; ahead was revolution: 'what shalle comme of those yt bee gaye with the goodes of the clergy . . . when a third mischefe commeth oute'.[3] Charles Wriothesley, one of the only observers of events to commit his thoughts to paper at the time, saw the suppression that spring of the last of the religious houses as a definitive dividing line: 'so that their is now but one order in the cleargies through this realm'.[4]

Historians have found it difficult to look on the years after 1540, the last years of Henry's reign, and those of his children, Edward and Mary, without the impression of new worlds being cut rapidly and roughly from the fabric of the old. From the Tudor period itself to the twentieth century it was an article of faith that these decades had witnessed sweeping transformations not only in the institution of the Church and the practice of religion but also in many aspects of economic and social life. Just as there was a new 'order of cleargie', in Wriothesley's phrase, the secular realm was said to be led by a new governing class, empowered by new property and wealth which was redrawing the profiles of the Tudor state and of provincial English society. Since then the old narrative has been repeatedly revised but also altered more in its emphasis than in its essentials. Change was by no means assured; sudden reversals were possible and inertia, which saw the old ways persist, cannot be underestimated. Yet the commitment of Henry, Edward and their respective regimes to a radical break with the past should not be doubted; and in their ways, Queen Mary and her advisors were well aware that their opportunity was not to rediscover the past but to describe an alternative future.[5]

Even as early as the spring of 1540 there were signs that the religious houses had given way to a new order. Perhaps especially visible in Wriothesley's London was a crowd of new clergy, 'which changed their habettes to secular priests'.[6] The surrender of eight of the capital's houses in just twelve months may have released as many as 150 individuals into city parishes which were not known to have been short of clergy.[7] Here, where the street plan (and permitted routes), open space and skyline had been defined by religious houses for more than 300 years, the first sight of new residents (and their very different occupations), who arrived rapidly, spoke at once of a new era, even if it was years before they made any alteration to the outward shape of the buildings.

Wriothesley, cousin to the king's chancellor, Thomas Wriothesley, may have also been aware of another tangible transformation taking place in the capital buildings of the Tudor regime. The harvest of precious metals, jewels and decorative objects of high market value were stockpiled on an unprecedented scale. The Keeper of the King's Jewels was forever 'caryeng and conveyinge [them] to and fro as well by bootes as cartes [and in] coffers, basketts and baggs'. There was too much to be kept in the Jewel Tower in the precinct of Westminster Palace and the Keeper made room for them at home, only for 125 lbs to be 'loste and spoiled at the bourning of his house'.[8]

There were signals of a new departure from the footprint of the regulars, which might be read by the nation as a whole. Henry's progress to the north of his kingdom, which he began on the last day of June 1541, was regarded by foreign ambassadors as a display of might and has been interpreted by some historians as a thinly veiled act of aggression towards Scotland. By that summer, certainly coastal regions would have known that a new war machine was ready to be deployed. Eight state-of-the-art castles and a dozen barrack blockhouses had been raised from the Essex estuaries all the way to Pembrokeshire.[9] The Crown's force of retained troops had grown in the second half of the 1530s, especially in Ireland, but most conspicuous at the passing of the monasteries was its wherewithal to pay to raise a substantial force in short order.

When the invasion of Scotland was imminent in the autumn of 1542, it was possible to mobilise nearly 1,500 men at the outset and to have £2,000 in hand for their pay.[10] Now the Crown could also call on thirty gallant (i.e. battle) ships and crew; the pay and victuals of all were charged to the Court of Augmentations.[11] A new state of war with Scotland opened up in 1542 and then, in 1544, an English army entered France. Both rivals were defeated in the field and the new military leadership extinguished internal enemies of the regime in 1549. Kett's Rebellion began with the punishment of a man, Sir John Flowerdew, seen to be complicit in the closure of a monastery (Wymondham Abbey); it was finally defeated and dispersed by one (John Dudley, duke of Northumberland) whose wealth, political and public profile had been a consequence of the dissolution.[12]

Yet despite these dramatic novelties, for much of this time many features of the old world of the regulars remained in view. The new ambitions of the Crown were advanced not only as a result of the treasures and raw materials given up by the religious houses but also, to a greater extent over time, by the revenues generated from their properties – agricultural, commercial, industrial and ecclesiastical – whose occupiers and supervisors did not suddenly change. Provincial England did not all at once try to tear itself free from the old patterns of economic, social and local political life. New governance in towns, and lordship in their hinterlands, grew up in time, but often from the customary and documentary roots of the old world.

The buildings of the religious houses also stood and held their ground even in urban centres where space was always at a premium; and more than this, in many cases, their uses were not very much changed. For years, they continued to be places of parish worship and burial, schools and libraries, where books had not once shifted their shelf position since the dissolution itself. The personal records of property, last will and burial have revealed how often regulars were still in evidence: a Syon monk published in 1541 as he had done almost annually since 1530; a Franciscan added new entries to the annal of his convent; women who had lived together in a convent stayed together in a secular household.[13] Regular priests changed their habit but not substantially their role; and a new habit did not see them entirely subsumed into the ranks of the secular clergy.

Between Henry's death and the death of his son Edward six years later in 1553, regular clergy rose again into the hierarchy of the Church in England. There were more bishops trained in the tradition of the religious orders in 1549 than there had been at any time since 1536. Ten sees remained in monastic hands before 1553, including the two largest (York, Lincoln) and two of the new 1542 foundation (Bristol, Gloucester). These men were marked by their old tradition but they joined the movement of the times. Only a handful of them, and a tiny minority of the wider population of former religious, felt compelled to pledge themselves inviolably to the old world or the new. In this they were like the society that surrounded them. The impulses either for revolution or counter-revolution in these years were never strong or sustained. Monastic England remained in present sight but without the prospect of being restored.

The transformation that seized the Tudor imagination most of all was the immediate and remarkable enrichment of the Crown. Wriothesley documented the progressive 'augmentation' of the Crown, 'in as ample manner as the said abbottes and priors' over four years of suppression and surrender: £13,200 was his figure for 1536; then the 'shryne and goodes' of Thomas Becket, set in 'silver richly', were 'taken to the kinges' treasury', then 'all their goodes and implements' of the friars; finally 'divers other houses' and all shrines 'taken downe throughout England', which 'had to the kings treasurye in the Towre of London . . . amounted to great riches'.[14]

For his estimate of the king's reward from 1536, Raphael Holinshed (1577) raised his estimate by a factor of four, counting £320,000 for the value of the monasteries' lands and another £100,000 for the treasures of their churches and convent buildings.[15] In the vivid colour that comes more from legend than first-hand memory, John Stow (1592) pictured a particular vignette, 'the spoyle' of Thomas Becket's shrine at Canterbury 'which . . . filled two great chestes' such as '6 or 8' men could carry only one at a time.[16]

The next generation suspected these to underweigh the king's reward. 'Speed [was] standing on slippery ground [and] tread[ing] only on figures and not on numbers at length', opined Thomas Fuller, who depicted King Henry as glutton duly gorged 'sucked up' and making a succession of 'rich meals'.[17] At the end of the decade Wriothesley caught the impression of the Crown now with cash in an open hand: a new cohort of gentlemen of the household received £8 'a peece out of the court of augmentation'.[18] Rumours of a prodigal king ran also at street level. 'The kingis grace had a horse lode of plate,' claimed 'a fellow callyd William Wodlow', at Winchcombe, 'and porcion of everye riche man of the town', in February 1540. Wodlow conjured an image of common thievery: 'two malt syffes full of plate' were brought to the tollbooth at Tewkesbury, 'taken from the rich men of the same town for the kingis highnes'.[19]

Later historians have hesitated to scrutinise the numbers very closely at least in part because they shared Fuller's concerns about the accuracy of the available records, of the valuation of 1535, and often of post-dissolution returns. There has long been an awareness also of the momentum of these years. There was perhaps no one point in time at which the wealth of the Crown might be judged to have been transformed. The new wealth which commentators saw awarded by statute in 1536, and by the drift of surrenders at Easter 1540, was no more than notional at those moments in time. Property acquisitions were cumulative over the four years in which religious houses were closed, and beyond; the ghost of monastic proprietors haunts account books at least as far as 1541–42, the second accounting year after the dissolution was complete. The retrieval of the treasure was even more protracted. John Williams, Keeper of the King's Jewels, was still receiving deliveries from the commissioners who had emptied sacristies as late as 1545–46, almost a decade after they had begun their task;[20] of course, the delay, and the position of the commissioner as a go-between, naturally raises the question of whether what arrived was more than a fraction of what originally passed out of the precinct. The traffic in receipts made the rewards of the Crown patchy and unpredictable and its effects were compounded by the king's ongoing expenditures. As Fuller again was one of the first clearly to observe, Henry began spending as soon as the first of the spoil arrived: 'Alas! What the crown possessed . . . was nothing to what he passed away!'[21]

A measure of the change in the fortune of the Crown is best begun with the treasure – the jewels, plate, precious works of art and coin (some of it already raised from the sale of these pieces) taken from the diverse collections of the religious houses that are certain to have passed into royal possession. Inventories of these items were compiled at the end of Henry's reign and again subsequently, and crucially an account of their weight and value was rendered by Keeper Williams in response to an inquiry in 1551. Certainly, these were the first visible rewards of the dissolution; clearly, as at Tewkesbury, their transport across the country did not pass unnoticed.

The first receipts recorded in Williams's account date from late April 1537, when more than seventy pounds of gold, silver gilt and silver plate was delivered from Merton Priory in nearby Surrey.[22] This entry was for stand-out items and it is very likely that other loads of treasure had reached London from the first months of the circuit in 1536. Even before the suppression statute was made law, silver-gilt crucifix and other plate from Tilty Abbey had been passed into the hands of Richard Cromwell.[23] In the summer Richard Southwell had carried away not only 'plat juells and stuffe' from Walsingham Priory but also 'instruments potts belowes flyers of suche straunge colers', the tools of the gold- and silversmith's trade.[24]

In December, John Gostwick answered Cromwell's request with the calculation that £2,159 of plate remained in the Jewel House, £3,870 in the hands of Robert Lord and £400 in his own.[25] The depositions of prisoners taken in Lincoln provide an oblique glimpse of the movement of valuable treasure: it seems to have been widely known that Matthew Mackarell was passing plate worth £100 from Barlings through his personal network in the weeks before the trouble began at the beginning of October.[26] Robert Aske established his good faith with the network of rebel houses by providing a spice plate from Watton Priory.[27]

When order was restored in the spring, the receipt of notable treasures gathered pace. On 28 May 1537 Gregory Conyars delivered to Thomas Avery, Cromwell's servant, a remarkable trove of treasures 'to the use of the kings highnes', recovered from the coffers of James Cockerell of Guisborough, now attainted and executed for his role in the rising. At the head of a list including five gilt goblets, three gilt salt cellars, fifteen silver spoons and garnets mounted in silver were four gold rings, one with a 'great saphure', two 'lesser saffires' and the other with an 'emythyst'; not the accustomed plate of an Augustinian prior but the war chest of a prospective rebel.[28]

The total value of the plate received by the end of the reign, calculated from the figures cited in these original accounts, was a little over £415,000. Of this there was more than 900 pounds of gold.[29] When the largest and wealthiest of the Benedictine foundations were surrendered in the last months of 1539 they brought vast returns: Winchester gave up the greatest volume, more than 950 pounds in weight; Glastonbury was not far below at 860 pounds.[30]

The value remained a matter of mass rather than money until such time as it could be sold. This inevitable check on the king's reward was visible from the outset. Before the end of 1536 John Gostwick warned Cromwell that 'there is plate lately receved . . . of the augmentacions whiche cannot be converted into redy money'.[31] Two years on and Williams's account recorded deliveries to the Royal Mint in two kinds, cash of almost £19,000 but also approaching 1,000 pounds of plate as yet unsold.[32] Treasure lying unsold in London was matched by large quantities of high-value building materials left on site. From Leicester Abbey a little over £300 had been raised from the sale of livestock and bells, but what the Crown had expected to be the best currency, the lead, said to be worth £1,000, had found no buyer.[33]

The volume of the treasure taken into custody created a constant demand for carriage and storage which wore away at the overall value of the return. The new offices of the Augmentations were no better prepared practically than any other part of their operations. A great chest was purchased in 1539 for £22 10s, almost exactly the total value of the Augustinian priory at Bradley (Leicestershire) suppressed under the statute of 1536.[34] New storage in the city was commandeered at Elsing Spital at Cripplegate; by 1540 a new purpose-built storehouse was called for at a cost of £30.[35] The attentions of the custodians required their own reward. Gostwick had observed as early as 1536 that 'persones be gredy of money with open mouths'.[36] For the survey of the jewel house in 1545, the accounts record the purchase of some twelve tuns of Gascon wine.[37] It seems the king was aware of the delicate balance of benefit and cost and already in 1539 was inclined to call for certain treasures to be kept in situ, although losses on site were as likely as losses on the road.

The enhancement of the Tudor monarchy with treasure was not itself a break with the past. King Henry's father, after the Battle of Bosworth, may have found the Westminster Jewel House largely an empty space, but over the next twenty years he replenished it, and his principal palaces, at a cost of some £200,000.[38] No inventory of Henry VII's acquisitions survives but in his will he directed that 'the grettest ymage of our Lady that we nowe have in our Juelhouse' should be sent to his new Lady chapel at Westminster Abbey; he believed there was enough of a surplus for his executors to sell jewels and plate to underwrite his funeral commemorations up to 20,000 marks.[39] The change his son Henry VIII achieved was one of scale. Inventories made months after his death have been preserved and they describe as many as 3,700 individual pieces of precious metal plate and jewellery necessarily distributed along the chain of royal palaces in and around the capital, the Tower, the Charterhouse, Greenwich, Westminster Palace, Hampton Court, Nonsuch (near Epsom, Surrey) and Oatlands (near Weybridge, Surrey).[40]

Henry VII had been a judicious investor whose preferences for the form and function of decorative art were conventional. His son, however, held something of a magpie's eye and from the regulars' centuries-old hoards he created a new cabinet of royal curiosities. The inventories made after Henry VIII's death record such singular treasures as an elephant's tooth, ostrich feathers, and objects believed to have been fashioned from a unicorn's horn; three of these last had been taken from the sacristy at Winchester Cathedral Priory (see Fig. 29).[41] The king also made a collection of clocks and dials; the first of fifteen timepieces was 'fayer . . . standing upon a myne of silver . . . garnyished with diverse counterphet stones and perles'. It is possible that some of them had been taken from the greater abbeys and priories, pioneers of clock-time; one conjured an image of early science, 'metall graven . . . with the planettes in imagerie'.[42] There was no ready market for these rare and costly pieces and it may be that the closure of religious houses created a royal horologium by default.

The dissolution had created one particular royal collection which Henry VII had not known. By the time the inventories were made in the summer of 1547, there was established at Westminster Palace a new 'upper library'.[43] The Tudors had acquired books as much as any educated and pious family of the social elite, but it seems it was their scrutiny of the regulars' resources and their repossession of them that spurred the curation of a permanent collection, housed at the heart of the principal royal palace. Books were the first monastic treasures to be taken by the Crown in any bulk. Most of those that were now found at Westminster had been demanded almost a decade before the dissolution began, during the preparation of the case for the king's divorce.[44] The visitors of 1535 occasionally took hold of texts thought to be suspect or otherwise unusual, although most acquisitions made after 1534 may have come from John Leland who boasted to the king 'I have conserved many good authors, the which otherwise had ben lyke to have peryshed'.[45] The first surviving inventory of the Westminster library, compiled in 1542 perhaps only shortly after the collection was settled there for the first time, captures the scale of the accessions: at least 195 volumes derived from the libraries of forty-three monasteries and friaries.[46]

To these contents of the treasure houses can be added the cash receipts. Coin came in quickly. Before any furnishings, buildings or land were sold, the commissioners recovered cash sums which the houses had kept in hand. At Leicester Abbey they took into custody £506, more than they were able to raise from plate, stock and bell metal combined.[47] Transactions completed locally at or around the moment of dissolution prompted cash flow in several parallel streams that might remain live for months, even years. Contents other than precious treasures, including decorative objects, such as plate and vestments, which because of their material, age or condition did not merit dispatch to London, were sold on site together with domestic furnishings.

At Michaelmas 1538, Thomas Pope, treasurer of Augmentations, recorded a total for the sales of almost £7,000, more than the total annual revenue of the wealthiest of monasteries. Until the turn of 1540, fines levied for a house to continue, first in dispensation of the terms of the 1536 statute, latterly applied to all that remained standing, amounted to a discrete cash stream. It was a measure of the number and scale of the fines paid by smaller houses in order to evade the statute that Pope's account for 1538 recorded almost £6,000. The final receipts may have fallen some way below the potential return as, by the spring of that year, houses chose voluntary surrender before these cash sums were paid.[48] Where they were made above board, houses faced fines for any new lease. For the two years from April 1536, some £1,000 was received in lease fines.[49]

These cash flows were easily eclipsed by the return from sales of lands taken into the custody of the Crown at the point of closure. These transactions began at the outset of the suppressions. The sale of a select portion of the endowment might be concluded almost at once. The Hertfordshire estates of Holywell Priory delivered an immediate return to the Crown in 1537 under its sale to Sir Thomas Audley for £85.[50] For many others, a seller's market was confected, by the king personally as much as either Cromwell or Richard Rich, and the price to purchase was raised to a multiple of the annual revenue. Sir Edward Baynton settled on a figure of £1,200 for a portion (twenty manors) of the estates of Stanley Abbey, five times the annual value recorded in 1535.[51] The sudden turnover of estates unseen for centuries invested these endowments with a value in their own neighbourhood that ensured the ready supply did not suppress the demand. It was possible for the Crown to set its price, far above the level that any private proprietor might command. To secure his interest in a portfolio of properties from Louth Park, Sir Thomas Burgh was compelled to accept a purchase price of £3,213 17s 2½d, almost twenty times the total value of the house in 1535.[52] In principle the return to the Crown from such sales was immense but it was a rare buyer who could muster more cash than a percentage instalment. Sir William Sharington settled terms for Lacock Abbey with a down payment of just £100. Like the monastic treasure, much of the value of land sales to the Crown was deferred.[53] Not all of these purchases were completed, allowing the Crown to profit from abortive as well as completed sales.

By the end of the accounting year in 1538, Treasurer Pope posted transactions totalling £71,616 16s 1½d.[54] The gross profit is remarkable at a time when fewer than half the religious houses had been suppressed or surrendered, but its net value was much reduced after the fees of agents and others and outstanding debts and liabilities were settled: the true value to the Crown in this year was less than £24,000, as some 67 per cent of the gross profit was lost to the administration of the sale. Yet the cost of cash sales was in large part offset by their frequency.

This flow of cash continued, and in the next year of dissolutions, to Michaelmas 1539, it grew further. Sales made directly by the king reached more than £44,000 gross, those devolved to Cromwell and others more than £36,000; now the net figure was almost twice that of the previous year. The total receipts recorded at the year's end stood at £131,836 5s 10d.[55] In 1542, £51,951 was passed to the Keeper of Westminster Palace; the next year the gross return on all sales topped £91,000, almost 15 per cent more than had been realised in 1539–40.[56]

These tangible returns, weighed in or counted out and visibly so, stood in contrast to the property wealth which in principle the dissolution had passed to the Crown. The potential value of all the estates, urban property, infrastructure and churches of 850 monastic foundations certainly exceeded the face value of the treasure that was in Crown hands by 1540. The sum of the Valor assessments was £162,000 and their coverage was far from complete, and while they failed to count some of the charges on these properties at the same time it seems likely that they did not always discover the full extent of their worth. The difference between the gross and the net income that might be raised from such a domain cannot be counted reliably. From the surveyors' own figures, it would appear to be in the region of 16 per cent, but even as properties were being claimed by the king's commissioners new liabilities were found. As the number of surrenders rose over the summer of 1538, Chancellor Rich ordered the receivers in the Western March to make their own survey of charges on all lands of religious houses; less than two and a half years after the valuations had been returned to Westminster, the regime acknowledged that the work needed doing again.[57]

The recipients of annuities, corrodies and pensions sometimes stepped from the wings onto the main stage of the suppression or surrender. In August 1539, Margaret Scotson reminded the receivers holding the property of Barlings Abbey, attainted nearly three years before, of her 'dewe' of a corrody, the quarterly value of which was £4.[58] Beneficiaries continued to trouble the regime with their claims to the very end of the reign, and beyond. In the second year (1548–49) of the young King Edward, the regime was reminded of the continued 'lyvyng and abydyng' of Emme Dygger, 'late of the monastery of Bysstyr [Bicester]' entitled to a pension of 100s.[59]

The traffic was heavy even before the full extent of illicit and counterfeit leases issued over the course of the decade had been recognised. The possible gain was compromised also by the tendency to transact properties from the very moment they were placed under royal authority. The exchange, grant and sale of particular properties and portions of properties began at the time of the first suppression circuits; while it was overseen by Cromwell and the king himself it was not strictly orchestrated by either of them. The commissioners, local lordship and the monastic communities themselves were able to initiate negotiations which at times the regime was obliged to adopt. The 'great labour' of John Scudamore over fees and leases for which he was thanked warmly by Francis Talbot, 5th earl of Shrewsbury, in October 1538 was surely not unusual.[60] The pace of the process, the distance of central government, and the diverse and subdivided form of many properties made it inevitable.

It was not a pure transfer of all of the revenue which the regulars may have known but by the measure of royal income at the end of the Middle Ages it represented a vast dividend. Given the unsteady course the closures followed from the spring of 1536, there was no sudden injection of new funds into the exchequer. Perhaps only at the turn of the financial year in 1539 (April), when the first treasurer of Augmentations, Thomas Pope, was succeeded by Edward North, was the scale of the change clearly perceptible. In the eighteen months from the first suppressions under the statute of 1536, the return from monastic lands amounted to a little less than £28,000.[61]

After four and a half years as treasurer, at Michaelmas 1543 North reported that the total received from lands was £177,806, a figure from which can be calculated an annual return of almost £40,000. This did represent a transformation of the value of the Crown estate. At the accession of Henry VII in 1485 the total annual return had been no more than £42,000. His purchase of political loyalty had necessarily reduced his resource by as much as 36 per cent by 1491. He had bequeathed solvency to his son but nothing in reserve.[62] It was only after monastic endowments began to be added to the royal domain that Henry VIII's personal income surpassed that of his father twenty-five years before. During Treasurer North's first years at Augmentations (1539–43), the dissolution added to the revenue from property roughly 100 per cent of the figure received at the foundation of the dynasty six decades before.

Yet the moment when the revenue gains began to be calculated fully was also when they began to recede. It is often said that the financial advantage which the dissolution gave to the Crown was soon squandered by the spending of the king's last decade.[63] Yet there were challenges to and constraints on income inherent in the settlement of the dissolution itself. It had been apparent even before the statute of 1536 that the appropriation of the monastic estate was only possible if it was pursued in partnership with the proprietorial, commercial and industrial interests in provincial England: suppression or surrender committed the Crown to the continued redistribution of monastic property by grant and sale. Like his father before him, Henry VIII was obliged to use his windfall to secure his regime for now and for the future. The possession of the monastic estate was a structural gain in so far as it expanded the royal domain in England and Wales, but it also represented a structural loss since, in the extinction of the religious houses, it cut from the Crown's resources a source of tax revenue on which it had relied for 300 years.

By the time of Henry's death in 1547 it may be estimated that the return from the clerical subsidy, the levy on the income of all church institutions, granted at regular intervals at royal request, had fallen by as much as 60 per cent. The total revenue from three post-dissolution years, 1543, 1545 and 1548, was £126,000; only a little less than this had been raised in 1523, when all rateable religious houses remained in place.[64] The perspective of the recusant Nicholas Harpsfield was not, in this respect, distorted: 'the people is now more charged . . . with subsidies' without abbeys 'out of which was wont the prince to be furnished'.[65]

There is no doubt that the cash flow from the dissolution was channelled into the new enterprises of the king's final years. Keeper Williams's account of the treasures records a total sum of £3,078 7s 7d required to see the carriage and train of Anne of Cleves safely from Calais to Greenwich in the final weeks of 1539. The same account records the staggering figure of £10,285 8s 4d to be 'saveley conveyed to Ireland' in May 1541 to meet the costs of 'cotes [for] men of were ... transportacion ... araye and other chardges' for the 'king's majesties warre'.[66] The prospect of offensive wars on two fronts (France and Scotland) consumed more of the monasteries' material remains. Just as their sites were made quarries, their old treasures stored in the jewel houses were mined as the raw material for petty cash.

The Keeper's account summarises a series of large payments made in the accounting years 1538–39 and 1539–40 for 'rigging' and 'apparelling for new' the king's ships, for the victualling of their crew at Portsmouth and the king's army at Southampton. The total expenditure exceeded £7,700.[67] The second of these years saw a further £2,000 demanded from the Keeper for the repair of the castle and town at Berwick-upon-Tweed.[68] The volume of treasure retrieved may have been large enough to put pressure on storage, but the account suggests that quantities were converted quickly for the purposes of the Mint. In November 1538, just about the halfway point in the dissolution, the Keeper dispatched to the Mint a sum of £18,942, raised from the sale of treasure and 10,329 ounces of plate to be recycled.[69]

'All this income,' Fuller reflected, 'rather stayed the stomach than satisfied the hunger of the king's exchequer.'[70] Two financial years after the last of the religious houses was closed, in the spring of 1542, the regime was again compelled to look for loans. A pro forma was drafted for the terms of personal loans from 'dyverse faythfull and loving subiects' of 'their own free will and full consent lovingly consented to advance' for 'dyverse greate and urgent causes'; 550 subjects now entered into terms: every one of the bishops and the full complement of the king's chaplains.[71] Another three years and commercial credit was required. Negotiations with the Fuggers, the German bankers who were creditors to the royal houses of sixteenth-century Europe, opened in 1545; a year later the king's obligation to them already stood at more than 150,000 Flemish pounds.[72]

The king's new wealth may have been more apparent than real but there was no doubt that in the wake of the dissolution he was possessed of a new magnificence.

On the day that Thomas Cromwell was executed at Tower Hill, Henry made his third marriage to Catherine Howard at Oatlands, a red-brick palace of multiple gables and symmetrical turrets, whose remodelling had been completed only months before with money and material from the monasteries. It was the first of two new palaces into which the king quickly channelled his new resources as the dissolution continued to unfold. Nonsuch, only a dozen miles from Oatlands, was begun in April 1538, and ready to be adopted as a royal residence in 1541. Even as it was almost ready for use that spring, labourers were still 'occupiede at Marten [Merton Priory] in settinge fourthe stuff redy to be caryed'.[73] Monastic fabric and funds were also employed for the further refinement of Hampton Court, its buildings, 'hewyng dores wyndoes chymneys', contents, 'making tables forms and stoles' and grounds, 'digging uppe gardyns'.[74] At the end of 1538 total expenditure on the palaces stood at £767 15s 2d; three years later and the outstanding account for labour at all three sites was £1,442 10s, almost half as much again as the annual revenue of Merton itself.[75]

These palaces are generally seen as giving expression to the ambitions of the Tudor monarchy after the Reformation: indomitable lordship and cutting-edge Renaissance style to challenge any European rival. Yet if the frame is widened beyond these three Surrey palaces, there was much in the source and style of Henry's late magnificence that seemed anchored in the pre-dissolution world. Two monastic palaces which had been heartlands of Tudor royalty and family since before 1509, Greenwich, with a friary church standing within it, and Sheen, with an adjacent Carthusian convent, remained among the principal residences. A new monastic environment was now added, as St Augustine's Abbey, just beyond the city wall at Canterbury, was converted for the king's use. James Needham, surveyor of the king's works, was dispatched there in mid-October 1539 to begin to plan the conversion, with the ample expenses for the month's work of £500.[76]

There does seem to have been a sense in which Henry garnered some of the sites with general royal or particularly personal associations. Initially he held in his possession the abbeys and precincts of Glastonbury, Reading, St Albans, Syon, Waltham and Woburn, some of them having been a preferred stop in his progresses; some, because of the fate of their abbots, a symbol of his triumph over papal monarchy. The royal occupation of these sacred sites could not fail to stir the public imagination. Perhaps the tale told with relish by Nicholas Harpsfield had been widely enjoyed: when Henry's corpse lay at Syon en route for Windsor, 'the fat and the corrupt putrefied blood dropped out' drawing 'a dog lapping', apparently fulfilling the promise of his opponent's curse that he would be another Ahab (1 Kings 21:19).[77]

The continuities in the king's associations with religious houses were matched in the patterns of occupation and ownership countrywide. Generally, the grants, leases and sales of sites, their buildings and estates made as the closures continued, and in the years immediately following, were to those already with a profile in the same region, and often with a prior connection the house. Arthur, Lord Lisle's pursuit of a poor priory such as Frithelstock, in which he persisted from the moment he received news of the suppression statute in March 1536, reflected the property interest in North and West Devon that had come to him by his second marriage.[78] Sir Edward Baynton, among the first to have confirmed the purchase of the major portion of a monastic estate, Stanley Abbey, in February 1537, was established as a Wiltshire landlord, his seat at Bromholm scarcely more than six miles from the precinct of the monastery.[79]

Certainly not every new proprietor was a neighbour of the house but typically their sphere of interest was still broadly local. Sir Thomas Cheyney, grantee of Minster-in-Sheppey, was of Kentish origins although his marriage into a mercer dynasty and his offices had made him a city of London figure.[80] The original home of the Parrs was Kendal (Cumbria) and Sir William's purchase of Byland was a westward extension of his northern interest.[81] Even when monastic property was given as a reward to lesser servants in the royal household, it seems there was some consideration of local connections. John Ogan of the household, grantee of the site of Taunton Priory, was a member of a Somerset family.[82]

Early grantees not infrequently held formal ties to the house as hereditary founder, principal patron, chief steward (or all three). Thomas West, Baron de la Warr, took possession of the priory at Boxgrove, which had been under the protection of his Sussex family for almost a century. Thetford Priory was made a mausoleum for the Howard family and in 1538 Thomas, duke of Norfolk, took it permanently into his care. In the wake of the suppression statute there was a widespread expectation that these patronal positions would become the guiding principle of any redistribution. 'Yt wolde be thowght I weyre smalley regarded,' Sir William Parr had written to Cromwell in May 1537, reminding him of his hope to have Jervaulx Abbey, of which he was founder: 'Shuld [I] not obteigne in thius my sute', '[it] shulde redownde to my dyhonestye and great reproche'.[83] There was no automatic recognition of the claims of the founder or principal patron and grants or licences to lease or to purchase were made to them selectively. It is doubtful there was a deliberate intent to provoke a confrontation with the local lordship; the concern may have been quite the opposite, not to upset the balance of power. That Parr was disappointed in his claim on Jervaulx may have owed much to the value of its estates, approaching £500 per year, more than twice the return on Byland.[84]

The first beneficiaries of the monastic estate were not men whose status in society, political or public life was either new or only now becoming established. Many of the most substantial allocations made as the government's policy unfolded between 1536 and 1539 were to figures who had always stood at the head of the Tudor regime. George Talbot, earl of Shrewsbury, was not projected centre-stage by his grant of Rufford Abbey in 1537.[85] Having defended the dynasty man and boy, rather he took it as his long-service souvenir. Charles Brandon, duke of Suffolk, the king's companion for almost three decades, received his first reward from the monastic estate in April 1537 (Leiston Priory).[86] Thomas Howard, duke of Norfolk, took his first just a month later (Buckenham and Coxford priories); more followed at the turn of the year (Bungay and Castle Acre).[87]

The principal officers of the Crown were among the very first to receive grants from the Court of Augmentations. Thomas Audley, the king's chancellor, received St Botolph's Priory, Colchester, scarcely eight weeks after the suppressions began.[88] Just a month later, his colleague, the treasurer, Sir William Fitzwilliam, received the grant of Waverley, the earliest of England's Cistercian abbeys.[89] Chamberlains John de Vere, earl of Oxford, and Sir William Sandys, received their first priories (Colne, Mottisfont) four weeks on.[90] Thomas Wriothesley, for whom royal favour was rising in the first year of suppressions, was among the first to see great largesse. He received lands from Quarr in the winter of 1537; Beaulieu directly at its dissolution in the summer of 1538; a year later, he had stepped around and ahead of rival claimants to take Titchfield Abbey.[91] Their combined valuation in 1535 was more than £1,000.[92]

Cromwell himself had made only modest acquisitions in the first two years of closure, the foundations for his own domain in south-east England, with the wide coastal stretch of estates belonging to Michelham Priory and the sites of the Cluniac priory at Lewes. The prospect of further territory, of higher value, at Launde and St Osyth, arose only in April 1540, eight weeks before his final arrest.[93]

Taking possession of sites, most of which they had known in the past as patrons, at first the Tudor leadership seemed inclined to assimilate their old identity virtually unaltered. 'The nobilities in my tyme have swelled so much,' reflected William Turner, 'that all the houses that theyr fathers and they have buylded wyll not holde them but they must also have byshoppes ... deans [and] parsons houses.'⁹⁴ Four of the largest sites retained by the Crown to the end of Henry's reign and beyond were kept empty and untouched, to the frustration of covetous courtiers. It was the illicit removal of fabric – stone, lead – and furnishings from Sheen, Syon, Glastonbury and Reading that were headline accusations against the Lord Protector, Edward Seymour, duke of Somerset, in October 1549.⁹⁵

When Henry made a new progress north in the spring of 1541, the route he followed still led from one monastic setting to another: Sir William Parr at Pipewell Abbey, Sir John Byron at Newstead and Richard Whalley at Welbeck.⁹⁶ Richard Rich made St Bartholomew's Priory his main residence and, apparently, did not think to remodel the interior which until 1540 had accommodated an Augustinian prior. Indeed, he seemed glad to offer his guests monastic comfort, 'a bedde of the hardest for your wife and yourself'.⁹⁷ The Londoner John Luccas, grantee of the buildings and site of St John's Abbey, Colchester, reanimated the domestic buildings with activity no different from that of the former household of canons. His 'mylche beastis' were found 'fedyng upon the ... demayne', while his wife presided over the brewhouse 'for the necessaire brewinge of her drinke', 'the pastrye house and ovens for baking of her bred pyes pasties', and 'the mylke house for her chese butter and suche like'.⁹⁸

The Crown's most loyal prelates who had shaped the Reformation policy were also present in this first phase. In the course of an exchange of property with the Crown, Archbishop Cranmer took estates from the endowment of West Malling Abbey;⁹⁹ Rowland Lee received the grant of Stafford Priory;¹⁰⁰ Richard Ingworth was rewarded with his former house of King's Langley; Robert Fuller received selected properties from the domain of St Bartholomew's Priory, Smithfield, which had first been envisaged as an endowment for his own abbey at Waltham.¹⁰¹

Almost all of Cromwell's principal agents who had shouldered much of the administration of the dissolution had received a monastic portion by Easter 1540. Richard Rich was granted the whole site of St Bartholomew's Priory at Smithfield as well as estates from the endowment of Faversham Abbey. Thomas Legh received Calder Priory, which he had pressed for from the outset on the grounds of his family connections.[102] His settlement seemed to imprison him in the dissolution episode. At Legh's death in 1545 his home and income were monastic in origin; even his new career was marked by these associations as he had been chosen as the MP for Wilton. He placed his will in the hands of the leading dissolution men still living, Thomas Cranmer, Richard Rich and Robert Warmington, who were responsible for one of the drafts of the injunctions for the royal visitation.[103] The exception among Cromwell's agents was John Prise; in an undated appeal to his master, which has been assigned to 1540, he pressed him 'to doo [him] good as the kindest father wolde . . . his derest childe' for his 'riding of his graces affaires and . . . other sample services'. By contrast with Legh he asked only for the lease of his Herefordshire farm to be confirmed in 'like state and terme . . . as I had of the late house of Gioucester'.[104]

From the outset sales of monastic property reached a wider social and geographical catchment. By 1541 a cross section of propertied society was represented: city merchants and wealthy tradesmen; landowning gentry from high to relatively low; office-holders; Justices of the Peace; Members of Parliament and the principal officers of civic government. Yet few if any of these found their status in the ownership of some or other part of a former monastery. Michael Dormer, who bought Kenilworth Abbey's manor of Hughenden (Buckinghamshire) in 1539 for the sum of £387, more than half its Valor figure, had been a city alderman since 1531, the same year in which he was elected Master of the Mercers' Company.[105] His property portfolio did not provide him with a position; it secured it. In the same year he married a wealthy widow, with whom he established a school foundation in the name of her husband. Two years later he was chosen as London's Lord Mayor.[106] Richard Fulmerston of Ipswich, who purchased land which had been in the possession of Thetford's Austin Friary, could not claim such prosperity at the time but was already a committed servant of the Norfolk cause in Thomas Howard's affinity.[107] His landholding was one component of the independent sources of income he was securing in the course of the 1530s, from which he might launch a public career. A decade on and he had been elected MP for Southwark.

These were not men who rose rapidly, still less without any trace. Their trajectory, such as it was, was set out before they were presented with the option to buy these properties. The release of monastic property may have lubricated the cogs of social mobility and status in public life but it did not replace what was a well-established machine.

If there was a new caste of proprietor projected out of the shadows in these early acquisitions of property it emerged from inside the Tudor regime. From the first grants made in 1536 as far as Henry's death in 1547, the population of the royal household – office-holders, servants and other paid retainers – was disproportionately represented in the distribution of monastic resources, buildings and land, offices and annuities. Here there were gentlemen, such as William Herbert (grantee of Wilton Abbey), pledged to the personal service of the king;[108] those appointed to crown offices, such as Sir William Kingston, Constable of the Tower of London at the execution of Anne Boleyn (grantee of Flaxley Abbey);[109] household staff such as Richard Greenway, Usher (grantee of Missenden,[110] and William Hatton, Clerk of the Larder (Whalley);[111] and those providing professional services to the monarch ad hoc, such as Morgan Wolff, the king's physician (Chepstow).[112]

The gentlemen were not without property but the monastic grants they received did raise their status and project it further, into regions where they had no prior profile. Herbert's homeland was Herefordshire and while the earldom he won was the Pembroke title he claimed through his father, the source of wealth was the Wiltshire domain he was now awarded. Similarly, for a crown appointee such as Kingston, a windfall from the dissolution appeared to enhance a position already established. His family were already settled at Painswick twenty miles east of Flaxley, and although he developed a mansion house on the site, it was in the old family parish that he was buried in 1540. The household servants and prosperous professionals may have been set on a different course, at least for a time. Greenway was established at Missenden to the end of Mary's reign. Yet it may be wrong to think that their lack of profile as proprietors presented an upset in the neighbourhood of their grants. Dr Wolff's descent on Chepstow may not have been the arrival of a prosperous incomer but the return of a prodigal native.

Almost as soon as the first transfers of monastic property were made there was mounting alarm in provincial society. It was less the shock of a new order than what was perceived by many to be the sudden tremors threatening the collapse of the old, as the established framework of lord, tenant, labourer, and the responsibilities and rights of each, were roughly unravelled by appropriations and assigns. The draft of a bill intended for the commons, which is likely to date from the period between

1536 and 1539, may have given voice to a viewpoint that was already present at Westminster: 'playnlye ... a gret hurt and decay ys therby come to thys [our] relam ... a gret empoverisching of many ... poore obedient subiects'.[113]

The bill did not reach the statute book but its anxieties were not very far removed from those that informed the provisions of the second statute concerning the suppression of religious houses which won parliamentary approval in April 1539. Its primary purpose was not to set out a schedule for future closures but rather to recover control over those already in train. The monastic estate now across the kingdom 'renounced lefte forsaken' and 'gevynge uppe' was to 'come to his Highnes by the same authoritie ... [to] hold possesse and enjoy ... in as large and ample manner and forme as the late ... monasteries'.[114] New grants or leases made within a year of the final end of a given foundation were to be nullified, with special scrutiny given to those concerning parts of the property which had not customarily been put out to farm, and to woodland. Yet renewals entered into with existing leases where the terms were unchanged were honoured; and sales made under the authority of the Crown were all recognised. It also asserted that churches that might be transacted in the dispersal of estates were to be confirmed in the jurisdiction of the diocesan. The result would be for the whole 'or any parcel thereof' to be 'retayned ... [as] at the days of their suppression'.[115]

The rhetoric of petition and policy document is not readily tested in the evidence of particular neighbourhoods. The aftermath of closure and the years that followed are better documented in the case of many houses than as much as a quarter-century before. It is only for a handful that there is a cartulary or register recording their own last transactions in the making of grants, leases and scales, and most of these relate to wealthy foundations whose holdings of property were by no means representative.

Ministers' accounts, those made by agents of the Crown when it first took possession, have been preserved for a wider cross section but by their very nature they offer nothing more than an objective assessment of the present disposition of a property at that particular moment in time. They cannot trace the relationship between landlord and tenant over time, still less can they capture the experience of either as it unfolded two, three or more years after the monasteries' lordship was dissolved.

The records of subsequent transactions can sometimes offer some indication of the current conditions of tenure, and of the surrounding context, although often their perspective is as much retrospective as the customary forms are reaffirmed. To the end of the reign, and beyond, it is often only in cases of conflict, an appeal against or prosecution of one or other party, that a dynamic community becomes visible at all.

There can be little doubt that in some instances the change of landlord soon disturbed the established pattern of local life, particularly for tenants and labourers. Less than six months after the passing of the suppression statute, in August 1536 one Mr Edgar, tenant of Huttoft, a farmstead which had formed part of the estate of Markby Abbey, appealed to Cromwell about the conduct of the new proprietor, Sir William Skipwith, Lancashire MP: 'I wold to God the said Maister Skipwith his belly and guts were stuffed with all the tythe corne this yere gaddred in steves ... and then I truste he wolde have rest of craving for he hath the hole abbey and yet he wold once my said ferme.'[116]

The challenge to livelihoods came not from the turn from a clerical to a lay landlord but from an institution to an individual. 'The abbeyes tilled ... for the sustenacion of many men, women and children' was the fond memory of the recusant Richard Smith in 1554, but what he described before him now was not a great distortion, 'shepe and beastes are fedde there which do in a maner eate up men, women and children and do cause al things to be extreamely deare'.[117] The needs of a private proprietor, perhaps remote from the land they now owned, were entirely different from those of a corporation of many centuries' standing firmly embedded under local horizons.

Sent to Furness in the summer of 1537 to take the house and its domain into custody, Robert Southwell counselled caution, conscious that the climate that had provoked an uprising in the winter had not yet been dispelled and the country would not bear any more discontinuity: 'Beamonde [Beaumont] Grange is in occupation of 72 tall fellows,' he wrote and 'I beg these may not be expelled for any gentleman's pleasure'.[118] John London reflected on the contextual difference while still on circuit in January 1539, reporting from Northampton that '[while the regulars] were as yvill repairirs of ye lands as cowed be', 'gentillmen of the contrye take as much rent as they can extorte and do chardge the tenants with all maner of reparacyons'.[119]

This was no truer than for the most ubiquitous of all the incoming landlords, the Crown itself. In the wake of suppressions and surrenders, properties were placed in the custody of local paid officers. Some of these, perhaps a good many, had held the same positions under the monastery's lordship but the expectations on them, and their own exercise of their office, were necessarily different now their master was the Westminster government itself.

Not long after the surrender of the Cistercian abbey of Vale Royal in Cheshire (September 1538), the tenants of Over and Weverholme petitioned Cromwell that the bailiffs holding the manor on behalf of the Crown had 'lately inforsid and compellid [them] to do certeyen beanes [boons] ... by the space of to [two] abbots deis ... with waynes plowis and harowis in tymes of the ye and in harvest with hokis and making of hey' as well as meeting 'other chargis'; yet in the past service had been given 'off the frewill and gentylnes' of tenants, 'not of any dartie or prescribed customes', and were recompensed with 'bounteffull dyners' and 'grete releve and comfort of mete and drynke ... beside heybote howsebote and tymber'.[120]

It was to be expected that a private proprietor, the Crown or otherwise, would look to extract the maximum value from their property. The patterns of mutual support, in equipment and infrastructure, labour and food itself, which were formed around the religious houses perhaps for no other reason than their own persistence, were cut by the break-up of their domains, not least the separation of the principal site from its satellite estates. John Leland drew a picture of desolation at the 'bakke of the blake hille' at what may have been the former Valle Crucis grange of Buddugre'r (Denbighshire), 'where now shepherds kepe shepe' (see Fig. 30).[121]

The detachment of a new landlord upset the pattern of life as often because it led to neglect of the environment of an estate, its people and even its output. It is difficult to connect the material remains, such as monastic precincts, granges and other farmsteads, to a particular moment in time, but typically the datable evidence of debris and of earthworking suggests that there were years of unuse, decay and dereliction before there was repair or redevelopment. The expansion of the Crown estate was so sudden and so widespread geographically that it was always months, sometimes years before the occupation and use of an estate was properly understood.

A letter sent to the king's receiver at the Bolton Priory manor of Appletreewick may stand for many: the estate held a lead mine that remained live but this, its workers, the ore they mined, and their wage were new discoveries for the Crown: 'lede ore remayninthe yet there to oure use unsold ... We are enformyd that the leade mynes and leade ore within the said manor ... wilbe very commodious and profitable to us yerlie.'[122]

The inattention or inaction of incoming proprietors was identified as a new constraint on the local economy as early as 1539. The draft bill which may have been intended for the parliament of that spring again may have voiced an anxiety now rising across the kingdom. New owners, it suggested, should be compelled to use their acquisition productively 'or ells malke leasys' both of 'the mansion place or scyte of the monastery' and 'all the demaynes'.[123]

A new, unknowing landlord was not necessarily a threat to local livelihoods. There were many who held their monastic grants, leases and purchases as part of a large, diverse and dynamic portfolio; within years they had withdrawn or passed them on without interference either in the people or the physical fabric. For sitting tenants, the dissolution seemed suddenly to offer an unprecedented opportunity to dictate terms. John Colt and Robert Cragg were quick to capitalise on the febrile atmosphere surrounding Furness to claim land which they had coveted in the past; it was only on further investigation that it was revealed to have been a herdwick within the abbot's demesne.[124] William Hatton, royal grantee of a far-off grange of Whalley Abbey had no recourse but to the courts when the tenants he inherited took possession of a productive fishing weir.[125]

The change from an institutional to an individual landlord might be expected to have caused immediate disturbance to those rights and responsibilities that were part and parcel of many monastic properties, the principal sites as well as satellite manors. It was not only their retained labourers and their tenants but also the wider neighbourhood whose livelihood had been dependent to some degree on the watercourses and water sources, common pasture, woodland, seasonal fairs and markets operated under the authority of the house. Yet the few indications there are of the local conditions after the dissolution scarcely give a hint of the effect on these facilities. Many of the ancillary features of properties passed with them in grants, leases and sales. The notable exception was woodland which at first was reserved for the Crown itself; in time it was transacted as a discrete property. Claims over watercourses came to be subdivided as holdings were partitioned. The precincts of the largest monasteries and friaries were broken up into plots and with them passed precise sections of a channel, conduit or pipe. Already in 1538, the Court of Augmentations was confirming leases for tenements within the perimeter of the London Charterhouse, each of which was served by a channel that drew water from what had been the Great Conduit of the monastery.[126]

The status of fairs and markets, and the fixed stalls that religious houses had raised as rentable pitches, remains unclear. It seems plausible that those in the lee of the old foundation at first persisted at least as a time of year and a place in which to trade. The demolition of the north transept of the priory church of St Bartholomew's, Smithfield, early in the 1540s appears to have been to allow space for the summer's charter fair (24 August).[127] At Bodmin, the church of the Franciscan friary was kept and its modest but open interior space used as a covered market hall.[128] Monastic fabric became part and parcel of the new market opportunity at Coventry where a new cross was erected in 1541 with statuary from the rood screen of the Carmelite church built near it.[129] Those tied to manors further afield may have never returned. When burgesses of Wrington (Somerset) sought confirmation of the original rights of their town at the beginning of Elizabeth's reign they recalled the market there as a component of the old monastic lordship of Glastonbury Abbey; the implication was that it had not been seen since its dissolution twenty years before.[130] The stone cross of the old market at Milton seems to have been broken up and discarded only to be rediscovered when a later proprietor laid out a model village in the eighteenth century.[131]

The immediate fate of the diverse common rights, from firewood to fishing, is equally difficult to follow in the surviving documents. The permanent loss of old customary claims to resources with an obvious commercial value was always likely and it does seem that for some it happened almost at once. While the Crown's agents were still settling matters at Furness in the summer and autumn of 1537, tenants appealed to recover 'a fishing of salmons in the water of Lone [River Lune]'.[132] Yet it would be wrong to assume that the sudden end of the old quid pro quo was wholly unwelcome. Forty-five years later, the Crown's tenants at Furness commended the agreement reached with the king's commissioners which had seen their old customary boons compensated with a reduced, fixed rent.[133] There can be no doubt that land adjoining the principal monastic sites, manorial residences and granges came to be enclosed in the generations after the dissolution, but the archaeological surveys that have traced these developments can rarely if ever place them very precisely in time. It would be a mistake to assume that the creation of a field enclosure, chase or park was the hallmark of a post-dissolution landlord. When tenants of Binley, near Coventry, went to law over enclosure in 1544, it was to challenge an enterprise begun by the Cathedral Priory of Coventry as much as a decade before.[134] The battles over boundaries which brought religious houses and their tenants into the Court of Star Chamber at the turn of the century underline that a new landscape was being drawn long before.[135] It may be telling that even a vocal critic of enclosure, the MP John Hales, could declare after touring Somerset in the high summer of 1548 that 'people [are] well-disposed to the new order of things'.[136]

Since there was no sudden change in the supervision of these properties and their productive use remained the same, probably there was little if any change in their physical appearance. Yet the continuity may have seemed as jarring to the neighbourhood as any sudden transformation because it seems that some of these working sites were simply abandoned to dereliction. Barns in the precinct of Blythburgh Abbey were empty and fast falling late in the reign of Elizabeth when one Thomas Brock entered into a tenancy for a cottage standing there. His new home offered a barn 'now destroyed by the abbey churchyard'.[137] Landscape infrastructure was often entirely untouched. No one thought to fill the fishponds at Sempringham. They were still visible in the twentieth century.[138] There may have been some immediate benefits. At Glastonbury, where the commissioners found the abbot had held much of the pasture to himself, the commissioners let it out for a quarter-year while the king's pleasure was awaited. The fishery, however, with 'grett pikis, bremes, perche and roche', was left untouched; a frustration perhaps for locals.[139]

The preservation of some of the main features of the monastic landscape – field boundaries, closes, parks and woods, and working buildings – masked fundamental changes in its exploitation. These may not have been noticeable to those who knew the monasteries only as a landmark but they were surely seen at once by those who had owed them their labour or their land. The patterns of monastic landlordship, the distribution of its property among obedientiary departments, the proportion put in the hands of long-term tenants and the frequent turnover of demesne lands, now in, now out of direct management, were not replicated by new proprietors. Almost at once, the scale and scope of the agriculture and industry viable within the monastic framework was curtailed.

Perhaps the earliest, easily the most visible, evidence of a different approach was a fall in the size of livestock herds. Parliament had set a limit on the livestock grazed on any individual farm in 1534 and now the closure of the religious houses removed the largest of the institutional herds, which at their peak had topped 3,000.[140] Right up to its suppression, Wilton Abbey had run sheep flocks of more than 1,000 over its westward manors that extended almost twenty miles as far as the Dorset border. When Cecily Bodenham surrendered the abbey in March 1539, such numbers never passed that way again. Within a decade the effects of the change would have been visible in the downland over twelve miles from Broad Chalke to Semley, as slowly but surely the scrub crept back.[141] Fisheries, also, did not endure, at least not as the enterprise the monks had established. This may have been as much a matter of culture as cost. Writing at the end of Elizabeth's reign, John Taverner observed that now landlords favoured other alternatives to red meat such as chickens and rabbits.[142]

For a Tudor generation much occupied with the condition of their built environment, by the year of King Henry's death, they would have also seen grange establishments, well equipped with barns, workshops and even chapelries, abandoned as no longer viable. Cut loose from the *imperium* of a monastery, few of these could flourish. At Thorney, the inherent drainage problems of the site were no longer worth the while of the new proprietor to repair.[143]

Nor was every new proprietor inclined to carry the commercial risk of continuing the industry which had begun to take hold on monastic estates from south to north. On the last of his journeys before his health collapsed, John Leland had seen the abandoned salt mine at Combermere: 'the pitte yet hath salt-water but much filth is fallen into hit'.[144] Lead miners at the Bolton Priory manor of Appletreewick, now in the possession of the Crown, were forgotten entirely. They remained at the seam, the ore unclaimed and themselves without pay: 'the wages of the said poore people . . . for the dyggng and opteyning of the same ys yet to the same unpaid'.[145]

If the first changes of any kind to be felt in the countryside were challenges to tenure and the constriction of customary rights, it is tempting to see cities and towns standing in contrast as suddenly opened up to unprecedented opportunities. Urban historians have long debated the capacity of the dissolution to have been a catalyst for economic, social and political development. It has often been observed that towns whose governance had been held in the grip of a monastic lordship lost little time in petitioning for incorporation, a foundation charter for the town, a step said to be 'little short of revolutionary': a new beginning.[146]

Case studies have traced the emergence of a defined elite, confirmed in their status, if not created as such, by the opportunity to acquire and develop property and to grade, with none of the old restrictions. They have encouraged the view, first expressed just a century later in the wake of the Civil War, that the 1540s and 1550s were a golden age of civic independence, innovation and reform.[147] Yet the debate has been driven by the unavoidable evidence of towns that saw change only for the worse: the decline of trade, dilapidation of infrastructure and depopulation.

These conflicting viewpoints were apparent at the very moment that urban religious houses were given up to the Crown, even in the same town. In Coventry, the mayor and aldermen challenged the closure of the Franciscan convent, which offered space and service to the sick in time of plague; but in the same months that they made their formal representations to Cromwell, they presided over their fellow citizens helping themselves to furnishings and fabric of other monastic sites at the centre of the city.[148] With the prospect of dissolution coming to the kingdom's second city of York, the Council of the North seemed to hold the loss and the profit in a balance. In a letter addressed to Cromwell in November 1538 they regretted the likely loss of the Dominican convent, their usual headquarters in the city, 'a fayre and a goodlye large paleys' which 'standethe in mooste opene and commodious ayre', yet requested the 'leade stones glass and frames of tymber' of the Augustinian friary, to 'make [them] suche a house ... which ... wolde bee fytte and mete to receve his magestite'.[149]

Perhaps the one new opportunity shared by cities and towns even only of middling size was the infrastructure of their religious houses offered up at once for other purposes where the demand for adequate building and space was at a premium. Of course, there were wide disparities in the profile of these urban centres: London was a capital with a population approaching 50,000 before 1540; York, Bristol, Norwich all approached 20,000 permanent residents; Salisbury, Gloucester, Lincoln no more than half their size; Bury St Edmunds, St Albans fewer than 3,000; Abingdon, Battle, Malmesbury perhaps half this figure.[150]

But at each level the residential occupation and commercial use had outstripped the developed territory. Even in York, city of prelates and princes, the Council was wont to lament the 'contagyus' air, the 'corrupte and comen channels synkars and gutters'.[151] In the wake of the regulars' removal there was an early reach both for their buildings and their open ground. Again from York, Richard Leighton reported a sudden scramble for the lease of monastic sites for brewing, urged on by an abundance of Lincolnshire barley coming in 'by water', 'causeth everie ydle knave and vacabonde' to be 'ale typlers' and 'ther gettith hym an alehouse'.[152] Perhaps more common than a prompt for new trades, there was an expansion of those that were already established: rope at Ilminster (Somerset); woollen cloth at Malmesbury; wine and other imports at Bristol, Exeter, Newcastle and London; at Grimsby, 'ankers and cables with other necessaries belonging to shipes'.[153]

A new environment for business emerged ahead of any new system of urban government. There were immediate petitions for incorporation, that is the right, granted by royal charter, to govern themselves. The Ashridge house of Bonhommes had been surrendered for only a few weeks, and its prior was perhaps still in residence, when the burgesses of their manor of Hemel Hempstead secured their charter on 29 December 1539.[154] Boroughs which had lived wholly under the authority of independent abbeys did not break so quickly with their past. St Albans, just five miles to the west of Hemel, had been developed by the Benedictine abbey over the course of seven centuries. With the central site of the monastery retained by the Crown for six years after its surrender, and the steady redistribution of its property among landlords already established in and around the town, there was no concerted action for change for almost twenty years. The town was incorporated in 1553.[155]

Abingdon, a town which had also grown and prospered under the aegis of a Benedictine abbey, 'ran ... much as it had done before'.[156] Since the Court of Augmentations applied the proprietorial authority of the Crown at one remove and with the primary aim of maintaining revenue, its role was more often as an agent of continuity than immediate and profound change. The incorporation of Abingdon, which came as late as 1556, was less a new start for the town than a formal recognition of the course it had followed for the past twenty years.[157] It came when it did perhaps only because of the dissolution of Augmentations itself.[158]

The growth of independence in provincial England was incremental. Only nine boroughs had been chartered between the last of the dissolutions and the death of King Henry; during the short reign of his daughter there were almost three times as many.[159] It may be a mistake at any rate to regard the creation of a corporate body as in itself a watershed moment. The people of Reading, another town which had been in the shadow of a Benedictine abbey under royal patronage, may have regarded their charter (1542) only as a first milestone on their route towards the lived experience of a self-governing community.[160] In an environment where prospects were weighed in building materials, space and fresh air, it may have been only halfway through the reign of Elizabeth, when stone from the abbey was granted for the repair of the town, that locals may have felt they were on the threshold of a new era.

The historical view of urban fortunes has favoured an optimistic picture of new developments, perhaps because so many of the features of their old monastic world pass out of sight entirely. There is no account of the closure of the hospitals and almshouses that still operated under monastic jurisdiction. The dispersal of their officers and inmates is not recorded; still less the destinations of those dependent on this charity. A handful of those which had been under monastic jurisdiction were able to continue: St Nicholas's Hospital at Lewes was retained and maintained by local patronage; St Mary Magdalen at Colchester was incorporated into its parish organisation.[161] Larger towns and cities – Bury, Exeter, York – still held secular hospitals but the only talk of the potential challenge to welfare provision is heard before the dissolution took place. Nicholas Harpsfield opined that 'there were more holpen in the city of Canterbury in one day than be now in all Kent'.[162]

Acute need may have been visible first in smaller towns where a religious house had been the only source of social welfare. John Hamerton of Pontefract was wearied when he renewed his petition for the restoration of the town's hospital eighteen years after the last of the town's religious houses had been closed. 'We had in that towne one abbey, too [sic] collegys, a house of freers prechers,' he reflected, but now it is 'in great misery ghostly and bodily' and the needy 'ar nether relevyed'.[163] Perhaps there was an awareness of new circumstances in the instruction given by Alice Baldwyn in her will of 1545, to distribute £20 to the poor 'specially in Ayl[e]sbury where I think grede need is'. Alice had been abbess of Burnham (Buckinghamshire) and perhaps she was thinking of the effect of the loss of the Franciscan convent to the town.[164]

The grammar schools founded and funded by the monasteries were dissolved and dispersed at the same time as their other dependent foundations but there is no trace of the effects. The best measure of the loss to a town and its hinterlands are the efforts locally to see them restored. The school at Bruton was just twenty years old at the surrender of its abbot, one of the three patrons provided under its charter of 1519. Just over ten years later, a royal charter was secured for its re-foundation.[165] This formality and the new statutes that followed fifteen years later dispel any idea that a vestige of the old school had survived.

The new private interest that profited from dissolution did show an awareness of communal need. At Coventry, John Hales, grantee of the buildings of the Carmelites, led the foundation of a new school raised on the footprint of St John's Hospital. Hale paid £400 for the principal site and a further £320 for the grant of a grange which had been part of the endowment of Coventry Cathedral Priory.[166] City merchants in London led in the creation of Christ's Hospital school on the site of the Franciscans, 'to take oute of the striate all the fatherless [and] poore mens children'.[167]

The interest in schooling after the dissolution was conspicuous among former monastics themselves, perhaps with a greater awareness than most of what had been lost. By tradition, the young John Whitgift (b. *c.* 1530x31) was taught on the site of Wellow Abbey (Lincolnshire) by its former abbot, his uncle Robert, in the years (*c.* 1536–40) before he was sent to St Paul's.[168] William Hudson, canon of Alnwick, took the mastership of the town school in 1548.[169] William Barlow, prior of Bisham and long-standing Cromwellian ally, followed through on his critique of the state of learning in Wales and secured the grant of the Dominican church at Brecon for a collegiate foundation which secured the king's charter in January 1541 (see Fig. 31).[170] The archiepiscopal resources of Robert Holgate, archbishop of York, enabled him to form a tripartite foundation of schools at Hemsworth, his home town, Malton and York.[171] Holgate's suffragan, the former Augustinian, Robert Pursglove, planned schools at his home village of Tideswell (Derbyshire) and at Guisborough where he had been prior.[172] Richard Stevenage also looked to his old monastery, securing a licence in 1548 to set up a school in the old parochial chapel of the abbey of St Albans; a response perhaps to what had been a ten-year need in the town.[173]

The most immediate and enduring change to any community's social institutions occurred in their places of worship. By the end of Elizabeth's reign, converted cathedrals and parish churches were the most complete and conspicuous monastic buildings in England and Wales. As many as at least 100 remained in use for public worship; given the uncertain pace of change, early on there were possibly more.[174] Yet it would be a mistake to see in them the sign of a general continuity in the practice of public religion. These, thirteen cathedrals (at least for the short lifespan of Westminster) and perhaps another eighty churches were still a small exception to the general pattern; more than 80 per cent of the monastic churches in use in 1535 had been abandoned.

The typical picture of these sites in city, town and countryside after the suppressions began in 1536 was quite the opposite: closure, partial demolition, unregulated spoliation and, in due course, dereliction. Even some of those that were eventually converted at first followed this course of disuse and decay. The church at Romsey Abbey was almost certainly left unoccupied after its surrender in 1539 as the demolition of the Lady chapel seems unlikely if it had passed directly into parish hands. Their purchase was confirmed only in 1544.[175] The abbey church of St Albans passed into parish use fourteen years after the end of the monastery, by which time decorations and some fixtures may have already been removed.[176]

The permanent closure of more than 800 churches to any form of public worship between 1536 and 1540 cannot have failed to cause disturbance in their neighbourhoods. It is safe to say that every monastery and friary standing in 1535 was in use routinely for public worship. Benedictine and Augustinian churches had long since designated places, paths and porches for the full variety of lay devotions. The churches of the Cistercians and the friars, originally configured entirely for conventual religion, had been adapted to accommodate public masses at altars and shrines where oblations and chantry memorials might be sited. The investment of locals, and the wider network of patrons in monastic commemorations, had held at much the same level for the past thirty years. When these churches were given up to the custody of the commissioners, there was an array of votive objects, tombs and stipendiary teams of priests which had only just been installed. These were not the shell of an old world now passed. They were vital, and a good deal of their environment was new.

There are few indications of the immediate reaction. Cromwell's commissioners did not report confrontations; on the contrary, where they provide any witness to the social community at all they suggest that there was an immediate assault on the fabric of the buildings which they struggled to resist. Perhaps it was more from hope than first-hand experience that led these fervent reformers to picture popular iconoclasm. The preservation of fixtures, personal memorials as well as general furnishings in nearby parish churches would suggest that the motive was often more pragmatic, and sometimes a commitment to the history and traditions of the monastery itself. When, by whom and how the memorial brass of Thomas Nelond, prior of Lewes, was moved twenty miles over the South Downs to the parish church at Cowfold was never recorded; but since the priory church was razed to the ground in a matter of days it must have been carefully planned. The effects on the pattern of religious life depended on local circumstances. At Quarr, parish worshippers resumed their use of the nave of the abbey church after the commissioners were gone, at first taking advantage of the fact that one of the monks held a benefice nearby. By contrast, the people of Bordesley raised a complaint as far as Chancellor Rich because the closure of their monastery had robbed them of any incumbent and the next nearest church was unreachable when the fields were flooded.[177]

Burial, in general, is the matter on which the silence of the sources is most surprising. Monastic and friary churches and their precinct cemeteries had continued to offer the most and the best of the burial spaces in many neighbourhoods, urban and rural. The record of wills confirms that interment within their churches still held an appeal especially for families of high status with historic links and for a wider cross section who happened to live nearby. Generally, the remains recovered from their open cemeteries cannot confirm patterns of use to the precision of a particular decade. The shortage of space on monastery sites may have seen lay burials dwindle, although it seems that friary cemeteries continued to take lay burials beyond 1500.[178] There can be little doubt that their use was within living memory; there may have been some families for whom it had been a very recent event.

The sudden dereliction of these sites, and of the adjoining churches and chapels which certainly contained lay graves that were less than a decade old, must have meant an immediate disconnection as much psychological as physical. These open grounds were soon turned over to other uses, if not for new building, then for cultivation or grazing.[179] There is scarcely a trace of the personal impact. The practical consequences for communities, where the rights to burial had been a bone of contention from time immemorial, were surely acute. Still, the only glimpse of a reaction would suggest that the first thought of the lost graveyards was as a resource to be mined. Excavation has revealed evidence of the early robbing of graves in open grounds and in nave and choir positions within churches. Tombstones were more likely to be recovered for building materials than as memorials.[180] The timing of these acts in relation to the moment of the dissolution is difficult to determine, although associate deposits would indicate that they were within decades of the end.[181]

It may be that communities were more provoked by the fate of the particular fabric of monastic churches, recognised to be valuable, recyclable or personally important, than by the loss of the space itself. Certainly, in cities and larger towns major changes to parish arrangements were not unknown. The foundation of new institutions – colleges, schools – and the re-foundation of those already ancient – hospitals – had not infrequently required the redrawing of parish boundaries, the removal of a chapel or a discrete church and the merge of congregations. These would not have been so familiar to the social community of smaller towns, villages and their hinterland, although their size and geographical spread may have meant that they may have generated less traffic in the churches of outlying monasteries.

The general pattern of preservation of churches for parish use reflects these topographical differences: most were former Benedictine churches standing in urban or suburban locations with an established population; of the seventy Cistercian churches in England and Wales, all of which stood at some distance from any significant settlement, only one, at Holm Cultram, saw continuous occupation.[182] While it was remote, Holm stood at the gateway to Solway Firth and on the main east-west route north of the Lakes to the Irish Sea. The practical need of the resident population may have been the first and main consideration in community responses to the closure of monastic churches. In Reading the principal parish church of St Mary was refreshed and refined with materials from the abbey church, such as floor tiles, window glass and even piers pared away from the monks' choir.[183] The former parochial chapel of St Agatha, standing directly beside Easby Abbey, was retained for the use of the agricultural parish, too far downriver from Richmond to be affiliated to one of the town's parishes. Here the congregation worshipped only a few feet away from the unroofed church of their canons.[184] For the congregations of neighbouring parish churches and chapels the first change brought by the closure of a religious house was not to the building or its spaces but the clergy that served it. The parishoners of Bordesley complained to Richard Rich that their church had been left without staff after the surrender of the Cistercian abbey, and they were unable to reach any other because the surrounding area was prone to flooding. In the crowded quarters of cities and towns the experience may have been quite the reverse: almost overnight there came a drift of former religious reluctant to roam very far and ready to serve as stipendiary curates for chantry priests. By 1541 there were eleven of Bristol's canons and friars fulfilling these roles in city parishes.[185]

The jarring juxtaposition of old and new faced every Mass day by layfolk of St Agatha's was typical of the scene in the last years of Henry VIII and in the reigns of Edward and Mary. The institutional life of monasteries had been decisively shut down. Its disappearance had caused immediate disturbance wherever the houses had stood, held property or exercised jurisdiction, although the turbulence in tenure, labour and livelihood was rarely out of step with what had arisen when the monasteries were still in place. From the outset the story of the monastic past was overwritten by the schemes of new proprietors, urban corporations and parishes, but all of these fell far short of revolution. The only true novelty in the distribution of monastic estates was the turn from clerical to lay. In their social profile and their regional affiliation the new landlords were not new at all; they had always been there. Urban society was evolving in independence and identity even before the dissolution and after it continued on the same course, and at much the same pace. Parishes served their own interests opportunistically in the space left by religious houses much as they had done when they were occupied.

The impression of continuity in a changed landscape was cast above all by the living presence of the regulars themselves. The majority who left an enclosed life between 1536 and 1540 were still alive at the end of Henry's reign. If pension records are indicative, of those who had belonged to houses of twelve or fewer, typically no more than two or three had died within a decade of the dissolution; the rate of survival from houses above this level generally rose only in proportion. Where the ages of men and women were recorded at the assign of pensions, often as many as a third of the community were under the age of forty. If this proportion of the estimated total regular population lived another twenty years, then to the eve of the Elizabethan reformation there were as many as 4,000 in England and Wales who had known the professed life.

The men in the cohort might be said to have been the only members of post-dissolution society to have experienced an instant transformation. Their status had been formally changed from regular to secular clerk; almost all but the very old had secured licence to act as a secular priest. Yet in spite of the scramble for a 'faculty', these men had not suddenly flooded into the surviving institutions of the Henrician Church. As the closures of houses continued, diocesans had made it difficult for dispersed religious to step directly into the secular Church, prohibiting the preaching of those already displaced and proving reluctant to facilitate their licences or titles to benefices. In the first five years after the last of the dissolutions there may have been a very marked division in the fortunes of secularised religious between a minority who by negotiation or patronage took up a church living at or soon after their departure and a much larger number duly licensed who took up nothing at all or at least nothing permanent. In Bristol, a city of eighteen parishes, only one living inside the city held by a former religious by 1542; a further eleven had found roles as curates (4) or stipendiary priests (7).[186]

The registers of the largest dioceses do give the impression of a change in the traffic flow of ordinations and presentations in the first two years after the last of the houses had closed (1540–42).[187] It may be that monks and friars of several years' standing made the calculation that the pensions assigned to them were more valuable than the available benefices. It may be some proof of this that the first of the former religious to appear before the episcopal authorities were the youngest whose pensions, if they received them at all, did not amount to a livelihood. Richard Mercer, who presented himself to Bishop Longland for ordination to the priesthood in 1541, identified himself as a monk of Battle. His name does not appear on the abbey's surrender deed; if not a novice he may have been awaiting clothing.[188]

It does seem the situation changed dramatically in the second half of the decade. It is the case that most of the incumbents identified with any certainty as former religious first came into their benefices between 1544 and 1551; there was another upturn in the first two years of Queen Mary's reign, although this may reflect a return to duty of those whose service had been interrupted in the later years of Edward VI.[189]

The former religious who secured a parish living were only a fraction of those that found some occupation in the secular Church in the 1540s and 1550s. Before their own suppression was initiated by the statute that secured the new king's approval on Christmas Eve 1548 (1 Edward VI c. 14), chantry foundations had offered a settled living to the regulars now licensed as seculars in every part of the kingdom.[190] Where there was a concentration of these offices, in London and York and the largest of the provincial cities, it is likely they were more conspicuous in this capacity than as the pastor of a parish. In Bristol in 1548 there were at least seven, perhaps eight, former religious serving chantries, although another eight chantries in the city stood empty.[191] Beyond these conurbations the chantry posts were fewer and there was surely competition. By 1548 only nine out of ninety-eight pensioned religious in Durham had secured a chantry appointment; in five shires of the west March and Midlands (Gloucester, Hereford, Warwick, Worcester and Shropshire) forty-five religious can be identified as chantry priests; in Derbyshire there were only four.[192]

It has often been assumed that a chantry stipend was the rest-and-stay of older religious, unable to fulfil a parish role or to compete for the patronage that might offer one. Yet the records compiled in 1548 by the commissioners for the Court of Augmentations responsible for the enforcement of the statute – now known by the shorthand, Chantry Certificates – reveal priests of monastic and mendicant origin ranging from young to old. Thomas Kelyng, a former Cistercian serving a chantry at Bosbury (Herefordshire) in 1548, was in his eighth decade, and unable to ride or otherwise travel due to sickness, although he was still known as an organist. John Pickard, whom the commissioners found at the college of Irthlingborough (Northamptonshire), was then only thirty-three years old; when he had surrendered as a Carmelite friar a decade before he had been too young even for canonical ordination.[193]

The weight of the regulars in the rank and file of the church towards the end of the 1540s was matched in its hierarchy. By the last year of Henry VIII's reign, they were the dominant presence in the episcopacy: the northern province was governed by the Gilbertine Robert Holgate; two-thirds of the sees of the old foundation were in the hands of men who had first professed to the religious life; all but one of the incumbents of the new foundations – Bristol, Chester, Gloucester, Oxford and Peterborough – were monastics; only Westminster was different and there the dean was the last abbot. Their leadership was underpinned by at least eight suffragan bishops who were also former religious, and whose tenure of the role with one exception was unbroken since before they had changed their habits.[194]

Some of these stepped out at once from their former life as champions of the reformed Church. The Augustinian prior, William Barlow, had already held his bishopric for four years, and had assisted Cranmer, Latimer, Lee and other vocal advocates of reform in the compilation of the articles of the Bishop's Book. By the time the last of the monasteries were closed down he had begun a campaign of education and religious instruction in his Welsh diocese, 'the Welsh rudenesse [to] be framed to English civilite ... their corrupte capacyties easely reformed with godly intelligens'.[195] He may have also started to live a new priesthood, perhaps making a secret marriage even before 1540.

The new mantle of the Dominican John Scory (d. 1585), also a future bishop, came more suddenly: he had remained a friar as far as the surrender of his house but was then swept into Cranmer's circle as cathedral preacher at Canterbury and personal chaplain to the archbishop. He drew attention for his public preaching, which reinforced the Henrician programme and rejected the position of traditionalists and radicals.[196] Scory was influential before he held episcopal office; by contrast, Henry Holbeach, former prior of Worcester, advanced very rapidly, from suffragan of Bristol in 1540, Dean of Worcester in 1542, Bishop of Rochester in 1544 and finally Bishop of Lincoln in 1547, by which time he may have been on the brink of marriage.[197] Perhaps most prominent at the moment of monastic England's passing was the former Gilbertine, Robert Holgate, of all these men the closest to Cromwell. He entered the new era as President of the Council of the North; within five years he was also archbishop of York.

The reforms of the later 1540s and 1550s were taken forward, at least in part, under the leadership of former regulars. Yet their position at the apex of the Church, and that of many of their former colleagues in the lower tiers of the clergy, did not mean for all of them either the full embrace of Protestant values or the complete erosion of their original professed identity. Outwardly at least, their new careers were set in a recognisably monastic frame. Raised to the new see at Oxford, Robert King took up residence at a site he had known well as a monk, Gloucester College, the Benedictines' original *studium*.[198] Philip Hawford, former abbot of Evesham who succeeded Holbeach at Worcester in 1542, even after his preferment remained living at his old Evesham manor, surrounded by his personal library of books, and devotional objects, which he had collected as a monk.[199] Paul Bush, the Edington Bonhomme appointed to the new see at Bristol in the same year, carried with him the distinctive spirituality that had characterised his original brotherhood. The tomb effigy he commissioned for the choir of his cathedral depicted him in monastic tonsure.[200] The vignettes preserved in the Chantry certificates suggest clergy whose context was new but whose conduct and character were largely unchanged.[201]

In 1548 these men were known in their parishes for the same attributes that had defined them in their old precincts: their learning, teaching, music and pastoral care. Their recollection of their old monastic titles in their last testaments has often been seen as an expression of nostalgia but perhaps it reflected a view of their life as a continuum. They were clerks, erstwhile regulars, now seculars, but their impulse for learning and for the vocation of service was the very same.

Their detachment from any clearly defined notion of a watershed between old and new, and their separation from the partisan and political discourse that promoted it, is focused in a scene played out in 1544, at the centre of which was Thomas Way, former monk of Glastonbury Abbey. Way was a sixty-three-year-old monk when his monastery was forced into surrender in November 1539. Having lived under vows perhaps since the beginning of the century, it appears he had retired to the cathedral city just six miles from his old monastic world. He and his life history were well enough known five years later for him to be called as a witness in a dispute over property rights and money.[202] Now he spoke to the jurors with notable objectivity about his former home. He lent weight to the allegation of the plaintiff that his old abbot had been underhand in his management of the property and in the favour he had shown to his own kinfolk. Embezzlement had been one of the crimes for which he had been tried and executed. In his seventh decade, it seems that Way held in balance his past as a professed monk and his present as clerk, citizen and neighbour.

The experience of regular women may have been quite different. They knew no instant change of status. For them there was no counterpart to the opportunity to secularise; on the contrary, although they were dispersed from their house, they were not dispensed from their vows. So long as the old king lived, marriage was denied them; any early ambivalence had been removed by the prohibition in the Six Articles of 1539 (31 Henry VIII c. 14).[203] The pensions assigned to superiors at least held out the prospect of continuity, since they enabled an independent life not unlike the one they had known in their precinct lodgings. Yet so long as their vows remained, the rest were left somewhere between their old world and the new.

Those departing in 1536–37 without pensions were cast into a condition the same as a dependent spinster, except that for almost a decade there was absolutely no chance of their making a legal marriage. The opportunities for pensioned women were determined above all by the levels of the sums they received: a pension of £5, the equivalent to the poorest church living, only took them to the threshold of an independent life, although if they shared a household it might be assured. That their families continued to look to their material needs long afterwards suggests that vulnerability was their life sentence.

Just a year after the closures were completed William Martyn, a Wokingham clothier, foresaw that the pension granted to his daughter Elizabeth, 'that was professyd nonne', might 'fayle', and directed that she should have an annuity paid from the rent of his mill.[204] Probably the anxiety of Alice Baldwyn's father was no less because she had ended her career as a head of house, and he was a man of some means; probably it was familiar to many: 'I wold have my doughter more surely servid for term of her lyfe'. He went further than others could or would. By placing the 'rents, issues and profits of all . . . manors, land and tenements' in her hands, and appointing her his executor, he made her a gentlewoman.[205]

The prohibition of marriage for almost a decade after the dissolution acted to ensure that the majority of the former religious never made this most conspicuous change to their life. Charles Wriothesley had reported that 'above 300' priests and religious persons (regulars) 'presumed' to marry before the Six Articles were enacted.[206] Whether or not the number he counted was accurate, it seems likely that all of them at least publicly forswore their union for fear of prosecution. 'I perceive the kynges erudite iugement,' wrote John Foster in June 1539, and 'sett the woman to her frendys iii score myles from me and spedly'.[207] By 1547 perhaps there were fewer than a third of the former religious now of any age when the opportunity for marriage was likely to arise, since the youngest of them was, at the very least, approaching their thirties, middle age for many in the mid-Tudor population. In the diocese of Norwich, one of the only regions where the records provide an overall measure, 28 per cent of former regulars holding clerical office were deprived in 1555 for reasons of marriage: the raw figure was just eighteen.[208] A number of the men did now make a mid-life or late-life marriage. Quite possibly some of them were formalising relationships which had begun years before. In his will of 1551 Ralph Campion, a St Albans monk, there is a detachment from his wife, Joan, whom he treats as just another beneficiary on an equal footing to his own brother, and his godson, Albon. Perhaps he had not been married long enough not to look on his world like a bachelor. There were no children.[209] It may reflect a general pattern that, of twenty-eight monastic pensioners recorded living in Hereford diocese around 1554, only one was married: William Symes, who had been a thirteen-year-old novice at Gloucester, and not yet professed, when his monastic life was brought to a close.[210] Margaret Bashfurth, who had left Moxbury Priory (North Yorkshire) as early as May 1536, committed to a marriage only in 1550 when she may have been far into her fourth decade.[211]

The legal conflict, personal danger and social and emotional cost of enforced separation was surely a deterrent for those still living at the accession of Queen Mary. Women especially faced the danger of a second loss of a secure and stable household. If a home shared with other pensioned religious was open to them, then marriage risked not only punishment and desertion but also the loss of their most viable alternative. Many may have acted in the same way as Agnes Asleby, formerly of Nun Appleton, and Augustine Webber, of Glastonbury, both of whom did not wait for the new regime but arranged their own divorce. Webber acted with cool practicality: he left Hampshire where he had been married and moved 150 miles north to take a benefice unencumbered.[212]

Robert Persons disparaged just such conduct, 'only sen[ding] their concubines out of men's sight . . . before they said mass again'.[213] It is true that only a minority of regular men, now fervent reformers, defended their married priesthood: John Bale, now with children in tow, took flight. His fellow friar, Guy Eton, found refuge in Germany.[214] There were more who were prompted by Mary's Catholicism to reaffirm their belief in clerical celibacy. Robert Warton alias Perfey, bishop of Hereford, formerly Cluniac abbot of Bermondsey, had been close enough to the Edwardian regime to advise in the drafting of the 1550 prayer book but from 1554 he was assiduous in the identification and deprivation of married priests. The monk William Repps alias Rugg of Norwich was similarly repressive, provoking the Protestant George Joye to call him by the colour of his old coat, 'a drunken blacke monke', the fomenter of a 'pharisaicall faccion'.[215] Deprived himself, Robert Holgate publicly abjured the principle of clerical marriage, alleging that his own had been made under duress 'for feare the laite duke of Northumberlande [calling] him papiste'.[216]

Generally, the regulars who lived on into the middle years of the century showed a growing readiness to conform to the demands of the regime. Both open confrontations and conspiracies in favour of the monastic cause had continued as far as the summer of 1540 but they had faded completely before the next year when the king, his government and their resources were turned towards the prospect of war. It does seem that tales of diehard monastic men and women at once forsaking England for the Catholic cities of Europe are no more than defiant legend-making of the Counter-Reformation movement. In the case of Syon the story told carried some notable details, not least the name of the house, Falconklooster (Antwerp), where Katherine Palmer and an advance guard of sisters were said to have scouted for their new home.[217]

Yet there is no trace, in their own contemporary records, or those of the English authorities, of any traffic, let alone an exodus, in the winter of 1539–40. A cross section of canons, monks and friars had taken themselves into exile in the wake of the royal supremacy, albeit a number of them drifted back across the Channel or south of the Scottish border in the months that followed, perhaps tempted by the prospects of the uprisings of 1536–37. An expatriate Catholic opposition to the new Henrician Church was established in St Andrews (Scotland) and Leuven (Belgium) as much as two years before the dissolution was completed. Richard Marshall, a Newcastle Dominican, felt secure enough in his refuge at the University of St Andrews to pitch his own public argument against the royal supremacy in 1536; he continued to stir controversy in the Scots Church as far as the 1550s.[218]

Even the communities and congregations which from the first could not be reconciled to the rejection of Rome were reluctant to remove themselves from the Tudor realm. The Birgittine men and women remaining at Syon Abbey at its surrender in 1539 departed their house with much the same plans as many others: the prolific author, Richard Whitford, remained in London in the first instance; two of the women are known to have returned to a family home, while a small group under the former abbess, Agnes Jordan, shared a leased farmhouse in the Thames Valley where, by their own tradition, they were said to have improvised a chapel so as to continue a form of 'conventual' worship.[219] They cultivated a wider network of former regulars of other congregations which reached as far as Anthony Bolney, one-time sub-prior of Lewes.[220] But their social contact was the limit of their challenge to the dissolution for more than a decade. It was only after four years of further reform under Edward VI that they looked for a new life at Dendermonde in Catholic Flanders. Fewer than ten of them left the country.[221]

Former Carthusians who had escaped the earlier repression of their leadership also remained, at least as far as the death of Henry VIII. Maurice Chauncy, a member of the London convent whose memoir came to be enshrined as the Reformation history for his congregation, claimed that he and others tried to escape but found every port was watched. It may have been special pleading because in the event he and his colleagues remained at least as far as 1546–47.[222] This was in spite of the fact that Carthusians continued to fall under suspicion. The arrest of Nicholas Wilson, brother of John, prior of Mount Grace, renewed the regime's interest in the dispersed members of the network.[223]

It was the regulars that had taken up the cause of reform who at the outset were at odds with the new Henrician world. Before the dissolution itself was done, the Six Articles had dispelled any dream of radical change; Cromwell's own downfall a year later left those who had enjoyed his patronage especially exposed. Robert Barnes, a former Augustinian friar, was taken and burned at the stake just over a month after his erstwhile patron. Within eight weeks of Cromwell's passing, one protégé, Robert Ferrar, former prior of Nostell, had been imprisoned for his refusal to accept the Six Articles.[224] It was apparently Cromwell's death that decided John Bale's departure for Antwerp. John Hooper, former Cistercian of Cleeve and future bishop of Worcester, also fled before November 1540.[225]

Those radicals who remained in the last years of Henry VIII held themselves in open resistance. One Dundy, a former Observant, was among the 'heretics' in Kent parishes investigated by Cranmer in the summer of 1543.[226] John Cardmaker, former Franciscan ultimately executed during the Marian persecutions, held a prebend at Wells throughout the decade. He may have had the advantage of the detachment of elderly and infirm diocesans, John Clerk and William Knight.[227] The same may explain the persistence, in plain sight, of radicals such as the former Observant, John Lawrence, in a Norwich diocese, where William Rugg remained bishop until his death in 1550.[228]

The direction of the reforms under Edward VI acted to reconcile the surviving regulars who had embraced Protestantism. John Bale and John Hooper had both made a permanent return after the publication of the second prayer book of 1550. It was the turn of the regime also that aroused a Counter-Reformation impulse among former regulars. Not only did the remaining cliques of Birgittines and Carthusians now choose exile but also the regime began to confront the most unreformed ex-religious in the institutional Church. The aged William Rugg was pressured to resign his see in April 1550; his successor was Thomas Thirlby, who appears to have been moved from his see of Westminster for his conservative rule over a chapter comprised almost entirely of former Benedictine monks.[229]

The deprivation of another conservative, Edmund Bonner of London (1549), was followed by the arrest of one of his protégés, the former Benedictine, John Feckenham. Bonner had provided Feckenham with a living where he may have attracted attention for his traditionalist preaching. Cranmer now passed him through a sequence of punitive disputations with John Hooper and John Jewel. Feckenham had been no more actively in conflict with the state Church than most of his monastic peers. From prison, however, he began work on a refutation of the principle of the royal supremacy, the first monk to tackle the subject formally for nearly twenty years. Four years in custody under Cranmer's coercive correction changed him. Now he was a partisan of Counter-Reformation.[230]

Thirteen years after the final formal acts of dissolution the Tudor realm was placed under the rule of a monarch whose commitment to the old religious ways had never wavered. The succession of Henry VIII's eldest surviving child, Mary, after the death of her brother in July 1553 was by no means assured. It was as much of a minority coup as the plot that pushed Jane Grey towards the throne; it differed only in its success. Yet some unsettling of the changes in state, church and religion had long been anticipated. Before Henry's own death in January 1547, there was a widespread expectation that the transformations of institutions, property and buildings witnessed since 1534 would surely turn and turn again. The old king himself was said to have expressed some anxiety about the permanence of the suppression. In 1542 he pressured his loyal commander, Sir Andrew Windsor, into a property exchange to bring the estates of Bordesley back into royal ownership, 'in order to make the dissolution irreversible'.[231]

The direct action that erupted at the same time in Norfolk and the West Country in the summer of 1549 seemed to play out the scenes Henry had imagined. The Norfolk mob targeted sites of dissolution, and the properties of grantees, Wymondham and Mount Surrey, the mansion Henry Howard had raised on the ruin of a Norwich priory.[232] The western rebels circulated articles calling for a reversal of the reforms advanced since 1539. The Six Articles they wanted to be 'in use again as in Kyng Henry hys time', and 'abbey lands . . . [to] be geven again to . . . two chief abbeis . . . in every counte . . . there to be establyshed [as] place[s] for devout persons, which shall pray fore the king and the common wealth'.[233] Theirs was a vision of a monastic estate, reduced but retained in service to the regime, which the king and Cromwell had inclined towards ten years before.

The continued possession of old monastic property by the nobility and gentry families which had been their founders and lifelong patrons was only one reason why the changes of 1536–40 may not have seemed secure. The most conspicuous right across England and Wales was the continued presence of the infrastructure of former monasteries and friaries. Between Henry's last years and Mary's accession, it seems there was very little new building on these sites. Demolition was ad hoc, undirected, and often very slight. The ruin that onlookers of the 1540s and 1550s would have seen was largely the result of exposure and neglect, not widespread, deliberate destruction. Some of the most complete monastic precincts were those that had been an almost organic feature of cities and towns, such as the principal buildings of the London friars, and the abbeys of St Augustine's, Canterbury, Malmesbury, Shaftesbury and St Mary's, York. In these neighbourhoods, it must have appeared that the fate of the regulars had been a form of custody. They were still there, just in other hands.

Of course, also very visible were the regulars themselves. Perhaps no more than one-third of those dispersed after 1536 had died before 1553. It is possible that upwards of 7,000 of the original population remained. Even as the Edwardian reforms had gathered pace, and forces of conservatism were confronted, they had remained public figures. There were still eleven regular bishops in office at the time of Edward's death.[234] Perhaps in the lower ranks of the clergy it is also possible to see the first stirrings of an impulse to challenge which had been lacking in 1540 or 1547. Cranmer's prisoner, Feckenham, began to emerge as a representative voice for the regular conservative. In his preaching diary, the Carthusian Edmund Horde now copied out excerpts from Feckenham's published works.[235]

Nevertheless, Mary's success did not sway a sudden revival of monastic England. Perhaps the greatest obstacle was the viewpoint of the queen herself. Personally, Mary was committed to the institutions and customs of the original Roman Church. Like many of her generation, she had been exposed to the learned critiques of humanist divines. As a young woman, under the influence of her last stepmother Catherine Parr, she had even begun her own translation of Erasmus's *Paraphrases*, his retelling of the Gospels. Her religion carried the hallmarks of Christian humanism: it was textual, explicitly biblical, and above all personal. She had passed among regulars in her early life and witnessed their worship, but those associations had ended with the death of her mother, Katherine of Aragon, in 1536; at Beaulieu Palace (Essex) and Hunsdon (Hertfordshire) at the end of the 1530s she had been more removed from the remains of monastic England than her father.

Her spirituality was inspired by her own direct experience of the sacrament of the Mass. It was the restoration of this experience in the kingdom's churches and in the lives of her subjects that was Mary's priority for reform. The prerequisite was the readeption of the papal monarchy, the parliamentary price of which was the acceptance that there would be no complete reversal of the redistribution of church property that resulted from her father's reformation. Catholic worship would only be secured in a kingdom where the imperial authority of the Crown still seemed more imagined than real if the Henrician reorganisation of the Church was retained. The five new sees formed from monasteries must survive.

Robert Parkyn (d. 1570), curate of Adwick-le-Street (South Yorkshire), conjured a story of the return of monasticism by royal proclamation: 'all suche as had ben cloisterers ... were commandyde to take they habytte ... agayne'.[236] Mary did remember monastic England when she took power, yet her first thought was not of their collective possibility but of their individual service. She released John Feckenham from the Tower and appointed him as her personal chaplain and confessor and facilitated his placement in the deanship of St Paul's Cathedral. Her expectation was for the unreformed Benedictine to combine with her unreformed secular prelates, Cardinal Pole and Bonner, to form a front line of Catholic doctrine. Feckenham was soon put to work, sent to counsel Lady Jane Grey before her execution, and then John Throckmorton – a Gloucester gentleman and supporter of Henry Dudley's conspiracy of 1555 – to the same end.[237] These appearances as public pastor for the regime were dramatised in a printed pamphlet recalling his sorrowful departure from the cell of the nine-day queen: 'I am sure, quod he, that we two shal never mete. True is, quod she, unles god shal turn your hart.'[238]

It was a measure of the new regime's first priorities that the momentum for a monastic restoration originated outside of government. It stemmed from a source not directly connected to the dissolution itself. William Peryn was an erstwhile exile from Reformation England. He had been an opponent of Tudor policy since Henry's supremacy and had been abroad on and off for nine years. His own short life as a Dominican friar at Oxford was almost twenty years in the past.[239] He may have returned to London as early as 1553 when he was believed to be behind an agitation over the use of the buildings of the former Franciscan convent for a school foundation. It was said that Peryn found common cause with William Peto, a former Franciscan Provincial; even so, this was no fully formed plan for the revival of a friary, although the episode did reveal the presence of regulars, and their supporters, in the heart of the city: 'there were v or vi other poore fryers which had bene fryers ... before [and] woulde faine have bene restored to theire olde occupacions'.[240]

The Carthusian exile, Maurice Chauncy, returned to London with two others in June 1555. Like Peryn, they found supporters in the city and were able to create a common life of sorts in the chambers of the old Savoy Palace, given up to them by Sir Robert Rochester, Comptroller to the queen. Over the next two years another eight exiles crossed the Channel to join them.[241]

The re-emerging profile of regulars in the capital cannot have escaped the attention of John Feckenham at St Paul's. Conscious, no doubt, of a general sympathy to their cause within the regime, and knowing perhaps that Cardinal

Pole was in contact with exiles within months of Mary's accession, he was moved to act on Peryn's example and make a plea for his own congregation. In a letter to his master the Doge dated 19 March 1555, the Venetian ambassador, Giovanni Michiel, reported that 'last week', Dean Feckenham had processed before the queen, perhaps at Westminster, accompanied by fifteen men dressed in Benedictine habits.[242] More even than Peryn's demonstration in the city, it was a deliberate coup de théâtre. Michiel saw Mary moved by the spectacle and claimed that in that moment she convened a commission to consider a scheme for the re-foundation of a monastery. It elicited no clear response from the regime and in early June Feckenham seems to have seized on a public occasion to set out something of a manifesto. Preaching at the funerary rites for Queen Johanna of Aragon and Castile, he made an unmistakable call to arms:

> The bishoppes, priests and prelates of christes church having the flocke of christ committed to their great cure and charge ... must make their provision ... for the lost shepe which haue perished in ye late plague of errours and heresies: by a wise bringing of them backe againe into the folde and unite of christes church ... by a merciful binding and knitting of the woundes. Ye gentlemen and noble men which ... be very politike ... by your upright ministration of iustice and by the authoritie committed unto you ... defend God hys churches, byshopriches, cathedral churches [and] houses of religion.[243]

The new regime had not been entirely impassive in the face of such posturing. Even before Pole had arrived to take his place by the side of the new queen, he may have approached the Birgittine exiles at Dendermonde and encouraged them to consider a return.[244] Steeped in the governance of the Roman Church as cardinal and legate prominent in the Council of Trent, from the outset Pole thought of congregations and orders. If there was any impulse arising in Mary, it seems it was to recover the role of the regulars as pastors and the cult of their churches as a prompt for private devotion.

Late in her second year, when her fierce assault on heresy was already underway, she allowed the former Franciscan Provincial, William Peto, and a handful of other friars to return to the former Observant convent adjoining Greenwich Palace. It seems likely it was in connection with this train of thought that in early 1555 she may have called on Stephen Gardiner, bishop of Winchester, to summon two former Dominicans from Flanders, a command recalled in an uncatalogued letter of Pole's.[245] Yet by the spring the focus of her interest was the Franciscans. Their possession of the site was confirmed at Easter 1555. It was surely inevitable that Mary's patronage of regular religious should begin here, where her mother had hoped to be buried and she herself had been christened: the low-profile chapel standing in the lee of the palace where she had been born forty-three years before.

Mary's personal interest in the restoration of monasteries appears largely to have been satisfied by the reoccupation of Greenwich. A second colony of Observants did come to occupy their old site at Southampton some two years later, but it seems the Crown took no direct role. The site of the former convent was held by a cloth merchant with reversion to William Herbert, earl of Pembroke, and it appears it was his (in the words of the recorded letters patent) 'mind to restore the house to its ancient estate'. Royal authority was borrowed by Herbert only to prompt Thomas Bowes, a London merchant, to give it up with the promise of an export licence for 40,000 kerseys valid for the next three financial years.[246] Herbert was no recusant Catholic and his patronage was surely an expression of a purely political ambition; a personal piety might have persuaded him to restore the female community at Wilton, his principal residence.[247] His calculated favour for the queen's preferred order was rewarded with a continued status at court and ultimately the office of her executor. Perhaps it was his presence in this capacity that caused Mary to acknowledge the Southampton project with a donation of £200 for the support of a nascent community she had never seen.[248] It seems she was suspicious of any attempt for the renewed presence and profile of regular prelates to serve as a public or political platform. When Pope Paul IV named Prior Peto as a cardinal she prohibited the passage of his beretta of appointment into England; Peto himself was rendered a prisoner of royal patronage.[249]

The further ambitions for the return of monasticism belonged to Cardinal Pole and a handful of individuals in, or close to, the government, self-conscious in their commitment to the old ways. Pole himself had begun to contemplate a new monastery of Benedictines as much as a month before Feckenham's performance at court. He reached out to his Roman allies intending such a community to be affiliated to the reformed congregation of Monte Cassino in Italy.[250] His aspirations were well received but no formal agreement emerged. His preparations turned inward, towards Westminster, surely an acknowledgement of the force of the queen's own outlook, that the place for a new monastic England was in the principal churches and palace chapels of the monarchy itself. A new monastery at Westminster Palace might match the Escorial of Mary's Spanish husband Philip II. Finally, in November the secular chapter of Westminster was dissolved and on or around 21 November 1556 Feckenham and fourteen monks were 'putt in' and the next day 'whentt a prossessyon after the old fassyon in ther monkes wede'.[251]

It was at the instigation of Cardinal Pole, again charged by his international channels, that formal recognition was restored to the congregation of the hospitallers and the principal house at Clerkenwell was returned to them under letters patent issued in April 1557.[252] Sir Thomas Tresham, just thirty-three and with no preceding connection to their tradition, was named as Grand Prior. He was a Marian loyalist and it was an appointment less in monastic than political interest.[253] Tresham was surely a figurehead, a point of contact between the regime and the vestige of the old network of provincial commanders and preceptors who, together with the continental hierarchy, had lobbied the cardinal invoking the crusade against 'Turks and infidels'. As many as eight of the county outposts, reaching as far north as Shropshire and as far west as the Somerset–Dorset border, were named in the patent. Its language of a corporate body and its line of sight to a regional circuit of sites, if not communities, set this act apart from the circumstantial and contingent reoccupations which had already occurred. This impression was reinforced by the remarkable scale of the property the patent promised: as well as the buildings and site of Clerkenwell, the congregation was to take possession either at once or on reversion of many of the lordships, manors and lands countrywide which it had held before June 1540 and all of the church advowsons. Uniquely in Mary's counter-reformation, it was a mirror-image act to that of Henry VIII: he had suppressed the congregation by parliamentary statute; by this patent, in large part, it was returned.

The creation of a second friary, of Dominicans, in the buildings of the old Augustinian priory at St Bartholomew, Smithfield, looks to have been carried through by the champions of the regulars close to the queen. In December 1555 the site was vacated by Richard Rich, former chancellor, now out of office but not wholly out of favour. Probably his compliance was the result of those now leading the regime rather than a fiat from the queen herself. William Peryn himself presumably played an active part, his remonstrations over Christ's Hospital carrying him to the head of the circle of former friars at the heart of the city.

According to Charles Wriothesley, a handful of friars had reoccupied the principal buildings and presided over worship in the church by the spring of 1556.[254] Their coming together appears to have reawakened their network beyond the capital. Drawing up his will in August 1558, Robert Hill, former prior of the Dominican convent at Beverley, directed his executors to dispatch 40s to Richard Hargrave, Peryn's successor as prior now found 'for the use of religion and the health of my soul'; then he added 20s for commemorative masses.[255]

Meanwhile, the Comptroller of Mary's household, Sir Robert Rochester, championed the cause of the Carthusians, by 1555 a well-known if small presence in the city of London. Under the protective patronage of Rochester and Pole, the group made solemn vows in November and were said to have received royal letters of restoration as a corporate body on the last day of the year. Pole negotiated recognition from the General Chapter of Chartreux the following spring, although it was another year before they were put in possession of the former charterhouse at Sheen.[256]

The regime's formal recognition and patronage of the Carthusians offered a template for the treatment of autonomous networks of religious. In 1557 Pole also arranged for the settlement of women who had held on to their old identity since the dissolution of their former houses. He had probably known of the exiled Birgittines of Syon since 1554. By the summer of 1557 they had returned and received the formal grant of their old abbey buildings and its demesne lands. Seven women had remained in England since the dissolution, some of them living together, all of them remaining members of a common social circle.[257] They too were offered a formal enclosure of their own, at King's Langley, previously a convent of Dominican friars, although perhaps more importantly given the priority of the new monasticism, standing alongside a royal palace.

The creation of monasteries was slow, small-scale and almost exclusively confined within the network of royal palaces. Yet the notion of restoration also surfaced and was nurtured for a time in neighbourhoods across the kingdom. This was independent of the position and developing plans of the Crown, which would have been widely known for the first two years of the reign. Drafting his will in April 1555, a London ironmonger, Thomas Lewen, decided to put his town and country property in the hands of his Company of Ironmongers, 'until such time as a new monastery be erected at Sawtry ... of the same as were there in the old monastery before the suppression'. The Cistercian monastery there had been closed for almost twenty years. Lewen also bequeathed £5 from the income from his property to be paid annually 'to the friars Observant in the realm of England.'[258] Here was a vision that was not narrowly reactionary; rather it was for counter-reform: observant friars nationwide and evangelising monks. Lewen directed that once installed, the Ironmongers' Company should pay the abbot for four sermons to be delivered each year.

Nearly fifteen years after the town had purchased it for their parish church, one testator of Tewkesbury set aside funds 'if thys abbey be sett up againe'.[259] The incumbent of the parish church of Hinton St George (Somerset) bequeathed £2 to the 'edyfeynge of the abbeye of Glastonbury' and anticipated that he may himself live to see it 'payd'.[260] Gentry drafting wills in the region of St Albans also anticipated a restoration of the Benedictine abbey there, apparently responding to a proposal of the former abbot, to secure the church from the Crown.[261] Another former superior, Thomas Whytney, the last abbot of Dieulacres, dictating his will on 3 August 1558, thought it possible that his monastery 'be reedefyed and founded' during 'the space of sevyn yeres next after my decease' or, if not, during the life of his nephew, Nicholas, his executor. He bequeathed him a silver gilt chalice to be given up to the house as and when it returned.[262]

The expectations of provincial restorations seem to have faded almost as soon as they surfaced. Nor did the reality of religious life resumed generate any more lasting interest in the neighbourhoods surrounding them. Testators of Westminster in 1557–59 paid no attention to the return of their monastery. They may have had quite different sympathies. The will dictated by the Exchequer clerk, Richard Lyster, in November 1556 was witnessed by Thomas Kyrkham, a divine who had preached publicly that there was no substance in the Eucharist but bread and wine.[263] The reoccupation of Greenwich, Langley and Sheen also appears unremarked; here, the local outlook may have been that they formed part of the private religion of the royal palaces. Syon, already associated with Catholic exile, may have been regarded differently by the conservative interest. James Winnington, son of a Lancashire family committed to the old ways, secured rosary beads blessed by Abbess Katherine Palmer as a gift for his mother, Elizabeth.[264] Thomas Bonnde, a priest of Croston in the same county, made a grant of his share of tithes with a sum to be paid to Syon.[265] John Feckenham's personal profile may also have won him something of a social circle of supporters. Another member of the Winnington family met him on his arrival in the capital.[266] The slight profile of the Observants at Southampton prompted a small cash bequest from the parish physician and the promise of his personal library.[267] Only the Dominicans at Smithfield seem to have begun to build a network of benefactors. John Garet, city Salter, requested burial in the church of the Blackfriars and 12s to the order 'now being within the house of Great Saint Bartholomews'.[268] At the turn of the year, Richard Bartlett bequeathed 20s 'towarde the makynge of the churche wall'.[269] Two years on and barely twelve weeks before Mary's death, Robert Urmestone looked to be buried there.[270]

The flickering of interest in revived monasteries was stronger among the laity than among the former regulars themselves. 'Not a day passes,' wrote Ambassador Michiel excitedly to his master, 'without discovering persons ... replete with zeal and piety ... who retire to monasteries'.[271] '[They] restore unto theam agayne [and] ... that with outt delay,' recorded Robert Parkyn.[272] Yet both allowed hope to distort what was before their eyes. In a little over three years in total there were less than a hundred men and women who came forward to join these new communities. The largest cohort were the Birgittine women who came back to England from Flanders (Dendermonde). By the time of the Crown's formal grant in April 1557, there were twenty-four of them. There were a little over a dozen who first joined Feckenham at Westminster, and eleven who were named in the grant of Sheen. Seven women were named in the grant of the old priory at Langley.[273] The number of friars that entered Greenwich and Smithfield is not recorded; the domestic contingent may have been reinforced by foreigners: at the latter, one Spaniard, John of Vilagrassa, is known by name although it was later remembered that there were men from Germany and the Low Countries.[274]

The majority of these monks and nuns had been professed to the religious life before 1540. The Syon women had all been professed before the first surrender and had held together as a network before their resumption of conventual life in the winter of 1556–57. Twenty-one women were named in the charter of restoration dated 1 March 1557 although three were already dead before their formal enclosure at the house five months later; two more had died before the turn of the year.[275] There was a fleeting prospect of two new recruits, both reflecting the limited catchment of the new community: one was Thomas More's granddaughter, Margaret Clement, who in the event changed her mind; the other was the niece of Cardinal Pole.[276] The Langley women were all drawn from the original community of Dominican women at Dartford Priory, who, like their Syon counterparts, had since lived in interconnecting groups. Perhaps sixteen men who came to Westminster between 1556 and 1558 had been monks before; most of them were Benedictines, perhaps one or two Cistercians or Augustinian canons; all of them were at least forty years old when they returned.[277] The Carthusian community came together between 1554, when their prior, Maurice Chauncy, first returned to London, and at the moment of their grant, as many as half of those that took up residence came from elsewhere within England.[278] The two friaries stood apart as communities formed now, with patchy prior connections; some were new to England; some to the religious life itself. Thomas Bourchier, self-appointed spokesman of the new Observant colony at Greenwich, who would later write the history of their European odyssey in the years of reformation, was no more than a teenager in 1540.

Returning or new to the regular life, these men and women entered environments marked by twenty years of reformation. Just two of the churches, Greenwich and Smithfield, were more-or-less intact. The friary at Greenwich had never been a typical convent configured around a cloister; lacking the more conspicuous targets for defacement, the odd jumble of buildings seems to have been assimilated into the royal palace standing alongside. The church itself was a simple, low-profile space more like the chapel of a great household; outwardly it may not have appeared to be a target worth defacement. At Smithfield, St Bartholomew's church had been truncated but was still in use for parish worship.[279]

Each of the other sites stood in different degrees of damage and dereliction. Conspicuously, the hospitaller church at Clerkenwell had been for the 'most part ... body ... iles with the great bell-tower ... undermined and blown upp with gunpowder' three years before Mary's accession.[280] It seems the churches and convent buildings at Sheen and Syon had been partially demolished. In his custody (to 1552) Protector Somerset had turned Syon into a 'most beautiful' mansion house, the formal gardens of which must have required the clearance of at least part of the monastic ranges.[281] King Henry himself had raised a mansion house inside the precinct of Dartford Priory in about 1543; the church and convent may have been left derelict alongside, as was done elsewhere.[282] The buildings of Langley Priory had not been occupied since the surrender of the convent and a survey of 1553–54 saw the church, Lady chapel and cloister still standing but badly dilapidated 'bothe in tymber and tylinge' and the dormitory and refectory 'sore decayed'.[283]

In scarcely two years, there was a significant effort to restore both Sheen and Syon. In the will he drew up at the end of May 1557, Sir Robert Rochester provided two manors in Essex to the charterhouse on condition that a chantry in his memory was maintained in the parish church at Terling.[284] Since he died three days after the monks occupied the site in November it may be that building work began soon. The nave of the church was repaired enough for it to be used for the office; the chapter house was also restored and work may have begun on a new range of cells around a cloister.[285] A grant which Robert Southwell was licensed to make to the house in 1558 may also have been intended to underpin the project.[286] Another gentleman of the household and privy councillor to the queen, Sir Francis Englefield, was remembered as a patron of Syon and it may be that some repair of the church had begun there before the autumn of 1558.[287] Queen Mary's own will, drafted after Easter 1558, held in view building work that was already underway: 'lately . . . revivd and newly erected' she bequeathed £500 both to Sheen and to Syon 'to reedifye some part of ther necessary howses . . . and furnish themselves with ornaments'.[288] At the other sites there were only slight steps towards restoration. John Stow remembered that 'part of the quire . . . with some side chappels' at Clerkenwell were 'closed up at the west end and otherwise repaired' under the direction of Cardinal Pole.[289]

At Smithfield, it seems the friars began the reconstruction of a monastic aspect to a space that for now was shared with the parish community; it has been speculated that a new nave, chapter house, gate and even parochial chapel were begun, although the evidence is slight and the chance that construction had advanced very far in scarcely two years is slim.[290] The view of Greenwich drawn by Anton van den Wyngaerde in about 1562 gives a glimpse of a gatehouse which may have been new work (see Fig. 32). Perhaps these were 'the reparacyons and amendments' to which the queen bequeathed them £500.[291]

The belief that there was restoration work within Westminster Abbey has become something of a test of faith in the whole project. There seems to be no doubt that the restoration of the tomb and shrine of Edward the Confessor was underway as Henry Machyn understood it to be 'nuw set up' in April 1557.[292] There is also a tradition that Feckenham added the inscription to the tomb of Edward I that named him 'Malleus Scotorum', Hammer of the Scots.[293]

The new communities were given living space and at least the scope to practise their religion collectively but limited resources to sustain it for the long term. Only the grant for the monastery at Westminster amounted to an endowment, since the resources of the secular cathedral were reassigned, albeit with the liability for pensions to be paid to the departing canons. The integrity of the site and demesne estate at Syon had not been lost in their post-dissolution distribution and the Crown's grant conferred almost 400 acres of arable and grazing lands and commons.[294] The grant to the Carthusian group at Sheen described a domain of more than 100 acres, of gardens, closes, fields and meadows.[295] There were gardens, an enclosure and part of a manor at King's Langley; this may have had the scope of a home farm but certainly no more. Yet these were only the footprints for a foundation; absent from all three were the cash and the staff needed to exploit the property profitably.

The grant to Dominicans at Smithfield was confined to the former monastic precinct previously held by Richard Rich; the church itself had been partially demolished as early as 1543. There was nothing for the Greenwich friars beyond the buildings adjoining the palace, leaving them wholly dependent on the donations of the royal circle that lived alongside. The exiles had returned to circumstances much like those they had left in Flanders. Their continuance as a community would rely wholly on the goodwill of those around them.

It seems there was an awareness within the regime of the fragility of the foundations but it did not lead them to take further action with any speed. The queen's will proposed to award to Sheen and Syon 'mannours, londs, tenements, sometyme parcell of the[ir] possessions' yet still 'remaynng in our hands at the tyme of our decesse'. The 'clere valewe' of the release of these crown lands was to be only £100, no more than a gesture for foundations whose original Valor assessment was, respectively, between ten and twenty times that sum.[296] In what would prove to be Mary's final weeks a handful of new assigns were made, but given that the queen's decline had been obvious from the spring, it is difficult not to see these as desperate measures to buy time for institutions whose ultimate fate could hardly be in doubt. In September, preparations were made for the Dominican women at King's Langley to return to the sight of their original foundation at Dartford, forty miles to the south. They were granted the site and standing buildings of the old priory together with a portion of the demesne with £30.[297] In the first week of October a grant of outlying lands at Stanstead and Braintree was made to Syon in exchange for those nearby in Surrey. If these were the first steps in a fresh phase of endowments, they were stopped abruptly by Mary's death five weeks later.[298] In fact, the prudence of the patronage proposed in her will perhaps tells the true story: whatever her lifespan the political constraints on the re-endowment of monasteries were unlikely ever to ease.

It is very difficult to recover a clear picture of the monastic life that was resumed. The impression is of a tentative, even a tense, experience, caught between the practical obstacles that stood in the way of customary conventual observance, the expectations of courtly and civic patrons, and an uncertain attitude in the outside world. If the return of the religious had been Cardinal Pole's project rather than hers, Mary seems to have been quick to make a place for it in her devotional life but much like her father and grandfather, as a chantry on a grand scale. She was there for the first Easter weekend celebrated under her new regular dispensation, where she performed the Royal Touch after her observances in the conventual church.[299] Ambassador Michiel reported her return there for Christmas, where she heard vespers and was received in state.[300]

Such exclusivity may have left the friars somewhat vulnerable. There was an early tradition that William Peto himself 'as he was getting into a boat to return to Greenwich ... was set upon by an insolent Mobb, who pelted him with stones'.[301] Nonetheless, there are indications that both communities of friars found a wider catchment of devotees. Henry Machyn noticed Sydenham, a Greenwich friar, preaching at Trinity and dining afterwards with Sir Robert Oxenbridge, Constable of the Tower; and another unnamed friar preaching at the funeral of the city alderman, John Machell, at the church of St Mary Magdalen, Milk Street.[302] Peryn, as prior of the Dominicans, appeared as a public preacher at Paul's Cross, and at a private funeral.[303] Their commemorative services seemed to have resumed with something of their old style with 'torchys and gret tapurs'.[304] The benefactors drawn to them in 1556–57 may be a measure of how fast, and how far, they had returned to the pastoral life of city parishes.

There is no evidence of this kind either for Clerkenwell, King's Langley, Sheen or Syon, and it may be that these communities stayed largely self-contained. It was surely telling that when a wealthy resident of Clerkenwell, Richard Buckland, disposed of four tenements in his will drawn up in the summer of 1558, he described them as standing in the precinct of the 'late monastery'.[305] Ironically, the Carthusians may have formed more of a social affinity while they lived without a house of their own in the centre of the city. Here their improvised monastic life was visible at least to Machyn.[306] It is telling that the otherwise well-informed ambassador Michiel thought that the monks had not yet returned to Sheen as late as September 1556. News travelled slowly, even at an itinerant court, when there was little of substance to report.[307]

Given the traffic in clergy, laity and processions, and services at Westminster from 1556 to the time of Mary's death, it is tempting to think that abbey life had returned to its old ways. At a distance of 160 miles, the old Cistercian Thomas Whytney now living at Leek (Staffordshire) thought he saw his monastic life reborn. He was prompted to name Westminster's prior, Richard Eden, overseer of his will and to request burial 'in the monastery of Westmynster'.[308] The conferral of clerical orders on a number of young men is especially striking since it was the very hallmark of the health of a monastic community which the visitors had looked for as far back as 1535. It is difficult, however, to disentangle the new life of the professed community from the affairs of the secular Church and government that were still wrapped around it when they arrived. There is no doubt that the monastery itself did draw new recruits and a handful of them embarked on their preparation for priesthood as their predecessors had done. But the community was far from stable. The terms of the financial settlement, an income of £1,000 but a pension liability of £969, left the community close to debt from the first. Their only surviving account roll, from the cellarer, does show them living within their means.[309] Yet Machyn's story of their despoiling of Anne of Cleve's hearse, its velvet cloth and valance, presumably for sale, may suggest that the wolf was already at the door.[310] Not all of those that returned to their old monastic ways stayed for more than a few months. Some departed at news of attempts at restorations elsewhere. Feckenham himself may have kept the conventual life at arm's length. Certainly he was noticed in these three years as a public prelate. Machyn recorded him preaching 'goodlye' sermons at Paul's Cross in 1557 and 1558, 'and ther wher grett audience' of the city's 'worshepfulle'.[311] On a visit to London in 1558, Humphrey Winnington, member of the same family close to Katherine Palmer at Syon, was able to make a social call to his house.[312]

Six months after their reoccupation, there were signs of a renewed recognition of Westminster Abbey as a national church. In May, the 'quenes grace . . . and lords and knyghtts and gentylmen . . . whent a procession abowte the cloyster'.[313] Two months later the monastic community was placed at the head of the funeral procession for the former queen, Anne of Cleves, escorting her coffin from Chelsea to the abbey with 100 torches burning.[314] In November 1557 when Mary and Cardinal Pole appointed a new Grand Prior of the knights of St John and three new knights of Rhodes, Feckenham and his monks 'whent a procession . . . singing . . . and rond abowte the abbay'.[315] When a prisoner, Edward Vaughan, escaped from the Tower of London he claimed sanctuary and the advocacy of Abbot Feckenham. The response of the Privy Council was cautious, more so than it might have been twenty years before, inclined to promise that should Vaughan confess, 'the Sanctuary shalbe avaleable unto hym'.[316] Lent 1558, the traditional adornment of the abbey's Paschal Candle again held the attention of the city as it had done in years gone by.[317] Six weeks after the old queen's death, and six days before Christmas, a funeral rite for Emperor Charles V was performed at Westminster Abbey in preference to St Paul's Cathedral, 'saving of moch money to the quene's hignes'.[318]

The restored communities were not subject to another act of dissolution as such. In the wake of the queen's death their close(d) circle of courtier support was soon fractured. Cardinal Pole died from influenza just twelve hours after Mary. Sir Thomas Tresham made his will scarcely ten days later. In the opening lines he quoted Pole's patent of eighteen months before, 'purposing to revive and establish agayne the most godly religion and order'; the air of a plan aborted was unmistakable. He would only live for another three months.[319] Sir Francis Englefield took himself into exile in May the following year.[320] In spite of an almost immediate isolation, the regulars remained where they were for nearly seven months. Their last allies at court as the new monarch and her counsellors took control were the envoys of Catholic states, still present in spite of the transfer of power. According to the accounts kept by their own congregations, the cause of the Birgittine women and the Carthusian men was taken up by Spain's ambassador Gómez Suárez de Figueroa, duke of Feria (d. 1571). When his tour of duty ended in late May 1559, the religious crossed the Channel in his company, 'delivered', Maurice Chauncy reflected, 'from the snare of the fowler'.[321] There is no record of the steps taken by the new administration itself, to take either the sites or their small estates into custody. The only notice given to their leaving is found in the diary of the London clothier, Henry Machyn: they 'whent-away', he remembered, between 12 and 14 July 1559.[322] Since there were those in each group of religious who had been in exile before, they may not have waited for any prompt from the new queen. 'All other good relygyous peple' were reported as 'be yonde the seyes' by the spring of 1562.[323]

Machyn remembered 'the abbotte of Westmynster and the monks was reprevyd'.[324] The monks were still present at the time of Elizabeth's coronation in January 1559, although none of the first-hand accounts of the ceremony noticed their participation. The presiding prelate, and preacher, was Bishop Owen Oglethorpe of Carlisle; his surprising selection was as much a snub to the secular hierarchy as to Abbot Feckenham himself.[325] It may be that the ceremony marked the beginning of Elizabeth's rejection of any notion of a royal monastery, as the Catholic exile, Thomas Stapleton, claimed that before she was crowned she had observed the custom of an audience with the abbot. In that 'first and laste talke that ever he had with her in her palace' she 'hadde in remembraunce' a sermon he had preached before Queen Mary 'where he moved her highnes . . . to mercy, and to have consideration of the Quenes hignes that now is'.[326] Just over a week after the coronation, as she returned to Westminster to open her first parliament, Elizabeth's hostility was overt as she waved away the rank of monks as they prepared a customary torch-lit procession to accompany her into their church. 'Away with those torches,' she was heard to cry, 'we see very well.'[327]

In the wake of the coronation they were considered, and surely considered themselves, interlopers on the scene of the new regime. Feckenham received the customary summons to the first parliament in January as he joined the lords for the ceremonial opening, and he was confronted by a coruscating attack on his religion. According to the Mantuan envoy, Il Schifanoia, Bishop Richard Cox of Ely preached 'against the monks' for 'having caused the burning of so many poor innocents', urging the destruction of monasteries, and other symbols of the old religion.[328] The antiquarian, John Stevens, claimed on the authority of the Catholic historian, Nicholas Sander, that Elizabeth took this opportunity to try to reconcile Feckenham to her reform, proposing to allow his community to remain at Westminster if they recognised the royal supremacy and to provide him to the see of Canterbury.[329] If so, she failed. A manuscript fragment collected by the antiquarian Sir Robert Cotton contains a transcript, apparently of Feckenham's contribution to the debate on the bill that would become Elizabeth's Act of Uniformity. 'My very good lords,' he urged, must choose 'betwixt the true religion of God and the counterfeite', the former being that 'of most antiquitie' which 'did begin here in this realm 1400 years past in king Lucius his days' with 'holy monks . . . sent from . . . Rome'. He lamented the 'sudden mutation of subjects of this realm', as 'all things are changed and turned up sett down'.[330]

The monastic community at Westminster seems to have dispersed of its own accord, and was gone by early July. Feckenham remained in office and, apparently, in residence at Westminster Abbey, for a further ten months. Machyn remembered him being taken into custody in the Tower of London on 20 May 1560.[331] Just about three months later the Crown began to regrant the properties and revenues which the Marian government had given over for the support of these communities.[332]

There was a late and fleeting show of fight from the leadership of Mary's monasteries. In June 1562 Feckenham prevailed on Sir Richard Blount, Lieutenant of the Tower, to press the queen for greater freedom inside the precinct.[333] Around the same time he seems to have joined, if not initiated, an exchange of letters with Abbess Katherine Palmer and Prior Maurice Chauncy, now living with remnants of their communities respectively at Mariatroon, Dendermonde and Val de Grâce, near Bruges.[334] Their correspondence also drew in Englefield, also in Flanders, Edmund Bonner, deposed bishop of London now held in the Marshalsea Prison, and the dissident priest, John Payne (d. 1581). By late July it had been intercepted by the government, by which it was judged to be a 'treasonable' conversation concerning the restoration of Marian bishops and 'the old religion'.[335] Despite the discovery, by the following spring Feckenham had been released from the Tower, first into the custody of the new dean of the reformed Westminster Abbey, Gabriel Goodman, and then that of Bishop Robert Horne of Winchester. In these house-holds he continued to act, self-appointed, as the figurehead and voice of England's old monastic order. In 1565 he submitted a formal refutation of the royal supremacy to the queen's secretary of state, Sir William Cecil.[336] He placed it under the scrutiny of Edmund Grindal, bishop of London, the most strictly reformist of the senior prelates, who dismissed it as an undiluted assault on the very foundations of the state church. Feckenham was returned to the Tower. Bishop Horne made his treatise the subject of his own published defence of the royal supremacy, in 1566, apparently with the aim that a public pamphlet disputation might act to persuade the abbot to conform. Rather, it made him a focus for reactionary polemic.

The exiled papist priest, Thomas Stapleton, published a *Counterblast*, in 1567, 'proving the popes supremacy' in the name of 'My Lord Abbot of Wesminster, M. Feckenam'.[337] Feckenham himself rejoined the debate, apparently publishing a response to a reformer's sermon preached in the Tower. The result was his transfer from the Tower to the Marshalsea. Now, he retreated from public battles, although he remained in and out of custody until his final imprisonment in 1580, as the government alarm at the Catholic reaction intensified.[338] The same year witnessed the last public interest in the Marian religious remaining in exile, when Cecil, now Lord Burghley, received a petition from expatriate English Catholics to address the plight of the remaining sisters of Syon now exiled to Rouen and in 'great distress'.[339]

In 1541, from his Antwerp exile, Miles Coverdale, translator of the King's Bible and ally of Cromwell, mocked the conservatives in England whose reaction against reformation had sent him abroad. Their hostility to all these 'new fangles', he suggested, was like the behaviour of a prisoner suddenly sprung from his gaol, blinking and bewildered, 'a poore wretche . . . out of prison [left] to stande gasyng and gapyng'.[340] They were wrong to rail at a new world, he argued, for the 'popes power . . . masses for the deed and qycke . . . intercession of sayntes . . . and of the whole swarme of ydele relighious' were themselves 'nothing but new alterations'. The Tudor *Ecclesia Anglicana* was itself like an old world reborn, the 'antiquite and ancient age of our holy christen fayth'.

Coverdale's claim that an original Christian community had been created by 1540 was hardly convincing, but then neither was the conservatives' 'gasying and gapyng' over traditions transformed. Much of monastic England persisted in the last years of Henry VIII and onwards under the two different regimes of his son and elder daughter. The disendowment of religious did not suddenly change the distribution of power. The immediate beneficiaries were the same elites from which the monasteries' endowment had originated centuries before. The standing of the Crown itself was not transformed. There was a mark of Renaissance magnificence in the new royal palaces raised at Nonsuch and Oatlands, but this was more than counteracted by the diminished returns of the clerical subsidy. Regular men and women were forced to face change, but even some of the hallmarks of their monastic existence, such as chastity, communality and spiritual leadership, were not altered as much as might have been expected.

Yet none of this made the reversal of the events of 1536–40 the likely prospect that even Henry VIII was remembered to have feared in his final years. There were formidable legal and political obstacles, as the Marian regime acknowledged in its opening months. It was not only that favour for the new queen was very fragile, nor that the appetite of the political nation for sweeping statutory change was no stronger than Henry and Cromwell had judged it twenty years before; also the reassimilation of the regular estate had proved less than revolutionary and the grievances of land, labour and locality were not dramatically different from what was seen even before 1540. And there was another factor at work, the effects of which had influenced the course of events over a quarter of a century from the supremacy of Henry VIII to that of his second daughter. The people of England had long since made a separation between the fortunes of institutions and their own fundamental values. Thirty years of battles for the throne before the victory of the Tudors had not unsettled their investment in monarchy itself. For as much as a century and a half – since war in France had coincided with the first wave of the plague – churches had fallen derelict, been forcibly closed or transformed into colleges, but it had made no measurable difference to the practice of their faith. Abbeys featured in the landscape of their Christian history as far back as the tale of Joseph of Arimathea who came into England, but for most they had become the setting for a story of themes other than monasticism, its congregations and customs: patrimony, personal and communal identity, and the promise of salvation itself. In truth, people had begun to think of these places differently long before the Break with Rome.

EPILOGUE

The regulars of medieval England outlived the Tudor monarchy. The Crown's liability for their pensions continued at the Stuart succession and perhaps for a further five years. Jacobean England held a handful of men and women who had made a monastic profession before the autumn of 1539, in the south and the north; perhaps also elsewhere. Thomas Fuller claimed, at a distance of half a century, that the very last pensioner of all was living in Hampshire, although, of course, it may not have been the county of their profession.[1] The last undoubted sighting of any regular in the north country was of Isabel Coxson, Cistercian sister of Hampole Priory (South Yorkshire), just nineteen at the surrender of her house and, apparently, still hale at eighty-two in 1602.[2] It was claimed by Catholic missionaries that William Littleton, former monk of Evesham, was still living in 1603, 'now known by the nickname Parson Tinker'. If this man was the monk of this name, he would have been in his ninety-seventh year.[3] In 1606 a Yorkshire yeoman was able to describe the dress of a Cistercian in accurate detail; but this was no recent sighting, rather the remarkable recall that can come with great age. He had last seen this man eight decades before.[4]

Robert, alias Sigebert, Buckley, who had begun his monastic career at the recreated Benedictine community at Westminster in 1556, appeared, as an octogenarian, in London in November 1607. He was the main actor in a curious ceremony involving two native English converts to the regular life, professed at Padua and now returning to continue the papacy's mission to the Recusant minority. Buckley received them formally, or rather, he 'aggregated [them] to himself' and therefore 'to the whole English Benedictine body, the which by survivorship before remained in him alone'.[5] Remembered as a defiant demonstration of continuity, Buckley's role was proof of quite the opposite. Finally, the Henrician generation was gone.

When King Henry's youngest daughter, Elizabeth I, died at the beginning of Holy Week 1603, there cannot have been many more than half a dozen survivors of the 10,000 or so who had left the religious houses after 1536. But it was only as the queen's reign passed into a new century that they were no longer a noticeable presence in the mainland of her kingdom. In Elizabeth's decade of difficulty and disappointment that followed the defeat of the Spanish Armada (1588), the regulars were still to be seen and heard, certainly under local horizons, and news of them still reached as far her government. One of them at least remained its responsibility. Buckley was held with other Catholic prisoners at Wisbech Castle for eleven years until 1599 and then at Framlingham Castle (Suffolk), at least until the accession of James I/VI.

Not in custody, but quite possibly under the covert scrutiny of the Tudor regime, there were men and women professed as regulars in England now living in exile. A handful of survivors from the Birgittine abbey of Syon were (relatively) settled at Rouen from 1580 until 1594, when the community, now renewed by new recruits, removed to Lisbon.[6] Might there be grounds for suspicion of foul play from a fearful regime that an English priest travelling to visit them was set upon by thieves and murdered? Thomas Bourchier, friar of Queen Mary's Observant convent at Greenwich, had reached Rome from where he produced his history of mendicant martyrs since the year 1536.[7] It was reprinted twice (1586, 1589) just as Elizabeth faced the twin threat of covert Catholic missions and the Spanish fleet. Meanwhile, the queen's domain in Ireland raised a challenge of monastic survival and revival on a quite different scale. Nearly 200 monasteries and friaries remained or were renewed between 1542 and 1606. Even under the very eyes of the colonial administration in Dublin there had been acts of deliberate subversion.[8]

Elizabeth's government was also troubled much closer to home by the visible ties between the old monastic estate and gentry families now emerging as committed conservatives in religion. Several abbey sites became the focus of recusant networks and the native missionaries who served them. Ironically, the Tregonwells of Milton Abbey, whose mansion house had been the reward of a dissolution commissioner, protected priests passing in and out of the West Country; in the best chamber there was still 'one ffine table of our ladie' to welcome them.[9] To the north of this network, there were recusants concentrated around the old monastic sites at Montacute and Hinton.[10] The Browne family had made Battle Abbey such a haven for Catholic piety by Elizabeth's final decade that it became known as 'Little Rome'.[11]

Not under the government's gaze, but familiar in their own community, were former monks still serving as parish priests. Perhaps Richard Judson alias Baxby, vicar of Kirkbymoorside and originally a monk of Byland, was among the last of his kind when he resigned his living in 1592.[12] If so, it seems it was only a matter of two or three years since the congregations of a variety of provincial parishes had been called to worship, and coaxed to catechism conformity, with a priest who had once worn the cowl. In the early 1590s there were a number of religious women still living in the chaste independence that their pensions had provided for them. They were prominent enough in their neighbourhoods to be both the subject and object of wills. Mary Denys, who had surrendered the Benedictine priory at Kington St Michael in 1539, occupied a prominent town house in Bristol over-looking its new cathedral and former Augustinian abbey. Her death in 1592 cannot have passed without comment in that most confessionalised of cities.[13] Elizabeth Beaufeld, formerly of Bungay Priory, died in the last months of the century, sixty-three years after her convent was closed.[14]

Just how many of their former colleagues lived on alongside the few who have left some record can only be estimated. The unpensioned of 1536–37 can only be found by chance. Given the age ranges sometimes recorded, from mid-teenage upwards, it is quite possible that several from each house were still living beyond the 1570s. A pension register of 1566 reveals a very variable survival rate of pensioners from a variety of houses into the reign of Elizabeth, from as low as 10 per cent to as high as 75 per cent.[15] The fortunes of the friars have attracted less research than the monks, canons and nuns, their obscurity reinforced by their rela-tively limited presence in church livings. The former Trinitarian, Richard Burneston, still present in his old city of York in 1592, appears to be a rare exception.[16] A record of the status and age at death of the friars may never be found but it would be reasonable to assume that as the queen herself entered her seventh decade (1593), there were several dozen of them still in her midst.

This last age of Elizabeth might also be seen to mark the beginning of a change in the way in which the dissolution was understood. What had been a first-hand memory was now a matter of history. The generation that lived to the end of the century and beyond was the very first to be fully conscious of their separation from monastic and mendicant England, that 'whole rablement of this religious armie'.[17] Finally, after forty years and more, the material traces of their tradition had been transformed. After the last of his journeys before his health collapsed (January 1545), John Leland had passed back to the king the impression of institutions that were past but still present: 'there is almoste nother ... monasterie ... but I have seene them'.[18] Sites had stood empty, sometimes partially demolished but not removed. But as the Elizabethan government set itself in opposition to Catholic Europe between 1584 and 1589, a succession of new mansions arose from these old houses. Maybe it was now that most of the masonry was moved.[19] On his provincial journeys prior to the publication (1586) of his *Britannia*, William Camden passed through a different landscape: 'that temple is now become a private residence'.[20] It now appears that it was the ten years either side of 1600 that saw the most sustained investment in the standing remains of religious houses; only now did a residential outline efface, or replace, the old religious profile.[21]

John Stow's survey of London (1598) now required an effort of historical reconstruction: at East Smithfield 'there was sometime a monastery ... monks of the Cistercian or White Order'. Now 'clean pulled down', in its place was a bake-house for 'biskit' 'to serve her maiesties shippes'. Stow himself was a storehouse of arcane lore but he thought he should explain the finer points of the former regulars to his reader. 'Commonly,' he wrote of the Franciscans, 'of their habit [they were] called gray friars'.[22] In the crowded city, where the course of the streets mapped the precincts of the religious houses, such memories were not buried very deep, but in an open landscape it seems they were already passing beyond recall.

In his *Perambulation of Kent* (1576), William Lambarde saw that his county neighbours might wonder at the 'old house' on the road to Hythe, '... standing very neare to the towne ... now seeme[ing] but a base barn in your eie'. Yet, 'was it sometime an Imperiall seate of great estae and majestie. For it was the Saint Nicholas chappell, and he in papisme held the same empire that Neptune had in paganisme'.[23] Thomas Churchyard's *Worthines of Wales* presented a prospect of Tintern, for the first time, as an antiquity, 'as old a Sell, as is within that land'.[24]

Distance led late Elizabethans for the first time to consider the decline and fall of regular England as an historical moment. Perhaps the foundation was first set by John Bale, whose *Acts of the English votaryes* was extended for a new English readership only after the queen's accession (1560). Bale framed his annal in four ages, expressed with the memorable phrase-making of the practised preacher, 'of fast rising, faste building, fast holding, and fast fallynge'.[25] Following him, John Foxe had raised his *Monuments* (1563) for 'ye time of these 500 yeres, since Sathan broke lose', which he counted 'eftsones after the full thousand [years after Christ] was expired'.[26] Now, a new generation of antiquarians gave greater definition to a distinct epoch in the English experience. Lambarde represented it as a classical age, which flourished in antiquity, then fell:

> Let the souldiours of satan and superstitious mawmetri, howle, and cry out with the heathen poet [i.e. Lucan] *excessere omnes, aditis, arisque relictis, dii quibus imperium hoc steterat*: the gods each one, by whose good ayd this empire stoode upright are flowne, their entries and their altars eke, abandond quight.[27]

Camden saw a golden age which had soon tarnished, the character of the later regulars, and those in living memory, far removed from 'veterum monachorum'.[28] Michael Drayton (1563–1631) elaborated: 'Observe ... the difference twixt the more ancient times and our corrupted neighbour ages ... branded, and not uniustly, with dissembled bestiall sensualities of monastique profession.'[29] For the first time in print, he accounted the kingdom's monastic age 'a thousand lingering yeere'.[30] John Speed closed his *Historie* (1611) with a catalogue of religious houses, for readers both to follow their rise and to quantify their fall.[31]

Elizabeth's last decade saw popular print focus the particular drama of the dissolution. *The troublesome raigne of King Iohn of England*, presented by Her Majesty's Players and first circulated in 1591, quite apart from its ostensible subject, offered its audience a reminder of the Henrician reform:

> ... where I of Abbots, monkes and Friers
> Haue taken somewhat to maintaine my warres,
> Now will I take no more but all they haue.
> Ile rowze the lazie lubbers from their Cells,
> And in despight Ile send them to the Pope.[32]

In his *Crie of England* (1593), Adam Hill went so far as to narrate from the archival record, recalling readers to when 'King Henry of blessed memorie did visit the Abbies of England by Thomas Lee, Richard Leighton and Thomas Bedel ... beinge doctors of the law, in the yere of our lord God 1538 and in every abbie were found some to be sodomites, others to be adultrers, some ... harlots'.[33]

This historical perspective was not only described in print. From the privacy of his Yorkshire rectory, Michael Sherbrook traced for himself the age of the monastery, a 'space of a 1000 years and above ... that is, ever since the first receiving of Christ's faith in England'.[34] A burgess of St Albans, John Shrimton, bracketed the monastic antiquity of his town with its visible traces of Roman Verulamium and at the turn of the century searched for both in script and stone.[35] His impulse was shared by Sir John Oglander, whose purchase of Quarr in 1607, and wealth, prompted the first step towards a monastic archaeology. 'Inquyred of divors owld men where ye greate church stood', he 'hired some to digge to see wethor [he] might finde ye fowndation'.[36] Sir John Danvers, the new owner of Bradenstoke Priory, appears to have expressed his historical sensitivity in stone, recreating the vaulting of the already ruined building.[37] There was a hint of this sensibility at the heart of the reformed Church. The manual of procession customs maintained at Durham Cathedral was marked around the century's end with the comment, 'In oulde tyme'.[38]

The new sense of history did not unsettle the conviction of the rightness of the dissolution. Adam Hill was not the only polemicist of these years inclined to invoke its history to persuade those, growing weary under the ageing Elizabeth, of the benefits of a kingdom reformed. 'Many do lament the pulling downe of abbayes, they say it was neuer merie world since,' admitted Francis Trigge in his *Apologie or defence of our days* (1589), '[but] the sinnes of Sodomah raigned amongest them'. He declared:

> Our kings which haue pulled downe the abbeyes and expelled their Munkes, are also famous and in great estimation. Wee may saye: O thrise happie and faire Sunneshine dayes of ours, the which all the cloudes of ignorance being dispersed, all the vailes of superstition being rent in peeces, all the monumentes, and pillers of Idolatrie being pulled downe, haue Iesus Christ the true Sonne

of righteousnes, of saluation and trueth, moste clearely shining, and with his beames most plainly glistering in them.[39]

The anonymous editor of *A world of wonders*, a translation of Henri Estienne's assault on the Roman Church, published in the (likely) last year of a living religious (1607), set out an historical verdict for his English readers: 'if the life of our Ministers be compared with that of their Friers, it will be found to exceed theirs as farre as Yorke doth foule Sutton, to vse a Northerne phrase. And that if holinesse of life be a true note of the Church, ours will be found Apostolical, theirs Apostatical.'[40] Michael Drayton mined Estienne's French for an epitaph of his own, 'Les moins deuoint estre de fils de putains' (The monks became whoresons).[41] In spite of their fascination for their history, the antiquarians were equally unequivocal. 'In excess,' Camden concluded, 'they consumed the goods of the church and inheritance of the poor.'[42] In Wales, Humphrey Lloyd and David Powel likewise commended the end of 'all this baggage and superstition'.[43] It does appear that distance and the disappearance of any representatives of the old order, lent a fresh appeal to the old tales and tropes. 'The blincking Syr Johns' and 'lazie abby men' were as prominent in the popular prints of the 1590s as they had been at any time since the 1530s, in every form, from the plays of *King Johan* and *Arden of Faversham*, both of which made their scenes inside the precinct, to epigrams, pulpit polemic and the printing-house perennial, the 'merrie iests' of Robin Hood.[44]

However, the Elizabethans' belief in the Reformation triumph did not now obscure their view of other effects of dissolution. Even as the old allegations of a corrupt order flourished, there was a new lament for the assault that spelled its end. In William Camden a sense of loss deepened over time. In the Latin of his first edition of *Britannia* (1586), the approach and the tone was of detached reportage. He described for his readers only the scale and scope of the change, when a long-celebrated foundation (monasterium fuit longe celebratissimum), with the richest (opulentissimum) of architecture was put down (reducti), razed (demolitum) and left as rubble (in ruderibus).[45] Yet nearly a quarter of a century later when he revised the book, he expressed a commitment to, even a passion for, their cause:

I hope without offence I may speake the truth many religious places, monuments of our fore fathers pieetie and devotion to the honor of God, the propagation of Christian faith and goodlearning, and also for the reliefe and maintenance of the poore and ompotent to wit monasteries or abaies and prio-ries . . . a sudden flood (as it were) breaking thorow the banks with a maine streame . . . which whiles the world stood amazed, and England grone thereat . . . most goodlyt and beautiful houses, and those goods and riches which the Christian pieitie of the English nation had consecreated unto god . . . were in a moment as it were dispersed, and (to the displeasure of noman be it spoke) profaned.[46]

John Speed wrote less in sadness than in anger at 'the sudden deluge of those tempestuous times', and he determined to '[lay] to the Readers view a great part of this kings ill, the waste of so much of Gods reuenewe (however abused)'.[47] His outlook now was at one with Catholic historians. The first Jacobean edition of Nicholas Harpsfield's *Historia Anglicana ecclesiastica* mirrored the *Historie* with a catalogue of 'monasteries and other holy temples' (sacrarum aedium) that King Henry VIIII 'destroyed, tore up or utterly abandoned'.[48]

For the first time, this generation weighed the cost of the closure to the commonweal. 'Be ashamed,' urged Robert Some in 1582, for 'making foule havock . . . with the spoyle and ruine of churches.'[49] There was equal dismay at the general disarray and dereliction of the townscape. The Londoner Stow conveyed the daily frustration of the city following the closure of the 300-year-old Augustinian friary and the loss of the footway from All Hallows to Moorgate that 'forced [them] to go about' by a different route.[50] In his county of small towns, William Lambarde wrote of the 'lament and pitie [of a] generall decay'. 'For where wealth is at commaundement, how easily are buildings repaired? And where opinion of great holynesse is, howe soone are cities and townes advaunced to great estimation and riches. And therefore no marvaile, if wealth withdrawn and opinion of holynessee removed, the places tumble headlong to ruine and decay.'[51] Sir John Oglander ended his memoir with a simple aphorism of his own coinage: 'tyme pulleth downe greate thinges and setth up poore thinges'.[52] Spoliation was imprinted on the Elizabethan imagination. 'Into a monastere' went Edmund Spenser's knight errant, Calidore, in the *Faerie Queene*, completed in 1589, 'where he him found despoyling all with maine and might.'[53]

It has long been doubted that this generation spoke sincerely as they found. The turn-of-the-century economy carried with it the inflation of previous decades and was not yet freed from earlier pressures on employment and the food supply. It was not a period of collapse either in the urban environment or in the countryside. Lambarde may have been wrong to diagnose a 'generall decay'. Yet, as landscape and archaeological data of Reformation sites had been collated under the nation-wide Historic Environment Record, there is an emerging impression of a lengthy hiatus during which much of the infrastructure of the former religious houses remained little used or wholly untouched. Lambarde may have been right to see provincial England as tumbledown. This changed, or began to change, perhaps as the century turned. By the time Stow's *Survey of London* was published in 1598, on the precincts of the regulars there was now more activity housed in new buildings than in the standing remains of the old. In the decades that followed many of the remaining frames and facades of the old houses were covered over for new purposes, from the great nave of the London Greyfriars to the simple hall of the Franciscans facing the high street at Bodmin. Churches recovered for use ad hoc now saw their first formal rebuild. On the eve of the Civil War (1634), the Cistercian church at Abbey Dore was reconsecrated, under the patronage of a Scudamore descendant of Sir John, the Cromwellian commissioner.[54]

The last Elizabethans were also the first fully to count and to characterise the social cost. Those who witnessed the dissolution had hoped for much. 'Y wasse . . . as glade as any man of thys reame of the suppressycon,' wrote Sir Roger Graynfield in 1539, 'ye rekyn before thys they were tayrs a waye of the welth of thys reame'.[55] Yet scarcely a decade later and the polemicists spoke of prospects spoiled. 'Howe these lecherouse locustes have used theyr king,' spat John Bale.[56] Thomas Ruddoke railed at 'al fermours or owners of abbey lands being dissolved [who] ought and shold be contributours and helpers to the living of their person or vicar'.[57] The *Decaye of England*, a broadside published in 1552, pictured a husbandry grotesquely distorted by private enterprise pursuing profit:

> only [a] great multitude of shepe, to the vtter decay of houshold keping, mayn-tenaunce of men, dearth of corne, and other notable dyscommodityes . . . By reason cottages go downe in the contre, where as pultrye was wont to be breade and fedde, now there is nothyng kept there but shepe.[58]

The recent experience of social and economic change was the recurrent theme of Camden's portraits of provincial England: Colchester, where the corpse of the

Benedictine abbot had dangled from his gatehouse, was now a picture of civic success, 'elegant, bustling and delightful' (elegans, frequens amoena); Shrewsbury, which had held no fewer than four religious houses within its walls, prospered with fresh purpose (hodie vero urb est eximia frequens mercium copisoa); the removal of the friars from the coastal towns of Rye and Milford Haven (Pembrokeshire) appeared to have marked a new beginning: one had been renewed (refloruit), the other was noble 'like no other in Europe'.[59] But there were provincial towns (oppida) which in his estimation undoubtedly were diminished: the 'incomparable magnificence' of the abbey at Bury St Edmunds had been erased; Evesham was no more the well-favoured site of a renowned foundation (oppidum satis elegans notum monasterio); Camden even saw Ely as somewhat downgraded, since a great crowd of monks were replaced by a dean, prebends and a 'nursery of letters' for boys (decanus, praebendarii, ludus literarius in quo ... pueri ... aluntur).[60]

His tone was of measured detachment but now others were disposed to make it a matter of public and political complaint. Sir Everard Digby rounded on the post-Reformation proprietors, 'so besotted with the love of themselves ... their own goodes, their own lands ... that the kingdome of heaven to them is but a dreame'.[61] His public judgement was echoed in the personal papers of his peers. 'The estate of the realm hath come to more misery since King Henry his time than ever it did in all the time before.'[62] The Wyatt family chronicle recalled 'many as could smell [the revenues] were in short time fattened. Many who bere [were?] servants ... were shortlie Masters ... Some of them were so fine and nice that they might no longer piss in pewter.'[63] The popular play of the 1590s was *The Lamentable and true tragedie of M. Arden of Feveresham* (1592), the scandalous tale of a dissolution grantee murdered by his cheating wife.[64]

Here Camden's testimony may carry the greatest weight. By the 1580s, when he made his tours, neighbourhoods were different after the departure of their religious and the closure of their house. But there was no uniform change, for better or for worse. Camden's sketches suggest that he saw now above all a sharp break with the past: small towns – such as Thetford – were less after the loss of their religious, while significant locations on any route map – such as Shrewsbury – were as lively as before, only with different forms of life. His snapshot of Great Walsingham might stand for many: the life of the locality had not been extinguished but it had been changed beyond recognition. Traffic in pilgrims was replaced by trade in crocuses.[65] It was this, the natural disorientation arising from a profound change in the most familiar of scenes, that fuelled a popular memory of neighbourhood decline. If there was one reason for a different scene at Cerne in the judgement of the Jacobean traveller, Thomas Gerard (1593–1634), it was not commerce – the 'weeklie market' and 'faires' continued as before – but the spectacle of change itself: it was a town touched by 'suppression'.[66] At the end of the same century, the people of Ravensthorpe (West Yorkshire) and Swine (Lincolnshire) expressed this to the visiting antiquarian, Abraham de la Pryme, that '[the houses] being pulled down was the reason of the towns falling into ruin'.[67] The high turnover of Reformation property in the first half-century after 1540 serves to reinforce the view that what challenged livelihoods was not absolute loss but persistent change. Patterns of exchange and purchase in provincial towns show that there was no stranglehold on land, buildings, development or commerce. In fact, corporations found the freedom to choose what they recovered and rebuilt. From Bury to Gloucester, Coventry and Carlisle, urban life was recast by locals as the first generation of grantees passed on.[68]

Camden, his fellow antiquarians and their gentlemen readership reflected on wealth and its sources, but there was a growing popular voice preoccupied with the very opposite. '[The] gret nombre of peple shall have no lands and pensions to maytayne them,' argued the author of *Piers Plowmans exhortation to the Parlyamenthouse*, 'therfore if more woorke be not prouided for theym what can ensue but extreame pouertie beggery and miserie?'[69] Not a Catholic apologist, still he recalled 'when the Abbays did stand that Husbandman whych had two or thre Sonnes, wold for the mooste parte finde one of them at Scoole for a yere [or] helpe his other brethern to some parte or their liuinge, but nowe there is no such refuge'.[70] In the godly *Motive to good works* (1593), Philip Stubbes weighed their reputation in the same way: 'The monasteries ... were afterwards most horribly abused by Popish locusts', but 'what, and how many almes houses, hospitalls, and spittles did they found for the reliefe of the poore, and indowed them with competent lands and liuelodes for mayntenance of them?'[71]

The printed polemics made public matter a complaint that probably had been audible in provincial England for years. As early as 1548 the people of Bury had appealed to the need for 'an hospitall for the poore and a schoole for the education of youth'.[72] The complaints were not unfounded. In the last decade of Elizabeth's reign it was demonstrable that the charitable doles, schools and hospital foundations of monastic England had not been succeeded by institutions of a comparable scale and scope. It was an irony not lost on Elizabethans, moreover, that some of those which had been established stood on monastic foundations, some – a school at St Albans and at Guisborough – under the headship of former monks.[73]

Towards the century's end, the sources point to effects of the dissolution of which contemporaries were not so acutely aware. The conformity of the regulars, which had presented a challenge to royal authority collectively since 1534, and individually for as much as a decade, remained unresolved. Public historians of Elizabeth's reign, such as Foxe and Stow, had themselves reached middle age before the last of the men who had professed earlier than 1540 appeared at a scaffold. The radical reformer, John Taylor alias Cardmaker, originally an Observant Franciscan, was burned at Smithfield in 1555.[74] In the same year, William Branch alias Fowler, a former monk of Ely, also died for a commitment to reform that had compelled him to stab the celebrant at the Easter Mass in St Margaret's Church, Westminster.[75] Also in 1555, Robert Ferrar, who had fallen under the suspicion of both the Edwardian and the Marian regimes, finally faced execution, 'burned with turves and soddes for lack of wood', after years in prison.[76]

That no other former regular met summary justice in the reign of Elizabeth was only fortunate, not for want of intent on the part of the Crown. After the queen's Reformation several unreconciled Benedictines and Cistercians at first remained in England; only their flight to Flanders, France and Scotland spared them from certain detention and possible death. Several more struggled over conformity, and their underlying dissidence led them into long-term imprisonment. Half a century after the first statute for the suppression, there were former monks and nuns in custody at London, York, Wisbech and Hull. Thomas Mudde had cheated a worse fate than death in custody (at York) since he became a fugitive in the wake of the Rising of the Northern Earls (1569) and was known to carry with him a relic of one of the pilgrim 'martyrs' of 1537.[77] Isabel Whitehedde, professed at Arthington (West Yorkshire) in the late 1520s, died a prisoner of Elizabeth at seventy-eight in 1587.[78]

None of the exiles lived to the very end of the century but their persistence in the religious life had propagated a new network of English regulars. Before the year of the Armada the rising generation of recusant Catholics were already drawn to the claustral profession. The very first of these, Robert Sayer (1560–1602), became a Benedictine at Monte Cassino in 1588.[79] When he first completed his *Memoriall* in manuscript in 1596, his fiftieth year, Robert Persons was confident that the 'many good colleges' in Catholic Europe could 'increase[e] our clergie'.[80] The first Catholic mission led by the new breed of expatriate monks arrived in England when James had been king for scarcely six months.[81] Before 1600, there were three houses of English regulars established in Flanders. A century on, there were as many as twenty-two right across the region of the Counter-Reformation.[82]

The dissolution left other unfinished business in Elizabeth's later years. The Tudor regime had been aware of the challenge of concealment – of property and the revenue arising from it – from the circuits of the commissioners of 1535. Perhaps the first impulse of the statute of 1539 had been to put a stay on the autonomous alienation of endowments. There had been much legal traffic and some localised successes. But it was apparent – perhaps more so after the disbanding of the Court of Augmentations and the transfer of its books to the Exchequer – that transactions undocumented and dues unpaid extended very far indeed. As late as the 1580s, it was still thought there was a case to answer for concealed livestock.[83] Elizabeth's reign was punctuated with proclamations to prompt the search and surrender of concealed property. The warrants to pursue the inquiries were as sought-after as any of the monopolies that a courtier might purchase. It was this, and only this aspect of the concealment problem, that seems to have caught public attention. The call of Robert Greene's *Upstart Courtier* (1592) was: 'what farme is there expirde, whose least thou doost not begge? what forfeite of penal statutes? What concealed landes can overslip thee?'[84]

The sequence of Elizabethan inquisitions forms a roll call of premier monasteries and friaries: Glastonbury (1573–74), Kirkstall (1597–98), Leicester Abbey (1583–84), London Minories (1585), Plympton (1572–73), Shrewsbury (1585–86).[85] In 1600 a royal commission convened to reach a final settlement.[86] It did not succeed. In the last months of the queen's life, Sir Edward Dyer, whose own family held the old Glastonbury manor of Sharpham, observed in a memorandum that 'leses which sundry abbots priors and such lyke religious persons have graunted ... for terme of lyffe ... long since expired ... at this day hold the same no other tytle'.[87] In the last year of a living religious, commissions for no fewer than fourteen counties were authorised by the Crown.[88] In 1609 King James attempted an amnesty 'that all his loving subiects shall partake of this grace to have all the states of their lands confirmed ... notwithstanding any of the defects of imperfections'.[89] But claims and counter-claims continued. The loss to the Crown of late monastery land was still under the eye of parliamentary commissioners on the brink of Queen Victoria's reign.[90]

It was from this time, close to the end of the century and of the Tudor regime, that it is possible to trace another consequence of the dissolution. This was not a legacy of the confrontations of 1534–40; rather it was an inheritance of the history of the religious houses as a whole. There was, perhaps, an early glimpse in the reported encounter of the Jesuit missionary, William Weston (1549/50–1615), and an elderly employee of Glastonbury Abbey in 1586.[91] The old man showed him a crucifix which he claimed to have saved from the monastery. It had been made to hold a holy relic, a nail from the cross of Christ, which had since been confiscated by John Jewel, bishop of Salisbury. The revelation of a souvenir still kept forty-seven years after the closure of the church is less remarkable than the story of it that the old man told. He was accustomed to carry it with him, he explained, as he climbed a 'high mountain' a few miles from Glastonbury – perhaps Montacute – where there were ruined buildings said to be the remains of the cell occupied by Joseph of Arimathea. He would 'ascend, out of a motive of religion and devotion, not on his feet, but on his knees, carrying with him the cross and the case of the nail, "as my safeguard"'. At the summit he thought he heard 'wailings and groans and the mournful voices of people in grief', as if to suggest that he stood at the entrance to purgatory.[92] Weston's testimony was intended to demonstrate the enduring Catholic piety of the Tudors' subjects. But perhaps above all it is indicative of a turn in the associations of religious houses at a distance of half a century and counting from their closure.

When their living presence passed away what remained of the religious houses was their legend. Yet this was more than the residue of old stories to which any personal, social and cultural connection was wearing very thin. Viewed from this generation forward, ever further removed from the economic, fiscal, political and even the confessional discourses that surrounded them for so long, it does seem that the historical record of these houses was being revised. Now it could serve as a vehicle for values that undercut sectarian divisions: of the antiquity of a locality and its social community; the roots of its identity and its cultural tradition at the heart of which lay its original Christianity.

John Aubrey's papers preserve several suggestive scenes: at the rectory of Haselbury (Wiltshire), a living once held by the abbot and convent of Glastonbury, it was the custom of each new incumbent on arrival 'to read prayers in a room in the old house, and to have a portion of mould given into his hand in a ground called the burying place'.[93] A 'grett pott or crock' was put in the grounds of the mansion at Lacock to greet visitors as 'a relic of ancient hospitality'.[94] At his boyhood home of Kington St Michael (Wiltshire), Aubrey recalled how, 'when . . . a boy', he was told his own history from the window fragments found in the old priory church, of 'King Ethelred and Queen', and of 'the Ladie Bodenham', former prioress, of whose 'picture' there was 'the greater part . . . remaynyng'; and by the 'Y' marked in the main street, the place of a cross, although it was long gone, and a Friday market where the nuns had found their 'fish egges and butter'.[95]

Clearly, these were not confined within Aubrey's Wiltshire. After the Restoration (1660) at Abbey Dore on the Welsh border it was remembered that the pastor, John Gyles, would 'read prayers under an arch of the old demolished church'.[96] Surely it was no coincidence that by the end of the seventeenth century, and of Aubrey's long life, the old vocabulary of the religious houses – abbey, priory, abbot, monk, nun and friar, among others – had lost much of its partisan or pejorative connotations and conveyed instead the impression of a common inheritance, of a sacred tradition reaching far into the remote past. Now, a new house on an old plot at Grantham was named 'The Nuns'.[97] A farmhouse formed from the only standing building on the site of Carrow was called 'Abbey'.[98] The hamlet of Llanfihangel, expanding on the edge of the old demesne of Llantarnam, became 'Y Fynachlog' (The Monastery).[99] These monasteries of the historical imagination would prove durable indeed.

NOTES

BL British Library
Bodl. Bodleian Library
HER Historic Environment Record
LP *Letters and papers foreign & domestic of the reign of Henry VIII*, ed. J. S. Brewer et al.,
   22 vols. in 35 (Longman, Green, Longman and Roberts: London, 1862–1932)
STC Short Title Catalogue
TNA The National Archives
WAM Westminster Abbey Muniments

Introduction

1. TNA, E322/252.
2. TNA, SC6/HENVIII/995.
3. Knighton, 1996, 57–8; *LP*, 15, 378.
4. *LP*, 15, 488. The college itself was transferred to the new secular chapter of Canterbury Cathedral in the autumn of 1540 under which it continued to serve as a house-of-studies until its surrender on 27 November 1545: TNA, E322/127.
5. Knowles and Hadcock, 1971, 61, 74, 178.
6. There were 173 Augustinian houses in 1535; the next largest constituency was the Benedictines, with 126: Knowles and Hadcock, 1971, 52–8, 137–45.
7. Fizzard, 2007, 251.
8. The preceptory at Shingay (Cambridgeshire) had been unoccupied already for more than a year after its preceptor, Sir Thomas Dingley, had been attainted and executed for his sympathy for the rebels of 1536: Knowles and Hadcock, 1971, 300–1; *LP*, 14/1, 1104.
9. *LP*, 15, 498; TNA, SP 1/162, fo. 78r.
10. Knowles and Hadcock, 1971, 301.
11. Davey and Roscow, 2010, 19.
12. *LP*, 14/2, 1036.

13. Of the religious houses of the English islands, only Farne's Benedictine priory is recorded by Knowles and Hadcock, 1971, 54. For the Channel Islands see Ogier, 1996, 41–2.
14. Bradshaw, 1974, 162–80.
15. Counted here are those houses closed after 1 January 1536 in England and Wales, drawn from Knowles and Hadcock, 1971, 58–309.
16. For example, the colony of Cistercians on the Wirral Peninsula at Stanlow (Cheshire) was deemed no longer viable for a permanent presence in the middle years of the fourteenth century: Knowles and Hadcock, 1971, 130, 132.
17. Dickinson, 1968, 66.
18. Knowles and Hadcock, 1971, 83–95.
19. For Henry VII's transformation of Westminster Abbey as an animated memorial to his dynasty see Tatton-Brown and Mortimer, 2003. For the college and school foundations of his age see Davis, 1993, 57–63; Underwood, 1989; Jones and Underwood, 1992, 203–31.
20. *Colyn Cloute*, 404–5, 421–2; Scattergood, 2015, 224.
21. Mayer, 1989, 124.
22. TNA, SP 1/54, fo. 202r; Bernard, 1996, 283.
23. TNA, SP 1/34, fo. 240r–v.
24. Warham expressed a general anxiety after the first of the suppressions in 1524; the next year it was more acute, and he feared some form of protest arising from Tonbridge: TNA, SP 1/134, fo. 132r; SP 1/35, fos. 48r, 50r.
25. Loades, 1968, 159.
26. Anon., 1830, 153–6 at 154.
27. Snape (Suffolk) had emptied before the end; at Pynham (West Sussex) there was only one resident; others, such as Bromehill (Norfolk), St Mary de Pré (Hertfordshire) and Wallingford had probably not risen far above five for some considerable time: Knowles and Hadcock, 1971, 76–7, 79, 150, 171, 265.
28. The scandal was uncovered when the Carthusian, Edmund Horde, visited the house as commissary of Bishop Attwater of Lincoln: Thompson, 1940–7, i. lxxvi–lxxviii.
29. For the estimated population of these houses see Knowles, 1959, 470; Knowles and Hadcock, 1971, 148, 150, 153, 161.
30. Sylvester, 1959, 5.
31. *LP*, 4/3, 6539.
32. Dated 2 and 12 November 1528: TNA, SC 7/63/22, 24.
33. Hay, 1950, 254–5.
34. These numbers and phases of closure are based on the data in Knowles and Hadcock, 1971.
35. Chester, Shrewsbury (with Morville), Worcester, Tewkesbury (with Deerhurst and St James, Bristol), Gloucester (with Ewenny), Thetford, Wangford, Waltham, Westminster, Rochester and Canterbury.
36. Herrtage, 1878, liii.
37. TNA, SP 1/79, fo. 44r.
38. BL, MS Cotton Vitellius B XXI, fo. 108r–v.
39. Hildebrandt, 1984, 284.
40. [Barlow], 1531, B3v, P3r. Royal proclamations against heresy disseminated these views: Heinze, 1976, 132–3.
41. TNA, SP 1/98, fos. 134v–7r.
42. Jakobson, 2021, 1; Ekroll, 2019, 151–3 at 151; Berntson, 2003, 28. The population of these houses can only be estimated but a mean figure of 12 for a house might not be unreasonable given that a number had dwindled to the point of being abandoned.
43. Grell, 1995, 71; Seesko et al., 2019; Chadwick, 2001, 153–5.
44. Chadwick, 2001, 151–80 at 162.
45. There were 20 men and women at Syon, 15 at Westminster, 12 at Sheen and 7 at King's Langley. The number of friars that returned to Greenwich and gathered at Smithfield is not recorded but it is doubtful that either saw more than ten: Giuseppi, 1937–9, iii. 348–54

(Westminster); 354–5 (Sheen); 403 (King's Langley); Nichols, 1848, 171; Knighton and Mortimer, 2003, 82–3. For the effort to re-establish monasteries during Mary's reign see below, 512–27.

46. Nichols, 1848, 138,
47. For these efforts at re-foundation see: Knowles, 1959, 438; Clark, 2000, 320–3; Knighton, 2006, 84; Litzenberger, 1998, 82; Knowles and Hadcock, 1971, 80, 135, 202, 217, 230–1, 285, 305. See below, 513–27.
48. Knighton, 2006, 83–91, for a very full summary of the complexities of who may have arrived at Westminster, if not, clearly, when; Cunich, 2007, 47–8.
49. John Wilson, former prior of Mount Grace, died at Sheen, and Prior William Peryn at Smithfield: Hendriks, 1889, 282; Nichols, 1848, 171.
50. BL, MS Egerton 2164. The hanged corpse of the attainted abbot is shown in the far distance of the scene. The survey itself was the work of the king's commissioners, Richard Pollard and Thomas Moyle.
51. Ellis, 1812, 606.
52. MacCulloch, 2018, 2.
53. Bale, 1544, ixv; Strype, 1721, 377.
54. Ellis, 1798, 54; Shaw, 2004.
55. Ingworth's will was dated 2 November 1544; it was proved on 18 December: TNA, PCC Prob 11/30/259.
56. Smith, 2008, 25, 80; TNA, PCC Prob 11/26/308, fos. 136v–137v; Prob, 11/28/229, fos. 95v–97r; Knighton, 2004; Bale, 1551, A iir.
57. For these post-dissolution careers see Carter, 2004a; Atherton, 2011; Knighton, 2011.
58. BL, MS 11041, documenting his duties as a commissioner in the western march and the Midlands from 1535 to the mid-1550s.
59. Higgs, 1998, 130.
60. Oxford, Bodl., MS Douce 363, fo. 94v. For Batman see Zim, 2011.
61. Corrie, 1844–5, i. 75, 123, 232, 474.
62. Hall, 1809, 821.
63. Holinshed, 1577, 1566–67.
64. Stow, 1592, 966, 974.
65. It is difficult to see in the reformers' persistent fixation the 'selective amnesia' which has recently been read into their polemics: Lyon, 2018, 201.
66. Bale, 1546, A ii.
67. Sander, 1585, 141.
68. Kingsford, 1908.
69. Speed, 1611, 778, 801.
70. Parsons, 1690, 2.
71. Dickens, 1959, 90.
72. Weever, 1631, 50.
73. Andrew Marvell, *Upon Appleton House*, xii, xiv–xv, xxxiv.
74. Fuller, 1845, iii. 358.
75. Ibid, 438, 442.
76. Guinn-Chipman, 2013, 125.
77. Pocock, 1865, 12.
78. *England's Reformation*, Canto I, 42.
79. Pugin, 1836, 3.
80. Carlyle, 1843, 38, 43.
81. Wright, 1843, vi.
82. Brewer et al., 1862–1932.
83. Froude, 1856–70, 359.
84. Gasquet, 1893, i. vii, 178, 210, 395; ii. 85, 163, 364; Crake, 1886, 256.
85. Coulton, 1950, 561, 729.

86. Knowles, 1959.
87. Hoyle, 1995a, 299.
88. Bernard, 2005, 475; Marshall, 2018, 226–7.
89. Bernard, 2011, 408; Marshall, 2018, 227.
90. MacCulloch, 2018, 449.
91. Ibid, 546–7 at 546.
92. Bernard, 2005, 574.
93. Everett, 2015, 133–4.
94. Borman, 2014, 56, 63, 158–71.
95. 'He gave them latitude . . . [and] lost control': Shaw, 2003, 321, 422.
96. 'Cromwell found himself supporting . . . the king decided': Ibid, 418.
97. Everett, 2015, 247.
98. Marshall, 2018, 61.
99. Shagan, 2003, 164, 187.
100. Walsham, 2011, 166–7, 273–96.
101. The pursuit of the archaeology of reformation has been the most valuable research development of the past twenty years. Heritage Gateway (https://www.heritagegateway.org.uk/gateway/), a portal to the Historic Environment Records of English counties, has revealed the wealth of site information still awaiting critical attention. Synthetic studies remain few: Gaimster and Gilchrist, 2003; Willmott, 2020.
102. For Ireland's dissolution see Bradshaw, 1974.

Chapter I The Legend of the Cloister

1. *Morte darthur*, XIII, 9–10: Malory, 1485, N viir–viiiv.
2. Ibid, preface, A iiv.
3. The adoption in western Europe of the first two of these technologies is very well known; for the third see now Gleeson-White, 2012.
4. Fergusson, 2011, 152.
5. Lincolnshire HER, 20552.
6. In 1527 Abbot William Bean appealed for contributions to the maintenance cost: Staffordshire Record Office, D603/A/ADD/757.
7. De Windt and De Windt, 2006, 18–19.
8. Somerset Heritage Centre, DD\X\RMN/3.
9. The monks' right to run a ferry and to sell victuals dated from 1318: TNA, PRO, SC 8/160/7968.
10. East Sussex HER, MES3997.
11. Jones, 1989, 87–9.
12. Toulmin-Smith, 1906–10, i. 210, 284.
13. Harvey, 1991, 71, 73.
14. Ibid, ii. 61.
15. Fuller, 1845, iii. 332.
16. Traskey, 1978, 150.
17. Williams, 2001, 262–3; Coppack, 1998, 123.
18. The wall remains named after Abbot John Penny (1496–1509): Leicester City Council Heritage Data, MLC 1782.
19. Emery, 2006, 148–9 at 149; Cockerham, 2004.
20. Northampton HER, 1160/9/5.
21. Weever, 1631, 718.
22. Thompson, 1997, 200.
23. Luders et al., 1810–28, iii. 531 (27 Henry VIII c. 1).
24. Kresen Kernow, AR 25/2.

25. TNA, SP 1/104, fo. 246v.
26. Sylvester, 1959, 143.
27. TNA, SP 1/116, fo. 20r.
28. Fuller, 1845, iii. 338.
29. Toulmin-Smith, 1906–10, iv. 17.
30. Elrington, 1968, 110–18 at 115.
31. Bristol Record Office, P/AS/D/HS B 7.
32. Higham, 1999, 174.
33. Manning, 1988, 46.
34. Miller, 2001, 22.
35. Michelmore, 1981, lxiii, lxxx.
36. TNA, SP 1/142 fo. 137r. See also Toulmin-Smith, 1907–10, v. 155.
37. Henry VIII, 1527, D viiir; Chertsey, 1502, b iiv, aa iiv.
38. Colet, 1530, C ir.
39. Anon., 1528, 108.
40. Wiltshire and Swindon History Centre, 1422/109.
41. TNA, SP 1/139, fo. 148v.
42. Toulmin-Smith, 1906–10, ii. 62.
43. Ibid, 52–3.
44. Anon., 1528, fo. 79r.
45. [Saltwood], 1533, B iiv.
46. *Eclogues*, IV, 836: White, 1960, 170.
47. Haigh, 1969, 56.
48. Toulmin-Smith, 1906, 123; Oxford, Bodl. Top. Gen C IV, p. 35.
49. Welander, 1991, 297.
50. Hare, 1999, 4–5.
51. The Glastonbury *Magna tabula* is now Oxford, Bodl., Lat hist. a 2; Krochalis, 2001.
52. Now BL, MS Cotton Nero D VII. It seems the book was displayed at the high altar.
53. The manuscript is now at Dublin, Trinity College, MS 177. A note of its showing to the king is found on the flyleaf.
54. Toulmin-Smith, 1906–10, ii. 74.
55. Ibid, 59–60.
56. Society of Antiquaries Library, MS 720.
57. 'corpus inveniunt putridum / attamen ornatum gladio capitisque corona ... scepta tenet / aurea vestis erat propior, quam serica texit / calcar erat pedibus annulus in digito': Cambridge, Corpus Christi College, MS 158, fo. 54v.
58. Clark, 2019a, 119.
59. Carley, 1996, 36–7 at 37.
60. Erasmus, *Colloquia*, 'Peregrinatio religionis ergo'; Holtze, 1892, i. 345.
61. Baskerville, 1940, 23.
62. Sharpe, 1890, ii. 614–28.
63. Toulmin-Smith, 1906–10, i. 134; Hearne, 1770, i. x.
64. Bradshaw, 1521, II, iii. 39–40.
65. For the witness of the sacrists' rolls see, for example, Westminster Abbey Muniments, 9485; 19700.
66. Kresen Kernow, ART/4/10.
67. Anon., 1511, A iiiiv.
68. Ibid, A iir.
69. Geoffrey of Monmouth, *Historia regum Britanniae*, VIII, 127: Reeve, 2007, 170.
70. *Morte darthur*, XXI, 10: Malory, 1485, ee iiir–v at ee iii.
71. *Morte darthur*, XXI, 10, 4: Malory, 1485, f vr.
72. *Morte darthur*, preface: Malory, 1485, iiv.

73. The legend of Lucius was transmitted through a wide variety of medieval histories, of the nation and of particular church foundations, but one of the formative versions was Geoffrey of Monmouth's *Historia regum Britanniae*, IV, 72: Reeve, 2007, 87–8.
74. Heale, 2005.
75. Krochalis, 2001; Riddy, 2001.
76. Caley et al., 1817–30, i. 189, 265.
77. Henry Bradshaw, *The holy lyfe and history of saynt Werburge*, II, iii. 58–60: Bradshaw, 1521, u. iiii.
78. TNA, SP 1/92, fo. 22r.
79. Caley et al., 1817–30, i. 56 (Tewkesbury), 203–4 (St Albans). For Neville's burial at Bisham see an early 16th-century account in BL, MS 45131, fos. 22r–v. For Jasper Tudor's burial at Keynsham see his will, TNA, PCC 11/10/591, fos. 257r–v at 257r.
80. Ritchie, 1966, 51.
81. BL, MS Cotton Cleopatra C II, fos. 210r–24v.
82. Blunt, 1875, 84–5.
83. Queen Elizabeth of York met her expenses from her own privy purse: Nicholas, 1830, 29.
84. Ellis, 1844, 62.
85. Jasper's grandson was Thomas Gardener, on whose monastic career see Pearce, 1916, 175; Smith, 2008, 154.
86. TNA, SP 1/80, fo. 118r.
87. Anon., 1499, iir–v.
88. Ritchie, 1966, 43.
89. Hearne, 1770, iii, 122.
90. The family's patronage of regular foundations was celebrated in a genealogical history copied in the front of a cartulary of the earldom preserved at Powderham Castle: Clark, 2018, 3, 18–19.
91. West Sussex Record Office, CHICTY/AY/112.
92. Thompson, 1994, 116–17, 121.
93. Clark, 2018, 19.
94. Raine and Clay, 1836–1902, iii. 246–8; 1869, iv. 209–12.
95. Colvin and Stone, 1965; Marks, 1984.
96. Now, Oxford, Bodl., MS Top Glouc. D 2.
97. North Devon Record Office, B190/1.
98. TNA, STAC 10/1/30.
99. Bristol Record Office, P/AS/D/HS B 7.
100. See below, 554, n. 42.
101. TNA, Prob. 11/27, fos. 194v–195r.
102. The glass is now installed in the church of St Michael, Plumstead (Norfolk): Pevsner and Wilson 2002, 639.
103. [Alcock a], 1497, A iiv.
104. [Barlow], 1531, l 1v; Anon, 1528, h viir.
105. TNA, PCC Prob 11/21/462, fos. 211v–212r.
106. http://english.nsms.ox.ac.uk/holinshed/texts.php?text1=1587_7832.
107. [Alcock a], 1497, A ivr.
108. Anon., 1520, A iiiv.
109. [Atkinson] 1504, Bviiiv.
110. [Alcock b], 1497 B ir.
111. Peacock, 1883, 52.
112. For example, Thompson, 1915–27, ii. 85 (Dunstable); 150 (Huntingdon); Jessopp, 1888, 107 (Blackborough); 198 (Norwich).
113. Thompson, 1915–27, ii. 86 (Dunstable); 120 (Gracedieu).
114. TNA, SP 1/32, fo. 234r.
115. TNA, SP 1/19, fo. 221r.
116. TNA, SP 1/233, fo. 65r.

117. TNA, SP 1/82, fo. 130r.
118. BL, MS Harley 218, fo. 47r.
119. Miller, 2001, 127.
120. TNA, SP 5/2, fo. 259r.
121. Geoffrey Chaucer, *The Monk's Tale*, l. 171; *The Nun's Priest's Tale*, l. 2851.
122. Miller, 2001, 128.
123. Rees, 2008, 39.
124. *Philip Sparrow*, l. 391; *Colin Cloute*, ll. 376, 385; Scattergood, 2015, 69, 223.
125. Kingsford, 1908, 11.
126. Miller, 1966, 338–9.
127. Anon, 1496, D ivr.
128. Koopmans, 2011, 203–10.
129. Collier, 1838, 47–8.
130. BL, MS Cotton Cleopatra E IV, fo. 316v.
131. TNA, SP 1/102, fos. 85r, 103v.
132. Ibid.
133. Ibid.
134. TNA, SP 1/138, fos. 45r–46r at 45v; *LP*, 13/2, 719.
135. Raine, 1839, 152–3 at 152.
136. TNA, SP 1/94, fo. 102r; Knowles, 1959, 369.
137. Bequeathed 12d in the will of John Wastell, dated 3 May 1515: Tymms, 1850, 113–14 at 114.
138. Lancashire Archives, DDKE/HMC/1.
139. *LP*, 2/1, 115.
140. *Morte darthur*, XIV, 3: Malory, 1485, P iv–P iir.
141. Clark, 2004b, 90.
142. TNA, SP 1/22, fo. 65r.
143. Thompson, 1997, 633–4.
144. *LP*, 9, 609.
145. TNA, SP 1/129, fo. 12r.
146. Clark, 2000, 324.
147. Vallans, 1615, 24, 324–5.
148. Fulman, 1684, 560.
149. Haigh, 1969, 5.
150. McSheffrey, 2017, 27–35.
151. Romilly et al., 1874, i. 191 (3); Clark, 2019a.
152. TNA, C1/49/49.
153. TNA, SP 1/131, fo. 120r.
154. TNA, C1/813/1–2.
155. Anon., 1542.
156. Trigge, 1589, B3r, C1r.
157. The use of 'possessioner' had originated in the anti-clerical writing of Lollards, but by the reign of Henry VIII the image was taken up in public tracts: Fyloll, 1537. See also Bigod, 1535, C viiir; Nicolson, 1537; Mayer, 1989, 87.
158. *Robin Hood and the Curtal Friar*, ll. 27, 29: Knight and Ohlgren, 2000, 460–4 at 461.
159. Anon., 1519, fo. iv.
160. Douglas Hamilton, 1875, 109.
161. BL, MS Cotton Tiberius B III, fo. 148r.
162. *Morte darthur*, XXI, 7: Malory, 1485, ee ir.
163. DDCR/3/1/1/1.
164. TNA, SP 1/45, fo. 37r.
165. Bale, 1550, fo. ix.
166. TNA, SP 1/85, fo. 100r.

167. Gloucestershire Archives, D1224/T/Box 7/bundle 4 (part).
168. Riley, 1867–9, iii. 4.
169. TNA, SP 1/100, fo. 94r.
170. Ridley, 1540, B2v.
171. TNA, SP 1/80, fo. 197r.
172. Luders et al., 1810–28, iii. 575–8 (27 Henry VIII 28).
173. *The Canterbury Tales*, General Prologue, ll. 147, 160, 165, 206.
174. *Philip Sparrow*, l. 123; Scattergood, 2015, 63.
175. Anon., 1528, E iiiv.
176. Anon., 1520, Aiir–v.
177. *Eclogues*, I, 293–4: White, 1960, 9.
178. Trigge, 1589, 1.
179. TNA, SP 1/153, fo. 78r.
180. Herrtage, 1878, lvi.
181. *Robin Hood and the Monk*, l. 75: Knight and Ohlgren, 2000, 39.
182. Letter dated 8 May 1535: TNA, SP 1/92, fo. 131r; *LP*, 8, 690.
183. Anon., 1516, fo. iv.
184. Anon., 1515, fo. A ivr.
185. Anon., 1530, fo. ir.
186. Canterbury Cathedral Archives, CC/JQ/307/xiv.
187. Poem 43, Psalm 55.
188. Peacock, 1883, 58.
189. [Fish], 1529, 4r.
190. 'Why I can't be a nun', ll. 244–7: BL, MS Cotton Vespasian D IX, fos. 177a–82b, 190a–b.
191. [Alcock b], 1497, Bir, Dir.
192. One of two seal imprints on a document of 1317: ECA/ED/M/233.
193. Devon Heritage Centre, ECA/ED/M/326.
194. *Pardoner and the frere*, ll. 54–6: [Heywood], 1533, A iv.
195. Bigod, 1535, Div.
196. Jessopp, 1888, 115.
197. TNA, SP 1/78, fo. 119r.
198. *LP*, 7, 1607.
199. TNA, E 36/154, 98.
200. TNA, SP 1/89, fo. 9r. See also 215.
201. *LP*, 3, 3189.
202. Tyndale, 1528, fo. xxir.
203. Wood-Legh, 1984, 38–9, 41.
204. [Heywood], 1533, A iiiir.
205. [Barclay], 1518, A iv–A iir.
206. Fragments survive 35 miles away in the windows of All Saints' Church, Brandeston.
207. Weever, 1631, 434.
208. BL, MS Cotton Cleopatra E IV, fo. 280r.
209. TNA, SP 1/156, fo. 95r.
210. BL, MS Cotton Cleopatra E IV, fo. 264r.
211. TNA, SP 3/12, fo. 81r.
212. Benese, *c.* 1537; Whitford, 1538.

Chapter II The Religious Profession

1. Downe and Rutter were named as novices in the deed of surrender, signed on 20 January 1540. Given the recent Christmas period it is reasonable to assume that they entered the house later in 1539: *LP*, 15, 87, 93.

2. Taylour and Crafford were named as novices in the surrender of the abbey signed on 21 January 1540, the day after the surrender of St Werbergh's. As in the cases of the novice men there, it may be assumed that these women had arrived at the house at the turn of the year: *LP*, 15, 93.

3. Burne, 1962, 154–5.

4. Logan, 2002. For another but not altogether different reading see Shaw, 2003, 315–26, 460–3.

5. Crowland Abbey (Lincs.) seemed set on a triennial cycle since either three or four candidates were presented for minor orders in 1514, 1517 and 1520: Lincolnshire Archives, DIOC/REG/25, fos. 8r–v, 120r–121r, 131v–132r. Peterborough Abbey presented five for minor orders in 1515, a new cohort of six in 1519, and a further four in 1522: ibid., fos. 112r–v, 127v: Lincolnshire Archives, DIOC/REG/26, fo. 5r. At the other end of the endowment scale, Chacombe (Northants.) had seen two men entering the priesthood in 1514, and then brought forward four to become acolytes in 1517: Lincolnshire Archives, DIOC/REG/26, fos. 8v, 122r. Wormsley Priory (Here.) presented at least two candidates annually in 1523–25, and then three further in 1528 and 1532: Bannister, 1921, 314–15, 317–18, 320, 325–6, 328.

6. Harper-Bill, 1987–2000, ii. 286–7, 296 (78–9, 83) (Launceston, Bodmin, Totnes, 1492); Gasquet, 1904–6, ii. 197 (Durford, 1494); Thompson, 1940–7, ii. 73 (Ashridge, 1530).

7. 'In hac nostra tempestate (mundo iam in suum finem declinante) perpauci sint atque rarissimi qui vite austeritatem et observantiam regularem cupiant': TNA, SP 1/32, fo. 231v.

8. Dobson, 1995, 148–9.

9. Oliva, 1994, 38–43 at 41–2.

10. Gasquet, 1894, 275.

11. Williams, 1997, 73.

12. Haigh, 1969, 13.

13. *LP*, 14/1, 59.

14. Borthwick Institute, Abp Reg 28 (Register of Archbishop Edward Lee, 1531–44), fos. 198r–v.

15. Aveling, 1955, 13.

16. Orme, 2006, 346–71.

17. TNA, SP 1/136, fo. 167r.

18. TNA, E 314/62.

19. TNA, SP 1/10, fo. 161v.

20. Oliva, 1994, 46.

21. Chitty, 1930, 39.

22. *LP*, 14/1, 680.

23. Smith, 2008, 463; Cocks, 1982–3, 6–7.

24. Caley et al., 1817–30, vi/1, 537, 540; vi/3, 1549.

25. Oliva, 1994, 54.

26. TNA, C 1/1/44.

27. Powderham Castle, Courtenay Cartulary, p. 62; Davies, 1908, 298–9.

28. Greatrex, 1997, 173–6.

29. Caley et al., 1817–30, vi/3, 1510–11.

30. TNA, PCC Prob 11/27/216, fo. 119r–v at 119r.

31. John Campion entered Westminster in 1503–4 when he participated in his first Mass: Pearce, 1916, 180.

32. TNA, C 137/73/43.

33. BL, MS Arundel 327, inscription on last written leaf.

34. Bristol Record Office, P.AS/D/HS/B 7; Burgess, 2004, 34–5.

35. Lee, 2001, 115.

36. Rogers, 1947, 197.

37. TNA, E 36/154/198–9.

38. Liveing, 1906, 251.

39. East Riding Archives, DDCR 3/1/1/1.
40. Jackson, 1862, 145; Smith, 2008, 660.
41. Suffolk Record Office, 449/2/30; MacCulloch, 1986, 136–7 at 137; Statham, 2003, xxv, 163, 222, 230.
42. Caley and Hunter, 1810–34, ii. 117.
43. 'my father with iiii of his brethren did gibarte ther lyves yn hys true and iuste quarrell': TNA, SP 1/95, fo. 49r. A second letter, making the same point, survives in SP 5/4, fo. 128r. See also Greatrex, 1997, 853–4.
44. Pearce, 1916, 37.
45. TNA, SP 1/96, fo. 34r.
46. Twemlow, 1921, 512.
47. Clark, 2013, 172.
48. Ward, 2004.
49. Queen Elizabeth is recorded sending a messenger to her in September 1502, six months before her own death: Nicholas, 1830, 50.
50. Laynesmith, 2004, 16, 127–8.
51. Edward Tudor may be identified as Edward Bridgewater, monk of Westminster, who died there in 1471. Jasper Tudor's grandson was Thomas Gardener whose first Mass as a monk of Westminster was celebrated in 1500: Pearce, 1916, 161, 175.
52. Aveling, 1955, 3.
53. Hickman, 2001, 367–8, no. 550.
54. St Clare Byrne, 1981, v. 15 (Letter 1088).
55. St Clare Byrne, 1981; TNA, SP 3/10, fo. 6r; ibid, 107–8 at 108 (Letter 551).
56. TNA, SP 3/13, fo. 85r.
57. Oliva, 1994, 49, n. 51.
58. *LP*, 3/1, 1277.
59. Oliva, 1994, 137.
60. BL, MS Cotton Cleopatra E IV, fo. 26r.
61. *LP*, 14/1, 1321.
62. Anon., 1528 G ivv.
63. BL, MS Cotton Cleopatra F II, fo. 238r.
64. Taverner, 1536 D viiiv.
65. Maxwell Lyte, 1908, 549–50.
66. Heath, 1973, 90.
67. Bale, 1550, fo. ix.
68. James, 1997, 176.
69. *Utopia*, II.: Miller, 2001, 122.
70. Anon., 1535, Exposition of Psalm LI.
71. Brady and Olin, 1992, 28.
72. Erasmus, tr. Paynell, 1532, 100.
73. Longland, 1527, B 5r; for London and Salisbury see *LP*, 13/2, 518, 808.
74. Oliver, 1846, 36.
75. Bateson, 1891, 22–3; Wood-Legh, 1984, 12.
76. Now Cambridge, St John's College, MS T. 9. 1.
77. Now BL, MS Cotton Appendix XIV.
78. Now Oxford, Bodl. MS Rawl. Liturg. G. 12.
79. Now San Marino, California, Huntington Library, MS 34 B 7.
80. TNA, E 135/2/45.
81. Now Oxford, Bodl. 4° Z. 33 Th.
82. Lupset, 1535, B ivv.
83. BL, MS Cotton Cleopatra E IV, fo. 198r.
84. Lee, 2001, 113.

85. For example, at Christ Church Priory, Canterbury, in the fourteenth century: Sheppard, 1887–9, ii. 137.
86. Perry, 1889, 307.
87. TNA, SP 1/52, fo. 154r.
88. TNA, SP 1/95, fo. 161r–v; Hodgkinson, 2013, 218.
89. TNA, SP 1/136, fo. 21r.
90. Mellor and Pierce, 1981, 37.
91. Skeeters, 1993, 169–70; TNA, SP 1/22, fo. 66v; for London and Salisbury see *LP*, 13/2, 518, 808.
92. TNA, SP 1/100, fo. 94r.
93. Oliva, 1994, 48–51 at 48.
94. Peacock, 1883, 57.
95. TNA, C 1/486/12.
96. *LP*, 2, 1450.
97. Sharpe, 1890, ii. 594–614.
98. TNA, C 1/1519/99.
99. TNA, E 326/7987.
100. TNA, C 1/68/126.
101. BL, MS Egerton 3137, fo. 208r.
102. France, 2012, 300–22 at 300.
103. Miller, 2001, 33.
104. BL, MS Cotton Cleopatra E IV, fo. 31r.
105. TNA, SP 1/99, fo. 201r.
106. Wood-Legh, 1984, 32. Cecily Sawnders was found to have lived at Goring Priory (Oxon.) unprofessed for nineteen years: Thompson, 1940–7, ii. 157.
107. Poster and Sherlock, 1987, 73.
108. East Sussex and Brighton and Hove Record Office, AMS5789/15.
109. See below, 104.
110. Jessopp, 1888, 61.
111. Ibid, 118.
112. TNA, SP 5/3, fo. 93r; Wood-Legh, 1984, 44.
113. Register of John Blyth, 334; Wood-Legh, 1984, 22.
114. Peacock, 1883, 53.
115. BL, MS Egerton 3137, fo. 208r.
116. TNA, SP 1/99, fo. 201r.
117. Heath, 1973, 133; Thompson, 1940–7, ii. 76.
118. TNA, SP 1/97, fo. 91r.
119. Tindal-Hart, 1966, 97–8; Tatton-Brown, 2015b.
120. Craster, 1907, 107.
121. Jessopp, 1888, 178; Dickens, 1951, 35.
122. 'Et regule in anglicis non exponuntur': Heath, 1973, 33.
123. Oxford, Bodl. MS Digby 200.
124. Ryle, 2004.
125. Aveling and Pantin, 1967, 68–72.
126. Kent History and Library Centre, Fa/Q1.
127. Gray, 2004.
128. TNA, SP 1/100, fo. 94r.
129. Lancashire Record Office, D603/A/Add/670.
130. TNA, SP 1/101, fo. 129v.
131. Canterbury Cathedral Archives, CCA-DCc-Register/R, Sede Vacante Register (1496–1508), fos. 40r–171v. For Hampton see Greatrex, 1997, 698. Manydon is not noted.
132. Jessopp, 1888, 169.

133. Cross and Vickers, 1995, 607.
134. TNA, SP 1/97, fo. 28r.
135. TNA, SP 1/98, fo. 122r; *LP*, 9, 632; Searle, 1974, 439–40 at 40.
136. Benedict, 1517, 1–2.
137. Collett, 2002, 37–8; Fox may have been encouraged in this view by the convents' own leadership: Thompson, 1940–7, ii. 90.
138. Dowling, 1990, 61.
139. Ibid, 63.
140. Lee, 2001, 136.
141. An 'eagerness to hear sermons', was modelled for women religious of this period in the life of St Birgitta herself: Powell, 2017, 49–50, 53. For other evidence of preaching to nuns see Gunn, 2018.
142. The inventory is now Essex Record Office, D/DP F234–5. See also Bell, 1995, 116–20.
143. Oxford, Bodl. MS Digby 200.
144. Oliver, 1846, 36.
145. Chitty, 1930.
146. East Sussex Record Office, AMS140/1.
147. Caley et al., 1817–30, vi/3, 1510–11. The text of the indenture is given apparently in full but without reference to the documentary source.
148. Kock, 1902, 150.
149. Peacock, 1883, 55.
150. BL, MS Cotton Vespasian F IX, fo. 190r; *LP*, 4/3, 6075.
151. Oxford, Bodl., MS Dodsworth, 99, fo. 200r; BL, MS Arundel 97, fo. 28v.
152. Thompson, 1940–7, ii. 70.
153. Pearce, 1916, 35.
154. TNA, SP 5/5; E322/16; Fowler, 1895, 64.
155. TNA, E322/244 (12 January 1539).
156. William Jerome was executed together with Robert Barnes and Thomas Garrett on 30 July 1540: Hall, 1809, 840.
157. Anon., 1513, A ivr.
158. James, 1997, 176.
159. Pearce, 1916, 21.
160. TNA, SP 1/100, fo. 94r.
161. BL, MS Lansdowne 205, fo. 21r.
162. TNA, REQ 2/2/104.
163. TNA, C1/874/21.
164. Evans, 1907–14, 205.
165. Wood-Legh, 1984, 49.
166. TNA, SP 1/116, fos. 44r–45r at 44v; *LP*, 10, 437.
167. See below, 184.
168. Peacock, 1883, 61.
169. Aveling and Pantin, 1967, 32–3 (Letter 25).
170. *LP*, 14/2, 206. For the number of monks passing through university in the sixteenth century see Cunich, 1997.
171. Gasquet, 1904–6, ii. 184–5.
172. Pearce, 1916, 179.
173. Smith, 2008, 649; Chambers, 1966, 1.
174. TNA, SP 1; Oliva, 1994, 193.
175. Gasquet, 1904–6, ii. 23.
176. *Philip Sparrow*, ll. 1, 9; Scattergood, 2015, 60.
177. Elyot, 1534.
178. Thompson, 1915–27, ii. 68 (Dorchester, 1441); Pantin, 1931–37, ii. 197–8 (Capitular statutes, 1444).

179. Perry, 1889, 308.
180. BL, MS Add. 50856, fo. 22r.
181. Nicholas Rewe, the monk resident there in 1492, failed to appear for a visitation not only because of the perils of the journey but because of the business of the house. There can be little doubt that this was less a matter of liturgy than of land: Harper-Bill, 1987–2000, ii. 292 (81).
182. TNA, SP 1/137, fo. 184r.
183. Tillotson, 1988, 212.
184. TNA, SP 1/ 85, fo. 100r–v.
185. Nichols, 1852, 34.
186. TNA, SP 1/51, fo. 150r.
187. Apparently an attribute of Abbot John of the Cell of St Albans (1195–1214): Riley, 1867–9, i. 232.
188. Canterbury Cathedral Archives, CCA-DCc-AddMS/129/5 (Inventory of 1454). Prior Thomas Goldston (d. 1517) provided a set of service books for the monks' choir, presumably with the expectation that the community performed the service from them: Greatrex, 1997, 175.
189. Thompson, 1940–7, iii. 100.
190. TNA, SP 1/19, fo. 169r; *LP*, 3, 606.
191. Perry, 1889, 306.
192. Bowers, 2007; Perry, 1888, 713.
193. *LP*, 11, 1056; Burgess and Wathey, 2000, 18.
194. Milsom, 2004.
195. Oliver, 1846, 381.
196. Bowers, 2003, 50–2.
197. *LP*, 2/1, 115.
198. Greatrex, 1997, 711.
199. TNA, SP 3/9, fo. 167r; *LP*, 10, 767.
200. Perry, 1889, 305.
201. Walcott, 1873, 322–40.
202. WAM, 5458; Hope, 1906.
203. TNA, SP 1/99, fo. 85v.
204. BL, MS Cotton Cleopatra E IV, fo. 105r.
205. French, 2001, 180.
206. Ridley, 1540, B2v.
207. Hockey, 1970, 201.
208. Gysborn's commonplace book is now BL, MS Sloane 1584.
209. TNA, SP 1/100, fo. 90r.
210. Hinde, 1952, 82.
211. Bigod, 1535, B viir.
212. French, 2001, 179.
213. TNA, SP 1/45, 110–11; Greatrex, 1997, 707.
214. *LP*, 13/1, 1051.
215. Oxford, Bodl. MS Laud 625; Thompson, 1949, 91.
216. Pearce, 1916, 178–9, 181.
217. Now, BL, MS Harley 308. His name and the dates of his offices are written on a parchment piece which may have been the volume's cover, fo. 1*.
218. It was usual for the main officers of the community to have use of their own 'exchequer' or 'checker' (scaccarium) in which to handle the business of their department. Some may have been a suite of rooms: the cellarer at Battle Abbey was assigned a chamber large and well-appointed enough to have a fireplace; at Norwich the cellarage occupied a range: Searle and Ross, 1967, 157; Dobson, 1973, 230; Gilchrist, 2005, 213.
219. Rogers, 1947, 197.

220. Examples of Fulwell's cellarer's seal survive from 1530–5: BL, CXXXIX.9, 16, 30–1, 73; Pearce, 1916, 181.
221. Cross and Vickers, 1995, 607.
222. Dickens, 1959, 96.
223. Jackson, 1862, 12.
224. Coppack, 2002, 97.
225. Mellor and Pearce, 1981, 15.
226. Whitford, 1532, fo. 181r; Rhodes, 1993, 19.
227. Hare, 1985, 164.
228. Proved 5 January 1540: TNA, PCC Prob 11/28/3, fo. 2r.
229. TNA, SP 1/19, fo. 169r; LP, 3, 606.
230. BL, MS Cotton Cleopatra E IV, fos. 249r, 336r.
231. Peacock, 1883, 61.
232. Harper-Bill, 1987–2000, ii. 75.
233. TNA, SP 5/4, fo. 27r.
234. Kresen Kernow, ART/4/10.
235. Coppack, 1998, 123–4.
236. Traskey, 1978, 150.
237. Hanna, 1988, xxxv.
238. TNA, SP 1/101, fo. 135r.
239. Nichols, 1795–1811, ii. 551.
240. TNA, STAC 2/19/158; 2/26/18.
241. TNA, SP 1/78, fo. 119r.
242. BL, MS Cotton Cleopatra E IV, fo. 43r.
243. Devon Heritage Centre, W1258 M1/1/6, fos. 14r, 18r, 19v.
244. Eclogues, I, 292: White, 1960, 9.
245. TNA, SP 1/5, fos. 5r–6v.
246. Grainger and Phillpotts, 2011, 68.
247. Harvey, 1993, 43–4.
248. Loades, 1968, 156.
249. Eclogues, I, 1117–18: White, 1960, 41.
250. TNA, SP 1/86, fo. 91r; LP, 7, 1307.
251. Lambeth Palace Library, MS 854.
252. BL, MS Add. 60577, fo. 76v.
253. Jessopp, 1888, 139.
254. Ibid, 97.
255. TNA, SP 1/96, fo. 116r.
256. Bullen, Crook, Hubbuck and Pevsner, 2010, 589.
257. TNA, SP 1/229, fo. 1r.
258. For example, in the illuminated capital of the abbey's copy of quadripartite indenture that underpinned the foundation of the Tudor Lady chapel: BL, MS Harley 1498, fo. 1r.
259. TNA, PCC, Prob 11/28/3.
260. TNA, SP 1/19, fo. 169r; LP, 3, 606.
261. LP, 4, 3678 (3).
262. Sharpe, 1889, i. 430–6.
263. LP, 10, 562.
264. For example, deposits on the site of the reredorter at Lewes Priory: Lyne and Gardiner, 1997, 67.
265. Perry, 1889, 312.
266. Shelby, 1976, 93–4.
267. Pantin, 1931–37, iii. 127.
268. Oxford, Bodl. MS Douce 302, fo. 35a.

269. Thompson, 1997, 175.
270. Canterbury Cathedral Archives, CCA-CC-J/Q/333/vii.
271. Ibid, CCA-CC-J/Q/337/i.
272. Perry, 1889, 308.
273. Cross and Vickers, 1995, 550–1.
274. Lincolnshire Archives, DIOC/BOX/92/5.
275. Canterbury Cathedral Archives, CCA-DCc-ChChLet/II/138.
276. Heath, 1973, 90.
277. TNA, SP 1/96, fo. 77r.
278. Pearce, 1916, 188.
279. *LP*, 16, 91.
280. Welander, 1991, 296.
281. Peacock, 1883, 58.
282. BL, MS Arundel 68, fo. 11v.
283. Welander, 1991, 299.
284. TNA, SP 1/89, fo. 104r
285. Cambridge: Jesus (1496); Christ's (1505); St John's (1511); Oxford: Brasenose (1512); Corpus (1519).

Chapter III A Regular World

1. Alice's petition to the queen is preserved as TNA, E 135/22/15. Since the precise date of the incident is not recorded the queen in question may have been Anne Boleyn, Jane Seymour or Anne of Cleves.
2. Essex HER, 31400.
3. Oswald et al., 2010, 44; Willmott, 2020, 15.
4. Lincolnshire HER, 40003.
5. For example, at Leicester Abbey: Burtt, 1866, 204–6 at 5.
6. For example, at West Malling: Tatton-Brown, 2001, 179–94; Sloane and Malcolm, 2004, 196–7. Roundels from Waltham Abbey are preserved in the collection of the Victoria and Albert Museum, 2011 to Q-1899; Allan, Henderson and Weddell, 2016, 248.
7. Cumber, 2010, 95. The proportion (70%) was almost identical at Bury St Edmunds: Tittler, 1998, 61.
8. For the priory's Kidderminster property see Wiltshire and Swindon History Centre, 1332/3/2/1/1; see also Caley et al., 1817–30, vi/2. 644.
9. Cumber, 2010, 44.
10. Dorset HER, MDO 2348.
11. Scott, 2001, 157–9.
12. Röhrkasten, 2004, 510.
13. TNA, C 1/27/391; 64/503; 824/21; STAC 2/21/109, 198.
14. Battle established market stalls by the main gate notwithstanding that there was a market-place at the opposite end of the high street: Searle, 1974, 426. For St Albans see Slater, 1998. For Norton and its Hinton inn see Somerset HER, 25577.
15. Baker and Holt, 2003, 282–3.
16. Bettey, 1989, 30.
17. Lincolnshire Archives, MLI83269; MLI83270.
18. Norfolk Record Office, KL/C 50/532.
19. Lincolnshire HER, 34204.
20. Oxfordshire HER, 2718; 13861; Allen, 1994.
21. Cheshire HER, SMR 19/4/2.
22. Silvester and Hankinson, 2015, 38.
23. Lincolnshire HER, 22390.

24. Gibson, 1995, 55; Dobson, 1995, 98; Brown, 1995, 38.
25. Hillaby and Hillaby 2006, 236–7.
26. Gilchrist, 2005, 190.
27. The friary was sited at New Street, yards from the harbour, although its full scope remains unclear: Historic England Monument, number 437564. Leland described Plymouth at length but his full account of the Greyfriars has been lost: Toulmin-Smith 1906–10, 212–15 at 213.
28. Canterbury Cathedral Archives, CCA-DCc-ChAnt/C/213 (1535).
29. Kingsford, 1908, i. 126.
30. TNA, SP 1/120, fo. 235r.
31. Mayhew, 2014, 102 and n.
32. Black, Giuseppi and Maxwell Lyte, 1897–1901, i. 307.
33. Searle and Ross, 1967, 140.
34. Smith, 1943, 199; Canterbury Cathedral Archives, CCa/Ddc/Cellarer; CCa/CC/Woodruff/54/18.
35. Tillotson, 1988, 169.
36. Somerset Heritage Centre, DD\X\RMN/1–2.
37. Fish, 1529, 2, fo. 2r.
38. Berkshire Record Office, D/EP/7/33; Cumber, 2010, 92–3, 313.
39. Oxford, Jesus College, MS 77, fo. 323r.
40. TNA, SP5/3, fo. 17r.
41. Cornwall, 1962, 57.
42. Wood, 2013, 81.
43. Caley and Hunter, 1810–34, i. 353.
44. Bateson, 1890, 562.
45. Searle and Ross, 1967, 159.
46. TNA, SP1/100, fo. 44r.
47. Tillotson, 1988, 150, 153, 159–60.
48. Coppack, 1998, 99–102, 107; Courtney, 1989, 99–143.
49. *LP*, 10, 1191 (4, 2).
50. TNA, C 1/44/213.
51. Wood-Legh, 1984, 295.
52. Chester Archive and Local Studies, ZZS/B/5, fo. 109r.
53. Jessopp, 1888, 58 (Walsingham); 61 (St Benet Hulme), 136 (Ipswich).
54. Harvey, 2006, 83.
55. Bowers, 2033, 49–50 at 50.
56. Oliver, 1846, 381; Snell, 1967, 74–5.
57. Riley, 1870–1, i. 13.
58. TNA, SP 1/102, fo. 99r.
59. Evans, 1941, 418.
60. BL, MS Cotton Nero D VII, fos. 105r, 106r–v, 108v, 112r.
61. Toulmin-Smith, 1906–10, i. 154.
62. Clark, 2000, 301–2.
63. BL, MS Cotton Cleopatra E IV, fos. 105r–11r.
64. TNA, SC6/HENVIII/929.
65. Cumber, 2010, 82.
66. Summerson, 1993, ii. 614–15.
67. Fish, 1529, fo. 2r.
68. Pocock, 1878, 299.
69. Tillotson, 1988, 163; TNA, SC6/3479, addenda (account of Cellaress Eleanor Halle).
70. TNA, SP 1/5, fo. 8r. For a comparable pattern of provisioning out-of-neighbourhood at Abingdon see Cumber, 2010, 91.
71. *LP*, 1/2 (2617), 28.

72. Searle, 1974, 365; Searle and Ross, 1967, 142, 157. No takers in 1465–66 but there were in 1512–13.
73. Gilchrist, 2005, 189.
74. Sloane and Malcolm, 2004, 220–1.
75. Gilchrist, 2005, 190.
76. Clark, 2004b, 82–90.
77. Riley, 1870–71, i. 115–16; id., 1872–73, i. 30; ii. 250; Brownbill, 1914, 113.
78. Holder, 2017, 53; Clark, 2019b, 292–5.
79. Röhrkasten, 2004, 561–2 at 561.
80. Holder, 2017, 55, 94, 117, 140.
81. Norfolk Record Office, DCN 45/32/22; 45/34/25.
82. Röhrkasten, 2004, 255.
83. Surrey History Centre, Z/407/L6.368.
84. *LP*, 19/2, 166 (40); Hill, 1956, 63.
85. Röhrkasten, 2004, 238.
86. TNA, 326/3217 (Deed dated 1462).
87. Clark, 2004a, 16–17.
88. *LP*, 4/2, 3582; TNA, SP 1/45, fo. 86r (Tynemouth); *LP*, 3, 2; TNA, SP 1/39, fo. 145r (Whitby); SP 1/53, fo. 163r.
89. Röhrkasten, 2004, 517.
90. Raine, 1836–1902, ii. 271.
91. Suffolk Record Office, HD 1538/345/1/10.
92. BL, MS Harley 144, fo. 52r–v.
93. Gilchrist, 2005, 141, 161–2.
94. Sloane and Malcolm, 2004, 141.
95. Bettey, 1989, 17.
96. Heath, 1973, 81.
97. Fresh grants made at Bath in the twelve months from March 1538 filled twenty leaves of Prior Holeway's register: BL, MS Harley 3970, fos. 13v–35r. At Bury there were tenancies being granted for terms of between thirty and sixty years almost month by month in 1538: BL, MS Harley 308, fos. 112r–v (June 1538); 120r (October 1538); 121r–v (November 1538); 138v–139r (March 1539). Fresh tenancy agreements can be tracked across the first three decades of the reign in the abbatial registers from Gloucester: Gloucester Cathedral Library, Register D and Register E, with some of the most frequent traffic at the last, between February and November 1538, e.g. fos. 144v–145v, 167v–168r, 184v–185r.
98. BL, MS Harley 308 (Bury St Edmunds); MS Harley 3970 (Bath); Baker and Holt, 2003, 295–6.
99. Dickens, 1959, 95.
100. Anon., 1528, Cr.
101. Manning, 1988, 45–6. See also below, 171.
102. TNA, STAC, 2/31/38.
103. Snell, 1967, 78.
104. TNA, SP 1/96, fo. 163r.
105. TNA, SP 1/23, fo. 229r.
106. Brownbill, 1914, 172.
107. TNA, SC 8/189/9412.
108. East Sussex Record Office, SAS/G16/6.
109. Merriman, 1902, Letter 176, ii. 43.
110. TNA, C 1/780/35–7.
111. Aveling, 1955, 4.
112. Brown, 2011, 247; Savory et al., 1982, iii/2, 254–55; Williams, 2001, 78.
113. Searle, 1974, 365; Thomas, Sloane and Phillpott, 1997, 81.
114. Kent History and Library Centre, Fa/A/C/1.

115. Sheppard, 1887–9, iii. 321–9.
116. Long-standing disputes were settled at Coventry (1487), Faversham (1510) and Gloucester (1518): Coventry Archives, BA/B/7/14/1; Gloucestershire Archives, GBR B/2/1–2; B/8/7; Kent History and Library Centre Fa/AZ1. For Battle see Searle, 1974, 433, 440.
117. Cumber, 2010, 53–4.
118. Caley and Hunter, 1810–34, ii. 117, 394; iii. 33 (Lacock, Holywell, Dore); Searle 1974, 433.
119. See below, 351–3.
120. The anchor-hold of this view is Duffy, 1992, elaborated and enriched by Duffy, 2001.
121. The phrase is Robert Tittler's: Tittler, 1998, 33–6. For the building of churches in the century before 1540 see Byng, 2017.
122. Koopmans, 2010, 201–10.
123. Fryde, 1996, 268.
124. For the number of Benedictine houses see Knowles and Hadcock, 1971. For monastic churches that served as parish churches see Heale, 2003; Heale, 2004, 301–4.
125. Haigh, 1969, 3.
126. Orme, 2010, 144.
127. TNA, SP 1/120, fo. 233r; SP 1/132, fo. 175r.
128. The story of the 'stoute butcher' at Sherborne who 'defacid' the church still resounded when Leland arrived more than a century later: Toulmin-Smith, 1906–10, ii. 48; French, 2001, 37–8.
129. Riley, 1872–3, i. 427.
130. Mayhew, 2014, 33, 76; Caley and Hunter, 1810–34, i. 335 (St John, Southover); Brown, 1995, 38 (St Lawrence, Reading). At Woburn, a parochial chapel, St Mary's, was served by secular chaplains: LP, 13/2, 981 (2).
131. Rosser, 1989, 255–63 at 256.
132. Williams, 1976, 35, 125.
133. For example, Coventry: Knight, 1986, 10.
134. TNA, SP 1/124, fo. 111r.
135. The will of John Boyefeld (1519) refers to a chapel of our lady within the parish portion of the church; that of Richard Hawkyns (1539) calls it 'oure' chapel distinct from that in the abbey: TNA, PCC, Prob 11/19/295, fo. 163v; 11/28/81, fo. 36r.
136. Coppack, 1998, 81–2.
137. The phrases appear in an inventory of the furnishings of Rievaulx Abbey in 1538–9: Coppack, 1986, 103–7.
138. McSheffrey and Tanner, 2003, 158.
139. For the evolution of friary churches see Holder, 2017, 178–89; Röhrkasten, 2004, 466–72. For a nationwide survey of Dominican sites see O'Sullivan, 2013, 19–20 and 32–362 (gazeteer).
140. Richard Andrew of Orford bequeathed 12d to this end in 1507: Suffolk Record Office, EE5/6/136.
141. Röhrkasten, 2004, 466–7; Holder, 2017, 197–8.
142. BL, MS Cotton Vitellius F XII, fos. 274r–316r. See also Röhrkasten, 2004, 467–8; Steer, 2017, 277, 281.
143. Toulmin-Smith, 1906–10, i. 163.
144. James, 1997, 105.
145. Hodgkinson, 2013, 230. There was, proportionately, a comparable disparity in bequests to friaries (56%) and monasteries (30%) in Suffolk in wills proved in the archdeaconry of Bury St Edmunds: MacCulloch, 1986, 135.
146. Dickens, 1951, 66.
147. Clark, 2019a, 97, 108.
148. Heath, 1973, 148.
149. Anon., 1542, A5v.
150. Scarisbrick, 1994, 162.
151. Anon., 1515; Bradshaw, 1521; Clark, 2004b, 90.
152. Evans, 1941, 404–5.

153. Spooner, 2015, 272–3.
154. *LP*, 9, 42.
155. TNA, E36/115, fos. 23r, 27r, 31r, 39r, 55r, 91r.
156. McSheffrey and Tanner, 2003, 21.
157. Northamptonshire HER, 1160/8/4.
158. *Eclogues*, I, 539: White, 1960, 17.
159. TNA, C 1/611/29.
160. TNA, C 1/71/104.
161. Baker and Holt, 2003, 296.
162. Luders et al. 1810–28, 551–3 at 51 (27 H VIII c. 22).
163. Clark, 2006.
164. BL, Arundel MS 68, fo. 11v; Kresen Kernow, AR/27/12.
165. Swanson, 2007, 145–7, 172–3.
166. Bowry's editions are classified as STC (2nd edn.) 14077 c. 53, 55, Brocden's as STC (2nd edn.) 14077 c. 122.
167. Printed by Pynson in 1528: STC (2nd edn.) 14077 c. 76.
168. Ridley, 1540, D2r. For the trade see Swanson, 2007, 270–6.
169. She wrote to Cromwell from there in the final months of her life: TNA, SP1/89, fo. 133r; *LP*, 16, 719.
170. Purvis, 1934, 123 (120).
171. TNA, C 1/298/13; C 1/483/2; TNA, PCC Prob 11/8/56, fo. 27r–v.
172. TNA, C 1/168/41.
173. Gunn, 2016, 259–60. The women of Holywell were major beneficiaries of Lovell's will and custodians of his commemoration: TNA, PCC Prob 11/23/9, fos. 214r–17v. See also Bull et al., 2011.
174. For a discussion of tertiaries see Röhrkasten, 2004, 466.
175. Douglas Hamilton, 1875, 50.
176. Robson, 1997, 24.
177. Rawcliffe and Wilson, 2004, 111.
178. Farnhill, 2001, 90.
179. Röhrkasten, 2004, 515–16; BL, MS Cotton Vitellius B X, fo. 6r; *LP*, 5, 818.
180. *LP*, 13/1, 1127.
181. Harvey, 2006, 70–2, 125–8.
182. TNA, C1/181/4.
183. Bigod, 1535, Aivr.
184. TNA, SP 1/100, fo. 90r.
185. TNA, E 40/6366.
186. Gasquet, 1904–6, i. 152; ii. 3.
187. Jessopp, 1888, 160.
188. Statham, 2003, xxxvi.
189. Frere and Kennedy, 1910, 19–24 at 20.
190. Caley and Hunter, 1810–34, iv. 250.
191. Addy, 1878, 129; Cox, 1875, 215–16.
192. *LP*, 4/1, 522 (1194).
193. Mayhew, 2006, 212.
194. Pevsner and Newman, 2002, 171.
195. TNA, SC6/HENVIIII/3515; see also Mayhew, 2006, 241.
196. Somerset Heritage Centre, DD/S/WH/355.
197. Olding, 2015, 21.
198. Evans, 1942, 69.
199. Westminster Abbey Muniments, 19837.
200. TNA, E 36/152, 31.
201. BL, MS Add. 5810.

202. *LP*, 12/1, 901; Bateson, 1890, 561–2.
203. *Eclogues*, V, 789–93: White, 1960, 209.
204. Anon., 1528, G viiiv.
205. Dickens, 1959, 94.
206. East Sussex Record Office, RYE /35/24.
207. The Salters' Company, H1/4/1/15.
208. Canterbury Cathedral Archives, CCA-DCc-ChAnt/S/399 (1486).
209. Harvey, 2006, 29, 33, 36–7.
210. Wenzel, 2005, 157.
211. For Rypon's preaching see Harvey, 2006, 27–31 at 31, 125–8.
212. TNA, SP 1/100, fo. 3r.
213. Summerson, 1993, ii. 616.
214. Anon., 1516, 5.
215. TNA, E41/244.
216. Corrie, 1845, ii. 260.
217. Röhrkasten, 2004, 462.
218. Bristol Record Office, P/AS/D/HS B 7.
219. Condon, 2003a, 95–7.
220. Fish, 1529, 2, fo. 2r.
221. East Sussex Record Office, AMS140/1.
222. Lincolnshire Archives, 2ANC3/A/41.
223. Aveling, 1955, 15.
224. Nottinghamshire Archives, DD/4P/48/72.
225. Hertfordshire Archives and Local Studies, ASA/AR1, fo. 16r.
226. TNA, C 1/858/20–1.
227. Dinn, 1995, 242.
228. Lincolnshire HER, 12650.
229. Dinn, 1995, 243.
230. TNA, PCC Prob 11/16/351, fo. 104r.
231. Colvin and Stone, 1965; Marks, 1984; Traskey, 1978, 149.
232. TNA, PCC, Prob. 11/13/337, fos. 108v–109r.
233. TNA, PCC, Prob. 11/27/36, fo. 22v; Cumber, 2010, 90.
234. For example, the prior of Stone (Staffordshire) acted as suffragan of Lincoln in 1493–96: Hibbert, 1910, 119.
235. McSheffrey and Tanner, 2003, 310.
236. Ellis, 1846, i. 247–8.
237. Mayhew, 2006, 221.
238. Haigh, 1969, 36.
239. Sharpe, 1889–90, 618.
240. Devon Heritage Centre, 1038M/T/4/36.
241. Dinn, 1995, 240.
242. Fish, 1529, 14, fo. 8r.
243. Ellis, 1846, i. 228–30 at 229.
244. *LP*, 12/1, 901; Bateson, 1890, 561–2; Hoyle, 2001, 47–8 at 47.
245. *LP*, 12/1, 901; Bateson, 1890, 561–2; Hoyle, 2001, 47–8 at 47.
246. TNA, SP 1/ 104, fo. 246v.
247. TNA, SP 1/136, fo. 161r.
248. *LP*, 11, 57.
249. Clark, 1989, 138.
250. TNA, E 315/272, fo. 66v; Caley and Hunter, 1810–34, i. 194.
251. BL, MS Cleopatra E IV, fo. 116v; Ibid, 170.
252. BL, MS Cotton Cleopatra E IV, fos. 116v–117r. TNA, E 315/272.
253. TNA, SP 1/134, fo. 261r.

254. TNA, SC6 3984; Copland, 1536, 5, fo. Aiiiv.
255. Loades, 1968, 156.
256. TNA, E 36/154, 106, 146.
257. Fish, 1529, 4, fo. 2v.
258. Caley and Hunter, 1810–34, i. 107.
259. Jessopp, 1888, 12.
260. The exchange was one of the transactions accorded papal approval in 1528: TNA, SC 7/63/11.
261. Harvey, 2006, 171–2, 174.
262. TNA, SP 1/102, fo. 135r.
263. Gottfried, 1982, 193.
264. TNA, STAC 10/1/30.
265. *LP*, 12/2, 549.
266. St Clare Byrne, 1981, v. 95 (Letter 1137).
267. Gottfried, 1982, 192–207.
268. Canterbury Cathedral Archives, DCc-ChAnt/C/1059.
269. Bowers, 2007.
270. Bowers, 1999, 195–9, 201–4; Orme, 2006, 281–3, 346–71.
271. Somerset Heritage Centre, T\PH\cl/1/5.
272. Traskey, 1978, 156–7.
273. Mayhew, 2006, 274.
274. St Clare Byrne, 1981, iii. 350 (Letter 688a).
275. BL, MS Cotton Cleopatra E IV, fo. 368r.
276. Smith, 1554, 19.
277. Kent History and Library Centre, Fa/Q/1.
278. East Sussex Record Office, DUK 569.
279. Nicholas, 1826, ii. 411–14 at 414.
280. Anon., 1542, D4r.
281. Nottinghamshire Archives, DD/CH/32/20 [1496].
282. TNA, PCC, Prob 11/30/259.
283. Jessopp, 1888, 3.
284. Ibid, 77.
285. Corrie, 1844, i. 287.
286. TNA, SP 1/45, p. 110; fos. 218v–19r.
287. Jessopp, 1888, 197 (Norwich Priory).
288. TNA, SP 1/45, fo. 219v.
289. TNA, SP 1/34, fos. 240r–48v.
290. Jessopp, 1888, 118.
291. TNA, SP 1/117, fo. 160r–v; *LP*, 12/1, 491.
292. Haigh, 1969, 59.
293. *LP*, 9, 717.
294. Nottinghamshire Archives, DD/CH/32/20 [1496].
295. TNA, SP 1/73, fo. 121r.
296. Perry, 1889, 307.
297. TNA, PCC Prob 11/23/8, fos. 215v–219r.
298. Greatrex, 1997, 373. The abbot of St Albans entered the Holy Trinity guild at Luton on the edge of the Liberty of the Abbey: Gough, 1906; Luxford, 2011.
299. Shakespeare Birthplace Trust, BRT1/3/80, BRT1/3/105.
300. Knight, 1986, 422–3.
301. Harvey, 2006, 159.
302. McMurray Gibson, 1989, 108–14.
303. TNA, STAC 2/15.
304. TNA, STAC 17/223, 383.

Chapter IV The Tudor Reformation

1. TNA, SP 1/49, fo. 102r; Knowles, 1958.
2. TNA, SP 1/49, fo. 102r.
3. Craster, 1907, 108.
4. Pearce, 1916, 175; Boffey and Payne, 2017.
5. Craster, 1907, 107.
6. Campbell, 1873, i. 216–17; Burtt, 1866; Martin, 1923.
7. Edward had set in train the foundation, securing papal approval, and a site in 1480: Burtt, 1866, 54–5.
8. Beckett, 1995.
9. Ibid, 122.
10. Brodie, Black and Lyte, 1914–16, i. 143.
11. TNA, E 327/190; E 179/363/326.
12. The charterhouses of Axholm, Coventry, Hinton, Hull and Sheen were awarded tax-free wine from inland ports in 1494 and 1506–7: Brodie, Black and Lyte, 1914–16, i. 460; ii. 509–10, 515.
13. Campbell, 1873, i. 390.
14. Brodie, Black and Lyte, 1914–16, i. 365 (1491); ii. 134 (1498), 270 (1502), 338 (1504), 386 (1504).
15. Clark, 2019a, 124–5.
16. Condon, 2003a, 60–1.
17. Twemlow, 1960, 14, 306.
18. Ibid, 1960, 202–8.
19. Campbell, 1873, i. 201.
20. Ford, 2001, 264; Voigts, 2017.
21. Ford, 2001, 213–14.
22. Hay, 1950, 26–7. In the early months of the year Henry had passed through Chertsey, Colchester, Thetford and Walsingham: Ford, 2001, 213–14.
23. Lambeth Palace Library, MS 371, fo. 122v.
24. Ford, 2001, 235, 242, 265, 273, 279.
25. Brodie, Black and Lyte, 1914–16, i. 306, 365.
26. Ibid, ii. 143.
27. Ledward and Latham, 1955–63, ii. 197 (viii, xii); Ford, 2001, 211, 224.
28. Jones and Underwood, 1992, 195.
29. The monk was John Cerne I: Greatrex, 1997, 681.
30. Powell, 2017, 225–6, 244–5.
31. Ibid, 172–87.
32. Morgan, 1995, 90.
33. Lambeth Palace Library, MS 371.
34. Condon, 2003a, 81–2.
35. Ledward and Latham, 1955–63, ii. 389.
36. Condon, 2003a, 95–7.
37. Ledward and Latham, 1955–63, ii. 197 (10); Hay, 1950, 32; Gairdner, 1858, 84; *LP*, 2/10.
38. Leland, 1906–10, iv. 204–7 at 207. For Hall and Hunton see Smith, 2008, 84–5.
39. The exequies for Arthur began at Ludlow and where he died, and where they were led by Abbot Richard Lye of Shrewsbury and Richard Barbur of Bordesley. They culminated in a funeral at Worcester Cathedral where the region's convents accounted for a good proportion of the 1,000 or so present: Houlbrooke, 2009.
40. Boffey, 2019, 113; Jones and Underwood, 1992, 236–8.
41. TNA, SP 1/229, fos. 1r–4v at 4v.
42. Campbell, 1873, ii. 504; Rymer, 1739–45, xii. 326, 337.
43. Brodie, Black and Lyte, 1914–16, i. 158; Lowry, 1983, 114–17.
44. Williams, 2001, 289.

45. Jones and Underwood, 1992, 33.
46. Pearce, 1916, 161.
47. Lee, 2001, 116; Weir, 2014, 380.
48. Brodie, Black and Lyte, 1914–16, i. 64.
49. Ibid, 221, 229.
50. Rymer, 1739–45, x. 438; Power, 1922, 189.
51. The grants continued at almost the same frequency from 1486 to 1489, and then still not infrequently into the early 1490s: Campbell, 1873, i. 249, 427, 458–9, 528, 547; ii. 156, 195, 204, 244, 247, 289, 302, 306, 323, 376, 404, 422, 451, 522–3; Ledward and Latham, 1955–63, i. 125, 193; Brodie, Black and Lyte, i. 428.
52. Brodie, Black and Lyte, 1914–16, i. 64, 472.
53. Ibid, 269, 373.
54. Condon, 2003a, 60.
55. Campbell, 1873, i. 455 (1486); ii. 326–7 (1488); Finberg, 1951, 215 (1501).
56. TNA, E 211/106; Brodie, Black and Lyte, 1914–16, ii. 625.
57. Campbell, 1873, i. 107, 404, 194–5, 206.
58. As reported by Marmaduke Huby, then bursar of Fountains Abbey at the end of the year: Talbot, 1967, 129 (no. 64).
59. Riley, 1867–9, ii. 405–6; Pantin, 1931–37, iii. 34.
60. Pantin, 1931–37, ii. 99–101.
61. Campbell, 1873, i. 256.
62. Beckett, 1995, 122.
63. Ibid, 123.
64. Condon, 2003a, 88.
65. Sledmere, 1914, 24–5.
66. Bernard, 2005, 228.
67. TNA, SP 1/1, fo. 30r.
68. *LP*, 2/2, i. 12; 2 (xi).
69. *LP*, 2/2, 2 (3).
70. *LP*, 1, 670; *LP*, 2/1, 1573.
71. TNA, SP 1/ 17, fo. 2r.
72. Holder, 2017, 47.
73. *LP*, 1/1 (11).
74. London Metropolitan Archives, Guildhall Library, MS 9531/9, Register of Bishop Richard Fitzjames, fos. 161r–5r.
75. *LP*, 2/2, 6.
76. *LP*, 2/1, 1141.
77. *LP*, 2/1, 2018; 2/2, 2.2, 2.3, 4.3, 6.2, 8.1–2.
78. *LP*, 1/1, 1365 (4).
79. Gribbin, 2001, 210.
80. *LP*, 1/2, 2715; *LP*, 1/1, 740.
81. BL, MS Arundel 26, fo. 28r; BL, MS Harley 3504, fo. 264b; *LP*, 2/2, 3849.
82. For example, *LP*, 2/2, 2 (10).
83. For example, *LP*, 1/2, 2862, 2772; 2, 2 (10); 3/1 (9); 3/2, 3695 (1).
84. Less than a year after his election in February 1512, Rowland received a cup with a gilt cover from the king: TNA, SP 1/229, fo. 110r.
85. *LP*, 1/2, 27; *LP*, 5, 1799; see also Oliver, 1846, 92.
86. *LP*, 1/2, 2402.
87. The king announced his intention to call upon the learned of his kingdom in a letter to Pope Leo X dated 21 May 1521: *LP*, 3/1, 327.
88. TNA, SP 1/22, fo. 207r.
89. TNA, SP 1/67, fo. 54r; BL, MS Cotton Titus B I, fo. 46r; SP2/1, fos. 1r, 66r; Clark, 2019a, 130–3.

90. For the case for the recession of lay patronage see Thompson, 1994, especially 116–21. For reflective critique see Bernard, 2012, 184–6 at 185.
91. HMC, 3rd Report, 47; Alnwick Castle, A.III.4, C.III.4a, C.VIII.1l, D.III.4.
92. Oliver, 1846, 377, 392.
93. TNA, PCC 11/10/615, fos. 266v–7v at 266v.
94. TNA, PCC, Prob 11/16/351, fos. 104r–5r.
95. Caley et al., 1817–30, iii. 52–3; Traskey, 1978, 149–50.
96. TNA, PCC Prob. 11/22/98, fos. 33r–35r.
97. Caley et al., 1817–30, vi, pt. 3, 1510–11. The text of the indenture is given apparently in full but without reference to the documentary source.
98. He was chief steward of Buckfast, Buckland, Forde and Plympton, whose respective 1535 valuations were £504, £279, £394 and £931: Caley and Hunter, 1810–34, ii. 304–5, 369, 376, 379; Savine, 1909, 271–2.
99. TNA, E 329/244; Jones, 1959, 993.
100. Caley and Hunter, 1810–34, i. 241, 256, 280.
101. *LP*, 14/1, 518; 1154.
102. Caley and Hunter, 1810–34, ii. 362.
103. TNA, C1/391/13.
104. Heath, 1973, 109.
105. *LP*, 1/2, 2910.
106. TNA, SP 1/12, fo. 149r.
107. Ledward and Latham, 1955–63, i, 296.
108. TNA, SP 1/7, fo. 161r.
109. BL, MS Cotton Cleopatra E IV, fo. 62r.
110. TNA, C 1/934/25.
111. *LP*, 5, 1557; 6, 1304; 8, 188.
112. TNA, SP 1/ 130, fo. 239r.
113. Gunn, 2016, 161.
114. TNA, PCC, Prob 11/22/232, fos. 97r–102r.
115. Ibid, Prob 11/26/199, fos. 95r–97v.
116. See above, 116.
117. Hertfordshire Archives and Local Studies, DE/FL/17102; Sutton, 1994, 211–13.
118. For the pre- and post-Reformation actions and connections of the Horde family, see Connolly, 2019, 151–4.
119. Erler, 2013, 67, 72.
120. See, especially, Lee, 2001, 142–9, 173–88, 209–10; Erler, 2002, 15–26; Powell, 2017, 217–18, 220–1.
121. Higgs, 1998, 101; TNA, SP 1/136, fo. 86r.
122. For these parliamentary manoeuvres see Aston, 1984.
123. The 1529 petition was as much a 'rant' as a bill; what resurfaced in 1534 reached as far as a written proposal but there is no record of it being put to the Commons; Hoyle, 1995a, 285, 291.
124. For Hunne see Brigden, 1989, 98–103. For the statute concerning First Fruits (26 Henry VIII c.3) see Luders et al., 1810–28, iii. 493–9.
125. TNA, SP 1/69, fo. 219r.
126. After a second issue in 1529 the text was next printed at Antwerp under the name of Henry Nycolson in 1546, classified as STC (2nd edn.) 1462.9.
127. TNA, C1/145/36.
128. TNA, S8/338/E1203; C 1/930/42; STAC 2/17/5; 2/17/394; 2/24/142; 2/28/107.
129. TNA, STAC 2/27/15.
130. Higham, 1999, 174–6.
131. Chester Archives and Local Studies, Zs/B/5/e.
132. Black et al., 1901–10, iii. 45–6.

133. Knowles and Hadcock, 1971, 83–6.
134. See, for example, the visitations undertaken by successive bishops of Lincoln: Thompson, 1915–27.
135. Smith, 2008, 16. A further case of intervention came in 1463–4 over Thomas Banys of Folkestone Priory: Harper-Bill, 1977, 42–3.
136. Smith, 2008, 393. There were comparable challenges at Bath Cathedral Priory (1452–3), Chertsey Abbey (1459–62), St Oswald's Priory, Gloucester (1447) and Montacute (1458): Ibid, 17, 31, 246, 430; Greatrex, 1997, 33.
137. Riley, 1872–3, i. 396–9 at 399.
138. Horrox, 2004.
139. The visitors appointed by the chapter of the Benedictines gave way to the bishop as early as 1300. By 1466 they readily followed the prompting of 'his compertis and processe': Pantin, 1931–7, i. 263–5 (no. 146); iii. 112–15 at 113 (no. 274).
140. Harper-Bill, 1987–2000, i. 50; Knowles, 1952; Harper-Bill, 1977, 46.
141. Harper-Bill, 1987–2000, i. 13–15; Brodie, Black and Lyte, 1914–16, i. 372–3.
142. Harper-Bill, 1977, 46–7. The second issue of *Quanta* is printed in Wilkins, 1737, iii. 630.
143. Harper-Bill, 1977, 49–56; Harper-Bill, 1987–2000, ii. 12–38, 62–98 (Bath and Wells, Exeter, Winchester); 1–11, 105–23 (Coventry and Lichfield); 127–54 (Worcester).
144. Talbot, 1967, 9 and n.
145. Ibid, 202–13 (Letters 100–1, 103).
146. Brodie, Black and Lyte, 1914–16, i. 66; Smith, 2008, 251.
147. Harper-Bill, 1987–2000, i. 38.
148. Finberg, 1951, 215.
149. Harper-Bill, 1987–2000, i. 38; Harper-Bill, 1977, 48–9.
150. For the record of Morton's visitations and other interventions in Canterbury see Harper-Bill, 1987–2000, ii. x–xiii, 82–4, 86–7, 127–34, 277–96, 347–55, 374–94, 396–403, 442–7, 458–73; iii. 293–327. For discussion see also Harper-Bill, 1977, 43. Pope Benedict issued canons for the Cistercians in 1335 (*Fulgens sicut stella*), the Benedictines in 1336 (*Summi magistri*) and the Augustinian or Black canons in 1339 (*Ad decorem ecclesiae*). Each of the congregations knew their canons as the Benedictina, by which name they have also been known collectively. *Fulgens* is printed in Cocquelines, 1740, iii/2, 203–13. For *Summi* and *Ad decorem* see Wilkins, 1737, ii. 585–616 (*Summi*); 629–51 (*Ad decorem*). See also McDonald, 1986.
151. Harper-Bill, 1987–2000, ii. 130, 380 (35–7, 107–8); Harper-Bill, 1977, 51–2.
152. Harper-Bill, 1987–2000, ii. 127, 129 (32–3, 34–5); Harper-Bill, 1977, 51.
153. TNA, PCC Prob 11/12/178, fos. 70r–71v at 70v; Leader, 1983, 223.
154. Jessopp, 1888, 4–7 at 4 (Norwich Cathedral Priory); 19 (Horsham St Faith); 22 (Wymondham Abbey).
155. Heath, 1973, 13.
156. Alcock, 1497b, A iiv.
157. Ibid, 11.
158. Wood-Legh, 1984, 24.
159. He addressed the abbesses of Nunnaminster, Romsey and Wherwell directly in his preface: Benedict, 1516, A iiv. Collett, 2002, 46–52.
160. He described the abbot's work as a 'collectanaea', and claimed he had shared it with 'omnes domos religiosos': Longland, 1527, M 1r–v at M 1v.
161. Peacock, 1883, 60 (Missenden); Thompson, 1940–7, ii. 117–18 (Dorchester Abbey), 185 (Leicester Abbey).
162. Longland, 1527, plate 10.l.
163. TNA, SP 1/39, fo. 49r.
164. Benedict, 1516, F ivr.
165. Wood-Legh, 1984, 34, 296.
166. Benedict, 1516, G iiiv. His insistence on this point was perhaps reinforced by his experience in his own diocese: Collett, 2002, 30–1.

167. Thompson, 1989, 74.
168. Bowker, 1981, 17.
169. Serjeantson and Adkins, 1906, 125–7 at 126.
170. Wiltshire and Swindon History Centre, D 1/2/14, Register of Bishop Edmund Audley of Salisbury, 1502–24, fos. 135r–6r.
171. Thompson, 1989, 73.
172. Thompson, 1949, 82–7; Smith, 2008, 462.
173. By 1518 the abbots of St Mary Graces and Croxden faced Wolsey in chancery over the matter: TNA, C1/539/35.
174. Talbot, 1967, 233–6 at 236.
175. Wolsey interposed himself in the chapter of the Augustinian canons convened at Leicester in 1518, dispatching a letter to be read to the heads of houses setting out his expectations for reform: Salter, 1922, 131–43. The Cistercians he approached through their congregational visitors, first Abbot Chard, and then Abbot Huby of Fountains, now de facto head of the English network: Talbot, 1967, 260–1, 265–6.
176. Wolsey arranged for coadjutors to the abbot in 1518: TNA, SP 1/232, fo. 138r; SP 1/19, fo. 78r. In 1521 Pace reported to Wolsey the king's audience with the prior seeking licence freely to elect an abbot: BL, MS Cotton Vitellius B IV fos. 204r–6r. Wolsey was confirmed as abbot in commendam in December 1521, although papal approval came only over the next eighteen months (November 1522, March 1523): LP, 3/2, 1843; TNA, SC 7/64/25, 29.
177. Hay, 1950, 302–3.
178. Underwood, 1989, 35–40; Jones and Underwood, 1992, 202–31; McConica, 1986, 7–29; Burgess, 2019, 23.
179. 'Dessipacionem et ruinam non solum nostrae religionis sed etiam monachorum monacharum ac monialium quasi per totam Angliam': Dickens, 1951, 47.
180. TNA, SP 1/34, fo. 240r.
181. 'Tradidere et ad firmam dimisere': Dickens, 1951, 47.
182. LP, 2/2 A48.
183. Allen, 1929, 110 (Letter 65).
184. TNA, SP 1/34, fo. 182r.
185. Collett, 1985, 2–6, 8–10.
186. Sylvester, 1959, 130.
187. Pantin, 1931–7, iii. 123–4.
188. Kresen Kernow, ART/4/15.
189. LP, 3, 1, 589; TNA, SP 1/31, fos. 177v–8r; TNA, SP 1/48, fos. 80r–v at 80v. See also Gwyn, 1990, 276–7.
190. Salter, 1922, 138–9.
191. Talbot, 1967, 13–14, 260, 263, 265–6.
192. Pantin, 1931–7, iii. 123–4.
193. Hay, 1950, 258–9.
194. For example, his reporting of appointments at Bicester and Notley: TNA, SP 1/47, fo. 208r.
195. Heale counts thirty elections in which Wolsey had a hand: Heale, 2016, 277–8. For an alternative estimate, and view, see Gwyn, 1990, 316–23.
196. TNA, SP 1/16, fo. 219r (Valle Crucis); SP1/29, fo. 133r (St John of Jerusalem, Clerkenwell); SP 1/52, fo. 152r (Bruern); SP 1/55, fo. 155r (Rievaulx); BL, MS Cotton Nero B VI, fo. 35r (Eynsham); BL MS Cotton Titus B I, fo. 314r (Reading); LP, 4/3, 22 (Glastonbury).
197. TNA, SC 7/63/30 (dated 31 Aug.).
198. TNA, SC 7/63/23.
199. TNA, SC 7/63/11 (dated 31 May).
200. Lemon, 1830, i. 380–3 at 383.
201. TNA, E 303/10354.
202. Heale represents the supervision of elections not only as the end of any self-determination but also the beginning of the end of monastic discipline: Heale, 2016, 308.

203. Kirby, 1996, Letters 75, 134 (85,129) 1496.
204. These were the names of the heads of the monasteries at Canterbury (Christ Church), Battle and Bury St Edmunds. See also MacCulloch, 1986, 136–7, 188; Searle, 1974, 332. See above, 143.
205. Allen, 1929, 107–8 at 108 (Letter 63).
206. Beckett, 1995, 125–6.
207. TNA, C 1/525/2; C 1/1501/56.
208. BL, MS Cotton Titus B I, 108/353.
209. TNA, SP 1/39, fo. 49r.
210. Manning, 1988, 45.
211. Canterbury Cathedral Archives, CCA, CCA-DCc-ChAnt/C/1232/15
212. Manning, 1988, 45.
213. Jones, 1957, 41.
214. Rawcliffe, 1978, 98.
215. Dobson, 1973, 328–9; Manning, 1988, 46.
216. Smith, 2008, 295–6.
217. TNA, SP 1/79, fo. 33r.
218. TNA, SP 1/78, fo. 119r–21v.
219. Salter, 1922, 142, 137.
220. Ibid, 143.
221. Gwyn, 1990, 318.
222. BL, MS Cotton Nero B VI, fo. 35r.
223. TNA, SP 1/52, fo. 91r.
224. BL, MS Cotton Nero B VI, fo. 25r.
225. Gribbin, 2001, 201–11; Salter, 1922, xiv; Gwyn, 1990, 274.
226. 'Nam his diebus plus solito moliuntur plures, eciam regni maiores, paulatim ad subiecci-onem ordinem vestrem trahere': Talbot, 1967, 131–7 at 134 (no. 66).
227. Pantin, 1931–7, iii. 124–36.
228. See above, 173.
229. TNA, SP 1/117, fo. 139r
230. Talbot, 1967, 220–5 at 223 (no. 109).
231. Eclogues, IV, 526–8: White, 1960, 159.
232. Gribbin, 2001, 208–9.
233. Kresen Kernow, ART/4/10.
234. Now, Cambridge, St John's College, Ii. 3. 39.
235. The verdict is Heale, 2016, 54.
236. Armstrong, 2004; Chibi, 2004; Cross, 2004c; Shaw, 2004.
237. Cambridge, Emmanuel College, MS 94; Lovatt, 1968, 106, 118; Smith, 2008, 338.
238. BL, MS Cotton Nero B VI, fo. 25r.
239. For examples, an apparently autograph letter preserved in BL, MS Cotton Nero B VI, fo. 25r–v, and his signature on another, TNA, SP 1/235, fo. 346r. For books of his personal library bearing what are surely his annotations see Cambridge, Clare College, G. 1; Oxford, Bodl., Rawlinson Q. d. 12.
240. LP, 4/2, 3129; Ryle, 2004.
241. Erler, 2002, 108.
242. Erasmus was resident at St Mary's College in the autumn of 1499: Mynors et al., 1974, 202–6 at 206.
243. TNA, SP 1/84, fo. 22r; Cox, 1532; Ryle, 2004.
244. Longland, 1527, B 1r–C 5v at B 5r.
245. Cambridge, Clare College, unclassified.
246. Now, Oxford, Bodleian. 4° Z 33 Th.
247. Lambeth Palace Library, MS 159; BL, MS Harley 4843.
248. See above, 78.

249. For these congregations see Clark, 2011, 298–304; Collett, 1985, 2–6, 8–10.
250. Lambeth Palace Library, MS 159, fos. 268v–71v at 270r, 271r.
251. Clark, 2014.
252. *LP*, 3/1, 873; BL, MS Cotton Caligula D VII, fo. 240r; BL, MS Cotton Vitellius B XII, fos. 8r, 40r, 43–4, 48r; TNA, SP 1/29, fo. 240; SP 1/33, fo. 136r; SP 1/37, fo. 130r; SP 1/40, fo. 100r; *LP*, 3/2, 2030, 3293; 4/1, 1244; 5, 589.
253. TNA, SP 1/45, fo. 218r.
254. Fryde, 1996, 268–9.
255. Ibid, 268; Snell, 1967, 77. The suffragan status of Prior Thomas Vyvyan of Bodmin was remembered in his epitaph.
256. *LP*, 2/1, 2535.
257. The difficulty here is the verdict of Heale, 2016, 198.
258. Powicke and Fryde, 1961, 271–2.
259. Fryde, 1996, 271–2; Heale, 2016, 378; Atherton, 2004.
260. Caley and Hunter, 1810–34, ii. 409–18; Fisher, 2018, 73–75; Baker and Holt, 2003, 282–3, 292.
261. Robert Reve, described both as clothier and yeoman, was steward of the manor of Chevington; Edmund Reve was tenant of the abbey manor of Hargrave; one Henry Reve held a tenancy from the hospital: Suffolk Record Office, 449/2/30; 449/2/292; E135/2/212, fo. 1r.
262. Searle, 1974, 398, 440.
263. TNA, SP 1/170, fo. 192r.
264. TNA, SP 1/78, fo. 119r–21v.
265. BL, MS Cotton Nero B VI, fo. 25r.
266. TNA, SP 1/69, fos. 54r–57r (1531).
267. Anon., 1830, 380–3 at 380.
268. Crosby, 2014, 338.
269. The Canterbury book is now Lambeth Palace Library, MS 159, fos. 268v–71v.
270. *LP*, iv, 3815; Davies, 2004.
271. Bernard, 2011, 402.
272. A payment of arrears owing to the prior made from Hampton Court was recorded among Cromwell's remembrances in 1533: *LP*, 6, 1370.
273. TNA, SP 1/66, fo. 138r.
274. Ibid, fo. 145v.
275. Set out in letters dated 3 November 1531 and 23 January 1532: SP 1/68, fo. 38r; SP 1/69, fo. 14r.
276. TNA, PCC Prob. 11/23/8, fos. 216r–v, 220r.
277. TNA, PCC Prob. 11/24/307, fos. 175v–176r.
278. TNA, PCC Prob. 11/26/199, fos. 95r–97v.
279. TNA, SP 1/46, fo. 71r.
280. TNA, SP 1/66, fo. 138r.
281. *LP*, 5, 686.
282. Ibid.
283. Cambridge, Corpus Christi College, 440–1 at 440.
284. Cromwell wrote to his wife, Elizabeth, from Bayham on 29 November 1525; a surviving account of the manor of Bayham compiled in the wake of its closure is partially written in his hand: *LP*, 4/1, 1845; 4/3, 57.
285. TNA, SP 1/68, fo. 38r.
286. BL, MS Cotton Titus B I, fo. 358r.
287. TNA, SP 1/74, fo. 150r.
288. BL, MS Cotton Titus B I, fo. 462v.
289. BL, MS Cotton Titus B I, fo. 358r.

290. BL, MS Cotton Vitellius B XIII, fo. 117r.
291. TNA, SP 2/1, fo. 116r.
292. TNA, SP 1/67, fo. 54r; SP 2/1, fo. 66r; *LP*, 5, 720.
293. 23 Henry VIII c. 21: Luders et al., 1810–28, iii. 388–92 (Westminster Abbey); c. 23 (Waltham), 395–7; c. 25 (St Albans), 400–3; c. 26 (St John of Jerusalem), 403–6; (Sheen), 406–9; *LP*, 5, 720.
294. *LP*, 5, 405, 508.
295. *LP*, 5, 720.
296. TNA, SP 1/73, fo. 7r.
297. *LP*, 5, 392, 439, 464, 470, 475, 506, 559, 1799; Evidence of traffic to and from Waltham: TNA, SP 1/57, fo. 194r.
298. *LP*, 5, 720.
299. TNA, SP 1/78, fo. 215r.
300. *LP*, 5, 1207 (25, 35).
301. TNA, SP 3/12, fo. 145r.
302. For examples, from the summer of 1531 to the autumn of 1532: TNA, SP 1/66, fo. 46r (fo. 133r (Malmesbury); SP 1/70, fo. 154r (Montacute); SP 1/71, fos. 23r, 50r (Bruton); SP 1/237, fo. 201r; *LP*, 6, 1209 (Wilton).
303. *LP*, 4, 3, 230.
304. *LP*, 5, 823; Davis, 1925, 129.
305. TNA, SP 1/57, fo. 55r (1530); SP 1/75, fo. 175r (1533); SP 1/113, fo. 8r (1536); BL, MS Cotton Cleopatra E IV, fo. 283r.
306. Bradshaw, 1974, 43–4.
307. Douglas Hamilton, 1875, 19.

Chapter V The King's Commissions

1. TNA, SP 1/92, fo. 22r.
2. The *Taxatio ecclesiastica* was commissioned by Pope Nicholas IV and carried out in 1291–2 across England, Wales and Ireland. See https://www.dhi.ac.uk/taxatio/.
3. TNA, SP 1/95, fo. 147r–v.
4. Luders et al., 1810–28, iii. 492.
5. 26 Henry VIII c.1: Luders et al. 1810–28, iii. 492.
6. *LP*, 7, 1482.
7. 25 Henry VIII c. 22: Luders et al., 1810–28, iii. 471–74.
8. LP, 7, 665.
9. TNA, SP 1/83, fo. 228r. Lee was installed on 23 April and arrived at Sheen on 7 May 1534.
10. BL, MS Cotton Otho C X, fo. 171r.
11. Smith, 2008, 51, 80, 267, 325, 463.
12. TNA, SP 1/238, fo. 78r.
13. Lehmberg, 1970, 184.
14. *LP*, 6, 1111.
15. TNA, SP 1/77, fo. 186r; SP 1/82, fo. 239r; *LP*, 6, 868.
16. *LP*, 7, 530; Thompson, 2004.
17. *LP*, 7, 665; Murray, 2004.
18. Pantin, 1931–7, iii. 124–36 at 124–5 (no. 284); 262.
19. TNA, E 328/26/xi (dated 1531).
20. Clark, 2007, 88.
21. St Albans Abbey's books of canon law and, perhaps, its celebrated chronicles, were consulted, and, it would appear, appropriated from as early as 1527: Carley, 2000, xxx–xli at xxxi, xli.
22. Clark, 2007, 88.
23. Lehmberg, 1970, 177.

24. TNA, SP 1/82, fo. 239r.
25. TNA, SP 1/131, fo. 181r.
26. Temys's words were recalled in Halls's chronicle. See also Lehmberg, 1970, 147–8.
27. TNA, KB 9/529/39; Elton, 1974, 225–6.
28. BL, MS Cotton Cleopatra E IV, fo. 93r–v at 93r. See also Rex, 1991.
29. BL, MS Lansdowne 97, fos. 148r–53v at 153r.
30. TNA, SP 1/82, fo. 11r.
31. TNA, SP 1/66, fo. 145v. Kidderminster died before 25 August 1534: Cunich, 2004.
32. *LP*, 4/3, 6513. See also BL, MS Add. 38656, fos. 3r–4v.
33. TNA, SP 1/65, fo. 26r–v at 26r. Pantin, 1931–37, iii. 262.
34. TNA, SP 1/84, fo. 100r.
35. TNA, SP 1/85, fo. 9r.
36. TNA, SP 1/92, fo. 22r.
37. TNA, SP 1/84, fo. 172r.
38. TNA, SP 1/185, fo. 35r.
39. TNA, SP 1/90, fo. 189r.
40. TNA, SP 1/132, fo. 76r.
41. TNA, SP 1/84, fo. 6r.
42. BL, MS Harley 419, fos. 112r–14r.
43. *LP*, 8, 79.
44. [Lydgate], 1534, Y iiv.
45. BL, MS Royal 5 E IX, at fo. 2v,
46. BL, MS Royal 7 E X; BL, MS Add. 32091, fo. 3r; TNA, SP 1/96, fo. 212r.
47. TNA, SP 1/98, fo. 131r.
48. Cambridge, Corpus Christi College, MS 59, fo. 1r, upper margin.
49. BL, MS Cotton Cleopatra C III.
50. Lambeth Palace Library, MS 20. Another, apparently Canterbury book saw the word 'papa' substituted with 'episcopus': Cambridge, University Library, MS Dd 1.10–11 (first volume only).
51. BL, MS Egerton 3759, fo. 77r.
52. Atherton, 2003, 172. For Prior Steward's copy of the *Liber Eliensis* see BL, MS Harley 3721. The St Albans *Gesta abbatum* appears to have lost some instances of the word 'Papa': Riley, 1867–69, i. 127n.
53. BL, MS Cotton Claudius E IV; Atherton, 2003, 172; BL, MS Add. 39758, fos. 161r–68r.
54. BL, MS Egerton 3098, fo. 25v.
55. TNA, SP 1/103, fo. 212r.
56. TNA, SP 1/82, fo. 11r.
57. TNA, SP 1/84, fo. 172r; SP 1/85, fo. 136r.
58. TNA, SP 1/92, fo. 26r.
59. TNA, SP 1/93, fo. 170r.
60. *LP*, 8, 609, 661; Bainbridge, 2004.
61. TNA, SP 1/83, fo. 228r.
62. TNA, SP 1/85, fos. 21r, 77r.
63. BL, MS Cotton Cleopatra E IV, fo. 49r.
64. BL, MS Cotton Cleopatra E IV, fo. 31r.
65. TNA, SP 1/77, fo. 94r.
66. BL, MS Cotton Cleopatra E VI, fo. 164r; TNA, SP 1/92, fos. 26r, 53r, 188v.
67. BL, MS Cotton Titus B I, fo. 424v.
68. Elton, 1972, 19. See above, n. 63.
69. TNA, SP 3/7, fo. 166r; Bourchier, 1582, 5, 26; *LP*, 7, 1670.
70. *LP*, 7, 50; BL, MS Cotton Titus B I, fo. 462r.
71. Lincolnshire Archives, DIOC/REG/26 (Register of John Longland, 1521–47), fos. 44r–v.
72. *LP*, 10, 284.
73. BL, MS Cotton Titus B I, fo. 424r.

74. TNA, SP 1/88, fo. 68r.
75. TNA, SP 1/113, fo. 66r.
76. TNA, SP 1/86, fo. 62r.
77. TNA, SP 1/85, fo. 115r.
78. An inventory of books kept in the Lady chapel was made at an unknown date in the middle of the decade: Canterbury Cathedral Archives, CCA-DDc Inventory/29. A copy of the letters of Anselm of Canterbury, a work not without echoes of the church-and-crown conflict, was taken into Cranmer's possession at this time: now Lambeth Palace Library, MS 59.
79. TNA, SP 1/83, fo. 182r.
80. TNA, SP 1/85, fo. 123r.
81. Luders et al., 1810–28, iii. 492, 493–9 at 495.
82. Cromwell was in regular demand as referee in the row that ran on from the early summer to the end of the year, as well-placed courtiers also took sides: TNA, SP 1/93, fo. 18r; SP 1/96, fo. 69r; TNA, SP 1/98, fo. 51r.
83. BL, MS Cotton Titus B I, fos. 427r–v.
84. BL, MS Cotton Cleopatra E IV, fo. 372v–3r.
85. BL, MS Cotton Cleopatra E IV, fo. 368r–v.
86. TNA, SP 1/92, fo. 137r.
87. BL, MS Cotton Cleopatra E IV, fo. 372v–3r.
88. TNA, SP 1/92, fo. 142r.
89. TNA, SP 1/92, fo. 11r.
90. TNA, SP 1/92, fo. 137r.
91. TNA, SP 1/98, fo. 72r; Savine, 1909, 10.
92. TNA, SP 1/91, fo. 175r–v.
93. *LP*, 8, 503.
94. TNA, SP 1/91, fo. 107v.
95. *LP*, 8, 530.
96. TNA, SP 1/92, fo. 137r.
97. TNA, SP 1/99, fo. 107r.
98. TNA, SP 1/99, fo. 25r.
99. TNA, SP 1/92, fo. 136r.
100. TNA, SP 1/89, fo. 133r.
101. TNA, SP 1/91, fo. 147r.
102. TNA, SP 1/92, fo. 148r (16 May); BL, MS Cotton Cleopatra E IV, fo. 369r (24 May).
103. TNA, SP 1/93, fo. 161r.
104. BL, MS Cotton Cleopatra E IV, fo. 309r.
105. TNA, SP 1/98, fo. 133r.
106. TNA, SP 1/93, fo. 185r.
107. BL, MS Lansdowne, 446, fo. 102r.
108. BL, MS Cotton Cleopatra E IV, fos. 344r, 367r; Savine, 1909, 36 and n.
109. Savine, 1909, 21.
110. Dorchester, Studley and Thame: Savine, 1909, 34.
111. Savine, 1909, 21.
112. Evans, 1941, 45 & n.
113. BL, MS Cotton Cleopatra E IV, fo. 368r–v.
114. TNA, SP 1/93, fo. 174r.
115. TNA, SP 1/191, fo. 147r.
116. At the turn of the year, Barlow was already conspicuous in the service of the Crown, as a member of the king's embassy to James V of Scotland, where he was described as the king's 'cownsalor' and 'servitour': TNA, SP 49/4, fos. 70r, 74r.
117. TNA, SP 3/7, fo. 79r; SP 1/92, fo. 13r.
118. *LP*, 7, 927 (38, 44).
119. TNA, SP 1/91, fo. 89v.

120 TNA, SP 1/93, fo. 194r.
121. TNA, SP 1/95, fo. 96v.
122. TNA, SP 1/95, fo. 96r.
123. TNA, SP 1/95, fo. 135r.
124. TNA, SP 1/92, fo. 139r; *LP*, 8, 1056.
125. TNA, SP 1/97, fo. 26r.
126. TNA, SP 1/94, fo. 182r.
127. Ibid.
128. TNA, SP 1/97, fo. 22r.
129. BL, MS Cotton Cleopatra E IV, fo. 56r.
130. TNA, SP 1/98, fo. 152r.
131. In the first parliament a proviso added to the bill against Peter's Pence, Lehmberg, 1970, 192.
132. TNA, SP 1/96, fo. 163r.
133. TNA, SP 1/83, fo. 85r.
134. BL, MS Cotton Cleopatra E IV, fos. 14r–v.
135. London Metropolitan Archives, Guildhall Library MS 1231, fos. 1–2r; Shaw, 2003, 281.
136. TNA, SP 1/101, fo. 153r.
137. Luders et al. 1810–28, iii. 492.
138. BL, MS Cotton Cleopatra E IV, fos. 15r–19v; Wilkins, 1737, iii. 786–9.
139. Pantin, 1931–37, ii. 82–9 (no. 158).
140. Wilkins, 1737, iii. 789–91.
141. BL, MS Cotton Cleopatra E IV, fos. 22r–5r; TNA, E36/116, fos. 19r–22r; SP 6/6, fos. 6r–11v. See also Shaw, 2003, 282–9; MacCulloch, 2018, 299–302, 653–4.
142. For Prise's initial backroom role see Shaw, 2003, 32.
144. For the suggestion that the sequence is a draft set of injunctions to be read alongside the others see Shaw, 2003, 282.
144. Pantin, 1931–37, iii. 124–36 (Process of visitation at Malmesbury Abbey, 1527). For the contested responses to visitation see the reply of the abbot of Thame, 1525: Lincolnshire Archives, DIOC/REG/27, fos. 103r–104r.
145. Cheney, 1931; Pantin, 1931–37, iii. 279–91 (no. 350: Whitby, 1366).
146. For examples, Pantin, 1931–37, iii. 134–6 (no. 284: Malmesbury, 1527); Heath, 1973, 1 (Tutbury, 1515x1516), 124–5 (Burscough, 1524).
147. For example, Heath, 1973, 147 (Burton, 1524); Wood-Legh, 1984, 24 (Dover, 1511); 294 (Christ Church, Canterbury, 1511x1512).
148. For example, Gasquet, 1904–6, ii. 66 (Beauchief, 1494); Heath, 1973, 88–9 (Henwood, 1524); 120–1 (Maxstoke, 1524); 134 (Shrewsbury, 1524); Jessopp, 1888, 3–4, 74 (Norwich, 1492, 1514); Thompson, 1940–7, iii. 9–10 (Littlemore, 1516), 116–18 (Dorchester, 1517).
149. Pantin, 1931–7, iii. 124–36 at 126–7 (no. 284).
150. For the papal canons *Summi magistri* (1336) which set out comparable requirements see Wilkins, 1737.
151. BL, MS Cotton Cleopatra E IV, fo. 26r.
152. Wilkins, 1737, iii. 789–91.
153. Wood-Legh, 1984, 293–7 at 294–6 (Christ Church, Canterbury).
154. Benedict, 1516; Collett, 2002, 31, 35, 47–9.
155. Thompson, 1989, 74.
156. TNA, SP 6/1, fo. 116r–v.
157. See Makowski, 1997.
158. BL, MS Harley 791, fos. 27r–v. See also Shaw 2003, 267–8.
159. BL, MS Cotton Cleopatra E IV, fo. 13r.
160. TNA, SP 1/94, fo. 182r.
161. TNA, SP 1/97, fo. 101r.
162. TNA, SP 1/98, fo. 40r.
163. BL, MS Cotton Cleopatra E IV, fo. 13r.

164. Bush, 2009, 266.
165. BL, MS Cotton Cleopatra E IV, fo. 13r.
166. TNA, SP 1/94, fo. 182r.
167. TNA, SP 1/95, fo. 155r.
168. TNA, SP 1/95, fo. 155r.
169. Robertson, 1975, 207.
170. BL, MS Cotton Cleopatra E IV, fo. 131r (*LP*, viii, 1005).
171. BL, MS Cotton Cleopatra E IV, fo. 162r.
172. TNA, SP 1/94, fo. 182r.
173. TNA, SP 1/98, fo. 20r.
174. TNA, SP 1/95, fo. 155r.
175. Ibid.
176. TNA, SP 1/95, fo. 48r.
177. BL, MS Harley 604, fo. 65r.
178. TNA, SP 1/97, fos. 147r, 155r.
179. TNA, SP 1/98, fo. 16r.
180. *LP*, 9, 5.
181. TNA, SP 1/98, fo. 16r.
182. TNA, SP 1/95, 121r.
183. TNA, SP 1/96, fo. 210r.
184. Ibid.
185. TNA, SP 1/95, fo. 121r.
186. TNA, SP 1/98, fo. 94r.
187. TNA, SP 1/98, fo. 16r.
188. TNA, SP 1/98, fo. 20r.
189. TNA, SP 1/94, fo. 207r.
190. TNA, SP 1/98, fo. 4r.
191. Ibid.
192. TNA, SP 1/98, fo. 5r.
193. TNA, SP 1/95, fo. 155r.
194. TNA, SP 1/98, fo. 152r.
195. TNA, SP 1/98, fo. 169r.
196. *LP*, 9, 303.
197. BL, MS Cotton Cleopatra E IV, fo. 145r.
198. TNA, SP 1/101, fo. 127r.
199. TNA, SP 1/99, fo. 85v.
200. TNA, SP 1/97, fo. 74r.
201. TNA, SP 1/98, fo. 16v.
202. BL, MS Cotton Cleopatra E IV, fo. 162r–v.
203. TNA, SP 1/98, fo. 54r.
204. BL, MS Cotton Cleopatra E IV, fo. 68r.
205. *LP*, 9, 822.
206. TNA, SP 1/96, fo. 64r.
207. TNA, SP 1/91, fo. 6r; BL, MS Cotton Cleopatra F I, fo. 260r.
208. *LP*, 9, 604; TNA, SP 1/98, fo. 84r; Frere and Kennedy, 1910, ii. 30–3.
209. *LP*, 9, 517; TNA, SP 1/99, fo. 52r.
210. TNA, SP 1/95, fo. 58r.
211. Ibid.
212. Ibid.
213. *LP*, 9, 1173. For Holgate see also Parrish, 2004.
214. BL, MS Cotton Cleopatra E IV, fo. 62r.
215. BL, MS Cotton Cleopatra F V, fo. 260r.
216. TNA, SP 1/99, fo. 66r.

217. TNA, SP 1/98, fo. 69r.
218. BL, MS Cotton Cleopatra E IV, fo. 262r.
219. Letter preserved in BL, MS Stowe 141, fo. 23r.
220. SP 1/97, fo. 28r. TNA, SP 1/96, fo. 161r.
221. TNA, SP 1/97, fo. 28r; SP 1/98, fo. 69r.
222. TNA, SP 1/98, fo. 42r.
223. TNA, SP 1/102, fo. 127r.
224. Ibid.
225. *LP*, 8, 81.
226. TNA, SP 1/96, fo.161r.
227. TNA, SP 1/97, fo. 22r.
228. Ibid.
229. TNA, SP 1/96, fo. 133r.
230. *LP*, 8, 865.
231. TNA, SP 1/97, fo. 22r.
232. BL, MS Cotton Cleopatra E IV, fo. 154r.
233. TNA, SP 1/98, fo. 54r.
234. Ibid.
235. Fuller, 1845, iii. 382, 387.
236. TNA, SP 1/98, fo. 16r–v.
237. Ibid.
238. TNA, SP 1/98, fo. 40r.
239. TNA, SP 1/96, fo. 53r.
240. Ibid.
241. TNA, SP 1/97, fo. 9r.
242. TNA, SP 1/99, fo. 130r.
243. *LP*, 9, 5.
244. BL, MS Cotton Cleopatra E IV, fo. 199r.
245. BL, MS Add. 11041, fo.
246. TNA, SP 1/93, fo. 13r; 1/96, fo. 116r; 1/98, fo. 25r; 1/99, fo. 66r.
247. TNA, SP 1/98, fo. 174r.
248. TNA, SP 1/101, fo. 161r.
249. TNA, SP 1/98, fo. 98r.
250. *LP*, 9, 375.
251. BL, MS Cotton Cleopatra E IV, fo. 47r.
252. *LP*, 9, 256.
253. Holme, 1572, Cir; Morison, 1536, Bivr–v.
254. Corrie, 1844, 123.
255. Holinshed, 1577, 1564.
256. Fuller, 1845, iii. 369.
257. TNA, SP 1/102, fos. 84r–104v. Excerpts from the comperts for houses in Staffordshire, Nottinghamshire, Yorkshire, Lancashire and Norfolk are preserved in two sequences in BL, MS Cotton Cleopatra E IV, fos. 185r–195r, and 195v–197r. For a full account of the fragments and an interpretation of the circumstances and aims which guided their compilation see Shaw, 2003, 342–85.
258. A. N. Shaw has shown that the excerpts for Norwich diocese carry a trace of an entry for Ely: Shaw, 2003, 117.
259. TNA, SP 1/97, fo. 60r. See also Shaw, 2003, 24, 31, 91, 93.
260. TNA, SP 1/97, fo. 28r.
261. Shaw, 2003, 335, 349.
262. BL, MS Cotton Cleopatra E IV, fo. 13v.
263. TNA, SP 1/98, fo. 54v.
264. BL, MS Cotton Cleopatra E IV, fo. 300r.

265. TNA, SP 1/98, fo. 38r–v at 38r.
266. Haigh, 1969, 26–7.
267. TNA, SP 1/102, fos. 84r–104v.
268. TNA, SP 1/102, fo. 101r.
269. TNA, SP 1/95, fo. 38v.
270. TNA, SP 1/98, fo. 54v.
271. TNA, SP 1/139, fo. 154r.
272. *LP*, 9, 661.
273. BL, MS Cotton Cleopatra E IV, fos. 264r–v.
274. Frere, 1910, ii. 12–13.
275. Gilchrist, 2005, 201.
276. Dodwell, 1996, 247.
277. TNA, SP 1/118, fo. 1r.
278. *LP*, 16, 91.
279. Caley and Hunter, 1810–34, ii. 117; Merriman, 1902, Letter 266. For example, Bishop Voysey's visitation of Exeter diocese: *LP*, 13/1, 1106.
280. TNA, SP 1/98, fo. 174r.
281. TNA, SP 1/99, fo. 86v.
282. TNA, SP 1/139, fo. 154r.
283. *LP*, 13/2, 421.
284. Abbot, 1604, 37.
285. TNA, SP 1/98, fo. 58r.
286. BL, MS Cotton Cleopatra E IV, fo. 53r.
287. TNA, SP 1/89, fo. 42r.
288. TNA, SP 1/97, fo. 130r; SP 1/99, fo. 115r.
289. TNA, SP 1/91, fo. 8r.
290. TNA, SP 1/96, fo. 107r.
291. TNA, SP 1/101, fo. 127r.
292. BL, MS Cotton Cleopatra E IV, fo. 198r.
293. BL, MS Cotton Cleopatra E IV, fo. 199r.
294. TNA, SP 1/118, fo. 4r.
295. TNA, SP 1/101, fo. 135r.
296. TNA, SP 1/101, fo. 136r.
297. TNA, SP 1/102, fo. 19r.
298. TNA, SP 1/101, fo. 58r.
299. TNA, SP 1/99, fo. 9r.
300. TNA, SP 1/96, fo. 116r.
301. TNA, SP 1/97, fo. 47r.
302. TNA, SP 1/98, fo. 71r.
303. TNA, SP 1/99, fo. 52r.
304. Oxley, 1965, 100.
305. TNA, SP 1/97, fo. 22r.
306. *LP*, 9, 816.
307. TNA, SP 1/94, fo. 201r.
308. TNA, SP 1/96, fo. 161r.
309. TNA, SP 1/97, fo. 47r.
310. TNA, SP 1/97, fo. 9r.
311. TNA, SP 1/96, fo. 53r.
312. TNA, SP 1/98, fo. 27r.
313. Chitty, 1930, 43; Lincolnshire Archives, DIOC/REG/26 (Register of Bishop John Longland, 1521–47), fo. 45r–v; Hinde, 1952, 66.
314. Borthwick Institute, Abp Reg 28 (Register of Archbishop Edward Lee, 1531–44), fos. 195v–98v.

315. TNA, PCC Prob 11/25/375, fo. 194v.
316. TNA SC6/HENVIII/929.
317. See below, 359.
318. *LP*, 8, 291 (61).

Chapter VI The Challenge of Conformity

1. TNA, SP 1/115, fo. 144r.
2. BL, MS Cotton Titus B I, fo. 384r.
3. TNA, SP 1/112, fo. 99v.
4. TNA, SP 1/143, fo. 115r.
5. Anon., 1533. The second phrase appeared in a (now incomplete) proclamation suppressing superstitious customs kept on the eve of St Laurence: Anon., 1541.
6. TNA, SP 1/85, fo. 123r.
7. TNA, SP 1/239, fo. 335r.
8. TNA, SP 1/99, fo. 160r.
9. Starkey, 1536, D ivr.
10. TNA, SP 1/73, fo. 7r.
11. For the numbers at Canterbury and across the Carthusian network see Knowles and Hadcock, 1971, 61, 134–5. For the dispersal of the Observant friars at and after 1534 see *LP*, 7, 1607.
12. *LP*, 12/1, 283, 5901, 1285; Hoyle, 2001, 393–411.
13. For their backgrounds see Cross, 2004a; Doggett, 2004a, 2004c; Ward, 2004.
14. Hall, 1809, 824–5.
15. Summerson, 1993, ii. 621.
16. Haude, 1995; Martin, 1995.
17. Clark, 2004b, 82–90.
18. Dunning, 2004; Cunich, 2004.
19. Kaufman, 1986, at 75, 79–84.
20. *LP*, 2/1, 1515.
21. Riley, 1872–3, i. 159, 168, 171–4, 388–95.
22. Giles, 1845, 70.
23. Hay, 1950, 106; BL, MS Royal 14 B VII; Gairdner, 1861–3, ii. 335–7; Caley et al., 1817–30, ii. 408.
24. TNA, SP 1/80, fo. 119v; Shagan sees only political impulses: Shagan, 2003, 81–5.
25. Manning, 1988, 45.
26. For example, an inquest of March 1506: Chester Archives and Local Studies, ZS/B/6a.
27. Manning, 1988, 45. See also TNA, STAC 1/2/58.
28. Mundy, 1913, 56–7.
29. Rawcliffe, 1978, 98.
30. Fishwick, 1907, 11–15.
31. Higham, 1999, 174.
32. The allegation originated with Thomas Legh, who was a cousin of the victim, James Laybourne: TNA, SP 1/79, fo. 53r; Smith, 2008, 419.
33. TNA, SP 1/116, fo. 11r.
34. TNA, SP 1/152, fo. 91r.
35. BL, MS Cotton Cleopatra E IV, fo. 58r; TNA, SP 1/52, fo. 146r.
36. Rymer, 1739–45, xiv, 180; *LP*, 5, 627 (18).
37. TNA, SP 1/34, fo. 240r.
38. TNA, SP 1/34, fo. 132r.
39. *LP*, 4/2, 4254; Rex, 2002, 41–2.
40. TNA, SP 1/154, fo. 75r; SP 1/53, fo. 178r.
41. Rex, 2002, 40–1. By 1528, friars attached to the Franciscan convent at Colchester were implicated in the spread of the new radicals: *LP*, 4/2, 4029, 4218.

42. TNA, SP 1/47, fo. 80r.
43. No printed copy of Tyndale's translation has been identified. For Monmouth's testimony see *LP*, 4/2, 4282. For a discussion of the context see Erler, 2002, 106, 109.
44. TNA, SP 1/114, fo. 46r. Another report of Bale's preaching in 1531 surfaced four years later: BL, MS Cotton Cleopatra, E IV, fo. 397r. Suspect preaching had been noted at Ipswich in 1528: *LP*, 4/2, 4029.
45. Greatrex, 1997, 438–9; Chambers, 1966, 52.
46. TNA, SP 1/22, fo. 207r.
47. Bettey, 1989, 8.
48. Aveling and Pantin, 1967, 106–7 at 106.
49. TNA, SP 1/47, fo. 10r.
50. TNA, SP 1/47, fos. 52v–53r at 53v, 65r.
51. *LP*, 3/2, 4125; Principe, 2004.
52. TNA, SP 1/69, fo. 77r.
53. Brown, 1997, 16–17.
54. TNA, SP 1/88, fo.18r.
55. BL, MS Cotton Galba B X, fo. 102r.
56. TNA, SP 1/98, fo. 48r.
57. Nichols, 1852, 380–1.
58. TNA, SP 2/1, fo. 49r.
59. Marshall, 2004. The trust may have been misplaced, since Sir John Markham reported a 'sumwhat sedycyus and sclaunderus' sermon preached at Newark by one of the Observants: TNA, SP 1/81, fo. 118r.
60. Chambers, 1966, 21, 34, 49, 67, 82, 133.
61. Ibid, 37.
62. TNA, SP 1/95, fo. 45r.
63. TNA, SP 1/85, fo. 20r; SP 1/93, fo. 170r.
64. TNA, SP 1/86, fo. 18r.
65. Knowles, 1959, 233, 235.
66. Douglas Hamilton, 1875, 28.
67. TNA, SP 1/132, fo. 76r.
68. TNA, SP 1/85, fo. 123v.
69. TNA, SP 1/85, fo. 123v; Da Costa, 2011, 18–19.
70. Horde's commonplace book is now in Dublin, Trinity College, MS 352. The excerpts are at fos. 159r, 198v. For a thumbnail sketch of the book and its contents see Connolly, 2019, 162–3.
71. TNA, SP 1/ 91, fo. 95r.
72. TNA, SP 1/77, fo. 186r; SP 1/119, fo. 183r.
73. TNA, SP 1/90, fo. 189r (Stratford Langthorne); SP 1/96, fo. 108r (Kingswood) 115r–116r; SP 1/95, fo. 118r; SP 1/98, fo. 131r (Waltham).
74. TNA, SP 1/95, fo. 118r.
75. Ibid.
76. TNA, SP 1/132, fo. 76r.
77. *LP*, 7, 140, 454, 1024; *LP*, 12/1, 34.
78. Nichols, 1852, 282.
79. Morison, 1536, C iiv.
80. TNA, SP 1/103, fo. 212r.
81. TNA, SP 1/104, fos. 227r–232v.
82. BL, MS Cotton Claudius E IV, fo. 160r.
83. TNA, SP 1/83, fo. 172r.
84. BL, MS Cotton Cleopatra E IV, fo. 43r.
85. TNA, SP 1/94, fo. 42r.
86. BL, MS Cotton Cleopatra E IV, fo. 130r.
87. TNA, SP 1/80, fo. 118r.

88. Whitford, 1532, fo. 74r; Da Costa, 2011, 23.
89. BL, MS Cotton Cleopatra E IV, fo. 198r.
90. LP, 8 (2), 25.
91. TNA, SP 1/89, fo. 123r.
92. TNA, SP 1/102, fo. 45r.
93. BL, MS Cotton Cleopatra E IV, fo. 130r.
94. TNA, SP 1/93, fo. 170r.
95. TNA, SP 1/104, fo. 227r; 1/132, fo. 76r.
96. TNA, SP 1/90, fo. 189r.
97. BL, MS Harley 604, fo. 60r.
98. Thornton, 2006, 113–14.
99. BL, MS Cotton Cleopatra E IV, fo. 233r.
100. *LP*, 8, 196: BL, MS Cotton Cleopatra E IV, fo. 233r(?).
101. BL, MS Cotton Cleopatra E IV, fo. 157r.
102. TNA, SP 1/91, fo. 157r.
103. TNA, SP 1/83, fo. 183r; *LP*, 8, 657.
104. TNA, SP 1/83, fo. 183r.
105. TNA, SP 1/192, fo. 121r.
106. TNA, SP 1/94, unfoliated.
107. Speight, 1994, 630.
108. This was the memory passed down to John Hooker (d. 1601), recorder of Exeter, himself only a child of about nine at the time: Devon Heritage Centre, ECA Book 51, fo. 343r. His account of the Reformation in the city is discussed in Lyon, 2018, 167–9.
109. TNA, SP 1/102, fo. 27v–28r.
110. BL, MS Cotton Cleopatra E IV, fo. 199v; TNA, SP 1/102 fo. 95r.
111. *LP*, 10, 207.
112. TNA, SP 1/104, fos. 160r–162r.
113. TNA, SP 2/1, fo. 310r–325r at 310r.
114. *LP*, 8, 327.
115. TNA, SP 1/106, fo. 222v.
116. Dutton had raised the alarm over the conduct of the canons as much as eighteen months before: BL, MS Harley 604, fo. 60r.
117. Hall, 1809, 820, 821.
118. Ellis, 1812, 605.
119. Fuller, 1845, iii. 378; Davies, 1968; Hoyle, 2001, 17.
120. *LP*, 11, 714.
121. *LP*, 12/1, 380.
122. TNA, SP 1/109, fo. 52r.
123. Douglas Hamilton, 1875, 56.
124. Nichols, 1852, 38.
125. Morison, 1536 B iir.
126. Hall, 1809, 820.
127. Hardyng, 1543, fo. 159v.
128. Hoyle, 2001, 12–16; Shagan, 2003, 127.
129. The reach and the numbers involved are spoken of in the depositions taken after the event: TNA, SP 1/109, fos. 1r–14v. For the episode at Legbourne see SP 1/110, fos. 142r–147r.
130. Alvingham (4 miles); Bullington (17 miles); North Ormsby (7 miles); Sixhills (11 miles): Knowles and Hadcock, 1971.
131. The trouble erupted in the small hours of the morning of Sunday and was reported by Sir Piers Dutton the following day: TNA, SP 1/108, fo. 14r.
132. TNA, SP 1/119, fo. 21r; fos. 73r–87v at 83v, 85r.
133. *LP*, 12/1, 1019, 1020.

134. For reference to these places see the confession taken from the rebel leader, William Stapulton: TNA, SP 1/115, fos. 247r–257r at 247r; Bush, 1996, 79, 139, 145, 149, 163.
135. TNA, SP 1/119, fos. 73r–87v at 84r.
136. TNA, E 36/118, fo. 115v; SP 1/115, fo. 260r; Bush, 1996, 377–8.
137. TNA, SP 1/258, fos. 258r–260v.
138. For example, the proclamation of Thomas Howard, duke of Norfolk, in his capacity as Lieutenant North of the Trent: TNA, SP 1/115, fo. 180r.
139. *LP*, 12/1, 392; Cross, 2018, 202–3.
140. TNA, SP 1/107, fo. 73r.
141. TNA, SP 1/115, fos. 247r–257v.
142. TNA, SP 1/111, fos. 66r–67r at 66r.
143. TNA, SP 1/126, fo. 115r.
144. For surviving reports of the forced reoccupation see: TNA, SP 1/116, fo. 11r. See also Haigh, 1969, 62.
145. Haigh, 1969, 65–7, 73.
146. Ibid, 77–9.
147. Caley et al., 1817–30, v. 569.
148. *LP*, 12/1, 1036.
149. Haigh, 1969, 62.
150. TNA, SP 1/109, fo. 1r–14v.
151. TNA, SP 1/116, fo. 166r.
152. *LP*, 12/1, 201, 370; Cross and Vickers, 1995, 395.
153. *LP*, 12/1, 201.
154. TNA, SP 1/115, fos. 209r–215r at 209v.
155. TNA, SP 1/109, fos. 1r–14v.
156. TNA, SP 1/119, fos. 85r–v.
157. Haigh, 1969, 61.
158. TNA, SP 1/108, fos. 185v–186r; Bush, 1996, 234.
159. Cross and Vickers, 1995, 395.
160. Haigh, 1969, 78.
161. TNA, SP 1/118, fo. 6r.
162. Haigh, 1969, 96–7.
163. TNA, SP 1/114, fo. 17r.
164. *LP*, 11, 1231.
165. *LP*, 12/1, 389.
166. *LP*, 12/1, 315.
167. BL, MS Cotton Cleopatra E IV, fos. 105r–111v; TNA, SP 1/112, fo. 91r.
168. Bettey, 1989, 25.
169. TNA, SP 1/121, fos. 31r–v at 31r.
170. TNA, SP 1/119, fo. 114r.
171. TNA, SP 1/121, fo. 85r.
172. John Amadas of Tavistock, one-time MP, was ordered to supply men to serve the Crown: TNA, SP 1/178, fo. 59r.
173. Speight, 1994. TNA, SP 1/118, fo. 247r.
174. TNA, SP 1/118, fos. 247r–248r.
175. TNA, SP 1/121, fos. 235r–236r; SP 1/124, fos. 83r–84r.
176. TNA, SP 1/101, fo. 126r.
177. *LP*, 3/2, 1134, 1172.
178. Summerson, 1993, ii. 622.
179. Hall, 1809, 822.
180. Stow, 1592, 968.
181. Hall, 1809, 823.
182. TNA, SP 1/124, fo. 132r.

183. BL, MS Cotton Cleopatra E IV, fo. 250v.
184. TNA, SP 1/124, fo. 132r.
185. Rex, 2002, 45.
186. BL, MS Cotton Cleopatra E IV, fo. 199r.
187. Ibid, E IV, fo. 116v–117r. This is the second of two dated letters of 8 August 1535 (TNA, SP 1/95, fo. 48r) and 31 January 1536. Two undated letters also survive: SP 1/95, fo. 49r; SP 1/97, fo. 272r. See also Greatrex, 1997, 853–4.
188. An undated fair-copy memorandum of allegations against Abbot Roger Rodden of Abbotsbury by one of his monks, William Grey, survives as TNA, SP 1/100, fo. 11r. Another similar schedule concerning Abbot Thomas Corton of Cerne is in SP 1/89, fo. 104r.
189. BL, MS Cotton Cleopatra E IV, fo. 198r.
190. TNA, SP 1/101, fo. 105r.
191. BL, MS Cotton Cleopatra E IV, fo. 60r.
191. TNA, SP 1/104, fo. 39r.
193. See below, 370–1.
194. *LP*, 14/1, 4; 14/2, 418.
195. BL, MS Cotton Cleopatra E IV, fos. 15r–19v at 18v (clause 50); Wilkins, 1737, iii. 786–9.
196. *LP*, 8, 822.
197. TNA, SP 1/92, fo. 104r.
198. *LP*, 10, 624.
199. TNA, SP 1/98, fo. 54v.
200. TNA, SP 1/239, fo. 335r.
201. TNA, SP 1/101, fo. 58r.
202. TNA, SP 1/103, fo. 35r.
203. TNA, SP 1/103, fo. 106r.
204. TNA, SP 1/141, fo. 131r.
205. TNA, SP 1/133, fo. 170r.
206. TNA, SP 1/123, fo. 140r; SP 1/116, fo. 26r.
207. TNA, SP 1/121, fo. 120r.
208. TNA, SP 1/95, fo. 66r.
209. TNA, SP 3/6, fo. 42r.
210. Weever, 1631, cx.
211. TNA, SP 1/101, fo. 109r.
212. Norwich Cathedral Priory ran 6,500 sheep in 1494. John Hales, mid-century clerk of the Hanaper, counted 3 million sheep across the country as whole: Rose, 2018, 24–36 at 24, 173. See also Youings, 1967, 312–14.
213. BL, MS Cotton Cleopatra E IV, fo. 255r.
214. TNA, SP 1/120, fo. 26v.
215. Ibid.
216. See above, 49, 72, 106–9.
217. TNA, SP 1/157, fo. 95r.
218. Counted in the larder at Tilty were 46 couple of saltfish, 22 couple of ling and 31 couple of stockfish: TNA, SP 1/102, fo. 138r. Sir William Fairfax rendered account for 53s worth of red and white herring wasted at North Ferriby Priory: TNA, SP 1/117, fo. 216r. At Butley Priory they found a fish-house and a 'sealbote': TNA, SP 1/129, fo. 139r.
219. TNA, SP 1/101, fos. 127r, 131v.
220. TNA, SP 1/142, fo. 198r.
221. TNA, SP 1/133, fo. 235r.
222. TNA, SP 1/101, fo. 109r.
223. TNA, SP 1/153, fo. 126r.
224. Carter, 2013, 156.
225. TNA, SP 1/101, fo. 109r.
226. TNA, C 1/1057/6–7.

227. TNA, SP 1/105, fo. 111r; SP 1/106, fo. 35r.
228. TNA, SP 1/122, fo. 198v.
229. TNA, SP 1/36, fo. 126r.
230. Haigh, 1969, 108; Hoyle, 1989.
231. BL, MS Harley, 144, fos. 31r–35r.
232. Derbyshire Record Office, D258/27/3/1.
233. TNA, SP 1/144, fo. 151r.
234. TNA, E 322/1/1.
235. TNA, SP 10/6, fo. 49r.
236. Thomas, 1992a, 69.
237. Merriman, 1902, Letter 184, ii. 52–3.
238. Wiltshire and Swindon History Centre 1332/3/2/1/19. The priory had been granted to Edward Seymour by letters patent dated 6 June 1536: *LP*, 10, 1256 (6).
239. West Yorkshire Archive Service, WYL150/962 (23/13).
240. TNA, C 1/930/42.
241. TNA, C1/1123/51. See also Davidson, 1843, 105–11; Baskerville, 1940, 200–1.
242. Statham, 2003, xxviii.
243. Baskerville, 1940, 200.
244. BL, MS Harley 308, fos. 124r–125v.
245. West Yorkshire Archive Service, WYL150/961 (13/14).
246. BL, MS Harley 3970, fos. 23v–34r (grant to organist at fos. 28r–29r).
247. See, for example, an indenture dated 10 March 1539: Sheffield Archives, BFM/478.
248. Sparks, 1978, 124–6.
249. Wiltshire and Swindon History Centre, 132/3.
250. TNA, SP 1/127, fo. 89r.
251. TNA, SP 1/128, fos. 87r–88r at 88r.
252. Erler, 2011.
253. Youings, 1967, 329.
254. BL, MS Cotton Titus B I, fo. 403r.
255. BL, MS Cotton Cleopatra E IV, fo. 238r.
256. *LP*, 14/1, 1355.
257. *LP*, 14/2, 256.
258. Epsam was remembered by Edward Hall as the last clothed monk in England; Thomas Fuller believed that he had been arrested three years before, therefore in 1537. There is no record of him in the authoritative list of Westminster monks: Pearce, 1916.
259. Wiltshire and Swindon History Centre, 1946/4/3J/2.
260. Merriman, 1902, Letter 335, ii. 248.
261. TNA, SP 1/153, fo. 126r.
262. Thornton, 2006, 113–14.
263. Pocock, 1878, 287.
264. TNA, SP 1/134, fo. 236r.
265. *LP*, 13/1, 845.
266. Mills, 1996, 25.
267. TNA, SP 1/104, fos. 227r–232v at 227r–v.
268. TNA, SP 1/107, fo. 140r.
269. TNA, SP 1/132, fos. 76r–85r; see also Doggett, 2004a.
270. The date of the executions is not recorded but might be surmised from the dating of the Ministers' accounts: Scott Thomson, 1933, 139.
271. Cross, 2004a; Doggett, 2004c; Ward, 2004.
272. Hall, 1809, 852.
273. Fuller, 1845, iii. 431–2.
274. TNA, SP 1/154, fos. 79r–99r.
275. Gasquet, 1893, i. vii, 178.

276. TNA, SP 1/153, fo. 25r.
277. TNA, SP 1/153, fo. 78r, 113r.
278. TNA, SP 1/55, fo. 50r.
279. TNA, SP 1/155; BL, MS Cotton Titus B III, fo. 446r.
280. TNA, SP 1/153, fo. 102r.
281. *LP*, 14/2, 206.
282. TNA, SP 1/13, fo. 193r; SP 1/150, fo. 93r.
283. TNA, SP 1/139, fo. 144r.
284. TNA, SP 1/154, fos. 90r–98r.
285. Higgs, 1998, 129–47 at 140.
286. John Valey or Faley: BL, MS Cotton Cleopatra E V, fo. 410r.
287. TNA, SP 1/150, fo. 138v.
288. TNA, SP 1/154, fo. 60r.
289. Stow, 1592, 977.
290. *LP*, 16, 370.
291. *LP*, 16, 146.
292. TNA, SP 1/158, fo. 88r.
293. TNA, SP 1/157, fo. 57r.
294. Wood, 2007, 61.
295. TNA, SP 1/158, fo. 116r.
296. *LP*, 16, 423.
297. Anon., 1542, A7r, B1v–2r, C4r, E6v–7r.
298. TNA, SP 1/163, fo. 38r.

Chapter VII Punysshid, Subprest and Put Downe

1. TNA, SP 1/105, fo. 274r.
2. TNA, SP 1/99 fo. 60r. Legh had discovered the deal with Woodhouse in late November.
3. Holinshed, 1577, 1571.
4. Hall, 1809, 819.
5. Hoyle, 1995a, 290–4.
6. Two draft texts survive, BL, MS Cotton Vespasian C XIV/2, fo. 147r, and TNA, SP 6/1, fo. 116r–119r; Elton, 1974, 71.
7. BL, MS Cotton Cleopatra E IV, fos. 258v–259r at 258v.
8. A. N. Shaw, at pains to prove their commitment to the cause, acknowledges their 'hurry' although still asserts that they did not 'cut any corners': Shaw, 2003, 229.
9. Letter dated 22 October 1535: TNA, SP1/98, fo. 48r–v at 48v.
10. TNA, SP1/98, fo. 71r.
11. TNA, SP1/98, fo. 14r.
12. TNA, SP1/98, fo. 71r.
13. BL, MS Cotton Cleopatra E IV, fo. 152r.
14. Ibid, fo. 130r.
15. TNA, SP 1/195, fo. 64r; BL, MS Cotton Cleopatra E IV, fo. 47r.
16. TNA, SP 1/101, fo. 126r.
17. BL, MS Cotton Claudius E IV, fo. 62r.
18. Merriman, 1902, Letter 136, 1–3 at 2.
19. 'The king is anxious to know the real inclination of the French king,' wrote Cromwell to Gardiner on 7 December: *LP*, 9, 8. The imperial ambassador Chapuys found the king eager to discuss his foreign affairs on 30 December: *LP*, 9, 1036. They are prominent also among the remembrances assigned by the HMSO editors to year's end 1535: BL, MS Cotton Titus B I, fo. 475r.
20. Lehmberg, 1970, 220.
21. TNA, SP 1/99, fo. 159r.

22. BL, MS Cotton Cleopatra E VI, fo. 232r.
23. BL, MS Cotton Titus B I, fo. 422r–v at 422r; TNA, SP 1/102, fos. 5r–6r.
24. TNA, SP 1/101, fo. 49r–v.
25. BL, MS Cotton Cleopatra E IV, fo. 136r–v at 136v.
26. *LP*, 10, 284.
27. TNA, SP 1/99, fo. 109r.
28. Ibid, fo. 113r.
29. Lambeth Palace Library, MS F I Vv, fos. 38v–43r; Chambers, 1966, 34–8.
30. For the Llŷn monasteries see Stöber and Austin, 2013, 43–4, 48. The canons of nearby Bardsey remained until 1537. The expulsion of Observant friars from Guernsey may have deterred any continuation at Herm. See Thornton, 2012, 30, 58n, 73. For Tresco see Snell, 1967, 23, 130. It may be telling that the surrender of the parent monastery of Tavistock does not specify an incumbent for the Scillian outpost: TNA, E322/236; *LP*, 14/1, 429. The archaeological record has not as yet clarified the timing of its decommissioning: Cornwall and Scilly Islands HER, 7324/7324.01.
31. TNA, SP 1/102, fo. 127r.
32. TNA, SP 1/137, fo. 146r.
33. BL, MS Cotton Cleopatra E IV, fo. 301r–v at 301v.
34. Ibid, fo. 131r; Letter dated 18 March 1536: *LP*, 10, 494.
35. St Clare Byrne, 1981, iii. 283 (Letter 646).
36. TNA, SP 1/102, 177r.
37. Oxford, Bodl. MS Douce 363, fo. 100v.
38. TNA, SP 3/6, fo. 144r; *LP*, 10, 339.
39. Luders et al., 1810–28, iii. 575.
40. Ibid, 576.
41. Corrie, 1844, i. 123.
42. TNA, SP 1/98, fo. 48r
43. TNA, SP 1/102, fo. 83r.
44. Shaw, 2003, 398.
45. Loades, 1968, 159.
46. TNA, SP 1/102, fos. 5r–6r.
47. Hoyle, 1995a, 284–90.
48. Pocock, 1878, 293.
49. Ives, 2004, 307–10. The force of the queen's own influence has been doubted: Bernard, 2005, 240.
50. Herrtage, 1878, xlvii–lxiii at liv, lvi.
51. Luders et al., 1810–28, iii. 575–8.
52. TNA, SP 1/106, fo. 189r; Merriman, 1902, Letter 163.
53. Loades, 1968, 159.
54. Ibid, 160.
55. Luders et al., 1810–28, iii. 584, 599–601, 623.
56. Ibid, 551, 558–62, 601.
57. Hall, 1809, 818–19; Grafton saw the fateful moment as parliament's creation of the supremacy itself: Grafton, 1543, fo. 159r; see also Holinshed, 1577, 1564.
58. Lisle began pressing Hussee to enquire after abbey grants as early as the end of April 1536. He was narrowing the field to Devon by the end of May and in early August Frithelstock had become the target. When Christmas came it still eluded him: St Clare Byrne, 1981, iii. 343–4, 372–3, 468–71, 482–4, 498–501, 505–6, 520–2, 524–7, 533–40, 570–1, 576–8 (Letters 684, 703, 753, 753a, 765, 774, 779, 784, 786–7, 792–4, 808, 813–14).
59. BL, MS Cotton Cleopatra E IV, fo. 271r.
60. *LP*, 10, 278.
61. TNA, SP 1/102, fo. 15r.
62. TNA, E 322/148 (Marton); E322/104 (Hornby).

63. LP, 10, 360.
64. TNA, E322/20 (Bilsington); E322/343 (Tilty).
65. Lehmberg, 1970, 227.
66. TNA, SP 1/103, fo. 13r; LP, 10, 547.
67. LP, 10, 562.
68. TNA, SP 1/102, fo. 123r.
69. BL, MS Cotton Cleopatra E IV, fo. 280r.
70. TNA, SP 5/3, fos. 107v–108r.
71. LP, 10, 1256.
72. BL, MS Cotton Cleopatra E IV, fo. 332r–v.
73. The surviving sequence of draft instructions has been assigned to 24 April but the texts themselves are undated: TNA, SP 5/4, fos. 133r–151v.
74. Letters were sent to Cromwell on 19 May, reporting the work of the past two days: TNA, SP 1/104, fos. 30r, 32r.
75. Burnet, 1865, iii, 222.
76. TNA, SP1/104, fo. 166r.
77. BL, MS Cotton Cleopatra E IV, fos, 336r, 342v–343r.
78. TNA, DL, 11/47.
79. BL, MS Cotton Cleopatra E IV, fo. 237r.
80. TNA, SP 1/103, fo. 59r.
81. St Clare Byrne, 1981, iii. 402 (Letter 714).
82. Bradshaw, 1974, 47–9.
83. TNA, E117/12/33 (1 June 1536).
84. BL, MS Cotton Cleopatra E IV, fo. 241r.
85. Sir Ralph Ellerker, leader of the Yorkshire commissioners, had reached Hull by 26 May and was heading north (from Swine) two days later: TNA, SP1/104, fo. 64r. Their circuit continued through June. Their accounts are collected in SP 5/2.
86. The defacing of houses in Bedfordshire was reported on 8 September: TNA, SP 1/106, fo. 48r.
87. TNA, SP 1/105, fo. 257r.
88. Freeman himself was in the south-east corner of the county by 7 September: TNA, SP 1/106, fo. 142r.
89. LP, 11, 889.
90. St Clare Byrne, 1981, iii. 505–6 at 505 (Letter 779).
91. BL, MS Cotton Appendix XXVIII, fo. 119r. The following spring it was reported that 'they [the rebels] put in canons at St Agatha's beside Richmond': LP, 12/1, 29.
92. TNA, SP 1/102, fo. 27r.
93. LP, 12/1, 311.
94. TNA, SP 1/102, fo. 27r; SP 1/108, fo. 165r.
95. TNA, SP 5/5, fos. 133r–134v; 145r–146v; 149r–151v.
96. TNA, SP 5/5, fos. 149r–151v.
97. TNA, SP 1/106, fo. 189r; Merriman, 1902, Letter 163, 31–2.
98. TNA, SP 1/104, fo. 210r.
99. TNA, SP 1/240, fo. 222r.
100. TNA, SP 3/12, fo. 116r.
101. TNA, SP 1/101, fo. 154r.
102. TNA, SP 1/112, fo. 205r.
103. TNA, SP 1/102, fo. 22r.
104. Gasquet, 1894, 275.
105. TNA, SP 1/103, fo. 28r.
106. TNA, SP 1/113, fo. 22r.
107. TNA, SP 1/95, fo. 12r.
108. TNA, SP 7/1, fo. 38r.
109. TNA, SP 1/104, fo. 32r.

110. BL, MS Cotton Cleopatra E IV, fo. 329r.
111. Ibid, fo. 249r.
112. *LP*, 13/1, 625.
113. TNA, SP 1/85, fo. 65r.
114. TNA, DL 29/23/3, m. 17d; *LP*, 11, 1417 (g.18); Haigh, 1969, 23.
115. *LP*, 11, 1217 (13).
116. *LP*, 11, 1417 (2); 13/1, 487 (3).
117. BL, MS Cotton Cleopatra E IV, fo. 249r.
118. TNA, SP 1/105, fo. 199r.
119. Bourchier wrote of Beeleigh: TNA, SP 1/102, fo. 217r; De la Warr of Boxgrove: BL, MS Cotton Cleopatra E IV, fo. 280r; Stafford of the priories of Fineshade and Worspring: BL, MS Cotton Cleopatra E IV, fo. 232r; Edgcombe of Cornworthy and Totnes: TNA, SP 1/103, fo. 21r.
120. TNA, SP 1/102, fo. 217r.
121. *LP*, 11, 517.
122. BL, MS Cotton Cleopatra E IV, fo. 280r.
123. TNA, SP 1/107, fo. 133r.
124. TNA, SP 1/104, fo. 248r.
125. TNA, SP 1/105, fo. 248r.
126. TNA, SP 1/108, fo. 14r.
127. TNA, SP 1/111, fo. 26r; SP 1/112, fo. 47r.
128. Merriman, 1902, Letter 166, 34.
129. TNA, SP 1/105, fo. 243r.
130. TNA, SP 5/3, fo. 13r.
131. Ibid, fo. 22r.
132. TNA, SP 1/105, fo. 243r.
133. Lambeth Palace Library, MS F I Vv, fos. 28v, 32r–33v, 34v–35r; Chambers, 1966, 23–9.
134. Cambridge, Corpus Christi College, MS 111, 319–33.
135. For example, Bindon (Dorset); Lacock (Wiltshire); Polsloe (Devon); Wymondham (Norfolk): Cambridge, Corpus Christi College, MS 111, 320, 332–3.
136. Cambridge, Corpus Christi College, MS 111, 327–8.
137. *LP*, 11, 4.
138. Cambridge, Corpus Christi College, MS 111, 319.
139. Ibid, 324.
140. Clark, 1989, 133.
141. Brown, 1997, 50.
142. Lambeth Palace Library, MS F I Vv, fo. 145v (Bury St Edmunds), 148v (Westminster), 154r (Reading), 157v (Milton), 162v (Winchcombe), 165r (St Mary Graces); Chambers, 1966, 104, 110, 113, 116, 118.
143. Lambeth Palace Library, MS F I Vv, fos. 114r–133v at 133r–v; Chambers, 1966, 83–96 at 95–6. Geoffrey Baskerville's view of the rapid distribution of faculties is misplaced: Baskerville, 1933, 202.
144. Lambeth Palace Library, MS F I Vv, fo. 128r; Chambers, 1966, 92.
145. TNA, SP 5/3, fo. 79r.
146. Nichols, 1852, 285.
147. TNA, SP1/104, fo. 32r.
148. BL, Stowe MS 141; BL, MS Cotton Cleopatra E IV, fo. 241r; TNA, SP 1/104, fo. 32r; *LP*, 14/1, 519; BL, MS Add. 11041, fo. 31r.
149. TNA, SP 5/1, fo. 235r–v.
150. TNA, SP 1/97, fo. 22r; TNA, SP 1/115, fos. 105r–106v; TNA, SP 1/113, fo. 165r. Leighton wrote 'I have not in all the worlde V libras [£5] sterling *ad totam familiam alendam* (for the support of the whole family)'.
151. TNA, SP 1/105, fo. 243r.

152. He pressed the grant of the demesne of Hagnaby Abbey (Lincolnshire): TNA, SP 1/136, fo. 28r.
153. For the process see Knowles, 1959, 478–9; Shaw, 2003, 458–9.
154. TNA, SP 1/103, fo. 186r.
155. TNA, SP 1/112, fo. 137r.
156. TNA, SP 1/114, fo. 26r; *LP*, 13/1, 1131. The need for the younger Scudamore was reiterated the following year: *LP*, 14/1, 1221.
157. TNA, SP 1/155, fo. 82r.
158. Dowling, 1990, 60–1.
159. Ibid, 57, 59.
160. *LP*, 10, 284.
161. BL, MS Add. 46701.
162. TNA, SP 1/241, fo. 256r.
163. TNA, SP 1/121, fo. 1r.
164. *LP*, 12/2, 911.
165. BL, MS Cotton Cleopatra E IV, fo. 182r; *LP*, 14/1, 871; Elton, 1974, 72–7.
166. Norfolk Record Office, LEST/NG2.
167. St Clare Byrne, 1981, iii. 500 (Letter 774).
168. Hall, 1809, 819.
169. Melancthon, 1536, X iiiv.
170. Latimer, 1537, 27.
171. TNA, SP 1/102, fo. 127r.
172. Whitford, 1537; Gwynneth, 1536.
173. Heale, 2004, 308.
174. Knowles and Hadcock, 1971, 52–8; Heale, 2004, 311–13. For the recall from the Durham dependency at Lytham see Haigh, 1969, 20.
175. Knowles and Hadcock, 1971, 52–3; Savine, 1909, 281–2.
176. TNA, SP 1/102, fo. 204r.
177. Clark, 2000, 309–11.
178. Smith, 2008, 33, 64–5, 78, 86–7.
179. Ibid, 261, 335–6, 339.
180. Ibid, 281, 294.
181. Nichols, 1852, 38–9.
182. TNA, SP 1/110, fo. 6r.
183. Luders et al., 1810–28, iii. 558–62 (27 Henry VIII c. 25).
184. TNA, SP 1/103, fo. 275r.
185. Ibid, fo. 52r.
186. Shropshire Archives, LB/5/2/257.
187. BL, MS Cotton Cleopatra E IV, fo. 141r.
188. Williams, 1997, 90.
189 TNA, SP 3/5, fo. 30r; SP 3/4, fo. 99r.
190. *LP*, 12/2, 1008; TNA, SP 1/241, fo. 280.
191. TNA, SP 1/103, fo. 34r.
192. BL, MS Cotton Cleopatra E V, fo. 395r; TNA, SP 1/117, fo. 152r.
193. TNA, SP 1/114, fo. 46r–v; SP 1/119, fo. 183r.
194. TNA, SP 1/117, fo. 16r; SP 1/127, fo. 78r; SP 1/141, fo. 241r.
195. Hall, 1809, 828.
196. Ibid; Holinshed, 1577, 1578.
197. TNA, SP 1/117, fo. 152v.
198. Nichols, 1859, 283.
199. Douglas Hamilton, 1875, 66.
200. TNA, SP 1/105, fo. 258r.
201. Devon Heritage Centre, 123M/0/2.

202. Traskey, 1978, 123; TNA, SC6 2316 (account for 28–29 Henry VIII, i.e. 1536–1538).
203. TNA, SP 1/5, fos. 8r–10r.
204. *LP*, 10, 124.
205. London Metropolitan Archives, Guildhall Library MS 9531/11 (Register of John Stokesley, bishop of London, 1530–9), fo. 131r.
206. Lincolnshire Archives, DIOC/REG/26 (Register of John Longland, bishop of Lincoln, 1521–47), fos. 51r–56r.
207. Herefordshire Record Office, Hereford Diocesan Registry, unclassified (Register of Edward Fox, bishop of Hereford, 1535–8), fo. 38r.
208. For example, at the London Minories, where the name of one Bridget, 'novice' was later crossed through: *LP*, 14/1, 680.
209. For example, at Wilton Abbey, where Anne Ashe received 40s and the next most junior women received £4: *LP*, 14/1, 597.
210. The account of John Forest's attitude was from his own colleague, John Laurence, and dated from late November 1537. Forest had courted attention by receiving the confession of public figures such as John, Lord Mordaunt: BL, MS Cotton Cleopatra E IV, fos. 161r–v, 164r.
211. *LP*, 13/1, 225.
212. Ibid, 926.
213. *LP*, 13/1, 335; TNA SP 1/134, fo. 114r.
214. TNA, SP 1/144, fo. 85r.
215. St Clare Byrne, 1981, v. 303–4 (Letter 1282); 328–9 (Letter 1305).
216. TNA, SP 1/127, fo. 127r.
217. TNA, SP 1/91, fo. 157r.
218. TNA, SP 1/139, fo. 17v.
219. Shropshire Record Office, LB/5/2/130.
220. Lowe, 2010, 101.
221. Frere, 1910, ii. 15–18 at 16 (Latimer, Worcester); 19–24 (Lee, Coventry and Lichfield).
222. Ibid, 53–60 at 54 (Shaxton, Salisbury); 65–6 at 66 (Cranmer, sede vacante, Hereford).
223. Holder, 2017, 115, 308.
224. BL, MS Cotton Cleopatra E IV, fo. 301r.
225. Suffolk Record Office, HD 1538/274/11.
226. Ibid, comparing C/3/10/2/3/8/5 (a lease of 1535), C/3/10/2/3/8/6 (an enfeoffment of 1537).
227. Lowe, 2010, 49.
228. TNA, SP 3/3, fo. 23r.
229. TNA, SP 1/136, fo. 163r.
230. TNA, SP 1/134, fo. 114r.
231. TNA, SP 1/134, fo. 123v.
232. Frere, 1910, ii. 44–52 at 48 (Lee, Hereford); 53–60 at 59–60 (Shaxton, Salisbury).
233. *LP*, 13/2, 133.
234. *LP*, 13/2, 133.
235. BL, MS Cotton Cleopatra E IV, fo. 229r.
236. Pollard, Wriothesley and John Williams reported dismantling the shrine of St Swithun at Winchester on 21 September: TNA, SP 1/136, fo. 164r–v. Latimer had seen to the removal of the Holy Blood of Hailes, among others, by 16 November: Sp 1/139, fo. 108v. A commission for Sussex was dispatched on 14 December: SP 1/140, fo. 87v–88r.
237. Ridley, 1538, E2r.
238. Hall, 1809, 826; Stow, 1592, 970.
239. Canterbury Cathedral Archives, CCA-DCc-ChChLet/I/81.
240. TNA, SP 1/124, fo. 111r.
241. TNA, SP 1/94, fo. 94r–v.
242. BL, MS Cotton Cleopatra E IV, fos. 141r, 143v.
243. Hunt, 2014, 308–9.
244. TNA, SP 3/12, fo. 81r.

245. Smith, 1943, 204–5.
246. TNA, SP 5/2, fo. 250r.
247. *LP*, 13/2, 1280.
248. *LP*, 13/2, 457 (3).
249. Ibid, 457.
250. Ibid, 1128.
251. TNA, SP 1/101, fo. 135r.
252. Clark, 2000, 311.
253. Cross and Frost, 2014, 109.
254. Bernard, 2011, 406–7.
255. TNA, E 322/22; *LP*, 13/2, 422. Another instance is the surrender deed of the monks of St Andrew's, Northampton: E322/93.
256. BL, MS Harley 3970, fos. 13v–14v. 17v–19v, 22r–26v, 27r–28r, 29r–30r.
257. TNA, E 118 11/122.
258. TNA, SP 1/144, fo. 151r.
259. TNA, E 314/62.
260. The loan was pursued after the dissolution by the monk in question, Richard Blake: TNA C1/1197/31.
261. TNA, SP 1/141, fo. 180r.
262. TNA, SP 1/242, fo. 64r.
263. Derbyshire Record Office, DDM 19/24.
264. The first of these books was recorded in the library of Balliol College, Oxford, but has since been lost. The second is now at Windsor, St George's Chapel, III. C. This carries what appears to be the same inscription, 'ex emptione 1538', together with a reference to the chapter house but does not name Sagar.
265. BL, MS Harley 3970, fo. 1v.
266. Leighton, 1883, 98.
267. Hall, 1809, 821.
268. *LP*, 13/2, 1280. For comparable payments in 1534 see TNA, SP/2, fo. 2r.
269. *LP*, 13/2, 1280.
270. TNA, SP 1/128, fo. 92r.
271. Ibid., fos. 37r, 85r–86v, 92r, 122r, 145r; 1/136, fo. 131r.
272. Ibid, fo. 13r.
273. Ibid, fo. 87r.
274. BL, MS Cotton Cleopatra E IV, fo. 86r.
275. Ibid, fo. 271r.
276. TNA, SP 1/139, fo. 154r.
277. TNA, SP 1/242, fo. 101r.
278. TNA, SP 1/138, fo. 45r.
279. TNA, SP 1/128, fo. 37r; SP 1/134, fo. 248r.
280. St Clare Byrne, 1981, v. 18–20 (Letter 1090), 30–1 (Letter 1098), 96–7 (Letter 1138).
281. BL, MS Cotton Cleopatra E IV, fo. 307r.
282. TNA, SP 1/157, fo. 39r.
283. TNA, SP 1/128, fo. 37r.
284. BL, MS Cotton Cleopatra E IV, fo. 284r.
285. TNA, SP 1/127, fo. 127r.
286. TNA, E 322/27.
287. TNA, E 322/29.
288. TNA, E 322/16.
289. San Marino, CA, Huntington Library, MS EL 9 H 15, fo. 117v.
290. Knowles, 1964, 776.
291. Lapidge and Winterbottom 1991, 31–3.
292. For example, TNA, E322/14 (Barking); E322/93 (Godstow).

293. For possible instances see E/322 (St Albans); E36/153, fo. 19r (Chester, Carmelites).
294. Hampshire Record Office, DC/B/12.
295. TNA, SP 1/5, fo. 10r.
296. TNA, E 314/78.
297. TNA, SP 1/157, fos. 90r–91r at 90v–91r.
298. BL, MS Add. 11041, fo. 68r–v.
299. TNA, E 40/5346.
300. At Winchester, after conducting the formal act of surrender, Ingworth seems to have buckled when a Franciscan prior pressed him for readmission with four other friars: TNA, SP 1/134, fo. 241r.
301. TNA, SP 1/135, fo. 87r; SP 1/136, fo. 21r.
302. Sparks, 1978, 108; TNA, E322/76.
303. BL, MS Cotton Appendix XXVIII, fo. 41v.
304. TNA, SP 1/143, fo. 7r. A letter from Ralph Sadler to Cromwell concerning the king's reading of ambassadors' dispatches is signed 'at Waltham' but undated: TNA, SP 1/143, fo. 19r.
305. *LP*, 14/2, 781.
306. BL, MS Cotton Cleopatra E V, fo. 346r.
307. BL, MS Cotton Cleopatra E IV, fo. 316r.
308. Ibid, fo. 291r.
309. TNA, SP 1/242, fo. 121r.
310. TNA, SP 1/134, fo. 302r.
311. TNA, SP 1/142, fos. 42r, 52r.
312. Ibid, 222r.
313. Ibid, fo. 101r.
314. Ibid, fos. 67r, 99r.
315. Ibid, fo. 151r.
316. TNA, SP 1/143, fo. 124r.
317. TNA, SP 1/144, fo. 5r.
318. Luders et al., 1810–28, iii. 733–9 at 733.
319. Ibid.
320. Ibid, 734–5.
321. TNA, SP 1/144, fo. 151r.
322. TNA, SP 1/143, fo. 146r; SP 1/152, fo. 86r.
323. TNA, SP 1/144, fo. 191r.
324. He wrote from Paris to Edmund Bonner on 1 March: TNA, SP 1/44; *LP*, 14/1, 416.
325. Douglas Hamilton, 1875, 106–7, 109.
326. TNA, SP 1/129, fo. 83v.
327. *LP*, 13, 2, 306.
328. TNA, SP 1/136, fo. 86r.
329. Cross and Vickers, 1995, 332; Knowles and Hadcock, 1971, 169.
330. Lincolnshire Archives, DIOC/REG/26, fo. 59v.
331. Borthwick Institute, Abp Reg 28 (Register of Archbishop Edward Lee, 1531–44), fo. 198r–v.
332. TNA, SP 5/1, fo. 8r.
333. Ibid.
334. BL, MS Cotton Cleopatra E IV, fo. 307r.
335. TNA, C 1/1073/31.
336. WAM 25103; Pearce, 1916, 190.
337. TNA, SP 1/154, fo. 60r.
338. TNA, SP 1/150, fo. 138v.
339. TNA, SP 1/151, fo.126r.
340. TNA, SP 1/152, fo. 51r.
341. TNA, E 36/154.
342. TNA, SP 1/152, fo. 84v.

343. Ibid, fo. 104r.
344. TNA, SP 1/154, fo. 132r.
345. TNA, SP 1/156, fo. 96r; Brown, 1997, 69–71. The similar scheme to retain St Mary Graces as a social resource for London was proposed by the city authorities in 1538: Grainger and Phillpotts, 2011, 58.
346. Heale, 2016, 331–8.
347. BL, MS Cotton Titus B I, fo. 443r–v.
348. TNA, SP 1/155, fo. 82r.
349. TNA, SP 1/154, fo. 13r.
350. Ibid, fo. 24r.
351. Hinde, 1952, 212.
352. BL, MS Cotton Cleopatra E IV, fo. 307r.
353. *LP*, xv, 359, 551.
354. William Alynger, his predecessor, had died in January 1540: TNA, PCC, Prob. 11/28/3.
355. Luders et al., 1810–28, iii. 733–9; Smith, 2008, 319.
356. Smith, 2008, 141, 503.
357. Douglas Hamilton, 1875, 109.
358. Ibid, 105.
359. Ibid, 1875, 120.
360. Hall, 1809, 840.
361. Hardyng, 1543, fo. 160r–v.
362. Baxter, 2016, 140.
363. Anon., 1540, 1.
364. *LP*, 15, 31, 259; see also Erler, 2013, 51–2.
365. *LP*, 14/2, 750.
366. TNA, SP 1/157, fo. 125r.
367. TNA, SP 1/160, fo. 132r. Perhaps Temple Bruer: *LP*, 16, 1088; 17, 137; Bradshaw, 1974, 162–80 at 162.
368. San Marino, California, Huntington Library, MS EL 9 H 15, fo. 17v.

Chapter VIII Nothing Endid

1. BL, MS Cotton Cleopatra E IV, fo. 277r–v; TNA, SP 1/130, fo. 124r.
2. Ibid, fo. 277r.
3. Mayhew, 2014, 60.
4. Corrie, 1844–5, i. 391.
5. Foxe, 1563, IV, 824.
6. MacCulloch, 1998, 100.
7. Dickens, 1959, 124.
8. Camden, 1587, 310.
9. Dickens, 1959, 121.
10. Camden, 1587, 309.
11. Oxford, Bodl. MS Douce 363, fo. 95r.
12. Marvell, *Upon Appleton House*, xxxiv, 271–2.
13. For an account of the works for Gregory Cromwell see MacCulloch, 2018, 440–1.
14. Toulmin-Smith, 1906–10, i. 272; Doubleday and Page, 1903, 122; Chitty, 1930, 44.
15. John London presided over the surrender of the Coventry friars at the beginning of October 1538; on 20 October the mayor and aldermen complained to Cromwell of his wanton destruction; a week later London, still on circuit, responded claiming that he had acted only within the limit of his commission: TNA, SP 1/137, fo. 238r; SP 1/138, fo. 45r.
16. Willmott, 2020, 25.
17. For such reading of the spoil see Thomas, 2006, 205. For the alternative view see Grainger and Phillpotts, 2011, 59.

18. 'the cytie of Maynchester that sore was defaced with warre of the Danys': Fabyan, 1516, Cvr.
19. TNA, SP 1/104, fo. 191r.
20. TNA, SP 1/240, fo. 36r.
21. 'upon the defacyng of the late monasterye of Boxley,' wrote Jeffrey Chamber in February 1538, 'I dare say . . . to be defaced agayne': TNA, SP 1/129, fo. 12r.
22. East Sussex HER, MES 3267.
23. TNA, SP 1/143, fo. 198r.
24. Anon., 1528, 1 1r.
25. TNA, SP 5/4, fo. 148r–151v at 148r.
26. Ibid, fo. 148r.
27. Ibid, fos. 149v–150r.
28. This is the claim of a fragment of an undated memorandum of John Freeman assigned in the State Papers to 1536: TNA SP 1/240, fo. 37r–v.
29. TNA, SP 5/4, fo. 151r.
30. Luders et al., 1810–28, 733–9.
31. Ibid, 733–9 at 738.
32. TNA, SP 1/143, fo. 183r.
33. See above, 284, 288, 291.
34. TNA, SP 1/137, fo. 238r.
35. TNA, SP 1/104, fo. 111r.
36. TNA, SP 1/129, fo. 83r.
37. BL, MS Cotton Cleopatra E IV, fo. 264r.
38. TNA, SP 1/142, fo. 137r.
39. TNA, SP 1/154, fo. 108r–v.
40. TNA, SP 1/117, fo. 31r.
41. TNA, SP 1/138, fo. 6r.
42. TNA, SP 1/133, fo. 241r.
43. BL, MS Add. 11041, fo. 26r.
44. TNA, SP 1/138, fo. 45r.
45. BL, MS Cotton Cleopatra E IV, fo. 267r.
46. TNA, SP 1/240, fos. 36r–37v at 36r.
47. Ibid, fo. 37r–v.
48. TNA, SP 1/122, fo. 202r.
49. TNA, SP 1/138, fo. 45r.
50. TNA, SP 1/134, fo. 243r.
51. TNA, SP 1/135, fo. 214r.
52. BL, MS Cotton Cleopatra E IV, fos. 319r–320r at 319v.
53. TNA, SP 1/135, fo. 213r.
54. TNA, SP 1/134, fo. 243r.
55. This was reported in depositions taken in East Yorkshire on 10 February: TNA, SP 1/115, fos. 247r–59v at 247r.
56. TNA, SP 1/116, fo. 76r.
57. Forde, Munby and Scott, 2019.
58. TNA, SP 1/138, fo. 45r.
59. TNA, SP 1/129, fo. 12r.
60. TNA, SP 1/138, fo. 45r; BL, MS Cotton Cleopatra E IV, fo. 264r.
61. TNA, SP 1/137, fo. 130r.
62. BL, MS Cotton Cleopatra E IV, fo. 267r.
63. TNA, SP 1/140, fo. 76r.
64. *LP*, 13/2, 88.
65. TNA, SP 5/5; *LP*, 17, 8; Shagan, 2003, 162–3.
66. TNA, SP 1/138, fo. 124r.
67. *LP*, 13/2, 229.

68. *LP*, 14/2, 418.
69. Lyne and Gardiner, 1997, 79, 139.
70. Gilyard-Beer and Coppack, 1986, 162–3; Willmott, 2020, 35–6. For a comparable picture at St Mary Graces see Grainger and Phillpotts, 2011, 62–3.
71. Coppack, 1998, 129.
72. TNA, STAC 2/29/1 1509–57.
73. TNA, E101/459/22.
74. LP, 13/2, 342.
75. Hockey, 1970, 237.
76. LP, 13/2, 168.
77. TNA, SP 1/142, fo. 167r.
78. E 315/172/41; Hibbert, 1910, 237–9.
79. TNA, SP 5/3, fo. 98r–v.
80. St John Hope, 1906, 232.
81. BL, MS Stowe, 141, fo. 37r.
82. Sparks, 1978, 112.
83. See above, 314–15.
84. TNA, SP 1/242, fo. 32r.
85. BL, MS Cotton Cleopatra E IV, fo. 252r.
86. TNA, SP 5/2, fo. 27r.
87. TNA, SP 1/120, fo. 235r.
88. St John Hope, 1906, 233.
89. TNA, SP 5/4, fo. 27r; St John Hope, 1906, 233.
90. Hare, 1985, 184; Greene, 1989, 53–4 (Norton Priory).
91. Greene, 1989, 50–3 at 50. For comparison see also Ryder, 1959, 1 (Kirkstall).
92. Devon Heritage Centre, W1258 M1/1/6.
93. TNA, SP 1/135, fo. 215r.
94. TNA, E 36/115, fos. 1r, 9r, 10r, 11r, 141r, 153r.
95. TNA, SP 1/141, fo. 235r.
96. Myres 1933, 211.
97. TNA, SP 1/120, fo. 235r.
98. Oxford, Bodl. MS Douce 363, fo. 94v.
99. TNA, SC6/HENVIII/3116.
100. Marmalade was among the sweetmeats put before the guests at the funeral of Abbot John Islip in 1532; Caley et al., 1817–30, i. 278; 4 lbs of marmalade was provided for revels to entertain an embassy from the king of France at Greenwich, 1518: *LP*, 2/2, 1215.
101. Mellows, 1940, 25.
102. TNA, SP 1/136, fo. 119r.
103. TNA, SP 1/139, fo. 148r.
104. TNA, SP 1/136, fo. 119r.
105. TNA, SP 1/120, fo. 235r.
106. Schroder, 2020, 264–5.
107. BL, MS Cotton Cleopatra E IV, fo. 136r.
108. BL, MS Add. 11041, fo. 68r–v.
109. TNA, SP 1/136, fo. 119r.
110. TNA, SP 1/129, fo. 91r.
111. *LP*, 14/2, 236.
112. *LP*, 13/2, 457.
113. BL, MS Cotton Titus B I, fo. 446r; TNA, SP 1/5, fo. 2r.
114. TNA, SP 1/157, fo. 125r.
115. Franciscans at Stafford bought vestments at the moment of surrender: BL, MS Add. 11041, fo. 86v.
116. TNA, SP 1/141, fo. 235r.

117. TNA, SP 1/5, fo. 6r.
118. TNA, PCC Prob 11/37/129, fos. 64–65v at 65r.
119. TNA, SP 1/140, fo. 143r. Abbot John Harwood of Vale Royal also asked Thomas Holcroft for the organs from his own chapel: SP 1/136, fo. 96r.
120. BL, MS Cotton Claudius E IV, fo. 324r.
121. 'The seconde time we came to New Colege . . . we fownde all the gret quadrant courte full of the leiffs of Dunce [Duns Scotus]', Leighton to Cromwell, 12 September 1535: BL, MS Cotton Faustina C VII, fo. 210r–v.
122. For example, at Bath Cathedral Priory, where he seized and sent on a copy of the life and miracles of the Blessed Virgin, which he likened to *The Canterbury Tales*: TNA, SP 1/95, fo. 38r.
123. TNA, SP 5/3, fo. 79v.
124. William Forrest acquired an early manuscript of theological works, now BL, MS Burney 357, and a hymnal, now at Oxford, St John's College, MS 60. See also Edwards, 2019.
125. Willmott, 2020, 38.
126. James, 1997, 104.
127. The house was surrendered at the turn of the year. The books are now, respectively: Oxford, Bodl., MS Bodley 602; Oxford, Keble College, A 62.
128. For the deed of surrender see TNA, E322/193. The psalter, formerly Dublin, Chester Beatty Library W 34, was sold to a private collector in 1968.
129. BL, MS Add. 59616.
130. Erler, 2013, 131–43 at 137.
131. Cross and Vickers, 1995, 146.
132. Cross, 1989, 282–3; Cross, 2001, 77–9.
133. TNA, SP 1/138, fo. 124r
134. TNA, SP 1/143, fo. 138r.
135. TNA, SP 1/138, fo. 124r.
136. Ibid, fo. 124; *LP*, 14/1, 3.
137. TNA, SP 1/134, fo. 248r.
138. TNA, SP 1/128, fo. 37r.
139. TNA, SP 1/143, fo. 138r–v.
140. TNA, SP 1/137, fo. 107r.
141. *LP*, 13/1, 375, 1019.
142. TNA, SP 1/242, fo. 37r.
143. *LP*, 13/1, 1019 (1. ii–iii; 2. iii–v; 3. ii).
144. Lambeth Palace Library, MS 109, fo. 161r.
145. Thomas, 2006, 205–6.
146. Lincolnshire HER, 54217.
147. *LP*, 13/2, 342.
148. Gasquet, 1894, 274; St John Hope, 1906, 239.
149. Hare, 1985, 26. For the apparent burial of glass debris see Christie and Coad, 1980, 201; Lyne and Gardiner, 1997, 29–30; Thomas, 2006, 210; Coppack and Keen, 2019, 158.
150. Weever, 1631, 107, 428.
151. TNA, SP 5/4, fo. 148v.
152. For examples, see E36/154.
153. TNA, SP 5/3, fo. 13r.
154. BL, MS Cotton Cleopatra E IV, fo. 291r.
155. East Sussex Record Office, Rye/60/5, fo. 140r; Butler, 1865, 128.
156. TNA, SP 1/120, fo. 235r.
157. TNA, SP 1/135, fo. 63v.
158. TNA, SP 1/140, fo. 76r.
159. BL, MS Stowe 141, fo. 37v.
160. TNA, E315/248/1.
161. *LP*, 13/2, 839; BL, MS Add. 11041, fo. 78r–v.

162. TNA, SP 5/2, fo. 111r.
163. TNA, SP 1/130, fo. 20r.
164. Willmott, 2020, 23–9 at 28.
165. BL, MS Stowe 141, fo. 37r–v.
166. *LP*, 13/1, 1115 (13).
167. Aston, 1973, 242.
168. Hampshire Record Office, 44M69/G8/13.
169. Ibid, 44M69/G8/14.
170. BL, MS Cotton Titus B I, fo. 403r.
171. For example, at Bristol, E 117/14/35.
172. TNA, E 117/14/32.
173. TNA, C 1/1253/20–3; see also E 117/13/3.
174. Lambeth Palace Library, MS 109, fo. 161r.
175. BL, MS Add. 11041, fos. 94r–112r.
176. Holinshed, 1577, 1564.
177. Coppack, 1998, 126.
178. BL, MS Cotton Titus B I, fo. 469r.
179. Oxford, Bodl., MS Douce 363, fo. 95r.
180. TNA, SP 1/153, fo. 126r–v at 126r.
181. Tatton-Brown, 1991, 80. TNA, SP 1/153, fo. 82r.
182. Howard, 2003, 223.
183. TNA, SP 1/116, fo. 277r.
184. Hare, 1999, 20–1.
185. Yorkshire HER, monument number 11085.
186. Doggett, 2002, 51–52.
187. Lincolnshire HER, 30039.
188. Pevsner and Cherry, 2002, 91–93; St John Hope, 1906, 231.
189. Pevsner and Cherry, 2002, 120; Pevsner, 2002, 189, 330.
190. Doggett, 2002, 54, 128–9, 195.
191. BL, MS Cotton Cleopatra E IV, fo. 267v.
192. TNA, SP 1/136, fo. 73r. The Blackfriars was among the earliest grants to a civic authority, confirmed on 25 June 1540: Norfolk Record Office, 4a/3/19.
193. *LP*, 16, 305 (13).
194. *LP*, 19/1, 278, (27); Harbottle and Fraser, 1987, 23–4.
195. TNA, E 36/154.
196. Röhrkasten, 2004, 502.
197. Bliss and Twemlow, 1902, 366; Haigh, 1969, 3 and n.
198. Page, 1897–98, 99–101.
199. Hillaby, 2006, 257.
200. Their repossession cost them £100: *LP*, 19/1, 141 (57); Hare, 1999, 16–17.
201. TNA, SP 15/8, fo. 252r.
202. Prior John Draper had begun his campaign as early as 1538, when he set out before the king the case that Christchurch 'is a very poore towne' set 'in an angle . . . [of] not commodiouse countrey' whose church is 'notonly . . . for poore religiouse men but also is the parish church for the towne': TNA, SP 1/132, fo. 176r.
203. Dorset Record Office, DC/CC/G/1.
204. Pevsner and Wilson, 2002, 494–97; Williams, 1991.
205. St John Hope, 1906, 235; Hare, 1999, 23.
206. Fowler, 1895, 69.
207. Williams, 1997, 96–7.
208. Willmott, 2020, 42–6.
209. Doggett, 2002, 51.
210. Stow, 1908, ii. 202.

211. TNA, SP 1/158, fo. 79r; Essex Record Office, D/DJg L25.
212. TNA, SP 1/158, fo. 79r.
213. Gloucestershire Archives, P201/CW/3/2.
214. Hutchins, 1861–70, i. 354.
215. Williams, 2001, 91.
216. Leach, 1988, 50.
217. Thompson, 1949, 73; Guinn-Chipman, 2013, 9–10.
218. Scarisbrick, 1994, 160–1.
219. Nichols, 1852, 48.
220. Soden, 2003, 283.
221. Harbottle and Fraser, 1987; Willmott, 2020, 83.
222. 'Printed in the house of the late Greyfriars of London': STC, 2nd edn., 2971.5.
223. TNA, SP 1/134, fo. 124v.
224. Hey, Luscombe and Liddy, 2011, 18.
225. Hill, 1956, 92.
226. TNA, SP 1/158, fo. 99r.
227. East Sussex HER, MES 2301.
228. Schofield, 1993, 39; see also Schofield and Lea, 2005, 178.
229. Toulmin-Smith, 1906–10, i. 132.
230. TNA, E322/302; Fergusson and Harrison, 1999, 182, 188.
231. Long, 1888, 199.
232. Tatton-Brown, 2001.
233. Brown, 2011, 89, 256–58.
234. Maxwell Lyte et al. 1924–9, i. 245 (June 1547).
235. Fergusson and Harrison, 1999, 177, 180, 187; Coppack, 1998, 129.
236. For example, at Stanley and Rievaulx: Brown, 2011, 255.
237. Nichols, 1852, 48.
238. Leicestershire HER, MLE 17874.
239. Toulmin-Smith, 1906–10, i. 153, v. 160.
240. Baxter, 2016, 139–40.
241. Weld *et al.*, 1972, plate 58; Hopton, 1993.
242. Fergusson and Harrison, 1999, 180.
243. *LP*, 20, 1.
244. Traskey, 1978, 174.
245. In the decade after the dissolution Twyne wrote up the learned dialogue on the early history of Britain which he had begun with the abbot of St Augustine's and one of his monks, who 'revealed' his knowledge of antiquity to him: Twyne, 1590, 8; Clark, 2004b, 88.
246. Hay, 1938, 106–9.
247. TNA, PCC, Prob. 11/31/530, fos. 305r–307r.
248. Kingsford, 1908, i. 298; TNA, SP1/167, fo. 123r; SP10/1, fo. 67v.
249. Brown and Bentinck, 1873, 543.
250. Lambarde, 1576, 235.
251. See above, 282.
252. Gilchrist, 2005, 208–13.
253. Toulmin-Smith, 1906–10, i. 104.

Chapter IX Changes of Habit

1. TNA, SP 1/135, fo. 126r.
2. Ellis, 1811, 701.
3. Hooper, 1915.
4. Luders et al., 1810–28, iii. 430–2.
5. Taverner, 1536.

6. Morison, 1536, B iiiv–Bivr.
7. Collier, 1838, 28.
8. TNA, SP 1/85, fo. 21r.
9. TNA, SP 1/95, fo. 144r.
10. TNA SP 1/131, fo. 256r; Erler, 2013, 45–6.
11. TNA, SP 1/100, fo. 70r.
12. TNA, E322/279.
13. LP, 12/1, 380.
14. TNA, SP 1/129, fo. 53r.
15. BL, MS Cotton Cleopatra E IV, fo. 319v.
16. Douglas Hamilton, 1875, 82.
17. MacCulloch, 2018, 460.
18. TNA, SP 1/242, fo. 103v.
19. For an estimate of the total population see Rigby, 1995, 215.
20. TNA, SP 1/130, fo. 87r.
21. Oxford, Bodl. MS Douce 363, fo. 95r.
22. Dickens, 1959, 123, 125.
23. The suppression took place on 11 August: TNA, SC6/HENVIII/4517.
24. Augustinian: Barlinch, Bisham, Guisborough, Hartland, Newburgh, Northampton, St James; Benedictine: Chester, Rochester, Sherborne, Winchester, Worcester; Cistercian: Beaulieu, Biddlesden, Buckfast, Coggeshall, Conway, Cwmhir, Fountains, Sibton, Vale Royal, Valle Crucis; Premonstratensian: West Dereham, Titchfield; Benedictine women: West Malling (1536); Nun Appleton (1539/40); Wherwell (1535): Smith, 2008, 33, 62, 70, 86–7, 261, 267–8, 274, 281, 285, 294, 332, 343, 345, 370, 380, 434, 437, 487, 494, 587, 592, 669, 676, 704.
25. BL, MS Cotton Cleopatra E IV, fo. 234r.
26. TNA, SP 5/3, fo. 17r.
27. BL, MS Cotton Cleopatra E IV, fo. 139r; TNA, SP 1/102, fo. 103r.
28. See above, 87.
29. Harrington, 2004. Their presence is witnessed in the will of one of their number, William Alynger, Provisor of the College, proved on 5 January 1540: TNA, PCC Prob. 11/28/3, fo. 2r.
30. TNA, E101/76 (Evesham); TNA, SP 1/157, fo. 95r (Gloucester).
31. Thomas Wilberton and William Wisbech: Greatrex, 1997, 461–2.
32. TNA, SP 1/106, fo. 25r.
33. TNA, E322/208; Lincoln register.
34. For example, for Roche Abbey: TNA, SP 1/141, fo. 235r; LP, 13/1, 1115.
35. 31 Henry VIII c. 13, ii.: Luders et al., 1810–28, 733–9 at 733–4.
36. BL, MS Cotton Titus B I, fo. 398r.
37. TNA, SP 1/140, fo. 100r.
38. TNA, SP 1/135, fo. 45r at 45r.
39. Ibid, fo. 45r–v at 45r.
40. TNA, SP 1/122, fo. 196r.
41. Chambers, 1966, xliv.
42. Surrey History Centre, z/407/MSLb.545.
43. TNA, SP 1/240, fo. 18r.
44. Seven monks each from Swineshead and Vaudey had seen their faculties issued on 4 August 1536, but their brethren, and their colleagues from Kirkstead, Louth and Revesby, not for another nine or ten months: Chambers, 1966, 67, 95–6, 102, 128.
45. LP, 12/1, 380.
46. For a brief account of the administrative shortcomings see Chambers, 1966, li–lii, lv–lvi. Taken in the round the surviving records do not bear out Geoffrey Baskerville's view that 'no time was lost in furnishing these obligatory documents': Baskerville, 1933, 202.
47. TNA, SP 1/104, fo. 249r.
48. Chambers, 1966, 98.

49. BL, MS Cotton Cleopatra EIV, fo. 302r
50. Ibid.
51. TNA, SP 1/144, fo. 85r.
52. TNA, SP 1/135, fo. 85r.
53. TNA, SP 1/134, fos. 114r, 123r; 135, fo. 85r; BL, MS Cotton Cleopatra E IV, fo. 269r.
54. For example, Peter of Mainz, one of the Franciscans present at Llanfaes in 1538. Perhaps also Johannes de Coloribus, one of the Dominicans at Truro and Innocent Tutty among the Franciscans at Salisbury: LP, 13/2, 138, 405, 518.
55. TNA, SP 1/135, fo. 213r; LP, 13/2, 32.
56. TNA, SP 1/104, fo. 197r.
57. TNA, SP 1/133, fo. 170r.
58. TNA, SP 1/136, fo. 96r.
59. TNA, SP 1/128, fos. 85r–86r at 86r.
60. BL, MS Cotton Cleopatra E IV, fo. 283r.
61. BL, MS Harley 3970, fo. 31r–v.
62. LP, 13/1, 1485.
63. LP, 10, 1191 (4, 1).
64. Caley et al., 1817–30, v. 470; *decrepita et non abilis ad equitandum, neque eundum.*
65. LP, 10, 1191 (4, 1); Thorpe, 1982; Smith, 2008, 662.
66. LP, 14/1, 575.
67. BL, MS Cotton Cleopatra E IV, fo. 269r. Warden Baskerfield secured a living at Westcote (Oxon.) by 1539: Baskerville, 1929, 21.
68. Cambridge, Corpus Christi College, MS 111, 319–33.
69. Blackborough, Bruisyard, Carrow, Crabhouse, Flixton, Thetford: Cambridge, Corpus Christi College, MS 111, 321. For the northern province, ibid., 326–8.
70. Cambridge, Corpus Christi College, MS 111, 326–7, 330–1.
71. Ibid, 319.
72. Ibid, 319, 321, 323–4, 331–2.
73. Ibid, 325.
74. Ibid, 321, 324, 327.
75. Ibid, 319–20, 324.
76. Ibid, 319.
77. TNA, SP 5/4 fo. 109r; SP, 1/104, fo. 226r; SP, 5/3, fo. 22r.
78. BL, MS Cotton Cleopatra E IV, fos. 342v–343r.
79. TNA, SP 1/104, fo. 248r.
80. Page, 1906, 421.
81. Savine, 1909, 285.
82. TNA, E315/288/16; Savine, 1909, 277.
83. TNA, E315/232, fo. 17r; Savine, 1909, 273.
84. BL, MS Cotton Cleopatra E IV, fo. 327r.
85. TNA, E315/232, fo. 17r; Savine, 1909, 273.
86. TNA, SP 1/118, fo. 181r.
87. LP, 14/2, 208.
88. BL, MS Cotton Cleopatra E IV, fo. 250r.
89. TNA, SP 1/127, fo.146r.
90. Dickens, 1940, 416; see also Heath, 1969, 147–74 at 173.
91. TNA, SP 5/4, fo. 148r.
92. TNA, SP 5/1, fo. 23r.
93. Ibid, fo. 91r.
94. TNA, SP 1/117, fo. 84r.
95. Hodgett, 1962, 202.
96. TNA, SP 1/154, fo. 140r
97. LP, 13/2, 1128.

98. *LP*, 14/1, 207.
99. *LP*, 14/1, 31, 276, 312.
100. *LP*, 14/2, 462, 476.
101. *LP*, 141/2, 401; Savine, 1909, 278.
102. TNA, PCC, Prob. 11/37/218, fos. 127r–v.
103. Ibid, 11/37/403; SP 1/143, fo. 146r.
104. TNA, SP 1/134, fo. 163r.
105. TNA, SP 1/140, fo. 143r.
106. Savine, 1909, 283; TNA, SP 1/132, fo. 58r.
107. TNA, SP 1/154, fo. 140r.
108. *LP*, 14/2, 641.
109. *LP*, 14/1, 341. Their annual values assessed in 1535 were respectively £819 and £309: Savine, 1909, 272, 287.
110. BL, MS Cotton Titus B I, fo. 119r.
111. TNA, SP 1/242, fo. 72r.
112. *LP*, 14/1, 161.
113. Caley et al., 1817–30, v. 429.
114. Merriman, 1902, Letter 278, 159.
115. *LP*, 14/2, 646.
116. TNA, SP 1/155, fo. 127r.
117. *LP*, 14/1, 75.
118. Hockey, 1970, 230–1.
119. TNA, SP 1/129, fo. 53r.
120. BL, MS Cotton Cleopatra E IV, fo. 238r.
121. TNA, SP 1/126, fo. 135r.
122. Dickens, 1940, 411.
123. The potential of the Calais friary preoccupied Lisle in his letters to his agent Hussee for much of 1539: TNA, SP 3/4, fo. 109r.
124. Easton, £6: E315/232, fo. 22v; Thelsford, £5: *LP*, 13/2, 707.
125. *LP*, 13/2, 354; TNA, SP 1/136, fo. 119r.
126. Chauncy, 1890, 71; Cunich, 2007, 36.
127. TNA, SP 1/129, fo. 53r.
128. TNA, SP 1/142, fo. 180r.
129. Douglas Hamilton, 1875, 86.
130. As reported by John Hussee to Lisle: TNA, SP 1/152, fo. 79r.
131. Richard Tracy, *A supplycacion to our moste soueraigne lorde Kynge henry the eyght Kynge of England of Fraunce and of Irelande [and] moste ernest defender of Christes gospell, supreme heade under God here in erthe next [and] immedyatly of his churches of Englande and Irelande.* STC (2nd edn.) 24165.5. London, 1544.
132. Cross and Vickers, 1995, 4, 35, 37–8, 88, 107, 110, 117, 122, 144, 149, 150–1, 162, 164, 176–7, 194, 203, 212, 238, 249, 259, 275–7, 289, 319–20, 341, 368, 388, 407, 425, 434, 449, 452, 457, 459, 475, 483, 498–9, 509.
133. Hampshire Record Office, 44M69/G8/18/61.
134. TNA, SP 1/134, fo. 118r.
135. TNA, SP 46/124, fo. 30r.
136. The record of incumbents is not nearly well enough preserved to arrive at an accurate count of the total, and the pattern of departures from regular institutions both before and after 1536 adds further to the difficulty: some chantry and parish priests found in and after 1540 had been monastic or mendicants in years, not months, gone by. The impression cast by Geoffrey Baskerville's pioneering analysis of the records of Norwich diocese should not be too readily applied to the country as a whole: Baskerville, 1933.
137. Seven monks of Westminster were passed over for canonries at the time of the re-foundation: Knighton, 2003, 17.

138. John Chambers, bishop of Peterborough, had been abbot there since 1528. William Benson, bishop of Westminster, had been abbot there since 1532. Paul Bush, bishop of Bristol, had been rector of the Edington Bonhommes; John Wakeman, bishop of Gloucester, had been abbot of Tewkesbury; Robert King, bishop of Oxford, had been abbot of Thame: Smith, 2008, 59, 74, 80, 339, 617.

139. *LP*, 13/1, 1115 (4): Norwich; 16, 678 (53): 700: Canterbury; 802 (11): Carlisle; Winchester; 878, (25): Durham; 947 (36): Rochester; 1227 (11): Ely; 17, 71 (28): Worcester; Houlbrooke, 1996, 507.

140. TNA, SP 1/159, fo. 92r.

141. Summerson, 1993, ii. 625.

142. John Capon, Bangor (1534), Salisbury (1539); John Hilsey, Rochester (1535); William Repps alias Rugg, Norwich (1536); William Barlow, St David's (1536); Robert Wharton alias Perfew, St Asaph (1536); Robert Holgate, Llandaff (1537). For the new suffragans see above, 197, 345.

143. BL, MS Add. 11041, fo 47r.

144. The three are described as 'scolers' of St Bernard's College in the will of the provisor, William Alynger, proved on 5 January 1540: TNA, Prob. 11/28/3. For their presence at the surrender of Hailes see *LP*, 14/2, 771.

145. Emden, 1974, 277, 481–2.

146. Fizzard, 2008, 245; *LP*, 12/2, 1320–21.

147. For Peryn and Palmer see Erler, 2013, 113, 121–3.

148. Dasent, 1890, ii. 97–8.

149. Ibid.

150. An undated memorandum placed by the HMSO editors in 1534 records 7 friars absconded to Scotland and 18 overseas: TNA, E36/153, fos. 2v–3r; *LP*, 7, 1607. Bishop Tunstall reported fresh escapees across the northern border when the rising of 1537 was put down: Anon., 1830–52, v. 122.

151. TNA, SP 1/44, fo. 68r.

152. *LP*, 15, 96.

153. Dasent, 1890, i. 161.

154. Both Robert Barnes and Miles Coverdale had left the country, respectively, for Antwerp and Hamburg in 1528; Trueman, 2004; Daniell, 2004; Rex, 2002, 40–2.

155. King, 2004.

156. Dobson, 1995, 153.

157. Foxe, 1563, Book V, 1180–2, 1205–6.

158. Foxe, 1563, V, 1180–1182, 1205, 1727; Freeman, 2004; Greaves, 2004.

159. Chambers, 1966, xlii–xliii.

160. BL, MS Cotton Cleopatra E IV, fo. 284r.

161. Sherlock, 2018, 308.

162. This, at least, is the impression of the albeit patchy record of these closures: for example, *LP*, 10, 1191 (4–5) (Polesworth); TNA, SP 5/2, fo. 73r (Redlingfield, Norfolk, where 79-year-old Katherine Fletcher was found to be blind and deaf).

163. Wiltshire and Swindon History Centre, P5/1588/19.

164. TNA, PCC, Prob. 11/29/199, fo. 10v.

165. Oliva, 1994, 202.

166. Butler, 1977.

167. Cross and Vickers, 1995, 575.

168. Ibid, 595–6.

169. Rose-Troup, 1935, 48.

170. John Reve, former abbot, Thomas Ringstead, former cellarer, and Thomas Stonebarn.

171. TNA, PCC Prob. 11/37/187, fo. 85r–v.

172. TNA, PCC, Prob, 11/30/654, fos. 346v–347r.

173. Ayscough, Thorold and Dickens, 1940, 389. For the allocation of pensions to the abbot and monks of the island's abbey of Rushen see Davey and Roscow, 2010, 135.
174. Oliva, 1994, 196.
175. Somerset Heritage Centre, T/PH/cl/1/6.
176. Palmer, 1928–30, 61–2.
177. Nichols, 1852; Erler, 2013, 38–65.
178. Clark, 2000, 315–16, 326.
179. TNA, PCC, Prob. 11/26/308, fos. 17v–18v; Smith, 2008, 25.
180. Clark, 2000, 315–16, 326.
181. Aveling, 1955, 8.
182. BL, MS Harley 604, fos. 200r–v.
183. TNA, Prob. 11/31/24, fo. 13r.
184. TNA, Prob. 11/30/146, fos. 75r–v.
185. Cross, 1989, 28–30 at 29.
186. Cross and Vickers, 1995, 171–2, 174, 189, 195, 197.
187. Ibid, 22.
188. Williams, 2001, 87.
189. Cross and Vickers, 1995, 577; West Yorkshire Archaeology Advisory Service, Monument number 13976.
190. Lee, 2001, 124.
191. TNA, PCC, Prob. 11/31/24, fo. 13r.
192. TNA, PCC, Prob. 11/28/19, fo. 11v.
193. '... otherwise called John Stonywell by the grace of God Bischopp of Polotensis': TNA, PCC Prob. 11/37/402, fos. 218v–219r at 218v.
194. Lee, 2001, 122.
195. Fuller, 1845, iii. 462.
196. Jane Forget's tomb slab survives at St Michael's Church, Mere; Butler, 1977.
197. Westminster Abbey Muniments.
198. TNA, SP 5/3, fo. 34r.
199. TNA, SP 5/2, fos. 250r–251r.
200. *LP*, 13/2, 839.
201. TNA, SP 5/2, fo. 118r–v; 250r–251r.
202. Ibid, fo. 249v.
203. Ibid.
204. Proctor, 2018, 300.
205. TNA, SP 5/2, fo. 22r.
206. TNA, E36/154, fo. 126.
207. *LP*, 14/2, 542.
208. *LP*, 13/2, 839.
209. *LP*, 13/2, 839.
210. TNA, SP 5/4.
211. When she made her will there were at least two, perhaps more women in her household. Piccope, 1857, 54–6 at 55.
212. TNA, PCC Prob. 11/37/218, fo. 18r–v.
213. Mayhew, 2014, 430.
214. *LP*, 14/2, 401.
215. Somerset Heritage Centre, T/PH/cl/1/25.
216. TNA, REQ 2/3/235.
217. Douglas Hamilton, 1875, 43.
218. *LP*, 13/2, 839 (9).
219. *LP*, 13/1, 433 (iv).
220. TNA, E 36/154, 126, 134, 106.
221. TNA, SP 1/125, fo. 46r; 1/131 fo. 120r; McSheffrey, 2017, 11, 23, 142.

222. Loades, 2003, 82.
223. *LP*, 17, 258 (v).
224. TNA, C 1258/29–30.
225. *LP*, 16, 91.
226. Mayhew, 2006, 428.
227. TNA, SP 1/102, fo. 104v (Crabhouse).
228. West, 1774, 126.
229. St Clare Byrne, 1981, v. 15 (Letter 1088).
230. *LP*, 16, 1500 (17).
231. See above, 109.
232. *LP*, 14/1, 68.
233. The Bordesley salter cheerfully confirmed his debt was clear until the next season, for 'salte ys wont to be made alweys betwene Estur and Pentecoste': BL, MS Add 11041, fo. 48r.
234. TNA, SP 1/5, fo. 5r–6v.
235. In a letter to John Scudamore he complained there had been no time 'to resoun with my credyters' because the commissioners 'dyd tarye bot on day'. He declared 'nether law ne justyce' bound him to pay now since 'the kynge . . . be oure successor': BL, MS Add. 11041, fo. 68r–v.
236. See above, 459.
237. *LP*, 10, 226 (26).
238. *LP*, 13/2, 839.
239. Summerson, 1993, ii. 628.
240. For example, some of the earliest grants of sizeable endowments, such as Tintern to Henry Somerset, 2nd earl of Worcester, in March 1537: *LP*, 12/1, 795 9 (16).
241. *LP*, 12/2, 1008 (19).
242. *LP*, 13/1, 887.
243. *LP*, 1/1, 1519.
244. *LP*, 13/1, 646 (66).
245. *LP*, 15, 144 (22).
246. *LP*, 13/1, 1115.
247. Blanchard, 1970, 435.
248. Dickens, 1951, 46–7: omnes terras et redditus ad eandem spectantes et pertinentes ad laicorum manus ut fertur tradidere.
249. TNA, SP 1/242, for. 32r.
250. TNA, C 1/969/37.
251. East Sussex Record Office, SAS/CO/3/13/981.
252. Hoyle, 1989, 122–3.
253. *LP*, 13/1, 1504.
254. TNA, SP 1/127, fo. 59r–v, 60r.
255. TNA, SP 1/129, fo. 98r–v at 98r.
256. TNA, SP 1/120, fo. 235r.
257. TNA, SP 1/143, fo. 11r.
258. TNA, SP 1/135, fo. 63r.
259. TNA, SP 5/5, fo. 58r.
260. The lease was dated 16 June 1536. The abbey was surrendered 28 months later on 16 October 1538: Shropshire Archives, 972/1/1/374; TNA, E322/128.
261. Knighton, 2003, 32–3.
262. Thompson, 1949, 142.
263. TNA, SP 1/153, fo. 126r–v at 126v.
264. *LP*, 7, 1157.
265. Fizzard, 2008, 243.
266. Youings, 1967, 329; Breay, 1999, 74–5.
267. *LP*, 1547, 302 (17).

268. Breay, 1999, 420–21; Hertfordshire Archives and Local Studies, DE/B2067B/E34.
269. Wood, 2013, 81.
270. Knighton, 2003, 20–1.
271. BL, MS Harley 144, fo. 27v.
272. Haigh, 1969, 78.
273. De Windt and De Windt, 2006, 148.
274. Birmingham City Archives, MS 3525/ACC 1935–043/437922.
275. Parsons, 1690, 5.
276. Ibid, 6.
277. Ibid, 5.
278. Ibid, 21.

Chapter X The Old World and the New

1. TNA, SP 1/103, fo. 218r.
2. The draft is found in BL, MS Cotton Cleopatra E IV, fos. 215r–220v; Elton, 1974, 72–7.
3. Oxford, Bodl. MS Douce 363, fo. 95r.
4. Douglas Hamilton, 1875, 112.
5. While Mary was determined to undo the Edwardian reformation of the clergy, particularly the permission to marry, she showed no inclination for a wholesale restoration of a medieval penitential Church: Loades, 2006, 15, 18–19, 24.
6. Douglas Hamilton, 1875, 112.
7. From the turn of 1539 to Easter 1540 the Faculty Office registers recorded the names of nearly 50 London regulars receiving formal dispensation to change their habit. Notably absent from the list were the bulk of Augustinian, Dominican and Franciscan friars, some of whom may have stood in limbo: Chambers, 1966, 161, 182–3, 192, 201, 204, 209.
8. Williams, 1836, 93, 104.
9. TNA, SP 1/143, fos. 1r–2v.
10. Gunn, 2018, 104; *LP*, 17, 779.
11. *LP*, 19/1, 368. Payments made in April 1544 of £2,351 for the Paymaster of the king's ships and £2,298 for victualling.
12. Wood, 2007, 61, 71, 77–8.
13. Whitford's book was *Dyvers Holy Instructions*, STC (2nd edn.) 25420. The continuator of the Greyfriars chronicle cannot be identified with any certainty: Erler, 2013, 38–65, 131.
14. Douglas Hamilton, 1875, 42–3, 86–7, 88.
15. Holinshed, 1577, 1564.
16. Stow, 1592, 972.
17. Fuller, 1845, iii. 330–1, 466–7.
18. Douglas Hamilton, 1875, 112.
19. TNA, SP 1/157, fo. 125r.
20. Williams, 1836, 57.
21. Fuller, 1845, iii. 442.
22. Williams, 1836, 11.
23. TNA, SP 1/102, fo. 135r.
24. BL, MS Cotton Cleopatra E IV, fo. 275r.
25. TNA, SP 1/112, fo. 55r.
26. TNA, SP 1/117, fo. 160r–v. For a summary note of the same allegation see also BL, MS Cotton Cleopatra E IV, fo. 245r–246r at 245v.
27. TNA, SP 1/111, fo. 49
28. TNA, SP 1/120, fo. 213r–216v at 213r.
29. Schroder, 2020, 275.
30. Williams, 1836, 37–8, 41.
31. TNA, SP 1/112, fo. 55r.

32. Williams, 1836, 55.
33. BL, MS Cotton Cleopatra E IV, fo. 252r.
34. Savine, 1909, 276.
35. Schroeder, 2020, 273.
36. TNA, SP 1/112, fo. 55r.
37. Williams, 1836, 101.
38. Wolffe, 1964.
39. Condon, 2003b, 132.
40. BL, MS Harley 1419/1.
41. The inventories are preserved in two pairs of manuscript books, now in London, Society of Antiquaries MS 120 A-B and BL, MS Harley 1419/1–2. For the objects referenced here see in particular BL, MS Harley 1419/1, fos. 187v, 189r; the provenance of the unicorn horn staffs is confirmed in an inventory of church furnishings at Winchester, copied in Cambridge, Corpus Christi College, MS 111, 356.
42. BL, MS Harley 1419/2, fos. 192r–193v at 192r–v.
43. The arrival of books and other contents on 27 May 1542 was recorded in a general inventory of the palace's furnishings: LP, 17, 267.
44. Carley, 2000, xxxi–xxxvi, xli–ii.
45. Ibid, xlvi.
46. Ibid, 318–21.
47. BL, MS Cotton Cleopatra E IV, fo. 252r.
48. LP, 13/2, 457.
49. Ibid.
50. LP, 12/2, 1027.
51. LP, 12/1, 311; Savine, 1909, 285.
52. LP, 13/2, 457; Savine, 1909, 277.
53. For Sharington's agreement see TNA, WARD 2/28/94D/9 (16 July 1539).
54. LP, 13/2, 457.
55. LP, 14/2, 236.
56. LP, 18/2, 231.
57. LP, 13/2, 168.
58. TNA, SP 1/153, fo. 18r.
59. TNA, SP 46/124, fo. 54r.
60. LP, 13/2, 1013.
61. LP, 13/2, 457.
62. Hoyle, 1995b, 76.
63. 'The sad truth is that no minister of Henry VIII ever invented a way of providing him with enough money for his inflated overseas ambitions': MacCulloch, 1995, 6.
64. Hoyle, 1995b, 93.
65. Pocock, 1878, 299.
66. Williams, 1836, 78–83 at 83, 84–6 at 86.
67. Ibid, 88–9.
68. Ibid, 90–1.
69. Ibid, 55.
70. Fuller, 1845, iii. 108.
71. TNA, SP 1/168, fos. 137r–v, 138r–v.
72. LP, 21/1, 1250.
73. LP, 13/2, 342; LP, 14/2, 236; BL, MS Cotton Appendix XXVIII, fo. 69r.
74. BL, MS Cotton Appendix XXVIII, fo. 67r.
75. TNA, SP 1/242, fo. 105r; BL, MS Cotton Appendix XXVIII, fo. 69v; Savine, 1909, 283.
76. LP, 14/2, 236 (10).
77. Pocock, 1878, 203.
78. Grummit, 2004.

79. Wall, 2004.
80. *LP*, 12/2, 1311 (16).
81. James, 2004.
82. *LP*, 16, 1500 (2).
83. TNA, SP 1/120, fo. 218r.
84. Savine, 1909, 286.
85. *LP*, 12/2, 1008 (9); see also Nottinghamshire Archives, DD/SR/225/77.
86. *LP*, 12/1, 1103 (11).
87. *LP*, 12/1, 1103 (11, 26); 12/2, 1311 (24, 30).
88. *LP*, 10, 1015 (26).
89. West Sussex Record Office, Cowdray 5177 (20 July 1536); *LP*, 11, 202 (37).
90. *LP*, 11, 202 (29, 45).
91. *LP*, 12/2, 1150 (7).
92. *LP*, 13/1, 1487; 1519.
93. *LP*, 12/2, 1008 (3); 13/1, 384 (74); *LP*, 15, 611 (8).
94. Turner, 1555, 48–9.
95. TNA, SP 10/9, fo. 102r.
96. *LP*, 16, 677.
97. Letter to Sir Thomas Arundell, dated 6 October 1540: TNA, SP 1/163, fo. 61r.
98. TNA, PCC Prob 11/38/199, fos. 138v–139r.
99. *LP*, 15, 613, (32).
100. *LP*, 14/2, 435 (12).
101. *LP*, 16, 1500 (17).
102. *LP*, 13/1, 1519 (71); 16, 728; Shaw, 2004.
103. TNA, PCC, Prob 11/30/648, fos. 348v–350r.
104. TNA, SP 1/157, fo. 206r.
105. *LP*, 14/2, 236.
106. *LP*, 16, 1395.
107. *LP*, 16, 678.
108. TNA, E 326/12419; *LP*, 16, 720; Sil, 2004.
109. *LP*, 12/1, 795 (42). Kingston was granted the lease of the inner cloister of the London Dominicans on 6 May 1540 for an annual rent of 60s: Surrey History Centre, LM/345/99. See also Lehmberg, 2004.
110. *LP*, 16, 726.
111. *LP*, 13/1, 384 (33).
112. *LP*, 13/1, 1520; 14/1, 1354, (47).
113. BL, MS Cotton Cleopatra E IV, fos. 215r, 216r.
114. Luders et al., 1810–28, iii. 733–9.
115. Ibid, iii. 733–9.
116. TNA, SP 1/106, fo. 20r.
117. Smith, 1554, 19.
118. *LP*, 12/2, 205.
119. TNA, SP 1/142, fo. 31r.
120. TNA, SP 1/141, fo. 65r.
121. Silvester and Hankinson, 2015, 24.
122. TNA, E 314/20/10.
123. BL, MS Cotton Cleopatra E IV, fo. 216r.
124. TNA, SP 1/153, fo. 67r.
125. TNA, C 1/1009/14–17.
126. *LP*, 21/1, 1537.
127. Webb, 1921, i. 263–4.
128. Cornwall and Scilly Islands HER, 4354.10.
129. Woodfield, 2005, 156.

130. TNA, C 2/Eliz/G3/39.
131. Dorset HER, MDO9033.
132. TNA, SP 1/111, fo. 119r.
133. West, 1774, 121–9 at 126–7.
134. TNA, C1/1188/28–33.
135. For examples, TNA, STAC 1/258 (assault and damage to property: Fountains Abbey, 1499–1500); TNA, STAC 1/1/34 (disputed rights: Eynsham Abbey, 1502–3); STAC 2/19/102 (enclosure: Leicester Abbey); STAC 2/21/109 (trespass: Peterborough Abbey).
136. Lemon, 1856, 33 (9).
137. Suffolk Record Office, HA30/312/82.
138. Lincolnshire HER, 30039.
139. TNA, SP 1/153, fo. 126r–v.
140. Allinson, 1958, 100; Miller, 1991, 190.
141. Hare, 2011, 88.
142. Currie, 1990, 22–46.
143. Thomas, 2006, 188.
144. Toulmin-Smith, 1906–10, iv. 4.
145. TNA, E 314/20/10.
146. Tittler, 1977; idem. 1998, 8–10, 153.
147. Withington, 2005, 28.
148. See above, 390–1.
149. TNA, SP 1/138, fo. 135r–v.
150. For summary estimates of urban populations in this period see Jack, 1996, 173.
151. TNA, SP 1/138, fo. 135r–v.
152. TNA, SP 1/158, fo. 99r.
153. TNA, SP 1/137, fo. 146r.
154. Hertfordshire Archives and Local Studies, DE/HL/14388. For the appointment of the first bailiff see LP, 14/2, 780 (44).
155. Tittler, 1977, 42.
156. Cumber, 2010, 3.
157. Tittler, 1977, 41.
158. 'an affirmation of the community's ability to run its own affairs': Cumber, 2010, 3–4, 122, 127–8.
159. Tittler, 1998, 162.
160. Berkshire Record Office, R/IC1/6; Tittler, 1977, 42.
161. Willmott, 2020, 91–2.
162. Pocock, 1878, 298.
163. TNA, SP 15/17, fo. 132r–v.
164. TNA, PCC Prob 11/31/179, fos. 37v–38r.
165. Dated 1 May 1550: South West Heritage Centre, DD/BRU/1/1/4.
166. LP, 20/1, 1335 (39).
167. Lempriere, 1904, 11.
168. Sheils, 2004.
169. Hay, 1938, 107.
170. LP, 16, 468.
171. Holgate's endowment for his school at Hemsworth included property which had belonged to the Carthusian priory at Mount Grace: TNA, C 146/7628.
172. The licence for the foundation of Christ's School Tideswell was dated 18 November 1559: Collingridge, 1939, 289–90.
173. TNA, HL/PO/PB/1/1548/2& 3E6n53.
174. For a survey of these churches see Willmott, 2020, 71–80 at 73, 79.
175. LP, 19/1, 141 (57); Hare, 1999, 16–17.
176. By local tradition, stained glass in the nearby parish church of St Peter's was taken from the abbey church. For the sale of the church to the town see Caley et al., 1817–30, ii. 208.

177. Hockey, 1970, 235; Shakespeare Birthplace Trust, DR 3712/Box 125/7.
178. For example, St Mary Graces, where the western cemetery fell out of use by the end of the 15th century: Grainger and Phillpotts, 2011, 98, 101–3. The London Carmelite and Crutched Friars created new space for their lay cemeteries at the end of their history although the traffic in burials there is not easily documented; the Augustinian friars sited their preaching cross there, which would seem to affirm continued activity: Holder, 2017, 114, 138–9, 157.
179. For example, at St Mary Graces: Grainger and Phillpotts, 2011, 59.
180. Ibid, 62–3.
181. Woodfield, 2005, 73, 83; Forde, Munby and Scott, 2019, 33, 55, 65–7.
182. Grainger and Collingwood, 1929, 153–63.
183. Garry and Garry, 1893, 4–6, 22.
184. North Yorkshire HER, MNY20482.
185. Shakespeare Birthplace Trust, DR 3712/Box 125/7.
186. Baskerville, 1927, 94, 97; Skeeters, 1993, 155, 160–1, 163, 172, 175, 177–8, 180, 194.
187. The register of Bishop John Longland of Lincoln shows a significant drop in the number of candidates presented at ordination ceremonies, from between 30 and 50 in 1538 to 16 in March 1540 and 13 in March 1541. No ceremonies were convened in the year from March 1540: Lincolnshire Archives, DIOC/REG/27, fos. 57v–61r. For a comparable decline in the province of York see Cross, 1996, 8–9.
188. Lincolnshire Archives, DIOC/REG/26, fo. 61r.
189. For the ebb and flow of clerical candidates for benefices in these years see Cross, 1996, 12–13.
190. Luders et al., 1810–28, iv. 24–33.
191. Maclean, 1883–84, 232–3, 238, 242, 244, 252, 268.
192. Hay, 1938, 103–9; Clark, 1989, 144; Gill, 2010, 188.
193. Gill, 2019, 213, 217.
194. The regular bishops of the old foundation were Anthony Kitchen (Benedictine, Llandaff, 1545–66); William Repps (Benedictine, Norwich, 1536–50); Henry Holbeach (Benedictine, Rochester, 1544–7); Robert Wharton Alias Perfew (Cluniac, St Asaph, 1536–54); William Barlow (Augustinian, St David's, 1536–48); John Capon (Benedictine, Salisbury, 1539–57); Robert Holgate (Gilbertine, York, 1545–54). Those of the new foundation were Paul Bush at Bristol (Bonhomme, Edington, 1542–54); John Bird at Chester (Carmelite, Coventry, 1541–54); John Wakeman at Gloucester (Benedictine, Tewkesbury, 1541–9); Robert King at Oxford (Cistercian, Thame, 1541–7); John Chambers at Peterborough (Benedictine, Peterborough, 1541–56). The number is at least eight because the date of the death of John Bradley who held the suffragan title of Shaftesbury is unknown. In addition to the suffragans created in 1536–9 several who had held titles *in partibus infidelium* before 1536 lived on: John Draper (Winchester); William Fawell (Exeter); John Stonywell (York); Andrew Whitmay (Hereford and Worcester). For a summary list of suffragans see Heale, 2016, 378; Powicke and Fryde, 1961, 269, 271–2.
195. BL, MS Cotton Cleopatra E IV, fo. 316r.
196. Pettegree, 2004.
197. Bowker, 2004.
198. Doggett, 2004b.
199. Barnard, 1927–8.
200. Bettey, 2004.
201. For example, the former abbot of Milton (Dorset) styled Bishop of Shaftesbury, incumbent of Cannyng's chantry, Bristol: Maclean, 1883–4, 244–5. For further examples see Baskerville, 1933, 208; Gill, 2010, 133–4, 247; Gill, 2019.
202. Dated 24 April 1544, E135/2/32.
203. 'Preests after the order of presthode recyved as afore may not marye by the law of God . . . vows of chastitye or wydowhood by man or woman made to God advisedly ought to be observed': Luders et al., 1810–28, 739–43 at 739.

204. TNA, PCC Prob 11/29/199, fos. 83v–84v at 83v; Berkshire Record Office, D/EZ 104/1/1–2.
205. TNA, PCC Prob 11/31/179, fos. 37v–38r.
206. Douglas Hamilton, 1875, 103.
207. BL, MS Cotton Cleopatra E IV, fo. 140r.
208. Baskerville, 1933, 204.
209. TNA, PCC, Prob 11/35/202, fos. 121r–v.
210. Morgan and Morgan, 1962, 137.
211. Cross and Vickers, 1995, 606–7.
212. Ibid, 581.
213. Parsons, 1690, 20–1.
214. Rex, 2002, 48–9.
215. MacMahon, 2004; Joye, 1541, A ivv.
216. TNA, SP 2/6, fo. 133r; Dickens, 1941.
217. For the Syon legend see Fletcher, 1933, 37–8; Jones, 2015, 54.
218. Elton, 1972, 18–19; Cratty, 2018.
219. Fletcher, 1933, 37–8; Jones, 2015, 53–4.
220. Mayhew, 2006, 403.
221. Cunich, 2010, 71–2.
222. Cunich, 2007, 41 and n. 172.
223. *LP*, 15, 747.
224. Williams, 2004.
225. Newcombe, 2004.
226. *LP*, 18/2, 546.
227. Freeman, 2004. For Cardmaker's career see also Skeeters, 1993, 159.
228. Rex, 2002, 45–6; Lawrence, whom Foxe reported had 'entended to haue married [a mayde]', was executed at Colchester in March 1555: Foxe, 1563, V, 1181–2.
229. King, 2004; Newcome, 2004; C. S. Knighton represents the dissolution of the Westminster diocese as a pragmatic decision to restore authority to the see of London: Knighton, 2004.
230. TNA, SP 10/9, fo. 92r.
231. Gunn, 2016, 230–1.
232. Wood, 2007, 61, 63.
233. Rose-Troup, 1913, 220–1.
234. Bristol, Chichester, Gloucester, Llandaff, Oxford, Peterborough, Rochester, St Asaph, Salisbury, Worcester, York.
235. Dublin, Trinity College, MS 352, fo. 169v.
236. Parkyn, 1947, 83.
237. TNA, SP 11/8, fo. 26r; SP 46/162, fo. 176r.
238. Anon., 1554, 16.
239. Wooding, 2004. See also Erler, 2013, 115.
240. Lempriere, 1904, 66, 69–70.
241. Cunich, 2007, 43–5.
242. Brown, 1877, 30.
243. Feckenham, 1555, C ivv, C viiiv–D ir.
244. Fletcher, 1933, 40.
245. Anstruther, 1958, 3–4.
246. Giuseppi, 1937–9, iii. 372.
247. Herbert has been described as an 'habitual Erastian': Sil, 2004.
248. Rymer, 1739–45, xv. 117; Ruddock, 1945, 146.
249. Brown, 1877, 1024.
250. Ibid, 403.
251. Nichols, 1848, 118–19.
252. Giuseppi, 1937–9, iii. 313.
253. Carter, 2004b.

254. Douglas Hamilton, 1875, 134.
255. Borthwick Institute Archives, Prob. Reg. 15 pt III, fos. 103v–104r. See also Cross, 2018, 108.
256. Cunich, 2007, 43–6.
257. Lee, 2001, 19–23.
258. Sharpe, 1889–90, ii. 663.
259. Litzenberger, 1998, 82–3.
260. Page, 1911, ii. 96.
261. Knighton, 2006, 84–5; Clark, 2000, 332.
262. TNA, PCC Prob 11/40/398, fo. 36r–v.
263. TNA, PCC Prob 11/39/6, fo. 1v.
264. TNA, SP 46/8, fo. 184r.
265. Lancashire Archives, DDX 102/49.
266. TNA, SP 46/10, fo. 210r.
267. Ruddock, 1945, 146.
268. TNA, PCC 11/38/226, fos. 160v–161v at 161r.
269. TNA, PCC 11/40/280, fos. 194v–196v at 195v–196r.
270. TNA, PCC 11/41/6, fos. 5r–6r at 5r. The will was dated 27 July 1558; it was proved on 2 September.
271. Brown, 1877, 704.
272. Parkyn, 1947, 83.
273. Giuseppi, 1937–9, iii. 403.
274. Holder, 2017, 59.
275. The deed survives as Exeter University Library, MS 389/4120; Jones, 2015, 59; Powell, 2017, 248–9.
276. It is not recorded which daughter of the cardinal's brother, Sir Geoffrey (d. 1558); she was reportedly 'already with the nuns of Sion, and determined on taking the vows and living with them entirely' in November 1558: Brown, 1873–7, vi/3, 1287; Jones, 2015, 59.
277. Knighton, 2003, 83, 90.
278. Cunich, 2007, 44–8.
279. Holder, 2017, 61.
280. Kingsford, 1908, ii. 84–5.
281. Brown, 1873–7, vi/2, 704; Jones, 2015, 57.
282. Kent HER, TQ 57 SW 1042.
283. Doggett, 1991, 53. See also Hertfordshire HER, 97.
284. TNA, PCC, Prob 11/42A/105, fos. 117v–119v.
285. Cloake, 1977, 152–3, 170.
286. Knighton, 1998, 854.
287. Fletcher, 1933, 41.
288. Rymer, 1739–45, xv, 117.
289. Kingsford, 1908, 85.
290. Holder, 2017, 61–3.
291. Rymer, 1739–45, xv, 117.
292. Nichols, 1848, 132.
293. Clark, 2019a, 89.
294. Giuseppi, 1937–9, 291–2.
295. Ibid, iii. 354–5.
296. Rymer, 1739–45, xv. 117.
297. Giuseppi, 1937–9, iii. 417.
298. TNA, E 328/439.
299. Brown, 1877, 473.
300. Ibid, 771.
301. Parkinson, 1726, 253.
302. Nichols, 1848, 108, 171.

303. Ibid, 100, 119.
304. Ibid, 164.
305. TNA, PCC Prob 11/4/25, fos. 121r–123v at 121v.
306. Nichols, 1848, 110.
307. Brown, 1877, 634.
308. TNA, PCC Prob 11/40/398, fo. 36r–v at 36r.
309. Knighton, 2006, 92.
310. Nichols, 1848, 148.
311. Ibid, 140, 158, 168.
312. TNA, SP 46/8, fo. 210r.
313. Nichols, 1848, 137.
314. Ibid, 147–8.
315. Ibid, 159.
316. Dasent, 1893, vi. 128; see also 135, 251–2.
317. Nichols, 1848, 169.
318. TNA, SP 12/1, fo. 88r.
319. Tresham's will was dated 28 November. He died on 8 March: TNA, PCC Prob 11/42B/49, fos. 148r–150r.
320. Loomie, 2004.
321. Chauncy, 1890, xiii; Fletcher, 1933, 43; Cunich, 2007, 48; Jones, 2015, 61.
322. Nichols, 1848, 204. The memoir kept by the exiled Carthusians recorded their arrival at Bruges on 1 July 1559: Cunich, 2007, 48.
323. TNA, SP 12/23, fo. 138r.
324. Nichols, 1848, 204.
325. 'Proclaymed by a bishop Queene of England ... the trumpetts blowing': TNA, SP 15/9/1, fo. 18r. See also Nichols, 1848, 186–7.
326. Stapleton, 1567, fos. 27r–v.
327. Brown and Bentinck, 1890, vii, 15.
328. Ibid, 15.
329. Stevens, 1722, i. 289. Stevens gives no reference. Sander's *De origine ac progressu schismatis anglicanae*, written in 1585 and published in 1610, contains no such account.
330. BL, MS Cotton Vespasian D XVIII, fos. 86r–91v; Scott, 1809, i. 81–5 at 81, 84.
331. Nichols, 1848, 235.
332. A pension was granted from the revenues of the former monastery of Sheen on 5 August 1560: E135/1/22/143.
333. Lemon, 1856, i. 201 (40).
334. Fletcher, 1933, 43–4; Cunich, 2007, 49.
335. Lemon, 1856, i. 203 (60–1).
336. Ibid, 250 (23).
337. Stapleton, 1567, title page.
338. Knighton, 2004.
339. Lemon, 1856, i. 701 (114).
340. Coverdale, 1541, iiv–iiir.

Epilogue

1. Fuller, 1845, iii. 462.
2. Cross and Vickers, 1995, 568.
3. McCann and Connolly, 1933, 245.
4. Wood, 2013, 89.
5. McCann and Connolly, 1933, 177–8 at 178.
6. Knowles, 1959; Walker, 2006, 157.
7. Bourchier, 1582.

8. Bradshaw, 1974, 206; Murray, 2009, 257–8.
9. TNA, PCC Prob 11/48/167, fo. 131v.; Traskey, 1978, 179.
10. Anthony-Williams, 1975, 8–9.
11. Dimmock, 2014, 8–9.
12. Cross and Vickers, 1995, 105–6.
13. Mary Denys was remembered in the 1570 will of her brother Walter, of St Augustine's Green, Bristol: TNA, Prob PCC 11/53/260, fo. 199v.
14. Oliva, 1994, 191.
15. For example, Crowland, Spalding, Thornton, Nuncotham, Sempringham, St Katherine's Priory, Lincoln and Stixwould: BL, MS Harley 604, fos. 184–185v, 188r–189v, 194r–v, 198r–v.
16. Cross and Vickers, 1995, 504.
17. Lambarde, 1576, 170.
18. Hearne, 1744, i. xxii.
19. For example, see the site of Thorney Abbey: Thomas, 2006, 216.
20. Camden, 1587, 286; *illud templum . . . nunc, in aedes privatas conversum.*
21. Lincolnshire HER, 14505.
22. Kingsford, 1908, 34, 125.
23. Lambarde, 1576, 157–8.
24. Churchyard, 1587, B3v.
25. Bale, 1560, Dedicatory epistle.
26. Foxe, 1563, I, 17.
27. Lambarde, 1576, 267–8.
28. Camden, 1587, 333. The phrase, applied in Camden's description of the secularisation of Peterborough Abbey by Henry VIII, was added in the second edition of *Britannia*. In the first (1586, 288) he wrote only that 'Tunc enim exturbatis monachis Henricum VIII'.
29. Drayton, 1612, 187.
30. Ibid, 264.
31. Speed, 1611, 787–802.
32. Anon., 1591, 32.
33. Hill, 1595, 159.
34. Dickens, 1959, 89.
35. Ritchie, 1966.
36. Long, 1888, 199.
37. Heaton, 2020, 41–2.
38. Fowler, 1903, 52.
39. Trigge, 1589, 13–14, C2r–v.
40. Estienne, 1607, A 1v.
41. Drayton, 1612, 187.
42. Camden, 1587, 333.
43. Lloyd and Powell, 1584, 253.
44. For examples, Philip Stubbes, *The Theater of the Popes monarchie* (Thomas Dawson: London, 1585) STC (2nd edn.) 23399.3; [Anon.] *A merry iest of Robin Hood and of his life, with a newe play for to be plaied in May games* (Edward White: London, 1590) STC (2nd edn.) 13692.
45. Camden, 1587, 130, 234, 255, 288.
46. Camden, 1610, 163.
47. Speed, 1611, 778, 801.
48. Harpsfield, 1622, 741–79.
49. Some, 1582–83, A5r, A7r.
50. Kingsford, 1908, 176.
51. Lambarde, 1576, 267.
52. Long, 1888, 202.
53. *The Faerie Queene*, VI. xii. 23.
54. Sledmere, 1914, 26.

55. TNA, SP 1/152, fo. 204r.
56. Bale, 1551, 40; Part 2, fo. ixv, Biv.
57. Ruddoke, 1551, 1.
58. Anon., 1552, 10.
59. Camden, 1587, 46, 162, 337, 372.
60. Ibid, 255, 278, 326.
61. Digby, 1590, 2.
62. Dickens, 1959, 91, 96.
63. Loades, 1968, 161.
64. Anon., 1592.
65. Camden, 1587, 367.
66. Bettey, 1996, 79.
67. Wood, 2013, 70.
68. Statham, 2003, xxvii–xxix; Litzenberger, 1997, 49; Lowe, 2010, 99–102; Scarisbrick, 1994, 166–8; Summerson, 1993.
69. Anon., 1550, fos. A ivv–vr.
70. Ibid.
71. Stubbes, 1593, 45.
72. Statham, 2003, xxvii.
73. The last abbot of St Albans, Richard Bourman alias Stevenage, secured the precinct parish chapel of St Andrew for use as a school in 1549. Robert Pursglove, former prior of Guisborough, established a school under his own headship at Ashbourne (Derbyshire): Clark, 2000, 320; Cross, 2004b.
74. Foxe, 1563, V, 1,205–8.
75. The testimony recorded in Foxe tells that Branch had lived as a monk only as far as his ordination: Nichols, 1848, 85; Foxe, 1563, I,198–1,203; Merritt, 2005, 41.
76. Foxe, 1563, I,153–1,169 at 1,169; Cross and Vickers, 1995, 333.
77. Cross and Vickers, 1995, 135–6.
78. Ibid, 604.
79. Lunn, 1980, 16; Cooper and Rees, 2004.
80. Parsons, 1690, 57.
81. Lunn, 1980, 63.
82. Walker, 2010, 156.
83. Thomas, 1992b, 69.
84. Greene, 1592, C 1v.
85. E134/27 (Shrewsbury); E134 (Kirkstall); E178/653 (Plympton); 178/1021 (Glastonbury); 178/1245 (Leicester).
86. Thomas, 1992b, 181.
87. TNA, SP 12/286, fo. 103v.
88. TNA, SP 14/36, fos. 185r–6r.
89. Anon., 1609 Kitching, 1974; Guinn-Chapman, 2013, 53–7.
90. For example, in the royal commissions to examine real property (1828–32) and concerning charities (181–37).
91. Watkin, 1949, 85–6; see also Caraman, 1955, 110–12.
92. Watkin, 1949, 86.
93. Jackson, 1862, 58–9 and n.
94. Ibid, 90.
95. Ibid, 134–5, 139.
96. Sledmere, 1914, 25.
97. Thomas, 1992b, 181.
98. Norfolk HER, NHER 58529.
99. Proctor, 2018, 392.

BIBLIOGRAPHY

Primary Sources

Manuscript

Berkshire Record Office
D/EP/7/33   Records of the abbots of Abingdon
D/EZ/104/1/1-2   Probate of William Martyn, 1541
R/IC1/6   Charter of Incorporation, 1542

Birmingham City Archives
3525/ACC 1935-043/437922   Petition

Bristol Record Office
P/AS/D/HS B 7   Will of John Hawkes

Cambridge
Clare College
Unclassified   Rupert of Deutz

Corpus Christi College
59   Martin of Troppau, *Chronica pontificum*, Langdon Abbey
                                   or Merton Priory
111   Matthew Parker's Miscellany
440   Account of Elizabeth I's coronation

St John's College
Ii. 3. 39   Augustine of Ancona, Glastonbury Abbey
T. 9. 1   Psalter, Ickleton Priory

616

Canterbury Cathedral Archives
CCA-CC-J/Q/333/vii   Court of Quarter Sessions records, Canterbury
CCA-CC-J/Q/337/I   Court of Quarter Sessions records, Canterbury
CCA-CC-J/Q/367/xiv   Court of Quarter Sessions records, Canterbury
CCA-DCc-ChChLet/II/38   Letters, Christ Church Priory, Canterbury
CCA-DCc-ChAnt/C/213   Lease, 1535
CCA-DCc-ChAnt/C/1059   Court depositions, 1560
CCA-DCc-Add MS/129/5   Inventory of church plate, 15th-16th centuries
CCA-DCc/Cellarer   Cellarers' accounts, Christ Church Priory, Canterbury
CCA-DCc/Register/R   Sede vacante register, 1486–1508
CCA/CC/Woodruff/54/18   Orders and decrees

Chester Archives and Local Studies
Zs/B/5/e   Sheriffs' Court rolls
Zs/B/6/a   Sheriffs' Court rolls

Derbyshire Record Office
DDM 19/24   Lease of grange, Merevale Abbey, 1537
D258/27/3/1   Lease of Griffe Manor, 1537

Devon Heritage Centre
123M/0/2   Account, Montacute Priory
ECA/ED/M/326   Indenture
1038M/T/4/36   Petition, 1521
ECA Book 51   John Hooker
W1258 M1/1/6   Diary of daily foodstuff, Tavistock Abbey

Devon, Powderham Castle
Courtenay cartulary   Charters and genealogies of the Courtenay earldom

Dorset History Centre
DC/CC/G/1   Christchurch Borough charters

East Riding Archives
Dorset History Centre
DC/CC/G/1
DDCR 3/1/1/1

East Sussex Record Office
AMS140/1   Will of Sir John Dalingridge
AMS 5789/15   Charter
DUK 569   Will of John Pulton
D/DJ1/2
SAS/CO/3/13/981   Court roll, Combwell Priory
SAS/G16/6   Lease, Alciston
RYE/35/24   Mayoral Plead Book
RYE/60/5   Indenture

Essex Record Office
D/DJg L25   Waltham Abbey
D/DP F234   Inventory, Barking Abbey

Gloucestershire Archives
D1224/T/Box 7/bundle 4   Court roll, Syon Abbey
P201/CW/3/2   Petition, Stanley St Leonard

Hampshire Record Office
DC/B/12   Memorandum
44M69/G8/13   Grant, Bradenstoke Priory

Herefordshire Record Office
Hereford Diocesan Registry   Register of Bishops Charles Booth, 1516–35 and
unclassified   Edward Fox, 1535–38

Hertfordshire Archives and Local Studies
ASA/AR1   Archdeaconry Register of Wills
DE/B2067B/E34   Manorial accounts, Tyttenhanger
DE/FL/17102   Bargain and sale, St Albans, 1540
DE/HL/14388   Charter of incorporation, 1539

Kent History and Library Centre
Fa/Q1   Deed, Faversham Abbey
Fa/A/C/1   Mayoral register, Faversham

Kresen Kernow
AR/25/2   Letter of Sir John Arundell
AR/27/12   Fraternity grant, Bodmin Priory
ART/4/10   Miscellany, Tywardreath Priory
ART/4/15   Letter, Tywardreath Priory

Lancashire Record Office
D603/A/Add/670
DDKE/HMC/1   Miracle testimony, 1524
DDX 102/49   Conveyance, 1559

Lincolnshire Archives
DIOC/BOX/92/5   Visitation records
DIOC/REG/25   Register of Bishop William Attwater, 1514–21
DIOC/REG/26   Register of Bishop John Longland, 1521–47
DIOC/REG/27   Register of Bishop John Longland, 1521–47
2ANC3/A/41   Will of Lord Willoughby, 1526

Lincoln Diocesan Archive
Misc 9215

London, British Library
Additional 5810   Antiquities, Cambridgeshire
Additional 11041   Scudamore papers

Additional 17451	Rental, Glastonbury Abbey
Additional 21312	Conventual leases
Additional 32091	Tudor letters
Additional 38656	Declaration against the papal supremacy
Additional 39758	Chronicle and cartulary, Peterborough Abbey
Additional 46701	Cartulary, Stixwould Abbey
Additional 50856	Anthology, Durham Cathedral Priory
Additional 59616	Customary, Christ Church Priory, Canterbury
Additional 60577	Anthology, Winchester Cathedral Priory
Arundel 26	Tudor letters
Arundel 68	Register, Christ Church Priory, Canterbury
Arundel 327	Beatrice Burgh's book
Cotton Appendix XIV	Breviary
Cotton Appendix XXVII	Tudor letters
Cotton Appendix XXVIII	Royal household accounts
Cotton Caligula D VII	Tudor letters
Cotton Cleopatra C III	Chronicle, Whalley Abbey
Cotton Cleopatra E IV	Letters to Thomas Cromwell
Cotton Cleopatra E V	Reformation letters
Cotton Cleopatra E VI	Reformation letters
Cotton Cleopatra F II	Canon law
Cotton Galba B X	Tudor letters
Cotton Nero B VI	Tudor letters
Cotton Nero D VII	Book of benefactors, St Albans Abbey
Cotton Otho C X	Tudor letters
Cotton Tiberius B III	Benedictional, Christ Church Priory, Canterbury
Cotton Titus B I	Tudor letters
Cotton Titus B III	Tudor and Stuart letters
Cotton Vespasian C XIV/2	Royal letters
Cotton Vespasian D IX	Winchester miscellany
Cotton Vespasian D XVIII	Mid-Tudor miscellany
Cotton Vespasian F IX	Tudor letters
Cotton Vitellius B IV	Tudor letters
Cotton Vitellius B X	Tudor letters
Cotton Vitellius B XII	Tudor letters
Cotton Vitellius B XIII	Tudor letters
Cotton Vitellius B XXI	Tudor letters
Egerton 2164	Survey, Colchester Abbey
Egerton 3098	Inventory, Shaftesbury Abbey
Egerton 3137	Cartulary, Blackborough Priory
Egerton 3759	Gradual, Crowland Abbey
Harley 144	Rental, Kirkstead Abbey
Harley 218	Thomas Cleobury's miscellany
Harley 308	Register, St Edmund's Abbey, Bury
Harley 419	Chronicle, St Augustine's Abbey, Canterbury
Harley 604	Commissioners' accounts
Harley 791	Tudor letters and papers
Harley 1419/1	Inventory of Henry VIII, 1547–48
Harley 3504	Records of royal ceremonial
Harley 3739	Cartulary, Waltham Abbey
Harley 3721	Augustine of Hippo

Harley 3970	Register, Bath Priory
Harley 4843	Anthology of Durham Saints' lives
Lansdowne 97	Burghley papers
Lansdowne 446	Strype's Miscellany
Royal 5 E IX	Letters
Royal 7 E X	Anthology, Abingdon Abbey
Royal 14 B VII	Fines
Sloane 1584	Anthology, Coverham Abbey
Stow 141	Letters

London, Lambeth Palace Library

20	Martyrology, Christ Church, Canterbury
59	Anselm of Canterbury
109	Lead sales from St Mary's Abbey, York
159	Saints' lives, Christ Church Priory, Canterbury
371	Chronicles, Reading Abbey
854	Register, Winchcombe Abbey
F I Vv	Faculty Office Register

London Metropolitan Archives

Guildhall Library MS 1231	Reformation memoranda
Guildhall Library MS 9531/9	Register of Richard Fitzjames, bishop of London, 1506–22
Guildhall Library MS 9531/11	Register of John Stokesley, bishop of London, 1530–39

London, The National Archives

DL	Duchy of Lancaster
E36	Treasury receipts
E40	Augmentations Office, Feoffments
E117/11/32	Inventory of vestments and plate, St Albans Abbey
E135	Exchequer accounts
E179	Augmentations Office, First Fruits
E314	Augmentations Office, Surveys
E322	Deeds of surrender
E326	Augmentations Office, Ancient Deeds
E327	Augmentations Office, Ancient Deeds
PCC Prob 11	Wills
SC6	Ministers' and receivers' accounts
SP1	Commissioners' accounts
SP2	Commissioners' accounts
SP3	Commissioners' accounts
SP4	Commissioners' accounts
SP5	Commissioners' accounts
SP8	Royal letters
SP12	Royal letters
SP14	Royal letters
STAC	Star Chamber records

Norfolk Record Office

DCN, 45/32/22; 34/25	Indentures
KL/C 50/532	Indenture

LEST/NG2   Survey, Walsingham Priory
4a/3/19   Grant, Norwich Blackfriars

North Devon Record Office
B190/1   Letter of John Dynham

Nottinghamshire Archives
DD/4P/48/72   Will of John Stoner, 1532
DD/CH/32/20   Deed, Henry, Lord Grey
DD/SR/225/77   Grant of Rufford Abbey, 1537

Oxford, Bodleian Library
4° Z 33 Th.   Erasmus, Merton Priory
Douce 363   Stephen Batman's miscellany
Lat hist. a 2   Magna tabula, Glastonbury Abbey
Laud Misc. 625   Rental, Leicester Abbey
Rawl. Liturg. G. 12   Prayerbook, Pilton Priory

San Marino, California
Huntington Library
MS EL 9 H 15   Martyrology and customs of Ashridge, Bonhommes
MS EL 34 B 7   Processional, Chester Abbey

Sheffield Archives
BFM/478   Indenture

Shropshire Archives
LB/5/2/130   Obit of Alice Lane, 1537
LB5/2/257   Deed, 1536
972/1/1/374   Lease of Wildmore Grange, 1536
6000/6294A   Grant to Abbot Thomas Butler, 1538

Somerset Heritage Centre
DD\X\RMN/3   Deed, Old Cleeve
T\PH\cl/1/5   Charter, Bruton School
T\PH\cl/1/25   Indenture, Glastonbury Abbey

Staffordshire Record Office
D603/A/ADD/757   Letter from Abbot William Bean of Burton-on-Trent, 1527

Suffolk Record Office
449/2/30
449/2/292   Deed
EE5/6/136   Will of Richard Andrew, 1507
HD/538/345/1/10   Grant
HA30/312/82   Indenture

BIBLIOGRAPHY

Surrey History Centre
LM/345/99   Lease of London Blackfriars, 1540
Z/407/L6.368   Indenture
Z/407/MSLb.545   Letter

West Sussex Record Office
Cowdray 5177   Grant of Waverley Abbey, 1536
CHICTY/AY/112   Will, Giles Bull

West Yorkshire Archive Service
WYL150/962 (23/13)   Indenture, Fountains Abbey
WYL150/961 (13/14)   Indenture, Fountains Abbey

Wiltshire and Swindon History Centre
D 1/2/14   Register of Bishop Edmund Audley of Salisbury, 1502–24
P5/1588/19   Inventory and will of Jane Forget, 1588
132/3   Indenture, Lacock Abbey
473/227   Indenture, Stanley Abbey
1332/3/2/1/1   Charter, Maiden Bradley Priory
1332/3/2/1/19   Leases, Maiden Bradley Priory
1422/109   Legal document

York
Borthwick Institute
Abp Reg 28   Register of Archbishop Edward Lee, 1531–44
Prob. Reg 15 pt III   Probate Register

Print

George Abbot, *The reasons which Doctour hill hath brought for the upholding of papistry, which is falsely termed the Catholike religion*. J. Barnes: Oxford, 1604. STC (2nd edn.) 37.

Abstracts of Star Chamber proceedings relating to the county of Sussex. Henry VII to Philip and Mary, (ed.) P. D. Mundy, Sussex Record Society, 16 (1913).

Accounts of the cellarers of Battle Abbey, 1275–1513, (ed.) E. Searle and B. Ross. Sydney University Press: Sydney, 1967.

Accounts of the feofees of the town lands of Bury St Edmunds, 1569–1622, (ed.) M. Statham and D. MacCulloch, Suffolk Record Society, 46 (2003).

Acts of the Privy Council of England. New Series: 1542–1558, (ed.) J. R. Dasent, 6 vols. HMSO: London, 1890–93.

[John Alcock a] *Abbaye of the Holy Ghost*. Wynkyn de Worde: London, 1497. STC (2nd edn.) 13609.

[John Alcock b] *Spousage of a virgin to Christ*. Wynkyn de Worde: Westminster, 1497. STC (2nd edn.) 286.

[John Amundesham] *Annales monasterii S. Albani a Johanne Amundesham monacho ut videtur conscripti (AD 1421–1440) quibus praefigitur Chronicon rerum gestarum in monasterio S. Albani (AD 1422–1431) quodam auctore ignoto compilatum*, (ed.) H. T. Riley, 2 vols. Rolls Series, 28/5 (1870–1).

[Anon.] *A balade agaynst malycyous sclaunderers*. John Gough: London, 1540. STC (2nd edn.) 1323.5

[Anon.] *Certayne causes gathered together, wherin is shewed the decaye of England onely by the great multytude of shepe, to the utter decay of householde keeping maytenaunce of men*. S. Mierdman: London, 1552. STC (2nd edn.) 9980.

[Anon.] *The complaynt of Roderyck Mors, sometime a gray fryer, unto the parliament howse of Ingland.* Wolfgang Kopfel: Strasbourg, 1542. STC (2nd edn.) 3759.5.

[Anon.] *The confession of the faith of the Germaynes exhibited to the moste victorious Emperour Charles the V in the councell or assemble holden at Augusta the yere of our Lorde 1530. To which is added the apologie of Melancthon.* Robert Redman: London, 1536. STC (2nd edn.) 908.

[Anon.] *The copy of the commaundement generall by the abbot of euyll profytes.* Peter Treuerys: London, 1530. STC (2nd edn.) 5743.

[Anon.] *Cronycles of Englonde with the dedes of popes and emperours, and also the descripcyon of Englonde.* Wynkyn de Worde: London, 1528. STC (2nd edn.) 10002.

[Anon.] *The dyetery of ghostly helthe.* Wynkyn de Worde: London, 1520. STC (2nd edn.) 6833.

[Anon.] *A dyaloge describing the originall ground of these Lutheran faccyons and many of theyr abuses compyled by Syr Wyllyam Barlow chanon.* Wyllyam Rastell: London, 1531. STC (2nd edn.) 1461.

[Anon.] *A goodly prymer in englyshe newly corrected and printed with certeyne godly meditations and prayers added to the same, very necessarie [and] profitable for all them that ryghte assuredly understand not yet latine.* John Byddell for Wyllyam Marshall: London, 1535. STC (2nd edn.) 15988.

[Anon.] *Here begynneth the lyfe of the blessed martyr Saynte Thomas* [Becket]. Richard Pynson: London, 1520. STC (2nd edn.) 23954.

[Anon.] *Here begynneth a lytell treatyse or booke named Johan Maundeuyll knight born in Englonde in the towne of saynt Albone speketh of the ways of the holy londe towarde Jherusalem & of marueyles of Ynde & of other dyuerse countrees.* Wynkyn de Worde: London, 1499. STC (2nd edn.) 17247.

[Anon.] *Her begynneth a mery geste of the frere and the boye.* Wynkyn de Worde: London, 1513. STC (2nd edn.) 14522.

[Anon.] *Here begynneth the orcharde of Syon in the whiche is conteyned the revelacyons of seynt Katheryne of Sene with ghostly fruytes and precious plantes for the helthe of mannes soule.* Wynkyn de Worde: London, 1519. STC (2nd edn.) 4815.

[Anon.] *Here begynneth the pystell & gospels of the sondayes and festyvall holy days.* Richard Grafton: London, 1540. STC (2nd edn.) 2971.5.

[Anon.] *Here foloweth a life taken out of a boke which sometyme Theodosius the Emperour founde in Iherusalem in the pretorye of pylate of Joseph Armathy.* Wynkyn de Worde: London, 1511. STC (2nd edn.) 14806.

[Anon.] *The lamentable and true tragedie of M. Arden of Feversham in Kent who was most wickedlye murdered by the meaes of his disloyall and wanton wife.* Edward White: London, 1592. STC (2nd edn.) 733.

[Anon.] *A mery gest how a sergeaunt wolde lerne to be a frere.* Julyan Notary: London, 1516. STC (2nd edn.) 18091.

[Anon.] *The myracles of oure blessyd lady.* Wynkyn de Worde: Westminster, 1496. STC (2nd edn.) 17539.

[Anon.] *Of this chapell se here the fundacyon bylded the yere of crystes incarnacyon a thousande complete syxty and one the tyme of sent Edward kyng of this region.* Richard Pynson: London, 1496. STC (2nd edn.) 25001.

[Anon.] *Piers Plowmans exhortation to the Parlyamenthouse.* Anthony Scoloker: London, 1550. STC (2nd edn.) 19905.

[Anon.] *A proclamacion devised by the kynges hygnes with the aduyse of his counsayle, that his subiectes be warned to auoyde in some cases the daunger and penaltie of the statute of provision and premunire.* Thomas Berthelet: London, 1533. STC (2nd edn.) 7779.

[Anon.] *A proclamation signifying his Maiesties pleasure, to confirme by all meanes the estates of his subiects against all defects in their assurances, and all concealed titles.* Robert Barker: London, 1609. STC (2nd edn.) 8432.

[Anon.] *Rede me and be nott wrothe for I saye no thynge but trouth I will ascende makynge my state so hye that my popous honoure shall never dye.* Johann Schott: Strasbourg, 1528. STC (2nd edn.) 1462.2.

[Anon.] *The troublesome raigne of King Iohn King of England . . . also the death of King Iohn at Swinstead Abbey as it was sundrie times publikely acted by the Queenes Maiesties players in the honourable citie of London*. Sampson Clarke: London, 1591. STC (2nd edn.) 14644.

[Anon.] *This is the table of the historye of Reynart the foxe*. William Caxton: London, 1481. STC (2nd edn.) 1212.

A proclamation deuysed by the kings maiesty, by the advyse of his hyghnes counsel the xxii day of Iuly in the xxxiii yere of his maiesties reygne. Thomas Berthelet, 1541. STC (2nd edn.) 7795.

[William Atkinson] *A ful deuout and gostely treatyse of the imitacion and folowyngeye blesseyd lyfe of our most mercyful sauiour cryst compyled in laten by the right worshypful Doctor Mayster Iohn Gerson and translate into Englysshe the yere of our lord M d ii by mayster Wyllyam atkynson doctor of diuiuite*. Wynkyn de Worde: London, 1504. STC (2nd edn.) 23954.7.

[John Bale] *The actes of Englysh votaryes comprehendynge their unchast practyses and examples by all ages, from the worldes begynnynge to thys present yeare, collected out of their own legendes and chronycles by Iohan Bale*. S. Mierdman: Antwerp, 1546. STC (2nd edn.) 1270.

[John Bale] *The apology of Iohan Bale agaynste a ranke papyst anuswering both hym and hys doctors, that neyther their vowes nor yet their priesthode areof the Gospell, but of antichrist Anno Dⁱ MCCCCCL*. S. Mierdman: London, 1550. STC (2nd edn.) 1275.

John Bale, *An epistle exhortatorye of an Englyshe Christiane unto his derelye beloved contreye of Englande against the ompouse popyshe byshoppes therof*. Widow of C. Ruremond: Antwerp, 1544. STC (2nd edn.) 1291.

[John Bale] *The first two partes of the actes or unchast examples of the Englysh votaryes gathered out of their owne legenades and chronycles by Johan Bale*. For John Bale: London, 1551. STC (2nd edn.) 1273.5.

John Bale, *Kynge Johan. A Play in two parts*, (ed.) J. P. Collier, Camden Society: London, 1838.

[Alexander Barclay] *The eclogues of Alexander Barclay: from the original edition by John Cawood*, (ed.) B. White, Early English Texts Society. Oxford University Press: Oxford, 1960.

[Alexander Barclay] *Here begynneth a ryght frutefull treatyse, intituled the myrrour of good maners conteynyng the iiii vertues called cardynall, compiled in latyn by Domynike Mancyn*. Richard Pynson: London, 1518. STC (2nd edn.) 17242.

[Benedict of Nursia] *Here begynneth the rule of Seynt Benet*. Richard Pynson: London, 1516. STC (2nd edn.) 1859.

[Benedict of Nursia] *Three Middle English Versions of the rule of St Benet*, (ed.) E. A. Kock, Early English Text Society, Original Series, 120 (1902).

[Richard Benese] *This boke sheweth the maner of measurynge all maner of lande as well of woodlande as of lande in the felde and comptyng the true nombre of acres of the same. Newlye invented and compyled by Syr Richard Benese chanon of Marton Abbay besyde London*. James Nicolson: London, c. 1537. STC (2nd edn.) 873.

Francis Bigod, *A treatise concernynge impropriations of benefices*. Thomas Godfray: London, 1535. STC (2nd edn.) 4240.

Bishop Geoffrey Blythe's visitations, c.1515–1525 (ed.) P. Heath, Staffordshire Record Society, Historical Collections, 4:7 (1973).

Thomas Bourchier, *Historia ecclesiastica de martyrio fratrum ordinis divi Francisci dictorum de observantia*. Jean Pouppy: Paris, 1582.

[Henry Bradshaw], *Here begynneth the holy lyfe and history of Saynt Werburge very frutefull for all christen people to rede*. Richard Pynson: London, 1521. STC (2nd edn.) 3506.

Bullarum privilegiorum ac diplomatum Romanorum Pontificum amplissima collectio, Tomus tertius, pars secunda. A Gregorio X ad Martinum V, scilicet ab anno 1271 ad 1431, (ed.) C. Cocquelines. Jerome Mainard: Rome, 1741.

Gilbert Burnet, *History of the Reformation of the Church of England*, (ed.) N. Pocock, 7 vols. Clarendon Press: Oxford, 1865.

Calendar of Close Rolls, Edward III: Volume 10, 1354–1360, (ed.) H. C. Maxwell Lyte. HMSO, London, 1908.

Calendar of Close Rolls, Henry VII, 1485–1509, (ed.) K. E. Ledward and R. E. Latham, 2 vols. HMSO: London, 1955–63.

Calendar of Close Rolls preserved in the Public Record Office, prepared under the superintendence of the Deputy Keeper of the Records, (ed.) H. C. Maxwell Lyte. HMSO: London, 1955–63.

Calendar of Papal Registers, Volume 4. 1362–1404, (ed.) W. H. Bliss and J. A. Twemlow. HMSO: London, 1902.

Calendar of Papal Registers relating to Great Britain and Ireland, Volume 11. 1455–1464, (ed.) J. A. Twemlow. HMSO: London, 1921.

Calendar of Papal Registers, Volume 14. 1484–92, (ed.) J. A. Twemlow. HMSO: London, 1960.

Calendar of Patent Rolls preserved in the Public Record Office, prepared under the superintendence of the Deputy Keeper of the Records. Edward IV–Richard III, 1461–1485, (ed.) J. G. Black, M. S. Giuseppi and H. C. Maxwell Lyte, 3 vols. HMSO: London, 1897–1901.

Calendar of Patent Rolls preserved in the Public Record Office, prepared under the superintendence of the Deputy Keeper of the Records. Edward VI, 1547–53, (ed.) H. C. Maxwell Lyte, 6 vols. HMSO: London, 1924–9.

Calendar of Patent Rolls preserved in the Public Record Office, prepared under the superintendence of the Deputy Keeper of the Records. Elizabeth I, Volume 1, 1558–60, (ed.) J. Collingridge. HMSO: London, 1939.

Calendar of Patent Rolls preserved in the Public Record Office, prepared under the superintendence of the Deputy Keeper of the Records. Henry VI, 1422–61, (ed.) J. G. Black, 6 vols. HMSO: London, 1901–10.

Calendar of Patent Rolls preserved in the Public Record Office, prepared under the superintendence of the Deputy Keeper of the Records. Henry VII, 1485–1509, (ed.) R. H. Brodie, J. G. Black and H. C. Maxwell Lyte, 2 vols. HMSO: London, 1914–16.

Calendar of Patent Rolls preserved in the Public Record Office, prepared under the superintendence of the Deputy Keeper of the Records. Philip and Mary, 1553–58, (ed.) M. S. Giuseppi, 4 vols. HMSO: London, 1937–9.

Calendar of State Papers. Domestic Series. Edward VI, Mary I, Elizabeth, 1547–80, Volume 1, (ed.) R. Lemon. Longman, Brown, Green, Longman and Roberts: London, 1856.

Calendar of State Papers. Domestic Series. Mary I, 1553–58, (ed.) C. S. Knighton. HMSO: London, 1998.

Calendar of State Papers and manuscripts relating to English affairs existing in the archives and collections of Venice and in other libraries of northern Italy, V–VII, 1534–80, (ed.) R. L. Brown and G. C. Bentinck. Public Record Office: London, 1873–90.

Calendar of wills proved and enrolled in the court of Husting, 1258–1688, (ed.) R. R. Sharpe, 2 vols. HMSO: London, 1889–90.

William Camden, *Britannia siue Florentissimorum regnorum Angliae, Scotiae Hiberniae et insularum adiacentium ex intima antiquitate chorographica description*. STC (2nd edn.) 4504. Ralph Newbery: London, 1587.

Thomas Carlyle, *Past and Present*. Chapman and Hall Ltd: London, 1843.

The cartularies of Southwick Priory, Part 1, (ed.) K. Hanna, Hampshire Record Series, 9. Hampshire Record Office: Winchester, 1988.

The cartulary of Chatteris Abbey, (ed.) C. Breay. The Boydell Press: Woodbridge, 1999.

George Cavendish, *The life and death of Cardinal Wolsey*, (ed.) R. Sylvester, Early English Text Society, 243 (1959).

Chapters of the Augustinian Canons, (ed.) H. E. Salter, Oxford Historical Society (1922).

[Maurice Chauncy] *The history of the sufferings of eighteen Carthusians in England: who refusing to take part in the schism, and to separate themselves from the unity of the Catholic church, were cruelly martyred*. Burns and Oates: London, 1890.

[Maurice Chauncy] *The various versions of the Historia aliquot martyrum Anglorum by Dom Maurice Chauncy*, (ed.) J. Clark, intr. P. Cunich, *Analecta Cartusiana*, 86 (2007).

[Andrew Chertsey] *Here foloweth a notable treatyse and full necessary to an crysten men for to know and it is named the Ordynarye of Crystyanyte or of Crysten men.* Wynkyn de Worde: London, 1502. STC (2nd edn.) 5198.

The chronicle of John Hardyng, (ed.) H. Ellis. F. C. and J. Rivington et al.: London, 1812.

Chronicle of the Greyfriars of London, (ed.) J. G. Nichols, Camden Society, 53. Royal Historical Society: London, 1852.

Chronicles of the White Rose of York: a series of historical fragments, proclamations, letters and other contemporary documents relating to the reign of King Edward the Fourth, (ed.) J. A. Giles. Bohn: London, 1845.

'Chronicle of the years 1532–37 written by a monk of St Augustine's Canterbury', in *Narratives of the days of Reformation, chiefly from the manuscripts of John Foxe martyrologist*, ed. J. G. Nichols. Camden Society. Royal Historical Society: London, 1859, 279–86.

The Churchwardens' accounts of the parish of St Mary's Reading, Berks, 1550–62, (ed.) F. N. A. Garry and A. G. Garry. E. Blackwell: Reading, 1893.

Thomas Churchyard, *The worthiness of Wales wherein are more then a thousand several things rehearsed*. G. Robinson: London, 1587. STC (2nd edn.) 5261.

[John Colet] *The sermon of Doctor Colete made at the conuocation at Paulis*. Thomas Berthelet: London, 1530. STC (2nd edn.) 5550.

Collectanea Anglo Premonstratensia. Documents drawn from the original register of the order, now in the Bodleian Library, Oxford, and the transcript of another register in the British Museum, (ed.) F. Gasquet, 2 vols. Royal Historical Society: London, 1904–6.

Concilia magnae Britanniae et Hiberniae a synodo Verolamiensi AD CCCCXLVI Londoniensem AD MDCCXVII accedunt constitutions et alia ad historiam ecclesiae Anglicanae spectantia, (ed.) D. Wilkins, 4 vols. R. Gosling: London, 1737.

[Robert Copland] *The hye waye to the spyttell hous*. Robert Copland: London, 1536. STC (2nd edn.) 5732.

[Miles Coverdale] *The old fayth an euydent probacion out of the holy scripture, that the christen fayth (which is the right, true, old and undoubted faith) hath endured sens the beginnyng of the worlde*. M. Crom: Antwerp, 1541. STC (2nd edn.) 4070.5.

Leonard Cox, *The art or crafte of rhetoryke*. Robert Redman: London, 1532. STC (2nd edn.) 5947.

The diary of Henry Machyn, (ed.) J. G. Nichols, Camden Society, 42 (1848).

Everard Digby, *His dissuasive from taking away the lyvings and goods of the church. Wherein all men plainely behold the great blessings which the Lord hath powred on all those who liberally have bestowed on his holy temple: and the strange punishments that have befallen them which have done the contrarie*. Robert Robinson and Thomas Newman: London, 1590. STC (2nd edn.) 6842.

Documents illustrating the activities of the general and provincial chapter of the English Black Monks, 1215–1540, (ed.) W. A. Pantin, 3 vols., Camden Society, 4th Series, 41, 44, 47. Royal Historical Society: London, 1931–7.

[Thomas Elyot] *A svvete and deuoute sermon of holy saynt Ciprian of mortalitie of man. The rules of a christian lyfe made by Picus erle of Mirandula, bothe translated into englyshe by syr Thomas Elyot knyghte*. Thomas Berthelet: London, 1534. STC (2nd edn.) 6157.

Desiderius Erasmus, *Colloquies*, (tr.) C. R. Thompson. University of Toronto Press: Toronto, 1997.

[Desiderius Erasmus] *De contemptu mundi. The disipisyng of the worlde compiled in Latyn by Erasmus Rot. and translated in to englyshe by Thomas Paynell*. London, 1532. STC (2nd edn.) 10470.8.

[Desiderius Erasmus] *The correspondence of Erasmus: Letters 1–141 (1484–1500)*, (ed.) R. A. B. Mynors, D. F. S. Thomson and W. K. Ferguson. University of Toronto Press: Toronto, 1974.

[Desiderius Erasmus] *Desiderii Erasmi Roterodami Colloquia familiaria et Encomium moriae*, (ed.) O. Holtze and O. Brandstetter: Leipzig, 1892.

[Desiderius Erasmus] 'Life of Jerome / Hieronymi Stridonensis vita', in *The edition of St Jerome*, ed. J. F. Brady and J. C. Olin, 61. University of Toronto Press: Toronto, 1992.

[Desiderius Erasmus] *A ryght frutefull epistle deuysed by the most excellent clerke Erasmus in laude and prayse of matrimony translated in to Englyshe by Rychard Tauernour*. Robert Redman: London, 1536. STC (2nd edn.) 10492.

[Henri Estienne] *A world of wonders: or an introduction to a treatise touching the conformitie of ancient and modern wonders or a preparative treatise to the Apologie for Herodotus*. Richard Field for John Norton: London, 1607. STC (2nd edn.) 10553.

Exhortacion to the people instructyng theym to unitie and obedience. Thomas Berthelet: London, 1536, STC (2nd edn.) 23236.

[Robert Fabyan] *Newe cronycles of Englande and of Fraunce*. Richard Pynson: London, 1516. STC (2nd edn.) 10659.

[Robert Fabyan] *The new chronicles of England and France; in two parts*, (ed.) H. Ellis. F. C. and J. Rivington et al.: London, 1811.

Faculty Office Registers, 1534–1549: a calendar of the first two registers of the archbishop of Canterbury's Faculty Office, (ed.) D. S. Chambers. Clarendon Press: Oxford, 1966.

[John Feckenham] *Here in this booke ye have a godly epistle made by a faithful Christian. A communication between Feckna and the Lady Jane Dudley*. A Scoloker (?): London, 1554. STC (2nd edn.) 7279.5.

[John Feckenham] *A notable sermon made within S. Paules church in London . . . at the celebration of the exequies of the right excellent and famous princesse, lady Ione, Quene of Spayne*. Robert Caly: London, 1555. STC (2nd edn.) 10744.

[John Feckenham] 'The Oration of Dr Feckenham, abbot of Westminster, made in the Parliament House, anno 1539', in *A collection of scarce and valuable tracts on the most interesting and entertaining subjects but chiefly such as relate to the history and constitution of these kingdoms . . . particularly that of the late Lord Somers*, 2nd edn. (ed.) W. Scott. T. Cadsell et al.: London, 1809, 81–5.

[Simon Fish] *A supplicacyon for the beggers*. J. Graphaeus (?): Antwerp, 1529. STC (2nd edn.) 10883.

Foedera conventiones, literæ, et cujuscunque generis acta publica, inter reges Angliæ, et alios quosvis Imperatores, Regis, Pontifices, Principes, vel communitates, ab ineunte sæculo duodecimo, viz. ab anno 1101, ad nostra usque tempora, (ed.) T. Rymer, 20 vols. Jacob Tonson: Den Haag, 1739–45.

The Fountains Abbey Leasebook, (ed.) D. J. H. Michelmore, Yorkshire Archaeological Society, Record Series, 140 (1981).

John Foxe, *Actes and monuments of these latter and perillous dayes touching matters of the church, wherein ar comprehended and described the great persecutions and horrible troubles that have been wrought and practised by the Romishe prelates speciallye in this realme of England and Scotlande, from the yeare of our Lorde a thousande unto the tyme nowe present*. John Day: London, 1563. STC (2nd edn.) 11222.

The confutaycon of the first part of Frith's book with a dysputacyon before whether it be possyble for any heretike to know that hym selfe is one or not. And also an other, whether it be wors to denye directely more or lesse of the fayth, put forth by Iohn Gwynneth clerke. STC (2nd edn.) 12557. John Herford: St Albans, 1536.

[Jasper Fyloll] *Agaynst the possessyons of the clergye Harkyn what great auctorytes shall nowe folowe, for proffe thereof*. J. Skot: London, 1537. STC (2nd edn.) 11489.

Gesta abbatum monasterii sancti Albani a Thomas Walsingham regnante Ricardo secondo eiusdem praecentore compilata, (ed.) H. T. Riley, 3 vols., Rolls Series, 28 (1867–9).

[Robert Greene] *A quip for an vpstart courtier: or a quaint dispute between veluet breeches and clothbreeches wherein is plainely set downe the disorders in all estates and trades*. John Wolfe: London, 1591. STC (2nd edn.) 12300.

[Edward Hall] *Hall's Chronicle, containing the history of England during the reign of Henry the Fourth to the end of the reign of Henry the eighth*. J. Johnson, F. C. and J. Rivington et al.: London, 1809.

[John Hardyng] *The chronicle of Ihon Hardyng in metre from the first begynnyng of Englande, unto ye reigne of Edward ye fourth . . . with a continuacion of the storie in prose to this our tyme*. Richard Grafton: London, 1543. STC (2nd edn.) 12766.7.

Nicholas Harpsfield, *Historia Anglicana ecclesiastica a primis gentis susceptae fidei incunabulis ad nostra fere tempore deducta*. Richard Gibbon: Douai, 1622.

[Nicholas Harpsfield] *A treatise on the pretended divorce between Henry VIII and Catherine of Aragon, by Nicholas Harpsfield, LLD, archdeacon of Canterbury, now first printed from a collation of four manuscripts*, (ed.) N. Pocock, Camden Society. London, 1878.

Henry VII's London in the Great Chronicle, (ed.) J. Boffey, Medieval Institute Publications. Western Michigan University: Kalamazoo, MI, 2019.

[Henry VIII] *A copy of the letters wherin the most redoubted and mighty prince our soverayne lorde king Henry the Eight, king of England and of Fraunce defensor of the faith and lorde of Ireland made answere unto a certaune leter of Martyn Luther sente unto him by the same.* Rycharde Pynson: London, 1527. STC (2nd edn.) 13086.

[John Heywood] *A mery play between the pardoner and the frere, the curate and neybour Pratte.* Wyllyam Rastell: London, 1533. STC (2nd edn.) 13299.

Adam Hill, *The crie of England. A sermon preached at Pauls crosse in September 1593.* Edward Alde: London, 1595. STC (2nd edn.) 13465.

Historiae Dunelmensis Scriptores Tres, Gaufridus de Coldingham, Robertus de Graystanes et Willielmus de Chambre, (ed.) J. Raine, Surtees Society, 9 (1839).

Raphael Holinshed, *The firste volume of the Chronicles of England, Scotland and Ireland Conteyning, the description and chronicles of England, from the first inhabiting unto the conquest.* Henry Bynneman for John Harison: London, 1577. STC (2nd edn.) 13568.

Wilfrid Holme, *The fall and euill successe of rebellion from time to time wherein is contained matter, most meete for all estates to vewe.* Henry Binneman: London, 1572. STC (2nd edn.) 13602.

[Robert Horne] *An answeare made by Robert Bishoppe of Wynchester to a booke entituled the declaration of suche scruples, and staies of conscience touching the othe of the supremacy as M Iohn Fekenham by wrytinge did deliver unto the L. Bishop of Winchester with his resolutions made thereunto.* Henry Wykes: London, 1566. STC (2nd edn.) 13818.

[John Howes] *John Howes' MS, 1582. Being a brief note of the order and manner of the proceedings in the first erection of the three royal hospitals of Christ, Bridewell & St Thomas the Apostle*, (ed.) W. Lempriere. Christ's Hospital: London, 1904.

The injunctions of John Longland, bishop of Lincoln to certain monasteries, 1531, ed. E. Peacock, *Archaeologia*, 47 (1883), 49–64.

The itinerary in Wales of John Leland in or about the years 1536–39, (ed.) L. Toulmin-Smith. George Bell and Sons: London, 1906.

The itinerary of John Leland in or about the years 1533–43, (ed.) L. Toulmin-Smith, 5 vols. George Bell and Sons: London, 1906–10.

[George Joye] *The defence of the mariage of preistes agenst Steuen Gardiner bisshop of Wynchester, Wylliam Repse bisshop of Norwiche.* Jan Troost: Antwerp, 1541. STC (2nd edn.) 21804.

Kentish visitations of archbishop William Warham and his deputies, 1511–12, (ed.) K. L. Wood-Legh, Kent Archaeological Society, Record Series, 24 (1984).

William Lambarde, *A perambulation of Kent conteining the description, hystorie, and customes of the that shyre. Collected and written (for the most part) in the yeare 1570.* Ralphe Newberie: London, 1576. STC (2nd edn.) 15175.5.

Lancashire and Cheshire Wills and Inventories from the Ecclesiastical Court, Chester. First portion, (ed.). G. Piccope, Chetham Society, 33 (1857).

The last days of Peterborough monastery, (ed.) W. T. Mellows, Northamptonshire Record Society, 12 (1940).

[Hugh Latimer] *The sermon that the reuerende father in Christ, Hugh Latimer, byshop of Worcester, made to the clergie, in the conuocation before the parlyament began, the 9 day of June, the 28 yere of the reigne of our souerayne lorde Kyng Henry.* Thomas Berthelet: London, 1537. STC (2nd edn.) 15286.

[Hugh Latimer] *The works of Hugh Latimer, sometime bishop of Worcester, martyr, 1555*, (ed.) G. E. Corrie, 2 vols., Parker Society (1844–5).

[William Latymer] 'Chronicklle of Anne Bulleyne', (ed.) M. Dowling, Camden Society, 4th Series, 39 (1990), 23–65.

The ledger-book of Vale Royal Abbey, (ed.) J. Brownbill, Manchester Record Society, 68 (1914).

W. A. Leighton, 'The register of Sir Thomas Botelar, vicar of Much Wenlock', *Transactions of the Shropshire Archaeological and Natural History Society*, 6 (1883), 93–132.

[John Leland] *Johanni Lelandi antiquarii de rebus Britannicis Collectanea ex autographis descripsit ediditque*, (ed.) T. Hearne, 6 vols. G. and J. Richardson: London, 1770.

The letter book of Robert Joseph, monk-scholar of Evesham and Gloucester College, Oxford, (ed.) H. Aveling and W. A. Pantin. Oxford Historical Society: New Series, 19 (1967).

Letters from the English abbots to the chapter at Citeaux, 1442–1521, (ed.) C. H. Talbot, Camden Society, 4th Series. Royal Historical Society: London, 1967.

Letters and papers foreign & domestic of the reign of Henry VIII, ed. J. S. Brewer et al., 22 vols. in 35. Longman, Green, Longman and Roberts: London, 1862–1932.

Letters and papers illustrative of the reigns of Richard III and Henry VII, (ed.) J. Gairdner, 2 vols., Rolls Series, 24 (1861–3).

Letters of Richard Fox, 1486–1527, (ed.) H. M. and P. S. Allen. Clarendon Press: Oxford, 1929.

The Libraries of Henry VIII, (ed.) J. Carley, Corpus of British Medieval Library Catalogues, 7. British Academy and Oxford University Press: London, 2000.

The life and letters of Thomas Cromwell, (ed.) R. B. Merriman, 2 vols. Oxford University Press: Oxford, 1902.

Lincoln Wills, 1532–34, (ed.) D. Hickman, Lincoln Record Society, 89 (2001).

The Lisle Letters, (ed.) M. St Clare Byrne, 6 vols. The University of Chicago Press: Chicago and London, 1981.

Literae Cantuarienses. The letter books of the monastery of Christ Church, Canterbury, (ed.) J. B. Sheppard, 3 vols., Rolls Series, 85 (1887–9).

Humphrey Lloyd and David Powel, *The historie of Cambria now called Wales*. Rafe Newberie and Henrie Denham: London, 1584. STC (2nd edn.) 4606.

Lollards of Coventry, 1486–1522, (ed. and tr.) S. McSheffrey and N. Tanner, Camden Society, 5th Series, 23. Royal Historical Society: London, 2003.

[John Longland] *Tres conciones reuerendissimo Domino do Waramo Cantuariensi archiepiscopo totius Angliae primate merito nuncupatae*. Richard Pynson: London, 1527. STC (2nd edn.) 16790.

[John Longland b] *John Longland, Sermones Ioannis Longlondi theologie professoris . . . habiti coram illustrissimi regis Henrici opctaui, fidei defensoris inuictissimi summa maiestate, cui est a confessionibus*. Richard Pynson (?): London, 1527. STC (2nd edn.) 16797.

[Thomas Lupset] *An exhortation to yonge men perswading them to walke in the pathe way that leadeth to honest and goodnes writen to a frend of his by Thomas Lupsete*. Thomas Berthelet: London, 1535. STC (2nd edn.) 16936.

[John Lydgate] *Here begynnethe the glorious lyfe and passion of seint Albon prothomartyr of Englande, and also the lyfe and passion of saint amphabel which conyerted saint Albon to the faith of Christe*. John Herford: St Albans, 1534. STC (2nd edn.) 256.

[Sir Thomas Malory] *Le morte darthur*. William Caxton: Westminster, 1485. STC (2nd edn.) 801.

Materials for a history of the reign of Henry VII from the original documents preserved in the Public Record Office, (ed.) W. Campbell, 2 vols., Rolls Series, 60. Longman and Co.: London, 1873.

Memorials of Father Augustine Baker and other documents relating to the English Benedictines, ed. J. McCann and H. Connolly, Catholic Record Society, 33 (1933).

Memorials of King Henry the Seventh, (ed.) J. Gairdner, Rolls Series, 10 (1858).

Monastery and Society in the late Middle Ages: selected account rolls from Selby Abbey, Yorkshire, 1398–1537, (ed.) J. H. Tillotson. The Boydell Press: Woodbridge, 1988.

Monasticon Anglicanum, or the history of the ancient abbies and other monasteries, hospitals, cathedral and collegiate churches in England & Wales, collected & published in Latin by Sir William Dugdale and Roger Dodsworth and now epitomised in English, (ed.) J. Caley, B. Bandinel and H. Ellis, 6 vols. in 8. London, 1817–30.

Monasticon dioecesis Exoniensis being a collection of records and instruments illustrating the ancient conventual, collegiate and eleemosynary foundations in the counties of Cornwall and Devon, with historical notices and a supplement, (ed.) G. Oliver. P. A. Hannaford: Exeter; Longman, Brown, Green and Longmans: London, 1846.

Geoffrey of Monmouth. *The History of the Kings of Britain.* An edition and translation of the 'De gestis Britonum' [*Historia regum Britanniae*], ed. M. D. Reeve, tr. N. Wright, Arthurian Studies, 69. Boydell Press: Woodbridge, 2007.

[Sir Thomas More] *The correspondence of Thomas More,* (ed.) E. F. Rogers. Princeton University Press: Princeton, 1947.

Sir Thomas More, *Utopia,* (trans.) C. H. Miller. Yale University Press: New Haven and London, 2001.

[Richard Morison] *A lamentation in which is shewed what ruyne and destruction cometh of seditious rebellion.* Thomas Berthelet: London, 1536. STC (2nd edn.) 18113.3.

[James Nicolson] *The original [and] sprynge of all sects [and] orders wy whome, wha or were they beganne.* John Gough: London, 1537. STC (2nd edn.) 18849.

The obituary roll of John Islip, abbot of Westminster, 1500–1532 with notes on other English obituary rolls, (ed.) W. St John Hope. Vetusta monumenta, VII/4. Society of Antiquaries: London, 1906.

The Oglander memoirs. Extracts from the MSS of Sir J. Oglander, Kt, (ed.) W. H. Long. Reeves and Turner: London, 1888.

Original letters illustrative of English History, including numerous royal letters, 3rd Series, I, (ed.) H. Ellis. Richard Bentley: London, 1846.

A. Parkinson, *Collectanea Anglo-minoritica or A collection of the antiquities of the English Franciscans or Friers minors commonly call'd Gray Friers.* Thomas Smith: London, 1726.

[Robert Parkyn] 'Robert Parkyn's narrative of Reformation', *English Historical Review,* 62:242 (1947), 58–83.

Robert Parsons, *The Jesuit's memorial for the intended reformation of England under their first popish prince published from the copy that was presented to the late King James II.* Richard Chiswell: London, 1690.

The Plumpton Letters and Papers, (ed.) J. Kirby, Camden Society, 5th Series, 8. Royal Historical Society: London, 1996.

Poly-Olbion by Michaell Drayton Esqr. Humphrey Lownes for M. Lownes; Browne, Helme Busbie: London, 1612. STC (2nd edn.) 7266.

Post-Reformation Catholicism in Bath, Volume 1, (ed.) J. Anthony-Williams, Catholic Record Society, 65 (1975).

The pre-Reformation records of All Saints, Bristol, (ed.) C. Burgess, Bristol Record Society, 46, 53, 56 (1995–2004).

Privy purse expenses of Elizabeth of York: wardrobe accounts of Edward the Fourth with a memoir of Elizabeth of York. (ed.) H. Nicholas. William Pickering: London, 1830.

J. S. Purvis (ed.), *Monastic chancery proceedings (Yorkshire).* Yorkshire Archaeological Society, Record Series, 88 (1934).

Records of St Bartholomew's Priory and of the church and parish of St Bartholomew the Great West Smithfield, (ed.) E. A. Webb, 2 vols. Oxford University Press: Oxford, 1921.

The register or chronicle of Butley Priory, 1510–1535, (ed.) A. G. Dickens. Warren and Son: Winchester, 1951.

The register of the fraternity or guild of the Holy and undivided Trinity and Blessed Virgin Mary in the parish church of Luton in the county of Bedford from AD MCCCCLXXV to MCCCCCXLVI, (ed.) H. Gough. London, 1906.

The register of John Morton archbishop of Canterbury, 1486–1500, (ed.) C. Harper-Bill, 3 vols., Canterbury and York Society, 75, 78, 89 (1987–2000).

The registers of Cuthbert Tunstall, bishop of Durham, 1530–59, and James Pilkington, bishop of Durham, 1561–76, (ed.) G. Hinde, Surtees Society, 161 (1952).

Registra quorundam abbatum monasterii S. Albani qui saeculo XVmo floruere. Registra Johannis Whethamstede, Willelmi Albon et Willelmi Walingforde abbatum monasterii Sancti Albani, (ed.) H. T. Riley, 2 vols., Rolls Series, 28/6 (1872–3).

Registra Stephani Gardiner et Johannis Poynet. Episcoporum Wintoniensium, (ed.) H. Chitty, Canterbury and York Society, 37 (1930).

Registrum Caroli Bothe, episcopi Herefordensis, AD MDXVI–MDXXXV, (ed.) A. D. Bannister, Canterbury and York Society, 28 (1921).

Rerum Anglicarum scriptorum veterum, (ed.) W. Fulman. Oxford, 1684.

Laurence Ridley, *An exposition in the epistell of Iude the apostel of Christ wherein he setteth plainly before every mans eyes false apostels and tehyr craftes by ye which they have longe received simple Christian people.* Thomas Gybson: London, 1538. STC (2nd edn.) 21042.

Laurence Ridley, *A commentary in Englyshe upon Sayncte Paules epistle to the Ephesyans for the instruccyon of them that be unlearned in tonges gathered out of the holy scryptures and of the olde Catholyke doctors of the chyrche*. Robert Redman: London, 1540. STC (2nd edn.) 21038.5.

The Rites of Durham. Being a description or brief explanation of all the ceremonies, rites and customs belonging or being within the monastical church of Durham, before the suppression. Written 1593, (ed.) J. T. Fowler, Surtees Society, 107 (1903).

'Robin Hood and the Monk', (ed.) S. Knight and T. H. Ohlgren, in *Robin Hood and other outlaw tales*, ed. idem. TEAMS Middle English Texts Series, Medieval Institute Publications, Western Michigan University. 2nd edn., Kalamazoo, MI, 2000.

Thomas Ruddoke, *A remembraunce for the maintenaunce of the luynge of ministers and preachers now notablye decayed.* William Seres: London, 1551. STC (2nd edn.) 21435.5.

[Robert Saltwood] *A comparison bytwene iiii byrdes, the larke, the nyghtyngale, ye thrusshe the cuko, for theyr syngnge who shuld be chauntoure of the quere.* John Mychell: Canterbury, 1533. STC (2nd edn) 21647.

[John Skelton] *The complete English poems of John Skelton*, (ed.) V. J. Scattergood. Liverpool University Press: Liverpool, 2015.

Richard Smith, *A bouclier of the Catholike fayth of Christes church conteynyng divers matters now of late called into controversy by the new gospellers.* Rychard Tottell: London, 1554. STC (2nd edn.) 22816.

Robert Some, *A godlie treatise of the churche.* George Bishop, London, 1582–82. STC (2nd edn.) 22910.

[John Speed] *The historie of Great Britaine under the conquests of ye Romans, Saxons, Danes and Normans . . . with ye successions, lives, acts & issues of the English monarchs from Iulius Caesar to our most gracious soueraigne King Iames.* William Hall and John Beale: London, 1611. STC (2nd edn.) 23045.

[Thomas Stapleton] *A counterblast to M. Hornes vayne blaste against M. Fekenham wherein is set forth a ful reply to M. Hornes answer and to euery part therof made, against the declaration of my L. Abbat of Westminster, M. Fekenham, touching, the Othe of the Supremacy.* Jean Fouler: Louvain, 1567. STC (2nd edn.) 23231.

[Thomas Starkey] *England in the reign of King Henry the Eighth. Part 1 Starkey's Life and Letters*, (ed.) S. J. Herrtage, Early English Texts Society, Extra Series, xxxii (1878).

Thomas Starkey, *A dialogue between Pole and Lupset*, ed. T. F. Mayer, Camden Society, 4th Series, 37. Royal Historical Society: London, 1989.

State papers published under the authority of His Majesty's Commission, ed. R. Lemon, 11 vols. London, 1830–52.

Statutes of the realm, ed. A. Luders et al., 11 vols. in 12. Dawsons of Pall Mall: London, 1810–28.

John Stevens, *The history of the antient abbeys, monasteries, hospitals, cathedral and collegiate churches, being two additional volumes to Sir William Dugdale's Monasticon Anglicanum.* 2 vols. Thomas Taylor et al.: London, 1722.

John Stow, *The Annales of England faithfully collected out of the most autenticall authors, records and other monuments of antiquitie, from the first inhabitation until this present yeere*. Rafe Newbery: London, 1592. STC (2nd edn.) 23334.

John Stow, *A Survey of London. Reprinted from the text of 1603*, (ed.) C. L. Kingsford. Oxford, 1908.

John Strype, *Ecclesiastical memorials relating chiefly to religion and the reformation of it, shewing the various emergencies of the church of England under Henry the eighth*, Volume 1. John Wyat: London, 1721.

[Philip Stubbes] *A motive to good works or to true Christianitie indeed*. Thomas Man: London, 1593. STC (2nd edn.) 23397.

[Thomas Swinnerton] *A litel treatise ageynste the mutterynge of some papists in corners*. Thomas Berthelet: London, 1534. STC (2nd edn.) 23551.5

Testamenta Eboracensia or, wills registered at York, illustrative of the history, manners, language, statistics &c. of the province of York, from the year MCCC downwards, (ed.) J. Raine and J. W. Clay, 5 vols., Surtees Society, 4, 30, 45, 53, 79, 106 (1836–1902).

Testamenta vetusta being illustrations from wills, of manners, customs as well as of the descents and possessions of many distinguished families. From the Reign of Henry II to the accession of Queen Elizabeth, (ed.) N. H. Nicolas, 2 vols. London, 1826.

Three chapters of letters relating to the suppression of monasteries edited from the originals in the British Museum, (ed.) T. Wright, Camden Society, 26. J. B. Nichols and Son: London, 1843.

Richard Tracy, *A supplication to our moste sovereigne lord kynge henry the eyght*. Thomas Dawson?: London, 1585. STC (2nd edn.) 24166.

Francis Trigge, *An apologie or defence of our days against the vaine murmurings & complaints of manie wherin is plainly proved that our days are more happie & blessed than the days of our forefathers*. John Wolfe: London, 1589. STC (2nd edn.) 24276.

Tropenell Cartulary being the contents of an old Wiltshire Muniment Chest, (ed.) J. S. Davies, 2 vols. (1908).

Tudor treatises, (ed.) A. G. Dickens, Yorkshire Archaeological Society, Record Series, 125 (1959).

William Turner, *A new booke of spirituall physik for dyverse diseases of the nobilitie and gentlemen of Englande*. Marcus Antonius Constantius: Basel?, 1555.

William Tyndale, *The obedience of a Christen man and how Christen rulers ought to governe, where in also, if thou marke diligently thou shalt fynde eyes to perceave the crafty conveyance of all iugglers*. J. Hoochstraten: Antwerp, 1528. STC (2nd edn.) 24446.

William Vallans, *The honourable prentice: or, this taylor is a man shewed in the life and death of Sir John Hawekwood, sometime prentice of London . . . also of the merry customes of Dunmow, where any one may freely have a gammon of bacon that repents not marriage in a yeere and a day*. J. Beale for Henry Gosson: London, 1615.

Valor ecclesiasticus temp Hen VIII auctoritate regia institutus, (ed.) J. Caley and J. Hunter, Record Commissioners, Texts and Calendars, 6 vols. George Eyre and Andrew Strahan: London, 1810–34.

Polydore Vergil, *Anglica Historia*, (ed.) D. Hay, Camden Society, New Series, 74. Royal Historical Society: London, 1950.

Polydore Vergil *Three books of Polydore Vergil's English History, comprising the reigns of Henry VI, Edward IV and Richard III*, (ed.) H. Ellis. Camden Society: London, 1844.

Visitation articles and injunctions of the period of the Reformation, (ed.) W. H. Frere and W. M. Kennedy, 2 vols. Longman, Green and Co.: London, 1910.

Visitations in the diocese of Lincoln, 1517–31, (ed.) A. H. Thompson, 3 vols., Lincoln Record Society, 33, 35, 37 (1940–7).

Visitations of the diocese of Norwich, AD 1490–1532, (ed.) A. Jessopp, Camden Society, 43. Historical Society: London, 1888.

Visitations of Religious Houses in the diocese of Lincoln, 1420-49, (ed.) A. H. Thompson, 3 vols., Lincoln Record Society, 7, 14, 21 (1914–29).

M. E. C. Walcott, 'The inventories of Westminster Abbey at the Dissolution', *Transactions of the London and Middlesex Archaeological Society*, 4, part 3 (1873), 313–64.

J. Weever, *Antient funerall monuments within the united monarchie of Great Britain, Ireland and the islands adiacent with the dissolved monasteries theirin contained: their founders, and what eminent persona have beene in the same interred.* Thomas Harper: London, 1631. STC (2nd edn.) 25223.

T. West, *The Antiquities of Furness; or an account of the royal abbey of St Mary in the Vale of Nightshade near Dalton-in-Furness.* J. Robinson and J. Ridley: London, 1774.

William Weston, The autobiography of an Elizabethan, tr. P. Caraman. Longman, Green and Co., London, 1955.

[Richard Whitford] *Here begynneth the boke called the Pype, or tonne, of the lyfe of perfection. The reason or cause wherof dothe playnely appere in the processe.* Robert Redman: London, 1532. STC (2nd edn.) 25421.

[Richard Whitford] *A werke for housholders or for them that haue the guydynge or gouernaunce of any company. Gadred and set forth by a professed brother of Syon, Richard Whitforde: and newely corrected [and] prynted agayne with an addicion of polici for housholding, set forth also by the same brother.* STC (2nd edn.) 25425. Robert Redman: London, 1537.

[Richard Whitford] *A dayly exercice and experience of deathe, gathered and set forthe by a brother of Syon Rycharde Whytforde.* Robert Redman: London, 1538. STC (2nd edn.) 25415.

[Sir John Williams] *Account of the monastic treasures confiscated at the Dissolution of the various houses in England*, (ed.) W. B. D. D. Turnbull. Abbotsford Club: Edinburgh, 1836.

Wills and inventories from the registers of the commissary of Bury St Edmund's and the archdeacon of Sudbury, (ed.) S. Tymms, Camden Society, 49: London, 1850.

Charles Wriothesley, *A chronicle of England during the reigns of the Tudors from AD 1485 to 1559*, (ed.) W. Douglas Hamilton, Camden Society, New Series, 11. Royal Historical Society: London, 1875.

The papers of George Wyatt esquire of Boxley Abbey in the county of Kent. Son and heir of Sir Thomas Wyatt the Younger, ed. D. M. Loades, Camden Society, 4th Series, 5. Royal Historical Society: London, 1968.

York clergy wills, 1520–1600, II. City Clergy, (ed.) C. Cross, Borthwick Texts and Calendars, 15 (1989).

Secondary Sources

Addy, S. O. (1878), *Historical memorials of Beauchief Abbey.* James Parker and Co.: Oxford and London.

Allan, J., Henderson, C. G. and Weddell, P. J. (2016), 'A summary of the archaeological evidence for the late medieval friary', in N. Orme, 'The Franciscan friars of Exeter', *Proc. Devon Archaeol. Soc.*, 74, 235–51.

Allen, T. (1994), 'A medieval grange of Abingdon Abbey at Dean Court Farm, Cumnor', *Oxoniensa*, 59, 219–47.

Allinson, K. J. (1958), 'Flock management in the sixteenth and seventeenth centuries', *Economic History Review*, 11:1, 98–112.

Anstruther, G. (1958), *A hundred homeless years. English Dominicans, 1558–1658.* Blackfriars Publications: London.

Armstrong, C. D. C. (2004), 'Stephen Gardiner (c. 1495–1555)', *Oxford Dictionary of National Biography.* Oxford University Press: Oxford.

Astill, G. (2011), 'The changing monastic cloister: excavations in the south range of Bordesley abbey', *Archaeological Journal*, 168: 285–404.

Aston, M. (1973), 'English ruins and English history: The Dissolution and the sense of the past', *Journal of the Warburg and Courtauld Institutes*, 36: 231–55.

Aston, M. (1984), 'Caim's castles: Poverty, politics and disendowment', in *The church, politics and patronage in the fifteenth century*, (ed.) R. B. Dobson. Alan Sutton: Gloucester, 49–57.

Atherton, I. (2003), 'The dean and chapter: Reformation to Restoration, 1541–1660', in *A history of Ely Cathedral*, (ed.) P. Meadows and N. Ramsay. The Boydell Press: Woodbridge, 169–92.

Atherton, I. (2004), 'John Salisbury (1501/2–73)', *Oxford Dictionary of National Biography*. Oxford University Press: Oxford.

Atherton, I. (2011), 'Scudamore family (per. 1500–1820)', *Oxford Dictionary of National Biography*. Oxford University Press: Oxford.

[John Aubrey], Wiltshire: The topographical collections of John Aubrey, FRS, AD 1659–70, with illustrations, (ed.) J. E. Jackson. Wiltshire Archaeological and Natural History Society. Devizes, 1862.

Aveling, H. (1955), 'The monks of Byland after the Dissolution', *Ampleforth Journal*, 60, 3–15.

Bainbridge, V. R. (2004), 'Richard Reynolds (d. 1535)', *Oxford Dictionary of National Biography*. Oxford University Press: Oxford.

Baker, N. and Holt, R. (2003), *Urban growth and the medieval church. Gloucester & Worcester*. Ashgate: Aldershot.

Barnard, E. A. B. (1927–8), 'Philip Hawford, pseudo-abbot of Evesham (1539), and dean of Worcester (1553–1557)', *Transactions of Worcestershire Archaeological Society*, New Series, 5, 52–69.

Baskerville, G. (1927), 'The dispossessed religious of Gloucestershire', *Transactions of the Bristol and Gloucestershire Archaeological Society*, 49, 63–122.

Baskerville, G. (1929), 'Elections to convocation in the diocese of Gloucester under Bishop Hooper', *English Historical Review*, 44:173, 1–32.

Baskerville, G. (1933), 'Married clergy and pensioned religious in Norwich diocese, 1555', *English Historical Review*, 48:189, 43, 64; 199–228.

Baskerville, G. (1940), *English monks and the suppression of the monasteries*, The Bedford Historical Series, 7. Jonathan Cape: London.

Bateson, M. (1890), 'Aske's examination', *English Historical Review*, 5:19, 550–73.

Bateson, M. (1891), 'Archbishop Warham's visitation of monasteries', *English Historical Review*, 6:21, 18–35.

Batho, G. (1967), 'Landlords in England', in *The Agrarian History of England and Wales, Volume IV 1500–1640*, (ed.) J. Thirsk. Cambridge University Press: Cambridge, 256–356.

Baxter, R. (2016), *The royal abbey of Reading*. The Boydell Press: Woodbridge.

Beckett, N. (1995), 'Henry VII and the Sheen Charterhouse', in *The reign of Henry VII*, (ed.) B. J. Thompson. Paul Watkins: Stamford, 117–32.

Bell, D. N. (1995), *What nuns read: Books and libraries in medieval English nunneries*. Cistercian Studies Series, 98. Cistercian Publications: Kalamazoo, MI.

Bernard, G. W. (1996), 'The fall of Wolsey reconsidered', *Journal of British Studies*, 35:3, 277–310.

Bernard, G. W. (2005), *The king's reformation: Henry VIII and the remaking of the English Church*. Yale University Press: New Haven and London.

Bernard, G. W. (2011), 'The dissolution of the monasteries', *History*, 96:324, 390–409.

Bernard, G. W. (2012). *The late medieval English church. Vitality and vulnerability before the break with Rome*. Yale University Press: New Haven and London.

Bernston, M. (2003), *Klostren och reformationen. Upplösingen av kloster och konvent i Sverige 1523–1596*. Artos and Norma: Malmo.

Bettey, J. (2004), 'Paul Bush (1489/90–1558)', *Oxford Dictionary of National Biography*. Oxford University Press: Oxford.

Bettey, J. H. (1989), *The suppression of the monasteries in the West Country*. Alan Sutton: Stroud.

Bettey, J. H. (1996), 'Early topographers, antiquarians and travellers in Dorset', in *Topographical writers in South-West England*, (ed.) M. Brayshay. University of Exeter Press: Exeter, 77–89.

Blanchard, I. W. (1970), 'Population change, enclosure and the early Tudor economy', *Economic History Review*, 23:3, 427–45.

Blunt, J. H. (1875), *Tewkesbury Abbey and its associations*. Simpkin, Marshall and Co.: London; W. North: Tewkesbury.

Boffey, J. and Payne, M. (2017), '*The Gardyner's Passetaunce*, the *Flowers of England*, and Thomas Gardyner, Monk of Westminster', *The Library*, 18:2, 175–90.

Borman, T. (2014), *Thomas Cromwell: The untold story of Henry VIII's most faithful servant*. Hodder and Stoughton: London.

Bowers, R. (1999), 'The almonry schools of the English monasteries, c. 1265–1540', in *Monasteries and Society in Medieval Britain*, (ed.) B. J. Thompson. Paul Watkins: Stamford, 177–222.

Bowers, R. (2003), 'The musicians and liturgy of the Lady Chapels of the monastery church, c. 1235-1540' in *Westminster Abbey: The Lady Chapel of Henry VII*, (ed.) T. Tatton-Brown and R. Mortimer. The Boydell Press: Woodbridge, 33–57.

Bowers, R. (2007), 'An early Tudor monastic enterprise: Choral polyphony for the liturgical service', in *The culture of medieval English monasticism*, (ed.) J. G. Clark, *Studies in the History of Medieval Religion*, 30. The Boydell Press: Woodbridge, 21–54.

Bowker, M. (1981), *The Henrician Reformation: the diocese of Lincoln under John Longland, 1521–1547*. Cambridge University Press: Cambridge.

Bowker, M. (2004), 'Henry Holbeach (d. 1551), bishop of Lincoln', *Oxford Dictionary of National Biography*. Oxford University Press: Oxford.

Bradshaw, B. (1974), *The dissolution of the religious orders in Ireland under Henry VIII*. Cambridge University Press: Cambridge.

Brigden, S. (1989), *London and the Reformation*. Clarendon Press: Oxford.

Brown, A. (1995), *Popular piety in late medieval England: The diocese of Salisbury, 1250–1550*. Clarendon Press: Oxford.

Brown, A. (1997), *Robert Ferrar. Yorkshire monk, Reformation bishop and martyr in Wales (c. 1500–55)*. Inscriptor Imprints: London.

Bull, R., Davis, S., Lewis, H. and Phillpotts, C. (2011), *Holywell Priory and the development of Shoreditch to c. 1600. Archaeology from the London Overground East London line*. MOLA monograph Series, 53. London.

Bullen, M., Crook, J., Hubbuck, R. and Pevsner, N. (2010), *The Buildings of England: Hampshire: Winchester and the north*. Yale University Press: New Haven and London.

Burgess, C. (2019), 'Fox's choice: founding a secular college in Oxford', in 'Renaissance College: Corpus Christi College, Oxford, in context, 1450–1600', *History of Universities*, 32:1–2, 22–39.

Burgess, C. and Wathey, A. (2000), 'Mapping the soundscape: church music in English towns, 1450–1550', *Early Music History*, 19, 1–46.

Burne, R. V. H. (1962), *The monks of Chester. The history of St Werbergh's Abbey*. SPCK: London.

Burtt, J. (1866), 'Original documents: charter of Henry VII to the Franciscan friars at Greenwich and an inedited seal of the warden', *Archaeological Journal*, 23, 54–9.

Burtt, J. (1870), 'Survey of the abbey of St Mary de Pratis, nigh Leicester, tempore Henry VIII', *Archaeological Journal*, 27, 204–6.

Bush, M. (1990), '"Enhancements and importunate charges": an analysis of the tax complaints of October 1536', *Albion*, 22:3: 403–19.

Bush, M. (1991), '"Up for the Commonweal": the significance of tax grievances in the English rebellions of 1536', *English Historical Review*, 106:419, 219–318.

Bush, M. (1996), *The Pilgrimage of Grace: a study of the rebel armies of October, 1536*. Manchester University Press: Manchester.

Bush, M. (2009), *The pilgrim's complaint: A study of popular thought in the early Tudor north*. Ashgate: Farnham.

Butler, A. (1977), 'Ann Boroeghe, of Clerkenwell and Dingley', *Northamptonshire Past and Present*, 5, 407–12.

Butler, G. S. (1865), 'Notes on Rye and its inhabitants', *Sussex Archaeological Collections*, 17, 123–36.

Byng, G. (2017), *Church building and society in the later Middle Ages*. Cambridge University Press: Cambridge.

Carley, J. P. (1996), *Glastonbury Abbey. The Holy house at the head of the moors adventurous*. Gothic Image Publications: Glastonbury.

Carlson, E. J. (1992), 'Clerical marriage and the English Reformation', *Journal of British Studies*, 31:1, 1–31.

Carter, M. (2010), 'Remembrance, liturgy and status in a late medieval English Cistercian abbey: the mourning vestment of Abbot Robert Thornton of Jervaulx', *Textile History*, 41:2, 145–60.

Carter, P. R. N. (2004a), 'Richard Rich, first Baron Rich (1496/7–1567)', *Oxford Dictionary of National Biography*. Oxford University Press: Oxford.

Carter, P. R. N. (2004b), 'Sir Thomas Tresham (c. 1500–1559)', *Oxford Dictionary of National Biography*. Oxford University Press: Oxford.

Chadwick, O. (2001), *The early Reformation on the continent*. Oxford University Press: Oxford.

Chibi, A. A. (2004), 'John Stokesley (1475–1539)', *Oxford Dictionary of National Biography*. Oxford University Press: Oxford.

Christie, P. M. and Coad, J. D. (1980), 'Excavations at Denny Abbey', *Archaeological Journal*, 137, 138–284.

Clark, J. G. (2000), 'Reformation and reaction at St Albans Abbey, 1530–58', *English Historical Review*, 115, 297–328.

Clark, J. G. (2004a), *A monastic renaissance at St Albans: Thomas Walsingham and his circle, c. 1350–c.1440*. Oxford Historical Monographs. Clarendon Press: Oxford.

Clark, J. G. (2004b), 'Print and pre-Reformation religion: the Benedictines and the press, 1470–1540', in *The uses of script and print*, (ed.) J. Crick and A. Walsham. Cambridge University Press: Cambridge, 71–92.

Clark, J. G. (2013), 'Why men became monks in late medieval England', *Religious men and masculine identity in the Middle Ages*, (ed.) P. Cullum and K. Lewis. The Boydell Press: Woodbridge, 160–83.

Clark, J. G. (2014), 'John Stonywell [Stanwell] (d. 1553)', *Oxford Dictionary of National Biography*. Oxford University Press: Oxford.

Clark, J. G. (2018), 'Cistercian histories in late medieval England and beyond', in *Monasteries and histories in medieval Britain: Essays in honour of Janet Burton*, (ed.) K. Stöber, J. Kerr and A. Müller. University of Wales Press: Cardiff, 3–26.

Clark, J. G. (2019a), 'From Plantagenet tragedies to Tudor triumphs: Westminster Abbey, 1307–1532', in *Westminster Abbey: A church in history*, (ed.) D. Cannadine. Yale University Press: New Haven and London, 88–133.

Clark, J. G. (2019b), 'The small-town friaries of later medieval England', in *Church and city*, (ed.) D. Harry and C. Steer. Shaun Tyas: Stamford, 277–300.

Clark, R. (1989), 'Regular clergy of Derbyshire at the dissolution of the monasteries', *Derbyshire Archaeological Journal*, 109, 131–49.

Cloake, J. (1977), 'The Charterhouse of Sheen', *Surrey Archaeological Collections*, 71, 145–98.

Cockerham, P. (2004), 'Catacleuse, wood and plaster: Markers for the renaissance in early-modern Cornwall', *Journal of the Royal Institution of Cornwall*, New Series, 43–63.

Cocks, T. Y., 'The last abbot of Leicester', *Transactions of the Leicestershire Archaeological and Historical Society*, 58 (1982–3), 6–19.

Collett, B. (1985), *Italian Benedictine scholars and the reformation. The congregation of Santa Giustina of Padua*. Oxford Historical Monographs, Oxford University Press: Oxford.

Collett, B. (2002), *Female monastic life in early Tudor England: with an edition of Richard Fox's translation of the Benedictine rule for women, 1517*. The Early Modern Englishwoman 1500–1750: Contemporary editions. Ashgate: Aldershot.

Colvin, H. and Stone, L. 'The Howard tombs at Framlingham, Suffolk', *Archaeological Journal*, 122:1 (1965), 159–71.

Condon, M. (2003a), 'God save the king! Piety, propaganda and the perpetual memorial', in *Westminster Abbey: The Lady Chapel of Henry VII*, (ed.) T. Tatton-Brown and R. Mortimer. The Boydell Press: Woodbridge, 59–97.

Condon, M. (2003b), 'The last will of Henry VII: Document and text', in *Westminster Abbey: The Lady Chapel of Henry VII*, (ed.) T. Tatton-Brown and R. Mortimer. The Boydell Press: Woodbridge, 99–140.

Connolly, M. (2019), *Sixteenth-century readers, fifteenth-century books: Continuities of reading in the English Reformation*. Cambridge University Press: Cambridge.

Cook, G. H. (ed.) (1965), *Letters to Cromwell on the suppression of the monasteries*. John Baker: London.

Cooper, T. and Rees, D. (2004), 'Robert Sayer (1560–1620)', *Oxford Dictionary of National Biography*. Oxford University Press: Oxford.

Coppack, G. (1986), 'Some descriptions of Rievaulx Abbey in 1538–9: The disposition of a major Cistercian precinct in the early sixteenth century', *Journal of the British Archaeological Association*, 139:1, 100–33.

Coppack, G. (1998), *The White Monks: The Cistercians in Britain, 1128–1540*. Tempus: Stroud.

Coppack, G. (2002), 'Sawley Abbey: the architecture and archaeology of a smaller Cistercian abbey', *Journal of the British Archaeological Association*, 155, 22–144.

Coppack, G. and Keen, L. (ed.) (2019), *Mount Grace Priory: Excavations of 1957–1992*. Oxbow: Oxford and Philadelphia.

Cornwall, J. (1962), 'English county towns in the 1520s', *Economic History Review*, 15, 54–69.

Coulton, G. G. (1950), *Five centuries of religion. Volume IV: The last days of medieval monachism*. Cambridge University Press: Cambridge.

Courtney, P., Heron, G., McDonnell, G. and Jones, G. G. (1989), 'Excavations in the outer precinct of Tintern Abbey', *Medieval Archaeology*, 33:1, 99–143.

Cox, J. C. (1875), *Notes on the churches of Derbyshire. Volume I. The hundred of Scarsdale*. Palmer and Edmunds: Chesterfield.

Crake, A. D. (1886), *The last abbot of Glastonbury: A tale of the dissolution of the monasteries*. A. R. Mowbray and Co.: Oxford and London.

Craster, H. H. E. (1907), *A history of Northumberland. VIII: The parish of Tynemouth*. Andrew Reid and Co.; Simpkin, Marshall, Kent and Co.: Newcastle upon Tyne and London.

Cratty, F. (2018), '"To whom say you your Pater noster?": Prayer on the eve of the Scottish Reformation', *Reformation & Renaissance Review*, 20, 18–34.

Crosby, B. (2014), 'Music across the centuries', *Durham Cathedral: History, fabric & culture*, (ed.) D. Brown. Yale University Press: New Haven and London, 333–45.

Cross, C. (1996), 'Ordinations in the diocese of York, 1500–1630', *Patronage and recruitment in the Tudor and early Stuart church*, (ed.) M. C. Cross, Borthwick Studies I. History, 2, Borthwick Institute of Historical Research, York, 1–19.

Cross, C. (2001), 'A Yorkshire religious house and its hinterland: Monk Bretton Priory in the sixteenth century', in *Christianity and Community in the West*, (ed.) S. Ditchfield, St Andrews Studies in Reformation History. Ashgate: Aldershot, 72-86.

Cross, C. (2004a), 'Hugh Cook (d. 1539)', *Oxford Dictionary of National Biography*. Oxford University Press: Oxford.

Cross, C. (2004b), 'Robert Pursglove (1503/4–1580)', *Oxford Dictionary of National Biography*. Oxford University Press: Oxford.

Cross, C. (2004c), 'Edward Lee (1481/2–1544), archbishop of York', *Oxford Dictionary of National Biography*. Oxford University Press: Oxford.

Cross, C. (2018), 'Friars, the Pilgrimage of Grace, and the dissolution of the Dominican and Franciscan priories in sixteenth-century Beverley', *Yorkshire Archaeological Journal*, 90:1, 96–110.

Cross, C. and Frost, J. A. (2014), 'A prior and his church: Alvered Comyn and Wragby church in the reign of Henry VIII', *Northern History*, 51/1, 183–9.

Cross, C. and Vickers, N. (1995), *Monks, friars and nuns in sixteenth-century Yorkshire*. Yorkshire Archaeological Society: York.

Cummings, B., Law, C., Riley, K. and Walsham, A. (ed.) (2020), *Remembering the Reformation*. Routledge: Abingdon.

Cunich, P. (1997), 'Benedictine monks at the university of Oxford and the dissolution of the monasteries', in *Benedictines in Oxford*, (ed.) H. Wansborough and A. Marrett-Crosby. Darton, Longman and Todd: London, 155–84.

Cunich, P. (2004), 'Richard Kidderminster (c.1461–1533/4)', *Oxford Dictionary of National Biography*. Oxford University Press: Oxford.

Cunich, P. (2007), 'Maurice Chauncy and the Charterhouses of London and Sheen Anglorum', in the various versions of the *Historia aliquot martyrym Anglorum maxime octodecimo Cartusianorum sub rege Henrico octavo*, (ed.) J. Clark. Institut für Anglistik und Amerikanistik, Universität Salzburg: Salzburg, 1–58.

Cunich, P. (2010), 'The brothers of Syon', in *Syon Abbey and its books: reading, writing and religion, c. 1400–1700*. The Boydell Press: Woodbridge, 39–81.

Currie, C. K. (1990), 'Fishponds as garden features, c.1550–c.1580', *Garden History*, 18:1, 22–46.

Da Costa, A. (2011), 'The king's great matter: negotiating censorship at Syon Abbey, 1532–4', *Review of English Studies*, 62, 15–29.

Daniell, D. (2004), 'Miles Coverdale (1488–1569)', *Oxford Dictionary of National Biography*. Oxford University Press: Oxford.

Davey, P. J. and Roscow, J. (2010), *Rushen Abbey and the dissolution of the monasteries in the Isle of Man*. Isle of Man Natural History Society Monographs, 1.

Davidson, J. W. (1843), *The History of Newenham Abbey in the county of Devon*. Longman and Co.: London.

Davies, C. S. L. (1968), 'The Pilgrimage of Grace reconsidered', *Past and Present*, 41, 54–76.

Davies, C. S. L. (2004), 'Richard Fox (1447/8–1528)', *Oxford Dictionary of National Biography*. Oxford University Press: Oxford.

Davis, E. J. (1925), 'The beginning of the Dissolution: Christchurch, Aldgate, 1532', *Transactions of the Royal Historical Society*, 4th Series, 8, 127–50.

Davis, V. (1993), *William Waynflete. Bishop and educationalist*. The Boydell Press: Woodbridge.

Dent, E. (1877), *Annals of Winchcombe and Sudeley*. John Murray: London.

De Windt, A. R. and De Windt, E. B. (2006), *Ramsey: The lives of an English Fenland town, 1200–1600*. Catholic University of America Press: Washington DC.

Dickens, A. G. (1940), 'The Edwardian arrears in augmentations payments and the problem of the ex-religious', *English Historical Review*, 55:219, 384–418.

Dickens, A. G. (1941), 'Archbishop Holgate's apology', *English Historical Review*, 56, 450–9.

Dickinson, J. C. (1968), 'The buildings of the English Austin Canons after the dissolution of the monasteries', *Journal of the British Archaeological Association*, 3rd Series, 31:1, 60–75.

Dimmock, M., Hadfield, A. and Quinn, P. (2014), 'Introduction: contesting early modern Sussex', *Art, Literature and Religion in Early Modern Sussex*. Ashgate: Farnham and Burlington, VT, 1–15.

Dinn, R. (1995), '"Monuments answerable to men's worth": Burial patterns, social status and gender in late medieval Bury St Edmunds', *Journal of Ecclesiastical History*, 46:2, 237–55.

Dobson, R. B. (1973), *Durham Priory, 1400–1450*. Cambridge University Press: Cambridge.

Dobson, R. B. (1995), 'Canterbury in the later Middle Ages', *A history of Canterbury Cathedral*, (ed.) P. Collinson, N. Ramsay and M. Sparks. Oxford University Press: Oxford, 69–153.

Dodwell, B. (1996), 'The monastic community', in *Norwich Cathedral: Church, city diocese, 1096–1996*, (ed.) I. Atherton, E. Fernie, C. Harper-Bill, and H. Smith. Hambledon Press: London and Rio Grande, 231–54.

Doggett, N. (1991), 'The demolition and conversion of former monastic buildings in Hertfordshire at the Dissolution', in *Hertfordshire in History. Papers presented to Lionel Munby*, (ed.) D. Jones-Baker, Hertfordshire Publications: University of Hertfordshire Press, Hatfield, 47–64.

Doggett, N. (2002), *Patterns of re-use: The transformation of former monastic buildings in post-Dissolution Hertfordshire, 1540, 1600*, BAR, British Series, 331.

Doggett, N. (2004a), 'Robert Hobbes (d. 1538)', *Oxford Dictionary of National Biography*. Oxford University Press: Oxford.

Doggett, N. (2004b), 'Robert King (d. 1557)', *Oxford Dictionary of National Biography*. Oxford University Press: Oxford.

Doggett, N. (2004c), 'Richard Whiting, abbot of Glastonbury (d. 1539)', *Oxford Dictionary of National Biography*. Oxford University Press: Oxford.

Doubleday, A. and Page, W. (ed.) (1903), *A history of the county of Hampshire and the Isle of Wight. Volume 2*. Archibald Constable and Co.: Westminster.

Duffy, E. (1992), *The stripping of the altars: Traditional religion in England*. Yale University Press: New Haven and London.

Duffy, E. (2001), *The voices of Morebath: Reformation and rebellion in an English village*. Yale University Press: New Haven and London.

Dugdale, W. (ed.), Dodsworth, R., Caley, J., Ellis, H., Bandinel B. and Taylor, R. C. (1817–30), *Monasticon Anglicanum: a history of the abbies and other monasteries, hospitals, frieries and cathedral and collegiate churches*. Longman, Hurst, Rees, Orme and Brown: London.

Dunning, R. W. (2004), 'Richard Bere (c. 1455–1525)', *Oxford Dictionary of National Biography*. Oxford University Press: Oxford.

Edwards, A. S. G. (2019), 'William Forrest, poetry, politics script and power', *Sederi. Journal of the Spanish Society for English Renaissance Studies*, 29, 163–78.

Ekroll, O. (2019), 'Thrown to the wolves? The fate of Norwegian monasteries after the Reformation', in *The Dissolution of Monasteries. The case of Denmark in a regional perspective*, (ed.) P. Seesko, L. N. Kallestrup and L. Bisgaard. University Press of Southern Denmark: Odense, 151–68.

Ellis, H. (1798), *History and antiquities of the parish of Saint Leonard Shoreditch and the liberty of Norton Folegate in the suburbs of London*. J. Nichols: London.

Elrington, C. R. (1968), 'The borough of Tewkesbury: introduction', in *A history of the county of Gloucester, 8: Cleeve, Deerhurst and Tibblestone hundreds, Tewkesbury and Warminster hundreds and Tewkesbury borough*. (ed.) idem, Oxford University Press: Oxford.

Elton, G. R. (1972), *Policy and police: The enforcement of the Reformation in the age of Thomas Cromwell*. Cambridge University Press: Cambridge.

Elton, G. R. (1974), 'Parliamentary drafts, 1529–40', *Studies in Tudor and Stuart politics and government*. Cambridge University Press: Cambridge, 62–81.

Emden, A. B. (1974), *A biographical register of the University of Oxford, AD 1500–1540*. Clarendon Press: Oxford.

Emery, A. (2006), *Greater medieval houses of England and Wales, 1300–1500. Volume III: Southern England*. Cambridge University Press: Cambridge.

Erler, M. (2002), *Women, reading and piety in late medieval England*. Cambridge University Press: Cambridge.

Erler, M. (2011), 'A possible Syon book owner after the Dissolution: William Mownselowe, 1543', *Notes and Queries*, 256, 202–4.

Erler, M. (2013), *Reading and writing during the Dissolution: Monks, friars and nuns, 1530–58*. Cambridge University Press: Cambridge.

Evans, A. (1941), 'Battle Abbey at the Dissolution: income', *Huntington Library Quarterly*, 4:4, 393–442.

Evans, A. (1942), 'Battle Abbey at the Dissolution: expenses', *Huntington Library Quarterly*, 6:1, 53–101.

Evans, E. H. (1907–14), 'Communication concerning an early sixteenth-century manuscript and certain printed matter found in the watching loft, St Albans Abbey Church, in January AD 1912', *Transactions of the St Albans and Hertfordshire Architectural and Archaeological Society*, 204–8.

Everett, M. (2015), *The rise of Thomas Cromwell: power and politics in the reign of Henry VIII, 1485–1534*. Yale University Press: New Haven and London.

Farnhill, K. (2001), *Guilds and parish community in late medieval East Anglia, c. 1470–1550*. York Medieval Press: York.

Fergusson, P. (2011), *Canterbury Cathedral Priory in the age of Becket.* Yale University Press: New Haven and London.

Fergusson, P. and Harrison, S. (1999), *Rievaulx Abbey: Community, architecture, memory.* Paul Mellon Centre for Studies in British Art. Yale University Press: New Haven and London.

Finberg, H. P. R. (1951), *Tavistock Abbey: A study in the social and economic history of Devon.* Cambridge University Press: Cambridge.

Fishwick, Lt.-C. (1907), *The history of the parish of Lytham in the county of Lancaster.* Chetham Society, New Series, 60.

Fizzard, A. (2007), 'Shoes, boots, leggings, and cloaks: The Augustinian canons and dress in later medieval England', *Journal of British Studies*, 46:2, 245–62.

Fizzard, A. (2008), *Plympton Priory: a house of Augustinian canons in south-western England in the late Middle Ages.* Brill: Leiden.

Fletcher, J. R. (1933), *The story of the English Bridgettines of Syon Abbey.* Syon Abbey: South Brent.

Forde, D., Munby, J. and Scott, I. R. (2019), *Torre Abbey, Devon: The archaeology of the Premonstratensian Abbey.* Oxford Archaeology Monographs, 29. Oxbow Books: Oxford.

Fowler, J. C. (1895), *The Benedictines in Bath during a thousand years: A sketch founded upon authentic records.* Western Chronicle Co.: Yeovil.

France, J. (2012), *Separate but equal: Cistercian lay brothers, 1120–1350.* Cistercian Publications, 246. Liturgical Press: Gethsemani, KY.

Freeman, T. S. (2004), 'John Cardmaker (c. 1496–1555)', *Oxford Dictionary of National Biography.* Oxford University Press: Oxford.

French, K. L. (2001), *The people of the parish: Community life in a late medieval English diocese.* University of Pennsylvania Press: Philadelphia, PA.

Froude, J. A. (1856–70), *A History of England, from the fall of Wolsey to the death of Elizabeth*, 10 vols. J. W. Parker and Sons: London.

Fryde, E. (ed.) (1996), *Handbook of British chronology*, 3rd edn. Cambridge University Press: Cambridge.

Fuller, T. and Brewer (1845), *Church-history of Britain*, (ed.) J. S. Brewer. Oxford University Press: Oxford.

Gaimster, D. and Gilchrist, R. (ed.) (2003), *The archaeology of reformation, 1480–1580: Papers given at the archaeology of reformation conference, February 2001.* Maney: Leeds.

Gasquet, F. A. (1893), *Henry VIII and the English Monasteries: An attempt to illustrate the history of their suppression*, 2 vols., 5th edn. John Hodges: London.

Gasquet, F. A. (1894), 'Overlooked testimonies to the character of the English monasteries on the eve of their suppression', *Dublin Review*, 115, 245–77.

Gibson, M. (1995), 'Normans and Angevins, 1070–1220', *A history of Canterbury Cathedral*, (ed.) P. Collinson, N. Ramsay and M. Sparks. Oxford University Press: Oxford, 38–68.

Gilchrist, R. (2005), *Norwich Cathedral Close: The evolution of the English cathedral landscape.* The Boydell Press: Woodbridge.

Gill, S. (2019), '"Of honest conversation and competently learned": The dissolution of the chantries (1548) and chantry priests of the East and West Midlands', *Midlands History*, 44:2, 205–21.

Gilyard Beer, R. and Coppack, G. (1986), 'Excavations at Fountains Abbey, North Yorkshire, 1979–80: the early development of the monastery', *Archaeologia*, 108, 147–88.

Gleeson-White, J. (2012), *Double entry: How the merchants of Venice created modern finance.* Allen and Unwin: London.

Gottfried, R. S. (1982), *Bury St Edmunds and the urban crisis: 1290–1539.* Princeton University Press: Princeton.

Grainger, F. and Collingwood, W. G. (1929), *Register and records of Holm Cultram*, Westmorland Antiquarian and Archaeological Society Record series, 7. T. Wilson & Son: Kendal.

Grainger, I. and Phillpotts, C. (2011), *The Cistercian Abbey of St Mary Graces, East Smithfield, London.* Museum of London Archaeology, Monograph 44, London.

Gray, M. (2004), 'Anthony Kitchin (1477–1563), bishop of Llandaff', *Oxford Dictionary of National Biography*. Oxford University Press: Oxford.

Greatrex, J. (1997), *A biographical register of the English cathedral priories of the province of Canterbury, c. 1066–1540*. Oxford University Press: Oxford.

Greaves, R. L. (2004), 'John Rough (c.1508–1557), protestant martyr', *Oxford Dictionary of National Biography*. Oxford University Press: Oxford.

Greene, J. P. (1989) *Norton Priory: the archaeology of a medieval religious house*. Cambridge University Press: Cambridge.

Greene, J. P. (2000), 'The impact of the dissolution of the monasteries in Cheshire: The case of Norton', in *Medieval art and architecture at Chester*, British Archaeological Association Conference Transactions, Leeds, 152–66.

Grell, O. P. (1995), 'The Catholic Church and its leadership', in *The Scandinavian Reformation from evangelical movement to institutionalisation of reform*, (ed.) O. P. Grell. Cambridge University Press: Cambridge, 70–113.

Gribbin, J. (2001), *The Premonstratensian canons in late medieval England*. The Boydell Press: Woodbridge.

Griffiths, R. A. (2004), 'Bridgwater, Oxford and Whitland Abbey in 1491', *Studia Celtica*, 38, 125–9.

Grummit, D. (2004), 'Plantagenet, Arthur, Viscount Lisle (b. before 1472, d. 1542)', *Oxford Dictionary of National Biography*. Oxford University Press: Oxford.

Guinn-Chipman, S. (2013), *Religious space in Reformation England: Contesting the past*. Taylor and Francis: London.

Gunn, C. (2018), 'Anonymous then, invisible now: the readers of a sermon a dames religiose', in *Nuns' literacies in medieval Europe: The Antwerp dialogue*, (ed.) V. Blanton, V. O'Mara and P. Stoop. Brepols: Turnhout, 251–70.

Gunn, S. J. (2016), *Henry VII's new men and the making of Tudor England*. Oxford University Press: Oxford.

Gunn, S. J. (2018), *The English people at war in the reign of Henry VIII*. Oxford University Press: Oxford.

Gwyn, P. (1990), *The king's cardinal: The rise and fall of Thomas Wolsey*. Barrie and Jenkins: London.

Haigh, C. (1969), *The last days of the Lancashire monasteries and the pilgrimage of grace*, Chetham Society, 3rd Series, 17. Manchester University Press: Manchester.

Harbottle, B. and Fraser, R. (1987), 'Blackfriars, Newcastle on Tyne after the dissolution of the monasteries', *Archaeologia Aeliana*, 15, 23–149.

Hare, J. (1985), *Battle Abbey: The eastern range and the excavations of 1978–80*. Historic Buildings and Monuments Commission for England, Archaeological Report, 2. English Heritage: London.

Hare, J. (1999), *The dissolution of the monasteries in Hampshire*. Hampshire County Council: Winchester.

Hare, J. (2011), *A prospering society: Wiltshire in the later Middle Ages*. University of Hertfordshire Press: Hatfield.

Harrington, D. (2004), 'Christopher Nevinson [Nevynson] (d. 1551)', *Oxford Dictionary of National Biography*. Oxford University Press: Oxford.

Harvey, B. F. (1993), *Living and dying in England, 1100–1540: The monastic experience*. Oxford University Press: Oxford.

Harvey, M. (2006), *Lay religious life in late medieval Durham*. Regions and Regionalism in History, 6. The Boydell Press: Woodbridge.

Harvey, P. D. A. (1991), *Medieval maps*. British Library: London.

Harward, C., Holder, N., Phillpotts, C. and Thomas, C. (2019), *The medieval priory and hospital of St Mary Spital and the Bishopsgate Suburb: Excavations and Spitalfields Market, London E1 1991–2007*. Museum of London Archaeology: London.

Haude, S. (1995), 'The silent monks speak up: the changing identity of the Carthusians in the fifteenth and sixteenth centuries', *Archiv für reformationsgeschichte*, 86, 124–40.

Hay, D. (1938), 'The dissolution of the monasteries in the diocese of Durham', *Archaeologia Aeliana*, 15, 64–114.

Heale, F. (2005), 'What can King Lucius do for you? The Reformation and the early British church', *English Historical Review*, 593–614.

Heale, M. (2003), 'Monastic-parochial churches in England and Wales, 1066–1540', *Monastic Research Bulletin*, 9, 1–19.

Heale, M. (2004), *The Dependent Priories of Medieval English Monasteries*. The Boydell Press: Woodbridge.

Heale, M. (2016), *Abbots and priors in late medieval and Reformation England*. Oxford University Press: Oxford.

Heath, P. (1969), *The English parish clergy on the eve of the Reformation*. Studies in Social History. Routledge and Kegan Paul: London.

Heaton, M. (2020), 'The ghost of Kane: Bradenstoke Priory, William Randolph Hearst and the birth of cultural chauvinism in Britain', *Transactions of the Ancient Monuments Society*, 64, 32–43.

Heinze, G. W. (1976), *The proclamations of the Tudor kings*. Cambridge University Press: Cambridge.

Hendriks, L. (1889), *The London Charterhouse: Its monks and its martyrs. With a short account of the English Carthusians after the Dissolution*. Kegan, Paul, Trench and Co.: London.

Hey, D. Liddy, L. and Luscombe, D. (2011) (ed.), *A monastic community in local society: the Beauchief Abbey cartulary*, Camden Fifth Series, 40. Royal Historical Society: Cambridge, 2011.

Hibbert, F. A. (1910), *The dissolution of the monasteries as illustrated by the suppression of the religious houses of Staffordshire*. Pitman and Sons: London.

Higgs, L. M. (1998), *Godliness and governance in Tudor Colchester*. The University of Michigan Press: Ann Arbor.

Higham, J. (1999), 'The relationship between the town of Peterborough and the abbey from 1200 to the Reformation', in *Monasteries and society in medieval Britain*, (ed.) B. J. Thompson. Paul Watkins: Stamford, 155–76.

Hildebrandt, E. (1984), 'Christopher Mont: Anglo-German diplomat', *Sixteenth-Century Journal*, 15, 281–92.

Hill, J. W. F. (1956), *Tudor and Stuart Lincoln*. Cambridge University Press: Cambridge.

Hillaby, J. G. and C. (2006), *Leominster minster, priory and borough, c. 660–1539*. Friends of Leominster Priory with Logaston Press: Leominster.

Hockey, S. (1970), *Quarr abbey and its lands, 1132–1631*. Leicester University Press: Leicester.

Hodgett, G. A. J. (1962), 'The unpensioned religious in Tudor England', *Journal of Ecclesiastical History*, 13:2, 195–202.

Holder, N., Betts, I., Röhrkasten, J., Samuel, M. and Steer, C. (2017), *The friaries of medieval London from foundation to dissolution*. The Boydell Press: Woodbridge.

Hooper, W. (1915), 'The Tudor Sumptuary Laws', *English Historical Review*, 30: 119, 433–49.

Horrox, R. (2004), 'Peter Courtenay (c. 1432–1492)', *Oxford Dictionary of National Biography*. Oxford University Press: Oxford.

Houlbrooke, R. (1996), 'Refoundation and Reformation, 1538–1628', in *Norwich Cathedral: Church, city diocese, 1096–1996*, (ed.) I. Atherton, E. Fernie, C. Harper-Bill and H. Smith. Hambledon Press: London and Rio Grande, 507–39.

Houlbrooke, R. A. (2009), 'Prince Arthur's Funeral', in *Arthur Tudor, Prince of Wales: Life, death and commemoration*, (ed.) S. J. Gunn and L. Monckton. The Boydell Press: Woodbridge, 64–76.

Howard, M. (2003), 'Recycling the monastic fabric: beyond the Act of Dissolution', in *The Archaeology of Reformation, c. 1480–1580*, (ed.) D. R. Gaimster and R. Gilchrist, Society for Post-Medieval archaeology monograph, 1. Maney: Leeds, 221–34.

Hoyle, R. W. (1989), 'Monastic leasing before the Dissolution: The evidence from Bolton Priory and Fountains Abbey', *Yorkshire Archaeological Journal*, 61, 111–37.

Hoyle, R. W. (1995a), 'The origins of the dissolution of the monasteries', *Historical Journal*, 38:2, 275–305.

Hoyle, R. W. (1995b), 'War and public finance', in *The reign of Henry VIII: Politics, policy and piety*, (ed.) D. MacCulloch. Macmillan: London, 75–100.

Hoyle, R. W. (2001), *The pilgrimage of grace and the politics of the 1530s*. Oxford University Press: Oxford.

Hunt, D. (2014), 'The shrine of St Cuthbert', in *Durham Cathedral: history, fabric and culture*, (ed.) D. Brown. Yale University Press: New Haven and London, 303–13.

Hutchins, J. (1861–70), *The history and antiquities of Dorset*, 4 vols., 3rd edn. John Bowyer, Nichols and Son: London.

Ives, E. (2004), *The life and death of Anne Boleyn*. Blackwell: Oxford.

Jack, S. M. (1996), *Towns in Tudor and Stuart Britain*, Social History in Perspective. Macmillan: London.

Jackson, J. E. (ed.) (1862), *Wiltshire: The topographical collections of John Aubrey, 1659–70, corrected and enlarged*. Wiltshire Record Society: Devizes.

Jackson, R. (2006), *Excavations at St James Priory, Bristol*. Oxbow Books: Oxford.

Jakobsen, J. G. G. (2021), 'A brief history of monasticism in Denmark (with Schleswig, Rügen and Estonia)', *Religions*, 12: 469, 1–20.

James, S. E. (2004), 'Parr, William, marquess of Northampton (1513–1571)', *Oxford Dictionary of National Biography*. Oxford University Press: Oxford.

James, T. (1997), 'Excavations at Carmarthen Greyfriars, 1983–90', *Medieval Archaeology*, 41, 100–94.

Jarrett, B. (1921), *The English Dominicans*. Burnes, Oates and Co.: London.

Jones, B. (1989), 'The Dominican friars of Haverfordwest: Their sites and lands before and after the dissolution of the monasteries', *Journal of Pembrokeshire Historical Society*, 3: 77–91.

Jones, D. (1957), *The church in Chester, 1300–1540*, Chetham Society, 3rd Series, 7. Manchester.

Jones, E. A. (2015), *England's last medieval monastery: A history of Syon Abbey, 1415–2015*. Gracewing: Leominster.

Jones, E. D. (1959) 'Vaughan family of Clyro, Rads', *Dictionary of Welsh Biography*, Honourable Society of Cymmrodorion: London.

Jones, M. K. and Underwood, M. (1992), *The King's Mother: Lady Margaret Beaufort. Countess of Richmond and Derby*. Cambridge University Press: Cambridge.

Kaufman, P. I. (1986), 'Polydore Vergil and the strange disappearance of Christopher Urswick', *The Sixteenth-Century Journal*, 17:1, 69–85.

Kellar, C. (2003), *Scotland, England and the Reformation, 1534–61*. Clarendon Press: Oxford.

King, J. N. (2004), 'John Bale (1495–1563)', *Oxford Dictionary of National Biography*. Oxford University Press: Oxford.

Kitching, C. J. (1974), 'The quest for concealed lands in the reign of Elizabeth I', *Transactions of the Royal Historical Society*, 5th Series, 24, 63–78.

Knighton, C. S. (1996), 'The reformed chapter, 1540–1660', in *Faith and fabric: A history of Rochester Cathedral*, ed. N. Yates, with the assistance of P. A. Welsby. The Boydell Press and Friends of Rochester Cathedral: Woodbridge, 57–76.

Knighton, C. S. (2003), 'King's College', in *Westminster Abbey reformed, 1540–1640*, (ed.) C. S. Knighton and R. Mortimer. Ashgate: Aldershot and Burlington, VT, 16–37.

Knighton, C. S. (2004), 'Thomas Thirlby (c. 1500–1570)', *Oxford Dictionary of National Biography*. Oxford University Press: Oxford.

Knighton, C. S. (2006), 'Westminster Abbey restored', in *The Church of Mary Tudor*, (ed.) E. Duffy. Ashgate: Aldershot and Burlington, VT, 77–105.

Knighton, C. S. (2011), 'Petre, Sir William (1505/6–1572)', *Oxford Dictionary of National Biography*. Oxford University Press: Oxford.

Knowles, D. (1952), 'The case of St Albans Abbey in 1490', *Journal of Ecclesiastical History*, 3:2, 144–58

Knowles, D. (1959), *The religious orders in England: The Tudor Age*. Cambridge University Press: Cambridge.

Knowles, D. and Hadcock, R. N. (1971), *Medieval religious houses: England and Wales*. 2nd edn. Routledge: London.

Knowles, M. D. (1958), '"The matter of Wilton", 1528', *Bulletin of the Institute of Historical Research*, 31: 83, 92–6.

Knowles, M. D. (1964), 'Notes on a bible of Evesham Abbey', *English Historical Review*, 79: 313, 775–8.

Koopmans, R. (2011), *Wonderful to relate: Miracle stories and miracle collecting in high-medieval England*. University of Pennsylvania Press: Philadelphia.

Krochalis, Jean (2001), 'Magna Tabula: The Glastonbury Tablets (Parts 1 and 2)', in *Glastonbury Abbey and the Arthurian tradition*, (ed.) J. P. Carley. D. S. Brewer: Woodbridge, 435–567.

Lapidge, M. and Winterbottom, M. (1991), *Wulfstan of Winchester, the life of St Æthelwold*. Oxford Medieval Texts, Clarendon Press: Oxford.

Laynesmith, J. L. (2004), *The last medieval queens: English queenship 1445–1503*. Oxford University Press: Oxford.

Leach, A. (1988), *Furness Abbey: A history and illustrated guide*. Fletcher and Robinson: Ulverston.

Leader, D. K. (1983), 'Professorships and academic reform at Cambridge, 1488–1520', *Sixteenth-Century Journal*, 14:2, 215–27.

Lee, P. (2001), *Nunneries, learning, spirituality in late medieval English society: The Dominican priory of Dartford*. York Medieval Press: Woodbridge.

Lehmberg, S. E. (1970), *The reformation parliament, 1529–36*. Cambridge University Press: Cambridge.

Lehmberg, S. E. (1977), *The later parliaments of Henry VIII, 1536–47*. Cambridge University Press: Cambridge.

Lehmberg, S. E. (2004), 'Sir William Kingston (c. 1476–1540), courtier and administrator', *Oxford Dictionary of National Biography*. Oxford University Press: Oxford.

Litzenberger, C. (1997), *The English Reformation and the laity: Gloucestershire, 1540–80*, Cambridge Studies in Early Modern British History. Cambridge University Press: Cambridge.

Litzenberger, C. (1998), 'The coming of Protestantism to Elizabethan Tewkesbury', in *The Reformation in English towns*, (ed.) P. Collinson and J. Craig. Macmillan: London, 79–93.

Liveing, H. G. D. (1906), *Records of Romsey Abbey: an account of the Benedictine house of nuns, with notes on the parish church and town (AD 907–1558)*. Warren and Son: Winchester.

Loades, D. (2003), 'The sanctuary', in *Westminster Abbey reformed, 1540–1650*, (ed.) C. S. Knighton and R. Mortimer. Ashgate: Aldershot and Burlington, VT, 75–93.

Loades, D. (2006), 'The personal religion of Mary I', in *The Church of Mary Tudor*, (ed.) E. Duffy. Ashgate: Aldershot, 1–29.

Logan, D. (2002), 'Departure from the religious life during the royal visitation of the monasteries, 1535–36', in *The religious orders in pre-Reformation England*, (ed.) J. G. Clark. The Boydell Press: Woodbridge, 213–36.

Loomie, A. (2004), 'Sir Francis Englefield (1522–1596)', *Oxford Dictionary of National Biography*. Oxford University Press: Oxford.

Lovatt, R. (1968), 'The *Imitatio Christi* in late medieval England', *Transactions of the Royal Historical Society*, 18, 97–121.

Lowe, B. (2010), *Commonwealth and the English Reformation: Protestantism and the politics of religious change in the Gloucester Vale, 1483–1560*. Routledge: London.

Lowry, M. J. C. (1983), 'Caxton, St Winifred and the Lady Margaret Beaufort', *The Library*, 6th Series, 5:2, 102–17.

Lunn, D. (1980), *The English Benedictines, 1540–1688: From Reformation to Revolution*. Burns and Oates: London.

Luxford, J. (2011), 'The Charterhouse of St Anne, Coventry', in *Coventry: Medieval art, architecture and archaeology in the city and its vicinity*, (ed.) L. Monckton and R. K. Morris, British Archaeological Association Conference Transaction, 33. Maney: Leeds, 240–66.

Lyne, M. and Gardiner, M. (1997), *Lewes Priory excavations by Richard Lewis, 1969–82*. Lewes Priory Trust: Lewes.

MacCulloch, D. (1986), *Suffolk and the Tudors: Politics and religion in an English county, 1500–1600*. Clarendon Press: Oxford.

MacCulloch, D. (1998), 'Worcester: a cathedral city in Reformation', in *The Reformation in English towns, 1500–1640*, (ed.) P. Collinson and J. Craig. Macmillan: London.

MacCulloch, D. (2018), *Thomas Cromwell: A life*. Allen Lane: London.

Maclean, J. (1883–4), 'Gloucestershire chantry certificates', *Transactions of the Bristol and Gloucestershire Archaeological Society*, 8, 229–308.

Makowksi, E. M. (1997), *Canon law and cloistered women: Periculoso and its commentators, 1298–1545*. Catholic University Press of America: Washington DC.

Makowksi, E. M. (2011), *English nuns and the law in the Middle Ages: Cloistered nuns and their lawyers, 1293–1540*. The Boydell Press: Woodbridge.

Manning, R. B. (1969), *Religion and Society in Elizabethan Sussex*. Leicester University Press: Leicester.

Manning, R. B. (1988), *Village revolts: Social protest and popular disturbances in England, 1509–1688*. Clarendon Press: Oxford.

Marks, R. (1984), 'The Howard tombs at Thetford and Framlingham: New discoveries', *Archaeological Journal*, 141, 252–68.

Marshall, P. (2004), 'John Forest (c.1470–1538), Franciscan friar and martyr', *Oxford Dictionary of National Biography*. Oxford University Press: Oxford.

Marshall, P. (2018), *Heretics and believers: A history of the English Reformation*. Yale University Press: New Haven and London.

Martin, A. R. (1923), 'The Greyfriars of Greenwich', *Archaeological Journal*, 30, 81–114.

Martin, D. D. (1995), 'Carthusians during the Reformation era: *Cartusia nunquam deformata, reformari resistens*', *Catholic Historical Review*, 81, 41–66.

Mayhew, G. (2014), *The monks of Saint Pancras: Lewes Priory. England's premier Cluniac monastery and its dependencies, 1076–1537*. Lewes History Press: Lewes.

McConica, J. J. (ed.) (1986), 'The rise of the undergraduate college', in *The History of the University of Oxford. 3. The Collegiate University*, (ed.) idem. Oxford University Press: Oxford, 1–68.

McDonald, P. (1986), 'The papacy and monastic observance in the later Middle Ages: The *Benedictina* in England', *Journal of Religious History*, 14:2, 117–32.

McMurray Gibson, G. (1989), *The theater of devotion: East Anglian drama and society in the late Middle Ages*. University of Chicago Press: Chicago and London.

McSheffrey, S. (2017), *Seeking sanctuary: crime, mercy and politics in English courts, 1400–1550*. Oxford University Press: Oxford.

Mellor, J. and Pearce, T. (1981), 'The Austin Friars, Leicester', *Council for British Archaeology Research Reports*, 35.

Merritt, J. F. (2005), *The social world of early modern Westminster: Abbey, court and community, 1525–1640*. Manchester University Press: Manchester.

Miller, C. A. (1966), 'Erasmus on music', *The Musical Quarterly*, 52:3, 332–49.

Miller, E. (1991), 'Yorkshire and Lancashire', *The Agrarian History of England and Wales. III 1348–1500*, (ed.) E. Miller. Cambridge University Press: Cambridge, 182–93.

Mills, D. (1996), 'The Chester mystery plays: Truth and tradition', in *Courts, counties and the capital in the later Middle Ages*, (ed.) D. E. S. Dunn, Fifteenth Century Series, 4. Sutton and St Martin's Press: Stroud, 1–26.

Milsom, J. (2004), 'Thomas Tallis (c. 1505–1585)', *Oxford Dictionary of National Biography*. Oxford University Press: Oxford.

Morgan, N. J. (1995), 'The *scala coeli* indulgence and the royal chapels', in *The reign of Henry VII*, (ed.) B. J. Thompson, Harlaxton Medieval Studies, 5; Paul Watkins: Stamford, 82–103.

Morgan, F. C. and Morgan, P. E. (1962), 'Some nuns, ex-religious and former chantry priests living in the diocese of Hereford (c. 1554)', *Transactions of the Woolhope Naturalists' Field Club*, 32/1, 135–48.

Murray, J. (2004), 'George Browne (d. in or after 1556), Church of Ireland archbishop of Dublin', *Oxford Dictionary of National Biography*. Oxford University Press: Oxford.

Murray, J. (2009) *Enforcing the Reformation in Ireland. Clerical resistance and political conflict in the diocese of Dublin, 1534–1590*. Cambridge University Press: Cambridge.

Myres, J. N. L. (1933), 'Butley Priory, Suffolk', *Archaeological Journal*, 90:2, 177–281.

Newcombe, D. G. (2004), 'John Hooper, (b.1495x1500)', *Oxford Dictionary of National Biography*. Oxford University Press: Oxford.

Nichols, J. (1795–1811), *The history and antiquities of the county of Leicester*, 4 vols. in 8 pts. J. Nichols: London.

Norrie, A. (2019), 'The bishop and the queen; or, why did the bishop of Carlisle crown Elizabeth I?', *Northern History*, 56, 25–45.

Oates, J. C. T. (1958), 'Richard Pynson and the Holy Blood of Hayles', *The Library*, 5th Series, 13: 269–77.

Ogier, D. M. (1996), *Reformation and society in Guernsey*. The Boydell Press: Woodbridge.

Olding, F. (2015), 'Church and settlement: St Mary's priory and the archaeology of the town', in *An anatomy of a priory church: the archaeology, history and conservation of St Mary's Priory church, Abergavenny*, (ed.) G. Nash. Archaeopress: Oxford, 13–28.

Oliva, M. (1994), *The convent and the community in late medieval England: Female monasteries in the diocese of Norwich, 1350–1540*. Studies in the History of Medieval Religion, 12. The Boydell Press: Woodbridge.

Orme, N. (2006), *Medieval schools: From Roman Britain to Renaissance England*. Yale University Press: New Haven and London.

Orme, N. (2010), *The Victoria History of the Counties of England: The County of Cornwall. II. Religious History to 1560*. Institute of Historical Research. The Boydell Press: Woodbridge.

O'Sullivan, D. (2013), *In the company of preachers: The archaeology of medieval friaries in England and Wales*. Leicester Archaeology Monograph, 23. University of Leicester: Leicester.

Oswald, A., Goodall, J., Payne, A. and Sutcliffe, T.-J. (2010), *Thornton Abbey, North Lincolnshire. Historical, archaeological and architectural investigations*. Research Department Report Series, 100. English Heritage: Portsmouth.

Owen, D. (2003), 'Ely 1109–1539: priory, community and town', in *A history of Ely Cathedral*, (ed.) P. Meadows and N. Ramsay. The Boydell Press: Woodbridge, 59–76.

Oxley, J. E. (1965), *The reformation in Essex to the death of Mary*. Manchester University Press: Manchester.

Page, W. (1897–98), 'The parochial chapel of St Andrew formerly attached to St Albans Abbey', *St Albans and Hertfordshire Architectural and Archaeological Society Transactions*, I/II, New Series, 84–106.

Page, W. (1906), *A history of the county of Norfolk: Volume 2*. Constable: London.

Page, W. (1911), *The Victoria history of the county of Somerset*. Volume 2, Ecclesiastical History. London: Archibald Constable for the University of London.

Palmer, W. (1928–30), 'The nunnery of Swaffham Bulbeck', *Cambridge Antiquarian Society*, 31, 30–65.

Parrish, H. L. (2004), 'Robert Holgate (1481/2–1555)', *Oxford Dictionary of National Biography*. Oxford University Press: Oxford.

Peacock, E. (1883), 'Injunctions of John Longland, bishop of Lincoln, to certain religious houses in his diocese, 1531', *Archaeologia*, 47, 49–64.

Pearce, E. H. (1916), *The monks of Westminster being a register of the convent from the time of the Confessor to the dissolution*. Cambridge University Press: Cambridge.

Perry, G. G. (1888), 'The visitation of the monastery of Thame, 1526', *English Historical Review*, 3 (1888), 704–22.

Perry, G. G. (1889), 'Episcopal visitations of the Austin canons of Leicester and Dorchester, Oxon.', *English Historical Review*, 4:14, 304–13.

Pettegree, A. (2004), 'John Scory (d. 1585), bishop of Hereford', *Oxford Dictionary of National Biography*. Oxford University Press: Oxford.

Pevsner, N. (2002), *The buildings of England: Bedfordshire and the county of Huntingdon and Peterborough*. Yale University Press: New Haven and London.

Pevsner, N. and Newman, J. (2002), *The buildings of England: Dorset*. Yale University Press: New Haven and London.

Pevsner, N. and Wilson, B. (2002), *The buildings of England. Norfolk I. Norwich and North East*. Yale University press. New Haven and London.

Pevsner, N. and Cherry, B. (2002), *The buildings of England: Wiltshire*. Yale University Press: New Haven and London.

Pfaff, R. (2009), *The liturgy in medieval England*. Cambridge University Press: Cambridge.

Poster, J. and Sherlock, D. (1987), 'Denny Abbey: the nuns refectory', *Proceedings of the Cambridge Antiquarian Society*, 76, 67–82.

Powell, S. (2017), *The Birgittines of Syon Abbey: Preaching and print*. Texts and Transitions, 11. Brepols: Turnhout.

Power, E. (1922), *Medieval English nunneries, c. 1275 to 1535*. Cambridge University Press: Cambridge.

Powicke, F. M. and Fryde, E. B. (1961), *Handbook of British Chronology*, Royal Historical Society Guides and Handbooks, 2. 2nd edn. Royal Historical Society: London.

Principe, L. M. (2004), 'William Blomfild (fl. 1529–1574)', *Oxford Dictionary of National Biography*. Oxford University Press: Oxford.

Pugin, A. W. (1836), *Contrasts: A parallel between the noble edifices of the fourteenth and fifteenth centuries and similar buildings of the present day*. Published by the author: London and St Mary's Grange, near Salisbury.

Rawcliffe, C. (1978), *The Staffords, Earls of Stafford and Dukes of Buckingham, 1394–1521*. Cambridge Studies in Medieval Life and Thought, 3rd Series, 11. Cambridge University Press: Cambridge.

Rawcliffe, C. and Wilson, N. (ed.) (2004), *Medieval Norwich*. Hambledon: London.

Rees, E. A. (2008), *A life of Guto'r Glyn*. Y Lolfa: Talybont.

Rex, R. (1991), 'The execution of the Holy Maid of Kent', *Historical Research*, 64, 216–20.

Rex, R. (2002), 'Friars in the English Reformation', *The beginnings of English Protestantism*, (ed.) P. Marshall and A. Ryrie. Cambridge University Press: Cambridge, 38–59.

Rhodes, J. T. (1993), 'Syon Abbey and its religious publications in the sixteenth century', *Journal of Ecclesiastical History*, 44:1, 11–25.

Riddy, F. (2001), 'Glastonbury, Joseph of Arimathea and the grail in John Hardyng's Chronicle', in *Glastonbury Abbey and the Arthurian tradition*, (ed.) J. P. Carley. D. S. Brewer: Woodbridge, 269–84.

Rigby, S. H. (1995), *English society in the later Middle Ages. Class, status and gender*. Macmillan: Basingstoke.

Robson, M. J. (1997), *The Franciscans in the medieval custody of York*, Borthwick Paper, 93. Borthwick Institute: York.

Rodwell, W. (2011), 'Combe Abbey: From Cistercian abbey to country house', in *Coventry: Medieval art, architecture and archaeology in the city and its vicinity*, (ed.) L. Monckton and R. K. Morris. British Archaeological Association Conference Transaction, 33. Maney: Leeds, 286–303.

Röhrkasten, J. (2004), *The mendicant houses of medieval London*. Vita regularis. Abhandlungen, Bd 21: Münster.

Romilly, J. (ed.) (1874), *Fourth report of the royal commission on historical manuscripts. Report and Appendix*, 2 vols. Eyre and Spottiswode: London.

Rose, S. (2018), *The wealth of England: The medieval wool trade and its political importance, 1100–1600*. Oxbow Books: Oxford.

Rose-Troup, F. (1913), *The western rebellion of 1549: an account of the insurrections in Devonshire and Cornwall against religious innovations in the reign of Edward VI*. Smith, Elder: London.

Rose-Troup, F. (1935), 'Lists relating to persons ejected from religious houses', *Devon and Cornwall Notes and Queries*, 18, 45–8.

Rosser, G. (1989), *Medieval Westminster: 1200–1540*. Clarendon Press: Oxford.

Ruddock, A. (1945), 'The Greyfriars in Southampton', *Proceedings of the Hampshire Field Club and Archaeological Society*, 16:2, 137–46.

Ryder, M. L. (1959), 'The animal remains found at Kirkstall Abbey', *The Agricultural History Review*, 7:1, 1–5.

Ryle, S. F. (2004), 'Leonard Cox (b. c. 1495, d. in or after 1549)', *Oxford Dictionary of National Biography*. Oxford University Press: Oxford.

Sander, N. (1585), *De origine ac progressu schismatis anglicanae*, (ed.) E. Rishton. Cologne [rect. Rheims].

Savine, A. (1909), 'English monasteries on the eve of the dissolution', in *Oxford Studies in Social and Legal History*, (ed.) P. Vinogradoff. Oxford University Press: Oxford, 1–304.

Savory, H. N. et al. (1982), *The Royal Commission on Ancient and Historical Monuments in Wales. An Inventory of the Ancient Monuments in Glamorgan. Volume III: Medieval Secular Monuments. Part II: Non-defensive*. HMSO: Cardiff.

Scarisbrick, J. J. (1994), 'The dissolution of St Mary's priory', in *Coventry's first cathedral: The cathedral and the priory of St Mary. Papers from the 1993 symposium*, (ed.) G. Demidowicz. Paul Watkins: Stamford, 158–68.

Schofield, J. (1993), 'Buildings in religious precincts in London at the Dissolution and after', in *Advances in monastic archaeology*, (ed.) R. Gilchrist and H. Mytum. British Archaeological Reports, British Series, 227. BAR Publishing: Oxford, 29–41.

Schofield, J. and Lea, R. (2005), *Holy Trinity Priory, Aldgate: An archaeological reconstruction and history*. Museum of London Archaeology Service Monographs, 24. English Heritage and Museum of London: London.

Schroder, T. (2020), *A marvel to behold: Gold and silver at the court of Henry VIII*. The Boydell Press: Woodbridge.

Scott, I. (2001), 'Romsey Abbey: Benedictine nunnery and parish church', *Monastic Archaeology*, (ed.) G. Keevil, M. Aston and T. Hall, 150–60.

Scott Thomson, G. (1933), 'Woburn Abbey and the dissolution of the monasteries', *Transactions of the Royal Historical Society*, 16, 129–60.

Searle, E. (1974), *Lordship and community: Battle abbey and its banlieu, 1066–1538*. Pontifical Institute of Mediaeval Studies. Studies and Texts, 26: Toronto.

Seesko, P., Kallestrup, L. N. and Bisgaar, L. (ed.) (2019), *The Dissolution of Monasteries: The case of Denmark in regional perspective*. University Press of Southern Denmark: Odense.

Serjeantson, R. M. and Adkins, W. R. D. (1906), *A history of the county of Northamptonshire. Volume 2*. Archibald Constable and Co.: London.

Shagan, E. H. (2003), *Popular politics and the English Reformation*. Cambridge University Press: Cambridge.

Shaw, A. N. (2004), 'Sir Thomas Legh (d. 1545)', *Oxford Dictionary of National Biography*. Oxford University Press: Oxford.

Sheils, W. J. (2004), 'John Whitgift (1530/31?–1604)', *Oxford Dictionary of National Biography*. Oxford University Press: Oxford.

Shelby, L. R. (1976), 'Monastic patrons and their architects: A case study of the contract for the monks' dormitory at Durham', *Gesta*, 15:1, 91–6.

Sherlock, P. (2018), 'Monuments and memory', in *Early Modern Women's Writing*, (ed.) P. Phillippy. Cambridge University Press: Cambridge, 292–314.

Shrimpton, J. (1966), *The antiquities of Verulam and St Albans*, (ed.) C. I. A. Ritchie. St Albans and Hertfordshire Architectural and Archaeological Society: St Albans.

Sil, N. P. (2004), 'William Herbert, first earl of Pembroke (1506/7–1570)', *Oxford Dictionary of National Biography*. Oxford University Press: Oxford.

Silvester, R. J. and Hankinson, R. (2015), *The monastic granges of East Wales: A scheduling enhancement project*. Clwyd Powys Archaeological Trust Report no. 1340.

Skeeters, M. C. (1993), *Community and clergy: Bristol and the reformation, c.1530–c.1570*. Clarendon Press: Oxford.

Slater, T. R. (1998), 'Benedictine town planning in medieval England: The evidence from St Albans', *The church in the medieval town*, (ed.) T. R. Slater and G. Rosser. Ashgate: Aldershot, 155–76.

Sledmere, E. and C. E. (1914), *Abbey Dore, Herefordshire, its building and restoration*. Jakeman and Carver: Hereford.

Sloane, B. and Malcolm, G. (ed.) (2004), *Excavations at the priory of the hospital of St John of Jerusalem, Clerkenwell, London*. Museum of London Archaeology Service, Monograph 20.

Smith, D. M (ed.) (2008), *Heads of religious houses, III, 1377–1540*. Cambridge University Press: Cambridge.

Smith, R. A. L. (1943), *Canterbury Cathedral Priory. A study in monastic administration*. Cambridge University Press: Cambridge.

Smyly, J. G. (1922), 'Thomas Gardiner's history of England', *Hermathena*, 19:43, 235–48.

Snell, L. S. (1967), *The suppression of the religious foundations of Devon and Cornwall*, Wordens of Cornwall: Marazion.

Soden, I. (2003), 'The conversion of former monastic buildings to secular use: the case of Coventry', in *The archaeology of Reformation, c.1480–1580*, (ed.) D. Gaimster and R. Gilchrist, Society for post-medieval archaeology, monograph 1. Maney: Leeds, 280–9.

Sowerby, T. A. (2010), *Renaissance and reform in Tudor England: The careers of Sir Richard Morison*. Oxford University Press: Oxford.

Sparks, J. A. (1978), *In the shadow of the Blackdowns: Life at the Cistercian abbey of Dunkeswell and on its manors and estates, 1201–1539*. Moonraker Press: Bradford on Avon.

Speight, H. (1994), 'Thomas Cromwell and the governance of south-west England', *The Historical Journal*, 37, 623–38.

Spooner, J. (2015), 'The Virgin Mary and white harts great and small: the fourteenth-century wall-paintings in the chapel of our lady of the pew and the muniment room', in *Westminster: The art, architecture and archaeology of the royal abbey*, (ed.) T. Tatton-Brown and W. Rodwell. British Archaeological Association Conference Transactions, 29/1. Maney Publishing: Leeds, 262–90.

Stanley, A. P. (1890), *Historical memorials of Westminster Abbey*, 7th edn. John Murray: London.

St John Hope, W. (1900), *Fountains Abbey, Yorkshire*. J. Whitehead and Sons: Leeds.

St John Hope, W. (1906), 'The making of Place House at Titchfield, near Southampton in 1538', *Archaeological Journal*, 63, 231–43.

Steer, C. (2017), 'Burial and commemoration in the London friaries', in N. Holder et al., *The friaries of medieval London: From foundation to dissolution*. The Boydell Press: Woodbridge, 272–92.

Stöber, K. and Austin, D. (2013), 'Culdees to Canons: the Augustinian houses of North Wales', in *Monastic Wales: New approaches*. University of Wales Press: Cardiff, 39–54.

Summerson, H. (1993), *Medieval Carlisle: The city and its borders from the late eleventh century to the mid-sixteenth century*, 2 vols. Cumberland and Westmoreland Antiquarian and Archaeological Society: Kendal.

Sutton, A. F. (1994), 'Lady Joan Bradbury (d. 1530)', in *Medieval London Widows, 1300–1500*, (ed.) C. Barron and A. F. Sutton. Hambledon: London, 209–38.

Swanson, R. N. (2007), *Indulgences in late medieval England: Passports to paradise?* Cambridge University Press: Cambridge.

Swynnerton, C. (1921), 'The prior of St Leonard of Stanley, co. Gloucester in the light of new discoveries documentary and structural', *Archaeologia*, 71, 199–227.

Tatton-Brown, T. (1991), 'The buildings and topography of St Augustine's Abbey, Canterbury', *Journal of the British Archaeological Association*, 144:1, 61–91.

Tatton-Brown, T. (2001), 'The Buildings of West Malling Abbey', *Architectural History*, 44: 179–94.

Tatton-Brown, T. (ed.) (2015a), *Westminster Abbey: The art, architecture and archaeology of the medieval abbey and royal palace, vol. 1*. British Archaeological Association Conference Transactions, 39/1. British Archaeological Association: London.

Tatton-Brown, T. (2015b), 'The new work: aspects of the later medieval fabric of the abbey', in *Westminster Abbey: The art, architecture and archaeology of the medieval abbey and royal palace, vol. 1*. (ed.) T. Tatton-Brown, British Archaeological Association Conference Transactions, 39/1. British Archaeological Association: London, 312–24.

Thomas, C., Sloane, B. and Phillpott, C. (1997), *Excavations at the priory and hospital of St Mary Spital, London*. Museum of London Monograph Series, 1. Museum of London: London.

Thomas, D. (1992a), 'The Elizabeth crown lands: Their purposes and problems', in *The estates of the English Crown, 1558–1640*, (ed.) R. W. Hoyle. Cambridge University Press: Cambridge, 58–87.

Thomas, D. (1992b), 'The leases of crown lands in the reign of Elizabeth I', in *The estates of the English Crown, 1558–1640*, (ed.) R. W. Hoyle. Cambridge University Press: Cambridge, 169–90.

Thomas, J. (2006), 'The evidence for the dissolution of Thorney Abbey: Recent excavations and landscape analysis at Thorney, Cambridgeshire', *Journal of Medieval Archaeology*, 50, 179–241.

Thompson, A. H. (1949), *The abbey of St Mary of the Meadows Leicester*. Edgar Backus: Leicester.

Thompson, B. J. (1994), 'Monasteries and their patrons at foundation and dissolution', *Transactions of the Royal Historical Society*, Sixth Series, 4, 103–25.

Thompson, S. (1989), 'The bishop and his diocese', *Humanism, reform and the Reformation: The career of Bishop John Fisher*, (ed.) B. Bradshaw and E. Duffy. Cambridge University Press: Cambridge, 67–80.

Thompson, S. (2004) 'John Hilsey (d. 1539), bishop of Rochester', *Oxford Dictionary of National Biography*. Oxford University Press: Oxford.

Thornton, T. (2006), *Prophecy, politics and the people in early modern England*. The Boydell Press: Woodbridge.

Thornton, T. (2012), *The Channel Islands, 1370–1640: Between England and Normandy*. The Boydell Press: Woodbridge.

Thorpe, S. M. (1982), 'Sir Richard Sacheverell', *The history of Parliament, 1509–1558*, (ed.) S. T. Bindoff, Secker and Warburg for the History of Parliament Trust: London.

Tindal-Hart, A. (1966), 'The Reformation and its aftermath, 1474–1660', in *A house of kings: The history of Westminster Abbey*, (ed.) E. Carpenter. John Baker: London, 87–175.

Tittler, R. (1977), 'The incorporation of boroughs, 1540–58, *History*, 62:204, 24–42.

Tittler, R. (1987), 'The end of the Middle Ages in the English country town', *Sixteenth-Century Journal*, 18:4, 471–87.

Tittler, R. (1998), *Reformation and the towns in England: Politics and political culture, c. 1540–1640*. Clarendon Press: Oxford.

Traskey, J. P. (1978), *Milton Abbey: A Dorset monastery in the Middle Ages*. Compton Press: Tisbury.

Trueman, C. R. (2004), 'Robert Barnes (c. 1495–1540)', *Oxford Dictionary of National Biography*. Oxford University Press: Oxford.

Turner, S. (2007), 'Field, property and agricultural innovation in late medieval and early modern south-west England', in *Estate landscapes: Design, improvement and power in the post-medieval landscape*, (ed.) J. Finch and K. Giles. The Boydell Press: Woodbridge, 57–76.

Twyne, J. (1590), *De rebus Albionicis, Britannicis atque Anglicis, commentariorum libri duo*. Richard Watkins: London.

Underwood, M. (1989), 'John Fisher and the promotion of learning', *Humanism, reform and reformation: The career of Bishop John Fisher*. Cambridge University Press: Cambridge, 25–46.

Voigts, L. (2017), 'Plague saints, Henry VII and Saint Armel', in *Saints and cults in medieval England: proceedings of the 2015 Harlaxton Symposium*, (ed.) S. Powell, Harlaxton Medieval Studies. Shaun Tyas: Donington, 101–23.

Walker, C. (2006), 'Continuity and isolation: The Bridgettines of Syon in the sixteenth and seventeenth centuries', in *Syon Abbey and its books: Reading, writing and religion, c. 1400–1700*, (ed.) E. A. Jones and A. Walsham. The Boydell Press: Woodbridge, 155–76.

Wall, A. (2004), 'Baynton Family (per. 1508–1716)', *Oxford Dictionary of National Biography*. Oxford University Press: Oxford.

Walsham, A. (2011), *The reformation of the landscape: Religion, identity and memory in early modern Britain and Ireland*. Oxford University Press: Oxford.

Ward, J. C. (2004), 'Marshall [Beche], Thomas, abbot of Colchester (d. 1539)', *Oxford Dictionary of National Biography*. Oxford University Press: Oxford.

Ward, S. (2000), 'The friaries in Chester', in *Medieval archaeology, art and architecture at Chester*, (ed.) A. Thacker. British Archaeological Association Conference Transactions, 22. Maney: Leeds, 45–56.

Watkin, A. (1949), 'Last glimpses of Glastonbury', *Downside Review*, 67:1, 76–86.

Weir, A. (2014), *Elizabeth of York: The first Tudor queen*. Jonathan Cape: London.

Welander, D. (1991), *The history, art and architecture of Gloucester Cathedral*. Alan Sutton: Stroud.

Weld, J. W., Darby, H. C., Ralegh Radford et al., (ed.) (1972), *An inventory of Historical Monuments in the County of Dorset*. Volume 4 North Dorset. Royal Commission on Historical Monuments (England). HMSO: London.

Wenzel, S. (2005), *Latin sermon collections from later Medieval England: Orthodox preaching in the age of Wyclif*. Cambridge University Press: Cambridge.

White, A. (1993), 'Where was Beaumont?', *Contrebis*, 18, 54–6.

Williams, D. (1976), *White monks of Gwent and the border*. Hughes and Sons: Pontypool.

Williams, D. H. (2001), *The Welsh Cistercians*. Gracewing: Leominster.

Williams, G. (1991), 'Kidwelly Priory', *Sir Gâr: Studies in Carmarthenshire history: Essays in memory of W. H. Morris and M. C. S. Evans*, (ed.) H. Morris. Carmarthen Antiquarian Society: Carmarthen, 189–204.

Williams, G. (1997), *Wales and the Reformation*. Cardiff University Press: Cardiff.

Williams, G. (2004), 'William Barlow (d. 1568), bishop of Chichester', *Oxford Dictionary of National Biography*. Oxford University Press: Oxford.

Willmott, H. (2020), *The dissolution of the monasteries in England and Wales*. Equinox Publishing: Sheffield and Bristol, CT.

Withington, P. (2005), *The politics of commonwealth: Citizens and freemen in early modern England*. Cambridge Social and Cultural Histories, 4. Cambridge University Press: Cambridge.

Wolffe, B. P. (1964), 'Henry VII's land revenues and chamber finance', *English Historical Review*, 79, 225–54.

Wood, A. (2007), *The 1549 rebellions and the making of early modern England*, Cambridge Studies in Early Modern British History. Cambridge University Press: Cambridge.

Wood, A. (2013), *The memory of the people: Custom and popular senses of the past in early modern England*. Cambridge University Press: Cambridge.

Woodfield, C. (2005), *The church of Our Lady of Mount Cartmel and some conventual buildings at the Whitefriars Coventry*. British Archaeological Record, 389.

Wooding, L. E. C. (2004), 'William Peryn (d. 1558), prior or St Bartholomew's, Smithfield, and theologian', *Oxford Dictionary of National Biography*. Oxford University Press: Oxford.

Youings, J. (1967), 'The Church', in *The agrarian history of England and Wales, Volume IV 1500–1640*, (ed.) J. Thirsk. Cambridge University Press: Cambridge, 306–56.

Zim, R. (2011), 'Batman, Stephen (c. 1542–1584)', *Oxford Dictionary of National Biography*. Oxford University Press: Oxford.

Unpublished Dissertations

Brown, G. (2011), 'Stanley Abbey and its estates, 1151–c.1640'. University of Leicester, PhD.

Cumber, J. (2010), 'Tudor Abingdon: The experience of change and renewal in a sixteenth-century town'. University of Oxford, PhD.

De Beer, L. (2018), 'Reassessing English alabaster carving: Medieval sculpture and its contexts'. University of East Anglia, PhD.

Fisher, R. (2018), 'Three English cathedrals and the early reformation: a cultural comparison of Hereford, Worcester and Gloucester'. University of Bristol, PhD.

Ford, L. (2001), 'Conciliar politics and administration in the reign of Henry VII'. University of St Andrews, PhD.

Gill, S. M. (2010), 'Managing change in the English Reformation: The 1548 dissolution of the chantries and clergy of the midland county surveys'. University of Birmingham, PhD.

Harper-Bill, C. (1977), 'An edition of the register of John Morton, archbishop of Canterbury, 1486–1500, with a critical introduction'. King's College London, PhD.

Hodgkinson, B. W. (2013), 'Withering on the vine: The connectivity between the people of Lincolnshire and their monastic houses, 1500 to 1540'. University of Nottingham, PhD.

Knight, M. (1986), 'Religious life in Coventry, 1485–1558'. University of Warwick, PhD.

Lyon, H. K. (2018), 'The afterlives of the dissolution of the monasteries, 1536–c.1700'. University of Cambridge, PhD.

Proctor, E. (2018), 'The topographical legacy of the medieval monastery: Evolving perceptions and realities of monastic landscapes in the southern Welsh marches'. University of Exeter, PhD.

Robertson, M. L. (1975), 'Thomas Cromwell's servants: The ministerial household in early Tudor government and society'. University of California at Los Angeles, PhD.

Rowland, E. (1989), 'The popular reformation in County Durham'. University of Durham, PhD.

Shaw, A. N. (2003), 'The *Compendium compertorum* and the making of the suppression act of 1536'. University of Warwick, PhD.

INDEX

Bartholomew, St, cult of at Crowland 45
Bartlett, John 238
Barton, Elizabeth (*c.* 1506–34), called 'Holy
    Maid of Kent' 36, 214, 219, 267,
    270, 275, 277, 280, 348–9
Barton, Geoffrey, abbot of Lilleshall (1498–
    1516) 187
Barton, Thomas, abbot of Colchester (1523–
    33) 214
Barwicke, Richard, monk of St Mary's
    Abbey, York 454
Baryngton, Robert, abbot of Walden (1533–
    35?) 274
Bashfurth, Margaret, nun of Moxbury
    507
Basil, St, of Caesarea (330–379 CE) 176
Basing, William, prior of St Swithun's,
    Winchester (1536–39) 366
Basingwerk Abbey (Flintshire) 103, 414
  abbot of *see* Pennant, Nicholas
Baskerfield, Edward 214, 434, 601n
Baskerville, Geoffrey 589n, 600n, 602n
Bassett, James 65, 460
Bateman, John, Carthusian 273
Bath 133, 413, 448
  bishop of (and Wells) 211, 225, 281
  Cathedral Priory at 87, 113, 217, 252–3,
    319, 346, 561n, 569n, 597n
  diocese of 174, 196, 226
  prior of 305, 358–9, 432 *see also* Holeway,
    William
Batman, Stephen 11, 381, 547n
Batmanson, John, prior of the London
    Charterhouse (1529–31) 48
Battle (East Sussex)102, 104, 495
    Abbey 72, 76, 78, 90, 101–2, 106, 108–9,
    111, 114–16, 121, 127–8, 141, 197,
    217, 228, 346, 363, 503, 532, 557n,
    559n, 561n
    abbot of 76, 197 *see also* Hamond, John
    cellarer 106
    egg-collector of 106
Bayham Abbey (East Sussex) 5, 142, 181,
    201, 205, 272, 325, 384, 572n
Baynton, Sir Edward (*c.* 1495–1544), Queen's
    vicechamberlain 477, 483
Beauchamp, Margaret 157
Beauchief Abbey (South Yorkshire) 126, 415,
    576n
Beaufeld, Elizabeth, nun of Bungay 532
Beaufort, Edmund (1406–55), 2nd duke of
    Somerset 35

Beaufort, Lady Margaret (1443–1509),
    countess of Richmond and Derby
    155, 157, 187
Beaulieu Abbey (Hampshire) 45, 204, 211,
    270, 459, 462, 484, 600n
  abbot of 204
Beaulieu Palace (Essex) 512
Beauvale (Nottinghamshire), Charterhouse
    at 35, 70, 111, 153, 156, 168, 199,
    206–8, 215, 219, 261, 363
  prior of 199, 363 *see also* Wartre, Nicholas;
    Woodcock, Thomas
Bebe, John, abbot of Dale (1510–38) 303
Becket, Thomas, archbishop of Canterbury
    (1162–70) 50, 55, 217, 311, 354,
    400, 442, 472
Beckington (Somerset) 304
Bede, St (673/74–735), of Monkwearmouth
    194, 359
Bedford (Bedfordshire), Franciscans at 351,
    401
  suffragan bishop of 196, 344
Bedfordshire, county of 75, 238, 329, 588n
Bedlingfield, Edmund, patron of
    Redlingfield Priory 453
Bedyll, Thomas (*c.* 1486–1537), archdeacon
    of Cornwall (1534–37) 214, 220,
    246, 260, 277, 281, 318
Bee, Brian, monk of Axholme 276
Beeleigh Abbey (Essex) 90, 394
Beerley, Richard, monk of Pershore 258
Beeston Priory (Norfolk) 76, 334
  prior of 334 *see also* Hudson, Richard
Bele, Thomas, of St Mary's College, Oxford
    196
Bell, Sir Thomas, mayor of Gloucester 353
Bells 42, 103, 127, 331, 369, 403, 407,
    413–14, 475
Benedict, of Nursia, St, rule of 50, 67, 74,
    76–7, 177–8, 236, 240
Benedict XII, pope (1334–42) 174, 569n
Benedictina, canons for monastic reform 175,
    182, 184, 569n
Benedictines, congregation of in England
    515, 520, 531, 541, 545n
  General Chapter of in England 196, 569n
Benett, William 64
Benson, William, abbot of Westminster
    (1533–40) 10, 85, 205, 212, 603n
Berden Priory (Essex) 430
Bere, Richard, abbot of Glastonbury (1493–
    1525) 157, 193, 269–70